Daffodil, Snowdrop  and Tulip Yearbook 2008-2009

An annual for amateurs and specialists growing and showing daffodils, snowdrops and tulips

in association with

The Royal Horticultural Society

LONDON

Published in 2008 by
The Royal Horticultural Society,
80 Vincent Square, London SW1P 2PE

All rights reserved. No part of this publication may be reproduced in any form or by any means, without permission from the Publisher

ISBN 978-1-902896-93-9
© The Royal Horticultural Society 2008

EDITORIAL COMMITTEE

M S Bradbury (*Honorary Editor*)

Mrs W M Akers

J L Akers MBE

J W Blanchard VMH

C D Brickell CBE, VMH

B S Duncan MBE

J Gibson

Mrs S Kington

Lady Skelmersdale

Opinions expressed by the authors are not necessarily those of the Royal Horticultural Society

Printed by Alden Press UK, Witney, Oxfordshire

Contents

Editorial	6
Wisley daffodil trials	
by Sue Drew	8
Narcissus 'Cedric Morris'	
by John Blanchard	10
Narcissus 'Cecil Nice'	
by Brian Mathew	12
Narcissus provincialis: a minor problem	
by James Akers	14

SYMPOSIUM ON THE WORLD DAFFODIL CONVENTION 2008

Introduction	
by Malcolm Bradbury	18
Daffodils in England 2008	
by Peter and Lesley Ramsay	19
A visit to Ballynahatty Road	
by David Adams	23
Three days in Holland	
by Mary Lou Gripshover	24

Recent developments in trumpet daffodils	
by Brian S Duncan	28
What will daffodil growers do without formalin? *by Gordon Hanks*	38
UK *Narcissus* crop improvement research: a rapid *Narcissus* micropropagation technique *by Helen Robinson, David Pink and Gordon Hanks*	42
John Sydney Birch Lea	
by John Gibson	46

AWARDS TO PEOPLE

The Peter Barr Memorial Cup 2008 awarded to Nancy Tackett and Ben Blake	48
MBE awarded to James Akers	48
ADS Gold Medal awarded to Peter Ramsay	49
KAVB Dix Medal awarded to N A Nijssen	50
KAVB Dix Medal awarded to Brian Duncan	50

Galanthomania, chipping and twin-scaling *by Colin Mason*	51
How I grow snowdrops *by Angela Whinfield*	54
Collecting snowdrops - some observations *by Chris Sanham*	57
Tulipa sylvestris subsp. *australis* *by Richard Wilford*	60
In search of tulips *by John Page*	61
Small-flowered tulip trial at Wisley *by Christine Skelmersdale*	64
Large-flowered tulip trial at Wisley *by Sue Drew*	67
World Tulip Summit 2008 *by Johnny Walkers*	70
Tulip Sour: *Fusarium oxysporum f.sp. tulipae* in tulips *by Marjan de Boer*	72
RHS show dates 2009	74
Hardy nerine study day *by John David*	75

BOOK REVIEWS

International Daffodil Register and Classified List 2008 *by Chris Brickell*	77
Common Snowdrop *by Alan Leslie*	78
Transcript of the Tenth Galanthus Gala *by Alan Leslie*	79
Gardening with Tulips *by John Page*	80
Buried Treasures *by John Page*	81
Spalding Flower Parade: the golden years *by Wendy Akers*	83

DAFFODIL, HYACINTH, SNOWDROP AND TULIP NOTES

Ralph B White Memorial Medal *by Malcolm Bradbury*	84

Definition of division 9 - poeticus
    daffodil cultivars *by Sharon McDonald*   84
Nomenclatural standards of daffodils in the
    RHS Herbarium *by Susan Grayer*   85
Hyacinth trial at Wisley
    by Malcolm Bradbury   86
A new snowdrop discovery - *G. plicatus*
    'E.A. Bowles' *by Michael D Myers*   86
A snowdrop tour
    by Ruby Baker   87
Correction   88

OVERSEAS SHOWS AND REPORTS
ADS National Show and Convention
    by Mary Lou Gripshover   90
Daffodils in New Zealand 2007   92
A whirlwind tour
    by Richard Perrignon   97

RHS EVENTS
Snowdrops at RHS shows 2008
    by Alan Leslie   99
RHS Early Daffodil Competition
    by John Goddard   103
RHS Daffodil Show
    by Jackie Petherbridge   106

RHS Late Daffodil Competition and
    Tulip Competition *by Reg Nicholl*   114

OTHER UK SHOWS
Daffodils, snowdrops and tulips at two
    AGS shows
        Harlow *by Mary Randall*   119
        Loughborough *by Robert Rolfe*   120
South East of England Daffodil
    Society shows *by Robert Wiseman*   122
The Daffodil Society Show
    by Gwynne Davies   123
HarrogateSpring Flower Show
    by Richard Smales   125
City of Belfast Spring Flower Show
    by Richard McCaw   127
Wakefield and North of England Tulip
    Society Annual Show *by James Akers*   129

Bulbs in the Spring Garden   130
Awards to plants for exhibition   131

RHS Daffodil and Tulip Committee 2008   133
Advisory Panel on Narcissus Classification   133

Index   134

ILLUSTRATIONS
Front cover
Narcissus 'Triple Crown' (*photo* M Sleigh/RHS) - see page 131
Back cover
Tulipa 'Monte Carlo' (*photo* Johan van Scheepen) - see page 50
Tulipa 'Rory McEwen' (*photo* James Akers) - see page 48
All other illustrations are described and attributed *in situ*

INDEX TO ADVERTISERS

ADS Annual Convention 2010	12	John Gibson Daffodils	41
American Daffodil Society, The	17	Mitsch Daffodils	inside back cover
Bramcote Bulbs	27	Ringhaddy Daffodils	inside front cover
Daffodil Society, The	102	Janis Ruksans	7
Daffodil Society of New Zealand,		Miniature Bulbs	89
The National	13	Walkers Bulbs	5

Editorial

The internet and the increasing affordability of travel continue to encourage a broader international perspective in leisure pursuits, to which gardening is no exception. This year we note in the *Yearbook* both the World Daffodil Convention and the World Tulip Summit, whilst snowdrop enthusiasts can point to the steady two-way flow of visitors to events in the United Kingdom, the Netherlands and Germany. Such contacts are clearly beneficial, not only in terms of mutually interesting holidays and friendships but also in helping the spread of new ideas and best practice. We hope that our coverage of these events will be enjoyed both by participants and by those who were unable to travel this year.

Articles by Sue Drew and Christine Skelmersdale highlight the significant increase in recommendations for Award of Garden Merit resulting from the culmination of one trial of daffodils at Wisley and two of tulips. Gardeners will also be fascinated by notes from John Blanchard and Brian Mathew on daffodils 'Cedric Morris' and 'Cecil Nice' respectively, and they will find Marjan de Boer's article on Tulip Sour instructive.

Readers interested in plant hunting will enjoy both James Akers' account of his search for daffodils in France and John Page's discussion of what is involved in finding and identifying wild tulips.

Daffodil enthusiasts will be particularly interested in Brian Duncan's comprehensive look at recent developments in trumpet daffodils and Gordon Hanks' discussion of the withdrawal of formalin. Helen Robinson, David Pink and Gordon Hanks report on research at Warwick HRI that seeks to increase stocks of new daffodils at a faster rate than can be achieved by natural increase and twin-scaling. John Gibson reminds us of John Lea and his exceptional daffodils.

Two well-known galanthophiles, Angela Whinfield and Chris Sanham, give interestingly different perspectives on their snowdrop collections and how they grow them; Colin Mason looks at the contribution twin-scaling can make to both propagating rare snowdrops and helping to contain the recent significant rise in their prices; and Michael Myers is excited by a new snowdrop discovery. As usual, Alan Leslie comments on many of the snowdrops seen at Vincent Square and given RHS awards this year.

A note by John David on the hardy nerine study day highlights the important role that the RHS can play in reducing the confusion caused by incorrectly named plants. That such problems are not confined to hardy nerines was unfortunately evident from the recent Wisley trial of small-flowered tulips, where it was clear that similar problems arise with several widely grown, botanical tulips.

This year, our comprehensive range of show reports is supplemented by a larger than usual range of book reviews and short notes about daffodil, hyacinth, snowdrop and tulip matters.

In a particularly busy year, I am grateful to all members of the Editorial Committee for their continuing support. I am particularly grateful to James and Wendy Akers for the many weeks they spend preparing printer-ready copy and distributing mail order copies of the finished work. Thanks are also due to Sally Kington for proofreading and for imposing a consistent house style on our articles; and to Gordon Hanks both for his own articles and for his expert advice elsewhere.

The publication of the *Yearbook* now involves an enormous input of voluntary effort. During the coming months we will be looking carefully at whether or how we can continue to manage this process without imposing too great a burden on only a handful of people.

Malcolm Bradbury

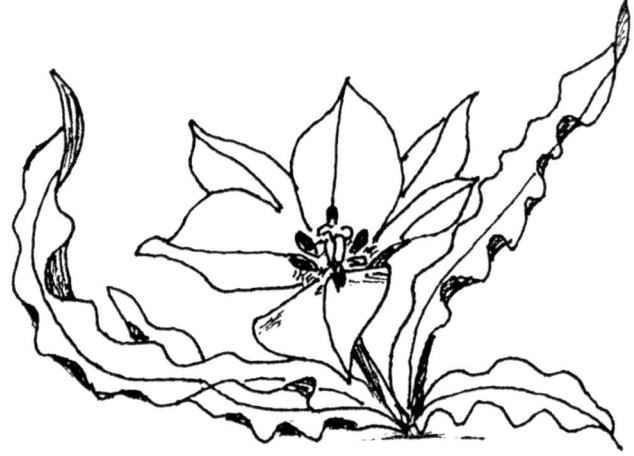

JĀNIS RUKŠĀNS BULB NURSERY

THE LARGEST SELECTION OF THE RAREST SMALL BULBS

A RICHLY ILLUSTRATED COLOUR CATALOGUE
FOR ONLY 5 US $ OR EURO BILL

Only cash or GB£ cheques please. No dollar or Euro cheques accepted

J. RUKŠĀNS, DR. BIOL. H.C.
P.O. STALBE, LV-4151 CĒSIS DISTR., LATVIA
FAX: +371-64133223
TEL: +371-29418440/+371-64133223
Email: janis.bulb@hawk.lv

Wisley Daffodil Trials
Sue Drew

The 22 entries in a trial of daffodils at Wisley were judged by the Daffodil and Tulip Trials Sub-Committee in 2007 and 2008 for the RHS Award of Garden Merit (AGM), using a scoring system out of 50 points based on the following criteria:

Maximum of 30 points for impact, grace and charm: i.e. colour; style and proportion; carriage and pose; bloom density

Maximum of 10 points for durability: i.e. weather resistance; flower life

Maximum of 10 points for constitution: i.e. plant health and vigour; plant habit

Entries 1-3 (miniature daffodils): these were grown on a plot that was single-dug prior to planting. No fertilizer was added to the site. A grit mulch was spread on top of the bulbs to aid drainage, deter slugs and maintain the cleanliness of the site.

Entries 4-22: manure was spread on their plot in July/August and subsequently rotavated with a tractor-mounted rotavator. Before planting, the ground was cultivated by hand.

All the bulbs were planted at the end of October 2006, spaced 15cm (6in) apart, in blocks of 25 double bulbs for each entry. Entries were examined for virus each spring and affected bulbs were removed.

The Trials Sub-Committee recommended that the following cultivars should receive the Award of Garden Merit subject to ratification by the Daffodil and Tulip Committee in October 2008.

Abbreviated comments from members of the Trials Sub-Committee are shown in italics and the number of flowering stems per ten bulbs relates to the second year.

N. 'Curlew' 7W-W
Raised by G E Mitsch, sent by Bloms Bulbs, Primrose Nurseries, Melchbourne, Bedfordshire MK44 1ZZ. *Very free flowering; flowers are well above the foliage.* Flowered for 24 days from 31 March 2008, with 34 flowering stems per 10 bulbs. Many of the flowering stems produced two flowers.

N. 'Garden Opera' 7Y-Y
Raised by Rosewarne EHS, sent by R E Body via Fentongollan Farm, St Michael Penkivel, Truro, Cornwall TR2 4AQ. *Super flower, a very impressive show. Star of the trial. Good longlasting flowers on strong flowering stems.* Flowered for 50 days from 20 March 2008, with 57 flowering stems per 10 bulbs. Produced three to five flowers per stem.

N. 'Warbler' 6Y-Y
Raised by G E Mitsch, sent by Bloms Bulbs. *A cyclamineus hybrid with a lovely, showy flower.* Flowered for 37 days from 27 February 2008, with 16 flowering stems per 10 bulbs.

N. 'Spring Essence' 7W-Y
Raised by G E Mitsch, sent by J S Pennings, Schorweg, 14 'De Bilt', 1764 MC Breezand, Netherlands. *Good low-growing, front of border daffodil.* Flowered for 34 days from 27 February 2008, with 19 flowering stems per 10 bulbs.

AGM subject to nomenclature
N. jonquilla var. henriquesii 13Y-Y
Selection from the wild, sent by J S Pennings. *Lovely garden plant, scented and free flowering.* Flowered for 87 days from 22 February 2008, with 62 flowering stems per 10 bulbs. Produced three to five scented flowers per stem.

Wisley Daffodil Trials

'Curlew'
(*photo* Sue Drew)

'Garden Opera'
(*photo* Sue Drew)

'Spring Essence'
(*photo* Sue Drew)

N. jonquilla var. *henriquesii*
(*photo* Sue Drew)

'Warbler'
(*photo* Sue Drew)

Narcissus 'Cedric Morris'

John Blanchard

The small yellow trumpet daffodil 'Cedric Morris' is quite widely grown by enthusiasts, is occasionally shown on trade stands and is offered in a few specialist catalogues. The story of its discovery more than 50 years ago has become folklore. Sometimes such stories improve by frequent telling, but in this case the original is quite splendid. Through the kindness of Kath Dryden, who was sorting the papers of the late E B Anderson (President of the Alpine Garden Society from 1948 to 1953), I have the original of a letter to him from the well-known painter Basil Leng, who found the original plants. A copy is reproduced in the box. From this it is clear that the find was almost certainly of a species, not a hybrid as has sometimes been suggested. It is also probable that the clump was the product of a number of seeds and not a single clone.

I do not know what happened to the bulbs sent to E B Anderson or Robert Gathorne Hardy, but I know that Sir Cedric Morris had some that he grew in his garden in Suffolk and generously distributed to several people including my father. It is likely that it was he who gave them to Beth Chatto, who registered the name in 1978 and obtained an Award of Merit for exhibition for the plant in the same year. The award cites it as a cultivar selection of *N. minor* and it is shown as such in the International Register, but I have always been doubtful. I think it is more like *N. asturiensis* than *N. minor*, particularly as it has the constriction of the corona midway along its length. The variation of *N. asturiensis* in north-west Spain is now better understood than it was three decades ago (see *Daffodils with Snowdrops and Tulips 2003-2004*) and the problem of comparison with *N. minor* is that the original description of that species by Linnaeus was from a cultivated plant of unknown origin. I have never seen *N. minor* in the wild but there are several references to it in Spanish literature, though these need to be checked as it is clear that some of them are to other species in Section Pseudonarcissus. As will be seen, Basil Leng went back later to try to see the plant again, but without success. Others have since made a fruitless search of the area but if it is still there I feel that the chance of seeing it would be remote unless one went at flowering time. How fortunate that Basil Leng found it when he did and that it has been brought into cultivation, as it is of great interest.

'Cedric Morris' (*photo* Jim Pearce)

The outstanding features of 'Cedric Morris' are its larger size and its earliness of flowering. The size of the flower is only a little larger than the variants of *N. asturiensis* commonly seen, but with upright stems of 20-25 cm it is more like variants in western Galicia. In cultivation it can be in flower before the end of October and is regularly out in the first half of November. Not surprisingly at this time of year it is longlasting, and flowers often persist well into January. It rarely, if ever, sets seed in cultivation, but this may be a consequence of its flowering time. It seems to prefer a soil on the acid side of neutral.

Narcissus *'Cedric Morris'*

Pavillon Thérèse
Chemin des Nielles
Antibes (A - M)
2.12.61

Dear Bertram

In 1955 I drove from St. Jean de Luz to Santiago de Compostela on my way to Portugal. This was between Christmas and New Year 1956.

The weather was warm and lovely all along the North coast of Spain and there were primroses out by the wayside.

If you have a map of Spain you will see that west of Oviedo the road to Coruña goes to the sea just before a fishing village called LUARCA and the sea road from Gijon joins it some few miles before Luarca. It was on the side of the road on a steep rocky bank facing south and near the viaduct of a railway that I saw a large clump of daffodils in full flower. I put my car close to the bank and tried to get at the clump by climbing on top of the car but was not successful. Just then a little girl appeared and saw what I was up to. She jumped on the car, then scrambled up the slippery bank of the hill and seized the whole clump with the idea of picking the flowers for me. What happened was that the whole clump and a lot of stones and earth came away and fell down onto the car.

So I got about 50 bulbs with leaves flowers and all and quite a lot of earth. I took this lump with me, all round the Iberian peninsular and finally returned here with it in February 1956 when it survived that month of snow and ice we had here.

During the summer when the bulbs had finally dried off I sent them to various friends in England. I did not keep any here as this climate is quite unsuitable.

Last spring I passed by that road again just before Easter, hoping to find some leaves of the daffodils, but everything including asphodels was already quite dried up owing to an exceptional dry period in all that region. There were even foxgloves in flower. Besides that the road had been widened, the bank had become a cutting and I could not recognise the place.

However I don't doubt that the Narcissus is growing in that region and presumably tends to flower in autumn or winter according to weather conditions and some one should go and search for it about now in the coast or near-coast region of Luarca where there is quite a nice hotel. But it needs quite a lot of enthusiasm as it rains so much all along there and though it probably doesn't get dark before 5.30 p.m. as it is so far west, there is that ghastly period till 9 or 9.30 p.m. before you can get your supper and go to bed and also quite a lot of bother getting breakfast in the morning. This is my excuse for not going there now to search the region for the daffodil myself. Of course I do not know if it flowers in November in its native haunts and was rather late when I happened on it in the last days of December 1955, but I gather from Cedric Morris and Robert Gathorne Hardy that it flowers with them as with you in November.

A knowledge of Spanish and a letter to the local school master and another to the Priest and perhaps the Chemist of Luarca might produce some useful information.

Lots of autumn rains here. I have a nice Portuguese mauve crocus out now and a small bright blue scilla from Tangier. Narcissus serotinus and viridiflorus both over and gone to seed.

Yours

Basil Leng

Narcissus 'Cecil Nice'

Brian Mathew

At the time of writing, in the second week of February, some promising buds are appearing once more on various small *Narcissus cyclamineus* hybrids. They are all attractive but a particular favourite is 'Cecil Nice', a bulb of which was given to me years ago by Chris Brickell. As with most of these hybrids involving *N. cyclamineus* it has proved to be an easily grown, very hardy, outdoor garden plant, although its small size - it is only about 10-15cm (4-6in) tall when in flower - also makes it ideal for an alpine house. The main point to remember if it is grown in pots is that the bulbs need watering from time to time when dormant in summer as, like the species itself, they will shrivel and die if too hot and dry.

This attractive cultivar is named after Cecil Nice who was employed from 1924 for 56 years at Nymans Garden in Sussex, taking over as Head Gardener from James Comber in 1953 and continuing in that position until he was over 70 in 1980. *The International Daffodil Register and Classified List* 1998 records *N.* 'Cecil Nice' as having been registered by John Blanchard in 1997, with the stated origin: 'believed to be a chance seedling from Sheffield Park.' This latter information is incorrect and has now been altered in the 2008 edition of the *Register*. The plant was actually found by David Masters growing in his garden when he took over from Cecil Nice as Head Gardener at Nymans. He has informed John Humphris, to whom I am indebted for passing on this information, that he then bulked it up and put it before the relevant committee but it failed to receive an award because of an insufficient number of flowering stems. He

Cecil Nice with *Rhododendron loderi* 'King George'
(*photo* A D Schilling)

also commented that after he left Nymans the area where it was growing was allotted to pigs! However, material had been distributed, so hopefully its continued existence is assured.

It was during Cecil Nice's time at Nymans that the now very popular *Magnolia* × *loebneri* 'Leonard Messel' was raised. Other plants named after him include *Magnolia* 'Cecil Nice', a hybrid of *denudata* and *M. sargentiana robusta*,

Narcissus 'Cecil Nice'

and *Rhododendron pocophorum* 'Cecil Nice'. His little *Narcissus* may not have the same dramatic appeal as these but is nevertheless a delightful cultivar well worth preserving. He was also interested in old roses and maintained a large collection of them at Nymans. This notable gardener of the 'old school' was an avid exhibitor at the RHS Shows in London and for his sustained contributions to horticulture during a long career was made an RHS Associate of Honour.

Archie Skinner, a great friend and colleague who was Head Gardener for the equally famous gardens at Sheffield Park, recalls that in addition to his horticultural skills Cecil Nice was a very good cook. The last plant Cecil saw before he died was *Gentiana sino-ornata*, taken by Archie on a visit to him in hospital.

Narcissus 'Cecil Nice' (*photo* Brian Mathew)

The National Daffodil Society of New Zealand

is the second oldest National Society in the world.

The Society produces three publications each year and is always ready to welcome as members daffodil enthusiasts from anywhere in the world. Keep up with what is happening 'down under' by becoming a member.

Details can be obtained by contacting the
SECRETARY, DENISE McQUARRIE, "BANNOCKBURN", NGATIMOTI, R.D. 1, MOTUEKA, NEW ZEALAND
Email: mcquarrie@paradise.net.nz   www.daffodil.org.nz

Narcissus provincialis: A Minor Problem

James Akers

Apart from very brief incursions from Andorra or the Spanish Pyrenees and a short trip two years ago when we saw *Narcissus poeticus* but were too late for *Narcissus provincialis*, Wendy and I had not visited France in search of wild daffodils. However a present of Eurostar tickets from our family prompted us to plan a trip in March of this year, with the initial destination of Avignon.

I was very surprised at how little had been written in recent years about *Narcissus* in France, and although John Blanchard was very helpful with potential sites, our main targets were identified as a result of internet research. Here the amount of data was extensive, with many recent and excellent photographs, including an ongoing schools project to identify all the sites of *Narcissus pseudonarcissus* countrywide. The number of different species and subspecies is less than can be found in Spain, but with just seven days allowed for the visit we opted to leave until another year the chance to see some unusual bulbocodiums in the western Gironde. Instead we chose to go east with the chance of finding *N. provincialis* and south-west for some of the rarer tazettas that have been seen there. With two weeks to go to our departure I had a stroke of luck when I came across a photograph of *N. minor* on the Club Alpine France site. As there was no indication of scale, but the flower was a white and yellow bicolor and nothing like the larger *N. asturiensis* which we have come to picture when *N. minor* is mentioned, I wrote to the site manager suggesting that it was probably *N. pseudonarcissus*. Within a few days I was contacted by the photographer Jacques Vincent-Carrefour who indicated that his photograph, taken near Grasse, was of *N. provincialis,* which French botanists consider synonymous with *N. minor*. More importantly, the day before we left he was able to provide me with two locations where they were already in flower. More of that later.

We arrived in Avignon just before midnight on 11 March and collected our hire car the following day. Our first excursion was to the north-west towards Mont Ventoux, where Esprit Requien had first cultivated his interest in daffodils, and where much later the Yorkshire cyclist Tommy Simpson met his death in the Tour de France. It is always risky making a trip to an area at the beginning of the flowering season, and unfortunately Mont Ventoux was still closed because of snow. We saw only one clump of *N. assoanus,* although the area was covered with *Hepatica nobilis* in a variety of shades and of much greater size than we can achieve in our garden.

The following day was much more fruitful. A triangular area north of the A9 between Nîmes, Vacquières and Montpellier has many recorded sites of *N. assoanus* and *N. dubius,* including several where they grow in close proximity. We saw thousands of *N. assoanus* growing on the roadsides and in the very warm sun they had attracted a number of butterflies and humming-bird moths anxious to sample the nectar. Despite many attempts, I was unable to get an acceptable photograph of a flower with a butterfly or moth. *N. dubius* was less common; however there were plenty to see on the barren hillside above the village of St Bauzille de Montmel. Although the majority were single bulbs having flowers with four or five florets, two clumps drew our attention.

Both had more upright and greener foliage than the type, which had very lax, almost grey leaves. The first clump had just two bulbs, each with two florets, one white and one yellow. The second clump was much larger but again there was a mixture of white and yellow florets. I believe these to be N. × *pujolii*, the wild hybrid between *N. dubius* and *N. assoanus*. A similar wild hybrid, N. × *koshinomurae*, also opens yellow with the florets fading to white. Having seen our three main targets of this area we chose to go no further west nor to go north to the Parc National des Cévennes, where these three flowers also grow along with *N. pseudonarcissus*, though at a greater altitude and later in the year.

Instead we drove eastwards the next day towards Grasse, via Aix en Provence and Monte Saint-Victoire, the mountain painted so often by Cézanne. We had seen photographs on the internet taken there in the same week in 2007 of both *N. assoanus* and *N. dubius,* but again the season was much later and we drew a blank. The mountain was carpeted instead with crocus just coming into bloom. We spent the night at Castellane and then next morning set off towards Grasse.

Narcissus provincialis

The first site where we knew that flowers could be found was at Col de Pilon, where we saw only one clump with white-perianthed flowers. However at the Bois de Gourdon we saw within the first 50m (54yds) in excess of a thousand flowers, virtually all from solitary bulbs. The wood is around 10 hectares (25acres) and although Jacques is not certain that *Narcissus* grows throughout the whole area, he feels that there are over 100,000 flowers to be found there. The flowers were clearly of two types, one a concolorous yellow, the other having a whitish perianth. Jacques had previously indicated to me that they were in approximately equal proportions; however in the area where we saw the flowers, the all-yellow type were in a minority. Pugsley drew attention to forms of *N. minor* growing near Grasse in his monograph published in 1933 [1], including ones in Kew Herbarium that were sent to Gay in 1820 and 1862. In 1938 he visited two areas to see them in flower, and in the following year, in a discourse on *N. minor* published in the Journal of Botany [2], described the all-yellow variant as a new

Narcissus × *pujolii?*
(*photo* James Akers)

Narcissus provincialis (*photo* James Akers)

species, *N. provincialis*, and that with the whitish perianth as *N. provincialis* var. *bicolorans*. Surprisingly, I have been unable to find any published usage of the latter name other than in the original Journal. The botanist Emile Burnat explored the Alpes-Maritimes at the end of the 19th and beginning of the 20th centuries and a catalogue of his herbarium [3] published in 1988 mentions what he called *Narcissus pseudonarcissus* subsp. *minor* (L.) Baker in two locations near Grasse, including the woods at Gourdon.

It is likely that the specimens at Kew from 1862 were from this source. In the *Flore Méditerrannéenne de la France*, to be published soon, this daffodil will be included as *N. pseudonarcissus* subsp. *provincialis*.

A roadside tazetta

On our return south-westward towards Avignon we came across a beautiful tazetta growing at the roadside in a wooded area. Being on a series of hairpins on a busy road meant that it was difficult to investigate further and the wind made photography quite difficult. A preliminary identification as *N. tazetta* subsp. *ochroleucus* was made, assuming that it was a genuine wild population.

Esprit Requien

We had allowed a full day at the end of our week in southern France to visit the Requien Museum in Avignon. We arrived there mid-morning and looked round the ground floor of the museum, which has wonderful rock specimens, sea shells and dinosaurs, all of them interests of the avid collector Requien. We were disappointed, however, with the lack of daffodil material. The upper floor of the museum has a library which is restricted to students, but I approached the information desk and asked whether it would be possible to see anything of daffodil interest up there. We were seen by a lady who apologised that the person able to give permission was absent and asked if we could return at 2pm that day.

After a visit to the Palais des Papes and a wonderful lunch we returned to be met by M. Pierre Moulet, Assistant to the Museum, who took us to an upstairs room in which was a table with a pile of folders. These were the *Narcissus* herbarium specimens of Esprit Requien and included the specimen for *Narcissus juncifolius*, from around 1810. Because the name *juncifolius* had already been used by Salisbury, the plant was subsequently named *N. requienii* by Loiseleur-Deslongchamps and now is known as *N. assoanus*. M. Moulet explained how Augustin Pyramus de Candolle,

N. ochroleucus?   *N. juncifolius* specimen
(*photos* James Akers)

who named Section Pseudonarcissus, had encouraged Requien's interest in botany while Professor of Botany at Montpellier, south-west of Avignon. De Candolle gave many of his own collected *Narcissus* to Requien for the Botanic Garden at Avignon, of which Requien was the curator. We were able to see some of the herbarium specimens of these.

Narcissus provincialis: *a Minor Problem*

M. Pierre Moulet and Wendy with herbarium specimens
(*photo* James Akers)

M. Moulet then produced another pile of *Narcissus* herbarium specimens, those of Loiseleur-Deslongchamps, which Requien had purchased in the early 19th century for 1,000F. Loiseleur-Deslongchamps, a doctor and amateur botanist from Paris, regularly visited southern France and corresponded with Requien. He is responsible for several *Narcissus* names, particularly of tazettas, including the aforementioned *N. ochroleucus*.

On the bicentenary of Requien's birth in 1788, an exhibition had been held at the museum in Avignon for which a biography was written [4]. This includes extracts of several of Requien's letters to de Candolle and Loiseleur-Deslongchamps and indicates how interesting it would be to spend more time at the museum examining in detail all the correspondence they have between Requien and fellow botanists.

Next year we hope to go to western France to look for some of the other *Narcissus* seen on the internet, including the white bulbocodiums.

[1] Pugsley, H.W. (1933). A Monograph of Narcissus, Subgenus Ajax. *Journal of the Royal Horticultural Society,* **58** (1).
[2] *Journal of Botany* **77**: 335 (1939).
[3] Charpin, A. & Salanon, R. (1985-1988). Matériaux pour la flore des Alpes-Maritimes. Catalogue de l'herbier d'Émile Burnat déposé au conservatoire botanique de la ville de Genève. *Boissiera,* **36**: 1-258 & **41**: 1-340.
[4] Moulet, Pierre (1989). *Esprit Requien (1788-1851), Essai de biographie.* Fondation Calvet, Avignon.

THE AMERICAN DAFFODIL SOCIETY
www.daffodilusa.org

invites you to join with over 1300 members around the world, to learn about the latest cultural information, hints on improving showing technique, and in-depth reports on the newest daffodils. All members receive our award winning *Daffodil Journal*, a quarterly publication.
ADS proudly offers our growing on line daffodil database, with photos, for your reference: www.DaffSeek.org

Support the work of ADS and become a member today! $20 annual dues, $50 for three years *(dollar bank drafts, made payable to ADS, please),* or use your credit card at www.daffodilusastore.org. Necessary additional international airmail postage, to send the *Daffodil Journal*, is $26 annually.
AMERICAN DAFFODIL SOCIETY, INC.
Jaydee Atkins Ager ~ Executive Director
jager@dishmail.net
PO BX 522   Hawkinsville, Georgia 31036-0522

Symposium on the World Daffodil Convention 2008

Introduction
Malcolm Bradbury

World daffodil conventions offer much more than simply seeing a lot of flowers whilst having a good holiday with like-minded enthusiasts. Delegates and enthusiasts in the countries they visit are not only exposed to new ideas but also create or strengthen friendships whose impact on the evolution of daffodil growing is felt for many years to come. The World Convention alternates at four-yearly intervals between Australia, Europe, New Zealand and the USA. In 2008 delegates could mix and match from its three venues in Europe: England, Northern Ireland and the Netherlands.

In this symposium a brief review of events in England, Northern Ireland and the Netherlands is followed by articles by delegates who were visitors to those countries: Peter and Lesley Ramsay of New Zealand write about England, David Adams, also from New Zealand, writes about Northern Ireland, and Mary Lou Gripshover of the USA writes about the Netherlands.

England

A party of 23 delegates from New Zealand and the USA made a pre-Convention tour of Kent that included visits to Noel Burr's daffodils at Rushers Cross, the village show at Lamberhurst and the South East England Daffodil Society Show at Maidstone.

On Monday 14 April they were joined in London by a further 34 delegates from Australia, Canada, England, Japan, New Zealand and the USA to meet exhibitors staging daffodils both for the competitive classes at the RHS Daffodil Show and for some displays arranged specially for the Convention.

After the Show had closed for the day on 15 April, delegates and exhibitors attended a reception hosted by the RHS, at which, after

Presentation of the Engleheart Cup by Lesley Ramsay to John Gibson, with Malcolm Bradbury
(*photo* James Akers)

Presentation of the Bowles Cup by Rod Armstrong to Tony James
(*photo* James Akers)

outlining how the role of the RHS as International Cultivar Registration Authority for *Narcissus* could be traced back to the Daffodil Conference of 1884, Colin Ellis launched the newly published *International Daffodil Register and Classified List 2008*. The President of the RHS, Peter Buckley, then presented the Peter Barr Memorial Cup to American delegates Nancy Tackett and Ben Blake in recognition of the international contribution to daffodils made by their development of the American Daffodil Society's website *DaffSeek*. A daffodil-packed day concluded with a dinner at the Civil Service Club attended by 78 delegates and other daffodil enthusiasts. During the dinner Rod Armstrong, Immediate Past President of the American Daffodil Society, made a surprise presentation of that Society's Gold Medal to Peter Ramsay. The dinner concluded with a thought-provoking talk by John Blanchard about the resilience of wild daffodils in the face of threats from human activity and the dangers caused by very inflexible rules used in the European Union to protect wild plants.

The London leg of the Convention ended the following day with a visit by many of the delegates to the RHS Garden at Wisley, which included a conducted tour, the opportunity to take part in judging the daffodil trials and a display by the RHS Herbarium of standard specimens of garden daffodils.

Northern Ireland

The Northern Ireland leg of the Convention took place between Thursday 17 April and Monday 21 April (when delegates left for the Netherlands). Highlights included the Belfast Spring Flower Show; a dinner at Belfast Castle hosted by the Belfast City Council Parks Service; and visits to Nial and Hilary Watson's home at Killinchy (Ringhaddy Daffodils) and Brian and Betty Duncan's home and gardens near Omagh.

The Netherlands

The Netherlands leg proved to be a crowded but truly memorable three days of visits. A comment from Jackie Petherbridge, a delegate from England, was that they were 'royally entertained.'

Back to England

A party of 27 delegates from the USA and New Zealand returned to England for a post-Convention tour. On Friday 26 April they met English daffodil enthusiasts at a dinner in Harrogate to mark the 30th Anniversary of the Northern Group of the Daffodil Society, where the much traveled Tony James gave an after-dinner talk about the importance of traveling and international collaboration. There was also a formal presentation to Ben Blake and Nancy Tackett of Vice Presidencies of the Daffodil Society, made by the Chairman of the Society, Jackie Petherbridge. After visiting Harrogate Show the following day, delegates viewed the daffodils at Coughton Court, visited Clive Postles to see his daffodils at Purshull Green and concluded with a visit to the RHS Garden at Wisley where the RHS Late Daffodil Competition was held.

Looking forward

World Daffodil Conventions are a win-win situation for delegates and enthusiasts alike in the countries concerned. If the normal rotation continues it will be 16 years before the Convention returns to Europe. All the more reason therefore to look forward to the 2012 World Convention, which will be held in Dunedin, New Zealand.

Editor's note: I am grateful to Terry Braithwaite, Richard McCaw and Jackie Petherbridge for their help in compiling this report.

DAFFODILS IN ENGLAND 2008
PETER AND LESLEY RAMSAY

The brief from the Editor for this article was very precise: please write about the flowers you saw in England and not the functions. So this precludes us from describing the warm welcomes and the magnificent hospitality we received from Maidstone in the South to Harrogate in the North. We were showered with hospitality; almost everyone in our group of 23 (17 Kiwis and 6 Californians) put on weight thanks to the wonderful dinners and lunches served up to us. All of us were quite overcome with the level of hospitality.

But enough of that - we know our brief, and apart from the few words which have just been written (which could have been extended to a full chapter), we will refrain from any more expressions of bonhomie and write only about the many wonderful daffodils seen in England. We are reasonably well qualified to write on this topic as we first visited England over thirty years ago. We have returned five times, and since our first small daffodil show in Walsall we have been fortunate enough to attend many of the major exhibitions as well as visit the plantings of English exhibitors such as John Lea, Clive Postles, John Pearson, George Tarry, Jim Pearce, Noel Burr, Tony Noton, Malcolm Bradbury and others.

There are four parts to this report. We begin with an account of what to us is a special feature of English shows, the ability of exhibitors to grow older varieties in a way which leads to them achieving first place in their classes and better. We will then comment on a group of cultivars which have been established for some time and are now confirmed in a category often referred to as 'bankers'. Next we identify a group of more recently registered flowers which appear to have joined the banker group. Finally we will describe some varieties which we did not note in our earlier visits and which, for us anyway, signal some important advances.

A caveat
Before proceeding, we would have to point out that this review is written from the perspective of exhibitors. We were looking for varieties which performed consistently well on the show bench and/or could be built into our breeding programme. We are, therefore, bound by the conventions of the judging manuals. Show winners are our cup of tea! Of course this does not preclude us from looking for new colour breaks or advances in the higher-numbered divisions. But what is being exhibited in the classes for twelve varieties, one stem of each, always attracts our attention first.

The oldies
Let's now be specific about the older varieties. At our first show of the tour, at Lamberhurst village, we were impressed by a lovely vase of 'Ringleader' (1972)* and a pot of the venerable 'Hawera' (pre-1928) both grown by Laurie Manser. 'Hawera' has special relevance for Peter as that was his birthplace in New Zealand, post-1928 of course! At Maidstone Len Olive produced the Lea-raised variety 'Gold Convention' (1978) to take Best Bloom in show. At Harrogate another Lea variety, 'Inverpolly' (1980), was Grand Champion for Colin Gilman.

'Inverpolly' at Harrogate
(*photo* Kirby Fong)

This was a superb flower, vying for the best seen on our tour and better. If our memories serve us correctly, it was even better than those we observed at John Lea's under seedling number all those years ago. Another oldie to achieve honours was the redoubtable 1953-registered cultivar 'Ice Wings' (Best Bloom divison 5 at Maidstone and Harrogate). It also gave us special pleasure to note the New Zealand-raised 'Trena' 6W-Y (1971) taking the honours at Harrogate; Mavis Verry would have been pleased!

One oldie, however, surpassed all of the above in terms of the number of honours earned. It was Best Bloom division 1 at Maidstone, London and Harrogate. Registered in 1964, it was of course the Tom Bloomer-bred 'Silent Valley' 1W-GWW. This variety continued a performance noted on our last visit; what a remarkable record it is achieving.

All of the above varieties have been grown here in New Zealand but, 'Trena' apart, are seldom seen on the show bench nowadays. Perhaps we discarded too early, but we do have the consolation of having many of them in the breeding of New Zealand varieties; 'Silent Valley', for example, is the pollen parent of 'Cover Story', Peter's best 1W-W to date.

The confirmed bankers

We now turn to the flowers which were viewed as bankers in 2005 and which have confirmed their places in that category. These include John Pearson's 'Sheelagh Rowan' (1989), of which Roger Braithwaite's 'five star' flower was deservedly Best Bloom in show at Wisley this year; 'Ombersley' (1985), which was included regularly in top classes; 'Moon Shadow' (1992), a fine small cup; and 'Cape Point' (1996), which with its clear colour is a top-notch pink. 'Altun Ha' (1987) is a world-renowned variety that confirmed that it is the best of its type. 'Best Friend' (1991) was noted down at several shows but our notes do state, 'excellent form but needs more colour!' 'Cherrygardens' (1978) was also seen in top form in several shows and at Noel Burr's home; it remains a very good performer in New Zealand as well.

The most successful double in this group was Brian Duncan's 'Dorchester' (1987). At its best this cultivar is stunning; we saw splendid specimens of it at several of the shows where it was in contention for top honours. This particular variety is an enigma to us. We recall the excellent group Brian produced to receive a First Class Certificate at the RHS Show the last time we were in London. We also remember the droll comment of one of the members of the Daffodil and Tulip Committee, 'let's make the award if Brian will tell us how he gets it without green backs!' Well, plenty of English growers managed to do just that, including Barry Hogg who produced a beautiful bloom to take the Best Double in show award at Harrogate. Regrettably it is a 'greenie' for most of us in New Zealand, although it has taken more than its share of premier bloom awards here.

More recent bankers

We turn now to the group of flowers which we first saw on our most recent visit in 2005 and which have moved into the group of bankers. 'Entrepreneur' 2W-GWP (2002) has to be one of the best pinks around and is definitely worthy of a place in this group. 'Chanson' 1W-P (1997), yet another pink, lived up to its reputation and is performing better than here. We will be patient! 'Lakeland Fair' 2W-GPP (1994) and 'Lakeland Snow' 2W-W (2001) also confirmed that they should be in everyone's collection.

Of this group, though, the outstanding flower had to be 'Astrid's Memory' 3W-Y (2003). The flower grown by Paul Payne which was Best Bloom in show at London was a beauty. It was, however, not the best example we saw in England. On our visit to the Old Cottage at Purshall Green Clive Postles showed us several pots of this exceptional variety. There were two flowers which were as near to perfect as we have seen: 90 points plus on our judging system! We also noted its sister seedling 'Moon Madness' 3W-Y (2006), which, though not quite as good, will seal its place in this group when more widely grown. The Australian trio of 'Tao' 3Y-O, 'Banker' 2Y-O and 'Terminator' 2Y-O are now regulars in the top classes. The last-named comes with a very rough cup in New Zealand but the specimen which took Reserve Best Bloom in show at London showed no signs of this characteristic.

The new contenders
One of the most exciting things about an overseas daffodil trip is finding new varieties which meet the criteria of show-worthiness detailed above. We have never been disappointed on earlier visits and were not this time either. Even though some of the improvements are in small increments, improvements they were. At Lamberhurst we noted two varieties for further investigation. The first of these was 'Just Joan' 2W-O, a Frank Verge-raised variety which, while it was registered some time ago, was one that we had not seen before. This was an unusual bloom which may not appeal to all judges because of its wine goblet-shaped cup, but we liked the peachy orange cup colour very much. The second was the Best Bloom in show, 'Wessons' 2Y-YOO (2007), raised by Noel Burr. This was a very smooth flower in a heavily populated division. At Maidstone a Michael Baxter seedling caught our eye, a beautifully rimmed 2W-YYR. In Frank Verge's winning Championship Class collection an impressive 1W-Y seedling was noted

This is a division which is weak in New Zealand and one in which we have been striving for improvements. We became even more interested when we discovered that Frank's variety was bred from 'Fiona McKillop'. We have turned to this cultivar in our own breeding programme and selected some promising types last year. Hope springs eternal in daffodil breeders' chests!

At the RHS Show in London the star was a weathered but beautiful Brian Duncan seedling 1W-O, numbered 3065. This produced the 'Wow' factor for us, and was the best of its type to date, with wonderful colour. 'Vivash' 4W-P (2007) was another of Brian Duncan's to impress. It was a bit on the small size, but the petals were beautifully formed. In John Gibson's winning Engelheart group we found another couple of very promising 1W-Ys. Seedling 43-10-98 was the better of the two, bred from 'Elmbridge' × 'Stormy Weather': another Kiwi connection. We also ranked his 2W-W, A17-92, very highly. Again its breeding interested us: 'Silversmith' × 'Silent Valley'.

The American-raised 'Vineland' 6Y-Y is by no means new, though we had not seen it before. A vase of three in Terry Braithwaite's winning entry had us reaching for our notebook. 'Jersey Roundabout' 4W-Y (2007) was noted at several shows but seemed rather variable in form. While split-corona daffodils are not really our thing we noted some improved varieties in this area. Perhaps the best was 'Maria Pia' 11aY-R (2006). This is one of the few areas where we would say that New Zealand has the edge, thanks to the sterling efforts of Colin Crotty. While miniatures are even less our thing we were very impressed with 'Little Kibler' 9W-GYR (raised in America about 1991 but registered in 2006); it was shown by Kathy Andersen, who had brought the bloom all the way from the USA.

On the other hand we have become very interested in intermediates. Two we noted were 'Piglet' 2O-R (Noel Burr, 2006), which had a rich coppery hue to it (we hope everyone remembers A A Milne here); and John Gibson's impeccable 2Y-R, which took the honours at London. Richard McCaw also produced a vase of three 2Y-Rs which showed a lot of promise and will have no trouble in meeting the size barrier.

At Harrogate most of the winners were well-proved varieties. However, we did note a promising 2Y-R in Roger Braithwaite's winning entry called 'Ruddy Rascal' (2004), another from Brian Duncan. Indeed, Brian has made major advances in this area. At Wisley Brian's 'Tropical Heat' (1996), not new but the first time we had viewed it in the flesh, was very impressive in several entries. We also identified his red-rimmed seedling 2627 as very promising and one to look out for in the future. 'Warwick Castle' 2Y-O (2004) was bred by Clive Postles and was, as is usual with his breeding, neatly formed and with excellent colour. We thought that this cultivar looked more like a division 3 to us and would hold strong prospects for breeding.

It became obvious at Wisley that breeders are looking to fill the gap which used to exist for late-flowering, all-yellow daffodils. 'Gamebird' (registered 2005) which won its single bloom class fell into this category. Another of Brian's which we identified as top of our 'wants list' was the beautifully coloured 'Cherry Glow' 3W-WWP (2006); being a division 3 only increased its value. While this article is starting to look like a Brian Duncan testimonial, the final flower noted was a splendid double named 'Greek Surprise' 4W-Y (2007). It will be a surprise to us if this does not continue to do well.

A brief ego trip

One of the most pleasing things for daffodil breeders is seeing their 'babies' doing well in another country. It was therefore a pleasure to note 'Blossom Lady', 'Cameo Joy' (which was the first winning flower we saw at Lamberhurst) and 'Cameo Mist' winning in their respective classes and others reaching the show bench and gaining minor placings. While these varieties have not reached the banker status as yet, when more widely grown we think they just might!

Conclusion

So there it is, another great visit to a nation where our favourite flower is still very popular. We were impressed with the quality and standard of exhibits and the number of people who are turning their hands to hybridizing. And we must note the magnificent displays put up by Johnny Walkers and his team at London and Harrogate. They were breathtaking both in scope and in bloom quality. Finally our thanks to all who made us so welcome. We hope to return soon!

Dates in brackets refer to the date the cultivar was registered.

A Visit to Ballynahatty Road
David Adams

Things have changed at Ballynahatty Road. Rathowan Daffodils is a past memory. Gone are the rows of named cultivars waiting for the bulbs to be sent to eager buyers all over the world. The field looks empty for the moment but I am sure that will not be for long. Brian Duncan is still doing plenty of daffodil crosses. There are six and a half rows of selected cultivars under trial. In the bulb shed and in a shade house, Brian grows pots of named cultivars to be used for show purposes. The skill of growing show flowers in containers reflects the preciseness evident in all Brian does.

Brian Duncan's seedling beds
(*photo* David Adams)

Some believe that the character of a man is shown in the state of his shed. Brian Duncan's tool shed is immaculate. Tools are clean and neatly hung. The empty bulb boxes are stacked away and not a speck of dirt is on the floor. This suggests a man who is organised, careful about what he does and detailed in his recording of seedling progress. Brian is ably

Brian Duncan's plunge beds
(*photo* David Adams)

supported by his charming wife Betty who welcomes visitors into their home, enables them to relax and provides an endless supply of tea and biscuits.

We observed a number of flowers marked as having been pollinated this year. The seed from these will be added to the two beds of year one seedlings. I guess that these seedlings should flower by 2012 and be commercially available in 2020. Brian Duncan plans to be around for a long time yet.

We counted seven rows of year two and three seedlings and anticipated there were about 14,000 seedlings in the rows. I was always told that around 5 per cent of seedlings are worth naming. This ratio will have improved now that better parents are available for hybridizing. This would suggest a probability of 70 additional pages in the next edition of the *International Daffodil Register and Classified List*.

There were six rows of year four and five seedlings, some of which had been marked for further trial. One assumes that these were first flowering. In addition to those marked for trial some had been pollinated. The flowers covered a number of divisions and colour codes. Those selected need to be very special to supersede the already famous cultivars raised at Ballynahatty Road.

Things have changed at Ballynahatty Road. The plunge beds have been filled and planted with miniature and species daffodils. In recent years Brian has spent many hours on the Iberian Peninsula studying daffodils in their wild habitat. He has built up a collection of species daffodils and has begun a breeding programme of smaller cultivars. At this stage most of his crosses have been interspecies but with the preciseness evident in his other work one would expect some wonderful crosses between species and cultivars to come.

What has not changed at Ballynahatty Road is the welcome to visitors. What has not changed is the breeding programme for new cultivars. Brian's cultural practices that ensure top quality exhibition flowers have not changed. From our visit it is clear that Brian Duncan and his cultivars will be around for a long time yet.

THREE DAYS IN HOLLAND
Mary Lou Gripshover

They were like a whirlwind, those fun-filled three days in Holland. We boarded the buses early each morning and returned to the hotel after 9pm each night. In between, we visited the flower auction at Aalsmeer, saw half a dozen growers, looked at quaint Dutch villages, enjoyed a dinner cruise on a canal boat in Amsterdam, viewed the Hortus Bulborum, which is a living museum of bulbous plants, and had half a day to roam through the magnificent Keukenhof Garden.

Aalsmeer Flower Auction

The first morning began with a trip to the Aalsmeer Flower Auction, where every morning tens of millions of flowers and plants change hands via the thirteen auction clocks. Through this system, 60,000 transactions take place between grower and buyer in the space of a few hours. By noon, the huge hall is empty, and the flowers are on their way to destinations around the world.

Flower auction display screens
(*photo* Mary Lou Gripshover)

'First of March'
(*photo* Mary Lou Gripshover)

The Hortus Bulborum
The Hortus Bulborum in Limmen is a treasure trove of historic and modern bulbous plants. Over 3,500 spring bulbs are on display in the fields in the shadow of a small medieval church. The Hortus was established in 1928, and in the first few decades the focus was on tulips, with only about 200 daffodil cultivars. But in about 1996, approximately 500 new daffodil cultivars were added, from the garden of the late Karel van der Veek, a well-known daffodil grower and collector. Being a man of action, Karel didn't ask; he got his three sons together, and 'just did it.'

Lots of flowers to see and people to meet
We visited the plantings of Carlos van der Veek, Arno Kroon, Jan Pennings, Hein Meeuwissen, and W F Leenen, as well as the firms of Kapiteyn and the CNB. In every case we were warmly welcomed by the entire family. Carlos still maintains over 2,500 daffodils that were collected by his father, Karel, along with his own extensive collection. I made note of 'First of March' 6Y-Y, an unregistered flower bred by Karel, and I spotted very small stocks of a few miniatures way in the back of the field including 'Medway Gold' 7Y-Y and 'Miss Klein'. Here, too, we met Theo Sanders from Germany, who had brought about 40 of his own small, colourful seedlings for us to see. Arno is a middleman between growers and exporters; he grows over 1,500 different bulbs so that people can see what is available.

At the Pennings' 'De Bilt', there were miles and miles of flowers: 'Chromacolor' as far as the eye could see; long ridges of *N. bulbocodium* in various shades of yellow; 'Kokopelli' looking good. Tucked away in the middle of all these flowers was a small planting of 'Little Bell' 5Y-Y. Ans Pennings' lovely flower arrangements graced the hall where lunch was served and an authentic Dutch street organ played music for our enjoyment.

Hein Meeuwissen grows smaller quantities of bulbs than most, and cultivates more of the smaller flowers. He says that by offering smaller quantities he gets to know his customers better. At Leenen's, we saw some of their new cultivars being tested. There were some impressive doubles, and we were told that no matter how good the flower was, if the stem was not strong enough to hold the flower up, the flower was discarded. There were also some seedlings from *N. viridiflorus* in bloom.

Kapiteyn is a family firm which breeds, grows and also sells bulbs, somewhat unusually in the business. The CNB is an organisation of middlemen who oversee the flower bulb business.

The Keukenhof Garden
The Keukenhof is the showplace of the Dutch bulb growers, and is absolutely

magnificent! The 32 hectares (80 acres) are filled with grand sweeps of flowering bulbs. Inside, the show tables to be judged were filled with great bowls of flowers. We were welcomed by Johan van Scheepen, Registrar of the KAVB, and were present at the 'baptism' of the new cultivar 'Sint (Saint) Victor'. We were privileged to be in attendance when the KAVB awarded the prestigious Dix Medal to Brian Duncan, to honour him for his outstanding hybridization work in daffodils.

Jan Pennings, writing in his opening remarks in the programme, said he hoped at the end we would say, 'It's been unforgettable.' Well, it certainly has been!

Internal and external displays at the Keukenhof Gardens
(*photos* Mary Lou Gripshover)

American Daffodil Society
Annual Convention 2010

There will be a Daffodil Convention at Murphys, California from 11-14 March 2010. The Northern California Daffodil Society (NCDS) and the Ironstone Vineyards will be co-sponsoring the Annual Convention of the American Daffodil Society (ADS). This will be an international event, a meeting of daffodil enthusiasts to bridge the years between the 2008 World Daffodil Convention in Europe and the 2012 World Convention to be held in New Zealand.

Four years is just too long between meetings of daffodil friends!
http://frodo.tackettblake.com/mailman/listinfo/murphys2010

2009 Catalogue
Available from March
Or visit our web site at

Exclusive to Bramcote Bulbs all **Clive Postles** new and recent releases, plus other top quality exhibition daffodil bulbs.
An extensive list of award winning daffodils. Divisions 1-13, miniatures, hybrids and Species, standard and species Tulips, plus other bulbs

Send 3 x 1st Class Stamps or US $1 for a catalogue or download off our website

Contact—Terry Braithwaite
105 Derby Road, Bramcote
Nottingham NG9 3GZ
Tel: + (44) 0115 9255498
E-mail rogerbb@lineone.net
www.BramcoteBulbs.com

Recent Developments in Trumpet Daffodils

Brian S Duncan

All-yellow trumpets.
In a recent discussion I had with a prominent Dutch daffodil breeder, he said, 'We don't need any more yellow trumpets, we have plenty - what we need is something new.' Obviously he was thinking primarily about the people engaged in the commercial daffodil trade, but his remarks caused me to wonder if the same could equally apply to specialists and exhibitors. Having said that, I am conscious of what a well-known scribe unwisely wrote over a hundred years ago - that daffodils had reached such a stage of perfection that continued breeding was unlikely to result in further improvement. However, the question remains 'Do we really need more yellow trumpets?'

When I think back to my own 'daffodil' beginnings (mid 1960s), my acquisitions were selected from the various popularity polls and show reports in both the RHS *Daffodil and Tulip Yearbook* and the Daffodil Society's *Journal*. I still remember with great pleasure my stable of all-yellow trumpets, which included 'Kingscourt', 'Arctic Gold', 'Banbridge', 'King's Ransom', 'Viking', 'Yellow Idol', 'Slieveboy', 'Cromarty', 'Ulster Prince', 'Golden Rapture', 'Comal' and 'Arkle'. How many of these are seen on the show bench today? How many are still available? I commend Ron Scamp who still lists at least five of them, but only three are still grown in Holland, namely 'Arctic Gold' (3.76 hectares [9.4 acres]), 'Arkle' (1.39 hectares [3.48 acres]) and 'Golden Rapture' (0.09 hectares [0.23 acres]).

So, what varieties have replaced those winning beauties of the past and what are the characteristics that distinguish them as 'improvements' or 'developments'? I have to confess that with yellow trumpets I find it more difficult to enthuse about great advancement than with some other kinds. Indeed changes have not been dramatic and may largely be the result of fashion or perhaps of some of the older stocks succumbing to virus or basal rot.

The Daffodil Society's *Summary of Prize-winning Cultivars* at the main English shows for the last two years puts 'Goldfinger' AM, AGM (1983) and 'Ombersley' (1996) clearly at the top of the list. 'Goldfinger' is consistent, longlasting and seldom has nicks in the very broad petals, which, though of great substance, are annoyingly incurved at the edge; it resists and resents any kind of manipulative grooming. I have not grown 'Ombersley' but I have observed it often during judging and it has all the required show qualities combined with great size; but it is in a very different style, somewhat like an improved 'Golden Rapture' AGM or 'Arkle' AGM. The third on the list in the past two years has been 'Rathowen Gold' - how or why I do not know! Though it was raised by Tom Bloomer, I think I was responsible for registering it, but only after considerable soul searching. It may have show qualities, and excellent size and colour, but with rather narrow petals it lacks elegance and style and is certainly not an improvement on most of those on my starting list. Interestingly, these three poll-toppers are all related: they all have 'Camelot' and 'Arctic Gold' AGM as grandparents.

Also in the *Summary of Prize-winning Cultivars* were 'Chobe River' (1985), 'Disquiet' (1993) and 'Ethos' (1993). All can be excellent, and my favourite is perhaps 'Chobe River', the result of deliberate crosses trying to re-establish dramatically flanged trumpets. With a generous flange and slightly waisted narrow trumpet it is a prettier bloom than many of its class. It inherited this elegance and broad perianth from its unusual grandparents ('Joybell' 6W-Y × 'Empress of Ireland' 1W-W), which also account for its paler than ideal colour. The Tasmanian 'Disquiet' might well be the yellow trumpet of the future. Several magnificent specimens have been shown at English shows, one of which I was certain would be Best Bloom in Show but to the amazement of myself and several others, and to the consternation of the exhibitor, only got second prize in its class; seemingly it was thought to be too big! Having grown it for a few years I can vouch for its consistency, and it seems to like our wet climate though I have been told it does not like warm dry conditions. 'Disquiet' is the new blood stud in my current yellow trumpet breeding programme. 'Ethos' is a flower I will continue to grow; it is a reliable journeyman without stirring the heart, though I saw a wonderful specimen in New Zealand shown by Kevin Kerr that made me proud to have raised it. 'Ethos' is somewhat similar to 'Disquiet' in form and has a much longer stem so I await the children from their mating with interest. One well-known London exhibitor prefers 'Ethos' to 'Goldfinger' because of the flatter petals. It was good to see that old favourites 'Viking' AGM (1956) and 'Comal' (1968) sneaked into the list of prize-winners.

What then of the future? Can we expect dramatic improvement or change of style? I suspect not, but I do hope we find that flowers with expanded, flared and frilled trumpets make a come-back. The current crop of fairly straightish trumpet cultivars has arisen because they have a lesser tendency to produce nicked petals and have therefore been much used as breeding parents, either deliberately or unconsciously. Personal preferences will ensure demand for both 'stove-pipe' and 'flanged' trumpets. I feel sure that other breeders have seedlings under trial as I do which are inching their way towards even more perfect and varied flowers, so that those currently at the top of the poll may fairly rapidly be replaced.

Amongst my own seedlings, the very different 'Gatecrasher', with a very generously flanged trumpet, and 2360 ('Francolin' × 'Gold Bond'), which has a straight trumpet, may have their moments of popularity and provide useful breeding material for the future.

'Gatecrasher'
(*photo* Brian S Duncan)

The new 'Temba', which has already two Best Bloom awards to its credit, is of formal style and epitomises consistency, which is likely to be the keynote for future breeding activity.

I have just checked my seedling records and I was surprised to find that I still have 17 selected 1Y-Y seedlings under trial. I think there are a few good ones in that lot but Mr W J Dunlop told me many years ago something that I have found to be true, that yellow trumpets were amongst the most difficult to assess because they varied so much from year to year. Nevertheless, my '50 per cent per year discard rule' still needs to be applied rigorously!

'Temba'
(*photo* Brian S Duncan)

In New Zealand, John Hunter's 'Sulphur Monarch' (1995) and Peter Ramsay's 'Centor' (2005) are winning prizes and showing promise.

The popularity of yellow trumpet daffodils is emphasised by the number of entries in the American Daffodil Society's excellent *Daffseek* facility on the internet. There are almost 1,900 cultivars listed and detailed. It would seem that every daffodil hybridizer in the world has bred and registered yellow trumpets and will continue to do so.

Yellow and red trumpets

Referring back to my beginnings again, I often heard people talk about 'red trumpets' and of course I aspired to grow them. Later, impetus was added when 'Hero', an advance in its time, hit the headlines with a £100 price tag. I did search out many of the originals and found them to be rather rough, disappointing and certainly not very 'red'. *Daffseek*, to which I referred above, tells me that only 7 of the 79 entries have been registered as red, all before 1970 and all being Backhouse cultivars with the exception of 'Oregon Trail' (Tribe 2004). Best known of the seven would be 'Desert Fox' and 'Sutton Court'. I well remember seeing and coveting 'Oregon Trail' as seedling 16/1 in Bill Tribe's field in 1994. Though not the ultimate, it was of better form and certainly the nearest to red that I had seen at that time. From earliest days one of my dreams was to produce a really good red trumpet, so I was most grateful to Bill Tribe (my worm-brother, but that's another story, involving Tequila!) for his generosity in letting me have one of the first bulbs of 16/1 as I had known it for so long; it has been the backbone of my breeding programme.

The first 1Y-O daffodils were registered just over 50 years ago in 1956 by W O Backhouse. The table shows the history of the development of division 1 daffodils with orange and/or red trumpets by charting some of the best known registrations by decade - again I am indebted to *Daffseek*.

Pre-1980	12	'Dalinda' 1956, 'Deseado' 1956, 'Red Curtain' 1956, 'Brer Fox' 1959, 'Red Arrow' 1968, 'Glenfarclas' 1976
1980s	9	'Jamboree' 1982, 'Hero' 1984, 'Hacienda' 1985, 'King's Grove' 1987, 'Corbiere' 1988
1990s	18	'Uncle Duncan' 1991, 'York Minster' 1991, 'Cheetah' 1996, 'Nederburg' 1997, 'Ruddynosey' 1997, 'Magic Lantern' 1998, 'Jimmy Noone' 1998, 'Aunt Betty' 1999, 'Boyne Bridge' 1999
2000s	20	'Chingah', 'Feline Queen', 'Thunderhead', 'Tyree' (all 2002), 'Dunstan's Fire' 2003, 'Cutting Edge' 2004, 'Kingstanding' 2004, 'Red Reed' 2004, 'Oregon Trail' 2004, 'Morab' 2005', 'Okakune' 2005, 'Proud Fellow' 2005, 'Pumpkin Ridge' 2005; 'Longitude' 2007, 'Resistasol' 2007, 'Royeleen' 2008

I have selected for inclusion in the above list only those with which I am familiar, those that have appeared as prize-winners or those about which I have read reports or seen pictures. I apologise for any omissions. The summary clearly shows that interest in orange and/or red trumpets is accelerating as progress is made in both form and colour. The record indicates that there are almost 20 breeders worldwide who have registered 1Y-Os since 1990; and Fred Silcock from Australia who is reputed to have some excellent flowers is not amongst that number. That surely means that we can expect fairly rapid progress and that soon 1Y-Os will be able to compete on equal terms with any other colour group.

The road to the current standards has been long and slow. We all owe a debt to the Backhouse family for providing the early breeding material. I acquired most of their flowers and later added 'Hero' and the Australian 'Hacienda'. George Tarry and John Reed in America were both working on red trumpets and each kindly let me have one or two of their seedlings which I have used in breeding. Problems encountered in breeding were that the largest flowers were rough, and the brightest and best formed were small and of questionable trumpet measurement.

For many years I have been saying that amongst my 'red trumpet' seedlings I had achieved my main objectives, namely good colour, good size, good form and full trumpet length. Alas, not all qualities are combined in the one bloom as yet! However, the building blocks are now there and a few seedlings in the pipeline show some advancement. I have been pleased that some recent introductions have been good enough to appear in winning early-season Engleheart Cup groups: 'Chingah', which is large, consistent and vigorous but is only mid-orange in colour; 'Feline Queen', similar but smoother and also lacking really vibrant colour; and 'Tyree', which has excellent colour and form but is slightly small and sometimes does not measure full trumpet.

Interesting flowers as future breeding studs, which I think might help to progress this group, are Noel Burr's 'Dunstan's Fire' for colour and 'Kingstanding' for sheer quality and size; Clive Postles' 'Cutting Edge' for colour and form; and perhaps strangely the 1Y-Y 'Disquiet' (see above), which has the trumpet maturing to orange and has size, smoothness and form to spare. Currently, the pollen of seedling 2866 ('Tyree' × 'Nederburg'), which shows a lot of promise, is being liberally spread around.

In New Zealand, the 2008-registered 'Royeleen' (Roy Wilcox), bred from 'Corbiere', is making a name for itself. It has wonderful size and form but has hardly enough colour.

Seedling 2866
(*photo* Brian S Duncan)

Finally, I think the so-called red trumpets are a most important group for development, not only for the specialist and exhibitor but also for commercial exploitation. Already we are finding that they are far more sun-resistant than most of their division 2 counterparts - a fact noticed by several Dutch visitors to my seedling beds. I think we should back-cross them to the most sun-resistant of the large cups to obtain flowers which just do not burn in the sun; what an exciting prospect! For how long have we been crying out for such flowers?

Yellow and pink trumpets

Though daffodils with yellow petals and pink coronas are a recent concept for many people, it may be surprising to learn that in the *International Daffodil Register* there are already

'Longitude'
(*photo* Brian S Duncan)

nearly 40 distinct cultivars listed. These have come from 18 breeders from around the world, the first to be registered being the unaptly named 'Red Conquest' 1Y-P from David S Bell of New Zealand in 1970. Bell registered a further four cultivars, all with 'Red Conquest' as a parent, but none of them seem to have made an impact on the world stage. Also early on the scene were H R Barr's 'Prophet' 1Y-YYP (1975), smooth but pallid, which I remember seeing as a breakthrough at a London show, and P and G Phillips' brighter but rather rough 'Chitose' 1Y-P, which I have grown; but I have not seen any noteworthy progeny from either of these flowers.

The real progress came in the late 1970s when Grant Mitsch in Oregon produced 'Memento', 'Lorikeet' and 'Fidelity' by crossing 'Rima' 1W-P with 'Gloriola' 2Y-W, both of which had Radcliff's 'Dawnglow' 1W-P in their pedigree.

My own chance seedling 'Rosegold' recorded as from 'Daydream' × 'Reverie', two reverse bicolors, had a spell of popularity in its class and has been a useful breeder.

The next generation brought the renowned 'American Dream' 1Y-P (1989) and 'American Heritage' 1Y-P (1993), both of which have excellent yellow and pink colouring and have been good enough to win Best Bloom awards at major shows.

More than a dozen cultivars have been registered this century, of which I confess I do not have intimate knowledge as many have occurred in far away places. Such well-known breeders as John Hunter (New Zealand), Fred Silcock (Australia), Dr John Reed, Dr Bill Bender and Steve Vinisky (all three USA) and W F Leenen (Holland) have all made contributions. Of my own recent introductions, I think 'Bronzewing' 1Y/W-P, with its unusual white central stripe in the petals, and 'Juano' 1Y-P show some exhibition promise and much needed vigour in this class, obtained through the influence of John Lea's 'Filoli'.

In addition to those recently registered, I have seen some excellent seedlings in the fields of Fred Silcock (near Melbourne) and David Jackson (Tasmania) and I have no doubt there are excellent things to come from other areas now that suitable breeding stocks are available. The yellow and pinks have arrived in all their glory and in full colour. They can hold their own with the best and even the many doubters are finding them acceptable, but watch this space - the best is yet to come!

'Juano'
(*photo* Brian S Duncan)

Reverse bicolor trumpets

I fear I may not be qualified to report progress in this category. I did grow 'Spellbinder', the first reverse bicolor trumpet to be recognised, registered by Guy L Wilson in 1944, also the subsequent Mitsch varieties 'Entrancement' and 'Nampa' (both 1958) and 'Honeybird' (1965). Then followed Carncairn's 'Gin and Lime'. But I confess that I found them all a bit disappointing. Either the colour contrast was not clearly defined or it took too long to develop and generally they were a pretty rough bunch. Then came 'Trumpet Warrior' (1990), beautifully smooth, consistent and well-contrasted, if slightly small. It seemed that the Mitsch family would continue to dominate the class that they had developed from the original 'Spellbinder'. However, in 1995 John Pearson registered a rival, 'Lighthouse Reef', which hit the show benches with a series of Best Bloom awards. These two, now being in the hands of quite a few growers, are vying for top position, but in the last ten years John Pearson has registered a further ten cultivars several of which have been winning prizes. Who knows which of these will emerge as leader of the band: 'Lubaantun' with its lovely yellow rim or 'Chesapeake Bay' (both 2001); Lazy River' (1998); 'English Caye' (1997); or the more recent 'Satchmo' (2004), which has wonderful contrast. Most, if not all of these have 'Camelot' in their background and that is a great plus for most growers, giving substance and vigour. However, the few I have tried have too much substance in my combination of wet climate and heavy clay soil and do not smooth out as I would like. But, my goodness, John Pearson has raised the bar in reverse bicolor classes, both in division 1 and division 2.

All-white trumpets

In this group I fear I am unable to point to any really significant development. I cut my teeth on cultivars 'Cantatrice', 'Kanchenjunga', 'Broughshane' and, when I could afford it, the wonderful, the magnificent, the superlative and as yet largely unsurpassed 'Empress of

'Lubaantun'
(*photo* John Pearson)

Ireland', all raised and registered by Guy L Wilson more than 50 years ago. This is incredible considering that *Daffseek* records 840 white trumpets, including 145 registered in the last 20 years and 45 since 2000 - all of which indicates that though breeders have been busy in this category it would seem that no dramatic development has taken place. Indeed, the white trumpet class used to be one of the great contests at the London and Daffodil Society shows when 'Empress of Ireland' vied with her children 'Panache', 'White Prince' and the Tom Bloomer whites, 'White Empress', 'White Majesty', 'White Star' and 'Silent Valley', all of which had the smaller but beautifully smooth 'Rashee' as seed parent.

In the Daffodil Society's *Summary of Prize-winning Cultivars* for 2006, 'Silent Valley' is the overwhelming leader, a fact which I find surprising as I was in on the early development of Bloomer white trumpets. Tom regarded 'Silent Valley' as a bit of a joker with its very long slender trumpet, and, as I did, much preferred 'White Star', which had many Best Bloom awards. Alas, 'White Star' only grows well in the cool north and is now seldom seen, whereas 'Silent Valley', with bulbs coming in directly from Holland, has hit the top spot. Its illustrious parent is still in second place, followed by John Pearson's 'Quiet Waters', a very smooth flower but one that I feel does not quite look trumpet in character.

A flower that impressed in New Zealand was 'Snowy Morn', registered way back in 1985 and bred by amateur Welly Monroe using 'White Prince' and the pink 'Passionale'.

Of newer things, 'Nightflight' (Postles 1996) had a great initial impact that caused many of us to put our hands in our pockets, but it seems to have faded from the scene. My current favourite is 'Bridal Chorus' (Mitsch 1992), which can be truly magnificent but is not quite consistent - which may be the same for other would-be usurpers of the crown of the 'Empress of Ireland', still the template of consistent white trumpet that had the form of 'Empress of Ireland', the glistening whiteness of 'White Empress' and the smooth texture and substance of 'White Star' - that remains an unfulfilled ambition.

'Empress of Ireland'
(*photo* Tony James)

White and yellow trumpets

With the not very impressive 'Bravoure' (Dutch origin 1974) topping the 2006 Daffodil Society *Summary of Prize-winning Cultivars*, followed by 'Apple Honey' (1995), 'Cristobal' (1968) and the Australian 'Clubman' (1995), one might wonder if any real progress is being made in this division. This is surprising as there has been so much breeding activity, with approximately 60 of the 600 cultivars being registered within the last 10 years; but it probably illustrates the difficulty in breeding top class 1W-Y flowers.

I have personally raised many hundreds of unsatisfactory seedlings from leading flowers of the past, going back to 'Preamble', which had a long reign, 'Pennine Way', 'Newcastle', 'Dunmurry', 'Chief Inspector' and the Australian 'Pontes'. Despite the many crosses, it was an open-pollinated seedling from 'Pontes' that produced 'Queen's Guard' (1997),

'Snowy Morn'
(*photo* Brian S Duncan)

my ideally formed trumpet daffodil of whatever colour or colour combination. Many years ago I wrote that I would like to raise a

'Queen's Guard'
(*photo* Brian S Duncan)

which, if I can be excused a little bias, may be the best 1W-Y to date.

It already has several Best Bloom awards to its credit and I think is a genuine step forward in this division - time will tell when it is more readily available. Meanwhile 'Pops Legacy' and 'Predator' should still give a good account of themselves.

Many of the progeny of 'Queen's Guard' show great promise and I have many selected seedlings under trial, with 'Fiona McKillop', 'Predator' and 'Chief Inspector' as the other parents. Perhaps the frustrating 1W-Y breeding difficulties are at long last behind us, largely through the influence of the Tasmanian bloodline created by David Jackson, who has long been a prolific breeder of bicolor trumpets. Some of his newer cultivars may well set new standards when more widely grown; we should look out for 'Macdalla' (2001) and 'Newcrest' (2005).

White and pink trumpets

When I started growing daffodils, pink trumpets were practically unknown in the United Kingdom. My research indicates that there is not a single 1W-P registration from any of the major British and Irish raisers, whether the Brodie of Brodie, J L Richardson, G L Wilson, W J Dunlop, J S B Lea or Sir Frank Harrison. By contrast, in Australia, particularly Tasmania, breeders such as C E Radcliff, S J Bisdee and the Jackson family have between them named over 80 cultivars since 1930. In those early days I imported 'Karanja' (Radcliff 1942) and 'Rima' (Mitsch 1954) to be followed by 'Eiko' (Phillips 1977), 'Brookdale' (Pannill 1978) and 'Melancholy' (Jackson 1980). None of these encouraged me to use them much as parents and it was not until I got 'Cryptic' from David Jackson that I really felt I had promising breeding material. However, Grant Mitsch used 'Rima' extensively and produced 'Fidelity', 'Memento' and most important of all 'At Dawning' 1W-P (1975), which when crossed with 'Graduation' 2W-WWP gave 'Pink Silk' (1980), the present run-away leader in the 1W-P section of the Daffodil Society's *Summary of Prize-winning Cultivars*. This was an inspired cross: 'Graduation' was a child of the leading white trumpet 'Empress of Ireland' and 'Accent' was the brightest of all pink daffodils at that time.

In second place was my own 'Edenderry', which combines David Jackson's 'Camden' 1W-P with 'Bright Flame', Barbara Abel Smith's flower with amazing colour and a longish cup. I think that 'Edenderry', if well grown, can win many more prizes but I favour 'Chanson' ('Verran' × 'Algarve') or 'Korora Bay' ('Dailmanach' × 'Cryptic') to outstrip it when they are more widely grown. These have replaced 'Cryptic', which has been a disappointing parent, as my 1W-P studs.

The challenge now is to add even deeper pink, even a red-pink colour, to these trumpet kinds. If the *Daffseek* picture is reliable perhaps Steve Vinisky has already done this with his 2002 registration 'Pink Passion', and John Hunter's 'Pink Topaz' looks as if it is a flower worth checking out. We can also be sure that David Jackson has some lovely things in the pipeline and I am keen to see his 'Pukka' (2002). However, David Jackson and Jamie Radcliff tell me that 'Pink Belladonna' (1992),

'Chanson'
(*photo* Kirby Fong)

raised by Des Tongs, is probably still the best 1W-P in the land of their origin. Perhaps we need to try it in the northern hemisphere.

I am not familiar with many of the twenty or so registrations since 2000 but any of these may be winners in future. Certainly the building blocks are in place and I expect rapid and exciting developments in pink trumpet daffodils.

White and orange trumpets
It will be noted that the subheading says 'orange' rather than 'red'. There are no 1W-R registrations and I think red trumpet daffodils with white petals are still a long way off, unless we get the red from pink breeding lines, which seems more likely.

The paucity of 1W-O flowers may be surprising when we consider that the orange colour in the trumpets of the quite numerous 1Y-R flowers has the same *N. poeticus* origin. Indeed I have seen in the wild a natural hybrid between *N. abscissus* and *N. poeticus* (*N.* × *montserratii*) which had a fairly long cup, so I suspect that early breeders tended to favour adding orange or red to yellow rather than white petals. It is idle to speculate what the early 1W-O registrations such as 'War Cloud' (Sir Heaton Rhodes 1912) and 'Quip' (Guy L Wilson 1938) looked like. Likewise for the Dutch introductions which followed between 1968 and 1984, of which all trace seems to be lost and nobody seems to have used them for further breeding.

The most exciting things came from Tasmania: Jamie Radcliff's 'Crucial Point', with its deep orange stove-pipe trumpet, which he followed with his 'Hawley' series - all bred from seedlings (including one of Fred Silcock's) so we do not have much of a clue about their backgrounds. 'Goldspie' (1999) had 'Crucial Point' as a parent. John Reed in America registered 'Scott Joplin' 1W-O in 2002, the best formed true trumpet in this category that I have seen. It has old 'Preamble' twice in its parentage and the 2W-O 'Johann Strauss', a vigorous and colourful, longish-cupped 2W-O but certainly not a show flower. So the double influence of 'Preamble' is important on two scores, quality and length of trumpet.

'Crucial Point'
(*photo* Kirby Fong)

Fred Silcock has been working for many years at Mount Macedon in Australia, primarily on every colour combination of trumpet daffodils and we have seen some promising orange-trumpet pictures, with both yellow and white petals. However, few get to see Fred's flowers, he seldom exhibits at shows and he is not yet prepared to release any of his newer recent developments. But news reaches us that he has the best flowers in this category and it is to be hoped that he will soon make them available for wider appreciation.

My own efforts have been minimal because of the scarcity of suitable parents. I have used the long-cupped 'Crown Gold' 2W-O from Elise Havens and the even brighter 'Lutana' 2W-O from Jamie Radcliff and crossed them with 'Queen's Guard' and 'Chief Inspector'. From these crosses there are a couple of seedlings that show some promise, at least for further breeding.

I pin a lot of faith on 'Scott Joplin' as a future parent, which I have crossed with my own seedlings, and in future I will also go back to 'Lutana' and 'Crucial Point' (if I can find it) for back-crossing. I also hope to add Mitsch Daffodils' 'Orange Supreme' to the breeding stock - it has trumpet ancestors! Once trumpet length has been truly established then we can risk using some of the deepest coloured 2W-Rs in breeding programmes.

I see exciting developments ahead and I think we may again find that sun resistance is better in these trumpet flowers than in the white and orange cultivars currently registered in division 2.

Conclusion

I do not pretend that the above notes are comprehensive as I cannot possibly have full knowledge of all developments throughout the world. Obviously there are unregistered seedlings in growers' fields that will emerge in due course and invalidate many of my comments. This is as it should be. No doubt others will have different opinions on the current situation and I trust breeders will pardon me for any glaring oversights.

What Will Daffodil Growers Do Without Formalin?

Gordon Hanks

Daffodil growers are alarmed by the prospect that they will not be able to dip their bulbs in formalin after 2008. Formalin has been an essential part of our battle against basal rot (base rot) and stem nematode (eelworm), probably the two most destructive conditions suffered by daffodils.

An effective treatment
In the 1930s it was demonstrated that dipping daffodil bulbs in cold water containing formalin for about 30 minutes soon after lifting was an effective way of managing basal rot caused by the fungus *Fusarium oxysporum f.sp. narcissi*. Around the same time, formalin was shown to be an effective pesticide for stem nematode (*Ditylenchus dipsaci*) at hot-water treatment (HWT) temperatures, usually 44.4°C (112°F); adding it to the HWT tank increases the speed of kill of 'free-swimming' nematodes. Professional (commercial) bulb growers have long been advised to dilute one volume of Commercial Formalin to 200 volumes with water (say, 1 litre of Commercial Formalin into 200 litres of water) and use this for dipping bulbs, whether as a cold dip (against basal rot) or HWT (against basal rot and stem nematode), as formalin is ineffective against nematodes at room temperature. Formalin for horticultural or agricultural use has been produced by various companies, is known as 'Commercial Formalin' and contains 38-40 per cent of formaldehyde. Few of us liked formalin's acrid smell and effect on nose and eyes, but with ventilation, protective clothing and common sense, any unpleasantness could be minimised or avoided. Research, and years of practical experience, testified to the benefits of dipping bulbs in formalin.

A change in the law within the European Union
The European Commission *Review Programme for Existing Active Substances* (i.e. pesticides) has resulted in drastic curtailment of the numbers of fungicides, insecticides and herbicides available to farmers and growers, and for amateur (home/garden) use the choice is even more restricted. Up to now, professional growers have been able to use formalin to help control basal rot and stem nematode. But in June 2007 the Commission withdrew authorisations for about 100 'miscellaneous' substances, including formalin, effective 22 December 2007 with a 'period of grace' (a 'use-up existing supplies-by date') of 22 December 2008. The year 2008 is therefore the last in which formalin may be used for horticultural/agricultural purposes in the European Union. Despite a vigorous campaign on behalf of United Kingdom bulb growers by the Horticultural Development Council and others, it proved impossible to reverse this decision, or even to obtain an 'Essential Use' derogation for a few years while alternative pesticides were sought. For further information on legislation, see the Pesticides Safety Directorate web-site http://www.pesticides.gov.uk/home.asp and follow the links to 'PSD Databases'. This decision by the Commission may be not unconnected with a conclusion of the International Agency for Research on Cancer, part of the World Health Organization, that formalin should now be considered 'carcinogenic to humans' rather than 'probably carcinogenic to humans', despite arguments that the evidence used to justify this decision was sparse (see the following websites):

www.iarc.fr/ENG/Press_Releases/archives/pr153a.html
www.formacare.org/fileadmin/formaldehyde/Word_docs/Scientific_Fact_Sheet_18.12.06_01.doc

The search for alternatives to formalin

When doubts were raised about the safety of formalin in the 1980s and its use was restricted in the USA and elsewhere, sporadic attempts were made to find an alternative to it for use in daffodil growing. Urgent trials funded by the Horticultural Development Council are now under way in a joint ADAS and Warwick HRI project led by Mike Lole and Gordon Hanks. Following the laboratory screening of various candidate materials, two promising products are being tested on a farm scale in summer 2008 at Kirton, and the results will be available in 2009-2010. Alternative methods of treatment that might obviate the use of pesticides or disinfectants altogether, such as microwave, dry-heat or UV treatments, were considered by researchers but rejected because of the high likely costs of development.

Possible alternatives to formalin

Without formalin, and as yet without any formalin substitutes, the following alternatives can be suggested.

1. Rely on HWT alone

As mentioned above, formalin is added to the HWT tank to increase the speed of kill of 'free-swimming' nematodes (those that leave the bulb and are carried round in the dip). It is not always appreciated that the high temperatures alone should be sufficient to kill nematodes in the bulb, formalin being added because the 'free-swimming' nematodes are relatively more resistant to heat. With no formalin or formalin-substitute available, it will be more important than ever to ensure that HWT is properly done. This means:
(a) keeping to the correct HWT temperature and timing regime (see Box 1);
(b) not storing bulbs at warm temperatures (20°C [68°F] or above) and not allowing bulbs to dry out before HWT, both of which encourage multiplication of nematodes and their change into 'wool', a resistant form that appears like pinheads of off-white wool on the outside of the bulb near the base and escapes into the HWT dip.

2. Rely on HWT alone but use a hotter HWT

Even the regular HWT regime can damage flowers and leaves slightly, but this disadvantage is more than outweighed by the benefits of pest and disease control. Any increase in temperature or duration of HWT can increase damage. Nevertheless, many commercial growers do use hotter HWT - the standard Dutch HWT for stocks known to be infested with stem nematode is three hours at 47°C (116.6°F). In the United Kingdom a treatment at 46°C (114.8°F) for three hours can be used, though in this case bulbs are warm-stored and pre-soaked before HWT, which limits the damage caused. Using hotter HWT would be entirely at the owner's risk. It would be crucial to know that the tank temperature was calibrated, controlled and monitored accurately.

3. Rely on HWT and add a fungicide

Where the concern is to control basal rot and other fungal diseases as well as nematodes, it is likely that a fungicide is added to the HWT tank. Although various fungicides have been added with this in mind, only Storite Clear Liquid (containing thiabendazole) is approved for the purpose, though it would be the material of choice if there were a choice! Storite is available only to commercial growers. As always, the directions on the label, especially regarding the rate of usage, recently revised, should be followed. By coincidence, this material was originally introduced as a nematicide in animal husbandry, and trials showed that, when mixed with formalin, it gave better control of stem nematode than using formalin alone. Using a fungicide could be combined with using a hotter HWT (see 2).

4. 'Jet 5' quick dip

The horticultural disinfectant 'Jet 5' (containing 5 per cent peroxyacetic acid [aka peracetic acid] and 25 per cent hydrogen peroxide) is used for cleaning surfaces and equipment. It was tested as an HWT additive for controlling basal rot spores and stem nematodes, and was found to be as effective as formalin for both purposes when used at the appropriate dilution under experimental conditions, with tanks made up fresh and used only once [1]. Anecdotally 'Jet 5' was used by bulb growers, but it was found that the dip rapidly lost its effectiveness under practical conditions. Since no further information was forthcoming from the agrochemicals industry, this use could not be recommended. The EC review that withdrew approval for formalin also withdrew approval for peroxyacetic acid, though in this case the United Kingdom was allowed a derogation until 31 December 2010 for its use, they said, as 'an agricultural fungicide/nematicide and as a disinfectant for plant protection purposes' on flower bulbs. However, the relevant approval states 'flower bulbs . . . must be immersed for one minute in a 50:1 dilution of proprietary 5% w/w peroxyacetic acid formulation.' The temperature of dipping is not stated, and the effectiveness of such a quick dip has not been tested experimentally, though any effects would be almost entirely superficial. At some stage the treated bulbs would also need to receive HWT for control of nematodes and pathogens within the bulb. Daffodil bulbs should never be cold-dipped without formalin or an alternative, since fungal diseases will be spread in the dip.

5. Rely on cultural controls

Unfortunately, options 1 to 4 are available only if there is access to HWT facilities and professional pesticides. Without these advantages, 'cultural controls' will be needed (see Box 2) until alternative materials or methods become available.

Addendum

During the preparation of this article the fungicide 'Cercobin WG' (containing thiophanate-methyl) was granted specific off-label approval (SOLA) for use as a 30 minute dip against *Fusarium* diseases in ornamental bulbs by professional growers. This material is of the same class of fungicides as 'Storite', so daffodil bulbs may benefit from a cold dip shortly after lifting. Certain restrictions apply when using an *off-label approval*, for example they are applied at the grower's risk. To avoid the possible spread of nematode, formalin (or in the immediate future an alternative) should be added to cold dips.

Box 1: Daffodil HWT essentials
- HWT bulbs at the correct time - mid-July (south-west United Kingdom) to early August (east and north United Kingdom), and certainly no later than late August
- Earlier treatments are usable and may give better control, but there will be some damage to next year's flowers and leaves
- Ensure accurate temperature calibration, control and monitoring of the dip
- Tank design - ensure high and even flow rates within the tank
- Control the formation of foam (avoid sucking air into pumps; use an anti-foam preparation)
- Use the standard treatment of three hours at 44.4°C (112°F), timed from when the water temperature regains 44.4°C after the bulbs have been added to the tank or (at your own risk) a higher temperature (up to 47°C [116.6°F])
- Add a non-ionic wetter and (if basal rot control is required) Storite Clear Liquid at the recommended rates (these may only be available to professional growers)
- After HWT, ensure rapid ventilation, cooling and surface-drying of bulbs
- Plant bulbs promptly (or store at 17-18°C [62.6-64.4°F]) with a good air flow until planting

Box 2: Cultural controls to help nematode and basal rot control in daffodils
- After lifting, surface-dry the bulbs rapidly in a few days using a high air throughput and air temperatures no higher than 20°C (68°F), e.g. choose a cool period for bulb lifting or stack bulbs in trays in a windy position. This is especially important when dealing with basal rot-susceptible cultivars
- Do not allow bulbs to dry out excessively as this will encourage stem nematode to change into the resistant 'wool' stage
- Store bulbs at 17-18°C (62.6-64.4°F) with a good air flow; higher temperatures will encourage stem nematode multiplication and basal rot spread
- Consider planting later in September when soil temperatures have fallen
- Do not use a high rate of nitrogen fertiliser as it encourages basal rot
- Observe a long rotation period (minimum of six years) between daffodil crops
- Inspect leaves regularly for signs of stem nematode ('spikels') and, if found, remove and destroy all plants within 1m (3ft 4in)
- Consider early lifting (before soil temperatures rise to summer levels)

[1] Hanks, G.R. & Linfield, C.A. (1999). Evaluation of peroxyacetic acid disinfectant in hot-water treatment for the use control of basal rot (*Fusarium oxysporum f.sp narcissi*) and stem nematode (*Ditvienchus dipsaci*) in *Narcissus*. Journal of Phytopathology, **147**: 271-279.

Gordon Hanks was a bulb specialist at Warwick HRI, Kirton, Lincolnshire and is now a part-time freelance consultant.

John Gibson
Daffodils

Top quality bulbs
of exhibition, miniature,
and specie daffodils

Write, Phone or Email
for a free copy of our
new catalogue

14 Waverley Road
Kettering. Northamptonshire.
NN15 6NT

Tel : 01536 523350
Email : gibbo.john@ntlworld.com

UK *Narcissus* Crop Improvement Research
A Rapid *Narcissus* Micropropagation Technique

Helen Robinson, David Pink and Gordon Hanks

The United Kingdom *Narcissus* industry is the largest in the world, producing bulbs and flowers both for the home market and for export to Europe and the USA. A significant problem for the industry is the slow multiplication rate of *Narcissus*, meaning that it can take between 25-30 years to produce sufficient bulbs for the commercial release of a new variety. The Department for the Environment, Food and Rural Affairs (Defra) is currently funding a project at Warwick HRI (HH3729SBU - Crop Improvement of Narcissus) to increase the rate of multiplication by using a micropropagation system. The aim is to produce up to 1,000 bulbils from a single bulb in 18 months.

The microprop system under development uses small, clear plastic bioreactors called Rita ® Bioreactors that were developed by Cirad (Fig. 1). They work on a temporary liquid immersion system whereby the liquid growth media in the bottom chamber is forced up to the tissue in the top chamber by pumping sterile air through the central filter. This continues for the duration of the immersion time, when the pump switches off, allowing the media to return to the bottom as the air pressure equilibrates through the second offset filter (Fig. 2).

Explants

The explants or starting material for the bioreactors are bulbils taken from cultures called shoot clusters (Fig. 3). Shoot clusters are produced under sterile conditions from bulbs that have been stored at 15°C (59°F) for at least three months then prepared by removing the brown scale leaves and cutting back a lot of the old brown basal plate. The bulbs are given hot-water treatment for 30 minutes at 50°C (122°F) to activate fungal spores easily accessible by the water. The neck of the bulb is then cut off to reveal last year's dead flower unit, the new terminal bulb unit (TBU), which produces the next flower, and any daughter TBUs that might be present. The bulb can be cut open down the line of the old flower unit and the new TBUs removed (Fig. 4). The TBUs are surface-sterilized in a 10 per cent bleach solution for 30 minutes on a shaker to kill any pre-germinated fungal spores activated by the heat treatment, then they are rinsed thoroughly in sterile distilled water. The explants or starting material for the shoot clusters can now be cut out of the TBUs and are about 1cm (0.4in) high, made up of scale leaves, leaf base and flower scapes attached to about 1.5mm (0.17in) of basal plate; it may be possible to obtain three of them from a variety with a big bulb like 'Golden Harvest'. These explants are then put on to a special growth medium which promotes shoot multiplication. It can take up to four months for good shoots to grow, which are then cut off and placed on fresh growth medium. Once established, they are the shoot clusters which provide the starting material for the bioreactors. They need to be re-cultured every eight weeks by cutting back the green shoots to 1cm (0.4in) of the bulbil, cutting the bulbil in half and transferring to fresh media.

Optimising the bioreactors

To optimise the conditions in the bioreactor system, we have experimented with single, double or triple bulbil explants, with the

UK Narcissus *Crop Improvement Research*

Fig. 1 Rita Bioreactor
(*all photos* Helen Robinson)

Fig. 2
Diagrammatic representation of media flow in Rita Bioreactor. Liquid growth media in the bottom chamber (1) is forced up to the tissue in the top chamber by pumping sterile air through the central filter (2). This continues for the duration of the immersion time (3), when the pump switches off and the media returns to the bottom as the air pressure equilibrates through the second offset filter (4)

Fig. 3 Shoot cluster culture

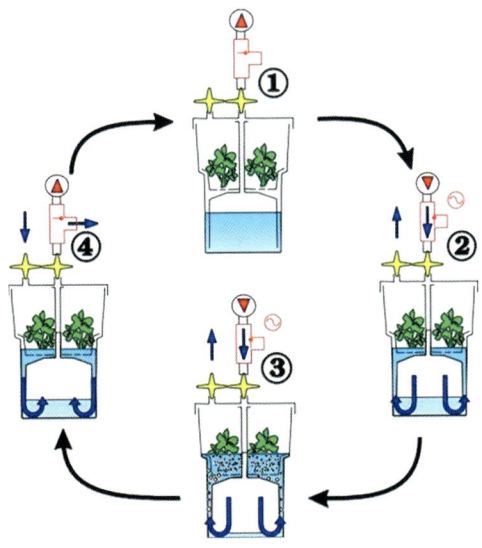

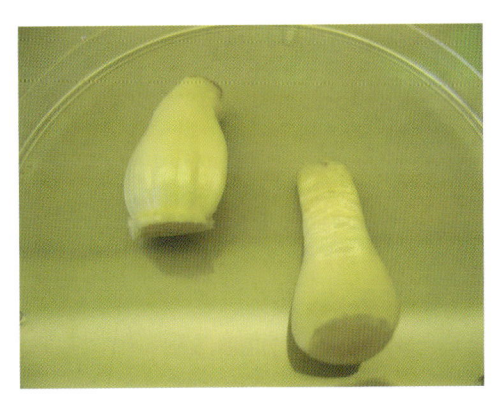

Fig. 4 Terminal base units extracted from *Narcissus* bulbs

number of explants per bioreactor (one, two, four, eight or sixteen), with the number of immersions per day, the temperature of the growth room containing the bioreactors and the growth substances in the growth medium. From this we have developed an optimised system starting with eight single bulbil explants per bioreactor which are immersed ten times a day and grown at a temperature of 16°C (61°F). Some varieties respond better than others by producing more bulbils, and we have experimented into the use of a compound called Ancymidol to increase multiplication rates. This is a growth retardant that has been found to prolong bud division in *Hosta*. From the results it appeared that for 'Saint Keverne', which generally produces a lot of bulbils, there was no increase in bulbil production with Ancymidol, whereas for 'Golden Harvest', which usually gives lower numbers of bulbils in bioreactors, Ancymidol significantly improved bulbil production. We are now trialling this compound with other, more modern varieties of *Narcissus*.

Weaning bulbils into soil

After two rounds of culturing on the multiplication liquid media the bulbils are given a bulbing liquid media step for six weeks. This has twice the amount (60g [1.67oz]) of sucrose in it and is designed to make the bulbils grow larger and produce roots. Once they get to around 1cm (0.4in) in diameter, they can be weaned into a compost mix of two parts peat-based compost developed at the Glasshouse Crops Research Institute and one part John Innes No.1 potting compost in small pots in the glasshouse or a Dutch Light frame. We still have to carry out work to improve the acclimatisation rate of the bulbils and to determine how quickly they can be grown from 1cm (0.4in) to the 3-4cm (1.2-1.6in) size that *Narcissus* growers can put into their nursery beds. However, although some varieties respond better than others, the micropropagation system we have developed can be successfully used to multiply *Narcissus* varieties more rapidly. To test it, new varieties obtained from growers and breeders are now being trialled in the optimised bioreactor conditions. For them, the rate of increase ranges from 4 to 12-fold.

Does tissue culture induce any change?

Because there are reports of tissue culture causing genetic change, the shoot cluster-derived bulbils from the bioreactors will need to be assessed for uniformity. This will be done by observing the characteristics of plants when they flower and by a technique called Amplified Fragment Length Polymorphism (AFLP), which is similar to that used by forensic scientists when they construct a DNA profile to identify criminals. So far we have not produced any bulbs that have flowered from shoot clusters in the bioreactors. However, in a previous project bulbils were produced through a different form of tissue culture called callus culture in the bioreactor system. These were planted out into the Dutch Light frame for assessment (Figs 5 and 6) and have been growing long enough to flower. We have assessed these and also tested them using a colorimeter to measure the colour of flower parts and leaves. The colorimeter is a specialized machine similar to those used to measure the colour in DIY stores when paint is being mixed to match a sample of material, etc. For both 'Saint Keverne' and 'Golden Harvest' callus culture appeared to produce no significant variation, the tissue culture bulbs looked very similar to bulbs produced by traditional techniques and there was no significant difference in their DNA profiles. This work will be repeated on the shoot cluster-derived bulbs when they flower, but all the evidence is that if change does occur, it is more likely to be from callus cultures than other forms, so we do not expect there to be any problems.

Fig. 5 Tissue culture bulbs growing in Dutch Light frames

Fig. 6 Comparison of 'tissue culture' and 'natural' bulbs

John Sydney Birch Lea
John Gibson

John Lea of Stourport belonged to an old Worcestershire family and was descended on his mother's side from the renowned botanist Sir Joseph Hooker. He was born in 1911. Although an accident with explosives at school caused him to lose the thumb and forefinger of his right hand, he became an accomplished engineer. Unable to join the military during the war, he worked in Birmingham on defusing unexploded bombs. It was when hostilities ended that John started attending the Midland Daffodil Society's Show, rapidly becoming a leading exhibitor and winning most of the major trophies.

John Lea started to hybridize daffodils as early as 1946, using the best available cultivars as seed parents and gratefully receiving gifts of pollen from Lionel Richardson and other leading breeders. He was fastidious in research, record keeping and analysis of what outcomes he was seeking when making a cross. Every cross was the product of study, reasoning and experience. He rarely pollinated more than four flowers of a cross and only occasionally repeated a cross. The quality and significance of the 130 registered daffodils raised by John Lea were a remarkable achievement given the small scale of his programme, the limited land available at Dunley Hall and the fact that until his retirement in 1971 he could only attend to his hobby at the weekends. At the RHS Daffodil Show he won the Engleheart Cup for one stem of twelve different daffodils raised by the exhibitor in 1971, 1973 and continuously between 1975-84; he was the first Englishman to defeat the Richardsons in this contest for 40 years.

John Lea is remembered today by many enthusiasts for the improvements he made to the intensity, depth and purity of colour in exhibition daffodils from divisions 1-4 and for raising arguably the first significant division 1 daffodils of exhibition quality with yellow perianths and either orange/red or pink trumpets. However, as has become clear since his death, John Lea's lasting legacy is a select group of cultivars that have proved to be good parents when used worldwide by contemporary hybridizers.

Some important daffodils raised by John

A very graceful, all-white, large-cupped daffodil resulting from the 'Ave' × 'Early Mist' cross John Lea made in 1953 was **'Canisp'**. 'Best Bloom in show on five occasions at RHS daffodil shows and competitions, 'Canisp' did much to establish his reputation as a major hybridizer of show daffodils.

In 1955 he bred two good all-white flowers 'Ben Hee' and 'Inverpolly' (see page 20). It was 'Inverpolly' which, when crossed with pollen from a pink-cupped seedling, resulted in **'Dailmanach'**, a successful show flower and exceptional parent used by many hybridizers to

'Canisp' in 1983
Best Bloom in London when shown by Noel Burr
(*photo* George Tarry)

improve the white perianths of pink-cupped daffodils. Meanwhile, 'Inverpolly' still shows its class and impeccable form as an exhibition flower after 50 years, winning the Grand Champion award this year at Harrogate Show.

John Lea's many superb yellow and orange/red daffodils included 'Bunclody', 'Loch Naver', 'Loch Hope', 'Achduart', 'Torridon' and **'Loch Lundie'**, the latter proving to be a key source of vigour and strong colour. He was also a successful raiser of white and red daffodils, of which 'Borrobol', 'Halgarry', 'Hartlebury', 'Invercassley', 'Cairntoul' and 'Royal Marine' are particularly well-known. An unusual success in 1976 was in three small-cupped daffodils, 'Dunley Hall', 'Evesham' and 'Loch Alsh', raised from a single pod of seeds.

In 1968 John Lea made two key breakthroughs. In his quest for division 1 flowers with orange/red trumpets, he raised **'Glenfarclas'** 1Y-O, a borderline trumpet of the required size and colour. He also raised **'Gold Convention'** 2Y-Y, an all-yellow trumpet that varied between divisions 1 and 2 and had exceptionally good form; this was perhaps his most celebrated flower. Both flowers have proved to be important parents used extensively by many hybridizers. In 1988 Clive Postles named and registered **'Corbiere'**, a wonderful yellow and orange trumpet raised by John from 'Gold Convention' × 'Glenfarclas' that did much to establish the credibility of such flowers as exhibition daffodils. Similar comments can also be made about John Lea's yellow and pink trumpet daffodil **'Filoli'**, another one named and registered by Clive Postles.

John Lea's legacy

John Lea died unexpectedly whilst on holiday in Scotland in 1984. Fortunately for daffodil enthusiasts and gardeners, his daffodil stocks and seedlings were not lost. His friend and fellow hybridizer Clive Postles took over the collection and continued to select and introduce many fine new daffodils from it.

Several Lea flowers still form the benchmark for exhibition daffodils, with 'Dailmanach', 'Gold Convention', 'Corbiere' and 'Achduart' leading the prize-winning cultivars in their respective categories in 2007. A number are good garden plants, with the RHS giving the Award of Garden Merit (AGM) to 'Aberfoyle', 'Ben Hee', 'Glenfarclas', 'Gold Convention', 'Grasmere', 'Loch Owskeich' and 'Special Envoy'. Above all, John Lea's work with daffodils has given contemporary hybridizers new options to explore and key parents with which to work.

As part of the World Daffodil Convention, a display of Johns Lea's daffodils in the Lawrence Hall at the RHS Daffodil Show illustrated his hybridizing work. Prominent amongst the exhibits were outstanding vases of 'Evesham', 'Dailmanach', 'Gold Convention' and 'Corbiere'. Great credit is due to Sharon McDonald, International Daffodil Registrar, and all the team involved in putting on the display.

'Gold Convention' in 1991 Best Bloom in London when shown by Paul Payne (*photo* George Tarry)

Awards to People
Malcolm Bradbury

During the last year Nancy Tackett and Ben Blake of the USA have been awarded the Peter Barr Memorial Cup by the Royal Horticultural Society (RHS) and been made Vice Presidents of the Daffodil Society; James Akers of England has been awarded the MBE in the Queen's Birthday Honours List; the American Daffodil Society (ADS) has awarded its Gold Medal to Peter Ramsay of New Zealand; and the Royal General Bulb Growers' Association (KAVB) has awarded J F Ch Dix medals to N A Nijssen of the Netherlands and Brian Duncan of Northern Ireland. In their varied ways, each of these people has 'made a difference' to horticulture and to the popularity and enjoyment of daffodils and tulips. We offer our congratulations to all of them and briefly highlight their key achievements.

Nancy Tackett and Ben Blake

Nancy Tackett and Ben Blake are well known to daffodil enthusiasts for their ongoing work both on *Daffnet* and the ADS website. However, in a major new contribution to the daffodil world they have taken Steve Vinisky's disc of the ADS *Illustrated Data Bank*, supplemented it with material from the *ADS Data Bank* and the *International Daffodil Register* and created *DaffSeek*, the daffodil photo database sponsored by the ADS. Given its extensive photographic content and ease and speed of use, *DaffSeek* has proved a great help to daffodil growers, hybridizers and enthusiasts.

The Peter Barr Memorial Cup is awarded annually by the RHS on the recommendation of the Daffodil and Tulip Committee to 'someone who has done good work of some kind in connection with daffodils.' Whilst making the award to Nancy and Ben at a reception in London to mark the publication of the *International Daffodil Register and Classified List 2008,* the President of the RHS, Peter Buckley, commented on the now rather archaic wording used to describe such a significant contribution to the development and enjoyment of daffodils. He also noted that this was the first time since the inception of the award in 1912 that it had been awarded to a team of two. Nancy and Ben were also honoured at Harrogate by being made Vice Presidents of the Daffodil Society.

Presentation to Nancy and Ben by Peter Buckley
(*photo* James Akers)

James Akers

James Akers is well-known to readers for the many weeks he voluntarily spends each year preparing printer-ready copy of the *Yearbook*, for subsequently holding stocks of the publication and for distributing it by mail order. Readers will also have seen his interesting articles on tulips and accounts of his searches for wild daffodils. Members of the Daffodil Society will be well aware of the significant contribution he has made over many years to the editing and preparation of their publications. However, it is for 'voluntary service to tulip horticulture' that James was awarded the MBE in the Queen's Birthday Honours List this year. When I telephoned to offer my congratulations, James' first reaction was to point out the strong and longstanding involvement and support he had received from his wife Wendy.

James became interested in tulips because of his father, who had joined the Wakefield and North of England Tulip Society before the Second World War. He won his first prize as an exhibitor at the Society about 60 years ago, and returning north in the 1970s, after working in the south of England for a decade, became an active member. He has been an officer for 30 years, formerly as treasurer and now as secretary and editor. James grows 3-4,000 Florists' tulips and with a few other stalwarts of the Society distributes bulbs to members, bulbs that have not been commercially available for 50 years. He is also an active hybridizer of Florists' tulips, and 'Rory McEwen' (see back cover) is perhaps the best-known of his raising. James is author of two books: *The English Florists' Tulip*, co-authored with two other members of the Society, and *The English Florists' Tulip: Into the 21st Century*. James was very heavily involved with the Society both in setting up a Gold Medal-winning exhibit on the genus *Tulipa* at the RHS in 2003 and in organising the 'Old Flames' exhibition of tulip paintings and artefacts at the Yorkshire Sculpture Park in 2006.

James joined the RHS Daffodil and Tulip Committee in 1993 primarily as a 'tulip' member. Highlights of his contribution to committee business have included visits to the Netherlands in the 1990s to help assess tulips for the RHS Award of Garden Merit, representing the committee at the first World Tulip Summit in Ottawa in 2002 and chairing the working group on a very successful Tulip Day held in 2003.

Peter Ramsay

At the World Daffodil Convention dinner in London, Rod Armstrong, Immediate Past President of the ADS, presented that Society's Gold Medal for services to the daffodil, to Peter Ramsay. Peter is a past president of the National Daffodil Society of New Zealand and currently edits their publications. He is a well-known hybridizer of daffodils mostly from divisions 1 to 4 and for many years was a partner with Max Hamilton in Koanga Daffodils. A meticulous and very successful exhibitor, Peter is a well-respected show judge and his assessments of daffodils, published worldwide, have a dedicated following. Above all, Peter and his wife Lesley have used their

James Akers
(*photo* Wendy Akers)

Peter Ramsay
(*photo* Mary Lou Gripshover)

many daffodil visits to Australia, the Netherlands, the United Kingdom and the Unites States both to promote close links between enthusiasts and to spread awareness of the flowers and the growing practices that they have encountered.

N A Nijssen
At the annual meeting in the Netherlands of the KAVB Commission on Nomenclature, the Chairman of the KAVB, Sjaak Langeslag, presented the J F Ch Dix Medal to N A Nijssen to honour his outstanding work as a tulip hybridizer. Mr Nijssen worked as hybridizer at A Nijssen and Sons, Sandpoort, and raised the very successful, double yellow tulip 'Monte Carlo' AGM 1993. A popular forcing tulip of which over 700 hectares (1,750 acres) were grown when at its peak in 1997-8, 'Monte Carlo' (see back cover) was then the most widely grown tulip in the world. Indeed, 185 hectares (457 acres) are still grown today.

'Monte Carlo' gave rise to many sports, including 'Abba', 'Viking' and 'Monsella'. The well-known tulips 'Ohara', 'Cairo', 'Carola' and 'Ted Turner' AGM 1999 were also raised by N A Nijssen. He was an active member of the KAVB's Tulip and Gladiolus Committee and his collection of seedlings was passed to Vertuco Ltd, a group of companies hybridizing tulips.

The Dix Medal is awarded by the KAVB to 'someone who has done outstanding work in the field of hybridization of bulbous crops.' It is named after John F Ch Dix, an early pioneer in modern commercial tulip hybridization.

Brian Duncan
During the World Daffodil Convention in the Netherlands, the Chairman of the KAVB, Sjaak Langeslag, also presented the Dix Medal to Brian Duncan of Northern Ireland, honouring his outstanding work as a daffodil hybridizer. The raiser of about 500 registered daffodil cultivars, Brian is a well-known exhibitor of show daffodils, past chairman of the RHS Daffodil and Tulip Committee and

Presentation of the Dix Medal by Sjaak Langeslag to Mr Nijssen
(*photo* Johan van Scheepen)

frequent participant in daffodil events worldwide. In their citation, the KAVB drew particular attention to the many cultivars of his that are grown commercially in the Netherlands because of their suitability for forcing and growing. They also commended his active role in spreading his knowledge of daffodils and his ideas about hybridizing them.

Brian Duncan
(*photo* Johan van Scheepen)

Galanthomania, Chipping and Twin-Scaling

Colin Mason

Looking back at catalogues from the 1970s, when admittedly there were only a limited number of snowdrop varieties offered for sale, the top price for a bulb was £1.50. Even allowing for inflation, prices have soared. Up to 2007, top-rated snowdrops were changing hands at £50 a bulb, and when single bulbs were auctioned they fetched about £70. Snowdrop sellers are sometimes accused of avarice and profiteering, to which their defence is that demand for the choicest varieties is such that they have to try to limit it by increasing prices.

This year, things have really got out of hand. Two bulbs have been sold on eBay, one at £130, the other for over £200. The moment a newly named variety gets publicity, there is huge demand for it, regardless of price. But for most enthusiasts, the exotic varieties are now simply out of reach. We have not reached the frenzy of tulipomania - yet - but seem to be heading that way. Something can be done, and ought to be done, to slow things down.

The natural increase of snowdrops by offsets is too slow. Increase by seed is quicker, but the resulting bulbs will not be true to type.

Use of tissue culture (micropropagation) to increase numbers involves skilled staff working in a laboratory environment. Recent research to develop tissue culture for snowdrops, funded by the Horticulture Development Council (HDC), has been very successful [1]. Species and hybrids of *Galanthus nivalis*, *G. elwesii* and *G. plicatus* were used in this study. The project arose from the demand both for large quantities of ordinary snowdrops to fill a gap in the gardening market and for small quantities of the rarer hybrids.

Chipping and twin-scaling

It is likely to be some time before tissue-cultured snowdrops are available, and there will always be enthusiasts wishing to multiply their own bulbs. Fortunately, propagation by twin-scaling, or in the case of snowdrops, what is known as chipping, can in time supply their demands. The technique has been known for a surprisingly long time. H P Traub published work on the propagation of *Hippeastrum (Amaryllis)* by 'stem cuttage' in the 1930s [2]. In his 1959 book *Dwarf Bulbs for the Rock Garden* [3], E B Anderson attributes 'chipping' to T H Everett, to whose book *The American Gardener's Book of Bulbs* [4] he refers. It does not seem to have been practised much in those early days, perhaps because of a more limited interest in snowdrops, uncertain results with the fungicides then available, and the use of peat as the growing medium before vermiculite became available.

The modern technique of twin-scaling bulbs is based on a 1982 Growers' Bulletin from the Glasshouse Crops Research Institute [5]. The procedure has been published many times, and is therefore not repeated here [6]. It was widely used on snowdrops in the mid-1980s, and unlike tissue culture can be easily carried out by amateurs on the kitchen table, with cheap materials, simple equipment, reasonable eyesight and a steady hand! Methods vary slightly, but most of us have used vermiculite and a fungicide containing the active ingredient carbendazim, though the latter is being withdrawn. The use of a fungicide is essential if the rotting of chips or twin-scales is to be avoided, and several other fungicides are available to commercial growers and a more limited range to amateur growers.

It is usually advocated that only healthy bulbs are selected for chipping, because any fungus or virus disease will be passed on. In practice, however, we often have no choice but to work with diseased or damaged bulbs, particularly those affected by the fungus *Stagonospora curtisii*. In fact, many rare varieties on the point of dying can be saved, so long as there is part of the base plate remaining and the central stem is still healthy.

If I acquire a rare snowdrop variety I invariably chip it when the leaves die down. I find this much safer than hoping the bulb will survive the next dormant season. All varieties can be chipped, though some slow-growing types, such as *G. cilicicus* and the 'spikies' [7], take longer to grow after chipping. It took me three attempts with *G.* 'Boyd's Double' before I succeeded. In a very few cases, perhaps three or four per cent, the process fails altogether at the first attempt. This is usually due to a diseased bulb or one that has not had the chance to build up strength after flowering.

When chipping, I nowadays peel off the brown tunic or outer scales before cutting off the roots. If, as is often the case, there are one or more offsets half-formed, these can be cut away carefully with a piece of base plate attached and sometimes a root or two. It is important not to tear offsets off, as they will break away above the base plate. Potted up in pockets of sharp sand in normal snowdrop compost, they will usually grow into flowering bulbs in a couple of years, adding insurance against the rare event of a failure in the chipping process.

The number of chips which can be cut depends on the size of bulb. With the tiniest bulbs, only 5mm (0.2in) diameter after stripping off the tunic, six to eight chips can be cut. For an average-size bulb of 15-18mm (0.6-0.8in) diameter, 15 to 20 chips can be obtained, depending on whether one prefers to cut fewer thicker chips or more numerous thin ones. For the largest bulbs it is possible to divide the larger chips into twin-scales, and obtain 30 or more pieces. We used to discard the top of bulbs when chipping them, but recently it has been found that new bulbs can grow from 'pips' which form on the top, and they can go into the vermiculite with the normal chips.

It is gratifying to find in nearly all cases that bulblets have formed on all the chips at the potting-up stage; though occasionally a small percentage is still 'blind'. In theory bulblets form at the junction of the bulb scale and base plate, but occasionally one or more additional pips will appear along the edge of the chip. These cannot be separated from the chip, which is simply potted up with the rest. I do not know if these odd growths eventually form bulbs.

The photograph shows the growth from chips in one year. Often bulblets do not put up a leaf in the first growing season, but will do so in the second year. Bulblets from large chips should reach flowering size in three years, whereas those from fine-cut chips will take

Snowdrop chips
(*photo* Colin Mason)

four. Attrition during these growing years reduces the final yield of flowering bulbs to 75-95 per cent of the original number of bulblets. It follows that, from a single bulb of a new variety, re-chipping after the first three years, it takes at least six years to have even a small quantity to give away or sell. There is no evidence that repeated chipping weakens the stock, in fact it is often found that chipping puts vigour back into the variety I must emphasise that the figures quoted are only from my experience; I do not know what other people obtain - possibly quite different results.

In theory, vegetative propagation by chipping should produce identical clones of the original variety. However, in very rare cases with hybrids, only two in my experience, a proportion of the bulbs produced revert to the features of one of the varieties in the original cross. For example, some five per cent of *G.* 'South Hayes' bulbs flower with no marks on the outer segments and without the characteristic 'pixie hat' shape. These bulbs do not come true in later years. Even odder things can happen to liven things up, as the inset to the photograph shows, where one chip bears yellow stamens..

Conclusion

Chipping is a very satisfactory method of propagation for the quantities of snowdrops required by enthusiasts, and the objective of this article is to encourage more people to try it. If, for one reason or another, they cannot do it themselves, I urge them to entrust the rarer varieties to experienced 'chippers'. Some people are afraid, if they do this, that they will not get all the progeny back, though this would be tantamount to theft. Owners of bulbs will very often agree that the chipper may keep one or two or even 50 per cent of the progeny in return for their services. In the case of private owners, if the chipper has a customer base, it can be agreed that a percentage of sales is remitted. In the case of very rare varieties 'owned' by friends in the snowdrop trade, if I am entrusted with a bulb to chip, I have long made it my practice to offer all surplus progeny back, and I believe this approach has encouraged rare varieties to become more widely available.

I thank the HDC for permission to refer to their snowdrop project, and Gordon Hanks for his helpful comments on the text.

[1] Selby, C., Staikidou, I., Hanks, G.R. & Hughes, P. (2005). *Snowdrops: Developing cost-effective production methods through studies of micropropagation, agronomy and bulb storage*. Final Report on Project BOF 48, Horticultural Development Council, East Malling.

[2] Traub, H.P. (1935). Propagation of *Amaryllis* by stem cuttage. *Yearbook of the American Amaryllis Society*, **2**: 123-126.

[3] Anderson, E.B. (1959). *Dwarf Bulbs for the Rock Garden*. Thomas Nelson, London. See also Alpine anthology. Bulb cuttings. *AGS Bulletin*, March 1962, 12-13.

[4] Everett, T.H. (1954). *The American Gardener's Book of Bulbs*. Random House, New York.

[5] Hanks, G. & Phillips, S. (undated). *Twin-Scaling*. GCRI Growers' Bulletin No. 6, Glasshouse Crops Research Institute, Littlehampton.

[6] For example: Hanks, G. (1991). Chips off the old bulb. *The Garden*, **116** (8) 442-446; Wiltshire, T. (2003). *Galanthus* Conservation Project: Dumlugöze, Turkey, *Daffodil, Snowdrop and Tulip Yearbook 2003-2004*, 44-46; Mackenzie, R. (2003). Twin scaling snowdrops and miniature daffodils. *Daffodil, Snowdrop and Tulip Yearbook 2003-2004*, 47-48.

[7] Snowdrop enthusiasts use the informal term 'spiky' to refer to mutant doubles with multiple narrow segments facing upwards, such as 'Boyd's Double' and 'Hanning's Horror'; they are either loved or loathed!

Further details may be obtained from Fieldgate Twinscaling: cmason@twinscaling.com

How I Grow Snowdrops
Angela Whinfield

Ian and I have lived at Snape Cottage for 20 years, and I have grown snowdrops in the garden for the last 18 of them.

Plant history, natural history, colour and form are the things which interest me and have influenced the development of the garden since our arrival here, but the site itself is the reason the garden has evolved as it has. The ancient rural landscape of Dorset is visible from the house, and I have made a garden which, hopefully, sits happily in that landscape and blends rather than jars with it.

Our garden
The garden slopes gently towards the south-east with a long view over the fertile Blackmore Vale, Thomas Hardy's 'Vale of Little Dairies'. The soil is a sandy loam with a pH of 7.3. Its main feature from a gardening point of view is that most of the 0.27 hectare (0.67 acre) site is blessed with an underground network of natural springs. I never water the garden - all plants are simply planted in the aspect which suits them best. Snowdrops love moist soil. Indeed, *G. nivalis* grows in carpets outside the cottage, and the happiest clumps are in the ditches either side of the lane, which are often 225mm (9in) deep in water.

We are lucky to have a variety of aspects and situations. In addition to dry shade, and well-drained soil in sun, there are large areas of moist soil, both in sun and shade. It is this moisture that most of the garden hybrid snowdrops revel in, although the *G. elwesii* types are planted in slightly drier, more open situations, wherever there is room.

Snowdrop cultivation
All varieties are lifted, divided and replanted on average every three years. When replanting, I replace congested clumps with seven or nine of the largest bulbs, spaced 75mm (3in) apart and 75mm (3in) deep. Each new planting receives a small handful of bone meal to provide some extra nourishment. All plants are carefully and clearly labelled!

I dead-head all snowdrops in the borders. This prevents seedlings occurring and therefore some potentially exciting finds, but it keeps the named cultivars accurately preserved. I have, however, planted duplicates of my favourite snowdrops in the front garden, on the lane and in the meadow areas. I encourage these to seed as freely as they wish and hope for something special to appear one spring.

Since our arrival in 1987, I have top dressed the garden every autumn with fish, blood and bone and then a generous 100mm (4in) mulch of our own compost [1]. We start cutting down and preparing the spring areas in October using our own compost on the north-east corner and all along the west-facing wall to the deep-shade beds further down. The snowdrop collection is planted throughout these areas and receives shelter from silver birch, *Ilex* 'Scotica', medlar, apple, crab apple and hawthorn as well as various old-fashioned shrubs. I also have a large number of *Helleborus* × *hybridus*, many obtained from the nursery of Mrs Ballard in the 1980s and 90s. I use each hellebore as a 'marker' for snowdrops that I plant at north, south, east and west, with the hellebore in the centre. This has worked very well indeed, so far. Other plants of association include hepatica, for which, in my experience, good drainage is the most important requirement and they thrive near tree trunks or on raised beds; *Cyclamen hederifolium*; numerous ferns; and *Narcissus* 'Bowles's Early Sulphur'. The hermaphrodite Butcher's Broom (*Ruscus aculeatus*) - from East Lambrook - is always smothered in large red berries for our Snowdrop Sundays. The long winding stems and yellow, netted leaves of *Lonicera japonica aureoreticulata* give added interest when draped over the Ruscus.

I am fascinated by the names and stories surrounding the gardeners who have gone before us, and am always thrilled to be given a plant with the assurance that 'This came from Mrs Fish, who received it from Mr Bowles.' Such plants forge a link with the gardeners of yesteryear and I particularly treasure plants handed down in this way. Snowdrops seem to be especially associated with tales of (often eccentric) people long gone.

Some snowdrops planted in special groups
I plant some of my snowdrops in special groups, partly to remind me where they are most likely to be, but also because I feel pleasure in the continuity with previous gardeners. For example, my *Helleborus* × *hybridus* 'Bowles' Yellow', which I received many years ago from Myddelton House (E A Bowles' former garden at Enfield), is surrounded by snowdrops associated with Mr Bowles himself. Similarly, I have a 'Cornish Corner' containing as many of Phil Cornish's exquisite introductions as I can find: 'Hoverfly', 'Lapwing' and 'Elfin' grow alongside 'Jessica' and 'Teresa'. There is a piece of the front garden which contains the four snowdrops associated with James Allen of

'Dodo Norton' (above), 'Jessica' (below left) and 'Lapwing' (below) (*photos* Angela Whinfield)

Shepton Mallet: 'Merlin', 'Magnet', 'Robin Hood' and 'Galatea'. Nearby grow 'S. Arnott' and 'Atkinsii' and 'Bitton' as these are associated with contemporaries of Allen and date from the early part of the 20th century.

I have a special little 'Lambrook Corner' where *Galanthus* 'Margery Fish', 'Walter Fish', 'Dodo Norton' (see photo on previous page), 'Lambrook Greensleeves' and the newly named 'Sir Henry Boyd Carpenter' all grow contentedly together. Nearby is *G.* × *allenii* which came originally from Mrs Fish. My life was altered by reading Mrs Fish's *Cottage Garden Flowers* in 1980! We live only half an hour from her old home, East Lambrook Manor, and I am lucky to have enjoyed special friendships with the various owners and gardeners there for almost 30 years.

West Porlock in Somerset was at different times the home of E B Anderson, Norman Hadden and Walter Butt. Snowdrops associated with these plantsmen have been grouped here at Snape Cottage in my Oval Bed on the western slope of the garden. A gardening friend of mine, George Chiswell, generously gave me some bulbs he had found in 1990 as tiny unflowered seedlings in E B Anderson's rented woodland. These I numbered 1-10, with the prefix WP for West Porlock. Of these, numbers 1 and 8 were deemed worthy of naming, and have been named 'Seagull' and 'White Wings' by Mr and Mrs Chiswell. *Galanthus* 'Seagull' bears a plump, shapely, pure white flower of the 'Mighty Atom' persuasion, whilst 'White Wings' is not dissimilar to 'Modern Art' in its inner and outer segment staining. In the early 1990s I was also given a most beautiful and interesting *G. rizehensis*-type which throws four and five-petalled flowers which make an elegant, dainty mound in the garden. This, too, is a West Porlock snowdrop as it came from Margaret Billington who owned Bales Mead, the former home of E B Anderson.

G. plicatus 'Cyril Warr'

I am surprised how many garden visitors draw my attention to a large *G. plicatus* type that grows against our west-facing wall.

This was the first snowdrop I noticed. In 1976 my family bought a gamekeeper's cottage at Woolland and we became friendly with the elderly Dorset man who lived in the carter's cottage opposite. His name was Cyril Warr and he had lived on the Woolland Estate all his life. I was very fond of him.

In the spring I noticed some snowdrops with huge leaves and pearldrop-like flowers growing all round Cyril's cottage garden. They were also in the churchyard, and the more I looked the more I saw that they were tucked into hedgerows and cottage gardens in our little part of Woolland. I also noticed from the churchyard that the sons of the Scott-Williams family who lived in Woolland House in Victorian times served in the Crimean War.

When I learnt more about snowdrops I read about the connection between *G. plicatus* and the Crimea (soldiers returning brought bulbs home with them). I have absolutely no proof that this is how they came to be growing so profusely at Woolland, but it seems possible. Before I realised the folly of naming snowdrops without verification, I had passed it around as *G. plicatus* 'Cyril Warr'.

[1] Our home-made compost consists of all waste from the garden except woody prunings and roots of arum, enchanter's nightshade, ground elder and bindweed. The stacked heap is turned into an empty bay at the end of the year, then covered and left for a year to decompose before being used on the garden. I have never used leafmould here.

Angela Whinfield has created a plantsman's garden at Snape Cottage, Bourton, Dorset SP8 5BZ. See www.snapestakes.com for opening times. Snowdrops are only available by mail order (send s.a.e. for list).

Collecting Snowdrops – Some Observations

Chris Sanham

Our garden lies on the sandstone ridge that runs through Sussex and on into Kent, and much of the garden where I now grow *Galanthus* was previously used as an orchard. Although I did not realise it when we moved there in 1999, what I had inherited was an ideal site for growing snowdrops, with fresh ground that had not previously been used for garden cultivation and sandy soil that provided excellent free drainage - both vital ingredients for maintaining a healthy collection and helping to reduce the build-up of disease.

Growing snowdrops
One of the first lessons that I learnt was that there is no agreed 'perfect' way to grow *Galanthus* - if you ask the same question of a thousand different snowdrop growers, you are just as likely to get a thousand different answers! Probably the most sensible piece of advice that I received was that 'the best thing to do is to try a few and see what happens' - a good general rule in gardening!

I have tried to learn as much as possible from other people's experiences and I have taken what seemed to me to be the most important elements and applied them to the growing conditions that I have; what I mention below are therefore things that work for me in my garden.

In the early years I planted all of my *Galanthus* directly into the ground and then laid down a good covering of coarse grit, both to mark the exact location of the bulbs and also to prevent the snowdrop flowers from being splattered with mud when it rained. The only feed given was a top dressing of bone meal before they came into growth each year.

With the very dry summers of recent years, the initial growth of the autumn flowering species has often been stunted, with flowers opening just barely above the surface, and it has become necessary to start watering in late August to create the right conditions for full growth. It seemed to me therefore that if I applied it thickly enough the coarse grit might also act like a mulch and help to keep the bulbs moist during the dry summer months. This would in part replicate conditions in the wild, where, for instance, *G. reginae-olgae* tends to have its bulbs and roots down deep between rocks, in shady places where they can stay cool and moist. I also thought that the coarse grit might, in some small way, help to discourage the activities of slugs and snails, but I suspect that this was just wishful thinking on my part!

As my collection grew I realised that, partly through constraints of space, I would have to change this approach of planting directly into the ground, particularly as it became clear that the bulbs of many forms of *Galanthus* had a tendency to 'wander', with the danger of intermingling with the bulbs of their neighbours.

It was then that I heard about the lattice pots used for growing pond plants, which offered the potential for containing this wandering habit whilst also enabling the roots to grow naturally into the surrounding soil through the holes in the pot. I decided to experiment by planting some bulbs in these pots, using my own 'mix', then planting the pots in the ground. Whilst this offered the immediate benefit of stopping bulb 'wander', allowing different forms to be grown closer together, I quickly realised that there were other substantial benefits, as follows:

Controlled feeding - by getting my 'mix' right, I could ensure that the plants got the balanced feed they needed, year on year, with minimal need for supplementary feeding.

Easier to lift bulbs - most galanthophiles that I know hate digging up bulbs because of the risk of damage. By growing them in lattice pots, I find it is so much easier when lifting dormant bulbs, and it even helps when lifting 'in the green', because you know exactly where they are and can greatly minimise damage to the bulbs and their roots.

Regular checking of the health of the bulbs - because I have to lift the lattice pots and replenish the 'mix' regularly, I can take the opportunity to examine the bulbs carefully, get early warning of any signs of problems and, where necessary, take immediate corrective action before the bulb is too far gone.

I now plant all of my new plants in lattice pots and am gradually transferring to pots the bulbs that were originally planted directly in the ground.

I should not move on without talking about my 'mix', but I must emphasise that this is what works for me, in my growing conditions, and is not intended in any way to be prescriptive. What I have tried to do is devise a mix that provides both quick release and slower release fertiliser for the plants, whilst at the same time ensuring that the soil remains free-draining. It comprises two parts sharp sand, two parts John Innes No. 3 [1] and one part multi compost [2] - for those snowdrops that are known to require a more acidic soil, or a chalkier soil, I adjust accordingly. Since changing to this mix, I have had consistently good results: the plants generally show strong growth, flower well and have good natural division.

Following the very heavy and prolonged rains in the summer of 2007, when the bulbs were sitting in saturated soil for long periods, at a time when they would normally expect to be dry and dormant, I found that I had a higher than usual incidence of bulb rot and *Stagonospora curtisii*. So this year I have further improved the drainage by adding one part coarse grit to the mix and, when potting/re-potting, I now put the bulbs on a bed of sharp sand to try and prevent them from sitting in wet soil in their dormant period. With increasingly unpredictable weather patterns, this will probably not be the last adjustment that I will make.

Keeping the collection healthy
I have mentioned disease and this is a constant challenge for snowdrop growers - do not assume that your snowdrops will not be hit by disease, or that if they are then it must be someone else's fault. Whilst measures should be adopted to guard against introducing disease into the collection, the best way to prevent it is to do everything possible to ensure the good health of your own plants. I have already mentioned the importance of ensuring that they are fed well, and this cannot be overstated in helping to keep them healthy. It is equally important that the soil is free-draining and that the bulbs do not sit in soggy conditions when they are dormant.

Good hygiene is essential - none of us wants to spread disease around our own collection, or for that matter to pass it on to anyone else, so at various times of the year, when it is necessary to handle the snowdrops, and always when I am dealing with plants that I suspect may have a problem, much washing of hands takes place between handling different plants, while any tools used are dipped in Jeyes Fluid or a similar garden disinfectant. I know that some of the commercial growers go one step further and use different sets of tools for different parts of their growing area.

Newly acquired plants are carefully examined for any sign of a problem and then all of them are routinely held in quarantine for at least a year, irrespective of where they came from. Indeed, some could remain in quarantine for up to three years if the source of the plants had had any 'problems' in the past. Only after a minimum of a year, and after checking that they appear to be healthy, are newly acquired snowdrops then planted out amongst the main collection.

Here I must touch upon the vexed question of fungicides, which are a general problem for private gardeners due to the lack of available products. Furthermore, fungicides may be curative or preventative and are not necessarily both. Whilst some growers routinely spray with fungicide two or three times annually, to provide some protection against infection, there are limits to what can be done to save infected plants and in most cases, particularly where the plant is a common form, the best course of action is to lift and destroy both the plant and the surrounding soil. If the infected plant cannot be removed immediately then, as a holding measure, I isolate the plant and the surrounding soil by dusting them with Bordeaux Mixture, to help stop the infection from spreading. If a modest spraying programme is envisaged, the fungicides used should be as varied as possible, using different classes of fungicides so as to reduce the likelihood of fungicide resistance occurring.

Constant visual examination is essential when the plants are in growth and I check daily for any signs of problems. Any plant that looks in any way out of the ordinary is suspect and the policy that I operate is 'if in doubt, chuck it out', on the basis that it is better to do this than to take a chance and put the rest of the collection at risk. If disease is found, or suspected, both plant and surrounding soil are immediately removed and destroyed. A plant from a different genus is then put in its place and the surrounding *Galanthus* are given a precautionary drenching in fungicide. Care is needed here, in that many other bulbous species may be attacked by the fungi likely to attack snowdrops.

The only exception to my policy of destroying infected plants is with rare plants that have been attacked. These I will attempt to save. Any infection on the leaves and stem must be cut out and any infected bulb scales must be peeled back until the bulb is 'clean'. Then the plant must be soaked in fungicide and, when it is dry, dusted with sulphur powder and potted up in sharp sand so as to minimise conditions for re-infection and to encourage strong root growth. The plant is then kept in quarantine, with further applications of fungicide after about two weeks and during the next growth cycle. If the plant remains in sharp sand for an extended period, it is sensible to give it some liquid feed. I then cross my fingers and wait, because while many of the plants treated in this way appear to recover, success is by no means guaranteed. The surgery that I have described can be quite traumatic, not least for the surgeon (!), and is best left to an expert, particularly one who has access to an effective fungicide. If damage to the infected bulb is extensive, twin-scaling is the best option, and in expert hands good results have been achieved, saving rare plants that might not otherwise have survived. There is of course no treatment for plants attacked by virus.

As soon as I can, and in order to reduce the risk of total loss of rare forms still further, I plant bulbs of the same form in more than one place in the garden, get a bulb twin-scaled and, as a last line of defence, place 'back up' bulbs with trusted friends.

I keep a log of 'problems' so that any trends can quickly be detected: e.g. in plants grown in a particular part of the garden, or in plants coming from a particular source, etc.

My final observation is that you should not underestimate the amount of time that is involved in building and maintaining a collection of snowdrops. As I have found, it is an addictive all-year-round hobby. Is this what is meant by 'White Fever'?

[1] See www.johninnescompost.org
[2] The multipurpose compost that I use is a mix of peat, sterilised loam, horticultural sand and trace elements, that contains enough nutrients for the first four to six weeks.

Chris Sanham became a National Collection Holder of Galanthus *earlier this year, the year in which the NCCPG is celebrating its 30th anniversary.*

Tulipa sylvestris subsp. australis

Richard Wilford

With a vast natural distribution, extending from the south-western tip of Europe and the north of Africa to the steppes and mountains of Central Asia, it is hardly surprising that *Tulipa sylvestris* varies from one end of its range to the other. These may be gradual differences, not significant enough to merit naming a new species, but when grown side by side, forms from different parts of the range can look distinct.

In Northern Europe, *T. sylvestris* is best known for its large yellow flowers held on stems over 30cm (1ft) tall. The tepals are up to 7cm (2.6in) long, often reflexed at their tip and stained green on the back. This is a stoloniferous plant that has spread over the centuries and become naturalized as far north as Scotland and Scandinavia, where it misses the hot, dry summers of its real home and often fails to flower, producing plenty of leaves but relying on stolons to increase.

Further south, around the Mediterranean, are smaller forms, more elegant but still unmistakably *T. sylvestris*. One variation from the hills and mountains of southern Europe and North Africa has flowers backed not with green but with violet or rusty red. It is a smaller plant than most forms of *T. sylvestris*, with a lower leaf less than 12mm (0.5in) wide, outer tepals up to 37 × 9mm (1.5 × 0.4in) and inner tepals up to 38 × 16mm (1.5 × 0.6in). This tulip was named *T. australis* in 1799 but is now treated as a subspecies of *T. sylvestris*.

Flowering bulbs of *T. sylvestris* subsp. *australis* were shown by Kew to the Daffodil and Tulip Committee and then the Rock Garden Plant Committee on 11 March 2008, and received a Preliminary Commendation as a Flowering Plant for Exhibition. The slender brown stems were around 8.5cm (3.4in) tall and held solitary yellow flowers with outer tepals 30 × 8mm (1.2 × 0.3in) and inner tepals 27 × 12mm (1.1 × 0.5in). The filaments were yellow and the anthers orange-yellow. The curved, glabrous, channelled leaves were dark green with a grey bloom. The longest reached 25cm (1in) but was only 7mm (0.3 in) wide.

This tulip had been collected as seed in Morocco in 1994 during an expedition led by the University of Reading. The plants were found in open woodland near the town of Melilla in north-east Morocco, on the road to Cap des Trios Forches.

At Kew the bulbs are grown in a fairly deep, 12cm (4.8in) diameter clay pot, which is housed under an unheated frame to keep the bulbs dry in summer. Repotting is carried out every year in August or September and a gritty, loam-based mix is used, topped with a grit mulch. The bulbs are placed around half way down the pot. The pot is plunged in sand, to protect it from temperature extremes, especially freezing, and to aid watering by allowing moisture from the sand to pass through the clay sides, preventing the soil drying too quickly.

Tulipa sylvestris subsp. *australis* can also be grown outside. Given a free draining spot and plenty of sunshine, it should flower as reliably as it does in a pot. However, the protection afforded by a cold frame does prevent damage to the flowers if our spring weather is not up to scratch.

Tulipa sylvestris subsp. *australis* (photo Richard Wilford)

In Search of Tulips
John Page

Brian Mathew has amusingly drawn attention to the coincidence that so many of the *Crocus* species listed in his splendid monograph are to be found close to roads. The joke is a good one, but there is more to it than that. Roads by their nature seek out the most direct route from A to B, cutting through the landscape like a knife, and in the process they provide an invaluable cross section of a flora. Of course, that is only part of the story and fresh discoveries undoubtedly await those who forsake the roads and, properly equipped, strike out across country. Two approaches then: the one presupposing some form of vehicle and covering a relatively wide area, the other a carefully planned trek into uncharted territory. The former may yield excellent results to the practised eye, the latter is more likely to reveal something new. Whichever method one chooses for a particular plant, the literature - e.g. the published floras, articles in *The Plantsman* or in periodicals such as *The Alpine Gardener* - must be studied beforehand and details relating to such matters as habitat, flowering period and distributional range have to be absorbed. Increasingly, information via the web is becoming invaluable.

What have I found?

Angels fear to tread in tulip territory and to have any chance of arriving at a correct name we must have a good idea of which features of the plant need to be examined closely when the process of identification starts. Taxonomists find the genus notoriously difficult to identify and the amateur will often need a large slice of humility when working through a key and settling on a name. Our starting points could be many. If we choose the stamens, a hand lens with a minimum ten times magnification is called for. Is the base of the filament swollen or not? Is it hairy or glabrous (devoid of hairs)? Is the base of the young flower constricted or rounded? How would you describe the overall profile of the flower? Is it waisted, funnel-shaped, cup-shaped or bowl-shaped? How do the outer three segments of the perianth compare with the inners in terms of colour, length and tip shape? Does the flower have an internal basal blotch of a different colour? If so, what is the pattern? If black, does it have a yellow rim? And how does the blotch relate in size to the flower as a whole? How many leaves are there, how would you describe their appearance and how does their size differ from the base to the upper stem? Are the leaves bluish green (glaucous) or shiny green? In some instances, the bulb gives indispensable information. This would inevitably require excavation, possibly down to a depth of 30cm (1ft) or more [1]. The texture and colour of the bulb tunic are both significant (papery? black? brown? reddish?) and especially the presence or otherwise of hairs, whether around the base plate, lining the tunic or protruding from the neck. And what sort of hairs? Are they bristly, soft, woolly, matted, straight, crinkly, etc.? Do the bulbs produce stolons? Identification may be daunting then, but it is endlessly interesting, and of course by no means all of the diagnostic features mentioned here have to be taken into account. Where I know, for example, that several different tulip species might be encountered in a given area, I find it useful to draw up a bespoke key, i.e. one which includes only those morphological features which I need to consider. I should also add that I am finding the many images I take with my digital camera extremely helpful when I call them up on the monitor.

Spotting tulip habitats

If you are botanising from a car the ability to 'read' the topography is vital. Ideally, both sides of the road are covered and the driver is experienced enough to sense promising terrain and adjust his speed accordingly. In some Mediterranean countries the terrain is often intensively cultivated, and though as we shall see in the case of some tulips this may not be a bad thing, we normally need to spot accessible sites which have avoided the plough - knolls, ridges, ledges and the like. First and foremost, tulips require good drainage, but they must also have copious water when in active growth, which means we must think about where the rain goes when it reaches the ground. Different shades of green in the grasses, for example, can help here, and of course the lie of the land. In limestone areas, due to the porosity of the rock, water courses will be less easy to track down. Rock types determine soil colour and pH, so geological changes should be noted. Since many bulbs prefer a particular aspect, we must know where north is, be able to visualise the passage of the sun and note where the maximum shade will occur. Should a find be significant, we will need to have with us a Global Positioning System (GPS) in order to record elevation and grid references.

Some *Tulipa* species and their habitats

There is great joy to be had at the sudden glimpse of a tulip, the flash of scarlet or yellow pulsating amongst the background vegetation, displaying that unmistakeable outline and characteristic sturdiness. The genus *Tulipa* is remarkably catholic in its choice of habitat. Several species are described almost witheringly as 'weeds of cultivation', and technically I suppose they are, if we are content to define weeds as plants flourishing where they are not wanted. Agriculture has transformed the landscape of Cyprus and has devastated much of the flora, but the two principal tulips found on the island are closely associated with man's activities. *T. agenensis* may still be found (though it seems to be rarer now) in vineyards and orchards in the south-west, whilst *T. cypria* remains common enough in pastures west of Kyrenia for Turkish Cypriot children to hawk bunches of its flowers by the roadside.

Young Turks (Cypriot) hawking *Tulipa cypria*
(*photo* John Page)

Similarly, despite the rocky habitats implied by its specific epithet, *T. saxatilis* persists in meadows on the Cretan Lasithi plateau and decorates the tables of nearby tavernas. Lower down around Spili, *T. doerfleri* borders ploughed fields with its brilliant red. The levees thrown up by farmers in north west Turkey as they clear their fields of boulders create perfect habitats for *T. orphanidea*. In dells of *terra rossa* on cultivated land to the east of Ankara *T. sintenisii* occurs in thousands, its underground stolons relishing the loosened soil.

For some species then there are close links with the disturbed land and the good drainage of agriculture. The majority of tulips, however, have their homes among the screes and rocks, from sea-level to altitudes way beyond the reach of the farmer, habitats guaranteeing good aeration, insulation, freedom from waterlogging and virtually no competition. In the Mani peninsula of the Peloponnese, the lovely scarlet flowers of the low-growing *T. goulimyi* occur on warm, stony hillsides above the Mediterranean. By contrast, high passes in Turkey funnelling the strong winds over bare rocks often provide sites for the hardier brethren such as *T. julia* and *T. armena* var. *armena*.

Tulipa armena var. *armena*,
east of Istanbul, Turkey
(*photo* John Page)

Around 2,550m (8,500ft) on the Güzeldere Pass in the south-east of the country, *T. humilis* carpets thin turf amongst harshly exposed screes, flowering deep into June as the snow melts. Again close to the snowline, we find around Karaman a recent addition to the Turkish flora, *T. cinnabarina*. The tulip species enthusiast must acquire a wide range of terms for red if he is to do justice to their flowers, and it is easy to see why staff at the Gothenburg Botanic Garden, where this was first named, hit on 'cinnabarine', a shade close to vermilion. With its delicate form and yellow eye, it is very attractive. In the epicentre of tulip species, Central Asia, most of the representatives of the genus colonise rocks of varying degrees of roughness, with only shepherds and guided tours for company. At the opposite end of the distributional range, in Portuguese hills above the Atlantic, *T. sylvestris* subsp. *australis* grows on rock terraces above the roads, producing vast numbers of seedlings and the occasional yellow flower.

There are still fresh discoveries to be made. High in the Akamas Peninsula in Cyprus in the early nineties my wife Kate came across a stand of tulips resembling *T. orphanidea* that matched nothing in R D Meikle's *Flora of Cyprus* [2]. Had it been overlooked? Was it a new arrival? No bulbs were removed, but photographs were taken (see below). To the best of my knowledge, it has still to be described.

New tulip for Cyprus
(*photo* John Page)

If foreign trips are not for you, however, some consolation may be found in Clive Stace's *New Flora of the British Isles* [3], where you will learn that *T. sylvestris* subsp. *sylvestris* has naturalised itself in woods, meadows and neglected estates in England and Scotland. Likewise, the neo-tulipa *T. gesneriana* has escaped to waysides and tips from gardens in the south and if you are walking on rough ground on Tresco in the Scillies you might just come across the diminutive pink *T. saxatilis*.

[1] Do remember that if you remove bulbs, you are legally required to have both an import and an export licence.
[2] Meikle, R.D. (1985). *Flora of Cyprus*, **2**. The Bentham-Moxon Trust, Kew.
[3] Stace, C. (1997). *New Flora of the British Isles*, 2nd edition. Cambridge University Press, Cambridge.

Small-Flowered Tulip Trial at Wisley
Christine Skelmersdale

Tulips have a poor reputation for perenniality in the garden and are therefore often lifted after flowering or treated as annuals by gardeners [1]. However the experience of some members of the RHS Daffodil and Tulip Committee suggested that this disappointing trait was not universal: many of the smaller species tulips often form persistent and free-flowering clumps, some even spreading to create large patches. One has only to think of the example of the 2 square metre (22 sq ft) patch of *T. saxatilis* that flowers magnificently every April on the dry bank above the Portsmouth Field at Wisley. And in my own garden they have spread from an initial ten bulbs to a three metre (10ft) patch over the last 30 years.

The Committee decided to test their theory by having an invited trial of the species and near species tulips to check for persistence. All entries were also considered as possible Award of Garden Merit (AGM) candidates. Although the trial was held under the auspices of the Daffodil and Tulip Committee able assistance was given by members of the Joint Rock Garden Plant Committee (to whom any recommendations for AGM were also sent for ratification) and other specialists. In all, the trial included some 99 entries representing 71 different taxa. With a few exceptions the larger-flowered dwarf tulips of the *T. greigii* and *T. kaufmanniana* group were deliberately excluded as they were already subject to other trial procedures.

The bulbs, 25 in most cases, were donated by both trade and amateur bulb growers from across Europe. They were planted in the autumn of 2005 on a sloping bank at the top of the trials field and given a gravel mulch. They were then left undisturbed for three years apart from the roguing of diseased material. A record of their health and flowering was kept throughout each spring. The bulbs were then lifted after the third flowering season (in May 2008), cleaned, graded and counted.

There were appalling vagaries in the weather – the first year was one of the hottest and driest summers and was followed by one of the wettest on record. Spring 2008 then really tested the bulbs by alternating periods of nightly frosts followed by unseasonably warm weather. Considering that most of them are montane plants used to more uniform weather, it is not surprising that some succumbed to tulip fire or other fungal diseases and were removed before the end of the trial. In all, there was no data for some 21 entries (29 per cent), either through failure, incorrect nomenclature or disease. This does not mean that under more normal circumstances in the more benign conditions of a garden some of these subjects would not perform well, just that they did not perform well in this trial. *T. saxatilis* and *T. sprengeri* are good examples of such unexpected underperformance. Both are acknowledged as good garden plants but neither had the time in the trial necessary to establish a flowering colony, so they do not appear in the results.

Another useful result of the trial was to clarify some nomenclature (naming) problems current in the bulb trade. In some instances identical plants were entered under different names whilst in others distinct plants were entered under the same name. A detailed report on each entry and full results will be published by the Trials Office in due course.

Although the failures caused by the weather conditions were disappointing and resulted in some well-known favourites under-

Small-Flowered Tulip Trial at Wisley

Clockwise from top
'Honky Tonk'
(*photo* Caroline Beck)
'Magic Fire'
'Tinka'
'Starlight'
'Peppermintstick'
(*photos* Sue Drew)

performing, the trial was very successful overall. It was certainly very popular with garden visitors. The persistence results are summarised in the table below: 34 per cent (24 taxa of the original 71) showed reasonable persistence (group 1); 27 per cent (19 taxa) were positively persistent (group 2); and the remaining 10 per cent (7 taxa) actively increased (group 3). Nine new AGMs were recommended.

[1] This is done primarily because summers in the United Kingdom are much cooler and wetter than they are in Central Asia where their species ancestors originated.

Group 1 (-50 to +50 per cent)	**Group 2** (51 to 200 per cent)	**Group 3** (>200 per cent)
albertii	*biflora* (of commerce)	*batalinii* 'Bronze Charm'
clusiana	*bifloriformis*	*bifloriformis* 'Starlight' **R**
clusiana var. *chrysantha* **E**	*clusiana* 'Sheila'	'Girlfriend'
dubia 'Beldersai'	*humilis* 'Persian Pearl'	*kaufmanniana* 'Ice Stick'
hageri 'Splendens'	'Pink Charm'	'Lady Jane' **R**
humilis 'Eastern Star'	*linifolia* **E**	*praestans* 'Fusilier' **E**
'Odalisque'	*linifolia* 'Red Hunter' **E**	'Taco'
yellow base	'Little Beauty' **E**	
kolpakowskiana **E**	'Little Princess' **R**	
kurdica	'Magic Fire' **R**	
'Lady Guna'	*neustruevae*	
linifolia 'Apricot Jewel'	*orphanidea* 'Flava'	
'Bright Gem' **E**	Whittallii Group **E**	
'Honky Tonk' **R**	'Peppermintstick' **R**	
Maximowiczii Group	*polychroma* (of commerce) **R**	
'Red Gem'	*saxatilis* 'Lilac Wonder' **E**	
'Scarlet'	*sylvestris* * **R**	
'Yellow Jewel'	'Tinka' **R**	
orithyioides	*turkestanica* **E**	
'Piccolo'		
praestans 'Unicum'		
saxatilis		
schrenkii		
urumiensis **E**		

E = existing AGM
R = new AGM recommendation subject to ratification in the autumn
* = subject to clonal name

Large-Flowered Tulip Trial at Wisley

Sue Drew

The 49 entries in a trial of large-flowered tulips at Wisley were judged by the RHS Daffodil and Tulip Trials Sub-Committee in 2008 for the RHS Award of Garden Merit (AGM), using a scoring system out of 8 points based on the following criteria:

Maximum of 4 points for constitution and vigour; health; foliage

Maximum of 4 points for form and substance; colour; durability

A trial of *Impatiens* had previously been grown on the site and at the end of the flowering season in 2007 the plants had been broken up using a flail. The plot was then subsoil-rotavated to incorporate the resulting organic matter into the soil and break down any cultivation pan that might have started to form. No additional organic matter was added before planting the tulips. Bulbs were planted on 24-25 October 2007, spaced 15cm (6in) apart each way in blocks of 25 bulbs for each entry.

Recommended for AGM

The Trials Sub-Committee recommended that the following cultivars should receive an AGM subject to ratification by the Daffodil and Tulip Committee in October 2008. Abbreviated comments from members of the Trials Sub-Committee are shown in italics.

T. 'Beau Monde' Triumph Group

Raised by I V T Wageningen, Netherlands, and sent by C v d Veek, Belkmerweg 20a, 1754 GB Burgerbrug, Netherlands. *Early. Excellent tulip, standing up well with good weather resistance. Even blooms. Superb foliage.* Flowered from 3 April to 1 May, with 10 flowering stems per 10 bulbs.

T. 'Spryng' Triumph Group

Raised by I V T Wageningen, Netherlands, and sent by Maveridge International, Groensveldsdijk 44, 1744 GE St Maarten, Netherlands. *Has plenty of impact.* Flowered from 3 April to 1 May, with 10 flowering stems per 10 bulbs.

T. 'Angels Wish' Single Late Group

Raised by Vitauts Skuja, Latvia, and sent by J S Pennings, 'De Bilt', Schorweg 14, 1764 MC Breezand, Netherlands. *Big flowers on very sturdy stems. Starts with a greenish-yellow flush on reverse which turns to pure white. A lovely tulip.* Flowered from 14 April to 7 May, with 12 flowering stems per 10 bulbs.

T. 'Dordogne' Single Late Group

Raised by W Dekker and Sons, Netherlands, and sent by C v d Veek. *Very tall, longlasting, late-flowering tulip, good flower colour.* Flowered from 21 April to 9 May, with 10 flowering stems per 10 bulbs.

T. 'Menton' Single Late Group

Raised by W Dekker and Sons, Netherlands, and sent by Bloms Bulbs, Primrose Nurseries, Melchbourne, Bedfordshire MK44 1ZZ. *Very tall, late flowers. A lovely colour.* Flowered from 21 April to 12 May, with 10 flowering stems per 10 bulbs.

T. 'Moonlight Girl' Lily-flowered Group

Raised by Vitauts Skuja, Latvia, and sent by J S Pennings. *A superb tulip, flowers are good size, elegant and well proportioned.* Flowered from 1 April to 29 April, with 10 flowering stems per 10 bulbs.

T. 'Red Hat' Fringed Group

Raised by Vitauts Skuja, Latvia, and sent by J S

Daffodil, Snowdrop and Tulip Yearbook 2008-2009

Clockwise from top left
'Beau Monde'
'Spryng'
'Jazz'
'Angels Wish'
Committee assesment
'World Expression'
'Dordogne'
(*photos* Sue Drew)

Pennings. *An impressive colour, a good fringed tulip.* Flowered from 21 April to 12 May, with 18 flowering stems per 10 bulbs.

T. **'Pirand'** Fosteriana Group
Raised by H Vreeburg, Netherlands, and sent by C v d Veek. *Early. A super tulip with good impact and weather resistance.* Flowered from 18 March to 8 April, with 11 flowering stems per 10 bulbs.

Recommended for AGM subject to availability
T. **'Louvre'** Fringed Group
Raised by J A Borst, Noorderbrug 5, 1713 GA Obdam, Netherlands, and sent by J A Borst. *The flowers stand up well. They are fringed; they have good impact and are a lovely rich colour.* Flowered from 4 April to 1 May, with 10 flowering stems per 10 bulbs.

Recommended to retain their AGM
T. **'Barcelona'** AGM (H4) 1999 Triumph Group. Sent by Bloms Bulbs.
T. **'Don Quichotte'** AGM (H4) 1995 Triumph Group. Sent by C v d Veek.
T. **'Maureen'** AGM (H4) 1993 Single Late Group. Sent by C v d Veek.
T. **'World Expression'** AGM (H4) 1999 Single Late Group. Sent by World Flower BV, Burgermeester, Lovinkstraat 105, 1764 GD Breezand, Netherlands.
T. **'Ballade'** AGM (H4) 1993 Lily-flowered Group. Sent by C v d Veek.
T. **'Spring Green'** AGM (H4) 1993 Viridiflora Group. Sent by C v d Veek.
T. **'China Town'** AGM (H4) 1995 Viridiflora Group. Sent by J S Pennings.
T. **'Angélique'** AGM (H4) 1999 Double Late Group. Sent by Bloms Bulbs.
T. **'Orange Princess'** AGM (H4) 1997 Double Late Group. Sent by J S Pennings.

Public voting
The large-flowered tulip trial was extremely popular with visitors to Wisley Garden, and with the help of the Wisley Trials Garden Staff the Trials Office conducted a public vote between 22 April and 11 May 2008. A total of 193 votes were cast. The top 5 favourite tulips as voted for by the general public were as follows. ('Ice Stick' and 'Pirand' were not included, having finished flowering.)

T. **'World Expression'** Single Late Group, with 10.9 per cent of the votes
T. **'Dordogne'** Single Late Group, with 8.8 per cent
T. **'Red Hat'** Fringed Group, with 6.2 per cent
T. **'Grand Perfection'** Triumph Group, with 5.2 per cent. Sent by C v d Veek.
T. **'Jazz'** Lily-flowered Group, with 4.7 per cent. Sent by C v d Veek.

World Tulip Summit 2008

Johnny Walkers

Where has the time gone? It hardly seems possible that it is almost two years since I attended the World Tulip Summit in Australia and learnt that alcohol stunts your growth (*Daffodil, Snowdrop and Tulip Yearbook 2007-08*) yet here I am at the next one on 1-2 May 2008. This time it was the turn of the United Kingdom - or more precisely Spalding - to host the event. As it was timed to coincide with the 50th Spalding Flower Parade, which uses tulip heads to create stunning floats that parade through town, there should have been plenty to attract a full house. However, despite the attraction of the Flower Parade and a host of international speakers, the number of English delegates was disappointing.

Lord Taylor of Holbeach opening the Tulip Summit
(*photo* David Norton)

First-day speakers

To set the scene, the first session was an introduction to the South Holland area in Lincolnshire, covering the reclamation and draining of the Fens that created some of the best farm land in England, ideal for growing tulips and daffodils. The speaker was John Honnor, a retired drainage engineer who is still passionate about how the Fens were created by Dutch engineers over the centuries - with miles and miles of drainage dykes, some as wide as a small river and dug out by hand using spades and wheelbarrows! Maintaining the theme of history the next session was James Akers MBE talking about English florists' tulips. Again James is one of those people who are so enthusiastic about these old tulips and The Wakefield and North of England Tulip Society that the 30 minutes allocated to him were really not enough. The Society, dating back to at least 1836, keeps the tradition of florists' tulips and showing in beer bottles very much alive and James is full of anecdotes. How many realise that in the 19th century there were as many as 200 florists' tulip shows per year and that the Society has not missed a show since it started.

One thing that the organisers could not be accused of was failing to have a truly remarkable line-up of speakers. James was followed by Anna Pavord talking about 'The flower that made men mad!' No matter how many times one hears the story about tulipomania in the 17th century it is still almost impossible to imagine the prices people would pay for a single bulb - up to 10,000 florins - the equivalent of the cost of a house by the canal in Amsterdam. All this for a flower that basically has no scent! (At the same time, however, one realises that there is nothing new in the world, because if one reads dot-com bubble for tulipomania what is new?)

The holy grail for the burgers of Holland at that time of course was a flower with lots of feathering and colour variations (not realising that it was a virus that caused the feathering).

Whilst the holy grail for Karen Platt, who followed Anna, was the black tulip. Despite its name, 'Queen of Night' is of course not truly black but very deep purple. For years people have been trying to get the definitive black tulip and Karen gave a fascinating insight into whether we will ever get there without genetic modification. Karen was followed by Richard Wilford a regular contributor to this *Yearbook* with an insight into the tulips at Kew.

After lunch we were treated to another three excellent speakers, namely Dr John Page the specialist in alpine tulips, Sally Pettit of Cambridge University Botanic Gardens and James Armitage of Wisley. Despite the advice to plant tulip bulbs into well-drained moisture-retentive soil, Dr Page went on to describe some of the conditions where he has found tulips growing quite happily, including scree beds with barely any soil, moist wet meadows in Cyprus and deep mud in Greece. Even at the highest altitudes, water in the autumn and spring is most critical.

Sally Pettit again gave a most interesting insight into Cambridge University Botanic Garden and makes one realise the depth of knowledge and facility we have in this country to study the tulip. The Garden now covers an area of 16 hectares (40 acres) and holds the NCCPG species tulip collection with over 68 now cultivated.

James Armitage's report on the small-flowered tulip trial at Wisley was an eye-watering account of the problems that can affect any trial, with tulip fire affecting eight of the entries in 2007 and many more in this the final year of the trial (see page 64). James really confirmed what many gardeners know, that monoculture and poor weather are among the biggest challenges for any gardener.

Second-day speakers

The keynote speaker for the summit was Professor Bill Miller of Cornell University and we were treated to a fascinating session on the second morning. Professor Miller is funded entirely by the Dutch exporters and many students are involved in his work. The USA is of course a massive importer of Dutch bulbs for flower production during the winter and much work is involved in improving the quality and vase life of forced flowers. The major researchers in bulb crops are now the Netherlands, USA, Israel, Japan and Poland whilst the United Kingdom, Chile, China, Korea and South Africa are classified as minors in bulb research work. But whilst most countries are cutting back on research facilities for all crops, China is the exception. The results of Bill Miller's research are available on the Cornell University website.

The late morning sessions had speakers from the packaging world on how illustrating bulbs and tulips had changed over the years and from a Belgian artist on the inspiration he had got from tulips.

The finale of the two days came when delegates from twelve countries (including Afghanistan) talked about tulips and tulip festivals in their own countries.

Conclusion

The next summit will be in 2010 and will coincide with the Skagit Valley Tulip Festival in the USA. In 2012 the host countries will be the Netherlands and Belgium.

As I said, the line-up of speakers at Spalding this year was superb, the presentations were faultless. A pity there were not more attendees.

Tulip Sour: *Fusarium oxysporum f.sp. tulipae* in Tulips

Marjan de Boer

A tulip-specific form of the fungus *Fusarium oxysporum* causes dry rot in tulip bulbs. This disease is also called Tulip Sour because of the sour smell of *Fusarium*-infected bulbs. The smell is produced by *Fusarium oxysporum formae specialis tulipae*. Other formae speciales of *Fusarium oxysporum* cause rot in other bulbous crops such as *Narcissus*, *Hyacinthus*, etc.

F. oxysporum Schlecht. *f.sp. tulipae* causes devastating damage during the production, storage and transport of tulips, resulting in losses of up to €10 million per year. The main damage occurs during storage and transport. Not only is there direct loss of quantity and quality of the bulbs due to *Fusarium* dry rot, but damage is also caused by ethylene produced by the fungus. Ethylene has severe negative effects on the infected bulbs but even more on the healthy bulbs. These effects are resin release, open shoots, 'pole' plants (those with multistems), bud necrosis and desiccation of flower buds.

What do you see?
Infection by *F. oxysporum f.sp. tulipae* causes several symptoms which are visible on the bulb during storage and on the plant that eventually arises from the bulb.

Bulb symptoms
Fusarium-infected bulbs develop greyish brown spots during storage, occasionally with concentric rings and a clear yellow rim. They give off a distinctive, acid smell. When the infection is more severe (usually in more humid conditions) the infected tissue is covered with a layer of white to pinkish white mycelium (fungus threads).

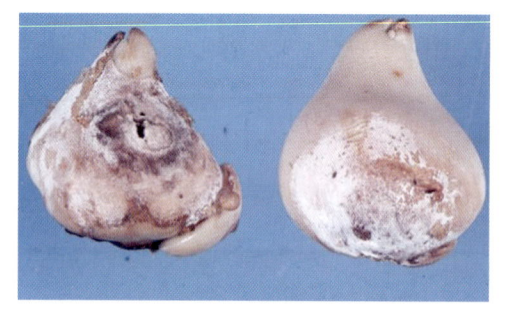

Infected bulbs
(*photo* Marjan de Boer)

Finally, the bulbs shrivel up and become loose in their tunics. Diseased bulbs can be infected by mites as a secondary infection. These bulbs pulverize to a granular mass and spread a typical musty smell [1].

Plant symptoms
No plants will emerge from heavily diseased bulbs. In less serious cases growth will be retarded, flower tips will turn yellow and flower buds will desiccate. Longitudinal dissection of a bulb clearly shows that the stem turns brown from the base upwards. Under specific circumstances such as a warm spring, plants can die off early in the season, leading to 'blue' plants.

Bulbs infected with *Fusarium* release ethylene into the soil, which may lead to retarded growth and even bud blasting in neighbouring plants [1].

How does the fungus behave?
In general *Fusarium oxysporum* survives in the soil by making special survival structures called chlamydospores, which can last for at least

eight years. Under optimal conditions chlamydospores germinate and infect the roots of plants. This way the fungus enters the vascular system, leading finally to wilting of the plant. In tulip bulbs, *Fusarium* probably enters through the roots or the base of the root crown, causing the specific bulb rot leading to production of spores called microconidia and macroconidia.

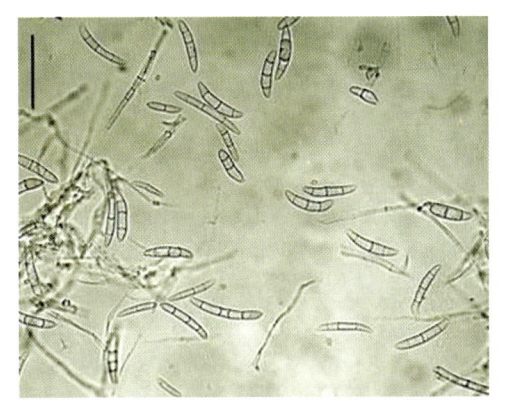

Tulip Sour fungus
(*photo* Marjan de Boer)

Another and more important way in which tulip bulbs are infected is during the processing of bulbs after harvesting. *Fusarium* spores (microconidia and/or macroconidia) are almost always present in stocks of tulip bulbs since one diseased bulb can produce millions of them.

During processing, several moments favourable to infection by *Fusarium* can occur. These are warm and humid conditions and wounds to the bulbs. Growers and export companies are advised to avoid such conditions during the processing and storage of bulbs, but it is not always possible.

Before the bulbs are planted, exported or prepared for gardening, the diseased bulbs are sorted out. But lightly infected bulbs or bulbs without visible latent infections are still present and can easily be sold, resulting in diseased plants in springtime.

What can you do about it?

*Try to plant the bulbs at soil temperatures below 10°C (50°F). The fungus in the soil and/or the bulb is not active at these temperatures.

* Avoid planting bulbs in places in the garden which can be moist and warm in spring and summer.

*Do not plant tulip bulbs in places where tulips have been grown in recent years. This precaution is not especially to avoid *Fusarium* infection from the soil, but mainly to avoid *Botrytis* infection.

*Plant healthy bulbs. Check the bulbs before planting them in the garden and discard any bulbs showing symptoms. It is very important to obtain high quality bulbs if not only *Fusarium* is to be avoided but also other fungal diseases.

* Due to latent or quiescent infections in the bulb it is not always possible to get rid of all infected bulbs. Consequently, in spring, the tulips should be watched carefully. Any plants with retarded growth or bulbs that do not produce a plant and/or a flower should be removed. This is not only because the new *Fusarium* spores produced by the diseased bulbs will infect the soil, but also because the ethylene produced by the diseased bulbs will cause retarded growth and malformed flowers amongst neighbouring healthy bulbs. Later in spring, if so-called 'blue' plants are observed, these plants should be removed as well.

*After the tulips die off naturally, usually at the end of June, it is best to dig them up. But before that, it is important to have dug and immediately removed all possible diseased plants and thus diseased bulbs, being new *Fusarium* sources. During handling of the healthy bulbs wounding must be avoided, also warm (19°-30°C [76°-86°F]) and humid conditions.

*Bulbs to plant again in autumn in the garden should be stored under dry conditions. This way new infection caused by humid conditions is avoided.

A 'blue' plant
(*photo* Marjan de Boer)

The control measures described are preventive measures based around planting healthy bulbs in healthy soil and removing diseased plant material. There are no measures such as fungicides that can be used to control the fungus in the bulb or in the soil.

Latent infections in commercial production

As mentioned earlier, growers and exporters are advised to avoid conditions favourable to *Fusarium* infection during processing and storage of the bulbs. Growers dip the bulbs in fungicides just before planting, so as to protect them for a few months against new infections from the soil or from spores that are still present on the bulb. However, fungicides applied by dipping do not reach the latent infections in the bulb. In recent years, these latent infections have caused the main problems with *Fusarium* in tulip bulbs.

Applied Plant Research (Flower Bulbs) in Lisse in the Netherlands is currently testing new methods to detect and control latent infections in bulbs. These are developed for growers and exporters.

[1] *Ziekten en Afwijkingen bij Bolgewassen* (trans. Diseases and Abnormalities in Bulbous Crops), *1: Liliaceae*. (3rd ed., 2000). Bulb Research Centre, Lisse

---

RHS SHOW DATES 2009

Ornamental Plant Competition	February 17 - 18	(Lawrence Hall, London)
Early Daffodil Competition and Hyacinth Competition	March 31 - April 1	(Horticultural Halls, London)
The Daffodil Show	April 7 - 8	(Hillside Centre, Wisley)
Late Daffodil Competition and Tulip Competition	April 28 - 29	(Hillside Centre, Wisley)

For further information contact the Shows Department, The Royal Horticultural Society Vincent Square, London SW1P 2PE (telephone 020 7630 7422)

Hardy Nerine Study Day

John David

Although *Nerine bowdenii* has been in cultivation in the United Kingdom for just over 100 years, it has become apparent that there are numerous variants and forms, some named, some not, and many incorrectly named. Consequently, it was decided to hold a study day to start to sort out what is in cultivation. The study day was supported by the RHS Herbaceous Plant Committee and the Nerine and Amaryllid Society, and was held at Wisley on 26 October 2007. Over 80 participants attended and brought cut flowers or plants of *N. bowdenii* and other nerines to show and discuss. We were particularly fortunate to benefit from the material supplied by the National Collection holder of hardy nerines, Margaret Owen, who, despite having staged an exhibit at Vincent Square two weeks earlier, managed to find plenty of interesting plants for the day.

The first half of the day concentrated on discussing the plants and started with learning about *N. bowdenii* in the wild. We were fortunate to have with us Graham Duncan, Specialist Horticulturist of the South African bulb collection at Kirstenbosch in South Africa and author of the guide book entitled *Grow Nerines* [1].

With his help we clarified the distinction between the original *N. bowdenii*, a native of the Eastern Cape, and the Natal Drakensburg population, commonly referred to as var. "wellsii". We then went on to consider the variants in cultivation and tackled some long-established problem names; we were assisted in this by Matt Bishop, who is not only an expert in snowdrops but also has a considerable knowledge of *Nerine*. One such question is the identity of *N. bowdenii* 'Mark Fenwick', which has received an AM and an FCC from the RHS although the true plant is rarely found. Much of what is in cultivation under this name is probably of hybrid origin or is from seed from the original. On show was a painting of the original plant in 1945, and with this we were able to decide which were the correct plants. Another problem was the identity of plants in cultivation under the name 'Alba'. The original 'Alba' was awarded an AM in 1919 and had pure white flowers with narrow petals. What is now cultivated under that name has pale blush pink flowers and should correctly be known as 'Pallida'. Perhaps one of the most surprising misidentifications to be discovered was *Nerine* 'Pink Triumph', which, when originally introduced, was a distinctive cultivar flowering in December through to January. There were plenty of plants on show under this name, all in flower and so, by definition, incorrect. It was established that 'Pink Triumph' is a hybrid with *N. undulata* as one of its parents, which is why it flowers so much later than *N. bowdenii* and its cultivars. Material of true 'Pink

John David, Graham Duncan and Matt Bishop (left to right) leading the discussion in the morning session.
(*photo* Linda Jones/RHS)

Triumph' remains to be traced but there is currently no name for plants being sold under this name. At the end of the session we had only covered some of the material on display but had made much progress in the correct naming of *N. bowdenii* and its cultivars.

In the afternoon there was a series of talks ably chaired by Captain Peter Erskine VMH. First of all, Graham Duncan gave us an insight into the species of *Nerine* in the wild, especially their ecology and distribution. The species can be grouped into those that grow in the summer rainfall region and those that occur in the winter rainfall areas, and this obviously affects the growth pattern and cultivation needs of the plants.

This was followed by a talk by John David, RHS Head of Botany, who revealed the history of the introduction of *N. bowdenii* into cultivation and how it came to be found to be sufficiently hardy to grow outside in the United Kingdom. The talk was illustrated with original letters from the collector's mother that had recently been discovered in the herbarium at Kew. Matt Bishop, Head Gardener at the Garden House in Devon, where the collection of nerines raised by the late Terry Jones is now held, talked about Terry Jones' breeding programme. Like others who have tried before him, Terry Jones was seeking to introduce the spectacular colours and glittering petals of *N. sarniensis* into a hybrid with *N. bowdenii* that would prove possible to grow outside. His success was apparent both from Matt's photographs and from the evidence of what has been tried in the garden.

The final talk was by Andrew Tompsett – no stranger to the daffodil world – who told us about the bulb physiology of nerines. He showed us how relevant this is to the successful flowering of these plants which, apparently uniquely, have two flower initials in the bulb at the same time, one of which is the flower for the current year and the other the flower for the following year. Flowering is affected by temperature and he provided information about the critical temperatures for the species commonly in cultivation.

The proceedings of the day are being written up for publication in a fully illustrated report that is due to be available from the RHS in autumn 2008. That the day was so successful was due in no small measure to the extraordinary hard work and organisation by Linda Jones (Secretary, Herbaceous Plant Committee) and the staff at Wisley who helped on the day. There is no doubt that outcomes from the day have already had an impact on the naming of *N. bowdenii* in cultivation.

[1] Duncan, Graham. *Grow Nerines.* Kirstenbosch Gardening Series, National Botanical Institute, Kirstenbosch, Private Bag X7, Claremont 7735, South Africa.

Nerine bowdenii at Wisley
(*photo* Barry Phillips/RHS)

Book Reviews

International Daffodil Register and Classified List 2008, compiled by Sally Kington. ISBN 978-1-902896-87-8. The Royal Horticultural Society, London, 2008. £40 (paperback, 1,412 pages)

The publication ten years ago of the *International Daffodil Register and Classified List 1998* was a major landmark in daffodil history, as well as highlighting the great importance of the registration of cultivar names in the genus *Narcissus*, for which the Royal Horticultural Society has long undertaken responsibility.

Since 1998 lists of new registrations of daffodil cultivar names have been published annually and, together with corrections and additional botanical and historical data gleaned by the Registrar, Sally Kington, the information obtained has been incorporated in this new edition of the Register, a very impressive tome containing 1,412 pages, published on 15 April 2008.

The detailed and comprehensive introduction provides the rationale for the entries in the Register and covers daffodil classification; cultivar registration; the scope of the Register; chromosome counts and the fertility they indicate; and the way in which the Register can be amended.

A new section in the introduction deals with first-flowering dates of cultivars and provides rationales for the use of these dates where these are known. Some amendments have also been made to the glossary, some of the illustrations of descriptive terms have been improved and all the illustrations have been digitised.

A further important and very useful addition is a list of the abbreviations for reference works cited in the Register, with titles spelt out in full.

No changes have been made in the new Register to the Horticultural Classification, but it is noted that international consultation on the definition of division 9 is ongoing. The cultivar name content in the Register has now expanded to over 29,000 (including over 2,000 unregistered names and some 1,400 synonyms), the increase to a large extent being accounted for by some 600 unregistered names obtained from show results and trade catalogues during recent years. Unregistered names are marked as such and are listed in the Register both to help prevent or minimise confusion between daffodils bearing the same cultivar name and to discourage or prevent further duplication of names.

Another new feature has been to list cultivar selections from species alphabetically under both the cultivar name and the botanical name. For example, while 'A.W. Tait' appears in its regular place under A, it also has a cross-reference under H, as *N. hispanicus* 'A.W. Tait'. This is a very helpful innovation when searching for the status of a particular cultivar.

Only minor amendments have been made to the Botanical Classification, but for the first time botanical names are listed separately from cultivar names in a new section between pages 1,365 and 1,386. The list of botanical names has been expanded considerably in order to try to lessen confusion over the identity of the taxa described; included are many former synonyms as well as some invalid names.

This list of botanical names was reviewed and amended by a Working Party constituted under the aegis of the former RHS Advisory

Panel on Narcissus Classification. Meetings were held regularly over a period of two and a half years prior to publication of the Register. It was clear from the report of the Working Party that there is a pressing need for thorough botanical revision of the genus, and it is hoped that this can be initiated and carried out before the next Register is due.

A further welcome innovation in this section is the inclusion of the reference works in which the botanical names accepted in the Register were originally published. Also provided for the first time is a list of the segregate genera such as *Ajax*, *Corbularia* and *Hermione* that were in the past considered distinct but are now regarded as synonymous with *Narcissus*.

While many individuals and organisations have been consulted and have provided information for the Register, the major credit for the production of this outstanding contribution to daffodil literature must be given to Sally Kington, modestly listed simply as compiler on the title page. Her diligence and persistence in ferreting out information worldwide during the last ten years has ensured that the 2008 edition of the *International Daffodil Register and Classified List*, with the much improved format and the greatly increased information and accurate data on *Narcissus* names, will become an essential reference work for use by all breeders, exhibitors and gardeners wherever daffodils are grown during the next decade.

Chris Brickell

The International Daffodil Register and Classified List at www.rhs.org.uk/plants/registerpages/intro.asp is updated with corrections and amendments at least monthly and with new registrations annually. New registrations are also published in annual Supplements obtainable from RHS Enterprises Ltd, RHS Garden Wisley, Surrey GU23 9QB, UK (telephone and credit cards (+44) (0)845 260 4505). Sharon McDonald, International Daffodil and Dahlia Registrar, is at the above Wisley address (tel. 01483 212 403, email sharonmcdonald@rhs.org.uk).

Common Snowdrop **(Galanthus nivalis L.)** *and its Diversity in Slovenia,* **by Joze Bavcon. ISBN 978-961-90262-5-0. Published by Botanicni vrt, Oddelek za biologijo, Biotehniška fakulteta, Ljubljana, 2008. €15 (paperback, 96 pages, including 26 colour plates).**

This is a little gem of a book but one that appears to be seriously flawed. It is a detailed account of all the variants of *Galanthus nivalis* that the author has discovered in the wild in Slovenia since 2001 and which have subsequently been cultivated in the Botanic Garden in Ljubljana. The text is presented first in Slovenian and then in an adequate English translation, the two halves separated by the 26 colour plates which alone make this a desirable addition to any galanthophile's library. Photographing snowdrops so as to show clearly the varied and subtle features that distinguish the myriad of variants is not easy, but the author has been successful in capturing almost a hundred different, named forms. These are divided up in relation to the type of variant concerned and although there is no index for the names and no cross-referencing from the text to the plate number, the majority of illustrations are at least in the same order as the text.

Cultivation has enabled the author to indicate which of the forms he observed in the wild are stable, which are only partially stable and which are not stable at all. He suggests that if one continues to search hard enough, even the most extreme variant will eventually be found to occur somewhere in a stable form. There is a useful summary of the main areas he has searched and the type of variants he has encountered in each one, as well as a brief but interesting account of the range of ecological conditions under which snowdrops are found in his country. The problems come when one considers that he seems to have named every distinguishable variant (whether known to be stable or not) but is not entirely clear whether in each case the name is intended to be attributable to an individual clone or to any plants of that type that are found. The latter situation is certainly the case in some instances. A system of formal Group epithets to bring together similar stable variants might indeed have been useful, but giving names to variants which are not stable is quite the reverse. All his epithets are presented as part of cultivar names but it seems that, based on this publication alone, none of them are formally established, since in two places in the text it is made clear that they are only provisional: 'for the sake of distinction single varieties had to be given provisional names' and 'a considerable number of forms have been determined, hereinafter provisionally described as new sorts.' There is little doubt that all this will cause a great deal of confusion, which is a great shame when this sort of carefully observed and meticulously recorded study is just what one would like to see undertaken for all snowdrop species.

The type of variants described include many that snowdrop lovers will be familiar with, including those varying in the number, size, shape and habit of the outer perianth segments, plus of course any amount of greening on the outers, not to mention split spathes and dangling pedicels, plus variations in inner segment shape, size and markings, variation in ovary shape and colour, as well as the presence of one or more petaloid bracts. The author has been unable, however, to find any good, stable yellows. Some of his plants are very beautiful and the green-suffused and exquisitely shaped "Tomišelj" would surely make even the most experienced galanthophile weak at the knees, and how could anyone resist something so evocatively and accurately described as is "Robcek" - 'as if a white handkerchief were hanging from a string'! However, even I might draw the line at "Spiralis" whose appearance I leave to your imagination!

As an account of the variation that can be found in a single species, this to be welcomed, but it leaves us with something of a nomenclatural headache.

Available from the author at Ljubljana Botanic Garden, Izanska C15, 1000 Ljubljana, Slovenia.

Alan Leslie

A transcript of the Tenth Galanthus Gala held at Concorde College, Acton Burnell, Shrewsbury, Shropshire on Saturday the 10th of February 2007. (18 one-sided, A4, un-numbered pages, plus 6 colour plates - published 16 February 2008).

This is the latest of these rather quirky records of the lectures given during a day of snowdrop indulgence, and as always is worth getting for the illustrations alone, some of which are the only published, pictorial record of the cultivars concerned. It is 'what it says on the tin', a transcript - so you get the largely unedited chit chat, badinage and fiddling about with slides that really would be better edited out. It is also hard to see why we should really want more than a page detailing the bidding for a number of auctioned bulbs. It would seem that with a bit more effort we could have had three much more coherent and in the long term more useful accounts if the authors had been persuaded to write up their presentations in a way more suited to the printed page. But that is the nature of this beast and it does not pretend to be otherwise. Mind you, on this occasion there is a solitary heading 'Introduction and welcome Joe Sharman' with nothing relevant to follow it; perhaps this was the result of some trenchant editing, but it might have been the opportunity to set the scene a bit since this Gala was the first to be almost snowed off, and it would have made sense of some of the references made in the talks to know this.

The record is primarily of

three talks: on the snowdrops of Ketton by Cliff Curtis, on the propagation and selection of *Galanthus reginae-olgae* by Melvyn Jope and on a melange of the new, the rare and the curious by Joe Sharman. All were thoroughly entertaining and informative. Cliff Curtis' account showed what can happen when a garden full of different snowdrops is left to get on by itself for perhaps a century or more and what several keen pairs of eyes can then pick out from amongst the resultant seedlings. In part this turned out to be quite a family affair with ones named after the lecturer, his wife ('Little Joan') and his daughter ('Sharron Louise'). The garden is famous for its self-sown *G. ikariae* and it seems likely that the much-coveted 'Chandler's Green Tip' came from here. (Well, someone paid £40 for it in the auction, so I think that indicates a coveted snowdrop!)

Melvyn Jope described how he has spent 25 years being fascinated by the autumn flowering snowdrop *G. reginae-olgae* and how over this time, starting with just a few bulbs, he has built up an unrivalled collection of variants of it, largely raised from seed. Many of these are indeed lovely plants and his presentation included all sorts of choice items; there is a nice picture in the transcript of the essentially poculiform 'Autumn Snow'. He gave some useful hints for those considering the challenge of attempting to twin-scale their bulbs, with the general recommendation that it was all pretty easy! Hygiene, sharp knives, attention to labelling at all stages, not being too greedy when chopping up the bulbs and knowing when and how to feed them all emerged as points to remember.

In the final lecture Joe Sharman made those attending doubt the evidence of their eyes - and indeed in some cases they were right to do so since he was having a bit of fun at times, having doctored the plants before taking their pictures! As part of the presentation he was trying to elicit from the participants suitable names for these and other genuine finds, and people proved to be remarkably inventive (if in a few cases going a bit near the bone). I hope some of the good names suggested will eventually get attached to some equally good plants. Here at any rate you can see *G. nivalis* 'Shrek', *G. elwesii* 'Kencott Ripple' and *G. nivalis* 'Quad' for the first time, although one wishes perhaps that this might be the first and last outing for the hideous pink-veined horror that is also illustrated. Would someone also please note that Joe wishes to join the 'immortals', as he put it in this talk, i.e. those after whom a snowdrop is named - so if you have something worthy (and it will need to be very good), please consider putting him out of his misery!

For future transcripts might it be a good idea to have at least a few words about the background of each lecturer?

Available from Joe Sharman at Monksilver Nursery, Oakington Road, Cottenham, Cambridge CB24 8TW at a cost of £10 (add £1 for postage and packing). Transcripts of earlier Galas can be had from the same source.

Alan Leslie

Gardening with Tulips **by Michael King. ISBN 0-7112-2539-7. Frances Lincoln, London, 2005. £25.00 (hardback, 192 pages).**

The author's starting-point is that tulips are suffering from an identity crisis. So often we meet them in our gardens as great slabs of dazzling colour, dominating borders and parterres, bedded out *en masse*, unchallenging and 'too easy to grow to be considered exclusive.' Convinced that they have a much wider role to play, Michael King sets out to change that image and to persuade us to use tulips more boldly, not in isolation, but in combinations with other bulbs, perennials, shrubs and trees. His plea is that we pay more attention to them as individuals and allow them a presence in the overall garden scheme that exploits their variety of form and vast colour range. From his base in Amsterdam he is well placed to appreciate that though the range of cultivars and species is enormous, some 90 per cent are destined for the cut-flower trade and opportunities in our gardens are being lost.

In the opening section on the anatomy of the tulip we are made aware of the consequences of the genetic instability that lies behind the remarkable diversity within the genus: 'The tulip's wild nature to change and adapt cannot be tamed and this allows it to continuously alter and offer tantalizing glimpses of new possibilities.' Hence the hundreds of cultivars we may choose from at any one time. The heart and soul of a tulip is of course the flower, its colour and its shape. How the two groups of interacting pigments determine that colour and how light affects the tepal surfaces are dealt with in considerable detail and presented in an easily digestible fashion.

An obligatory history of tulips in cultivation precedes a discussion of the 1996 Tulip Classification, which remains in current use. Divided into the conventional four Sections (Early Flowering, Mid-Season, Late and Species) each of the fifteen Groups is described in detail. To simplify matters, King chooses his top 20 classic tulips with each Group providing at least one, excluding the commercially banned Rembrandt tulips affected by virus. The selections have the secondary purpose of exemplifying the colour contributions that tulips can make to the spring garden. The radiant 'Apricot Beauty' is his favourite Single Early: 'The official colour description of salmon rose tinged with red hardly does justice to its subtle combination of peach and pink lightly reminiscent of blushing skin.' The Darwinhybrid 'Daydream' whose flowers open as buttercup yellow before changing to a warm glowing medley of light toffee-orange is his Mid-Season representative. The Lily-flowered 'Red Shine' with its tapering tepals epitomizes the elegant possibilities of the Late Section. The Species Section receives the full treatment it deserves. The spectacular 'Ancilla' bears the torch for the low-growing Kaufmanniana Group, whilst the scented 'Purissima' and the equally gorgeous 'Für Elise' illustrate the possibilities of the Fosteriana and Greigii Groups respectively. Declaring 'the more you grow tulips the more irresistible become the species,' the author sings the praises of a score or so attractive wild tulips which, given treatment normally afforded to alpines, deserve a place in our gardens. Most are best lifted and dried off in summer but the lovely *Tulipa sprengeri* may be left for years to spread by stolons undisturbed.

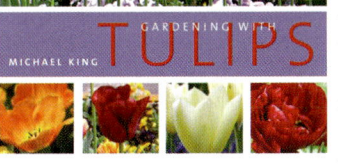

A welcome chapter of this in every respect highly recommendable book is on tulips in contemporary gardens, urging the reader to be more adventurous in the use of tulips and associated plants. Euphorbias are perfect partners, grasses such as *Calamagrostis × acutiflora* are good companions, as also are willows, dogwoods and various species of *Prunus*. The book concludes with two excellent essays on tulip colours and cultivation hints. The author's photographs illustrating over 400 different tulip cultivars and species are outstanding throughout.

John Page

Buried Treasures: finding and growing the world's choicest bulbs, by **Janis Rukšans**. ISBN 978-0-88192-818-1. Timber Press, Portland, Oregon, 2007. £30.00 (hardback, 383 pages, including 304 colour plates).

The idea of a lifetime spent digging up rare bulbs in the wild will doubtless raise eyebrows, but when the trowel is in the hands of an extremely knowledgeable and skilful plant hunter who, having identified his findings (well, most of them!), propagates and distributes seed, we may consider that he has performed a useful service. Unlike China and the Himalayas, which are well represented in plant-hunting literature, Central Asia has produced relatively little in the way of accounts in recent years. All the more welcome then is this detailed record of the author's adventures in the countries bordering on the Caspian Sea and beyond, no-go areas for Westerners throughout the decades of Soviet rule and potentially perilous still today.

The hot dry summers of these vast Central Asian hunting-grounds favour the growth of bulbs of course and their diversity is correspondingly great. Throughout this book we meet mouth-watering irises, alliums, bellevallias, colchicums, *Corydalis*, *Crocus*, fritillarias, muscaris, ornithogalums and scillas, amongst others.

The genus *Tulipa*

For most *Yearbook* readers, however, the main attraction is the genus *Tulipa*: the index makes reference to no less than 50 species and cultivars. Similarly, snowdrop enthusiasts will find 18 distinct though mostly brief mentions of *Galanthus* species and cultivars.

Few mountains in Central Asia that are known to hold special plants have escaped the author's attention, and when he finds his quarry he has no fear of challenging luminaries of the stature of Brian Mathew and Christopher Grey-Wilson on matters of identification (see his thoughts on *Crocus tauricus* and *Cyclamen kuznetzovii*). Nor is he willing to regard *Galanthus cabardensis* as a synonym of *G. lagodechianus* [1]. No surprise then when he remains loyal to *Tulipa karabachensis*, which he meets in the Zangezur range on Armenia's frontier with Azerbaijan. Richard Wilford [2] regards it as a variant of *T. armena*. The author is clearly his own man, but it would be wrong to suggest that he is instinctively at variance with the authorities. As we know only too well, tulips are immensely variable and the species boundaries are hazy to say the least. Given the right conditions, they are likely to crop up anywhere in the countries visited here, sometimes in huge numbers and frequently posing identification problems, to a point where in some cases the species rank appears of doubtful use. Hence the author's frequent reference to the widespread *Tulipa bifloriformis/turkestanica* aggregate. He is by no means sure of what he is looking at. In these journeys through remote regions, however, the tulip enthusiast has to envy him: in the Germab valley of Iran he finds *Tulipa micheliana* with its unique black basal blotch and deep-lying bulbs; over the border with Turkmenistan in the Kopet Dag there is abundant *Tulipa hoogiana*; on the heights of Sina in Uzbekistan it is *Tulipa greigii*; in Kazakhstan's Karatau range he meets yellow forms of the same, and the beautiful *Tulipa orthopoda* in the Berkara Gorge, terrain which also produced a mystery round bulb resembling *T. kaufmanniana* and awaiting identification. Tentatively labelled *Tulipa berkariense*, its clones include 'Morning Star' and 'Little Ilze'. The Zeravshan mountains of northern Tadzhikistan house *Tulipa fosteriana* in granite cracks, and the striking *T. korolkovii*. A river crossing leads to red and yellow forms of *T. butkovii*. Eroded sandstone in the Varzob Valley yields *T. hissarica*, and so on. These are but a few of his tulip finds and the reader will be out there in the mountains with Janis, savouring them all.

The author

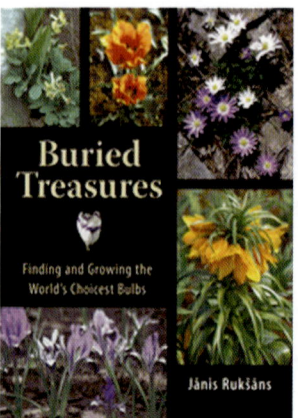

The author is a born survivor then, not only in the wilds of central Asia. In his native Latvia he combines journalism and the life of a nationalist politician with the daily grind of running a nursery. Even in the days of Russian domination, he was always adept at cultivating influential contacts in the West (Chris Brickell, Kath Dryden, Brian Duncan, Henrik Zetterlund, Jim and Jenny Archibald, Michael Hoog and Norman Stevens to name but a few), 'dangerous' individuals who attracted the attention of Soviet agents. He tells the story of a Siberian friend anxious to obtain from him samples of *Erythronium sibiricum* cultivars 'Olga', 'Zoya' and 'White Fang'. This led to an interrogation by the KGB who had intercepted the telegram and sensed a coded message.

Growing bulbs
The section on bulbs in the garden reflects the author's experience in Latvian conditions and contains much of interest to the grower. Low pH in a soil, he believes, promotes the formation of small bulbs and he recommends the addition of dolomitic lime. He advocates shallow planting of small bulbs and in the face of the prevailing wisdom uses a high nitrogen fertilizer in early spring to compensate for the leaching effect of the wet winter.

Conclusion
All in all, this book from a far corner of Europe fully deserves a place on the bulbgrower's bookshelf. Finally, a word of congratulation to the translators Gunta Lebedoka and Martins Erminass on a very readable text.

[1] See Bishop, M., Davis, A. & Grimshaw, J. (2001). *Snowdrops: A Monograph of Cultivated* Galanthus. The Griffin Press, Maidenhead.
[2] See Wilford, R. (2006) *Tulips: Species and Hybrids for the Gardener*. Timber Press, Portland, Oregon.

John Page

***Spalding Flower Parade - The Golden Years* by Doug Braybrooks. ISBN 978-1-84547-159-0 At Heart Ltd, Altrincham, 2007. 120 pages**
In 2008 Spalding held its 50th Flower Parade and this book celebrates the event by taking a look back over the years to the days soon after World War II when it all began.

In many ways they were innocent times: there were few cars; life was simple compared to our jet-setting, flat-screen-worshipping, internet-orientated lives today.

The Lincolnshire Fens have always been a special place with a special atmosphere. Until they were drained they were fertile but unusable. Once they came into cultivation they proved a wonderful bulb-growing area and the spectacle of fields of tulips growing *en masse* became a magnet for visitors each spring, particularly in the grey post-war years. How this developed into the world-famous flower parades, using the hand-cropped tulip heads to create great sculptures, is told with love and charm. The people who achieved the spectacular floats come to life, including the blacksmith Geoff Dodd who built the frames for 43 years from the designs of Adrianus van Driel and then later his son Kees. 'In an average year Geoff was using up to 14 miles of steel, 7,000 welding rods and 140,000 welds to produce a parade.'

Available from Lincolnshire Free Press and Spalding Guardian, The Crescent, Spalding PE11 1AB. £12.99 plus £2 postage and packing.

Wendy Akers

Daffodil, Hyacinth, Snowdrop and Tulip Notes

Ralph B White Memorial Medal
Malcolm Bradbury

The Ralph B White Memorial Medal is awarded annually by or at the discretion of the RHS Daffodil and Tulip Committee to the raiser of the 'best new daffodil cultivar exhibited to the Society during the year.' The medal was awarded in 2008 to Brian Duncan for Seedling 3065, a division 1 daffodil with a white perianth and an orange trumpet, raised from 'Queen's Guard' × 'Lutana' and since named 'Prime Target'. The flower was unplaced in its single bloom class at this year's RHS Daffodil Show due to a large split in its perianth. However, as will be clear from Brian's article on page 36, white and orange trumpet daffodils are at an early stage in their development and 'Prime Target' is a clear breakthrough in both colour and form.

'Prime Target'
(*photo* James Akers)

Definition of Division 9 - Poeticus Daffodil Cultivars
Sharon McDonald

A new consultation on the definition of division 9 was undertaken by the International Daffodil Registrar in 2007. Block votes on three options were invited from the RHS Daffodil and Tulip Committee (including trials and show schedule committees), the RHS Advisory Panel on Narcissus Classification (members including the six national daffodil registrars) and nine national daffodil societies, with the following results.

Option 1 - to retain the existing definition - 3 votes
Option 2 - to adopt a restricted definition proposed by Mary Lou Gripshover - 3 votes
Option 3 - to adopt a wider definition proposed by Max Hamilton - 2 votes

There were no stated abstentions but there were three non-respondents.

On the basis of this inconclusive vote the Registrar decided to retain the existing definition in the new edition of the Register, as publication was imminent, and to refer the matter back to the RHS Advisory Panel on Narcissus Classification (APNC). A note of explanation was added to the Register.

The APNC agreed that the way forward was for the Registrar, being new in post and new to the differences of opinion on the definition of division 9, to take a season to familiarise herself both with *N. poeticus* and with cultivars in divisions 9 and 3.

To this end the Registrar would welcome suggestions from individuals/societies as to which cultivars would be best to look at among those considered to be borderline between divisions 9 and 3. Pictures would be appreciated, as would measurements of perianth and corona lengths (including in the species).

This is just a brief synopsis of the situation. For more information, please contact Sharon McDonald, International Daffodil Registrar, RHS Garden Wisley, Woking, Surrey GU23 6QB, UK. (+44) (0)1483 212403. Fax (+44) (0)1483 211750. Email sharonmcdonald@rhs.org.uk

NOMENCLATURAL STANDARDS OF DAFFODILS IN THE RHS HERBARIUM (WSY)
SUSAN GRAYER

With around 200 new daffodils being registered annually, there is the potential to document them as nomenclatural standards.

A nomenclatural standard is a herbarium specimen (preferably) or a photograph; it provides a permanent record of the distinguishing characteristics of the cultivar in question and helps fix the name.

At the moment the RHS Herbarium (WSY) at Wisley has just over 4,500 standards, of which nearly 500 are daffodils. Ten of the daffodils are preserved as herbarium specimens, most of which have been collected from the RHS Trials. The overwhelming majority take the form of photographic images, most of which are sent in to the International Daffodil Registrar upon submission of the relevant registration form. The Registrar, Sharon McDonald, works closely with the Herbarium in the collection and curation both of the specimens and the photographs that provide daffodil standards.

An image is suitable for noting the form and colour of the cultivar (although this rarely matches exactly). It can greatly help with the formal description of the plant. However, nothing can substitute for a sample of the plant itself, which permits researchers to inspect characters not recorded by the photograph and in the future may even allow extraction of the DNA for genetic studies.

A successful nomenclatural standard comprises the following items:
• A sample of plant material: flower, stem, leaves and even bulb
• Photographs face-on and in profile, as the shape of the corona is frequently a diagnostic character of daffodils
• A reference for and photocopy of the first place of publication

Standard portfolio for
Narcissus 'Mallee'
(*photo* Susan Grayer/RHS)

More information on nomenclatural standards can be found on the RHS web pages, which include an A-Z of standard specimens held in the herbarium. The address is:
www.rhs.org.uk/learning/research/herbarium.asp
Standard specimens are now published annually in *Hanburyana*, a publication by the RHS Botany Department whose address is:
www.rhs.org.uk/learning/publications/hanburyana/index.asp
Please send material to:
The RHS Herbarium, RHS Garden Wisley, Woking, Surrey GU23 6QB

Susan Grayer is Herbarium Research Assistant (Standards) at Wisley.

Hyacinth Trial at Wisley
Malcolm Bradbury

A one-year trial of 27 hyacinth cultivars was held at Wisley in 2008 and was judged by members of the Daffodil and Tulip Trials Sub-Committee. This was the first modern trial of hyacinths held by the RHS and may even have been the first ever held by them. Following the trial it was recommended that the Award of Garden Merit (AGM) should be given to the following cultivars: 'Hollyhock' (double florets); 'Jan Bos', 'Miss Saigon' and 'Paul Herman' (single florets); and 'Blue Festival', 'Pink Festival' and 'White Festival' (multiflora). These recommendations were subject to ratification by the Daffodil and Tulip Committee in October 2008.

A New Snowdrop Discovery
Galanthus plicatus 'E.A. Bowles'
Michael D Myers

'E.A. Bowles'
The original clump at Myddleton House
(*photo* Michael Myers)

Okay, so I know what you are thinking, not another new snowdrop. The current vogue for snowdrops has led to a plethora of names in recent years. Some of these cultivars are novel and valuable additions to the range of plants currently grown, but all too often they are indistinct from existing varieties. The test of a truly exceptional new cultivar is that it is instantly recognisable and cannot be confused with anything else. If this is coupled with a desirability that instantly places it at the top of every galanthophile's desiderata, you then have a truly exciting snowdrop discovery. Such a plant I believe is *Galanthus plicatus* 'E.A. Bowles'.

As an enthusiastic galanthophile I try to attend some of the specialist snowdrop events that are held each spring. On 18 February 2004 I went to a Snowdrop Day organised by the RHS to coincide with their Early Spring Flower Show. The next day I took the opportunity to visit Myddelton House. The bulbs at Myddelton House are always a treat for a keen photographer and it was not long before a particularly large snowdrop in the middle of a border close to the house caught my eye. On closer inspection I realised it was a plicate (explicative) variety with large, rounded flowers, but could hardly believe my eyes when it turned out to be poculiform (all tepals of equal length and without green markings). I was not familiar with any poculiform *G. plicatus* cultivars and immediately tried to find one of the gardeners to ask about it. One of them, Brian, kindly offered to help but had not been aware of the snowdrop despite the fact it was in quite a prominent position; perhaps someone had selected it in the past and forgotten about it. Christine Murphy, the head gardener was unfortunately away, but thanks to Brian I left Myddelton House later that day with a single bulb and a broad grin.

My next step was to contact Joe Sharman

at Monksilver Nursery, a fellow galanthophile with a particular interest in the poculiform varieties. He too was unfamiliar with the snowdrop and promised to visit Myddelton House to check out the new find. At the same time I emailed Christine to suggest that if it were a new cultivar it might be appropriate to name the snowdrop after either the garden or its creator. Christine decided that 'E.A. Bowles' would be most appropriate; I fully agreed; and the cultivar was thus provisionally named. Although Bowles does have at least two snowdrops named for him (both *G. plicatus* forms), the best known cultivar does not have an obvious link since it commemorates his middle name, Augustus. *G. plicatus* 'Bowles's Large' (and 'Bowles's Late') are names sometimes attached to often mediocre forms of the species which may or may not have been distributed by Bowles. How fitting therefore that one of the greatest of all plantsmen and galanthophiles (he probably coined the term) should at last have such an exceptional cultivar, found at Myddelton House, named for him.

So why is *G. plicatus* 'E.A. Bowles' so exceptional? Well, it is unique in being the only poculiform variety of *G. plicatus* currently known in cultivation. The flowers seem to be stable, in that the inner tepals do not revert to being shorter or to having green markings as is seen in some poculiform cultivars of *G. nivalis*. The cultivar seems vigorous and healthy, with most flowering bulbs producing two flowering scapes. These are tall and upright (the first flower scapes are over 35cm (14in) tall, the second slightly shorter but they can abort before fully developed). The flowers are quite large, with the outer tepals being over 30mm (1.2in) long. The flowers are also quite late and longlasting, often until the end of March. In 2005 *G. plicatus* 'E.A.Bowles' started flowering before *G. plicatus* 'Baxendale's Late' but finished at the same time here in North Yorkshire. The leaves are typical of *G. plicatus*, being as long as the flower stems (37cm or 14.8in) and quite broad (2.5cm or 1in), with the margins 4-5mm (0.2in) along each edge folded downwards.

The above description is given from only a small sample of material and under certain growing conditions variability will most certainly occur. What is in no doubt however is that this cultivar is an exceptional snowdrop with a combination of highly desirable characteristics. *G. plicatus* 'E.A. Bowles' has been successfully twin-scaled by at least one grower and so in the not too distant future it should become available (at a suitably high price!) and may help raise funds for the garden at Myddelton House. The remaining bulbs at Myddelton House have been moved to a more secure position just in case there is anyone who cannot wait for them to become available legally (remember *Galanthus elwesii* 'Carolyn Elwes'). The cultivar received its first public showing at the 2005 Galanthus Gala in Beccles, where slides were shown by Joe Sharman, who just so happened was speaking on poculiform snowdrops. *G. plicatus* 'E.A. Bowles' was awarded a Certificate of Preliminary Commendation by the Joint Rock Garden Plant Committee on 12 February 2008 (see page 131).

I firmly believe that *G. plicatus* 'E.A. Bowles' will become as popular and coveted as its antithesis, namely *G. plicatus* 'Trym' (which has six 'inner' tepals rather than six 'outer' tepals). It is a fitting tribute to a much admired galanthophile.

A SNOWDROP TOUR
Ruby Baker

Galanthus galas are now annual events in both the Netherlands and Germany, though unlike ours not specialising solely in snowdrops. The Garden Tours (contact Monksilver Nursery) five-day trip to the Netherlands in February 2008 started with the three-day gala at De Boschoeve, Wolfhenze. A lecture was held each day and the 20 plant stands had a wide range of snowdrops, small daffodils and other bulbs, herbaceous plants, trilliums, books and memorabilia for sale. The garden was also open and there was a nursery nearby. The tour party had a full itinerary of visits to follow on with: to snowdrop gardens, wild populations, castle grounds, etc., in various provinces.

From the 1950s to 1987 enterprising bulbgrowers from the island of Texel took a bus (still on view) to France, returning with the *Galanthus nivalis* now grown in rows in the fields and sold as dry bulbs. The residue were planted in woods under alder and willow, in poor dune sand, and are now naturalised. These were happily explored and a few green-tips discovered; scattered *G. viridapice* were also noted in field populations.

All the visits on the trip were thoroughly enjoyed, but for snowdrops the accolade went to Annie Fallinger at Dordrecht, who has the Dutch National Collection of about 350 cultivars. The 0.13 hectare (0.3 acre) garden has sandy, peaty soil irrigated beneath by water from the adjacent dyke; the beautifully planted collection is set off by hellebores. In the United Kingdom low, clipped box hedges are sometimes seen as edgings; Annie uses a wide border of snowdrops for her beds (see left). This well-organized trip to the Netherlands was voted 'fantastic' by the participants.

Snowdrops as path-edging
(*photo* Ruby Baker)

CORRECTION

The picture of *N*. 'Quiet Waters' on page 41 of *The Daffodil, Snowdrop and Tulip Yearbook 2007-8* was taken by Tom Stettner and not as stated by John Pearson. Our apologies to both of them for this error.

Daffodils & Tulips
for exhibition and the garden
Large, miniature & species

Wins at the RHS, The Daffodil Society & AGS since 1975

New releases for 2009

visit **www.miniaturebulbs.co.uk**
or send 2 x 1st class stamps for our free catalogue

Ivor & Barbara Fox

Miniature Bulbs™
Choice Bulbs

The Warren Estate, 9 Greengate Drive, Knaresborough,
North Yorkshire   HG5 9EN   Tel/Fax: 01423 542819

Overseas Shows and Reports

ADS National Show and Convention 2008

Mary Lou Gripshover

The American Daffodil Society (ADS) held its 54th National Convention and Show in Richmond, Virginia, from 10-13 April 2008. Members laden with flowers began arriving on 9 April, in preparation for the show.

The National Show

Mother Nature was her unpredictable self, and early shows had fewer blooms than usual. However, nearly 100 exhibitors from around the world entered about 2,800 blooms to fill the benches by the time judging began on this one. It was good to see some new names appearing in the prize list, with Karen Cogar winning the Gold Ribbon for Best Bloom in show with 'Entente' 2Y-O taken from her winning Bozievich Collection. This collection of twelve varieties, one stem of each from at least four divisions, also included 'La Paloma', 'Kiwi Sunset' and 'River Queen'. Karen also used 'River Queen', along with 'Louise Randall' 2W-W and 'Peggy White' 2W-W, in her Purple Ribbon-winning collection of five white daffodils. She also won the ribbon for best collection of five historic (pre-1940) daffodils; included were 'Kansas' 1939 and 'Chinita' 1922.

Kathy Welsh, last year's big winner, repeated this year. She won the Quinn Medal for twenty-four varieties, one stem of each from at least five divisions; the Havens Medal for twelve varieties, one stem of each from at least three divisions, 5 through 10; the Red-White-Blue Ribbon for five American-bred daffodils; the English Award for five English-bred daffodils; the Carncairn Trophy for five daffodils bred in Ireland; the Northern Ireland Award; the Australian Award; the Dutch Award for one daffodil from each of five different decades, not necessarily raised in the Netherlands; and the Watrous Medal for twelve miniature daffodils. Ten daffodils appeared in two collections: 'Arrowhead', 'Lavalier' and 'Sugar Rose' 6W-GWP in the Havens and Quinn; 'Doctor Jazz' in the English and Quinn; 'Rockall' in the Carncairn and Quinn; 'Tycoon' 3W-WWY in the Australian and Quinn; 'Homestead' in the American and Dutch; 'Torridon' in the English and Dutch; 'Pixie Dust' 6W-W in the Havens and Dutch; and 'Mexico City' 2Y-O in the Quinn and Carncairn. Kathy's Watrous collection included three species, 'Yellow Fever' 7Y-Y, 'Sabrosa' and the newly registered 'Tiny Bubbles'.

The Throckmorton Medal for one daffodil from each of fifteen different RHS classifications and the New Zealand Award both went to Kathy Andersen. Prominent in her Throckmorton collection were 'Radar', an unregistered 1W-P from C E Radcliff; 'Terminator'; 'Pops Legacy'; 'Phoenician'; and 'Elusive' 3W-R. Her New Zealand collection included three Ramsay/Koanga seedlings along with 'Backchat' and 'Tinkerbell'.

Ginger Wallach won the Tuggle Medal (three stems of twelve varieties from at least three divisions), including 'American Classic', 'La Paloma' and 'Pink Silk'. Glenna Graves won the Maroon Ribbon for her collection of reverse bicolors, including an impressive bloom of 'Swedish Fjord'.

Overseas Shows and Reports

Rod Armstrong was the winner of the White Ribbon for Best Vase of Three Daffodils with 'Sugar Rose'. A bloom from this vase was also awarded the Fowlds Medal for Best Named Cyclamineus Hybrid in show. Rod also won the Miniature Bronze Ribbon for three stems each of five miniatures from at least three divisions. Rod's collection was a mix of old standbys 'Segovia', 'Minnow' and 'Xit' with newer cultivars 'Woodstar' and 'Mitimoto'.

The Olive Lee Bowl for Best Standard Flower in divisions 5 through 8 went to show chairman Delia Bankhead for her bloom of 'Sunday Chimes'. Elizabeth Brown won the Van Beck Medal for Best Historic Daffodil with 'Daphne' 1914, and the Historic Vase of Three Ribbon with 'Dreamlight' 1934. The ribbon for Best Intermediate Daffodil went to Jim Taylor for his bloom of 'April Joy' 2YYW-W, while the Rose Ribbon for Best Seedling went to Leone Low for her yellow/pink trumpet. The Small Growers Ribbon was awarded to Kristi Sadler, recently graduated from the Youth Section, for her bloom of 'Avalon'. Youth winners were Will Sadler, who had Best Bloom with 'Salome' and Best Collection of Five Daffodils. Madeleine Wallach had Best Vase of Three Daffodils with 'Rapture'.

Olivia Welbourn was awarded the Aqua Ribbon (one each of nine varieties from three divisions), which included the Miniature Gold Ribbon-winning 'Pequenita', along with 'Angel o' Music', 'Twinkle Boy' 12Y-Y, 'Heidi', 'Spoirot', and 'Smidgen' 1Y-Y. The Lavender Ribbon for Best Collection of 5 miniatures went to Mary Lou Gripshover, who also won the Miniature Rose Ribbon for 99-1 6G-Y, an open-pollinated Golden Bells Group seedling.

Edie Godfrey brought some of John Reed's early miniatures from Michigan. John won the Larus Trophy for three blooms of a miniature seedling with his 6Y-Y from 'Heidi' open pollinated. He also won the Miniature White Ribbon with three blooms of Crotty seedling 1-4-94, 6W-W. A bloom from this exhibit was later awarded the Gold Medal for Innovation in Daffodil Breeding. The medal goes to the hybridizer, so it was sent to Colin Crotty of New Zealand.

Elise Havens prevailed in the Challenge Section, winning with collections which were about half seedlings and half named cultivars. Her 'Little York' 2Y-P was included in several collections, and her MH7/11 ('American Dream' × 'Color Magic') 2Y-P was winner of the Bender Award for Best in Section. Elise also won the Mitsch Trophy with three blooms of OH4/3, another 2Y-P.

Ribbons for container-grown daffodils went to Ray Rogers and Kathy Welsh, while the Best in Photography Award went to Al Warfield.

The Convention

Later during the convention, Ray Rogers demonstrated his winning techniques for growing beautiful pots of daffodils, 'Preparing, Nurturing, and Showing Daffodils in Containers'. Kathy Welsh's topic 'How to travel with Show Flowers' was so popular that she demonstrated it in two sessions. Delia Bankhead gave a programme on 'New Developments in Miniature Breeding from Around the World', and Elise Havens headed a panel on 'Hybridizing Daffodils'. Ted Snazelle gave a programme on 'All you ever wanted to know about daffodils but were afraid to ask'. (Who knew that college professor Ted had such a sense of humour?) Bonnie Pega talked about 'Companion Planting for Daffodils'.

We enjoyed an evening at Lewis Ginter Botanical Garden, and toured four delightful private gardens. True to form, it rained on 'tour day', but that doesn't deter daffodil people.

The festivities ended with a chance to trip the light fantastic to music of the 1930s and 40s by the George Carroll Dance Band. It was a rousing end to another great convention. Come join us next year in Chicago so you can say, 'I was there!' and not 'I wish I'd been there.'

Daffodils in New Zealand 2007

Anon

With the Australasian Daffodil Championship and Convention coming to New Zealand, locals hoped for the bumper season that it turned out to be, with high quality flowers appearing on the show benches throughout the flowering period. The Championship was held in Hamilton, where the organisers had worked hard to make the occasion memorable. Publicity was circulated both within New Zealand and overseas. Rewards followed, with visitors from the United States, Northern Ireland, Tasmania, Victoria, New South Wales, ACT and Western Australia joining Kiwis from all over the country. Monetary backing from a range of sponsors and underwriting from the Northern Daffodil Club ensured that all had a good time. Visitors were met at the airport and bus stations by locals and transport was provided to and from the show venue throughout the three days. During staging, three lovely young hostesses and one handsome host, immaculately attired in black and wearing colourful daffodil vests, appeared with trays of complimentary wine, beer and juice. This was the first of many appearances by this group, ensuring that a party atmosphere was maintained throughout! The sponsorship also allowed the organisers to put on live professional entertainment throughout the show and at the three evening functions. Richard Ezell was at his humorous best as one of the after-dinner speakers, while the Andrews Sisters, and later the Soul Sisters had the whole party doing the Conga! A cultural performance by a youthful Maori kapahaka group was performed with such pride and intensity that it brought tears to the eyes of many visitors. On the other hand the efforts of 'volunteers' to perform a haka (a traditional Maori challenge) with the group proved to be hilarious. The show itself was high quality, not only on the competitive benches but also with wonderful floral art and displays of orchids, camellias and many other spring flowers. Free entry to the show plus clever publicity ensured record crowds. Along with the entertainment there were educational sessions - Wilf Hall on breeding tazetta hybrids, Nancy Tackett and Ben Blake on their inspirational programme, *Daffseek*, and Michael Brown on judging daffodils. Tours to local gardens and daffodil nurseries plus a river boat cruise on the Waikato proved to be popular. It all wound up on the Sunday evening with a complimentary Kiwi Barbecue funded by the Northern Daffodil Club and held by the pool at the home of Peter and Lesley Ramsay. The local food, which included smoked trout, mussel fritters, and a range of meats and vegetables plus magnificent home-made pavlovas from Lesley's kitchen, was supplemented by a range of quality donated wine from New Zealand's leading wineries. All of this led Brian Duncan to comment in an impromptu speech that this was the best convention that he had ever attended! Praise indeed from one of the world's leading convention attendees.

The last hurrah?

The year 2007 signaled the last year of shows for New Zealand's top exhibitors, Koanga Daffodils, who marked the occasion by going out on a high note. They exhibited at six shows and took Best Bloom in show at each. For the record, the blooms were 'Cameo Frost' 2W-W, Northern Daffodil Club table show; 'Impeccable' 2Y-Y, Morrinsville Horticultural Society Spring Show; 'Omeomy' 3Y-R, Australasian Convention Show; 'Moon Shadow' 3W-GYY, Cambridge Daffodil Show; 'Cameo Magic' 4W-W, South Island National Daffodil Show; and 'Cool Crystal' 3W-GWW, NDC Late Show. Surprisingly, all of these blooms were grown at the Ramsay's Matangi Nursery. Add to this Koanga's defence of the Australasian Open Championship, a win in the Australasian Open Seedling Championship, and many victories in collection classes at both National Shows and you can understand why this was a high note! They will be missed as a team but both Peter Ramsay and Max Hamilton intend to continue hybridizing and exhibiting, albeit on a much reduced scale. So, as the saying goes, the fat lady hasn't quite sung her last song yet!

The Australasian Daffodil Championship and North Island National Show

All of the above is just background to the main feature of the year. Ideal amounts of rain and sunshine helped produce flowers with excellent substance, size and form. The Australasian Championship and the North Island National Show at Hamilton on 14-16 September saw local exhibitors at peak bloom time and 2,362 blooms were staged. The fact that locals took first and second places in the Australasian Open Championship and all three places in the Australasian Seedling Classes speaks volumes. They had strong opposition: eight entries in the Championship and eleven in the Seedling class. Koanga's winning entries in both classes were, according to the judges, very clear winners. In the Open Championship, however, Miller Daffodils in second place and Kevin and Carol Kerr from Nelson were not far behind. There were also two strong entries from Australians Ian Dyson and Graham Brumley.

Koanga's winning entry had outstanding blooms of 'Blossom Lady' 4W-O (which was also unanimously awarded a First Class Certificate by the Floral Panel); 'Cameo Marie', a very reliable 3W-YYO; the vastly underrated 'Waihaha' 2W-P; 'Impeccable'; and 'Sulphur Monarch' 1Y-Y. The last mentioned flower is a clear shade of light lemon and a credit to its raiser, John Hunter. The winning entry was beautifully groomed and staged - it is reported that one of the Koanga team took almost two hours to prepare this entry, the seedling group and their winning entry in the North Island twelve, while the rest of the team were left to deal with their numerous other entries! The Miller Daffodils entry, in second place, lacked the colour and evenness of the winning entry but had some outstanding flowers. Jackson-bred 'Macdalla' 1W-Y, which has to be one of the best of its kind around, and their own 'Frontier Frills' 2W-Y caught our eye. Kevin and Carol Kerr continue to improve both the quality and size of their blooms. Their well-constructed group had six John Hunter-raised varieties including yet another very good 'Sulphur Monarch', while American-raised 'Trumpet Warrior' 1YYW-WWY was also noteworthy. The much repeated injunction 'read the schedule carefully' was not heeded by two growers with almost one hundred years of exhibiting experience between them. The consequence was the dreaded NAS (Not According to Schedule). It just goes to show that care must be taken, as Koanga found out at the next show of the season where their medal collection suffered the same fate! In the seedling classes Koanga and Millers were first and second again while Graham Phillips, another Waikato grower, came in third.

The Divisions 5-10 and 12 Championship saw John Hunter from Nelson scoring a meritorious win; all of his flowers were of his own raising. Second place went to a very welcome visitor from Tasmania, Rod Barwick, who traveled incognito, exhibiting under the name of Glenbrook Bulb Farm. We liked 'Tilly Titus' 5W-W in his entry. Koanga, who are not noted for exhibiting higher-numbered divisions, were third, but their entry did contain a very good stem of 'Fencourt Jewel' 8W-P which found its way to the premier table.

There were four entries in the Australasian Miniature Championship and this proved to be a close battle between the Malroze team from Southbridge in Canterbury and Glenbrook Bulb Farm. Unfortunately several of Rod's flowers were feeling the effects of the long journey from Tasmania, which left the door open for Malroze. One of their well-balanced and neatly presented entries, M65-18-7, was a miniature division 5 seedling which caught everyone's eye and ended up in the last group under consideration for Best Bloom in show. The Intermediate Championship went to Wanganui grower Wayne Hughes who is making the 'inbetweens' something of a

93

speciality. All blooms in the entry were of Wayne's own raising. He also won the Amateur Championship (nine quality entries) showing nice flowers of 'Fever Pitch' 2Y-R, 'Cameo Marie' 3W-YYO and 'Pillow Talk' 2W-W. Bob and Heather MacDonell were second, a very good result for recent recruits to daffodil growing. Mike Smith from Nelson was third, which again was creditable given the relatively small number of bulbs that he grows. Wayne was also the winner of the Amateur Seedling Championship from Tony Davis of Bowral, New South Wales.

With the best flowers being selected for the Australasian classes it would have been understandable if there had been a marked drop of quality in the North Island National Show classes. Certainly there was a slight drop-off but this was hardly discernible. Graham Phillips, who had a team including Brian Duncan to help him stage his vast collection of blooms, was the clear winner of the much sought-after NDS Raisers Cup. The rimmed variety 'Banda' 2Y-YYO (unregistered) was the outstanding flower in his entry. Having used their best blooms in the Australasian classes there was thought that Koanga might have been vulnerable in the Yarrow Trophy which requires twelve varieties, one stem of each. This did not prove to be the case, with the team producing another well-balanced set, including seven of their own raising. The collection class with most entries (seven) was for nine daffodils from division 6. Malroze have made this their property for several years and succeeded again with 'Rapture', 'Trena', 'Wings of Freedom' 6Y-Y and 'Golden Years' 6Y-Y. Perhaps the surprise of the day was the result of the class for nine double daffodils. Koanga had secured 21 successive wins in this class but were soundly beaten by John Hollever from Paraparaumu. John showed good flowers of 'Heamoor', 'Kiwi Solstice' and 'Neavesville Gold' 4Y-Y. Second was Graham Phillips and the well-beaten Koanga team was a distant third. The class for nine daffodils from division 8 saw the almost inevitable victory going to Wilf Hall from Levin. His entry consisted of six of his own raising and 'Compressus'. Brogden Bulbs from Hawera were second; we noted a nice bloom of the Byrne-raised 'Kahurangi' 8Y-YYO in the entry.

The Miniature Championship saw a new name engraved on the trophy - Sue Scott from Paraparaumu. This was a lovely wee entry which included 'Kokopelli', 'Sundial' and the best stem of 'Hawera' seen for some time.

The Amateur Collection classes were down on entries a little but the theme of good quality flowers continued. Wayne Hughes, who has signaled his intention to leave the Amateur ranks, won the major class, the Waikato Trophy, with a very well-balanced twelve. 'Pillow Talk' 2W-W, 'Botlar' 3Y-O and 'Cameo Marie' (having a great year) were the outstanding flowers. There were nine entries in the red cup classes where Wayne was again successful. One of the hardest trophies to win in the Amateur Collections Section is the Parr Trophy for six varieties. It was good to see Clive Denton of Cambridge, who oversaw the show construction and was the principal fundraiser for the event, get rewarded here. The six New Zealand-raised class went to Roy and Noeleen Wilcox with a nice set. One daffodil of their own raising 'Royeleen' 1Y-O (unregistered as yet), a 'Corbiere' seedling, created much interest as a significant improvement in this colour code.

The Amateur Multi-bloom and Single Bloom classes, the nursery of the future, were very well supported this year. There were thirteen entries in the class for three yellow trumpets which was won by first-year National exhibitor Ian Hook from Matangi, with three very tidy 'Centor' (an 'Akala' seedling). Corey Field from Opiki in the Manawatu took the next best supported class (twelve entries) for double daffodils; his entry had a lovely vase of 'Kiwi Magic'. The Single Bloom classes had a record 145 entries. It was pleasing to see ten individuals, many of them first-year exhibitors, winning classes.

The quality of the premier blooms was

Overseas Shows and Reports

'Royeleen' Best Amateur Bloom in show)
(*photo* Kirby Fong)

demonstrated by the number of growers involved - fifteen for the overall premiers and five Amateur awards each going to a different exhibitor. Ones that caught our eye were: 'Royeleen' shown by Brogden Bulbs and another flower of the same variety shown by its raisers Roy and Noeleen Wilcox from Hawera which was Champion Amateur Bloom (a first for them); a Hunter seedling 1Y-P grown by Kevin and Carol Kerr; Koanga's bloom of 'Impeccable'; the Burr-raised 'Cherrygardens' 2W-GPP shown by Graham Phillips; 'Omeomy' 3Y-R shown by Koanga; Bill Cowie's 'Heamoor' 4Y-Y; 'Party Girl' 4W-YYP, Canadian-raised and shown by Mike Smith; 'Ameeya' 4W-W shown by Graham Phillips; John Hunter's 'Flight Path' 6Y-W; and Glenbrook Bulb Farm's 'Weary Deary' 7W-P. The Best Overseas Grown Bloom in show award went to Ian Dyson from Melbourne for 'Waihaha' 2W-P.

After lengthy discussion, the Best Bloom in show award went on a split decision to 'Omeomy' (raised by Colin Crotty and exhibited by Koanga Daffodils) for the second year running. Reserve Best Bloom in show was 'Flight Path'.

The South Island National Show an anticlimax? Never

After the extravaganza of the Australasian Championship in Hamilton, some thought that the South Island National Show held in the small southern town of Winton on 29-30 September might be an anticlimax. However they forgot to tell the good people of the Winton Garden Club, who organised a wonderful finale. Held in two halls at the local High School, the show proved to be a spectacular event, with excellent flowers and genuine southern hospitality. It was obvious from the outset that the hosts believed that their visitors had not been well fed. Visits to the Home Science Room for all manner of taste treats became a regular feature. Add to this a spectacular dinner in an excellent garden setting and you will realize why the visitors avoided the bathroom scales for some weeks afterwards!

While the quality was not quite as high as in the North Island there were still plenty of very good flowers for the excellent public attendance to view. The Rhodes Silver Cup is a huge trophy and is sometimes referred to as the Baby's Bath. It calls for twelve varieties, three stems of each, New Zealand-raised. Last year Spud Brogden was the only entry but this year he had two strong competitors. As always his entry was immaculately presented with bright colours and the necessary size and substance. We noted 'Surfer Girl', a very tidy 3W-W; 'Mason Road', one of the best of the newer 2Y-Rs, and 'Wild Card' 3Y-W, still one of the best of its kind. The prestigious NDS Raisers Trophy went to Wayne Hughes, albeit narrowly from last year's winner Pleasant Valley Daffodils. The flowers in Wayne's entry were all under number and of fairly recent vintage. He will only get better!

Koanga Daffodils beat five other

competitors to win the International Class, in which nine of the twelve single blooms staged were of their own raising. The best of these were 'Lesley', a quality 3W-Y, 'Thumbs Up' 2Y-O and 'Cameo Magic'. 'Dailmanach', the renowned John Lea variety, also had the afficionados talking about its pure pink cup. Sometimes the oldies beat the newcomers! Also in their collection was the seldom-seen Duncan origination 'Cape Helles' 3Y-R. Its orange tones were very attractive. Kevin and Carol Kerr had to settle for second place although their entry was an improvement on the ones staged in Hamilton. They also included a good 'Cameo Magic', along with 'Centrefold' 3W-YYR and 'Navigator', a very tidy 2Y-O.

Michael and Marian Brown from Loburn regained the collection trophies for white trumpets and bicolor trumpets. The former was especially impressive, with fine examples of 'Snowy Morn' and 'Don Miller'. The Kerrs got their reward in the red cup and pink cup classes. Their pinks 'Applins', 'Dailmanach' and 'Polar Sky' were especially nice. Malroze also proved a point with wins in the American-raised, doubles and division 6 collection classes, thus completing the North/South Island double. They also retained the Miniature Daffodil Championship. Wayne Hughes continued his stellar run by winning the intermediate championship, this time very narrowly over Miller Daffodils. 'Petite Magic', a charming white and pink split-corona daffodil, attracted much comment from the public. Wayne also won the Amateur class for twelve varieties one stem of each, with 'Sulphur Monarch' (having a great year) and 'No Worries' 3W-WWY amongst his best flowers. Elsewhere in the Amateur classes Trevor Rollinson won the pinks and also the New Zealand-raised with well-grown flowers. The multi-bloom amateur classes were dominated by Judy and Gordon Phimister, signaling promotion next year, as will be the case for Bob Gordon who walked away with the single bloom trophy.

The premier table was dominated by Koanga Daffodils at their last National show. No fewer than ten premier certificates headed north. Of these, 'Lemon Spice' 3Y-Y, 'Barndance' 3Y-R with lovely clear colours and near perfect symmetry, a new 2Y-R (PR04:66) bred from ('Rabid' × 'Cowboy') × 'Cameo Flush', and an even newer 2W-Y (PR06:42) were interesting flowers.

Seedling PR04:66
(*photo* Kirby Fong)

Denise and Neil McQuarrie produced a spanking 'Kiwi Happy Prince' 2W-YYR; the Millers another excellent 'Macdalla'; Andrew Jenkins showed a very good 'Acumen' 2YYW-P; and Kevin and Carol Kerr demonstrated that a well-grown Purbeck 3W-YOO can still beat all others in its division. Winners of the Amateur Premier Bloom awards were division 1 Judy and Gordon Phimister with 'Golden Vale'; Wayne Hughes divisions 2 and 3 with a seedling 2W-W and 'Badbury Rings' respectively; and Andrew Jenkins division 4 with 'Cameo Magic'. Wayne's seedling was also Amateur Champion Bloom, a fitting farewell for Wayne from the amateur ranks.

The final two contenders for the Best Bloom in show award were both from Koanga

Overseas Shows and Reports

A Whirlwind Tour
Richard Perrignon

It was a whirlwind tour of Hobart in the Spring of 2007. Alas, I'd missed the Claremont Show, where I had hoped to catch up with Mike Temple-Smith and other luminaries of the Tasmanian daffodil fraternity. Never mind, there was still the Hobart Show on Friday 7 September. There was only one day to view it, before returning to Sydney to celebrate the 50th anniversary of my father-in-law's arrival in Sydney from Italy.

Of the many outstanding daffodils which graced the champions table at Hobart, two were particularly eye-catching. The first was the Champion Pink, 'Sally Malay' 2Y-P, staged by Pat and Phil Rowe. This delectable cultivar, with its perky poise, luscious pink cup and rich yellow perianth, seemed to look you right in the face. The second was the Reserve Champion - a brightly coloured 'Terminator' 2Y-O, staged by Jackson's Daffodils, whose trade stand was equally pretty. On this occasion, 'Terminator' was pipped at the post for Grand Champion by the Rowe's splendid bicolor cup, 'Flintlock' 2W-Y.

As readers of these pages will know, the writer is also a fan of the little daffodils. Though they are often in greater abundance at the earlier Claremont Show, this year the Hobart Show did not disappoint. The prizes for Champion miniature and Champion seedling were awarded to Kevin and Mary Crowe for their splendid seedling no. 6 of 2006. To crown the weekend, the Crowes also received the prestigious R H Glover Trophy from the Tasmanian Daffodil Council.

As one would expect, some fine miniatures were also staged by Glenbrook Bulb Farm. These included an elegant *Mitimoto*, a perfectly presented 'Ben'Bler' 10Y-Y - the same cultivar, if not the very bloom, that took Champion Division 10 the previous weekend at Claremont - and a stunning bloom of 'Olumbo', with a very generous yellow cup indeed, which was awarded this week's

'Kiwi Happy Prince'
(*photo* Kirby Fong)

'Cameo Magic' Best Bloom in show -
South Island National Show
(*photo* Graeme Miller)

Daffodils. The unanimous vote went to the Ramsay-raised 'Cameo Magic', with 'Dailmanach' being selected for Reserve Best Bloom in Show. Thus ended an era in the history of daffodil growing in New Zealand; next year will see many new names engraved on the major daffodil trophies in New Zealand!

'Sally Malay'
(*photo* Richard Perrignon)

'Ben'Bler' (magnif. × 5 approx.)
(*photo* Richard Perrignon)

champion Division 10. Remarkably, the most splendid example of 'Phalarope' I have ever seen failed to catch the judges' eye on this occasion. Could this have been the very bloom that won Grand Champion only days earlier at the Claremont Show?

Nowadays, the Hobart Show is staged in the City Hall. Grand though it is, its cavernous spaces, huge stage and multistorey seating seem to be designed for something rather less intimate than a daffodil show. I preferred the old Town Hall - a beautiful old Georgian edifice built of local sandstone, which housed the Hobart Show till about ten years ago. It was both intimate and elegant. Perhaps the show outgrew the old venue, but it would be worth the effort to squeeze back into it if the opportunity should ever arise.

After the show, there was time to rush back to Claremont and dine with my old friends, Rod Barwick and Ann Atkin at Glenbrook Bulb Farm. As always, I was greeted by a noble rooster on guard duty, and Rod's fearless watchdog, Justice, who will show anyone round the property for a pat. My favourite pink magnolia was in full bloom, and the pots were brimming with miniature seedlings. If the state of Rod's daffodil pots - or of the Hobart Show, for that matter - is any guide, the culture of daffodils in Tasmania continues to thrive.

As I write, it is July 2008. With snow falling only two days ago in the next suburb, it is one of the coldest Sydney winters I can remember. Soon, September will usher in the Spring once more. In the front yard, a pot of 'Welcome' 2Y-Y is in full bud. For decades, this sturdy cultivar has been a staple of the Australian cut-flower trade. The bulbs were given to Ida and the children by the kindly Alf Ladson last summer, when we visited him at his home in Wandin outside Melbourne. After the mandatory ride on Puffing Billy, we also visited Lyla Coles (Frank's widow) at Wantirna. Both Lyla and Alf, I am pleased to report, are in good health and spirits. The first blooms of 'Welcome' will be out before August. In the cold of winter, they shall be warm reminders of distant friends.

Editor's note: We apologise to both author and readers for the unavoidable shortening of Mr Perrignon's article in the last Yearbook *due to lack of space.*

Snowdrops at RHS Shows 2008
Alan Leslie

Two autumn flowering snowdrops
The cavalcade of snowdrop exhibits started earlier than usual, with the Joint Rock Garden Plant Committee being offered both *Galanthus reginae-olgae* and *G. peshmenii* at out-of-London meetings in October 2007. Mrs K Rimmer brought the former to a meeting in Glasgow on 6 October but failed to move the judges into award mode, whilst those bulb growers *extraordinaire* Bob and Rannveig Wallis had more success with their pan of *peshmenii* at Loughborough a week later, gaining an Award of Merit (AM) at the first time of asking.

Galanthus peshmenii 'Kastellorhizo'
(*photo* Chris Grey-Wilson)

Their stock originated with the 1974 Martyn Rix introduction (EMR 4041) from the tiny Greek island enclave of this species on Kastellorhizo. Here, rather atypically for a snowdrop, it grows in rock crevices and sometime occurs right down by the sea. The uniform nature of this stock and the fact that it seems to be distinct from all other collections in cultivation, which come from the populations on the Turkish mainland, has been used to justify the application of the cultivar epithet 'Kastellorhizo'. This does not necessarily mean that any plant from this island race will fall within this cultivar, which flowers with the leaves at least partially developed (unlike the Turkish plants) and has an apical heart-shaped mark on the inner segments. Some have suggested too that it is a bit more robust than the Turkish plants. *G. peshmenii* differs from *reginae-olgae* in its longer, narrower, more floppy leaves, which lack the pale central stripe of *reginae-olgae*, and in the reduced extent of the inner segment inner face markings.

January
The January RHS London Show saw many galanthophiles gather in the Hall looking for some snowdrop action and all knowing that in their gardens the season was already in full swing. The exhibits in the Hall really failed to reflect this, but Avon Bulbs and Foxgrove Plants had a few seldom-seen cultivars to test people's identification skills. Avon had Alan Street's 'Blewbury', an early-flowering, dwarf *nivalis* selection from the churchyard at Blewbury (Gloucestershire) - home of the better-known and much more distinctive 'Blewbury Tart'. It did have nicely rounded

flowers, a solid V-shaped bridge mark and a noticeably upright habit. Here too one was able to inspect 'Bess', named by Daphne Chappell for the late daughter-in-law of Helen Milford (of *Helichrysum milfordiae* fame), a probable *elwesii* hybrid with a single large apical V-shaped mark, the ends of the arms turned up at their tips. Foxgrove's most notable offering was *elwesii* 'Mary Biddulph', which as exhibited had a rather variable mid-green H-mark, long slender outers and a noticeably cylindrical ovary. Matt Bishop [1] describes the mark as in two separate parts (with the lower part also divided into two) so this may be one of those plants that can not quite make up its mind. It was originally christened 'Oliver Wyatt' by Mary Biddulph, after the donor of her plant, but once it was realised that this name was already in use, Daphne Chappell provided the new epithet to commemorate one of the original purveyors of the now famous snowdrop lunches.

Joint Rock had three snowdrops to consider that day and recognised the merits of two of them with awards: a Preliminary Commendation (PC) for Joe Sharman's *nivalis* 'Llo 'n' Green'; and an AM for Rod Leeds' *plicatus* 'Three Ships'. 'Llo 'n' Green' is an interesting plant originating from the Gorge de Llo in the eastern Pyrenees, characteristic of these Pyrenean snowdrops in flowering very early for a *nivalis* and like many of this provenance having a slight, pale, median stripe down the leaf. These features have suggested an association with *reginae-olgae* (otherwise not known further west than Sicily) but apparently DNA evidence does not support this and so they remain in *nivalis* for the time being. The strongly convex outer segments in this selection have 5-7 distinct green lines in the apical quarter below a pure white tip, and the inners sport a substantial, broad, deep green, apical bridge mark. Perhaps hardly Wagnerian in character, this is an engaging little plant when performing as it should. Its companion on the award bench is already a bit of a minor classic, a December flowering plicate selected by John Morley (himself a bit of a classic in the world of snowdrops!). It was found beneath 'an ancient cork oak at Henham Park, Suffolk in 1984' (Bishop *et al.*, 2001) and has since delighted all who can get their hands on a plant. You might well ask what it was doing in peak condition in mid-January and the answer lies in the fact that the plants exhibited were the first flowering of twin-scaled bulbs, which are often a bit later then normal. As Rod Leeds explained, this gave the opportunity for the Committee to see the plant, which otherwise would never come before them at its normal Christmas flowering time.

'Three Ships'
(*photo* Rod Leeds)

The flowers of 'Three Ships' have characteristic slightly puckered outer segments on a rather rounded flower (intimations of the effect G. *plicatus* achieves to even greater extent in the famous 'Diggory'); the flared inners have a large apical mark, extending especially along the margins towards the base. This is always a welcome gift for a fellow galanthophile! G. *elwesii* 'Zwanenberg' was the third of the trio on show on this occasion, exhibited by Mr Sharman, but this relatively undistinguished snowdrop is better as a good doer in the garden than on the show bench.

February
Fast forward now to February and a better, though by no means exceptional show of plants in the Hall: Avon Bulbs featuring

amongst others Elizabeth Parker-Jervis' discovery from the early 1970s of a double *elwesii* hybrid from the grounds of Kingston House at Kingston Bagpuize, which she christened 'Kingston Double', as well as the elegant French-origin *nivalis* 'Angelique'. Foxgrove provided their customary sumptuous carpet of species and cultivars, which on this occasion included the Irish aristocrat 'David Shackleton'; the almost all-green and much coveted Canadian G. *elwesii*, 'Rosemary Burnham'; and home-grown 'Curly' with its strongly recurved leaves and X-marked inner segments. Broadleigh Gardens had that epitome of the single-marked *elwesii*, John Morley's 'Comet', with big, beautifully proportioned flowers on long pedicels and a satisfyingly crisp, almost heart-shaped apical mark on its inners. This lovely snowdrop was apparently first noticed on the rock garden at Wisley and the name commemorates the appearance of the comet Kohoutek in 1972.

However, all this was eclipsed by the two awarded snowdrops, which quite stole the show on the day: 'Greenfinch' and 'E.A. Bowles'. What a splendid pair! Both gained PCs and will surely go on to get further accolades in the future. The former has been in limited circulation for a while, since its discovery by Richard Hobbs in the former Norfolk garden of Heyrick Greatorex in 1990, and was exhibited on this occasion under the unmistakable Cotswold colours of Dr Ronald Mackenzie. Its grey-green, plicate, arching foliage with broad wavy edge sets off flowers borne on tall stout stems. These flowers have long ovaries and inners with a large, heavy, dark green bridge mark around a deep apical notch; the outers have a distinct basal claw and a pinched-in tip but are otherwise strongly convex and bear an apical set of deep green lines that coalesce at their tips. The boldness and crispness of the marking make this an outstanding snowdrop. Green-tipped flowers are not that unusual nowadays, of course, but new poculiform snowdrops are uncommon and poculiform plicates rarer than the

'Greenfinch (above) and 'E.A. Bowles' (below) (*photos* Susan Grayer/RHS)

proverbial hen's teeth! So for almost everybody the appearance of G. *plicatus* 'E.A. Bowles', exhibited by Joe Sharman, was a delightful surprise and instantly went on every wish list! It originated in the garden at Myddelton House, which used to belong to the great plantsman and galanthophile after whom it is most appropriately named. Its broad, pale glaucous green leaves are held rather erect but are overtopped by large bulbous flowers with short oblong ovaries, each flower with a heavy green spathe and six pure white segments of equal length and no markings. 'E.A. Bowles' shows every sign of being a very vigorous, healthy garden plant and a great addition to any collection once it becomes available (start saving now!).

Also seen by Joint Rock on the same day was 'Ruby Baker', exhibited by Dr Mackenzie and named after the current doyenne of the snowdrop world by Robin Hill, in whose Irish garden Ruby had admired the original plant. This is a delightful convolute hybrid with strongly hooded leaves and bulbous pale green ovaries below well-formed flowers, whose inner segments sport a basal band and two apical 'pips' beside a deep sinus. It seems that Ruby now wishes she had drawn attention to something a little more distinctive! At the same meeting the Reverend Richard Blakeway-Phillips showed a pot full of 'Atkinsii' and Mr and Mrs Norman a hybrid seedling that spent so little time on public view that this reviewer had no time to see it at all.

March

The season was not quite yet done, as Professor John Richards put up *G. nivalis* 'Warei' for Joint Rock at the Harlow meeting on 1 March. No award was forthcoming, but this was an opportunity to see this sometime controversial triploid cultivar, differing from the better-known 'Viridapice' in having a much longer, almost leaf-like spathe and a slightly differently shaped apical mark on its inners. Both have green-tipped outers. Their separation has been a perennial source of argument whenever two or more galanthophiles come together, but hopefully this is now laid to rest by the detailed account in Bishop [1] - well that's the theory anyway!

It seems that as interest in snowdrops continues to grow and deepen, still more variations are coming to light, sometimes in species in which previously little variation was recognised. This, coupled with the first results of a few more hybridization programmes starting to flower, must mean that there will be more to fill these notes in the years to come.

[1] Bishop, M., Davis, A. & Grimshaw, J. (2001). *Snowdrops: A Monograph of Cultivated Galanthus*. The Griffin Press, Maidenhead.

THE DAFFODIL SOCIETY
(Founded 1898)

THE SPECIALIST SOCIETY FOR ALL DAFFODIL ENTHUSIASTS

Providing companionship, shared knowledge and advice, and information on growing and showing technique for over 100 years. Please join us.

Details from the Secretary:
Mrs Terry Braithwaite, 105 Derby Road, Bramcote, Nottingham NG9 3GZ   Email: rogerbb@lineone.net

RHS Early Daffodil Competition

John Goddard

Of all the daffodil events at the RHS, the Early Daffodil Competition relies most heavily on the vagaries of the weather. This year it was on 11-12 March and we had had very much a stop-start winter, with some early cultivars such as 'February Gold' blooming in January and then a long cold February holding back later flowers, making timing difficult even for those who grow in pots. There were just 16 exhibitors and a total of 205 daffodils.

Collection classes

Despite the weather we had nine entries in the collection classes. Class 1 for six cultivars from any division was won by John Goddard with a good colourful set comprising 'Predator', 'Sealing Wax' (registered as long ago as 1957), 'Jolly Good', 'Pink Silk', 'Pops Legacy', and 'Renovator'. Stan Ellison stepped up from the novice classes to come a very respectable second, his entry containing some very fine blooms if a little on the smaller side: 'Cryptic', 'Cape Cornwall', 'Osmington', 'Drayton', 'Heamoor' and 'Pink Silk'. Ron Scamp brought up the rear with a neat selection including 'Portloe Bay' and seedlings 889 2Y-O, 22 2Y-Y and 71-46-1 7W-Y, all of his own raising.

Class 2 for three cultivars three stems of each was also won by John Goddard, who showed 'Sealing Wax', 'Jolly Good' and 'Heamoor'. A bloom of the latter was chosen as Best Bloom in show. Ron Scamp had a nice refined 'Jack Wood' in his second-placed entry and Geoff Hollingdale a very pretty 'Lemon Silk' in his third-placed entry. He and his wife always come well prepared with their own collapsible table, lots of spare blooms, brushes and canes and all the extras that top exhibitors need to stage their flowers.

Division 6 cultivars are probably at their best in the early spring - or late winter if you prefer. Three vases each with three blooms of a distinct cultivar always catch the eye of the public, so Class 3 quite often is the star of the Competition. John Goddard's 'Rapture', 'Trena' and 'Warbler' beat Richard Tabor's 'Jetfire', 'Rapture' and 'Inca'. I also liked Ron Scamp's third-placed entry, which contained 'Kea' 6W-P and S508 6Y-O, both of high standard. There were no entries in Class 4 calling for seven blooms from division 1, which was not surprising at this time of year. This used to be a class for division 6, which is much more achievable for even the most serious exhibitor.

Single bloom classes

Eight entries for division 1 and top of the tree came Zara Evans, whose lovely 'Ristin' 1Y-Y beat John Goddard's 'Pink Silk' by a mile. 'Ristin' was raised over forty years ago in Tasmania and registered in 1979. It has also been the parent of many other cultivars and remains invaluable in very early shows. Well done Zara.

There were nine entries for large cups, with Stan Ellison showing 'Cape Cornwall', which was in contention for Best Bloom in show. Richard Hilson's well-formed 'Sealing Wax' came second, with John Gibson's third-placed 'Tingdene' 2Y-O looking promising though unfortunately not yet in commerce.

Flowers from divisions 3, 4 and 5 are a bit thin on the ground at this time of year, but Geoff Hollingdale found a nice early 'Park Springs' with plenty of colour. Zara Evans scored with 'Heamoor' (how useful this is), and 'Churchfield Bells' 5Y-Y won for Ron Scamp. The latter, 2007 registration was raised by amateur hybridizer Alec Harper from the fertile 'Limequilla' and the diploid *N. triandrus*. There were nine entries in the division 6 yellows and for once 'Rapture' was beaten into second and third by Brian Duncan's own 'Flashback' 6Y-Y, a cultivar in which the characteristics of *N. cyclamineus* are truly predominant. Division 6 whites had six entries, with a whole battery of 'Trena's of which John Goddard's was the best.

There were few blooms to highlight in the remaining single bloom classes. The split-corona daffodils were colourful, being won by Richard Tabor's 'Jack Wood', with Nial Watson showing a powerful 'Maria Pia'. Richard Hilson's stem of 'Cornish Chuckles' 12Y-Y beat several others, and the best of the last six classes were to be found in Class 17 for seedlings bred and raised by the exhibitor. John Gibson was placed first, second and third, with seedlings all under number, these were out of the top drawer, and we look forward to them being named.

Miniature and wild daffodils

Although there were not so many entries as last year, they could be said to have been of even higher quality. Brian Duncan and John Gibson had a rare old battle in this section. The general public were most intrigued by the different tiny forms on display, and some even questioned if they were daffodils.

In the bred and raised classes, Brian Duncan brought over from Northern Ireland some absolutely stunning examples in his quest for perfection. He won 'The Six' raised by the exhibitor with a fine collection that included 3047, a super flower bred from *N. cyclamineus* × 'Candlepower' which was Best Seedling and Best Miniature in show.

Brian also included *N. cyclamineus* × *N. jonquilla* var. *henriquesii*, 'Young Blood' × *N. dubius* and three others of similar vein in his collection. John Gibson just beat Brian in the three-vase class with seedlings all under number. The single bloom class had eleven entries nearly all Brian's although I spotted one from Malcolm Bradbury.

Seedling 3047
N. cyclamineus × 'Candlepower'
(*photo* Michael Shuttleworth Photography)

For the rest of these miniature classes, Brian took the three-vase class with his beloved 'Candlepower', 'Small Talk' and 'Norwester', together with three blooms of *N. cyclamineus* in Class 24. Single blooms of 'Norwester' and a *N. bulbocodium* seedling also scored. Not to be outdone, John Gibson won the class for three miniature species, three blooms of each, including the rarely shown *N. cantabricus* subsp. *monophyllus* in his set, and the single miniature species with a superb *N. cuatrecasasii*.

Novice classes

How nice to see entries here at the Early Competition. M Hill provided all five, of which 'Pink Silk' was his best. Four firsts and a second is a good start. Well done Mr Hill.

Other displays

Finally, I must mention the Avon Bulbs show stand, which was very interesting and informative, displaying thirteen gold medals won at Chelsea. I have no doubt 2008 will see another. Broadleigh Gardens (also Chelsea Gold Medal-winners) chose to show 42 vases of small and miniature daffodils displayed on a vacant show bench. The tiered staging showed them off very well. Just to add to the colour, H W Hyde produced a galaxy of colourful tulips, and Jan Pennings brought over from Holland 28 containers of gorgeous, scented hyacinths, which filled the whole hall with perfume.

The new Hyacinth Competition got off to a small but interesting start with four exhibitors. Jan Pennings showed some superbly grown recent introductions and Wendy Akers some distinctive and relatively rare historic hyacinths.

This was a very colourful show overall, at a time of year when we all want cheering up. Well supported by the public, we hope that the rumours of its demise in London are not true.

RESULTS

Class
1 Six Cultivars, any Division or Divisions, one bloom of each. (4) 1. J H J Goddard: Predator, Sealing Wax, Jolly Good, Pink Silk, Pops Legacy, Renovator 2. S Ellison: Heamoor, Pink Silk, Osmington, Cape Cornwall, Drayton, Cryptic 3. R A Scamp: Seedling 22, Seedling 71-46-1, Portloe Bay, Seedling B89, Queen Mum, Trigonometry
2 Three Cultivars, any Division or Divisions, three blooms of each. (3) 1. J H J Goddard: Jolly Good, Heamoor, Sealing Wax 2. R A Scamp: Boslowick, Swallow, Jack Wood 3. Mr & Mrs G Hollingdale: Salakee, Eaton Song, Lemon Silk
3 Three Cultivars Division 6, three blooms of each. (3) 1. J H J Goddard: Warbler, Trena, Rapture 2. R C Tabor: Inca, Rapture, Jetfire 3. R A Scamp: Seedling 505, Kea, Warbler
4 Seven Blooms Division 1 (0)
5 One Cultivar, Division 1, one bloom. (7) 1. Ms Z Evans: Ristin 2. J H J Goddard: Pink Silk 3. S Ellison: Pink Silk
6 One Cultivar, Division 2, one bloom. (9) 1. S Ellison: Cape Cornwall 2. R Hilson: Sealing Wax 3. J Gibson: Tingdene
7 One Cultivar, Division 3, one bloom. (2) 1. Mr & Mrs G Hollingdale: Park Springs 2. R A Scamp: Malpas
8 One Cultivar, Division 4, one bloom. (5) 1. Ms Z Evans: Heamoor 2. S Ellison: Heamoor 3. R A Scamp: Radjel
9 One Cultivar, Division 5, one bloom. (2) 1. R A Scamp: Churchfield Bells 2. Mr & Mrs G Hollingdale: Harmony Bells
10 One Cultivar, Division 6, yellow perianth, one bloom. (9) 1. B S Duncan: Flashback 2. R Hilson: Rapture 3. Mr & Mrs G Hollingdale: Rapture
11 One Cultivar, Division 6, white perianth, one bloom. (4) 1. J H J Goddard: Trena 2. Ms Z Evans: Trena 3. Mr & Mrs G Hollingdale: Trena
12 One Cultivar, Division 7, one bloom. (4) 1. R C Tabor: Crill 2. R A Scamp: Penstraze 3. J Gibson: Seedling K36/95
13 One Cultivar, Division 8, one bloom. (5) 1. S Ellison: Avalanche 2. Mr & Mrs G Hollingdale: Falconet 3. R A Scamp: Seedling H.8YY
14 One Cultivar, Division 11, one bloom. (4) 1. R C Tabor: Jack Wood 2. N Watson: Maria Pia 3. R A Scamp: Seedling 882
15 One Cultivar, Any other division, one bloom. (6) 1. R Hilson: Cornish Chuckles 2. J H J Goddard: Cornish Chuckles 3. R C Tabor: Cornish Chuckles
16 One Intermediate Cultivar from Divisions 1 to 4 or 11, one bloom. (3) 1. J S Pennings: Skilliwidden 2. R A Scamp: Seedling 1080 3. Mr & Mrs G Hollingdale: Topolino
17 One Cultivar Seedling under number, bred and raised by the Exhibitor, one bloom. (8) 1. J Gibson: 147/34/97 2. J Gibson: 2-4-90 3. J Gibson: 127-25-2000
18 Six Miniature Cultivars, bred and raised by the Exhibitor, one bloom of each (1) 1. B S Duncan: 3047 *N. cyclamineus* × Candlepower, 3241 Young Blood × *N. dubius*, 3232 *N. asturiensis* × Candlepower, 3100 *N. asturiensis* × Candlepower, 2940 *N. cyclamineus* × *N. henriquesii*, 3045 *N. cyclamineus* × Candlepower
19 Three Miniature Cultivars, bred and raised by the Exhibitor, one bloom of each (2) 1. B S Duncan: 3103 *N. cyclamineus* × Camborne, *N. asturiensis* × Candlepower, 3044 *N. cyclamineus* × Camborne 2. J Gibson: 158/M/11/04, 157/M/04, 156/M/11/04
20 One Miniature Cultivar, bred and raised by the Exhibitor, one bloom. (12) 1. B S Duncan: 3237 *N. cyclamineus* × Camborne 2. B S Duncan: 2937 *N. cyclamineus* × Camborne 3. B S Duncan: 3242 Silver Crystal × *N. dubius*
21 Three Miniature Cultivars, three blooms of each. (1) 1. B S Duncan: Candlepower, Small Talk, Norwester
22 Three Miniature Species or Wild Hybrids from Division 13, three blooms of each. (1) 1. J Gibson: *N. cyclamineus*, *N. cuatrecasasii*, *N. cantabricus* subsp. *monophyllus*
23 One Miniature Cultivar, three blooms (1) 1. J Gibson: Good Friend
24 One Miniature Species or Wild Hybrid from Division 13, three blooms (1) 1. B S Duncan: *N. cyclamineus*
25 One Miniature Cultivar (not Division 10), one bloom (3) 1. B S Duncan: Norwester 2. Mr & Mrs G Hollingdale: Tête-à-Tête 3. J Gibson: Roveroy
26 One Cultivar from Division 10, one bloom (1) 1. B S Duncan: *N. bulbocodium* 02/43
27 One Miniature Species or Wild Hybrid from Division 13, one bloom (2) 1. J Gibson: *N. cuatrecasasii* 2. B S Duncan: *N. henriquesii*
28 One Species or Wild Hybrid from Division 13 (other than miniature), one bloom (0)
29 One Cultivar, Division 1, one bloom (Novice class) (1) 1. Mr Hill: Pink Silk
30 One Cultivar, Division 2, one bloom (Novice class) (1) 1. Not awarded 2. Mr Hill: Unknown
31 One Cultivar, Division 3, one bloom (Novice class) (0)
32 One Cultivar, Division 4, one bloom (Novice class) (1) 1. Mr Hill: Woolaroo
33 One Cultivar, Division 6, yellow perianth, one bloom (Novice class) (1) 1. Mr Hill: Elfin Gold:
34 One Cultivar, Division 6, white perianth, one bloom (Novice class) (0)
35 One Cultivar, Any other Division, one bloom (Novice class) (1) 1. Mr Hill: Boslowick

RHS Daffodil Show

Jackie Petherbridge

There was much to celebrate and enjoy during the course of this year's RHS Daffodil Show held on 15-16 April: splendid displays of the flowers of British hybridizers; the animated company of overseas visitors in London as part of the World Daffodil Convention; a first-time winner of the prestigious Engleheart Cup; and the show benches and the Alpine Garden Society Show were pretty good too! Overall 1,112 daffodils were staged in 491 entries by 51 exhibitors in the competitive classes.

Special displays and trade stands
All the stops were pulled out to make this show a daffodil festival and there was much to see and talk about in both halls. In the Lawrence Hall Christine Skelmersdale is to be congratulated on an excellent educational display celebrating the life and work of Alec Gray. Christine is the custodian of the NCCPG National Collection of Alec Gray hybrids. This was a fascinating exhibition, meticulously researched, with excellent photographs and documents and even some of Gray's original pots. The living plant material covered a wide range of his blooms, with an interesting section showing several generations of flowers. It must have taken some time to prepare and stage and was well deserving of the Gold Medal it received.

Daffodil Registrar Sharon MacDonald and members of the Daffodil and Tulip Committee presented 22 vases of flowers from the hybridization programme of the late John Lea alongside a large display of blooms from current hybridizers in the United Kingdom. Anyone who has attempted a display of blooms at the RHS will know how difficult a task this can be, as the weather and transport problems often result in promised blooms failing to arrive. Fortunately this was not the case on this occasion although many flowers arrived on the morning, leading to some hasty and major rearrangement of the display and some derring-do from committee member Chris Yates as he scaled the exhibition tiers. It may not have met all the usual exhibition standards, but given the eclectic nature of the contributions it was a glorious display of blooms covering pretty nearly all divisions, colours and sizes of flower. A space was found for everyone who submitted flowers and the display solicited plenty of discussion and enjoyment.

Between the two displays was a delightful and complementary exhibition of original pictures from the Lindley Library, focusing on the daffodils used by John Lea and Alec Gray. There were some contemporary commissions but the considerable artistic talent of well-known daffodil growers such as E A Bowles and F W Burbidge were also revealed.

The show would be much the poorer without a showpiece trade stand and once again Johnnie Walkers' display of beautifully staged daffodils, Walkers@Taylors, made a huge impact on the hall, not least because it was 7.7m (25ft) long this year. There were 45 varieties on display and each bowl had around 30 blooms providing a vibrant wall of colour - another well-deserved Gold Medal exhibit. H W Hyde & Son received a Silver Medal for an attractive display of tulips.

In the Lindley Hall the Alpine Garden Society show benches seemed a little less full than usual but there were still some splendid exhibits and there were several very interesting and novel photographs to be seen. One final display of flowers deserves a mention. This was a collection of 52 older and often very graceful daffodils, many without a name, to be found in Acton Burnell churchyard in Shropshire. Names were being sought by Margaret Owen as part of an NCCPG project and it was pleasing to note that by the end of the first show day a number of these historic daffodils had been tentatively identified. Their proximity to the Engleheart Cup entries provided a thought-provoking perspective on how daffodils have evolved since the late 19th century.

Seedling classes

This year an international judging panel determined the outcome of the coveted Engleheart Cup and the scrutiny of flowers was thorough and exacting. Of the four exhibitors, John Gibson emerged a modest but well-deserved winner. In his twelve flowers there were four named varieties, 'Eastbrook Sunrise' 1Y-O, 'Draycote Water' 3W-W, 'Boughton Park' 1Y-Y and 'Dunchurch' 2Y-O. The remainder were seedlings, including 3-6-89, a 2Y-O that won the Best Seedling in show award. It has since been named 'Rowell Fair' and was raised from 'Craig Stiel' × 'Loch Naver'. Second-placed Brian Duncan was gracious in defeat but will be back next year, hoping to add to many earlier wins in this class. Ron Scamp was in third place and Richard McCaw's promising first entry in the Engleheart Cup was a very creditable fourth. A nicely balanced set of six seedlings gave Northern Ireland grower Derek Turbitt a Silver Simmonds Medal. In amongst Jeremy Wilkes' winning three seedlings, 3/98B, a 2W-YWW raised from 'Misty Glen' × 'Merlin', showed potential as an intermediate.

Alec Gray would have been pleased to see increased entries in the intermediate classes, given this gem of a quote brought to light by Christine Skelmersdale: 'I have always felt and said so in print a number of times that these [intermediate kinds] are by far the best both for the borders and pot culture. I believe they have classes for these in America but over here they are almost entirely neglected.' First place from nine entries and Best Intermediate was John Gibson's 57-3-95, a smooth 2Y-O with good form and a bright clear cup; it has since been named 'Eastbrook Beauty' and is certainly one to watch out for. Interestingly, 'Eastbrook Beauty' was raised from ('Loch Naver' × 'Ulster Bank') × 'Stanway, all standard-sized daffodils.

Brian Duncan's mastery of the miniature continues as he won the Alec Gray Trophy for 6 miniature hybrids as well as the subsequent three and single bloom classes. It is a shame there is not more competition for him. Brian's great strengths are his carefully selected species stock and his many years of hybridizing experience. The man has the keenest eye and he is having great fun with some of his crosses. Particularly attractive were 3245 (*N. asturiensis* × 'Telamonius Plenus') and 3135 (a two-headed 'Young Blood' × *N. dubius* seedling). What never fails to amaze me is the variation in sister seedlings. In class 108, 'Norwester' × *N. rupicola* produced a starry flower with a narrow yellow cup attractive in its own way but not as classy as 2845, a smooth, well-proportioned and reflexed bloom.

Open collection classes

Roger Braithwaite won the Guy Wilson Memorial Vase, with Derek Turbitt and Tony James in second and third place respectively. His were glorious flowers in size and substance, with 'Phoenician' and 'Sheelagh Rowan' catching my eye. Roger also had success in the twelve cultivars from four or more divisions class. His immaculately staged entry included 'Terminator' 2Y-R, Reserve Best Bloom in show and Best Bloom division 2. Rather oddly, the organisers placed this class completely out of sequence on the show bench and it was almost missed as a consequence.

'Vivash' 4W-P, a well-rounded pink double,

'Terminator'
(*photo* Michael Shuttleworth Photography)

earned Brian Duncan the Best Bloom division 4 award. It was staged in his winning entry in the class for three blooms of three double daffodils. Many of Brian's division 11 seedlings were also on display, and again two sister seedlings from a 'Diversity' × 'Trigonometry' cross attracted attention. Seedling 2885 had a soft pink and white perianth whilst 2956 was much deeper in tone.

Terry Braithwaite had three beautiful vases of Division 6 cultivars, all with good colour and form having received Terry's fine grooming. One of her three blooms of 'Vineland' was Best Bloom from divisions 5 to 10 and 12. She narrowly beat Brian Duncan into second place, whose entry included an eye-catching 6Y-O 'Surrey' × *N. cyclamineus* seedling.

Keith Harrop from Denton Chrysanthemum & Dahlia Society deserved some competition, as there were some very good flowers in this society exhibit. 'Sheelagh Rowan', 'Dailmanach', 'Jersey Roundabout', all flowers that were having a very good year, were included in this set of twelve.

Intermediates and miniatures

The attraction of well-grown intermediates can be in no doubt when you see such lovely flowers as 'Little Tyke' 1Y-Y, 'Brooke Agar' 2W-P and a distinctive 1Y-P 'American Heritage' cross, a winning combination for Brian Duncan. John Gibson's seedling 57-3-95 is very consistent, winning classes 122 and 188 when exhibited by Malcolm Bradbury and John Gibson respectively. When available it will be much sought for intermediate classes. However Noel Burr's 'Piglet', a striking 2O-R, was the big talking point. We look forward to future Pooh Corner registrations.

The miniature entries continue to go from strength to strength, with Brian Duncan and Terry Braithwaite exhibiting fifteen cultivars between them in classes 123, 124 and 126. Terry Braithwaite was delighted to win the class for six miniatures, three stems of each. Her 'Angel's Whisper', 'Xit', 'Sabrosa', 'Flomay', *N. triandrus* subsp. *triandrus* var. *concolor* and 'Snipe' showed good form and colour and immaculate staging. A good colour combination was also evident in Janine Doulton's winning collection of three stems each of 'Little Rusky', 'Yellow Xit' and 'Clare'.

However the best miniature cultivar of the show survived the journey from the USA to win first place for Kathy Andersen. It was 'Little Kibler', a perfect 9W-GYR that stole many hearts and was awarded Best Miniature in show. Congratulations too, to Mary Lou Gripsover, whose *N. rupicola* × *N. rupicola* subsp. *watieri* seedling jetted into third place.

Single blooms

There were some super blooms in these well-supported classes, the first-place blooms often standing out as shining examples of the cultivar. 'Ombersley' grown by John Peace had terrific form and substance and was clearly the best of the 21 entries. Ray Sedgewick, proving himself to be an exhibitor to watch, entered a fine 'Goldfinger', with 'Grafton Brook' 1Y-Y from John Gibson in third. John's winning 'Eastbrook Sunrise' had great size but 'Uncle

Duncan', again from John Peace, and 'Kingstanding' from Noel Burr were close behind in a class of eleven fine entries.

'Sargeant's Caye' exhibited by S Ellison was easily the best bloom in the 1Y-W class. I wondered if Nial Watson's winning 'Bronzewing' 1Y-P had been under consideration for a Best Bloom award. It had good proportions with a broad well-formed pink trumpet. It was certainly attracting favourable comments from the public. A flower bound for further success was a 1W-Y seedling from John Gibson. Seedling 44-10-98 has a striking yellow trumpet and substantial strong petals that ideally need to be smoother. Equally, despite its poor condition, a Brian Duncan seedling, 3065 1W-O raised from 'Queen's Guard' × 'Lutana', was much photographed because of its striking orange trumpet and was subsequently awarded the Ralph B White Memorial Medal (see page 84).

The winning flowers in the division 2 classes were all classic flowers. 'Gold Convention' was exhibited by Len Olive, 'Banker' by Mike Brook and 'Pacific Rim' by Geoff Ridley. John Blanchard can still spring a surprise and did so with a 2Y-P seedling 96/28A ('Filoli' × 'Rose Gold'). The reverse bicolor class was dominated by some fine John Pearson cultivars: 'Caribbean Snow', fully reversed and splendidly grown to a good size by Colin Gilman, with Ron Scamp and S Ellison placed second and third with 'Altun Ha'. I believe a newcomer to the London show bench was 'Colin's Joy' 2W-GWR, a New Zealand cultivar exhibited by Mary Lou Gripsover. This was just nudged into second place by a nicely formed 'Bandit' exhibited by P Barless, with Zara Evans' 'Kiltonga' third. It was nice to see one of my favourites, 'Cherrygardens', winning the W-P rim class for Noel Burr. 'Narrative' 2W-P, shown by Brian Duncan, looked good, as did 'Dailmanach', exhibited by John Goddard. This has been a good year for John Lea's premier pink.

'Sheelagh Rowan', awarded an FCC at the Daffodil and Tulip Committee later that day, was placed first and third in the 2W-W class, with Len Olive taking the first place. Zara Evans' entry, 'Nonchalant' 3Y-Y, had good colour, as did Roger Braithwaite's 'Tao' 3Y-O and Nial Watson's 'Badbury Rings'. However, Best Bloom division 3 and Best Bloom in show was an exquisite bloom of 'Astrid's Memory' 3W-Y grown by Paul Payne. John Peace coaxed great size and form to win a second place with old-timer 'Park Springs' and Richard McCaw's

'Astrid's Memory'
(*photo* Michael Shuttleworth Photography)

pretty 'Citrus Ring' came third. There were twelve exhibits in the class.

'Doctor Hugh' predominated in the 3W-O/R class but John Gibson seedling 145-17-95 stood out because of the unusual bright orange cup that clearly had two distinct shades - an interesting registration conundrum when the colour charts are consulted. Third-placed 'Feock', a flower exhibited by Mary Lou Gripsover, caught James Akers' eye, and 'Dena' 3W-WWP, exhibited by Nial Watson, caught mine, with its vivid reddish pink ring. A fine 'Draycote Water' with a beautiful green eye, a pleasing rounded form and a flat cup was a worthy winner of the 3W-W class for John Goddard.

There was an interesting mix of established favourites and seedlings in the division 4 classes. 'Jersey Roundabout' achieved a very creditable second against seedling 785 from Ron Scamp, and 'Blossom Lady' 4W-O saw off the 'Gay Kybo' challenge. All the 4W-P winners were 'Dorchester', with Brian Duncan not surprisingly growing the winning bloom. I wonder if 'Vivash' 4W-P will be the predominant flower next year?

It was pleasing to see some new and dainty division 5 blooms. Ron Scamp exhibited a three-headed W-Y seedling, 1-455, and Mary Lou Gripsover showed 85-2-X, a single-headed but very lovely 'Roseworthy' × *N. triandrus* seedling. However, a London show would not be complete without a first for Len Olive and 'Ice Wings'. Yet again his flowers had three good-sized but dainty blooms on a strong stem.

It was not a great year for division 6 flowers. Jim Davidson's journey from Scotland was worthwhile when he was awarded a first for his rarely seen Jefferson-Brown cultivar, 'Puppy' 6Y-Y, and Terry Braithwaite had a splendid 'Trena'. Ron Scamp's division 7s are always worth a second look and 'Penny Perowne' 7Y-Y was much admired, as was his two-headed seedling 774.

The outstanding division 8 cultivar was 'Falconet' 8Y-R exhibited by Geoff Ridley. The eight flowers with their red cups and glowing yellow-orange petals were nicely arranged and made a very pleasing exhibit. Havens' 'Unnamed Poet' won a first place for Reg Nicholl and with such reliable form and striking green, yellow, orange and red cup deserves a rather more respectful name.

'Menehay' and 'Bosvale' were winning blooms in the division 11 classes. A dainty, nigh on perfect *N. rupicola* and one of my all-time favourites, 'Stafford', were winning blooms for Janine Doulton in miniature classes 189 and 190.

Amateur classes

The Bowles Cup entry by Tony James was a showpiece of staging and proof yet again that those older varieties are worthy winners when well grown. Amongst his collection of 15 varieties were lovely vases of 'Park Springs', 'Purbeck', 'Golden Jewel' and last year's darling, 'Jersey Roundabout'. Mike Brook was the runner-up.

The Richardson Trophy was keenly fought with six quality entries. Colin Gilman emerged triumphant with an impeccably staged exhibit. His flowers were grown to a good size, were rich in colour and included some tried and tested favourites such as 'Gold Convention', 'Silent Valley', 'Cool Crystal' and 'Dailmanach'. 'Altun Ha', 'Crowndale' and 'Bluntingdon', a better choice than its father 'Doctor Hugh', completed the set, together with 'Moon Shadow', 'Sun Bronze' 2Y-O, 'Entrepreneur' and 'Arleston' 2Y-Y. Ken Dear's unplaced entry contained Best Bloom division 1, a superb 'Silent Valley'. Ray Sedgewick and Barry Hogg were amongst seven exhibitors entering the six daffodil collection class but were beaten by John Goddard. His set comprised 'Altun Ha', 'Doctor Hugh', 'June Lake', 'Goonbell' 2Y-Y, 'Ombersley' and 'Amazing Grace'. Jim Davidson also well deserved to win the class for five daffodils raised before 1980. His exhibit was fresh, colourful and beautifully staged, with 'Rose Royale', 'Ben Avon', 'Strines', 'Golden Amber' and 'Broomhill'.

Novice entries were well down in number but Frank Charlton who made the long journey from South Tyneside was well rewarded for his efforts with several wins including 'Silent Valley' which was Best Novice Bloom.

This was a much better year for most exhibitors, although some varieties grown for the collection classes were reported as coming to a standstill and thereby missing the London show but hopefully coming good for later shows. Certainly the colder conditions in Northern Ireland had been challenging for regular exhibitors.

RESULTS

Open classes
101 The Engleheart Cup Twelve, bred & raised by exhibitor, one bloom of each (4) 1. J Gibson: Eastbrook Sunrise, Draycote Water, Boughton Park, 155-52-99, 100-31-97, 3-6-89, 43-10-98, 112-19-99, 1-20-92, 14-1-97, Dunchurch, A17-92 2. B S Duncan: Chobe River, Harbour View, 2713, 2886, Chasseur, Honeybourne, Narrative, Arleston, Gold Ingot, Dorchester, Editor, Chingah 3. R A Scamp: 953, 322, 697, 930, 85-29-1, 788, 1-4-93, 352, 345, Poppy's Choice, Millennium Sunset, 962
102 Six, bred & raised by exhibitor, one bloom of each (3) 1. D Turbitt: DT9810, DT0416, DT0008, DT0315, DT0208, DT0514 2. N Watson: 283, 134, 181, 538, 183, 706 3. Not awarded
103 Three, bred & raised by exhibitor, one bloom of each (2) 1. J Wilkes: Arctic Rim, 6/02, 3/98B 2. Mrs M L Gripshover: TN39A, 85-7-7, 85-2-X
104 Three Division 11, bred & raised by exhibitor, one bloom of each (1) 1. B S Duncan: 2885, Maria Pia, Diversity
105 Three from divisions 5 to 10 & 12, bred & raised by exhibitor, one bloom of each (1) 1. B S Duncan: Kaydee, 2716, Lilac Charm
106 One Intermediate, divisions 1 to 4 or 11, bred & raised by exhibitor, one bloom (8) 1. J Gibson: 57-3-95 2. R McCaw: RAM86 3. B S Duncan: XEX00/48A
107 Six miniatures, bred & raised by exhibitor, one bloom of each (1) 1. B S Duncan: 3135 (Young Blood × *N. dubius*), 3245 (*N. asturiensis* × Telamonius Plenus) 3292 (Silver Crystal), 3053 (Norwester × *N. rupicola*), 3270 (*N. cyclamineus* × *N. asturiensis*)
108 Three miniatures, bred & raised by exhibitor, one bloom of each (1) 1. B S Duncan: 2845 (*N. rupicola* × *N. cyclamineus*), 3059 (Norwester × *N. rupicola*), 3053 (*N. rupicola* × *N. watieri*)
109 One Miniature, bred & raised by exhibitor, one bloom (3) 1. B S Duncan: 2846 (*N. rupicola* × *N. cyclamineus*) 2. B S Duncan: 2939 (*N. cyclamineus* × Camborne) 3. B S Duncan: 3244 (*N. asturiensis* × Telamonius Plenus)
110 The Guy Wilson Memorial Vase Six whites from divisions 1 to 3, three blooms of each (3) 1. R B Braithwaite: Phoenician, Cataract, Sheelagh Rowan, Castle Howard, Quiet Waters, Nice Day 2. D Turbitt: White Star, DT0411 (2W-W), Watership Down, DT9909 (1W-W), White Tea, Regal Bliss 3. A James: Silent Valley, Homestead, Misty Glen, Williamsburg, Silver Convention, White Tea
111 Twelve cultivars from four or more of Divisions 1 to 4 and 11, one bloom of each (1) 1. R B Braithwaite: Altun Ha, Entrepreneur, Jenna, Honeybourne, Bluntington, Ombersley, Pol Crocan, Best Friend, Tao, Lakeland Fair, Terminator, Gay Kybo
112 Three from one or more of Divisions 1 to 3, three blooms of each (2) 1. R G Sedgwick: Silent Valley, Loth Lorian, Regal Bliss 2. G H Hollingdale: Silent Valley, High Society, Angel
113 Three Division 4, three blooms of each (1) 1. B S Duncan: Dorchester, Vivash, Dunkery
114 Three Division 11, three blooms of each (1) 1. B S Duncan: 2885, 2956, Maria Pia
115 Three from divisions 5 to 10 & 12, three blooms of each (2) 1. Mrs T Braithwaite: Vineland, Kilstar, Rapture 2. B S Duncan: Lilac Charm, 2716, Georgie Girl
116 Three from one or more of divisions 1 to 3, with pink in corona, three blooms of each (0)
117 Three cultivars not in commerce, from any division or divisions, three blooms of each (0)
118 Seven blooms Division 4, in one vase (0)
119 Six raised outside Europe, one bloom of each (3) 1. M J Brook: Kinsman, Banker, Tristan's Memory, Busker, La Paloma, Disquiet 2. N Watson: Centrefold, Yum Yum, Twicer, Nonchalant, Grand Opening, Conestoga 3. J M Parkinson: Banker, Razadaz, Macdalla, Bright Candle, Swedish Fjord, Truculent
120 Twelve, representing divisions 1 to 4, one bloom of each (Horticultural Societies class) (1) 1. Denton Chrysanthemum and Dahlia Society: Arkle, Evesham, Goldhanger, Dailmanach, Sheelagh Rowan, Gold Bond, Bravoure, Cape Cornwall, Grasmere, Jersey Roundabout, Impeccable, Misty Glen
121 Three intermediates from divisions 1 - 4 and 11, three blooms of each (1) 1. B S Duncan: Little Tyke, 2553, Brook Ager
122 One Intermediate, Divisions 1 to 4 or 11, three blooms (3) 1. J Gibson: 57-3-95 2. G H Hollingdale: Skilliwidden 3. N A Burr: Piglet
123 Six miniature cultivars, species or wild hybrids, three blooms of each (2) 1. Mrs T Braithwaite: Xit, Angel's Whisper, Sabrosa, Snipe, Flomay, *N. triandrus* var. *concolor* 2. B S Duncan: Xit, Kokopelli, Hummingbird, Yellow Xit, *N. watieri*, *N. rupicola*
124 Three Miniatures from Division 13, three blooms of each (2) 1. Mrs T Braithwaite: *N. henriquesii*, *N. watieri*, *N. bulbocodium* 2. B S Duncan: *N. calcicola*, *N. cyclamineus*, *N. watieri*
125 Three miniature cultivars, three blooms of each (1) 1. Mrs J M Doulton: Little Rusky, Yellow Xit, Clare
126 One Miniature from Division 13, three blooms (2) 1. Mrs T Braithwaite: *N. cordubensis* 2. B S Duncan: *N. rupicola*
127 One miniature cultivar, three blooms (3) 1. Mrs K Andersen: Little Kibler 2. Mrs J M Doulton: Hawera 3. B S Duncan: Seedling (*N. rupicola* × *N. watieri*)
130 One Division 1, perianth yellow, corona yellow (21) 1. J Peace: Ombersley 2. R G Sedgwick: Goldfinger 3. J Gibson: Grafton Brook
131 One Division 1, perianth yellow, corona orange or red (11) 1. J Gibson: Eastern Sunrise 2. J Peace: Uncle Duncan 3. N A Burr: Kingstanding
132 One Division 1, perianth yellow, corona white with or without yellow rim (5) 1. S Ellison: Sargeant's Caye 2. J M Parkinson: Trumpet Warrior 3. Ms Z Evans: Lighthouse Reef
133 One Division 1, perianth yellow, corona any other colour or colour combination (4) 1. N Watson: Bronzewing 2. S Ellison: American Heritage 3. G Ridley: Memento
134 One Division 1, perianth white, corona yellow or white & yellow (6) 1. J Gibson: 44-10-98 2. J M Parkinson: Macdalla 3. B S Duncan: Queen's Guard
135 One Division 1, perianth white, corona white (14) 1. J Peace: Silent Valley 2. R G Sedgwick: Silent Valley 3. Ms A Peace: Chaste
136 One Division 1, perianth white, corona any other colour or colour combination (4) 1. N Watson: Edenderry 2. J H J Goddard: Chanson 3. C M van Hage: 3/08
137 One Division 1, perianth any colour. Not eligible for classes 126 to 132 (0)
138 One Division 2, perianth yellow, corona yellow (16) 1. L Olive: Gold Convention 2. J H J Goddard: Goonbell 3.

111

B S Duncan: 2713
139 One Division 2, perianth yellow, corona orange or red (22) 1. M J Brook: Banker 2. C.M.H Gilman: Sun Bronze 3. L Olive: Thumbs Up
140 One Division 2, perianth yellow, corona with orange or red rim (7) 1. G Ridley: Pacific Rim 2. R McCaw: RAM63 3. K Dear: Cape Cornwall
141 One Division 2, perianth yellow, corona containing pink (2) 1. J W Blanchard: 96/28a 2. J Wilkes: Acumen
142 One Division 2, perianth yellow, corona white, with or without yellow rim (11) 1. C.M.H Gilman: Caribbean Snow 2. R A Scamp: Altun Ha 3. S Ellison: Altun Ha
143 One Division 2, perianth orange, corona orange or red (3) 1. J Gibson: 2-4-90 2. J Wilkes: Creag Dubh 3. B S Duncan: 2969
144 One Division 2, perianth white, corona yellow or white & yellow (9) 1. L Olive: Cameo Mist 2. M J Brook: Corky's Song 3. R B Braithwaite: Honeybourne
145 One Division 2, perianth white, corona orange or red (8) 1. N Watson: Powerstock 2. Ms Z Evans: Star Glow 3. P G Barlass: Just Joan
146 One Division 2, perianth white, corona with orange or red rim (4) 1. P G Barlass: Bandit 2. Mrs M L Gripshover: Colin's Joy 3. Ms Z Evans: Kiltonga
147 One Division 2, perianth white, corona pink (14) 1. N A Burr: Cherrygardens 2. B S Duncan: Narrative 3. J H J Goddard: Dailmanach
148 One Division 2, perianth white, corona with pink rim (11) 1. P Payne: Warm Welcome 2. N Watson: Savoir Fair 3. R Hilson: High Society
149 One Division 2, perianth white, corona white (14) 1. L Olive: Sheelagh Rowan 2. J Gibson: Inverpolly 3. J H J Goddard: Sheelagh Rowan
150 One Division 2, perianth any colour. Not eligible for classes 134 to 145 (0)
151 One Division 3, perianth yellow, corona yellow (7) 1. Ms Z Evans: Nonchalant 2. K Harrop: Wychbold 3. J Wilkes: Citronita
152 One Division 3, perianth yellow, corona orange or red (7) 1. R B Braithwaite: Tao 2. B S Duncan: Ground Keeper 3. L Olive: Stanway
153 One Division 3, perianth yellow, corona with orange or red rim (8) 1. N Watson: Badbury Rings 2. R Hilson: Tehidy 3. R A Scamp: Badbury Rings
154 One Division 3, perianth yellow, corona white, with or without yellow rim (2) 1. N Watson: Chortle 2. J W Blanchard: Chortle
155 One Division 3, perianth orange, corona orange or red (4) 1. J M Parkinson: Tamar Lass 2. N Watson: Brodick 3. M J Brook: War Dance
156 One Division 3, perianth white, corona yellow or white & yellow (12) 1. P Payne: Astrid's Memory 2. J Peace: Park Springs 3. R McCaw: RAM165
157 One Division 3, perianth white, corona orange or red (8) 1. S Ellison: Doctor Hugh 2. J H J Goddard: Doctor Hugh 3. J Gibson: 145-17-99
158 One Division 3, perianth white, corona with orange or red rim (7) 1. N Watson: Cisticola 2. C.M.H Gilman: Shurdington 3. Mrs M L Gripshover: Feock
159 One Division 3, perianth white, corona containing pink (2) 1. N Watson: Dena 2. R A Scamp: Rosevine
160 One Division 3, perianth white, corona white (8) 1. R McCaw: Draycote Water 2. N Watson: Silver Crystal 3. R A Scamp: 311
161 One Division 3, perianth any colour. Not eligible for classes 147 to 156 (0)
162 One Division 4, single-headed, perianth yellow, corona segments yellow (6) 1. L Olive: Dream Team 2. N Watson: 641 3. M J Brook: Bela
163 One Division 4, single-headed, perianth yellow, corona segments orange or red (5) 1. R B Braithwaite: Crowndale 2. J H J Goddard: Crackington 3. L Olive: Crowndale
164 One Division 4, single-headed, perianth white, corona segments yellow or white (7) 1. R A Scamp: 785 2. P G Barlass: Jersey Roundabout 3. L Olive: Ameeya
165 One Division 4, single-headed, perianth white, corona segments orange or red (7) 1. L Olive: Blossom Lady 2. R G Sedgwick: Gay Kybo 3. B S Duncan: Rongoiti Gem
166 One Division 4, single-headed, perianth white, corona segments pink (5) 1. B S Duncan: Dorchester 2. J H J Goddard: Dorchester 3. G Ridley: Dorchester
167 One Division 4, single-headed, perianth any colour. Not eligible for classes 158 to 162 (2) 1. M R Bird: Sir Winston Churchill 2. R G Sedgwick: Yellow Cheerfulness
168 One Division 4, multi-headed, perianth any colour, corona segments any colour (0)
169 One Division 5, perianth yellow, corona white or coloured (7) 1. R A Scamp: 1-455 2. N Watson: Petanga 3. J M Parkinson: Liberty Bells
170 One Division 5, perianth white, corona coloured (1) 1. Mrs M L Gripshover: 85-2-X
171 One Division 5, perianth white, corona white (4) 1. L Olive: Ice Wings 2. R G Sedgwick: Ice Wings 3. N Watson: Mission Bells
172 One Division 6, perianth yellow, corona yellow or white (3) 1. J M Davidson: Puppy 2. B S Duncan: 3066 3. G Ridley: Rapture
173 One Division 6, perianth yellow, corona pink, orange or red (0)
174 One Division 6, perianth white, corona yellow (5) 1. Mrs T Braithwaite: Trena 2. Not awarded 3. G H Hollingdale: Trena
175 One Division 6, perianth white, corona pink, orange or red (5) 1. G Ridley: Lilac Charm 2. G H Hollingdale: Foundling 3. R G Sedgwick: Foundling
176 One Division 6, perianth white, corona white (1) 1. Not awarded 2. M S Bradbury: Jenny
177 One Division 7, perianth yellow, corona yellow (5) 1. R A Scamp: Penny Perowne 2. G H Hollingdale: Intrigue 3. I Fox: Marzo
178 One Division 7, perianth yellow, corona pink, orange or red (5) 1. R A Scamp: 774 2. J M Parkinson: Mowser 3. G Ridley: Suzy
179 One Division 7, perianth yellow, corona white, with or without yellow rim (0)
180 One Division 7, perianth white, corona white or coloured (1) 1. G H Hollingdale: Curlew
181 One Division 8, perianth yellow (3) 1. G Ridley: Falconet 2. Ms Z Evans: Highfield Beauty 3. J M Davidson: Highfield Beauty
182 One Division 8, perianth white (3) 1. S Ellison: Avalanche 2. G H Hollingdale: Geranium 3. G Ridley: Avalanche
183 One Division 9, perianth white (3) 1. R Nicholl: Unknown 2. L Olive: Sea Green 3. R A Scamp: 1012
184 One Division 10 or 12, any colours (5) 1. R Hilson: Odd Job 2. G H Hollingdale: Cornish Chuckles 3. Not awarded
185 One Division 11, perianth yellow (7) 1. R A Scamp:

RHS Daffodil Show

Menehay 2. J M Davidson: Jantje 3. N Watson: Pampaluna
186 One Division 11, perianth white (4) 1. Ms Z Evans: Bosvale 2. R A Scamp: 775 3. Mrs M L Gripshover: Mission Impossible
187 One, any of Divisions 1 to 3, reflexing perianth (4) 1. J H J Goddard: Clouded Yellow 2. P Payne: Seedling (Tudor Grove × Tudor Love) 3. M J Brook: Clouded Yellow
188 One Intermediate, Divisions 1 to 4 or 11 (3) 1. M S Bradbury: 57/3/95 2. Mrs M L Gripshover: Cinnamon Ring 3. R A Scamp: 1004
189 One Miniature, Division 13 (3) 1. Mrs J M Doulton: *N. rupicola* 2. B S Duncan: *N. rupicola* 3. G Ridley: *N. tazetta* 'Odoratus'
190 One miniature cultivar (3) 1. Mrs J M Doulton: Stafford 2. G Ridley: Chiva 3. Mrs K Andersen: Little Kibler
191 One, Division 13, NOT miniature (2) 1. B S Duncan: *N. nevadensis* 2. J M Davidson: *N. pseudonarcissus*

Amateur classes
192 Three, bred & raised by exhibitor, one bloom of each (3) 1. R McCaw: RAM165, RAM67, RAM92 2. D Turbitt: DT9810, DT9809, DT0102 3. J M Davidson: C86-40, A88-72, D87-37
193 One, bred & raised by exhibitor, one bloom (5) 1. C N Yates: 2-32-97 2. P G Barlass: PB98-1-3 3. M S Bradbury: 2008/5
194 The Bowles Cup Fifteen, from four or more divisions, three blooms of each (2) 1. A James: Jersey Roundabout, Corbiere, Williamsburg, Gold Bond, Pink Silk, Clouded Yellow, Purbeck, Oregon Pioneer, Harbour View, Golden Jewel, Royal Princess, Goldfinger, Park Springs, Misty Glen, Not recorded 2. M J Brook: Goldfinger, Doctor Hugh, Sherborne, Silent Valley, Camelot, Misty Glen, Pamplona, Ringleader, Menehay, Invercassley, Altun Ha, Parsifal, Achduart, Sandy Cove, Disquiet
195 The Richardson Trophy Twelve, representing Divisions 1 to 4 inclusive, one bloom of each (6) 1. C M H Gilman: Altun Ha, Dailmanach, Gold Convention, Silent Valley, Moon Shadow, Sun Bronze, Entrepreneur, Arleston, Banker, Bluntington, Crowndale, Cool Crystal 2. J Peace: Silent Valley, Cape Cornwall, Honeybourne, Ombersley, Gold Convention, Pol Crocan, Banker, Doctor Hugh, Royal Regiment, Liverpool Festival, Dorchester, Lennymore 3. Mrs J M Doulton: Dailmanach, Altun Ha, Honeybourne, York Minster, Banker, Evesham, Goldhanger, White Star, Park Springs, Zimplats, Dorchester, Samsara
196 Six, from three or more divisions, one bloom of each (7) 1. J H J Goddard: Altun Ha, Doctor Hugh, June Lake, Goonbell, Ombersley, Amazing Grace 2. B Hogg: Ombersley, Honeybourne, Pol Gooth, Corbiere, Banker, Dorchester 3. R G Sedgwick: Gold Convention, Misty Glen, Doctor Hugh, Hambledon, Lazy River, Pennyfield
197 Five AGM, from any of divisions 1 to 4, one bloom of each (1) 1. G H Hollingdale: Silent Valley, Verona, High Society, Rainbow, Doctor Hugh
198 Five, registered in or before 1980, one bloom of each (2) 1. J M Davidson: Ben Avon, Strines, Golden Amber, Broomhill, Rose Royal; 2. R Hilson: Cristobal, Angel, Aircastle, High Society, Gay Kybo
199 Three, Division 1, three blooms of each (0)
200 Three, Division 2, perianth yellow, three blooms of each (0)
201 Three, Division 2, perianth white, three blooms of each (0)
202 Three, Division 3, three blooms of each (0)
203 Three, Division 4, three blooms of each (0)
205 One, Division 6, three blooms (1) 1. G H Hollingdale: Foundling
206 One, Division 7, three blooms (1) 1. G H Hollingdale: Intrigue
207 One, Division 8, three blooms (0)
208 One, Division 9, three blooms (1) 1. Mrs E Bullivant: *N. poeticus* var. *recurvus*
209 One, Division 10 or 12, three blooms (0)

Novice classes
210 One, Division 11, three blooms (2) 1. G H Hollingdale: Boslowick 2. Mrs E Bullivant: Pink Shells
211 Six, from three or more divisions, one bloom of each (2) 1. F Charlton: Arkle, Silent Valley, Cristobal, York Minster, Carib Gipsy, Verona 2. B Hogg: Banker, Silent Valley, Doctor Hugh, Liverpool Festival, Goldhanger, Williamsburg
212 Three, Division 1, one bloom of each (1) 1. F Charlton: Arkle, Silent Valley, York Minster
213 Three, Division 2, one bloom of each (1) 1. F Charlton: Dailmanach, Carib Gipsy, Williamsburg
214 Three, Division 3, one bloom of each (1) 1. F Charlton: Loth Lorien, Angel, Verona
215 One, Division 1, perianth yellow, corona coloured (1) 1. F Charlton: York Minster
216 One, Division 1, perianth yellow, corona white, with or without yellow rim (0)
217 One, Division 1, perianth white, corona coloured (1) 1. F Charlton: Cristobal
218 One, Division 1, perianth white, corona white (2) 1. F Charlton: Silent Valley 2. Mrs K Andersen: Mountain Dew
219 One, Division 2, perianth yellow, corona yellow (0)
220 One, Division 2, perianth yellow, corona pink, orange or red (2) 1. B Hogg: Sealing Wax 2. Not awarded 3. Not awarded
221 One, Division 2, perianth yellow, corona white, with or without yellow rim (0)
222 One, Division 2, perianth white, corona yellow or white & yellow (0)
223 One, Division 2, perianth white, corona pink, orange or red (1) 1. F Charlton: Fragrant Rose
224 One, Division 2, perianth white, corona white (2) 1. F Charlton: Williamsburg 2. Mrs K Andersen: Homestead
225 One, Division 3, perianth yellow, corona coloured (0)
226 One, Division 3, perianth white, corona coloured (2) 1. B Hogg: Park Springs 2. Not awarded 3. Not awarded
227 One, Division 3, perianth white, corona white (0)
228 One, Division 4, single-headed (2) 1. F Charlton: Woolaroo 2. C M van Hage: 12/08
229 One, Division 4, multi-headed (0)
230 One, Division 5 (0)
231 One, Division 6 (0)
232 One, Division 7 (0)
233 One, Division 8 (0)
234 One, Division 9 (0)
235 One, Division 10 or 12 (0)
236 One, Division 11 (0)

113

RHS Late Daffodil Competition and Tulip Competition

Reg Nicholl

An unusually warm January and February caused daffodil growth to forge ahead, leading to predictions that the 'season' would be so early that there would hardly be anything to put on the benches come the Late Competition. As often happens, the predictions were way off mark and the event staged in the Hillside Events Centre at Wisley on 29-30 April was well supported, with 34 exhibitors staging 756 daffodils, the second highest total since the move from London. Given increasing support from local enthusiasts, the Late Daffodil Competition and the Tulip Competition have moved successfully to Wisley. However, the facilities need to improve considerably if trade stands or displays are to be accommodated in future, if entries continue to grow and if the public are to view the show in comfort.

Seedling 2627
(*photo* M Sleigh/RHS)

Seedling classes

Brian Duncan was the only entrant in the John Lea Trophy class which requires twelve blooms raised by the exhibitor. The outstanding flower in his collection was 2627, a superlative borderline 3Y-YYR raised from 'Pacific Rim' × 'Triple Crown' that was Reserve Best Bloom in show, Best Seedling under number and Best Bloom division 3. Brian also showed excellent flowers of 'Tropical Heat' 2Y-R and 'Coliseum' 2W-YYO. When more readily available, the latter may become the successor to 'Ringleader'.

Unusually for the six seedling class Mr C M van Hage staged six doubles, the best of which was Seedling 4/105, a neat white and pink bicolor.

Brian Duncan literally swept the board in the remaining seedling classes. Notable flowers were 2737 ('Diversity' × 'Trigonometry'), which as one would expect produced a superb pink split-corona with a markedly green eye; 2611, a 2W-P with a graduated coral-edged corona with rather pointed petals; and 3154, a neat all-yellow intermediate which was Best Intermediate in show.

Open collection classes

The Devonshire Trophy, which is a great attraction as it requires twelve blooms from three or more divisions, drew three entries and saw Roger Braithwaite win first place. He showed two relatively new cultivars, 'Warwick Castle' 2Y-O and 'Armidale' 3Y-O, which together with the now show-bench standard 'Sheelagh Rowan' were the outstanding flowers in his group. Robin Crouchman took the runner-up position and staged superb specimens of 'Altun Ha', 'Liverpool Festival' and 'Moon Shadow'. Unusually for him Brian Duncan only managed third place but included three doubles, one of which, 2437, a white and pink bicolor, was of almost circular form and very heavily petalled. Also in his collection were fine blooms of 'Mamma Mia' and 'Ribald' 2W-GPP. Dave Spencer and John Goddard were the only entrants in the Daffodil Society's Southern Championship third leg, which requires six cultivars one stem of each, with Dave Spencer winning both the class and the championship overall. Dave's outstanding flowers were 'Gay Kybo' and 'Henfield' 2Y-GOO.

Intermediate, miniature and wild daffodils

There were three very good entries in the class for three stems each of three miniature species daffodils, with Terry Braithwaite taking first prize. Her entry included the Best Miniature in show, a five-headed stem of *N. pachybolbus*. Janine Doulton came second and Robert Wiseman third. *N. jonquilla* featured in each of the three entries. Janine reversed the positions in the comparable class for miniature cultivars, her winning entry including the recently introduced 'Chiva'. Mike Bird staged a neat flower of 'Little Sentry' among his three blooms to win against seven other entrants in the miniature cultivar class.

Single bloom classes

There were twelve good entries in the all-yellow trumpet class, where Brian Duncan placed a cracking flower of his fairly new 'Gamebird' ahead of Dave Spencer's 'Goldfinger' and continued his winning ways with 2888, a well-reversed trumpet. However, even more outstanding was his strongly colour-contrasted seedling 2917, featuring a yellow perianth and orange corona. Many white-perianthed yellow trumpet cultivars have come and gone in recent years but Brian appears to have bred a future champion with his seedling 2878, which has both good poise and strong colour contrast. In second place, Fred Austin had a nice version of the American-raised 'Monticello', and to continue the international scheme Robert Wiseman showed a fine Australian-raised cultivar, 'Clubman'. It goes without saying that 'Silent Valley' will triumph in the all-white trumpets and not only did it do so for Roger Braithwaite, Len Mace and David Vivash respectively, but of the 14 entries in the class, twelve were 'Silent Valley'. 'Korora Bay' was another flower winning all three places in the 1W-P class, with Brian Duncan in pole position.

Invariably at shows, division 2 flowers are in the best-supported classes and so it was here. Roger Braithwaite's 'Goldhanger' was in immaculate form in the all-yellow class and Brian Duncan's and David Matthews' 'Tropical Heat' were intensely coloured and separated only by Geoff Ridley's 'State Express'. Even after celebrating its coming of age 'Altun Ha' has no peers and in a class which featured no less than nine of the 14 blooms of that name it took all the cards for David Matthews, Fred Austin and Len Olive respectively. The star of the all-white class and indeed of the whole show was Roger Braithwaite's stunning 'Sheelagh Rowan', accorded Best Bloom in show and hence also Best Bloom division 2.

'Sheelagh Rowan'
(*photo* M Sleigh/RHS)

Two other flowers that were of superb form were David Vivash's 'West Post' 2W-Y and the delightful, pink-cupped 'John Peace' 2W-P shown by Paul Payne.

Perhaps the most competitive class in the show was that for 3W-Y in which Roger Braithwaite's winning 'Moon Shadow' was of the highest quality. It was to triumph over the other 17 blooms shown, especially Brian Duncan's 'Jammin' and Ted Frost's 'Astrid's Memory' in the minor placings. Brian Duncan, however, won three other classes with 'Armidale', 'Doctor Hugh' and 'Repertoire' 3W-YYR, all excellent flowers.

The double daffodils received great support, with 'Spun Honey' making a clean sweep for David Matthews, Phil Barlass and Richard Tabor. The same thing happened to 'Gay Kybo', which dominated a class of 18 flowers; such was the close competition that the judges gave four cards to Messrs. Olive, Braithwaite, Spencer and Hillsom in that order. However, the most prominent flower, which received the Best Bloom division 4 award, was 'Greek Surprise' 4W-Y; it had immaculate form, substance and colour and was shown by Brian Duncan.

In the numerically higher divisions we saw 'Stratosphere' 7Y-O doing what it invariably does by winning two classes for Len Mace and Ted Perran due to its chameleon-like corona colouring, but it was Ted Perran who won the Best Bloom divisions 5-10 and 12 award. Richard Hillsom's fine stem of 'Tripartite' 11Y-Y was Best Bloom division 11.

Encouragingly, the Competition was well attended both by the general public and by World Daffodil Convention visitors, and a wealth of new and interesting seedlings suggests that the event has a bright future.

Tulips

Although it was a late season for tulips, this was probably the best-supported tulip show since the competition was restarted.

There were ten entries in the Walter Blom Trophy Class for a vase of nine blooms of one cultivar. Mr and Mrs Hollingdale were hoping for a hat trick of successes in this class but their 'Big Smile' had to be content with second place to J Fishenden's 'Golden Parade', with this exhibitor's 'Vivex' in third.

The class for three tulips of any other colour, well supported with eleven entries, was won again by Mr Fishenden, with a superb vase of 'Toyota' that deservedly won the Crystal Trophy for the Best Vase in the competition.

Results - Daffodils

Class
301 The John Lea Trophy Twelve Cultivars, Bred and raised by the exhibitor, one bloom of each (1) 1. B S Duncan: Treasure Hunt, Spin Doctor, Tropical Heat, Jammin, 2657 (2W-P), Armidale, Star Quality, Chobe River, Auchranie, Coliseum, 2627, 2611 (2W-P)
303 Three Cultivars, Bred and raised by the exhibitor, one bloom of each (0) 1. Not awarded
304 Three Cultivars Division 11, Bred and raised by the exhibitor, one bloom of each (1) 1. B S Duncan: Jodi, Tickled Pink, 2737 (4W-P)
305 Three Cultivars From Divisions 5 To 10 and 12, Bred and raised by the exhibitor, one bloom of each (1) 1. B S Duncan: 2/91 (7W-O), 2904 (7Y-Y), 2594 (7W-P)
306 One Unregistered Cultivar, Bred and raised by the exhibitor, one bloom (3) 1. B S Duncan: 2611 (2W-P) 2. B S Duncan: 2244 (2W-P) 3. B S Duncan: 2231 (2Y-P)
307 One Intermediate Cultivar, From Divisions 1 to 4 or 11 Bred and raised by the exhibitor, one bloom (3) 1. B S Duncan: 3154 (2Y-Y) 2. B S Duncan: Soler 3. C M van Hage: 3/302 (11W-P)
308 One Miniature Cultivar, Bred and raised by the exhibitor, one bloom (0)
309 The Devonshire Trophy Twelve Cultivars From Three or more Divisions, one bloom of each (3) 1. R B Braithwaite: Ruddy Rascal, Astrid's Memory, State Express, Sheelagh Rowan, Bluntington, Warwick Castle, Lakeland Fair, Summer Breeze, Sun Bronze, Moon Shadow, Armidale, Toby Holden 2. R Crouchman: Gold Convention, Claverly, Altun Ha, Doctor Hugh, Moon Shadow, Liverpool Festival, Royal China, Stanway, Mill Grove, Misty Glen, Arona, Gay Kybo 3. B S Duncan: 2619, Ribald, Mamma Mia, Palace Pink, Cape Point, Pincambo, Soprano, Zwynher, 2227, Dorchester, 2600, 2437
310 Seven blooms, Division 7, one or more cultivars, in one vase (4) 1. E Perren: Sun Disc 2. M S Bradbury: Stratosphere 3. Mrs J Doulton: Sun Disc
312 The Daffodil Society Southern Championship - Third Leg Six Cultivars, from three or more Divisions, one bloom of each (2) 1. D Spencer: Gay Kybo, Goff's Caye, Burning Bush, Moon Shadow, Inverpolly, Henfield 2. J Goddard: Legislator, High Society, Stanway, Pol Crocan, Goonbell, Silent Valley

313 Three Intermediate Cultivars From Divisions 1 to 4 or 11, three blooms (0)
314 One Intermediate Cultivar From Divisions 1 to 4 or 11, three blooms (4) 1. Mrs P R Cox: Bantam 2. B S Duncan: 2538 3. Mrs T Braithwaite: seedling
315 Three Miniature Species or Wild Hybrids From Division 13, three blooms of each (3) 1. Mrs T Braithwaite: N. intermedius, N. pachybolbus, N. jonquilla 2. Mrs J Doulton: N. jonquilla, N. rupicola, N. bulbocodium var. tenuifolius 3. R Wiseman: N. jonquilla, N. bulbocodium, N. rupicola
316 Three Miniature Cultivars, three blooms of each (5) 1. Mrs J Doulton: Stafford, Xit, Rikki 2. Mrs T Braithwaite: Little Sentry, Pixie's Sister, Chiva 3. Mrs P R Cox: Hawera, Segovia, Sun Disc
317 One Miniature Species or Wild Hybrid From Division 13, three blooms (1) 1. E Perren: N. jonquilla
318 One Miniature Cultivar, three blooms (8) 1. M R Bird: Little Sentry 2. Mrs T Braithwaite: Clare 3. Mrs P R Cox: Sun Disc
319 Division 1, Perianth Yellow, corona yellow Not recorded
320 Division 1, Perianth Yellow, corona White, with or without a yellow rim Not recorded
321 Division 1, Perianth Yellow, Corona in any other colour or colour combination Not recorded
322 Division 1, Perianth White, corona yellow or white & yellow Not recorded
323 Division 1, Perianth White, corona white Not recorded
324 Division 1, Perianth White, corona in any other colour or colour combination Not recorded
326 Division 2, Perianth Yellow, Corona yellow (14) 1. R B Braithwaite: Goldhanger 2. L Mace: Maya Dynasty 3. B S Duncan: Gold Ingot
327 Division 2, Perianth Yellow, Corona Orange or Red (13) 1. B S Duncan: Tropical Heat 2. G Ridley: Hot Gossip 3. D G Matthews: Tropical Heat
328 Division 2, Perianth Yellow, Corona with Orange or Red rim (10) 1. B S Duncan: 2627 2. R B Braithwaite: Fireblade 3. L Mace: Shangani
330 Division 2, Perianth Yellow, Corona White, with or without a yellow rim (14) 1. D G Matthews: Altun Ha 2. F G Austin: Altun Ha 3. L Olive: Altun Ha
331 Division 2, Perianth Orange, Corona Orange or Red (5) 1. M S Bradbury: Bionic 2. F G Austin: Bailey 3. P G Barlass: Limbo
332 Division 2, Perianth White, Corona Yellow or White & Yellow (6) 1. H D L Vivash: West Post 2. L Mace: Corky's Song 3. D Spencer: Holme Fen
333 Division 2, Perianth White, corona orange or red with colour predominant (4) 1. D G Matthews: Young Blood 2. D Spencer: Young Blood 3. Not awarded
334 Division 2, Perianth White, corona orange or red with colour not predominant (2) 1. B S Duncan: Coliseum 2. M S Bradbury: Conestoga
335 Division 2, perianth white, corona pink with colour predominant (19) 1. P Payne: John Peace 2. R B Braithwaite: Lakeland Fair 3. L Mace: Birky
336 Division 2, perianth white, corona pink with colour not predominant (15) 1. B S Duncan: Ice Dancer 2. D Spencer: Cherrygardens 3. Mr & Mrs G & V Ellam: Rainbow
337 Division 2, perianth white (15) 1. R B Braithwaite: Sheelagh Rowan 2. L Mace: Sheelagh Rowan 3. R Crouchman: Sheelagh Rowan
339 Division 3, perianth yellow, corona yellow (4) 1. J Goddard: Legislator 2. D G Matthews: Wychbold 3. S Ellison: Lemma
340 Division 3, perianth yellow, corona orange or red (12) 1. B S Duncan: Armidale 2. L Olive: Unknown 3. G Ridley: Stanway
341 Division 3, perianth yellow, corona with Orange or red rim (12) 1. L Mace: Badbury Rings 2. Mr & Mrs R Tabor: Triple Crown 3. J Goddard: Triple Crown
342 Division 3, perianth yellow, Corona white, with or without yellow rim (0)
343 Division 3, perianth orange, Corona Orange or Red (4) 1. D G Matthews: Bossa Nova 2. E Perren: Brodick 3. D Spencer: Bossa Nova
344 Division 3, perianth white, corona yellow or white & yellow (18) 1. R B Braithwaite: Moon Shadow 2. B S Duncan: Jammin 3. T R Frost: Astrid's Memory
345 Division 3, perianth white, Corona Orange or Red (10) 1. B S Duncan: Doctor Hugh 2. L Olive: Doctor Hugh 3. R B Braithwaite: Hartlebury
346 Division 3, perianth white, corona with Orange or Red rim (11) 1. B S Duncan: Repertoire 2. L Olive: Carole Lombard 3. G Ridley: seedling
348 Division 3, perianth White, Corona White (13) 1. L Olive: Achnasheen 2. P Payne: EJ540 3. H D L Vivash: Silver Crystal
350 Division 4, perianth and petaloid segments yellow, corona segments Yellow (9) 1. D G Matthews: Spun Honey 2. P G Barlass: Spun Honey 3. Mr & Mrs R Tabor: Spun Honey
351 Division 4, perianth and petaloid segments yellow, Corona segments Orange or Red (10) 1. L Mace: Crowndale 2. D G Matthews: Dunkery 3. L Olive: First Team
352 Division 4, perianth and petaloid segments white, corona segments Yellow or White (12) 1. B S Duncan: Greek Surprise 2. H D L Vivash: Serena Beach 3. E Perren: Unique
353 Division 4, perianth and petaloid segments white, corona segments Orange or Red (18) 1. L Olive: Gay Kybo 2. R B Braithwaite: Gay Kybo 3. D Spencer: Gay Kybo
354 Division 4, perianth and petaloid segments White, Corona segments Pink (5) 1. F G Austin: Duration 2. H D L Vivash: Hibernian 3. L Mace: Pink Paradise
356 Division 5, perianth Yellow, corona White or coloured (5) 1. Mrs T Braithwaite: Chipper 2. G Ridley: Hawera 3. E Perren: Hawera
357 Division 5, perianth white, corona coloured (1) 1. Not awarded 2. G Ridley: Katie Heath
358 Division 5, perianth white, corona white (8) 1. L Olive: Ice Wings 2. Mrs T Braithwaite: Sunday Chimes 3. Mrs P R Cox: Mission Bells
359 Division 6, perianth yellow, corona yellow or white (4) 1. F G Austin: Frogmore 2. Mrs T Braithwaite: Wheatear 3. Mrs P R Cox: Unknown
360 Division 6, perianth Yellow, corona Pink, Orange or Red (0)
361 Division 6, perianth white, corona Yellow (0)
364 Division 7, perianth Yellow, corona Yellow (6) 1. L Mace: Stratosphere 2. Mrs P R Cox: Stratosphere 3. F G Austin: Kokopelli
365 Division 7, perianth Yellow, corona Pink, Orange or Red (6) 1. E Perren: Stratosphere 2. T R Frost: Stratosphere 3. Mrs T Braithwaite: Stratosphere

366 Division 7, perianth yellow, corona white with or without a yellow rim (3) 1. T R Frost: Intrigue 2. Mrs P R Cox: Oryx 3. D G Matthews: Oryx
367 Division 7, perianth white, corona white or coloured (6) 1. L Olive: Ladies' Choice 2. Mrs T Braithwaite: An-Gof 3. Mrs P R Cox: Ladies' Choice
368 Division 8, perianth Yellow (1) 1. E Perren: Highfield Beauty
369 Division 8, perianth White (7) 1. S Ellison: Silver Chimes 2. E Perren: Silver Chimes 3. Mrs P R Cox: Silver Chimes
371 Division 10 or 12, Any colour combination (5) 1. G Ridley: Golden Bells Group 2. F G Austin: Golden Bells Group 3. Mr & Mrs G & V Ellam: Diamond Ring
372 Division 11, perianth Yellow (9) 1. R Hilson: Tripartite 2. L Olive: Tripartite 3. Mrs P R Cox: Gironde
375 Intermediate Cultivar from divisions 1 to 4 or 11 (11) 1. L Mace: Lauren 2. G Ridley: seedling 3. E Perren: Lauren
376 Miniature Species or wild hybrid from Division 13 (5) 1. Mrs T Braithwaite: *N. intermedius* 2. E Perren: *N. jonquilla* 3. R Wiseman: *N. × medioluteus*
377 Intermediate, Miniature & Wild Daffodils, Miniature Cultivar (13) 1. T R Frost: Hawera 2. M Ward: Sun Disc 3. Mrs T Braithwaite: Stafford
378 Species or wild hybrid from division 13 (other than miniature) (1) 1. R Wiseman: *N. poeticus* var. *recurvus*
379 Seven blooms, of one or more cultivars from any of divisions 1 to 3 (amateur class) (3) 1. R Wiseman: Overdraft (2), Suave, Holme Fen, Unknown, Tycoon, Silent Pink 2. R Hilson: Triple Crown 3. A Barrow: Golitha Falls, Rose Gold, Verona, Meissen, Goldfinger, Misty Glen, Unknown
382 Three cultivars, division 5, one bloom of each (amateur class) (2) 1. A Barrow: Lemon Drops, Hawera, Liberty Bells 2. R Wiseman: Ice Wings, Hawera, Chipper
383 Three cultivars, division 6, one bloom of each (amateur class) (0)
384 Three cultivars, division 7, one bloom of each (amateur class) (2) 1. R Wiseman: Kokopelli, Stratosphere, Bell Song 2. A Barrow: Stratosphere, Pipit, Hillstar
385 Three cultivars, division 8, one bloom of each (amateur class) (1) 1. A Barrow: Silver Chimes, Falconet, Hoopoe
386 Three cultivars, division 9, one bloom of each (amateur class) (2) 1. Mrs P R Cox: Poet's Way, Kamma, Blisland 2. R Wiseman: Blisland, Patois, Sea Green
387 Three cultivars, division 11, one bloom of each (amateur class) (1) 1. R Wiseman: Mitsch seedling, Pink Polynomial, Trigonometry
388 Division 1, perianth yellow, corona coloured (Novice class) (2) 1. A Barrow: Goldfinger 2. S M Lugg: Goldfinger
389 Division 1, perianth yellow, corona white (Novice class) Not recorded
390 Division 1, perianth white, corona coloured (Novice class) (2) 1. R J Munford: Bravoure 2. G Cooper: Bravoure
391 Division 1, perianth white, corona white (Novice class) Not recorded
392 Division 2, perianth yellow, corona Yellow (Novice class) (2) 1. Not awarded 2. Not awarded 3. R J Munford: Unknown
393 Division 2, perianth yellow, corona containing Pink, Orange or Red (amateur class) (4) 1. R Hedge: Pipe Major 2. R J Munford: Unknown 3. G Cooper: Lothario

394 Division 2, perianth yellow, corona white, with or without a yellow rim (Novice class) (1) 1. Not awarded 2. A Barrow: Helford Dawn
395 Division 2, perianth white, corona yellow or white & yellow (Novice class) (1) 1. Not awarded 2. Not awarded 3. R Hedge: Terracotta
396 Division 2, perianth white, corona Pink, Orange or Red (Novice class) (3) 1. R J Munford: Rainbow 2. A Barrow: Dancing Queen 3. S M Lugg: Rainbow
397 Division 2, Perianth white, Corona white (3) 1. M Ward: Cultured Pearl 2. A Barrow: Sheelagh Rowan 3. R Hedge: Sheelagh Rowan
398 Division 3, Perianth Yellow, Corona Coloured (Novice class) (3) 1. S M Lugg: Tehidy 2. R J Munford: Nonchalant 3. A Barrow: Stanway
399 Division 3, perianth White, Corona Coloured (Novice class) (3) 1. M Ward: Aircastle 2. R J Munford: Bainden 3. A Barrow: Crimson Chalice
400 Division 3, Perianth White, Corona white (Novice class) (3) 1. A Barrow: Verona 2. S M Lugg: Silverwood 3. R J Munford: Verona
401 Division 4 (5) 1. S M Lugg: Dorchester 2. A Barrow: Sherborne 3. M Ward: Gay Kybo
402 Division 5 (1) 1. A Barrow: Lemon Drops
403 Division 6 (1) 1. Not awarded 2. A Barrow: Reggae
404 Division 7 (3) 1. M Ward: Stratosphere 2. A Barrow: Intrigue 3. G Cooper: Pipit
405 Division 8 (3) 1. S M Lugg: Silver Chimes 2. R J Munford: Geranium 3. A Barrow: Silver Chimes
406 Division 9 Not recorded
407 Division 10 or 12 (1) 1. A Barrow: Toto

RESULTS - TULIPS

Class
1 Nine Blooms of one cultivar (10) 1. J Fishenden: Golden Parade 2. Mr & Mrs G Hollingdale: Big Smile 3. J Fishenden: Vivex
2 Three Double tulips (0)
3 Three White tulips (2) 1. Malcolm Bradbury:: Angel's Wish 2. Mrs T Braithwaite: White Dream
4 Three Yellow tulips (3) 1. Mr & Mrs G Hollingdale: Big Smile 2. J Fishenden: Golden Parade 3. Not awarded
5 Three Pink or Red tulips (7) 1. K Bacon: World's Favourite 2. J Fishenden: Parade 3. R Hedge: Pink Diamond
6 Three tulips any other colour (11) 1. J Fishenden: Toyota 2. R Hedge: Paul Scherer 3. Mr & Mrs G Hollingdale: Spring Green
7 Three Lily-flowered tulips (3) 1. G Cooper: Ballerina 2. Not recorded: Ballade 3. G Cooper: Ballade
8 Three Fringed tulips (1) 1. Mr & Mrs G Hollingdale: Lambada
9 Three Viridiflora tulips (2) 1. Not awarded 2. Not awarded 3. Not awarded
10 Three Parrot tulips (1) 1. Mr & Mrs G Hollingdale: Black Parrot
11 Three Darwinhybrid tulips (1) 1. K Bacon: Vivex
12 Five Kaufmanniana, Greigii or Fosteriana Tulips (0)
13 Three multi-headed Tulips (0)
14 Five blooms of one species tulip (1) 1. Mrs T Braithwaite: T. hageri
15 One species tulip, a pot or pan of at least five bulbs in bloom (0)

Other UK Shows

Daffodils, Snowdrops and Tulips at Two AGS Shows

Harlow
Mary Randall

The Alpine Garden Society's Early Spring Show, held this year on 1 March, seems to be a fixture at the Mark Hall School in Harlow, as is the excellent quality and variety of the entries. Many of these would not necessarily excite galanthophiles or tulipomaniacs, however the exhibitors come 'frae a' the airts' so, despite the early snowdrop season, there were still some good pans to admire.

Snowdrops

The 'common snowdrop' *Galanthus nivalis* showed its totally typical clump-forming growth to prove that easy garden plants can also look good on the show bench. 'Yellow' snowdrops currently carry almost as great a cachet as the more fancy 'greens'. The pot exhibited had originated in Northumberland, which seems to have been the main source of many of the yellow forms now in circulation. It is a much more fairy-like version of *G. nivalis*, with elegantly curving yellow spathes holding slim yellow ovaries from which hang delightfully fragile white 'drops' with neatly marked inners. I believe the *G. nivalis* Sandersii Group prefer a more acidic soil compared to the alkali-loving *G. nivalis*. The green-spathed, green-tipped bells of *G. nivalis* 'Viridapice' stood out in a bulbous class. To my eyes it is a more balanced flower than the larger *G. nivalis* 'Warei', and is certainly a good garden plant.

Galanthus plicatus 'Sophie North' made historical headlines for its naming after one of the victims of the Dunblane massacre. Doing well in Scotland and the North of England it has, unfortunately, proved less easy in the South. The pan staged was a very strong clump of well-formed flowers of good substance, some of the stems bearing two flowers. The inners, to my eyes, show a substantial green cross filled in at the base. *G.* 'Sophie North' was pot-grown in a mix of two parts John Innes compost [1] to one part grit. Finally, one of the 'greens', *G. plicatus* 'Trym', always seems to stand out, whether growing in the garden or in a pot. It is by no means a large flower but the slightly triangular shape and the cleanness of the green external mark make it quite spectacular. One can no longer call it 'unique' as it has proved to be a very fertile parent of a number of fascinating progeny bearing allied characteristics.

Daffodils

In the small six pan class was a little pot of my favourite daffodil, *Narcissus cyclamineus*. It is not normally seen as a pot plant, being so much happier in a fairly moist acid situation. I suppose it is the cyclamen effect of the deflexed petals which makes it so striking, together with the stiffly erect flower stems, not quite guardsmen on parade but a slightly comical military effect. No comic effect was perceived in the attractive pan of *N. atlanticus*. It is a sweetly scented, creamy white flower somewhat like *N. rupicola* subsp. *watieri* but a little taller and with a more bowl-shaped cup. Unlike the preceding *Narcissus* it requires the protection of an alpine house or bulb frame, with no overhead watering from the time in late spring when the foliage dies down until root growth resumes in late summer. The Tenby Daffodil, supposedly a Welsh native, made a welcome appearance. *N. obvallaris* is a vastly more substantial daffodil than any of the others mentioned but is nevertheless a good garden plant.

John Blanchard, the author of Narcissus: *A Guide to Wild Daffodils* (AGS 1990) is known to think that *N. alpestris* and *N. moschatus* may well represent one variable species. Be that as it may, *N. moschatus* is usually available from a number of specialist nurseries but one can rarely track down purchasable *N. alpestris*. Three forms were shown, one with the petals hanging somewhat listlessly like a Victorian lady having a fit of the vapours, the second more elegant in a pallid way and the third rather more robust with a touch of bicolor between petals and trumpet.

Moving on to the absolute star of the *Narcissus*, there was a wonderful pan of the engineered hybrid *N.* Eira Group 12W-W. The raisers being true bulb specialists and now adopted Welshmen, this pristine *Narcissus* has been given the Welsh name for snow. Having admired *N.* × *susannae* (syn. of *N.* × *litigiosus*), several people have attempted to recreate the cross using either the same parents (*N. cantabricus* subsp. *monophyllus* × *N. triandrus* subsp. *pallidulus*) or variants thereof.

Eira Group is a name applied to a look-alike grouping of seed-raised plants which arose from a deliberate cross made by the exhibitors between *N. triandrus* var. *triandrus* (not var. *concolor*) and a selected form of *N. cantabricus*. Seed was sown in October 1993 and the first flowers appeared early in 1997. The seedlings are fairly uniform both in vigour and appearance; the possibility of a second generation crop is remote, no seed having been set to date. Increase has been steady in an unheated alpine house. Water is withheld from the time that the narrow dark green leaves wither in May until root growth resumes in autumn. To stave off the threat of basal rot, to which miniature and small daffodils are horribly prone in some years, it is worth while dusting or drenching the bulbils with a fungicide during their annual repotting. Any bulbils that lack the firmness of their healthy counterparts should of course be discarded. It needs to be emphasised that this is not a clonal name but one applied to seedlings whose characters fall within the agreed published parameters.

Tulipa cretica

Lastly, and rather unexpectedly, one of our top orchid enthusiasts staged a lovely pan of *Tulipa cretica*. Like many of the bulbs mentioned it is a very delicate flower, with palest ethereal pink, starry petals centred with deepest gold and with golden anthers. A plant which is delicate both in bud and in flower, it appears to need nothing more than cold glasshouse treatment to be seen at its best, planted in a fairly standard John Innes mix with added grit.

How often do we find that our expert growers say, when asked what magic formula they use, 'Oh just an ordinary mix,' yet they always manage to produce such incredibly well-grown plants.

[1] See www.johninnescompost.org

LOUGHBOROUGH
ROBERT ROLFE

Alpine Garden Society (AGS) late winter and early spring Shows are often a good place to see unusual snowdrops, for the Society's membership includes many of the country's foremost *Galanthus* experts. The novelty this year at the Loughborough Show on 8 March was the species grown as *G. artjuschenkoae* that was shown three weeks earlier at the Caerleon event. Then again, green-marked snowdrops, some of them very recently discovered and newly named, have had a good run at the early RHS Westminster Shows. Some of the most striking are from continental Europe, and a highlight at Loughborough was *Galanthus nivalis* 'Virescens', whose history can be traced back to the second half of the 18th century when it was distributed by Professor Fenzl, Director of the Vienna Botanic Garden. It has never been widely grown, probably because its rate of increase is steady rather than spectacular. Like many snowdrops, it prefers the outdoor life, and indeed the exhibitor, Rosina Abbiss of Harpenden, had lifted the pristine clump from a shady, leafy spot in her garden. With this she easily won the class for a bulbous plant excluding *Narcissus* and *Fritillaria*

Galanthus nivalis 'Virescens'
(*photo* Robert Rolfe)

in her first year of exhibiting in the Open Section. Several stocks of similar appearance are apparently doing the rounds, a common snowdrop phenomenon. However, there was no reason to quibble over the identification of this potful, whose substantial flowers were delicately hatched light green from the ovary down two-thirds of the outer segment, leaving a white tip. With many green variants, of course, the proportion of green to white and the placement are reversed.

Another snowdrop of note, 'Augustus' (Della Kerr of Darlington), showed the sturdy merits of this *G. plicatus* seedling, put slightly in the shade perhaps by the very recent advent of the poculiform *G.* 'E.A. Bowles', whose name more explicitly commemorates the well-known snowdrop enthusiast (see pages 86 and 131). Nevertheless it remains a very attractive selection, with broad, glaucous leaves and sturdy stems carrying ribbed flowers, the outers generously concave, the inners with a deep green, H-shaped mark. As seen, it needed another year or two in which to form a clump, for the bulbs were rather spaced out in their pot, though in their prime and well-presented.

Daffodils

One never quite knows what to expect at this early March gathering, for it draws exhibitors out of hibernation over a very wide area: from Newcastle down to Kent, and across to Dorset and South Wales, in 2008 at least. One noted *Narcissus* grower was unable to make the trip this time, and coupled with a decidedly cold end to winter, this meant that despite a very buoyant entry in the Show overall, the half dozen miniature/dwarf daffodil classes the schedule includes were less keenly contested this time round. Bob and Rannveig Wallis of Carmarthen nonetheless brought with them an estate car full of plants, winning the Charnwood Forest Trophy for the most first-prize points in the Open Section. Among a host of bulb- and corm-dominated entries, especial mention should be made of their win in the three pans distinct, raised from seed class, where they showed *Fritillaria ariana* from seed collected in Afghanistan; a 2001 sowing of *Narcissus atlanticus* - derived from the original stock grown by Sir Frederick Stern, not the 1994 re-introduction; and an instructive, diverse pan of *N. asturiensis* × *N. cyclamineus*, sown in January 1999, the plants differing in the breadth of their trumpets and the horizontal through to fully swept-back perianth segments. Also notable was their large winning entry of three pans: *Narcissus bulbocodium* RRW 88.32, sourced by the exhibitors close to Tahanout in Morocco's High Atlas, with lemon-yellow, frilly-edged trumpets; *N. jonquilla* var. *minor* in promising but early flower; and *N. jonquilla* var. *henriquesii* with a mass of 25cm (10in) tall stems, topped by two or three long-tubed, heavily scented flowers. *N.* 'Eira' in their six pan from seed exhibit (upgraded to an RHS Award of Merit when shown at the Harlow Show the week before) also stood out. Raisings of comparable parentage (*N. triandrus* subsp. *triandrus* × *N. cantabricus*) were seen from early February to mid-April, with others annexing *N. triandrus* and - by deduction - *N. fernandesii*, from rich yellow through to almost white. A cream-flowered, subtly bicoloured raising shown at the AGS Chesterfield Show a month later formed a creditable end to the line. Disappointingly relegated to third place in the garden hybrid class, their enterprising *N. asturiensis* × *N. primigenius* cross inherited the

N. cyclamineus
(*photo* Robert Rolfe)

and even the offsets were presented in prime, floriferous condition, so that while the prize for best bulbous plant went to an early-stage *Erythronium*, in justice the award could have been attached to any of her several glowing entries.

N. triandrus × *?N. fernandesii*
(*photo* Robert Rolfe)

bicoloured facies of its Cantabrican pollen parent but was smaller still, at barely 10cm (4in) tall; the four flowers on display were uniform, and gave much promise, but judges are not always prescient, or willing to take a punt.

Some other newly-exhibited hybrids were also on display. Understandably *N.* 'Cornish Chuckles' AGM was passed over, for however well it performs in the garden, it tends to look out of place when pot-grown. The same fate befell *N.* 'Oz' 12Y-Y ('Jenny' × *N. jonquilla*, raised by Bill Pannill and first flowered in 1980) which as seen was too thin of trumpet and conversely too broad of petal to satisfy. Only the under-used *N.* 'Small Talk' 1Y-Y (a cultivar derived from *N. minor*, raised by Oregon daffodil breeder Grant Mitsch in 1965), which was shown by several exhibitors, provided a welcome debut. But all were eclipsed by several pans of that hardiest of all late winter, dwarf daffodils, *N. cyclamineus*, once again shown at its finest by Clare Oates of Scunthorpe. Her exhibits were uniform,

South East of England Daffodil Society Shows

Robert Wiseman

The Early Show

Despite the weather, the South East of England Daffodil Society show on 16 March was one of the best of our early shows. Although meant to be a prelude to the main show and a bit of a fun event, this one had over 20 exhibitors staging 264 blooms on the day, with a lot of healthy competition and with good quality flowers on display. Best Bloom in show was 77-92, a 1Y-Y seedling from Ron Allen; and Best Exhibit in show was a wonderful pot of *N. bulbocodium* var. *filifolius* from Janine Doulton. The only division not represented was division 9, which even had me beat this year, the first time I had not shown in this division since the start of our early show.

The Main Show

At our main show on 13 April we were joined by 30 World Daffodil Convention delegates, mostly from New Zealand and the USA and many of them joining our judging panels. This was a wonderful opportunity to put faces to people whom I had previously only read about or written to, also to greet acquaintances from previous meetings and trips. The alternating periods of warm and very cold weather that preceded the show meant that flower quality was much more variable than usual, as it was at the RHS Show a few days later. None the less, in a difficult season 48 exhibitors managed to stage 1,104 flowers on the day.

Collection classes

The South East England Championship, which requires one stem each of twelve distinct daffodils, attracted twelve entries. The winning places were hotly contested between David Matthews, Dave Spencer and Frank Verge, with Frank's meticulous attention to detail winning the day. He included particularly good flowers of 'Evesham', 'Honeybourne' and two of his own seedlings. Frank won not only the Championship but also Best Exhibit in show, a remarkable achievement as his bulbs were decimated last year and his winning collection came from fewer than 40 pots.

To mark the World Daffodil Convention we created a new class for three blooms of southern hemisphere daffodils. The class was won by Len Olive with very good flowers of 'Blossom Lady', 'Thumbs Up' 2Y-O and 'Cameo Joy', all raised by the partners of Koanga Daffodils in New Zealand, whilst second place went to Robert Wiseman with 'Terminator' 2Y-R, 'Machan' 2Y-Y and 'Macdalla' 1W-Y, all raised in Tasmania by Jackson's Daffodils.

The Ted Osborne Memorial Class for two vases of five blooms was won by Zara Evans, with good 'Goldfinger', 'Clouded Yellow', 'Lubaantun' and 'Wild Honey' amongst her flowers.

Best Bloom awards

Best Bloom in show and Best Bloom division 2 went to Len Olive for an outstanding 'Gold Convention'. Len also won the six bloom class, showing flowers of 'Thumbs Up', 'Dorchester', 'Silent Valley', 'Lakeland Snow' and 'Entrepreneur' alongside 'Gold Convention'. David Vivash took Best Bloom division 4 and Reserve Best Bloom in show with 'Dorchester'. Best Bloom division 1 came from Ray Sedgwick with 'Silent Valley', whilst Best Bloom division 3 was 'Best Friend' 3Y-YYO shown by Ian Johnson. Ian also took the Best Vase award with a superb exhibit of three 'Honeybourne'. Best Bloom divisions 5-11 was Dave Spencer's 'Ice Wings'. A 2W-YYO seedling raised by Mike Baxter and shown to good effect by David Matthews was Best Seedling in show.

Other classes

In the intermediary section, Best Bloom went to Alan Coles for the John Pearson-raised 'Monks Wood' 1YYG-Y; Alan also won the award for most points. Neil Lawrence took the Best Bloom honours with 'Hambledon' in the Novice classes, and the award for most points. For once Janine Doulton did not get it all her own way in the miniatures, as Robin Crouchman took the Best Vase award with 'Segovia', but she still took most points and the Championship.

The highlight of the day was the presentation of a Friendship Award to Frank Verge, by the President of the National Daffodil Society of New Zealand, Mrs Lesley Ramsay.

THE DAFFODIL SOCIETY SHOW
GWYNNE DAVIES

Daffodils always make people better, happier and more helpful; they are sunshine, food and medicine for the soul. (Apologies to Luther Burbank.) So it was for the 58 exhibitors and countless visitors at the Daffodil Society Show on the weekend of 19 and 20 April 2008, including the Mayor of Warwick who kindly presented the cups, trophies and awards.

Seedling classes

John Gibson, earlier winner of the Engleheart Cup in London, continued his success in classes for cultivars raised by the exhibitor in winning three cups: the Bourne Daffodil Cup for twelve cultivars, one bloom of each, where he showed 'Eastbrook Sunrise', 'Broughton Park', 'Draycote Water', 'Corby Candle' and a number of seedlings, including 103-9-98 2W-WWY, judged the Best Unregistered Seedling in show, and the author's favourite 1-20-92 2Y-Y; the Dr Lower Challenge Cup for three cultivars of trumpet daffodils, one bloom of each, including 'Coalbrookdale' and 'Grafton Brook'; and the Knight Challenge Cup for six cultivars, which also featured 'Coalbrookdale'.

Collection classes

Roger Braithwaite went 'nap' in winning five trophies. In the Cartwright Challenge Cup for twelve cultivars in commerce, representing not less than four divisions, one bloom of each, he included 'Claverley', 'Moon Shadow' and the Best Bloom division 3, 'Astrid's Memory'. John Peace was in second place, as last year, and included two cultivars, 'Altun Ha' and 'Ombersley', that Roger also showed.

The Williams Challenge Cup gave Roger more competition, with six exhibitors. Here six all-yellow cultivars were required, and Roger included 'Gold Convention', 'Arleston', 'Disquiet', 'Summer Breeze' 2Y-Y and 'Happy Valley', overcoming Keith Capper and John Peace in second and third places.

Six exhibitors competed for the Leamington Challenge Cup, six cultivars with orange and/or red in the corona, one bloom of each, with Roger's 'Cape Cornwall', 'Loch Alsh', 'Elusive', 'Dateline', 'Terminator' and 'Afficionado' 3W-O taking the honours. Evelyn Jane and Ron Parsons were in second and third places respectively.

The six cultivars of all-white daffodils, one bloom of each, for the Ernie Darlow Memorial Award attracted six entrants. The perennial runner-up, Derek Phillips, maintained his position in the class to Roger's winning six of 'Silent Valley', 'Inverpolly', 'Sheelagh Rowan', 'Cool Crystal', 'Nice Day' and 'Phoenician'. Evelyn Jane was third. The cultivars 'Silent Valley' and 'Regal Bliss' have become the basis for entries in this class.

The Walter Ware Challenge Vase, six cultivars with pink colouring in the corona, one bloom of each, easily became the fifth trophy for Roger, as he was the only entrant, with good examples of 'Sweet Georgia', 'Cape Point' and 'Entrepreneur'.

Not to be outdone by Roger, Terry Braithwaite won the James Barrington Memorial Award for six cultivars from not less than two of divisions 5, 6, 7 and 8, one bloom of each; Ted Perren and Frank Newbery taking the places. Terry was also successful with her miniature exhibit in the Warwick Trophy class for nine cultivars or species from not less than two divisions, beating Jackie Petherbridge and Janine Doulton with 'Segovia', 'Angel's Whisper', 'Yellow Xit', 'Clare', 'Xit', 'Sabrosa', 'Flomay', *N. bulbocodium* and a superb *N. pachybolbus*, which was declared Best Miniature in show.

The Miniature Challenge Trophy, three cultivars or species, three blooms of each in three vases, one cultivar per vase, attracted six strong entries. The well-deserved winner was Jeremy Wilkes with his 'Hawera', 'Segovia' and 'Sun Disc'; Jackie Petherbridge and Janine Doulton again took second and third places.

Best Bloom awards

The Best Bloom in show was 'Silent Valley', exhibited by John Peace, in the 1 W-W single bloom class, where just about every bloom was the same cultivar. The Australian-bred 'Banker', was Best Bloom division 2 in show and came from Ken Harrop's winning twelve in the Wootton Challenge Cup. The Best Bloom division 4 in show was 'Crowndale', shown by Len Olive in the single bloom class. The top multi-bloom vase, winner of the Bikini Trophy, was 'Banker', exhibited by John Peace and triumphant in the class for three blooms of one cultivar from division 2.

Harrogate Spring Flower Show
Richard Smales

Thirty delegates from the World Daffodil Convention chose to visit the Harrogate Show after the convention had officially ended. Not only did this mean that Harrogate became the only opportunity for many Daffodil Society members to meet the overseas visitors but the Daffodil Society and the Northern Group in particular were anxious to make them welcome and create a good impression with our flowers. We think we succeeded on both counts. Accommodation was arranged and the celebratory dinner in the hotel was a great success. The show ran from 24-27 April, and although the visitors did not get to it until the third day, the flowers had held well in the cool environment. Harrogate's many other floral offerings were there to covet too. So what did they see in the Daffodil Marquee?

First, there were two displays put on by the Northern Group. Our first attempt at a Society Stand showing the range of cultivars available won for us a Silver Medal. Then to commemorate 30 years of the Northern Group we had examples of the Grand Champion blooms over that time. It was a revelation to see that Paul Payne had been successful on nine occasions, a feat unlikely to be surpassed.

Collection classes

The North of England Championship was won by Roger Braithwaite from two other entrants, Ken Harrop and John Peace. Roger's 'Moon Shadow' went on to become Champion Bloom division 3 and his 'Inverpolly' was barely distinguishable from the one that became Grand Champion. These were three strong entries, any of which could have been champion in another year. Their growing, dressing, staging and attention to detail were skills honed by their exhibitors' lifelong involvement with chrysanthemums. Along with similarly minded colleagues they have raised the bar for daffodil showing, particularly with their collections. This cannot be a bad thing, and it provides a standard for us all to aspire to, but the traditional hobbyist can become disheartened. Not so long ago entries for the Championship were in double figures as we all sacrificed our best flowers in the hope of getting a minor placing. Since then it has all become more serious - you could almost say professional.

The first three places in the next class for six cultivars went to 'chrysanth' men', with Barry Hogg succeeding this time and his 'Dorchester' was Champion Bloom division 4. Nobody could find six cultivars from division 1 and we wonder if this reflects the dearth of good 1W-Ys. This is illustrated by looking at the single bloom class. The first three in the 1W-Y class were 'Cristobal', 'Newcastle' and 'Bravoure'. In contrast the show was awash with exciting 1Y-Y cultivars.

At least, in the class for six yellows, Wendy Akers managed third place behind two chrysanth' men, and similarly in the six whites second and third places went to the two stalwarts Ron Parsons and Ian Yeardley. To be fair, the winner Ken Harrop used only established well-known cultivars and his success was down to the attributes we have alluded to above. Each of the first three entries contained a 'Misty Glen' - one of the all-time dependables. Ron Parsons included 'Orkney' in his set, a promising new cultivar seen at several shows this season.

The Societies Class had the single entry from Denton C and D Society, who are repeating their many successes in chrysanthemum society classes. However, while we accept this was a collective effort, much of the credit must go to Ken Harrop, especially in view of his efforts elsewhere throughout the show.

Only Roger could find six cultivars with red or orange in the cup and again I suspect the imbalance in the available yellow perianths and white perianths is to blame. In the single blooms, the class for 2Y- with red predominant had thirteen entries, whereas the 2W- with red predominant had three, and the winner was 'Royal Regiment' registered in 1961. Even more markedly in the non-predominant classes there were ten entries in the yellow perianths but only a single entry, 'Ringleader' (1972), in the whites. The pattern is repeated in division 3 though not so obviously. There is a wide choice of yellows and in the white perianths 'Doctor Hugh' reigns supreme, but both here and in the non-predominant classes a breakthrough could be occurring with the arrival of 'Bluntington' and 'Shurdington' from the Clive Postles stable. Sister seedlings, and big bright impressive flowers, they are bred from 'Dunley Hall' and 'Doctor Hugh'.

Divisions 5-9 and miniatures

Only rarely do the chrysanth' men venture into divisions 5 to 8, where Terry Braithwaite rules the roost and most of her protagonists are ladies also. Prominent among these is Christine Yeardley, and in the class for six cultivars from divisions 5 to 8 she pushed Terry into second place. Her 'Ice Wings' was Champion Bloom division 5. Their tussle continued in the remaining classes. In the vases of three, Christine won with 'Falconet', one of which was Champion Bloom division 8. Terry's winning vase of 'Dainty Miss' contained the Champion Bloom division 7. This is a beautiful, ice-white but enigmatic flower: a Mitsch seedling, it has been around since 1966 but is rarely seen. It is a cross between *N. rupicola* subsp. *watieri* and a division 2 seedling, and though registered in division 7 would make a perfect division 3 intermediate. How can it be a jonquil when 'Xit' and 'Segovia' are classed as division 3? In the single blooms it was Sue Vinden's chance to shine and she won with 'Ice Wings', 'Trena', which was Champion Bloom division 6, and 'Itzim'.

It is in the miniatures where Terry really excels and she won four of the six classes she entered, displaying her professional versatility with multi-vase exhibits of species and cultivars alike. The range of combinations can be bewildering and there was at least one exhibitor who gave up when the schedule became too complicated.

Vases of three

The remaining classes for vases of three were very well supported and the first three classes were won by Barry Hogg, Colin Gilman and Ken Dear, with quality blooms of 'Ombersley', 'Altun Ha' and 'Triple Crown' respectively. Division 9 went to John Cosway for his vase of 'Blisland', which is fast becoming the poet to grow. It was the class for one bloom from each of divisions 1, 2 and 3, however, that created most interest. Ron Parsons won it and also the Jack Morley Memorial Trophy for Best Vase in that section. He included 'Tao' 3Y-O, a flower seen a lot this year and seeming to have a big future. It was in Colin Gilman's second-place exhibit though, that the star of the show was nestling. Grand Champion Bloom 'Inverpolly' was first flowered by John Lea in 1961 but not registered until 1980. We do not see it very often but that could change.

Single blooms

The single blooms were in line with what we have come to expect, with many exhibitors keeping their best for the collections. An exception was John Peace, who staged 'Silent Valley', Champion Bloom division 1. In doing so he repeated his achievement at Warwick. To include it as a single bloom class and in his collections, John must have planted a sackful! If you've found a winning formula why change it? Bulbs are cheap, so forget basal rot and buy in fresh next year. Some might find this approach cynical and straying beyond the average hobbyist's aspirations. I once attended a talk by a champion perpetual carnation grower. It turned out that he only grew nine varieties. Many would consider such a regime tiresome, but we have all grown a cultivar year after year without it earning its keep, and adhering to what wins for us is paramount.

Conclusion

In the end we are grateful to everyone who came along, including novices and beginners, for putting on such a wonderful display. Our special thanks go to our pals from the chrysanthemum world for showing us what can be achieved using the best of the old and the newer cultivars. Unfortunately, along with the higher standard a greater degree of competitiveness is creeping in. In the old days people seemed to be much more laid back and you 'won some and you lost some.' We all like to re-judge a show in a light-hearted way as we stroll along the benches looking at all the flowers. Nowadays exhibitors seem to converge on their own flowers and become obsessed with the judges' scores rather than the flowers. Feelings can run high and it is to be hoped that they never take to showing daffodils in midsummer or there will be no judges left. A parallel might be drawn with rugby league. Here the referee is called 'Sir', and whether right or wrong he demands respect at all times. The authorities are worried about the increase in dissent and indiscipline and attribute this to the increase in money in the game, making winning more important both for clubs and individuals. Surely we are not going to let this happen to us.

Tulips

The difference in growing conditions and seasonality between the north and south of England in 2008 could not have been better demonstrated than by visiting the tulip shows held at Wisley on 29 April (see page 116) and at Harrogate two days later. Whereas the former had its best show in recent years, the latter had its worst ever. At Harrogate in 2002 there were eleven exhibitors in the Tulip Championship of Great Britain for three vases of nine tulips, this year there were none. In the class for a single vase of nine there were 16 entries, this year there were only two. The effect on the show, as a colourful spectacle, of the loss of 47 vases containing nine tulips needs little imagination; and overall in only seven of the sixteen classes were the judges required to find a third-placed entry.

The lateness of the season was clearly shown in the class for a vase of nine, where Teresa Clements, who was the only exhibitor, won first and second place with 'Negrita' and 'Corsage'. These flowers from the Triumph and Greigii sections respectively would in a 'normal' season have flowered three weeks earlier. However, the loss of the larger but later flowers was compensated for by very good entries in the classes for species and small-flowered tulips. All three were won by Mrs Terry Braithwaite, who is already a major exhibitor of miniature and small daffodils.

The report of the Tulip Show was contributed by James Akers.

CITY OF BELFAST SPRING FLOWER SHOW
RICHARD MCCAW

The City of Belfast Spring Flower Show on 19-20 April 2008 welcomed delegates to the Northern Ireland leg of the World Daffodil Convention. Those who were judging assembled at the daffodil section on the Saturday morning.

The weather leading up to the Show was very favourable to the growers, if perhaps a little dry for the daffodils. All the enthusiasts from Ireland wanted to impress the travelling band of daffodil experts; hence exhibits were up 146 on 2007. It was good to see that 69 of these were in the novice section. With the number of blooms totalling over 1,200, this was one of the best shows for many years.

Open classes

The Championship of Ireland, which requires twelve distinct single blooms, was won by Brian Duncan with 'Arleston' 2Y-Y, 'Doctor Hugh', 'Honeyorange' 2O-R, 'Dorchester', 'Harbour View' 2W-P, 'Feline Queen' 1Y-O, 'Amazing Grace' 2W-P, 'Gold Ingot',

'Goldfinger', 'Camaraderie' 2W-YYO, 'Chingah' 1Y-O and 2919 2W-P ('Chanson' × 'Camden'), which was judged Best Bloom division 1. Second was Robert Curry who was having a brilliant year. He showed D2539, 'Silver Surf', 'Gold Ingot', 'Dorchester', 'Evesham', 'Entente' 2Y-O, 'Glen Alladale' 3W-WYO, 'Banker', 'Treasure Chest' 1Y-Y, 'Lisnamulligan' 3W-R, M Kerr seedling 10 and 'Cisticola' 3W-YYR. Third was Richard McCaw with 'Arid Plains' 3Y-R, 'Chasseur' 2W-P, 'Gold Ingot', 'White Star', 'Stoke Charity', D2225, 'Shangani' 2Y-YYR, 8-27-89, 'Surrey', 'Amazing Grace', RAM12 3Y-Y and a 2W-P seedling.

The Royal Mail Trophy for six varieties three stems of each had the same order of merit. Brian won with 'Paradigm' 4Y-R, 'Harbour View', 'Doctor Hugh', 'Temba' 1Y-Y, 'Gold Bond' and 'Alto' 2W-P. Robert was second with 'Dorchester', 'Ethos', 'Paradigm', 'Dunadry Inn' 4W-O, 'June Lake' and 'Ahwhanee'. Richard was third with 'Tyrone Gold' 1Y-Y, 'White Star', 'Chasseur', 'Lennymore', 'Arthurian' and 'Young Blood'.

The American Daffodil Society's Red, White and Blue Ribbon was won by Richard McCaw with 'Night Music' 4W-P, 'River Queen' 2W-W, 'Trumpet Warrior', 'Spring Morn' 2Y YPP and 'Geometrics' 2W-Y. Second was George Wilson, who included 'Star Trek' 3W-GYR, 'Independence Day' 4W-R, 'Silken Sails', 'Pipit' and 'Indian Maid'.

The Guy Wilson Trophy was won by Derrick Turbitt with 'White Star', 'Val D'Incles' and 'Silver Crystal', while Richard McCaw was second with 'White Star', 'Stoke Charity' and 'Quiet Waters'.

The International Award and South East of England Daffodil Society Medal for three vases of three blooms was won by Richard McCaw, who showed 'Colourful' 2Y-R, 'Crackington' and 'Badbury Rings'. Second was George Wilson with vases of 'Colourful' and 'Evesham'; 'Entente' 2Y-O, 'Lundy Light' 2Y-R and 'Badbury Rings'; and 'Cotchford' 1Y-Y and 'Greenodd' 3W-YYW.

The Daffodil Society Gilt Medal for one vase of three blooms of unregistered seedlings was won by Richard McCaw with seedling 3 2Y-R, seedling 12 3Y-Y and seedling 150 2Y-P. Second was Maurice Kerr with seedling 442/1 3W-GYOY.

Best Bloom and vase awards

Best Bloom in show and Best Bloom division 2 was 'Golden Flute' 2Y-Y, shown by Nial Watson in the single bloom classes. 'Badbury Rings' shown by Derrick Turbitt was Best Bloom division 3 and Brian Duncan's 'Dorchester' was Best Bloom division 4. The Best Seedling in show was Brian Duncan's 2495, a very full double raised from 'Serena Beach' × 'Gay Kybo'; and the Best Amateur Seedling was 97/18 2W-YYP shown by Derrick Turbitt. 'Patois' 9W-GYR shown by Richard McCaw was the Best Bloom from any other division and was given the W J Toal Award.

The Open Section Best Three Bloom Vase was 'Alto' from Brian Duncan, while Amateur Best Three Bloom Vase was 'Chickerell' 3Y-YYR from Derrick Turbitt. The very well-justified Best Three Bloom Vase in Show was 'Glasnevin' 2W-W from Raymond Copeland.

Amateur and novice classes

The Novice Championship of Ireland requiring twelve single blooms from three divisions was won by Raymond Copeland, who included 'Dorchester', 'Dispatch Box' 1Y-Y, 'Doctor Hugh', 'Savoir Faire' and 'Badbury Rings'. John Warren and Deirdre Cairns were second and third respectively.

With the hard work done, the daffodils scrutinised and a very fine lunch enjoyed by all that was hosted by Lord Mayor Jim Rogers, the World Convention delegates continued on their way to Holland, hopefully having enjoyed their time in Ireland as much as we enjoyed them being here.

Amateur Championship of Ireland

The Amateur Championship of Ireland was

held in Omagh and the winner was Robert Curry from Lisburn, with 'Dunley Hall', 'Honeyorange' 2O-R, Duncan seedling 3W-GYR, Duncan 2539 1Y-Y, 'Irish Rum' 2Y-O, 'Ice Dancer', 'Santana', 'Cape Point', 'Hibernian' 4W-P, 'Pacific Rim', Curry seedling 3W-GWW and D1547 3Y-R. Second was George Wilson with 'Sharnden' 1Y-Y, 'Astrid's Memory' 3W-Y, 'Skywalker' 2Y-YYR, 'Moyarget' 3W-Y, 'Star Quality' 3W-GYY, 'Lundy Light', DT9717 2W-YPP, 'Outline' 2Y-YYO, 'Altun Ha', 'Swan Vale' 1W-W, 'Carib Gipsy' and 'Korora Bay' 1W-P.

Silver Thread award

The Northern Ireland Daffodil Group Silver Thread award, for three vases of three blooms from at least three divisions, travelled to the South County Dublin Horticultural Society Show and was won by George Wilson, who travelled from Lisburn, with mixed vases of 'Contender' 2W-O, 'Matula' 1Y-Y, 'Chobe River', 'Fletching', 'Pink Silk', 'Party Girl' and the remaining vase of 'Uncle Duncan' 1Y-O, 'Sportsman' and 'Firehills' 2Y-O. Second was Deirdre Cairns, also with mixed vases of 'Dunkery', 'Uncle Duncan' 1Y-O, 'Pink Silk', 'Creag Dubh', 'Meldrum' 1Y-Y, 'Silver Convention' and a final vase of 'Cryptic' 1W-P, 'Sealing Wax' and an unknown 2Y-O.

WAKEFIELD AND NORTH OF ENGLAND TULIP SOCIETY ANNUAL SHOW
JAMES AKERS

After the disappointment of the tulip show at Harrogate it was feared that the 173rd Annual Florists' tulip show held at Normanton on 12 May would also suffer from a lack of entries. However there were 42 exhibitors, 7 more than in 2007 and possibly a record for the show.

Vase classes

There were four entries in the John Hardman Memorial Class for 18 tulips of the same variety. Three of them were Ken Bacon's 'Maureen', 'Roi du Midi' and 'Toyota' which were placed first, second and third respectively. As the number of flowers required reduces, so the number of entries increases: Barbara Pickering's 'Belle du Monde' beating four other entries in the twelve; Chris Bone's 'Maureen' first of 22 in the six; and Trevor Myers' 'Elegant Lady' winning the three from a mammoth entry of 36. So pristine were Trevor's flowers that the judge had no hesitation in awarding the vase the best exhibit in the section, a triumph of quality over quantity.

English Florists' tulips

Although the only exhibitor in the class for twelve breeders, Judy Baker was to be commended for managing to find twelve different varieties in such a difficult season. Unusually, breeder tulips were in much shorter supply than the rectified and there were only single entries in the nine and six breeder classes, both won by Judy, and five in the 'three' won by Barbara Pickering. Beryl Royles won the single breeder class with an unnamed seedling S45 that was later judged the Premier Breeder in show.

Malcolm Hainsworth, the Society's Chairman, was to be commended for winning for the first time the Needham Memorial Cup, the most challenging class in the show. His twelve rectified flowers included a good 'Lord Stanley' feather and a fine 'Sir Joseph Paxton' flame, a flower which has been the one to beat for over 150 years, but which has recently fared badly, seeming not to have adapted well to global warming. John Snocken was placed second, his best flower being a 'James Wild' which became Premier Feather in show. John was the winner of the nine and I managed to win the six rectified, including four newly broken flowers picked from the breeder bed.

With the number of new members now showing, it is very difficult to get out of the Novices. However Margery Walkington managed it this year in style, winning three of the five classes and coming second in another. Bob Taylor had the premier flower in the section although it was in a second-placed entry for breeder, flame and feather. 'Akers' flamed rarely produces a better-marked flower than its sister seedling 'Wakefield'; however on this occasion it was so well marked that in addition to being Premier Novice Bloom it was adjudged Premier Flame and then Premier Bloom in show. It has often been said in the past that the more experienced exhibitors kept the best bulbs to themselves rather than distributing them among the new members, but once again this was proved to be untrue, because in addition to Bob's fine flower, Roy Tetley's 'James Wild' won the single breeder class in this section and then was chosen as the Premier Breeder in show.

Trevor Myers, although still a novice, completed a good show day by gaining the trophy for most points in the Extra Open Section, and also had the Premier Bloom in this section, a fine 'Goldfinder' breeder.

Conclusion

Although not an outstanding show in respect of the quality of the Florists' tulips, it was nevertheless very encouraging to see so many members overcoming the difficult weather conditions this year to put on an excellent display.

BULBS IN THE SPRING GARDEN

WEDNESDAY 1 APRIL 2009

A DAY OF INTERESTING AND INSTRUCTIVE TALKS ABOUT GARDENING WITH SPRING FLOWERING BULBS

ROYAL HORTICULTURAL HALLS CONFERENCE CENTRE GREYCOAT STREET, LONDON SW1P 2QD

Organised by the RHS Daffodil and Tulip Committee this event offers an opportunity to hear from the experts about gardening with a comprehensive range of spring flowering bulbs. Speakers confirmed to date include Brian Mathew, John Page, Jan Pennings, Alan Shipp, Christine Skelmersdale and Johnny Walkers.

The programme, which starts at 10am, will conclude at 4pm to allow time to look round the RHS Flower Show. Tickets, which include coffee/tea at registration and mid-afternoon, are priced at £15.00. Further details and tickets are available by telephoning 0845 370 0148

Awards to Hardy Flowering Plants for Exhibition

GALANTHUS
Awarded by the Joint Rock Garden Plant Committee
Award of Merit
G. peshmenii 'Kastellorhizo' **AM** 13 October 2007. Exhibited by Dr and Mrs R Wallis, Llwyn Ifan, Porthyrhyd, Carmarthen SA32 8BP
G. plicatus **'Three Ships' AM** 15 January 2008. Exhibited by Mr R J A Leeds, Chestnuts, Whelp Street, Preston St Mary, Sudbury, Suffolk CO19 9NL

Certificate of Preliminary Commendation
G. **'E.A. Bowles' PC** 12 February 2008. Exhibited by Mr J L Sharman, Monksilver Nursery, Oakington Road, Cottenham, Cambridge CB24 8TW
G. **'Greenfinch' PC** 12 February 2008. Exhibited by Dr R Mackenzie, Barn Cottage, Shilton, Oxfordshire OX18 4AB
G. **'Lady Dalhousie' PC** 16 February 2008. Exhibited by Mr I Christie, Downfield, Westmuir, Kirriemuir, Forfarshire DD8 5LP
G. nivalis **'Llo 'n' Green' PC** 25 September 2008. Exhibited by Mr J L Sharman

HYACINTHUS
Awarded by the Daffodil and Tulip Committee
First Class Certificate
H. **'Blue Jacket' FCC** 19 May 2008. Exhibited by Mr J S Pennings, 'De Bilt', Schorweg 14, 1764 MC Breezand, Netherlands
H. **'Blue Tango' FCC** 19 May 2008. Exhibited by Mr J S Pennings

Award of Merit
H. **'Aiolos' AM** 19 May 2008. Exhibited by Mr J S Pennings
H. **'Hollyhock' AM** 19 May 2008. Exhibited by Mr J S Pennings
H. **'Miss Saigon' AM** 19 May 2008. Exhibited by Mr J S Pennings

NARCISSUS
Awarded by the Daffodil and Tulip Committee
First Class Certificate
N. **'Sheelagh Rowan' 2W-W FCC** 15 April 2008. Exhibited by Mr C N Yates, Melbreak, 44 Church Lane, Bicknoller, Somerset TA4 4EL

Award of Merit
N. **'Triple Crown' 3Y-GYR AM** 29 April 2008. Exhibited by Mr R Hilson, 8 Blackthorns, Lindfield, Haywards Heath, West Sussex RH16 2BB (see front cover)

Certificate of Preliminary Commendation
N. **'Good Friend' 6Y-Y PC** 11 March 2008. Exhibited by Mr S J Gibson, 14 Waverley Road, Kettering, Northants NN15 6NT
N. **'Jammin' 3W-GYY PC** 29 April 2008. Exhibited by Mr B S Duncan, Knowehead, 15 Ballynahatty Road, Omagh, County. Tyrone, BT78 1PN

Awarded by the Joint Rock Garden Plant Committee
Award of Merit
N. **Eira Group AM** 1 March 2008. Exhibited by Dr and Mrs R Wallis

Certificate of Preliminary Commendation
N. cantabricus subsp. *tananicus* **PC** 5 April 2008. Exhibited by the Regius Keeper, RBG Edinburgh, Inverleith Row, Edinburgh EH3 5LR

TULIPA
Awarded by the Daffodil and Tulip Committee
First Class Certificate
T. **'Ballerina' Lily-flowered Group FCC** 19 May 2008. Exhibited by Broadleigh Gardens, Bishops Hull, Taunton, Somerset TA4 1AE
T. **'Menton' Single Late Group FCC** 19 May 2008. Exhibited by Bloms Bulbs, Primrose Nurseries, Melchbourne, Beds MK44 1ZZ

T. 'Professor Röntgen' Parrot Group FCC
19 May 2008. Exhibited by Bloms Bulbs

Award of Merit
T. 'Barcelona' Triumph Group AM 29 April 2008. Exhibited by Mr R Blom, Birwell Lodge, Shelton, Huntingdon PE28 0NR.
T. 'Dordogne' Single Late Group AM 19 May 2008. Exhibited by Bloms Bulbs
T. 'Pink Panther' Parrot Group AM 19 May 2008. Exhibited by Bloms Bulbs

Awarded by the Joint Rock Garden Plant Committee
Certificate of Preliminary Commendation
T. *sylvestris* subsp. *australis* PC 11 March 2008. Exhibited by The Director, RBG Kew, Richmond, Surrey TW9 3AB

The above awards are for exhibition. Awards for garden merit (AGM) are on pages 8 and 67-69.

RHS Daffodil and Tulip Committee 2008

CHAIRMAN

Bradbury, M S, The Well House, 38 Powers Hall End, Witham, Essex CM8 1LS

VICE-CHAIRMEN

Duncan, B S, MBE, Knowehead, 15 Ballynahatty Road, Omagh, Co Tyrone, N Ireland BT78 1PN
Skelmersdale, Lady, Barr House, Bishops Hull, Taunton, Somerset TA4 1AE

MEMBERS

Akers, J L, MBE, 70 Wrenthorpe Lane, Wrenthorpe, Wakefield, West Yorkshire WF2 0PT
Blanchard, J W, VMH, Old Rectory Garden, Shillingstone, Blandford, Dorset DT11 0SL
Blom, R J M, Birwell Lodge, Shelton, Huntingdonshire PE18 0NR
Brandham, Dr P, Jodrell Laboratory, Royal Botanic Gardens, Kew, Richmond, Surrey TW9 3DS
Burr, N A, Rushers Cottage, Rushers Cross, Mayfield, East Sussex TN20 6PX
Gibson, S J, 14 Waverley Road, Kettering, Northamptonshire NN15 6NT
Hanks, G, 2 Malvern Close, Spalding, Lincolnshire PE1 2DQ
Nicholl, R, 17 Orchard Avenue, Rainham, Essex RM13 9NY
Pavord, Ms A, Sunnyside Farm, Loscombe, Dorset DT6 3TL
Pearson, A J R, Hofflands, Little Totham Road, Goldhanger, Maldon, Essex CM9 8AP
Pennings, J S, 'De Bilt', Schorweg 14, 1764 MC Breezand, Netherlands
Petherbridge, Mrs J, The Meadows, Puxton Road, Puxton, Somerset BS24 6TF
Scamp, R, 14 Roscarrack Close, Falmouth, Cornwall TR11 4PJ
Shipp, A K, 9 Rosemary Road, Waterbeach, Cambridge, Cambridgeshire CB5 9NB
Vandervliet, M, Bezurrel Farm, Relistan Lane, Gwinear, Hayle, Cornwall TR27 5HE
Vivash, H D L, 22 Gordon Road, Haywards Heath, West Sussex RH16 1EJ
Walkers, J, Volendam, Washway Road, Holbeach, Lincs PE12 8AH
Watson, N A C, Ringhaddy Lodge, Killinchy, Co Down, N Ireland BT23 6TU
Yates, C N, Melbreak. 44 Church Lane, Bicknoller, Taunton, Somerset TA4 4EL
Secretary McDonald, Ms S, RHS Garden Wisley, Woking, Surrey GU23 6QB

Advisory Panel on Narcissuss Classification 2008

Chairman Watson, N A C
Vice Chairman Duncan, B S, MBE
Blanchard, J W, VMH
Bradbury, M S
Breed, C V
Brickell, C D, CBE, VMH

Gripshover, Mrs M L
Kington, Mrs S
Nicholl, R
Scamp, R A
Secretary McDonald, Ms S
Ex officio David, Dr J

133

Index

Author

Adams, David
A visit to Ballynahatty Road — 23

Akers, James
Narcissus provincialis: a minor problem — 14
Wakefield and North of England Tulip Society Annual Show — 129

Akers, Wendy
Review: Spalding Flower Parade: the golden years — 83

Baker, Ruby
A snowdrop tour — 87

Blanchard, John
Narcissus 'Cedric Morris' — 10

Bradbury, Malcolm
Introduction: World Daffodil Convention — 18
Awards to People — 48
Ralph B White Memorial Medal — 84
Hyacinth trial at Wisley — 86

Brickell, Chris
Review: International Daffodil Register and Classified List 2008 — 77

de Boer, Marjan
Tulip Sour: *Fusarium oxysporum* f.sp. *tulipae* in tulips — 72

David, John
Hardy nerine study day — 75

Davies, Gwynne
The Daffodil Society Show — 123

Drew, Sue
Wisley daffodil trials — 8
Large-flowered tulip trial at Wisley — 67

Duncan, Brian S
Recent developments in trumpet daffodils — 28

Gibson, John
John Sydney Birch Lea — 46

Goddard, John
RHS Early Daffodil Competition — 103

Grayer, Susan
Nomenclatural standards of daffodils in the RHS Herbarium — 85

Gripshover, Mary Lou
Three days in Holland — 24
ADS National Show and Convention — 90

Hanks, Gordon
What will daffodil growers do without formalin? — 38
UK *Narcissus* crop improvement research — 42

Leslie, Alan
Review: Common Snowdrop — 78
Review: Transcript of the Tenth Galanthus Gala — 79
Snowdrops at 2008 RHS shows — 99

Mason, Colin
Galanthomania, chipping and twin-scaling — 51

Mathew, Brian
Narcissus 'Cecil Nice' — 12

McCaw, Richard
City of Belfast Spring Flower Show — 127

McDonald, Sharon
Definition of division 9 – poeticus daffodil cultivars — 84

Myers, Michael D
A new snowdrop discovery *G. plicatus* 'E.A. Bowles' — 86

Nicholl, Reg
RHS Late Daffodil Competition and Tulip Competition — 114

Page, John
In search of tulips — 61
Review: Gardening with Tulips — 80
Review: Buried Treasures — 81

Perrignon, Richard
A whirlwind tour — 97

Petherbridge, Jackie
RHS Daffodil Show — 106

Pink, David
UK *Narcissus* crop improvement research — 42

Ramsay, Peter and Lesley
Daffodils in England 2008 — 19

Randall, Mary
Daffodils, snowdrops and tulips at Harlow AGS show — 119

Robinson, Helen
UK *Narcissus* crop improvement research — 42

Rolfe, Robert
Daffodils, snowdrops and tulips at Loughborough AGS show — 120

Sanham, Chris
Collecting snowdrops - some observations — 57

Skelmersdale, Christine
Small-flowered tulip trial at Wisley — 64

Smales, Richard
Harrogate Spring Flower Show — 125

Walkers, Johnny
World Tulip Summit 2008 — 70

Whinfield, Angela
How I grow snowdrops — 54

Wilford, Richard
Tulipa sylvestris subsp. *australis* — 60

Wiseman, Robert
South East of England Daffodil Society shows — 122

page numbers in bold type indicate pictures

Galanthus
× *allenii* 56
Angelique 101
artjuschenkoae 120
Atkinsii 56,102
Augustus 120
Autumn Snow 80
Baxendale's Late 87
Bess 100
Bitton 56
Blewbury 99
Blewbury Tart 99
Bowles's Large 87
Bowles's Late 87
Boyd's Double 52,**53**
Carolyn Elwes 87
Chandler's Green Tip 80
cilicicus 52
Comet 101
Curly 101
Cyril Warr 56
David Shackleton 101
Diggory 100
Dodo Norton **55**,56
E.A. Bowles **86**,87,**101**,121, 131
Elfin 55
elwesii 51,54,80,100,101
Galatea 56
Greenfinch **101**,131
Hanning's Horror 53
Hoverfly 55
ikariae 80
Jessica **55**
Kastellorhizo **99**, 131
Kencott Ripple 80
Kingston Double 101
Lady Dalhousie 131
lagodechianus 82
Lambrook Greensleeves 56
Lapwing **55**
Little Joan 80
Llo 'n' Green 100,131
Magnet 56
Margery Fish 56
Mary Biddulph 100
Merlin 56
Mighty Atom 56
Modern Art 56
nivalis 54,80,87,102,119,131
Oliver Wyatt 100
peshmenii 99,131
plicatus 51,56,86,87,100,101, 119,121
Quad 80
reginae-olgae 57,80
rizehensis 56
Robin Hood 56
Rosemary Burnham 101
Ruby Baker 102
S. Arnott 56
Seagull 56
Sharron Louise 80
Shrek 80
Sir Henry Boyd Carpenter 56
Sophie North 119
South Hayes 53

Teresa 55
Three Ships **100**,131
Trym 87,119
Virescens 120,**121**
viridapice 88
Viridapice 102,119
Walter Fish 56
Warei 102,119
White Wings 56
Zwanenberg 100

Hyacinthus
Aiolos 131
Blue Festival 86
Blue Jacket 131
Blue Tango 131
Hollyhock 86,131
Jan Bos 86
Miss Saigon 86,131
Paul Herman 86
Pink Festival 86

Narcissus
A.W. Tait 77
Aberfoyle 47
abscissus 36
Accent 35
Achduart 47
Acumen 96
Afficionado 124
Ahwhanee 128
Akala 94
Algarve 35
alpestris 120
Alto 128
Altun Ha 21,109,110,114, 115,124,126,129
Amazing Grace 110,127, 128
Ameeya 95
American Classic 90
American Dream 32,91
American Heritage 32, 108
Angel's Whisper 108,124
Angel o' Music 91
Apple Honey 34
Applins 96
April Joy 91
Arctic Gold 28
Arid Plains 128
Arkle 28
Arleston 110,124,127
Armidale 114,116
Arrowhead 90
Arthurian 128
assoanus 14,15,16
Astrid's Memory 21,**109**,116, 124,129
asturiensis 10,14,107,121
At Dawning 35
atlanticus 119
Aunt Betty 30
Avalon 91
Ave 46
Backchat 90
Badbury Rings 96,109,128
Banbridge 28
Banda 94
Bandit 21,109,124
Barndance 96

Ben Avon 110
Ben Hee 46,47
Ben'Bler 87,**98**
Best Friend 21,123
Blisland 126
Blossom Lady 23,93,110,123
Bluntingdon 110,126
Borrobol 47
Bosvale 110
Botlar 94
Boughton Park 107
Bowles's Early Sulphur 54
Boyne Bridge 30
Bravoure 34,125
Brer Fox 30
Bridal Chorus 34
Bright Flame 35
Bronzewing 32,109
Brookdale 35
Brooke Agar 108
Broomhill 110
Broughshane 33
Broughton Park 124
bulbocodium 25,104
   var. *filifolius* 122
Bunclody 47
Cairntoul 47
Camaraderie 128
Camden 35,128
Camelot 28,33
Cameo Flush 96
Cameo Frost 92
Cameo Joy 23,123
Cameo Magic 92,96,**97**
Cameo Marie 93,94
Cameo Mist 23
Candlepower 104
Canisp **46**
cantabricus 120,121
   subsp. *monophyllus* 104,120
   subsp. *tananicus* 131
Cantatrice 33
Cape Cornwall 103,124
Cape Helles 96
Cape Point 21,124,129
Carib Gipsy 129
Caribbean Snow 109
Cecil Nice 6,12,**13**
Cedric Morris 6,**10**
Centor 30,94
Centrefold 96
Chanson 21,35,**36**,128
Chasseur 128
Cheetah 30
Cherry Glow 23
Cherrygardens 21,95,109
Chesapeake Bay 33
Chickerell 128
Chief Inspector 34,35,37
Chingah 30,31,128
Chinita 90
Chitose 32
Chiva 115
Chobe River 28,129
Chromacolor 25
Churchfield Bells 103
Cisticola 128
Citrus Ring 109
Clare 108,124
Claverley 124

Clouded Yellow 123
Clubman 34,115
Coalbrookdale 124
Colin's Joy 109
Coliseum 114
Color Magic 91
Colourful 128
Comal 28,29
Compressus 94
Contender 129
Cool Crystal 92,110,124
Corbiere 30,31,47,94
Corby Candle 124
Cornish Chuckles 104,122
Cotchford 128
Cover Story 21
Cowboy 96
Crackington 128
Craig Stiel 107
Creag Dubh 129
Cristobal 34,125
Cromarty 28
Crown Gold 37
Crowndale 110,124
Crucial Point **36**,37
Cryptic 35,103,129
cuatracasasii 104
Curlew 8,**9**
Cutting Edge 30,31
cyclamineus 12,104,121,**122**
Dailmanach 35,46,47,96,97, 108,110
Dainty Miss 126
Dalinda 30
Daphne 91
Dateline 124
Dawnglow 32
Daydream 32
Dena 109
Deseado 30
Desert Fox 30
Dispatch Box 128
Disquiet 28,29,31,124
Diversity 108,114
Doctor Hugh 109,110,116, 126,127,128
Doctor Jazz 90
Don Miller 96
Dorchester 21,110,122,123, 125,127,128
Draycote Water 107,109,124
Drayton 103
Dreamlight 91
dubius 14,15,104,107
Dunadry Inn 128
Dunchurch 107
Dunkery 129
Dunley Hall 47,126,129
Dunmurry 34
Dunstan's Fire 30,31
Early Mist 46
Eastbrook Beauty 107
Eastbrook Sunrise 107,108, 124
Edenderry 35
Eiko 35
Eira 121
Eira Group 120,131
Elmbridge 22
Elusive 90,124

135

Empress of Ireland 29,33, **34**,35
English Caye 33
Entente 90,128
Entrancement 33
Entrepreneur 21,110,123, 124
Ethos 28,29,128
Evesham 47,123,128
Falconet 110,126
February Gold 103
Feline Queen 30,31,127
Fencourt Jewel 93
Feock 109
fernandesii 121
Fever Pitch 94
Fidelity 32,35
Filoli 33,47,109
Fiona McKillop 22,35
Firehills 129
First of March **25**
Flashback 104
Fletching 129
Flight Path 95
Flintlock 97
Flomay 108,124
Francolin 29
Frontier Frills 93
Gamebird 23,115
Garden Opera 8,**9**
Gatecrasher **29**
Gay Kybo 110,115,116,128
Geometrics 128
Gin and Lime 33
Glasnevin 128
Glen Alladale 128
Glenfarclas 30,47
Gloriola 32
Gold Bond 29,128
Gold Convention 20,**47**,109, 110,123,124
Gold Ingot 127,128
Golden Amber 110
Golden Flute 128
Golden Harvest 42,44
Golden Jewel 110
Golden Rapture 28
Golden Vale 96
Golden Years 94
Goldfinger 28,29,108,115, 123,127
Goldhanger 115
Goldspie 36
Good Friend 131
Goonbell 110
Graduation 35
Grafton Brook 108,124
Grasmere 47
Greek Surprise 23,116
Greenodd 128
Hacienda 30,31
Halgarry 47
Hambledon 123
Happy Valley 124
Harbour View 127,128
Hartlebury 47
Hawera 20,94,124
Hawley 36
Heamoor 94,95,103

Heidi 91
Henfield 115
Hero 30,31
Hibernian 129
hispanicus 77
Homestead 90
Honeybird 33
Honeybourne 123
Honeyorange 127,129
Ice Dancer 129
Ice Wings 20,110,123,126
Impeccable 92,93,95
Inca 103
Independence Day 128
Indian Maid 128
Invercassley 47
Inverpolly **20**,46,47,124, 125,126
Irish Rum 129
Itzim 126
Jack Wood 103,104
Jamboree 30
Jammin 116,131
Jenny 122
Jersey Roundabout 22,108, 110
Jetfire 103
Jimmy Noone 30
Johann Strauss 36
John Peace 116
Jolly Good 103
jonquilla 115,122
var. *henriquesii* 8,**9**,104,121
var. *minor* 121
Joybell 29
Juano **32**
juncifolius **16**
June Lake 110,128
Just Joan 22
Kahurangi 94
Kanchenjunga 33
Kansas 90
Karanja 35
Kea 103
Kiltonga 109
King's Ransom 28
King's Grove 30
Kingscourt 28
Kingstanding 30,31,109
Kiwi Happy Prince 96,**97**
Kiwi Magic 94
Kiwi Solstice 94
Kiwi Sunset 90
Kokopelli 25,94
Korora Bay 35,115,129
× *koshinomurae* 15
La Paloma 90
Lakeland Fair 21
Lakeland Snow 21,123
Lavalier 90
Lemon Silk 103
Lemon Spice 96
Lennymore 128
Lesley 96
Lighthouse Reef 33
Limequilla 104
Lisnamulligan 128
× *litigiosus* 120
Little Bell 25

Little Kibler 22,108
Little Rusky 108
Little Sentry 115
Little Tyke 108
Little York 91
Liverpool Festival 114
Loch Alsh 47,124
Loch Hope 47
Loch Lundie 47
Loch Naver 47,107
Loch Owskeich 47
Longitude 30,**32**
Lorikeet 32
Louise Randall 90
Lubaantun **33**,123
Lundy Light 128,129
Lutana 37,84,109
Macdalla 35,93,96123
Machan 123
Magic Lantern 30
Mamma Mia 115
Maria Pia 22,104
Mason Road 95
Matula 129
Medway Gold 25
Melancholy 35
Memento 32,35
Menehay 110
Merlin 107
Mexico City 90
Minnow 91
minor 10,14,15,16,122
Miss Klein 25
Misty Glen 107,125
Mitimoto 91
Monks Wood 123
Monticello 115
× *montserratii* 36
Moon Madness 21
Moon Shadow 21,92,110, 115,116,124,125
Morab 30
moschatus 120
Moyarget 129
Nampa 33
Narrative 109
Navigator 96
Neavesville Gold 94
Nederburg 30,31
Newcastle 34,125
Newcrest 35
Nice Day 124
Night Music 128
Nightflight 34
No Worries 96
Nonchalant 109
Norwester 104,107
obvallaris 119
ochroleucus **16**
Okakune 30
Olumbo 97
Ombersley 21,28,108,110, 124,126
Omeomy 92,95
Orange Supreme 37
Oregon Trail 30
Orkney 125
Osmington 103
Outline 129

Oz 122
pachybolbus 115,124
Pacific Rim 109,114,129
Panache 33
Paradigm 128
Park Springs 103,109,110
Party Girl 95,129
Passionale 34
Patois 128
Peggy White 90
Pennine Way 34
Penny Perowne 110
Pequenita 91
Petite Magic 96
Phalarope 98
Phoenician 90,107,124
Piglet 22,108
Pillow Talk 94
Pink Belladonna 36
Pink Passion 35
Pink Silk 35,90,103,104,129
Pink Topaz 35
Pipit 128
Pixie Dust 90
poeticus 36,84
Polar Sky 96
Pontes 35
Pops Legacy 35,90,103
Portloe Bay 103
Preamble 34,36,37
Predator 35,103
Prime Target **84**
primigenius 121
Prophet 32
Proud Fellow 30
provincialis 14,**15**,16
var. *bicolorans* 16
pseudonarcissus 14,15
subsp. *provincialis* 16
Pukka 36
× *pujolii* **15**
Pumpkin Ridge 30
Puppy 110
Purbeck 110
Queen's Guard **35**,37,84,109
Quiet Waters 34,88,128
Quip 36
Rabid 96
Radar 90
Rapture 91,94,103,104
Rashee 33
Rathowen Gold 28
Red Arrow 30
Red Conquest 32
Red Curtain 30
Red Reed 30
Regal Bliss 124
Renovator 103
Repertoire 116
requienii 16
Resistasol 30
Reverie 32
Ribald 115
Rima 32,35
Ringleader 20,114,126
Ristin 103
River Queen 90,128
Rockall 90
Rose Gold 109

136

Rose Royale 110
Rosegold 32
Roseworthy 110
Rowell Fair 107
Royal Marine 47
Royal Regiment 126
Royeleen 30,31,94,**95**
Ruddy Rascal 22
Ruddynosey 30
rupicola 107,108,110
   subsp. *watieri* 108,119,126
Sabrosa 90,108,124
Saint Keverne 44
Sally Malay 97,**98**
Salome 91
Santana 129
Sargeant's Caye 109
Satchmo 31
Savoir Faire 128
Scott Joplin 36,37
Sealing Wax 103,129
Segovia 91,123,124,126
Serena Beach 128
Shangani 128
Sharnden 129
Sheelagh Rowan 21,107,108,
   109,114,**115**,124,131
Shurdington 126
Silent Valley 21,22,33,34,
   110,115,123,124,126
Silken Sails 128
Silver Convention 129
Silver Crystal 128
Silver Surf 128
Silversmith 22
Sint (Saint) Victor 25
Skywalker 129
Slieveboy 28
Small Talk 104,122
Smidgen 91
Snipe 108
Snowy Morn **34**,96
Special Envoy 47
Spellbinder 33
Spoirot 91
Sportsman 129
Spring Essence 8,**9**
Spring Morn 128
Spun Honey 116
Stafford 110
Star Quality 129
Star Trek 128
State Express 115
Stoke Charity 128
Stormy Weather 22
Stratosphere 116
Strines 110
Sugar Rose 90,91
Sulphur Monarch 30,93,96
Summer Breeze 124
Sun Bronze 110
Sun Disc 124
Sunday Chimes 91
Sundial 94
Surfer Girl 95
Surrey 108,128
× *susannae* 120
Sutton Court 30
Swan Vale 129
Swedish Fjord 90

Sweet Georgia 124
Tao 21,109,126
tazetta subsp. *ochroleucus* 16
Telamonius Plenus 107
Temba 29,**30**,128
Terminator 21,90,97,107,
   108,123,124
Thumbs Up 96,123
Thunderhead 30
Tilly Titus 93
Tingdene 103
Tinkerbell 90
Tiny Bubbles 90
Torridon 47,90
Treasure Chest 128
Trena 21,94,103,110,126
triandrus 104,110,121
   subsp. *pallidulus* 120
   subsp. *triandrus* var. *concolor*
   108
   var. *triandrus* 120,121
Trigonometry 108,114
Tripartite 116
Triple Crown 114,126,131
Tropical Heat 22,114,115
Trumpet Warrior 33,93,128
Twinkle Boy 91
Tycoon 90
Tyree 30,31
Tyrone Gold 128
Ulster Bank 107
Ulster Prince 28
Uncle Duncan 30,108,129
Unnamed Poet 110
Val D'Incles 128
Verran 35
Viking 28,29
Vineland 22,108
viridiflorus 25
Vivash 22,107,110
Waihaha 93,95
War Cloud 36
Warbler 8,**9**,103
Warwick Castle 22,114
Weary Deary 95
Welcome 98
Wessons 22
West Post 116
White Empress 33,34
White Majesty 33
White Prince 33,34
White Star 33,34,128
Wild Card 95
Wild Honey 123
Wings of Freedom 94
Woodstar 91
Wow 22
Xit 91,108,124,126
Yellow Fever 90
Yellow Idol 28
Yellow Xit 108,124
York Minster 30
Young Blood 104,107,128

Nerine
Alba 75
Mark Fenwick 75
Pallida 75
Pink Triumph 75

Tulipa
Abba 50
agenensis 62
Akers 130
albertii 66
Ancilla 81
Angels Wish 67,**68**
Angélique 69
Apricot Jewel 66
armena 62
   var. *armena* 62,**63**
australis 60,132
Ballade 69
Ballerina 69,132
batalinii 66
Beau Monde 67,**68**
Beldersai 66
Belle du Monde 129
berkariense 82
biflora 66
bifloriformis 66,82
Big Smile 117
Bright Gem 66
Bronze Charm 66
butkovii 82
Cairo 50
Carola 50
China Town 69
cinnabarina 63
clusiana 66
   var. *chrysantha* 66
Corsage 127
cretica 120
cypria 62
Daydream 81
doerfleri 62
Don Quichotte 69
Dordogne 67,**68**,69,132
dubia 66
Eastern Star 66
Elegant Lady 129
Für Elise 81
Flava 66
fosteriana 82
Fusilier 66
gesneriana 63
Girlfriend 66
Golden Parade 117
Goldfinder 130
Grand Perfection 69
greigii 64,82
hageri 66,118
hissarica 82
Honky Tonk **65**,66
hoogiana 67
humilis 63,66
Ice Stick 66,69
James Wild 129,130
Jazz **68**,69
julia 62
karabachensis 82
kaufmanniana 64,66,82
kolpakowskiana 66
korolkovii 82
kurdica 66
Lady Guna 66
Lady Jane 66
Lilac Wonder 66
linifolia 66

Little Beauty 66
Little Ilze 82
Little Princess 66
Lord Stanley 129
Louvre 69
Magic Fire **65**,66
Maureen 69,129
micheliana 82
Menton 67,132
Monsella 50
Monte Carlo 50
Moonlight Girl 69
Morning Star 82
Negrita 127
neustruevae 66
Odalisque 66
Ohara 50
Orange Princess 69
orphanidea 62,63,66
orithyioides 66
orthopoda 82
Peppermintstick **65**,66
Persian Pearl 66
Piccolo 66
Pink Charm 66
Pink Panther 132
Pirand 69
polychroma 66
praestans 66
Professor Röntgen 132
Purissima 81
Queen of Night 71
Red Gem 66
Red Hat 69
Red Hunter 66
Red Shine 81
Roi du Midi 129
Rory McEwen 49
saxatilis 62,63,64,66
Scarlet 66
schrenkii 66
Sheila 66
Sir Joseph Paxton 129
sintenisii 62
Splendens 66
sprengeri 64
Spring Green 69
Spryng 67,**68**
Starlight **65**,66
sylvestris 60,63,66
   subsp. *australis* **60**,63,134
Taco 66
Ted Turner 50
Tinka **65**,66
Toyota 117,129
turkestanica 66,82
Unicum 66
urumiensis 66
Viking 50
Vivex 117
Wakefield 130
World Expression 67,**68**,69
Yellow Jewel 66

137

CW01151721

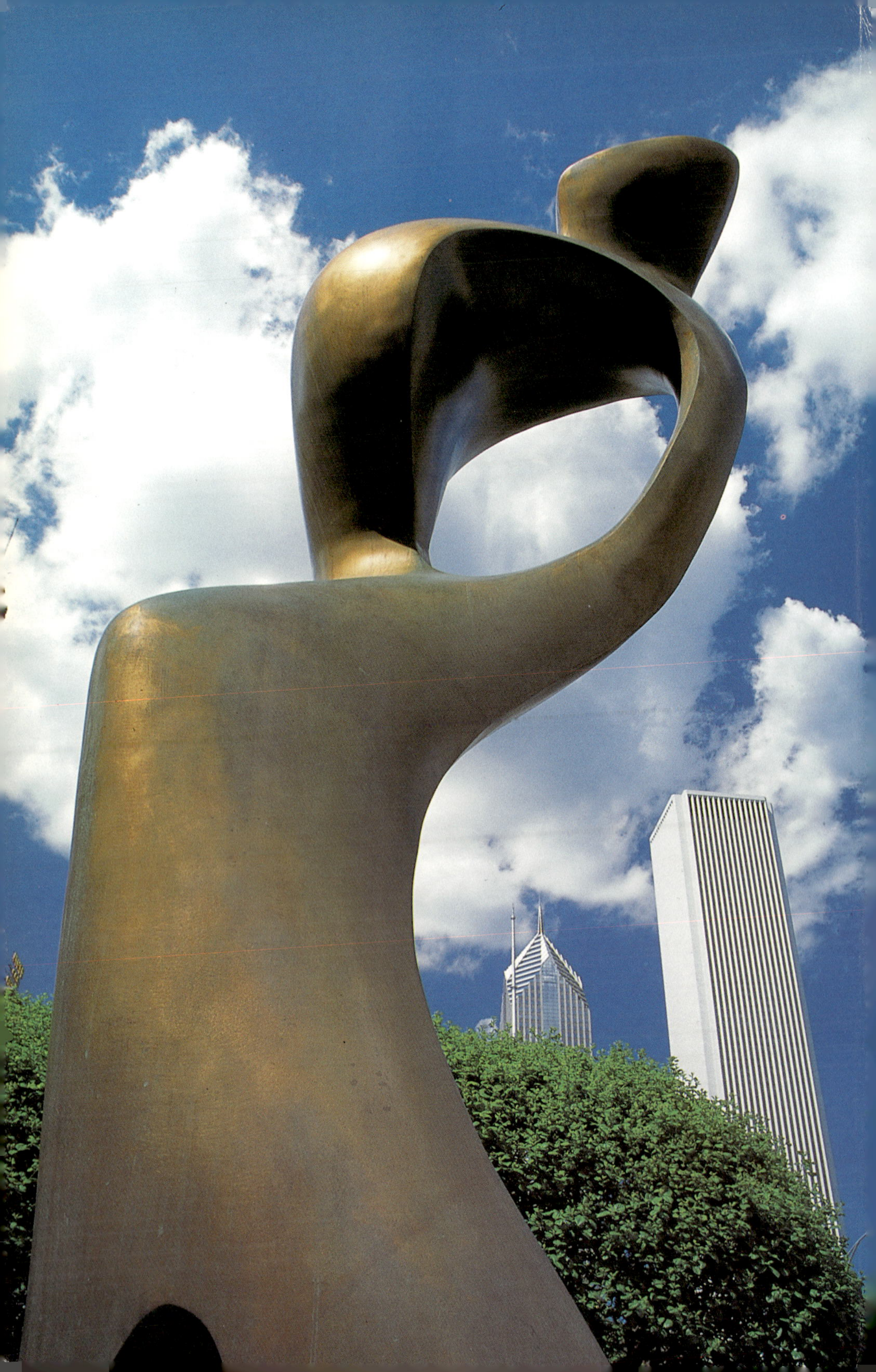

INSIGHT GUIDES

Created and Directed by Hans Höfer

CHICAGO

Edited by Tim Harper
Principal Photography by Chuck Berman
Editorial Director: Brian Bell

Houghton Mifflin

APA PUBLICATIONS

ABOUT THIS BOOK

Chicago has always been a city of strong impressions, a classic American town that is still distinctive among US metropolitan centers. It's not surprising, then, that Chicago came to the attention of Insight Guides, the award-winning travel series created by **Hans Höfer**, founder of Apa Publications. *Insight Guide: Chicago*, employing the photojournalistic techniques for which the series is renowned, examines not only the city's physical and cultural aspects but also the historical, social and economic factors that have made it unique.

Chicago is also a writers' town. The team that assembled this book span a wide variety of journalistic talent, from lifelong city natives and devoted transplants to informed outsiders looking in. The thread linking these writers and photographers is their fascination with Chicago, both its good and bad sides, and an unyielding interest in the city's effect on the human condition.

Project editor **Tim Harper** grew up 150 miles to the south, in Peoria, Illinois. To him Chicago was always the exciting, pulsing big city – of museums and shopping and baseball games in his early years and, later, of smoky clubs and ethnic restaurants and, yes, baseball games. Today, as a journalist and lawyer, he still occasionally wears his "No Lights in Wrigley Field" T-shirt, a reminder of the ill-fated 1980s campaign to keep the Cubs from hosting night games. Harper did much of the work on this book during trips to the Midwest as he and his wife, Nancy Bobrowitz, ferried their two children to visits with grandparents in Wisconsin and Peoria.

Martha Ellen Zenfell, editor-in-chief of the North American Insight titles, monitored and guided the project from her editorial base in London, England. A native of the American South, Zenfell has been the project editor of several Insight Guides herself, including books to Bermuda, the Greek Islands, New York and New Orleans.

Chuck Berman, the principal photographer of this book, is a veteran *Chicago Tribune* lensman known for his sharp attention to detail and his talent for composing feature photos with just the right touch of whimsy. His wife, **Barbara Brotman**, a *Tribune* writer, put together the chapters on the Magnificent Mile and the Black Sox baseball scandal. They live with their two children on the North Side.

Manuel Galvan, a *Chicago Tribune* executive and member of the John Dillinger Died for You Society, was this book's expert on Al Capone and other mobsters. Galvan, who became intimate with the city as he moved up through the ranks as a reporter, editor and member of the editorial board, also wrote the insider's look at nightlife and dining out in Chicago.

Tom Hardy, who analyzed Chicago's ever-windy political scene, is the political editor of the *Chicago Tribune*. As a South Sider – just like the Daleys and other Chicago mayors – he has grown up in the rough and tumble of Chicago politics, yet is still able to appreciate just how the Chicago political scene is sometimes unusual, occasionally funny and always remarkable. His wife, **Pam Hardy**, assembled the information-packed "Travel Tips" section, and keeps the various editions of this book up to date.

Tom McNamee, who is a native South Sider, now lives in Evanston, a leafy northern suburb, with his journalist wife Deborah Wood and their three children. He adapted his essay on Chicago's history from his work as a

Höfer

Harper

Zenfell

Berman

Brotman

Galvan

McNamee

reporter for the *Chicago Sun-Times*. McNamee, who also wrote the section on the North Side, is co-host of a popular Saturday-morning talk show on Chicago radio, and co-author of *Streetwise Chicago*, a guide to every street in Chicago and how it got its name.

Don Hayner, McNamee's co-host on the radio program and co-author of *Streetwise in Chicago*, is another *Sun-Times* reporter. As a lifelong resident of Beverly, a quintessential South Side neighborhood, his story on the South Side underscores the divisions between the different sides of town, both in terms of geography and attitude. He and his wife Dawn, his toughest editor, have two sons.

Joseph Epstein, whose witty and perceptive essay "A Hustlin' Town" looks at the people of Chicago, is the editor of *American Scholar* magazine. A lifelong Chicagoan who now lives in suburban Evanston, he is the author of several books, including a collection of essays called *A Line Out for a Walk*.

Carol Jouzaitis, who once aspired to be a Chicago police officer but instead became a business reporter at the *Tribune*, profiled the city's financial district and its lakefront – her own personal work- and playground. Now covering higher education, she lives near Wrigley Field and sneaks off to as many afternoon games as she can.

Stuart Silverman and his wife **Sondra Rosenberg**, freelance writers who often work together, shared a number of assignments for this book, including vivid descriptions of the Loop, the West Side, Chicago shopping centers and the famous suburb Oak Park. Silverman emigrated from the East Coast as a college lecturer, but in recent years has combined writing about food and travel with poetry and literary criticism. Rosenberg, a native of Austria, is a professor of humanities at Harold Washington College in Chicago. She also writes and broadcasts, notably on the arts and on travel.

Eileen Norris, who did double duty by looking at the rise and fall of the Playboy empire along with the rise and rise of the Oprah Winfrey empire, was born in Chicago and grew up on the South Side. She is a former *Chicago Tribune* reporter whose work has appeared in many major American magazines since she left the security of the newspaper to freelance.

Janet Neiman, who recounted some of Chicago's best-loved scandals and described its history of grass-roots liberal activism, is a Chicago freelance journalist who grew up in suburban Evanston and earned a graduate degree in urban studies from Loyola University. She writes for many local and national publications.

Lisa Goff, a former editor for *Crain's Chicago Business*, relied on her considerable experience in writing about urban design to discuss Chicago's famed architecture. She also wrote extensively on local real estate, economic development, retailing and politics during her years in Chicago. She is now based in New York City.

Fernando Jones is an up-and-coming bluesman and bluesologist. In the former role, he plays the guitar and harmonica with various groups around Chicago, including his own. In the latter role, his contributions to the "Chicago Blues" section of this book grew out of his self-published memoir, *I Was There When The Blues Was Red Hot*.

The text was proof-read and indexed by **Elizabeth Boleman-Herring**, and marshaled through a variety of Macintosh computers by **Jill Anderson**.

K2

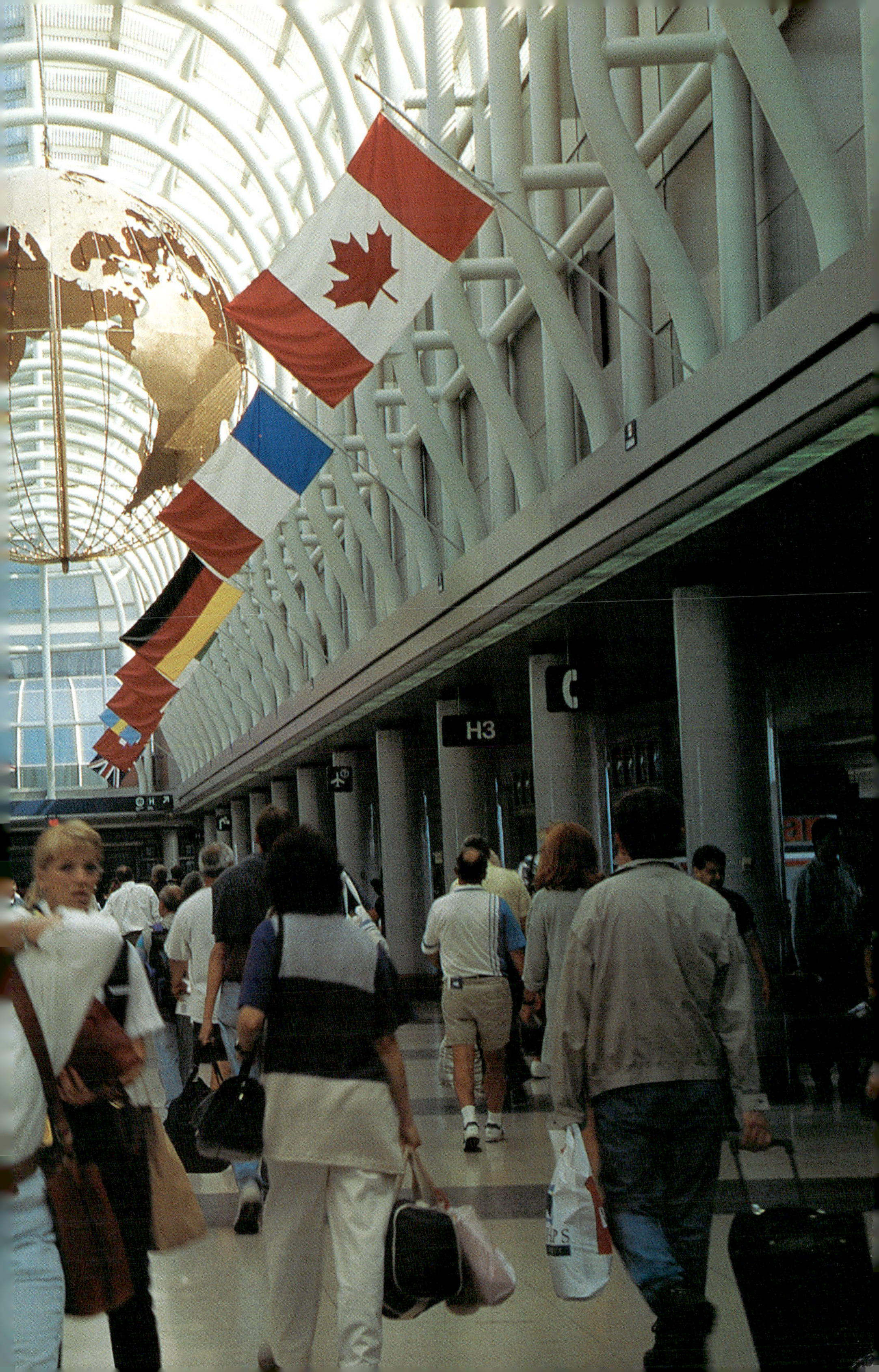

C
H3

CONTENTS

Introduction

The City of Broad Shoulders
by Tim Harper 23

History

From Swampland to Skyscrapers
by Tom McNamee 27

Decisive Dates
by Tim Harper 42

The Winds of Politics
by Tom Hardy 45

Schooled in Scandal
by Janet Neiman 51

People and Culture

A Hustlin' Town
by Joseph Epstein 59

Rooting Out Problems
by Janet Neiman 65

Voices of Chicago
by Tom McNamee 69

A Faded Playboy
by Eileen Norris 73

The Chicago Blues
by Fernando Jones 77

Blues Joints
by Fernando Jones 83

A Sports-Mad Town
by Tim Harper 87

An Architect's Phoenix
by Lisa Goff 95

Places

Introduction
by Tim Harper 109

Looping the Loop
by Stuart Silverman and
Sondra Rosenberg 113

Chicago in the Movies
by Tim Harper 123

The Financial District
by Carol Jouzaitis **127**

Cooler by the Lake
by Carol Jouzaitis **135**

Studs Terkel
by Tom McNamee **141**

The Magnificent Mile
by Barbara Brotman **145**

Shopping Centers
by Sondra Rosenberg **152**

The Gang's All Here
by Manuel Galvan **159**

The North Side
by Tom McNamee **166**

Urban Woodlands
by Janet Neiman **166**

Year-Round Performances
by Manuel Galvan **183**

Getting into "Oprah"
by Eileen Norris **191**

The West Side
*by Stuart Silverman and
Sondra Rosenberg* **195**

Tastes of Chicago
by Manuel Galvan **207**

Oak Park
by Stuart Silverman **217**

The South Side
by Don Hayner **225**

Day Trips
by Manuel Galvan **239**

Maps

Chicago 108
The Loop 114
The Lakefront 136
Chicago and Suburbs 168

TRAVEL TIPS

Getting Acquainted
The Place 250
Time Zones 250
Climate 250
The People 250
The Government & Economy ... 250

Planning the Trip
What to Bring 251
What to Wear 251
Entry Regulations 251
Health 251
Currency 251
Public Holidays 251
Getting There 252
Special Facilities 253

Practical Tips
Emergencies 254
Business Hours 254
Tipping 254
Religious Services 254
Media 255
Postal Services 255
Phones & Faxes 255
Tourists Information 256
Consulates 256

Getting Around
Orientation 256
From the Airport 257
Domestic Travel 257
Public Transportation 257
Walking & Cycling 257
Hitchhiking 258
On Departure 258

Where to Stay
Hotels 258
Bed & Breakfast 259
Youth Hostels 259

Eating Out
What to Eat 259
Where to Eat 259
Drinking Notes 263

Attractions
Culture 263
City 265
Suburbs 266
Tours 266
Recommended for Children 267
Diary of Events 268
Nightlife 269

Shopping
Shopping Areas 270

Sports & Leisure
Participant 271
Spectator 271

Further Reading
General 272
Other Insight Guides 272

Art/Photo Credits 273
Index 274

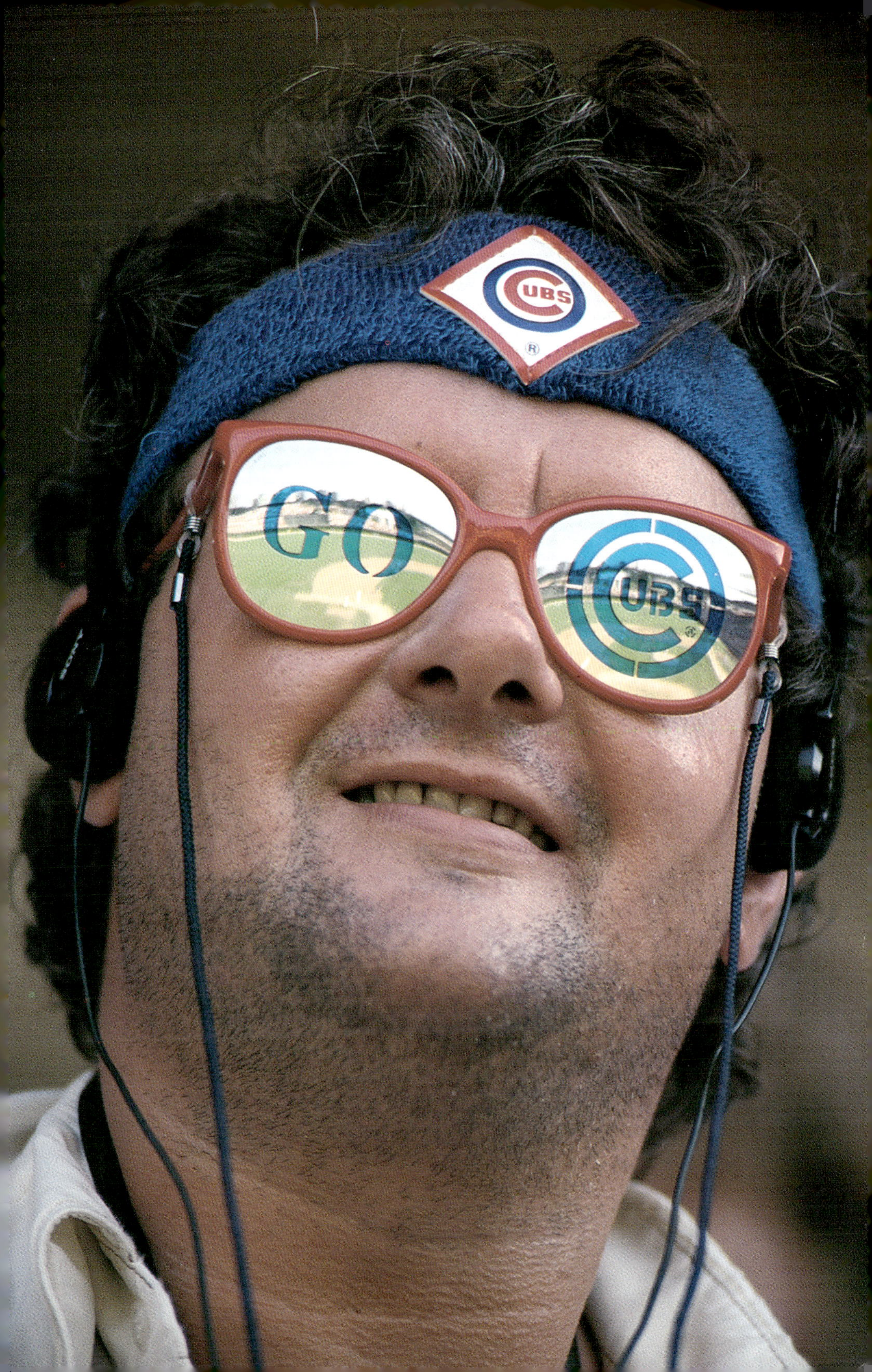
CUBS
GO
CUBS

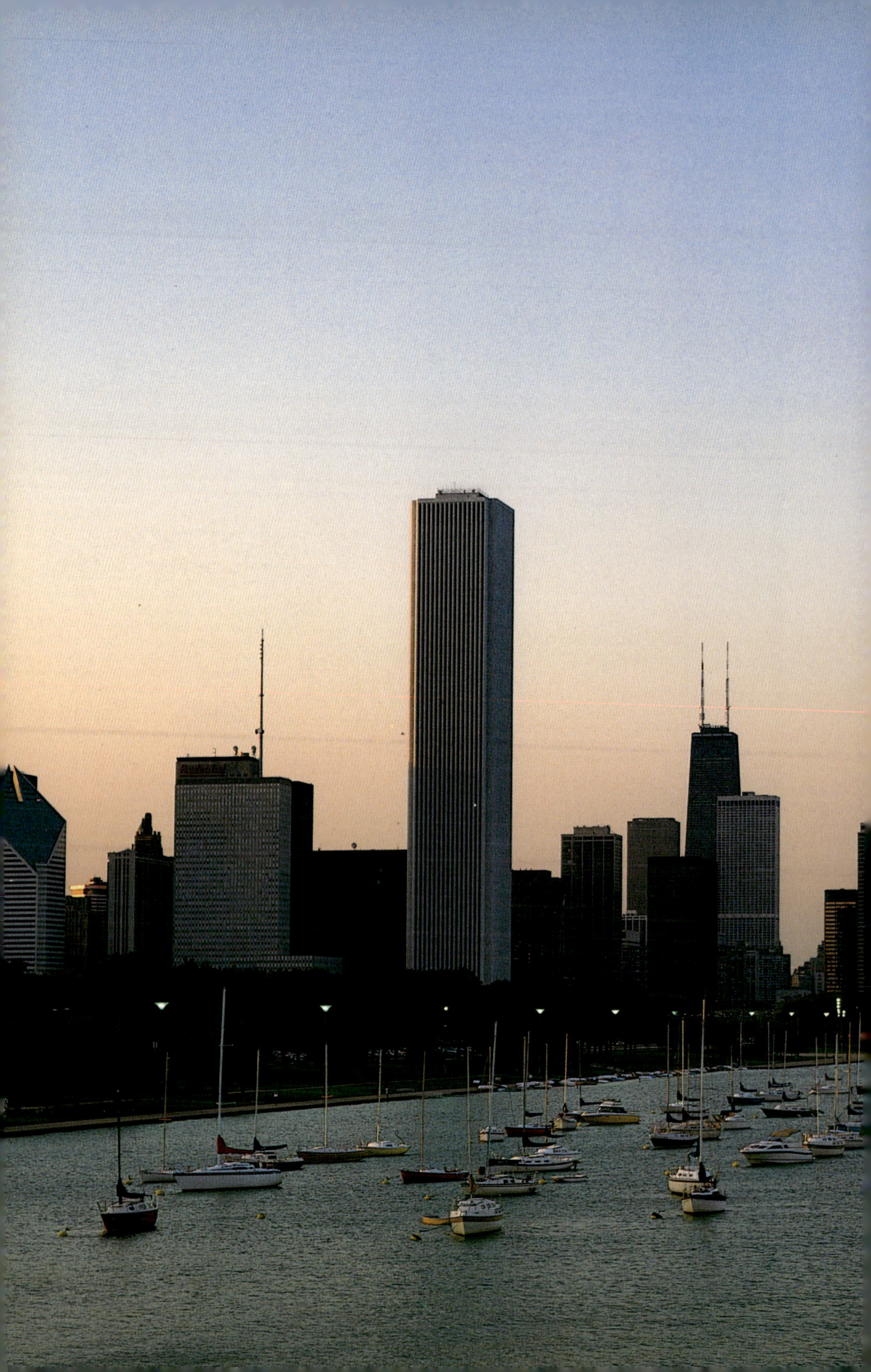

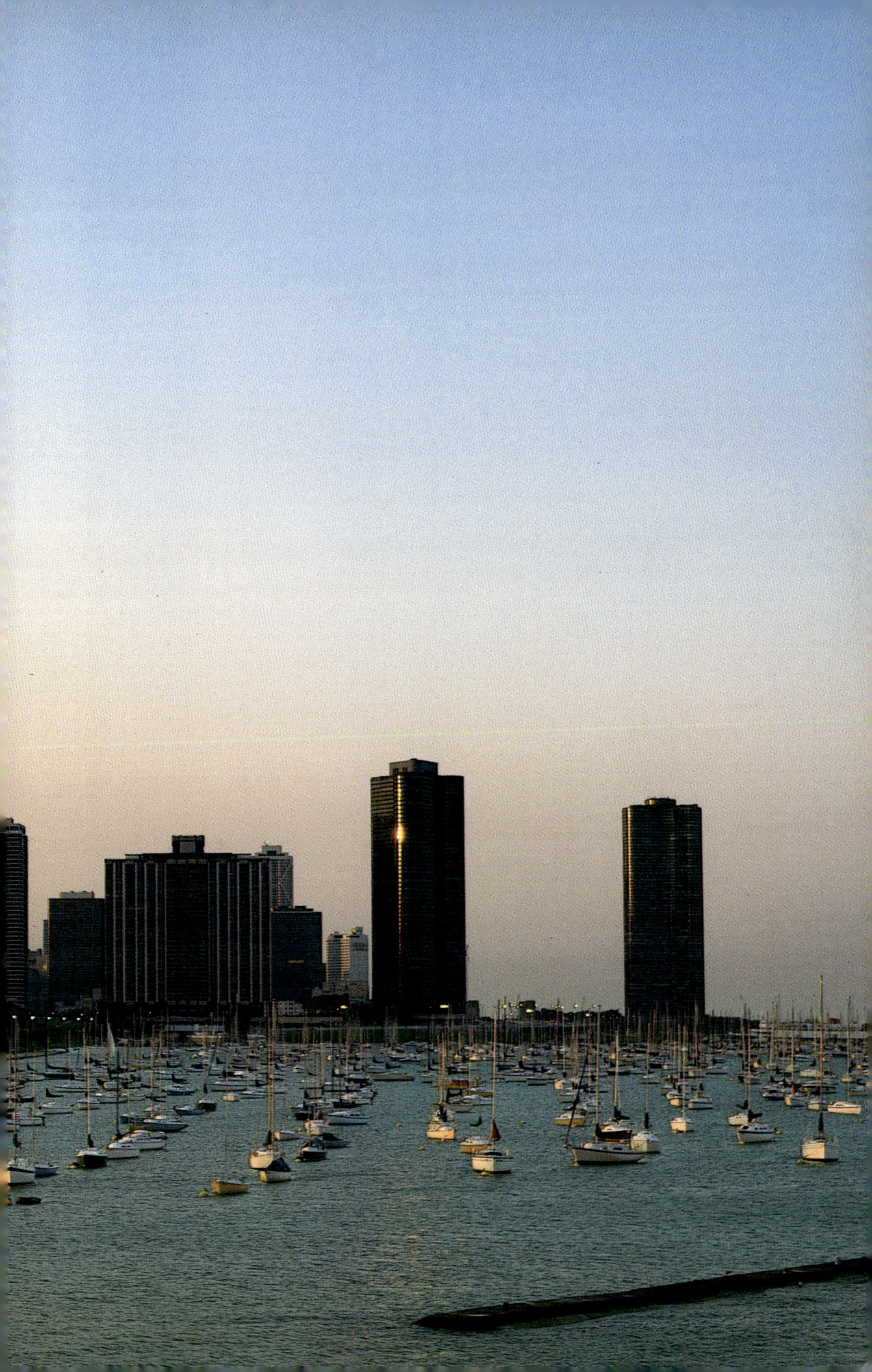

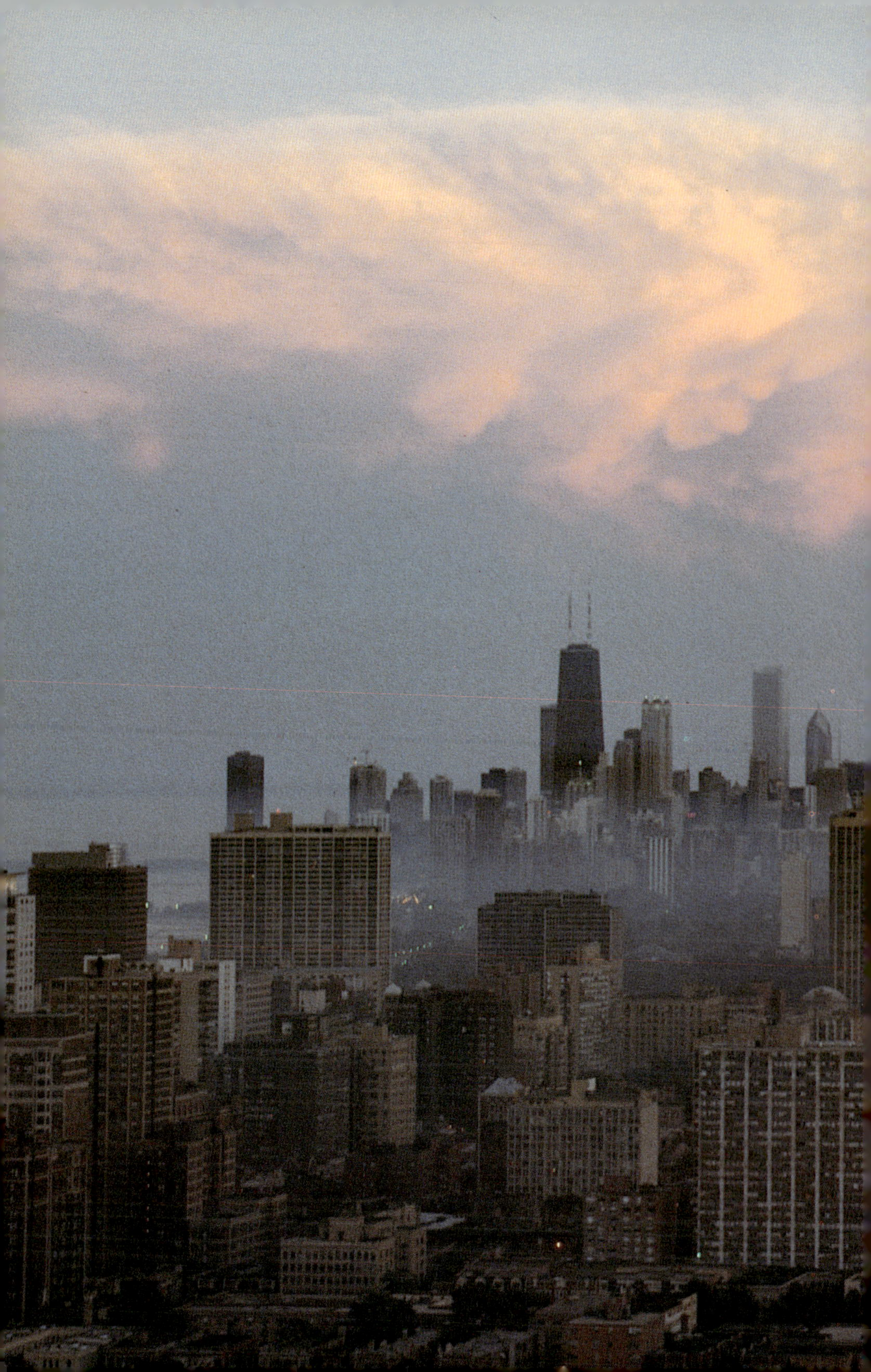

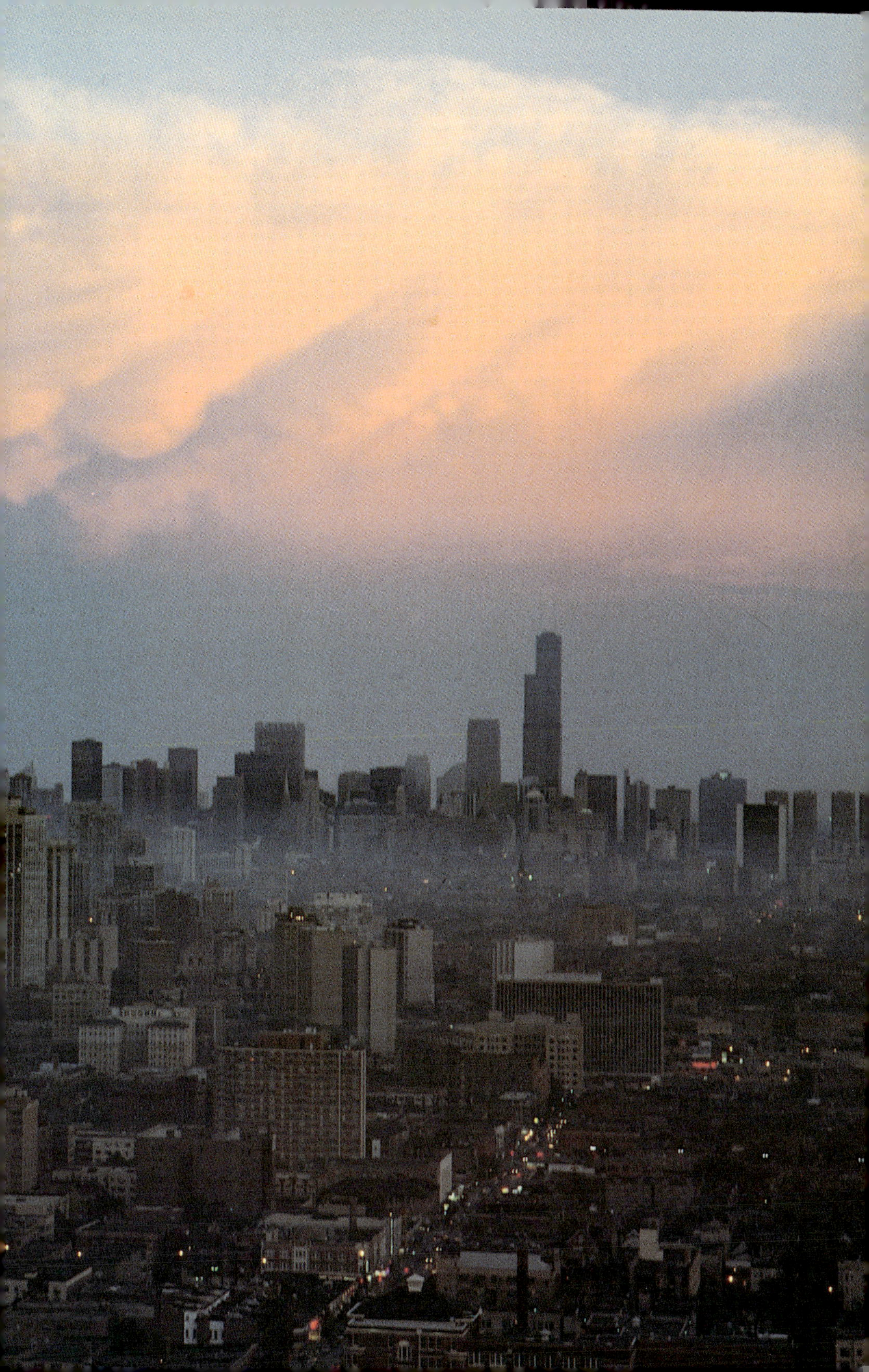

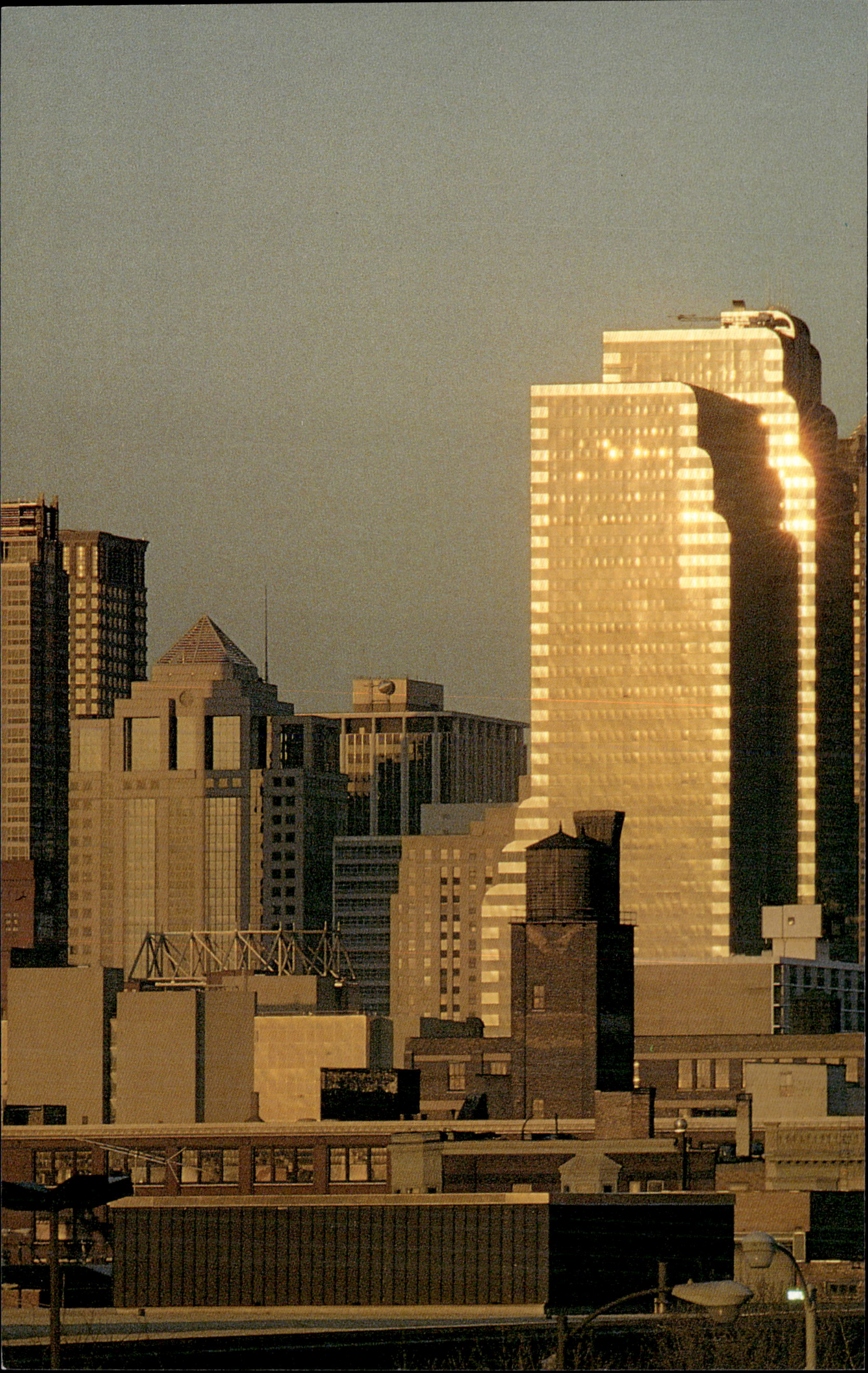

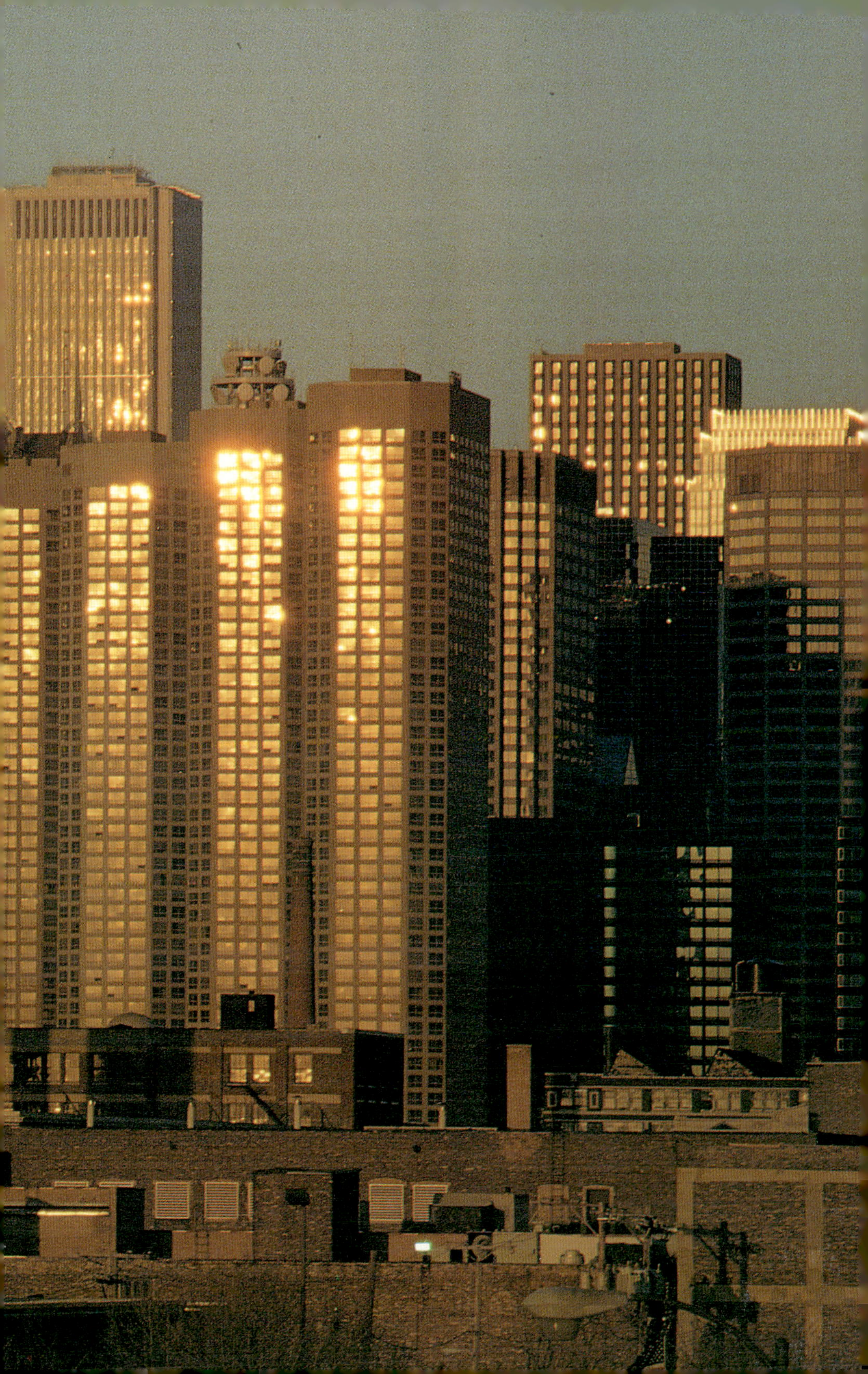

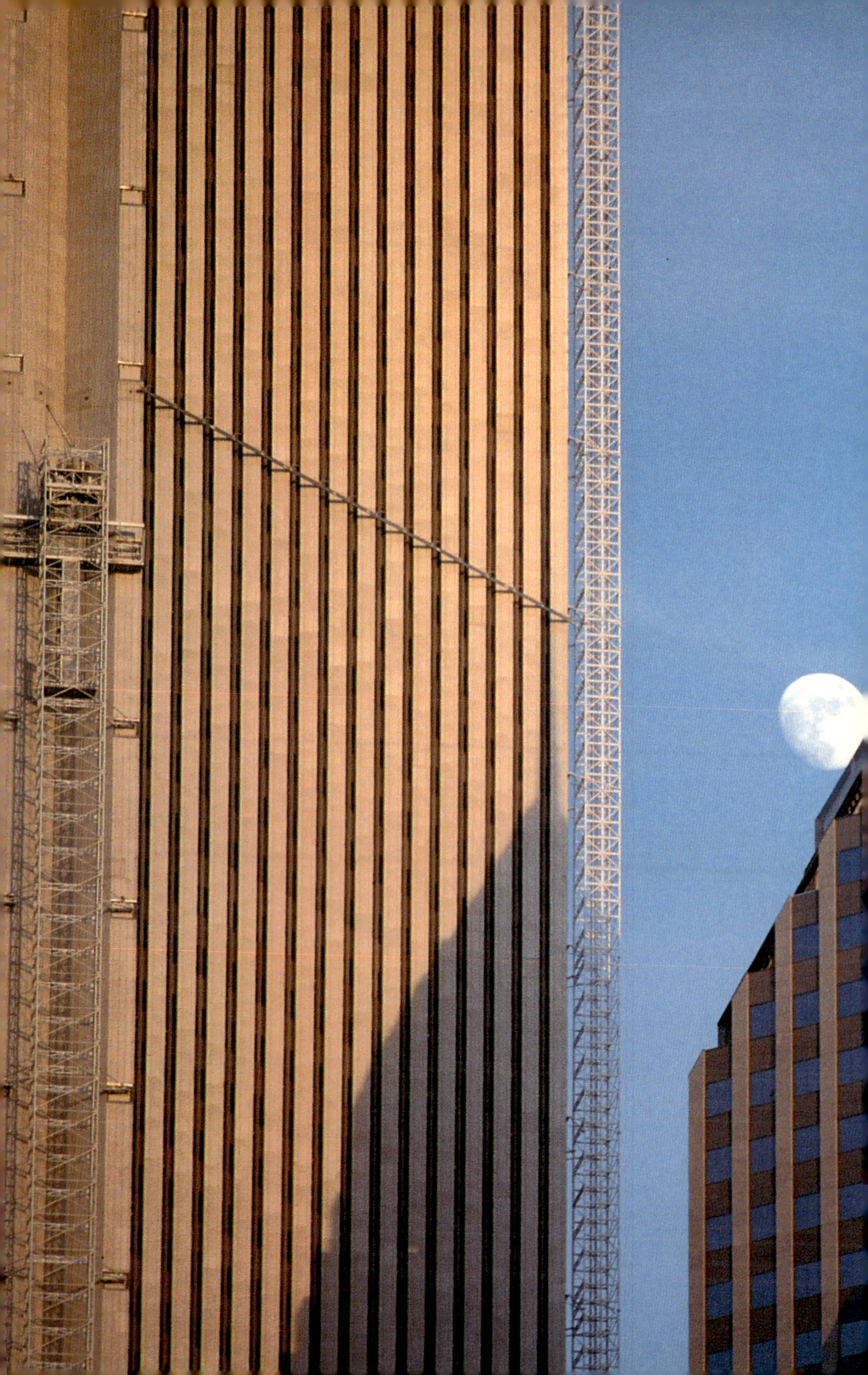

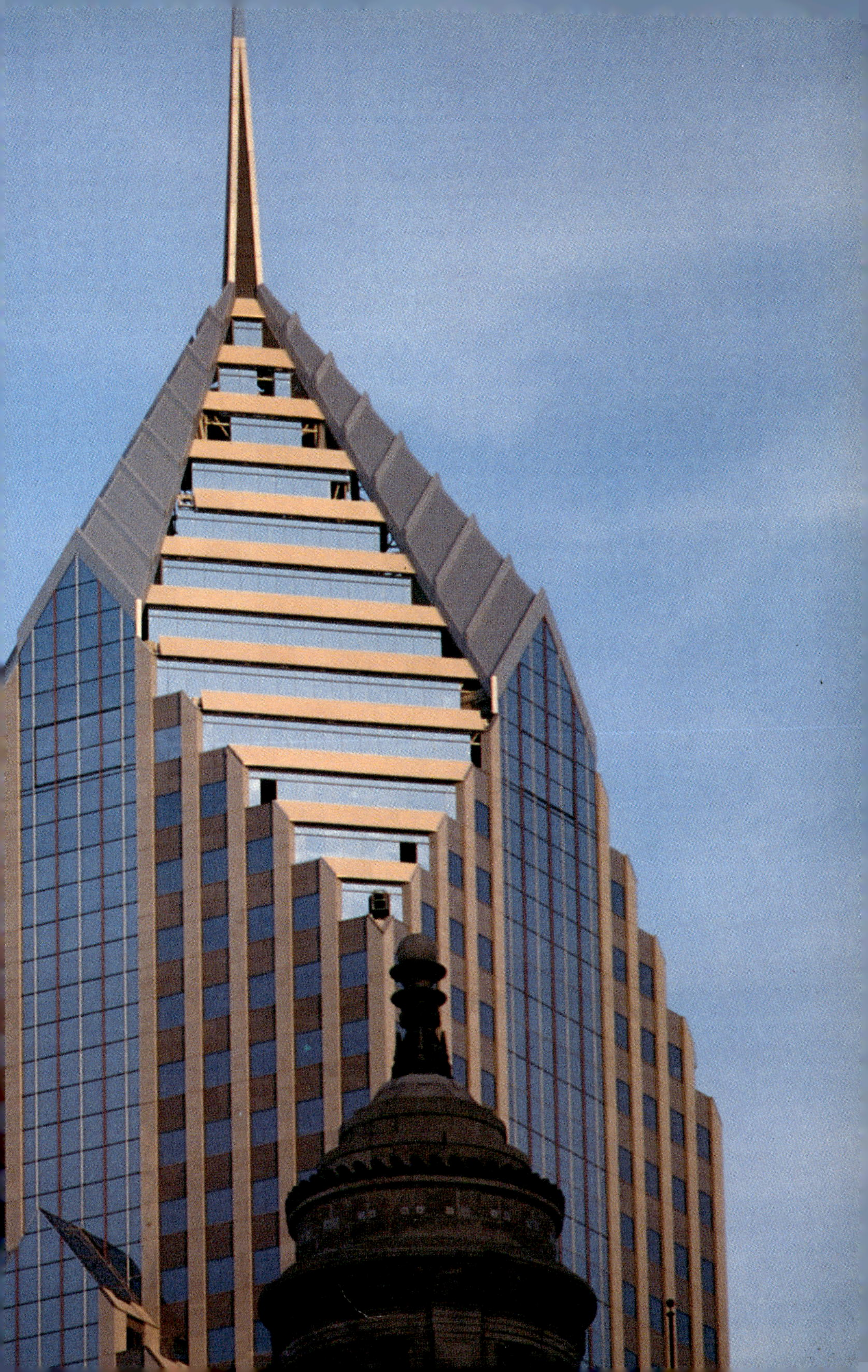

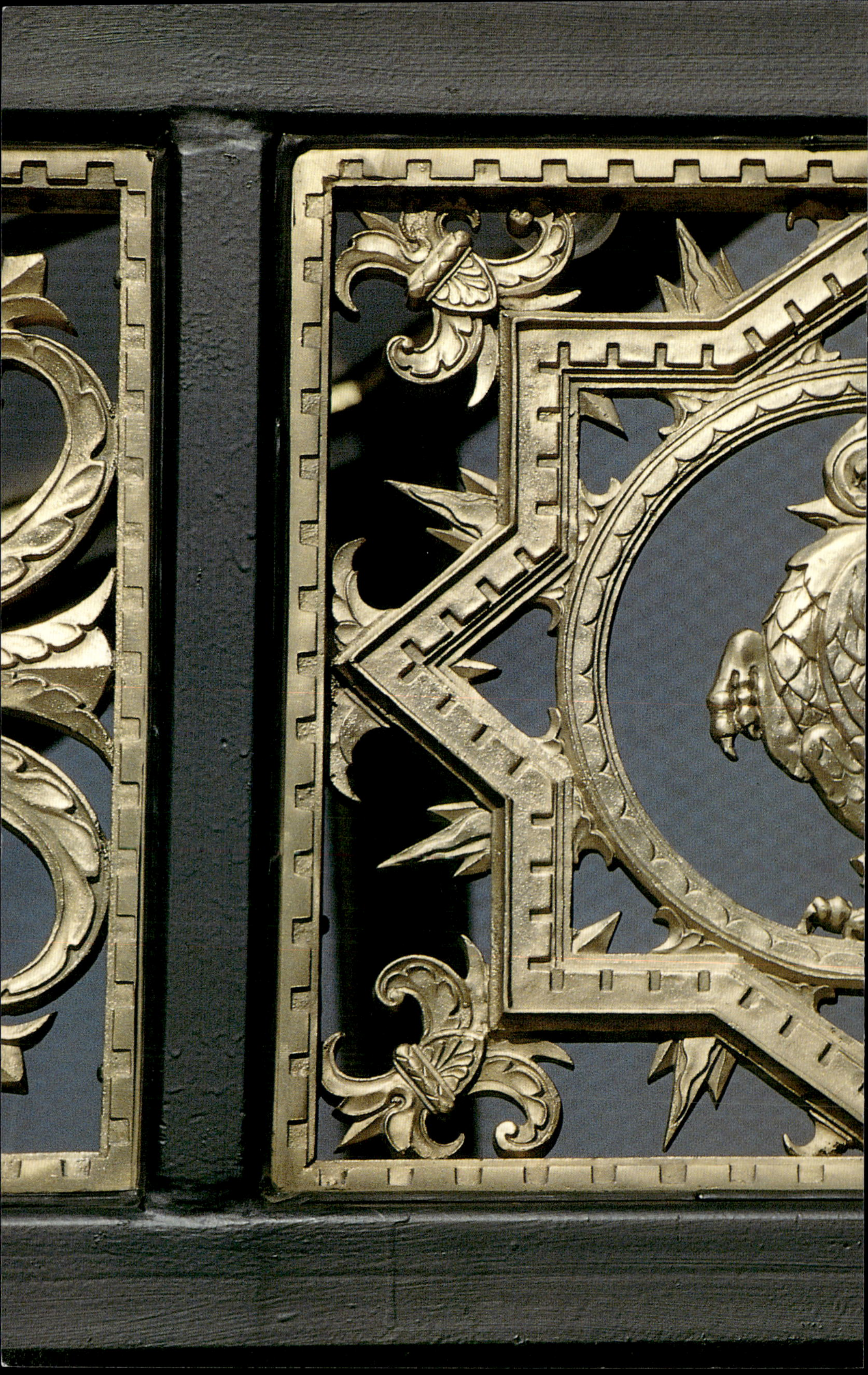

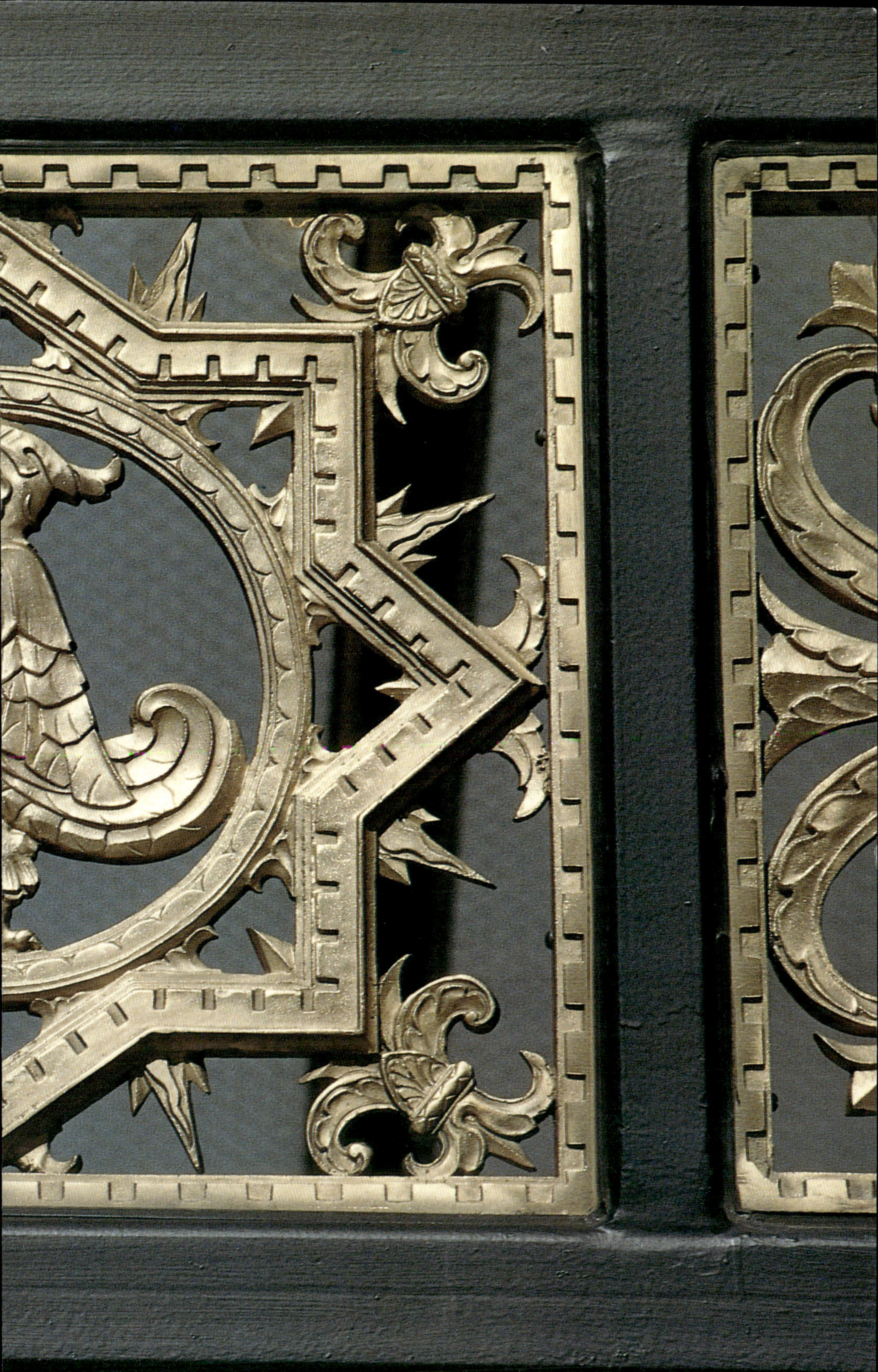

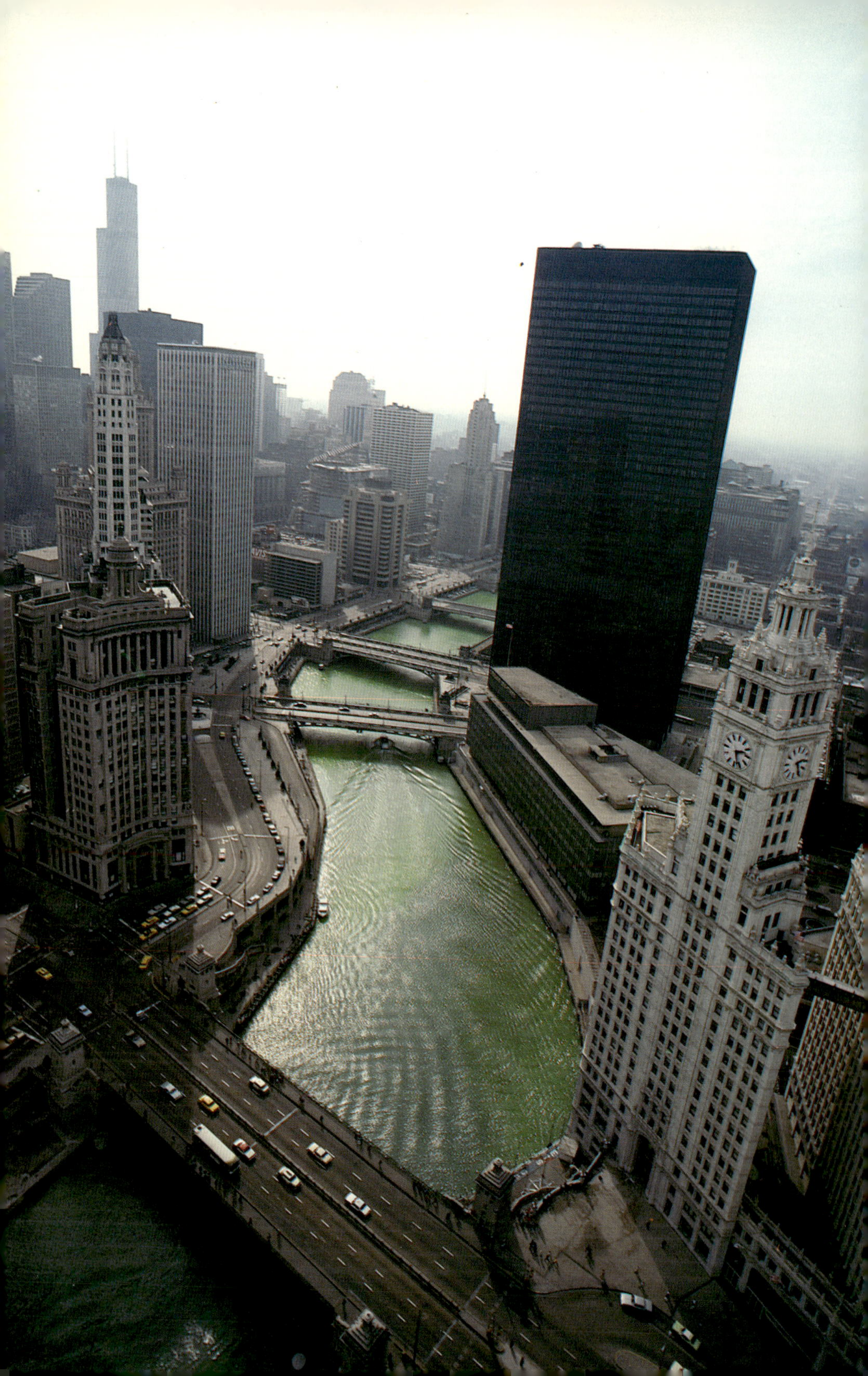

THE CITY OF BROAD SHOULDERS

Chicago is a city of strength – of bold visions, deep emotions, pungent flavors and decisive actions. Small wonder it was immortalized as "the city of broad shoulders," that it boasts three of the world's five tallest buildings and that its traditional food specialties include various forms of protein-rich red meat.

Many people like to characterize Chicago as the most American of all the big cities in the United States. With little of the pretension of New York and even less of the glamour of Los Angeles, Chicago is a city that was born of and still fits its geography. From flat prairies and swampland, Chicago in a remarkably short time became a world trade center, but has never been regarded as particularly cosmopolitan. Its financial markets and commercial enterprises influence economies all over the globe, but Chicago hardly considers itself "international" in the manner of European capitals and even smaller US cities such as San Francisco and New Orleans.

Chicago is a big, brassy, blowzy town where people, including strangers, tell each other what's on their minds. And in no uncertain terms. Chicago is known for its tough guys, for the machine-gun mobsters of the past and for the hardball politicians and manic financial traders of recent years. Today, politics and sports – not necessarily in that order – are the main topics of conversation in most Chicago social circles. But visitors need not try to initiate discussions about either political situations or sporting events – or anything else – that doesn't have some direct bearing on Chicago. A better conversational tack is to examine how events in Chicago may affect the outside world. Unlike other cities, Chicago doesn't depend on or need the outside world; everything a person could want, from a great education to a great pizza, is homegrown in the heart of the Midwest.

Even Chicago's remarkable literary history, where the lines between journalism and literature are blurred as perhaps nowhere else, is of a robust, take-no-prisoners style. And the music that came from the South Side, now known the world over as the Chicago blues, is driven by the hard edge and fast pace of a note-bending electric guitar.

Chicago is a town that outsiders, especially other Americans, often take for granted. It's not until they begin to learn of its complexities, of its many offerings to those of all interests and tastes, that visitors start to appreciate just how special Chicago is – and how much Chicagoans already appreciate it.

Preceding pages: downtown clock; Henry Moore sculpture; O'Hare arrival; tuned-in Cubs fan; Loop skyline; reflected glory; rising moon; brassy bird. **Left**, the Chicago River winds through the Windy City. **Following pages:** Chagall's *The America Windows*, Art Institute.

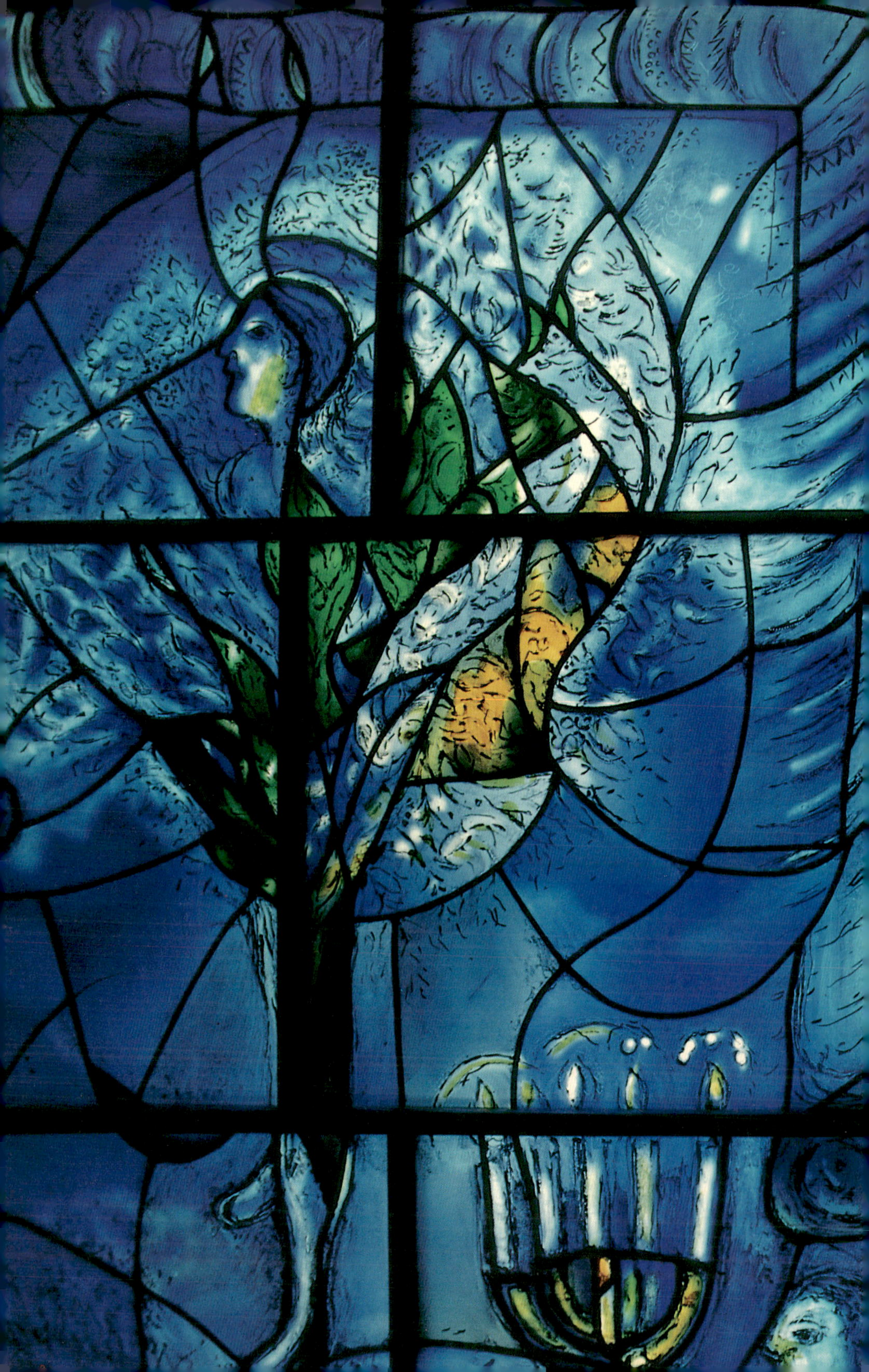

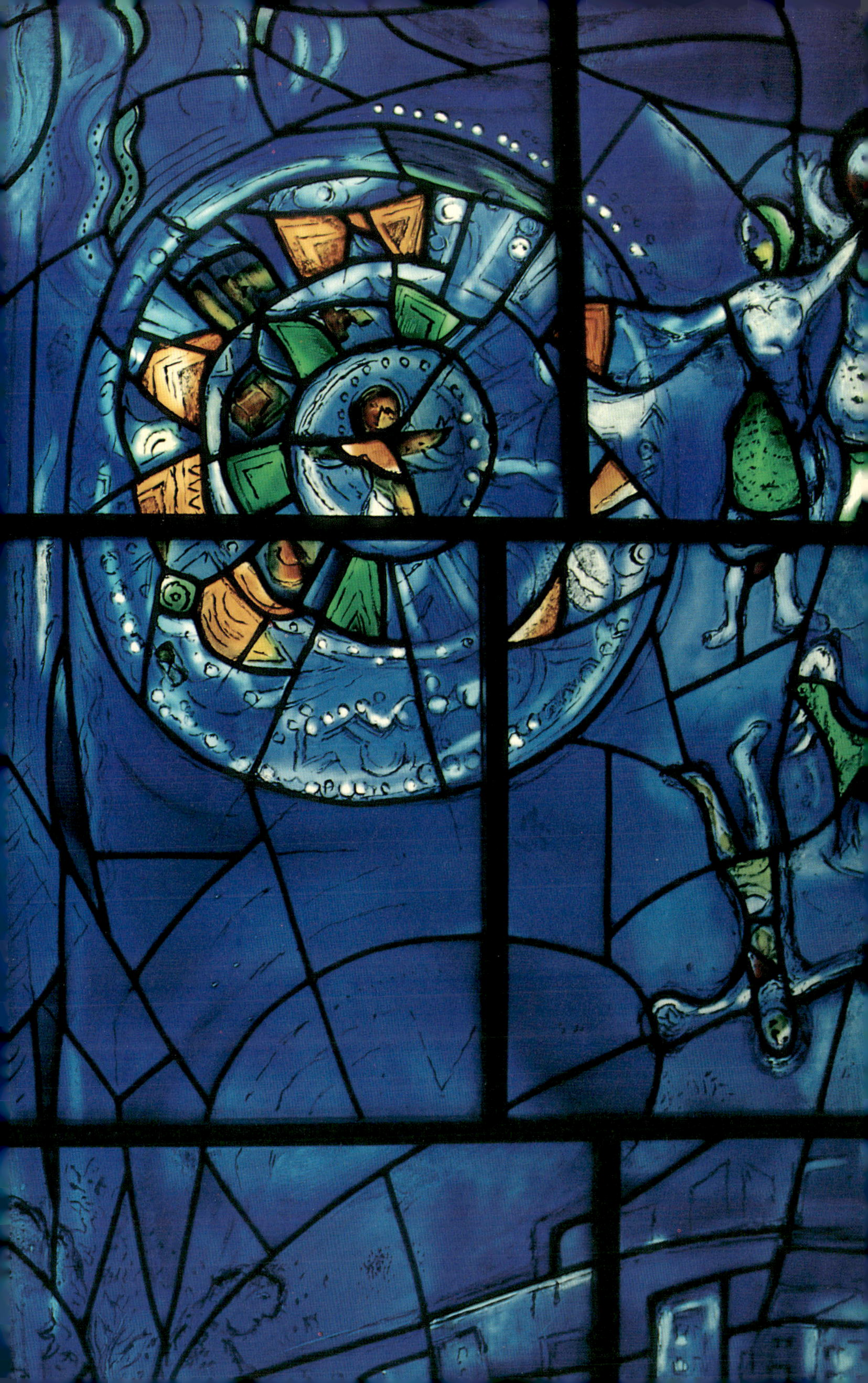

Jacques Marquette

From Swampland To Skyscrapers

Two French explorers with very different reasons for being in the New World are given the credit for being the first Europeans to set eyes on what is now Chicago. Louis Jolliet was searching for gold. Father Jacques Marquette was out saving souls. Splashing about in the marshlands together in 1673, they formed Chicago's prototypical dynamic duo: the man of plunder and the man of prayer, the getter and the giver. They represented two strains of men who one day would build this contradictory city, who would nail it together in a greedy man's haste, jack it up out of a prehistoric muck and reshape it like soft putty after it had endured cholera, fire and financial collapse.

Meatpackers and merchants: Jolliet was the forefather who begat meatpacker barons and merchant princes and condominium kings. Marquette was the forefather who begat social workers and community organizers and spirited advocates for the street-curb poor. At worst, they worked at cross purposes, the men on the make trampling all. At best, they joined in common cause, cash and compassion working together. A pretty park, for example, can soothe men's souls – and increase a real estate agent's profits. These are the types who built Chicago, transforming marshland into Big Shoulders.

Chicago is, above all, an American city, a mid-continental Uncle Sam of gold coasts and slums, of babbling tongues, of punch clocks and blues and verve. It owes that verve to generations of strong backs, to its precious few visionaries and to a few scoundrels, too. Lovely on its lakefront, shabby on its back streets, like a rusting Chevy in the alley, Chicago is a cauldron bubbling with contrasts, like the nation itself. It both nurtures and corrupts. Chicago, America's City. Incorporated March 4, 1837.

Twelve thousand years ago, Lake Chicago, a larger version of today's Lake Michigan, covered much of what is now the Midwest. As the great glacial lake receded, it left

Left, Marquette. **Right**, Pottawattomie chief.

behind vast, waving prairies and a shoreline swamp. America's native people – the Indians who were Chicago's first immigrants – embraced the swampland. They called it Checagou or Checaguar – or something close. It meant "wild onion" or "skunk," apparently a reference to the smell of rotting marshland onions that permeated the entire area. The name implied – and still implies – great strength.

From the beginnings of human inhabitation, the swamp was a place of action, a dealing and swapping ground. The Pottawattomies, traveling by canoe, traded furs and skins there. The swamp linked North America's two great waterways: the Mississippi to the southwest – via the Des Plaines and Illinois rivers – and the Great Lakes to the north and east. During spring rains, shallow-bottomed Indian canoes traversed the swamp, traveling about eight miles from the Des Plaines River to Lake Michigan for trading powwows.

Jolliet saw the big town coming. Paddling along, coasting past 10-foot-high prairie

History 27

grasses, he predicted to Marquette: "Here some day will be found one of the world's great cities." And a later explorer, Robert Cavalier, Sieur de La Salle, saw it, too. "This will be the gate of an empire," he said. "The typical man who will grow up here must be enterprising. Each day, as he rises, he will exclaim, 'I act, I move, I push.'"

America became a land where bustling, sophisticated cities and towns dotted the East Coast. Those cities' paved streets were lined with shops selling imported goods. People read newspapers every day and went to the doctor when they were sick or to the lawyer when they had a legal problem. Families attended church together on Sunday.

Only a few hundred miles to the west, however, were farmers and trappers and hunters who literally lived off the land and might go weeks without seeing a neighbor. Many believed that the country was getting too crowded if they could see the smoke from the next farm. For what few supplies and little companionship they needed, these self-sufficient frontiersmen depended on the small, scattered settlements and trading posts. There they would swap their vegetables or skins culled from the local animals for food and luxury items that they didn't grow or make for themselves at home.

Chicago was one such gathering place, growing from trading post to settlement to village to city largely because of a geographical location that allowed easy transport in all directions. Many of those who came to Chicago in the early days were not farmers or frontiersmen themselves. Some were misfits drawn by the prospect of fewer social and legal constraints in what was at that time the "Wild West." Many were dreamers who believed the West was going to grow dramatically, and then went west themselves to realize those prophecies. They came to Chicago to be big fish in a little pond, and then to make the pond bigger.

The fort: It was a black man who led the way. Jean Baptiste Point DuSable, the tall French-speaking son of a Quebec merchant and a black slave, established a trading post in 1779 on the north bank of the Chicago River at what is now Michigan Avenue. He erected Chicago's first permanent house. Later, he sold the house to another trader, John Kinzie.

Meanwhile, the white man's government began to force out the red man – in the name of progress, of course. General "Mad Anthony" Wayne in 1795 overran the Indians and forced the Pottawattomie tribe to cede huge tracts of Midwestern land, including "six miles square at the mouth of the Chickago River." It was prime real estate even then, a speculator's dream as swamps and forestland turned almost overnight into commercial property. The Indians, who had no concept of "owning" the land, were pushed out as white men sold each other pieces of paper they called "titles." The white man thus entitled himself to control and own the land.

Blue-coated US soldiers arrived from Detroit. In 1803, they built Fort Dearborn at what is now Lower Wacker and Michigan. Ordered to evacuate Fort Dearborn during the War of 1812 against the British, settlers and soldiers fleeing the fort were ambushed by Indians allied with the British. Fifty-two men, women and children from the fort were slain in what is now known as the Fort Dearborn Massacre. But the pioneering deluge was checked only briefly. The soldiers returned, Fort Dearborn was rebuilt, and 5,000 Pottawattomies were booted out for good. Scattered like bungalow dwellers in the path of a coming expressway, some Indians were relocated or drifted to government reservations, often hundreds of miles away; others tried to eke out a living on the edge of the white world, doing menial labor. A few Indian families and small groups became poor wanderers, seeking but never finding a place where they could carry on their traditional way of life. No matter what the Indians tried, however, Pottawattomie children and grandchildren became more and more absorbed into the white world. In effect, after the Fort Dearborn Massacre the traditional Pottawattomie tribe ceased to function as it had for generations.

Boom town: Things happened fast after that. In 1825, the Erie Canal was opened, creating a new water route between Chicago and the East to transport furs, grain, lumber and livestock. The Illinois Legislature plotted a course for the Illinois-Michigan Canal that would connect Lake Michigan and the Mississippi. Federal dollars paid for dredging a harbor. Chicago boomed, though it was less a town than a real estate lottery. A chunk of Lake Street property bought for $300 in 1833 – the year Chicago was incorporated as a village – was sold one year later for $60,000.

New wagons rolled in daily. Settlers from the East swelled the population from 50 in 1830 to 4,170 in 1837. Buoyed by immigrants from Ireland and Germany, within 30 years the population had topped 40,000. Traders and merchants came. So did saloon keepers and prostitutes. As with Jolliet, the lure was money. An early mayor, newspaper publisher "Long John" Wentworth, recalled in the 1880s: "We had people from almost every clime, and almost every opinion. We had Jews and Christians, Protestants, Catholics and infidels. Among Protestants there were Calvinists and Armenians. Nearly every language was represented. Some people had seen much of the world, and some very little."

Everything was new. Anything was possible. Audacious men blustered like the prairie winds. On March 4, 1837, in Vandalia, the southern Illinois community that was later replaced by Springfield as the state capital, the Legislature approved a charter that formally recognized Chicago, previously a vil-

Left, DuSable. Right, Fort Dearborn, 1803.

lage, as a city. The tallest building was two stories. Nobody had a basement. Nobody had gas. Nobody had a paved street.

In New York, the *Chicago American* reported that day, picketers were protesting against the price of bread. In Washington, contributions were being accepted for the construction of the Washington National Monument. Out in the brand-new city of Chicago, meanwhile, local businessmen were advertising 4,000 pounds of log chains, bushels of garden seed, Brandreth Vegetable Pills ("known to benefit persons of a bilious or costive habit of body") and even encouraging migration to smaller Midwestern towns ("Albion – One of the Healthiest Spots in Western America").

Two months later, in an election marred by brawls, a former New York state legislator named William B. Ogden defeated the early settler, John Kinzie, to become Chicago's first mayor. Ogden first stomped into town in the 1830s, steaming mad because a relative had purchased, sight unseen, a muddy tract along State Street for $100,000. Ogden wanted to dump the land and get on home. But after selling a third of the land for $100,000, he changed his mind. He stuck around. He got rich. Ogden was made for this town. He was part Jolliet and part Marquette, part money man and part civic man, a getter and a giver. In the course of piling up his fortune, he built the city's first drawbridge and first railroad – now called the Chicago & North Western.

Aspirations and action: Chicago's early history is replete with the doings of men with huge egos and boundless ambition. They left personal imprints (and sometimes skid marks) on an impressionable city. When "Long John" Wentworth, elected mayor in 1857, tired of the dogfights and sex shows in the red-light district, he personally led a posse of 30 cops and hundreds of citizens on a clean-up crusade. They demolished every disreputable house.

When Chicagoans tired of slopping around in the mud, a sanitation engineer named Ellis Sylvester Chesbrough proposed raising the level of the entire city. Sidewalks were promptly boosted up, turning ground floors into basements. George Pullman, the railroad man, then used armies of workmen to jack up the buildings themselves. And when Chicagoans tired of contracting cholera and dysentery from foul shoreline drinking water, city workers dug a two-mile tunnel out into the lake to tap clean water. For good measure, Chicago amazed the world in 1900 by making the Chicago River run backward. That feat, aimed at using fresh lake water to flush away the polluted, disease-carrying riverflow, was an engineering marvel of locks and channels that is still often studied today.

Chicago was leaving the provinces behind and emerging as America's crossroads. By 1856, Chicago was the hub of 10 railroad trunk lines. Raw materials brought by wagon, barge, ship and train were turned into products to build and feed the country – lumber from nearby forests, iron ore from Minnesota, livestock and produce from some of the richest farmland in the world. Chicago led the world in the transportation of cattle, grain and lumber. Grain elevators, jabbing the skyline, were the Sears Towers of the day.

As surely as one clever manufacturer knew how to turn out a product, someone else knew how to sell it. The mail-order giants Sears, Roebuck & Co. and Montgomery Ward & Co. were born in Chicago. Legendary merchants, whose names are still in evidence not only on Chicago hotels and department stores but in branches scattered across America's retail landscape, included Marshall Field, William Wieboldt, Potter Palmer, Samuel Carson and John Pirie. And, if the soul of Marquette was sometimes conspicuously absent, if the rascals sold spoiled beef and defective weapons to the Union Army, if the political booster boys seemed all too forgiving of City Hall corruption and 400 brothels – well, hell, to quote a future alderman, "Hinky Dink" Kenna: "Chicago ain't no sissy town."

Up in flames: Then came the fire. The Great Chicago Fire of 1871 started, according to the legend, on October 8 in Mrs O'Leary's barn, now the site of the Chicago Fire Department Training Academy. O'Leary's cow got the rap; it kicked a lantern, they said. The fire spread fast, an eyewitness describing it as "a vast ocean of flames, sweeping in mile-long billows and breakers over the doomed city." Three hundred people were killed; 100,000 were left homeless; 18,000 buildings were destroyed. Chicago's first city was in ashes.

So they built a second: this time a sturdier town of fireproof brick. Two days after the fire, W.D. Kerfoot, a spunky real estate

Left, displaced Indians, *circa* 1907. **Right**, the new Chicagoans, *circa* 1907.

History 31

agent, posted a sign on a shack: "All gone but wife, children and energy." Money was there to be made. No time to mourn. Chicago warn't no sissy town.

A civic ripening emerged out of the great fire's ashes. Architects, sensing unlimited opportunity, flocked to Chicago. They endowed the city with a touch of New World class, a skyline of state-of-the-art office buildings. Many of the post-fire classics, particularly those in the range of 14 to 18 stories high along South Dearborn Street, remain the relatively earthbound bulwarks of the steel-frame construction process that led to today's skyscrapers. Because it was continuing to grow so quickly as an industrial and commercial center, downtown Chicago needed big buildings, and ambitious architects with powerful new designs were given free reign to build toward the clouds. Three world masters led the charge: John Root, designer of the graceful Rookery and Monadnock buildings; Louis Sullivan, designer of the efficient Auditorium and Carson Pirie Scott buildings; and Sullivan's peerless protégé, Frank Lloyd Wright. Brilliant innovators, they established Chicago's tradition of architectural leadership. Mies van der Rohe, the father of unadorned steel-and-glass modernism, nailed it down. Helmut Jahn, iconoclastic creator of the rolling Xerox building and the hotly disputed State of Illinois Center, helped ensure its strength today.

Cultural birth: By 1890, Chicago was struggling out of an era of cut-throat Social Darwinism into an age of social reform. In the City Council, the avaricious "Gray Wolves," the bribery-wizened councilmen who picked over the bones of every public spending project for kickbacks ranging from jobs for relatives to cash for themselves, still divvied up the boodle. But more civic-minded Chicagoans demanded social justice, a bit of high culture, and such public amenities as spacious parks and an uncluttered lakefront. The 1890s saw the establishment of the Art Institute, stocked with Dutch Masters' paintings; the University of Chicago, founded with Rockefeller money on Marshall Field real estate; the Museum of Science and Industry, and the Columbian Exposition of 1893, a fabulously successful world's fair that introduced the Ferris wheel and the "shake" dancer Little Egypt. Her "exotic" bumps and grinds were undoubtedly modest by today's standards, but Little Egypt's act nonetheless drew condemnation from moralizing newspaper editors and clergymen who warned that she was instilling evil lust in the hearts and minds of her many male fans.

The Chicago Symphony Orchestra made its debut, although the conductor, Theodore Thomas, recruited from the New York Philharmonic, dared not offer many symphonies at first. Chicago's musical taste was too undeveloped; "light music" had to suffice as culture. Asked why he bothered to settle in Chicago at all, he explained: "I would go to hell if they would give me a permanent orchestra." Thomas was one of those rare men of scope and vision who made Chicago what it is today. There were also others.

There was A. Montgomery Ward, a stoical money man in the Jolliet mold who revealed the heart of a Marquette when he launched his 13-year court battle to save Grant Park from public buildings. City Hall, the press and the business community ganged up on the merchant, calling him an "obstructionist." But Ward legally established the principle that Chicago's entire lakefront should be preserved "forever open, clear and free."

Left, the Opera House after the fire, 1871. Right, Burnham's 1909 Plan for Chicago.

There was the architect Daniel H. Burnham, who enshrined the principle of a pristine lakefront in his famous city plan of 1909. No other plan has so influenced Chicago's growth. The Burnham Plan of 1909 resulted in the creation of a string of lakefront parks and beaches, including Jackson Park and Washington Park; the acquisition of a green belt of forest preserves on the city's periphery; the construction of Chicago's main post office, and the siting of the Eisenhower Expressway. Still, there was no pleasing everybody. An important councilman, Council Gray Wolf, growled: "The lakefront ain't no place for a park."

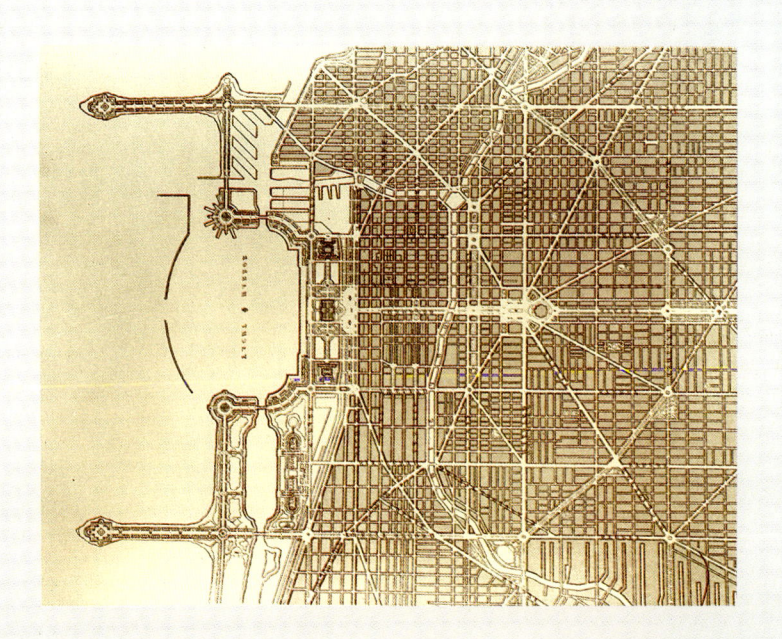

In many ways, Chicago's renowned social consciousness was a reaction against the city's legendary greed. In this town of extremes, with its unofficial "Where's mine?" motto, it made sense for the backlash against rampant capitalism to be a particularly selfless, far-reaching brand of humanitarianism.

Civic conscience: Social reform by 1890 was, in part, a survival tactic. Chicago seethed with labor unrest, and the city became an incubator for a national organized labor movement, then in its infancy. The class warfare, fueled by the loose alliance of young unions that were committed to better

History 33

working and living conditions for all laborers, spooked Prairie Avenue's Millionaires' Row. In the 1880s and 1890s, a nationwide campaign for the eight-hour day and the minimum wage triggered bloody confrontations. Thirteen men were killed in Chicago during one summer week. The National Guard was called out to quell a workers' riot outside Pullman's railcar plant. Seven policemen were killed in the Haymarket Riot of 1886. No one saw who threw the bomb, but four anarchists went to the gallows.

Pressures for social reform came from other quarters. From an emerging professional class stepped rebellious giants – social worker Jane Addams, attorney Clarence Darrow and muckraking journalist Upton Sinclair. Addams, a proper young woman from Rockford, walked among the shabby sweatshops and immigrant tenements on the city's Near West Side and decided to devote her life to helping the people there. Chicago's population had reached 1 million by 1890, including hundreds of thousands of Irish, Italian and Eastern European immigrants living in squalor within a whiff of the stockyards.

Addams' Hull House, a settlement house tending to the needs of immigrants at Blue Island and Halsted, became a model for the nation. Through the efforts of committed staff and concerned volunteers, it fought for an end to child labor, for factory inspections and a minimum wage. Jane Addams was some kind of crazy lady, according to the mavens of La Salle Street, Chicago's Wall Street – but, they had to admit, she was effective. Addams and her followers at Hull House and other settlement houses established throughout Chicago provided fresh clean milk for babies, taught immigrants English and set up day care centers for the children of working mothers. They provided a range of care and comfort that became a model for inner-city social welfare programs, from prescribing balanced diets for young families to describing how to open a bank account, enroll children in school or apply for a better job. These early social workers helped instill a sense of self-esteem and hope in an exploited, downtrodden class of menial laborers.

Others have followed in Addams' footsteps. In the 1950s and 1960s, Saul Alinsky, the patriarch of militant community organizers, fought City Hall with his Back of the Yards Council and the Woodlawn Organization. In the 1980s and into the 1990s, Douglas Dobmeyer, president of the Chicago Coalition of the Homeless, led ragged demonstrations outside the yuppie high-rises that have displaced the Skid Row poor.

Upton Sinclair was crazier still. In *The Jungle*, his muckraking exposé of the stockyards, he wrote of "the secret rooms where the spoiled meats went to be doctored." He told of workmen whose feet were eaten away by acids in the fertilizer rooms. And he repeated dark tales of other workers who had fallen into steaming vats, and gone out to the world as pure beef lard. Federal investigators checked out the allegations. All of these things are pretty much true, they said.

But there was much more to the stockyards than the horrible sanitary and working conditions. There were the living conditions, often no less unsanitary. Families, many of them immigrants from Europe, were crowded into narrow wooden rowhouses in the neighborhood known as the Back of the Yards. Many of the workers were rural Europeans who spoke little or no English. Many were unfamiliar with living in America after hearing from friends and relatives, earlier immigrants, about how easy it was to get a high-paying job, and about how wealthy Chicago was. What the immigrants didn't find out until they arrived was how hard they had to work, often in disgusting conditions; how much daily living cost, and how quickly those seemingly high wages disappeared; and how Chicago's vast wealth was accumulated and hoarded by a relative few who profited from the backbreaking labor of the new arrivals.

The Back of the Yards was a ghetto. Its "inmates" never escaped from the stink of animal manure, slaughterhouses and rendering plants. In hopes of raising enough money to escape, or merely to meet the rents charged for their substandard housing, often owned by the companies using the stockyards, men and women worked long hours, sometimes at two jobs. They often kept their children out of school in order to put them to work, too, so that the whole family might have enough money to move to a new neighborhood and find better jobs. These were the people, whose children worked long hours and didn't have the ways or means to keep their babies healthy, whom social reformers tried to help.

Left, back of the Union Stock Yard houses. **Right**, Union Stock Yard, 1866.

After World War I, an influx of blacks from the Southern states provided a new source of cheap labor to be exploited by the stockyards. Almost overnight, much of Chicago's South Side became predominantly black neighborhoods.

In its peak year of 1924, the Union Stock Yard, a square mile of land down by Canaryville, employed over 30,000 workers and received more than 18.6 million head of cattle and calves, sheep and hogs. But in 1971 the big yard closed. Omaha and Iowa could cut a pork roast cheaper.

Sinclair was in the vanguard of the Chicago literary movement in the years before the Great Depression. Other notables included Carl Sandburg, the poet who wrote so eloquently of the city; Theodore Dreiser, chronicler of big-city sins and small-town waifs, and Ben Hecht, the ex-newsman who told Broadway a secret: Chicago loves its rogues as much as its squares – sometimes more. Writing a bit later were James T. Farrell, Nelson Algren, Richard Wright and Saul Bellow.

Machine guns, politics: After World War I, Chicago's focus of power shifted from industrialists to politicians. While heirs to Chicago's great retailing and meatpacking fortunes ensconced themselves on the North Shore, crooked politicians and bootleggers plundered the city. The handful of social reformers were too focused on caring for deprived individuals to worry about the corruption of an entire political system, and they would probably have been no match for men with machine guns and briefcases anyway. In truth, most of the population didn't care about the corruption and booze smuggling – after all, anyone who made the right connections could always be assured of an easy job during the day and a hard drink at night. So the bootleggers dueled it out and more than 400 gangsters were killed over five years, including seven in the 1929 St Valentine's Day Massacre.

Bestriding the city during the Prohibition years – from 1920 to 1933 when a constitutional amendment outlawed alcoholic beverages of any sort throughout the United States – was that colossus of crime, Al Capone. Like many Chicagoans, he was an immigrant, born in Naples in 1899.

A one-time speakeasy bouncer who graduated to running houses of prostitution, Capone built a vast bootlegging empire that included importing real whisky from Canada and operating his own beer breweries right in the middle of Chicago. To keep his operations going, he made the bribery of officials at every level, from City Hall to cops on the beat, an everyday fact of life that still plagues Chicago.

Capone, whose business card identified him as a "Second-hand Furniture Dealer," was short and pot-bellied and not particularly physically imposing. But Capone was nicknamed Scarface for the parallel reminders of a knifing on his cheek, and he was a crudely brilliant and cunningly brutal organizer who ruled through a combination of fear and rewards, stick and carrot. Those who did what he wanted could get rich quickly. Those who refused requests could get dead even more quickly.

He often made his points in a most dramatic way, sending out carloads of gunmen with nonmusical violin cases or interrupting a black-tie banquet to kill a fellow diner, a disloyal lieutenant, with repeated blows to the back of the head with a baseball bat. Capone is listed in the *Guinness Book of Records* for the highest gross income ever accumulated by a private citizen in a single year: $105 million in 1927, when he was 28 years old.

Chicago in general boomed during the Roaring Twenties. Fortunes were made in the rising stock market. More big buildings went up. Flappers danced on speakeasy tables. Legal nightlife sparkled with dozens of vaudeville houses and legitimate theaters that featured both local groups and touring professional troupes. Most people tolerated crime as a part of everyday life, as long as it wasn't one of their relatives or friends who was cut down in the latest careless crossfire among rival hoodlums.

Capone was finally brought down by a group of federal agents, led by Eliot Ness and known as the Untouchables for their refusal to take bribes. Unable to pin murder or even bootlegging directly on the crafty Capone, Ness and his men instead went after the gangster for failing to pay taxes on his millions in illicit gain. Capone was convicted and went to prison. He died in 1947, quietly, in bed, of syphilis.

But Capone didn't invent political corruption in Chicago. Back in 1837, on the very day Chicago voted to become a city, wagonloads of non-resident Irish canal diggers, technically ineligible to vote, were lugged to

Left, Al "Scarface" Capone, 1931 mug shot. **Right**, officers survey gangland carnage.

History 37

the convention hall to cast their ballots. Consider just two stealing mayors. When Fred A. Busse died, he left behind a safe-deposit box full of stock in a company that sold the city its manhole covers. And when Prohibition-era Mayor William Thompson died, he left behind safe-deposit boxes containing $1,578,000 in cash, stocks, bonds and certificates. No one knows exactly how the mayor got so rich, or where that money came from. However, Al Capone always liked Thompson, to the point of keeping Big Bill's picture on his office wall.

Tony Cermak, the mayor who died stopping a bullet meant for President Franklin D. Roosevelt, dreamed up the political machine. Running as a Democrat against Thompson in the mayoral campaign of 1931, Cermak pieced together the first "balanced" party ticket – a Pole here, a German there, an Irishman here and there – and swept the white ethnic voting bloc. Only the blacks, still loyal to the party of Lincoln and Emancipation, backed Thompson. No surprise there: Chicago always has been a divided town – black here, white there, blood-red too often in between.

During the Civil War (1861–65), Irish canal diggers cheered Confederate victories. To celebrate, they poured out of Archer Avenue saloons and chased down blacks. In 1919, a black boy drifted into a white swimming area and was drowned when a white man on shore hit him with a stone. The ensuing riots left 37 more dead. "The slums take their revenge," Carl Sandburg wrote. It would be fire the next time. In 1968, Dr Martin Luther King Jr was shot in Memphis and America's cities exploded. Chicago's West Side burned.

In the 1930s, the Great Depression hit hard. In Chicago, out-of-work men and women marched in protest down State Street. Businessmen cried. One of the richest, Sam Insull, who made a billion dollars from his power and light companies, lost it all and fled to London, where he died penniless. And yet, weak-kneed Chicago toddled along still. The city threw another world's fair in 1933, a Century of Progress, and gave the world another sexy sensation, Sally Rand. Like Little Egypt at the Columbian Exposition 40 years earlier, Sally Rand was an exotic dancer whose titillating act drew mobs of men and made her notorious. Unlike Little Egypt, however, Sally Rand went on stage nude except for large stage props, usually fans but sometimes feather boas or even a large ball, that she maneuvered enticingly to provide provocative glimpses of bare flesh while avoiding "total revelation."

Their Daley bread: World War II jerked the nation out of its doldrums. Chicago worked, all out – grunted, groaned and sweated. What with all the bustle, nobody paid much notice when, in 1942, a team of physicists at the University of Chicago – an historically prestigious institution that claims more Nobel Prize winners than any other university in the world – built the first nuclear reactor. The scientists, working under the direction of Italian-American physicist Enrico Fermi in a grim basement beneath the university athletic stadium, toiled in secret through the early part of World War II. They rarely spoke of the practical applications of their work. In 1942, their "atomic pile," as they called it, created the first controlled nuclear chain reaction, and with it the technology for both nuclear power and the bomb.

By the 1950s, Chicago was more than 100

years old. It had moved through eras of settlement, furious growth, depression and war. One last period remained: the Era of Daley. Richard J. Daley. "Da Boss." He ruled Chicago for 21 years. Daley was a man far more complicated than any Jolliet or Marquette caricature. He was a getter, yes, but he sought power, not money. He was a giver, yes, but he sometimes gave you what you didn't want. He loved the city and showed his love in a way all his own – take it or leave it. Like the city's skyscrapers, Mayor Daley was a monument on the landscape, and, despite his excesses, his legacy has proven as durable as reinforced concrete.

He bulldozed whole communities, always against their wills, for expressways and plazas and universities. He plowed old ghettos and built segregating walls of high-rise public housing. Daley ran expressways toward the Loop, the downtown area circumscribed by the city's elevated trains. The business center thrived. But, by that time, the Loop's once-glittering nightlife was history. Daley played kingmaker to a president, withholding the 1960 Chicago vote to see how the election was going and then delivering the winning margin to John F. Kennedy. In 1968, at the height of the Vietnam conflict, Daley's cops beat up anti-war protesters outside the Conrad Hilton Hotel during the Democratic National Convention. "The whole world is watching," demonstrators chanted. Chicago hasn't had a big political convention since.

Back to the future: So what of Chicago today? A city that stands as a monument to those who first passed through – Jolliet and Marquette, the getter and the giver. More Gold Coast. More ghetto. More growth. More decay. Post-industrial Chicago is shuffling along, learning to compete again in a service-oriented economy. Businesses and people have followed the expressways into the suburbs, trading bad schools and racial strife for green lawns and safer streets. Steel mills are rusting and stock yards closed.

But where there is doubt, there is hope.

Left, Sally Rand has a ball. **Right**, Nobel laureate Saul Bellow. **Following pages**: Dearborn and Randolph Streets, 1909.

Chicago theater, all but dormant since the heyday of the 1920s, struts again. Old Loop railyards are new office buildings. Midway, once an aviation ghost town, roars again. New immigrant groups from the Far East, the Asian subcontinent, the Caribbean and elsewhere give old neighborhoods new life. School drop-out rates soar, but innovative schools churn out top-class scholars. The old political machine is losing people and power, and the long-oppressed black minority is coming into its own.

A black man, the late Harold Washington, became mayor and built his own version of the Chicago machine in the 1980s, paving the way for the 1990s streamlined political framework of "Richie" Daley, the son of Da Boss, who won the mayor's office and claimed what many stalwarts believed was his birthright. Saul Bellow, Chicago's Nobel laureate in literature, often commented on Chicago's history: "Cycles of prosperity and desolation… risings and fallings, so much death, rebirth, metamorphosis, so many tribal migrations."

Chicago is still a town of genius and guts and verve. And it still ain't a sissy town. Jolliet just might love it. Marquette might like it, too.

History 39

LAWYER

KOESTER & ZANDER   KOESTER & ZANDER
                 REAL ESTATE
        REAL   KOESTER
        ESTATE.   AND
                          ZANDER

                  KOESTER   KOESTER
                  &   &
                  ZANDER   ZANDER
                  REAL   REAL
                  ESTATE   ESTATE

THE CUNARD LINE   CUNARD LINE   HOLLAND-AMERIKA LINE

ELSTON AV

FREDRIKSEN ICE CO

FRANK M. HALLENBECK PHOTO.

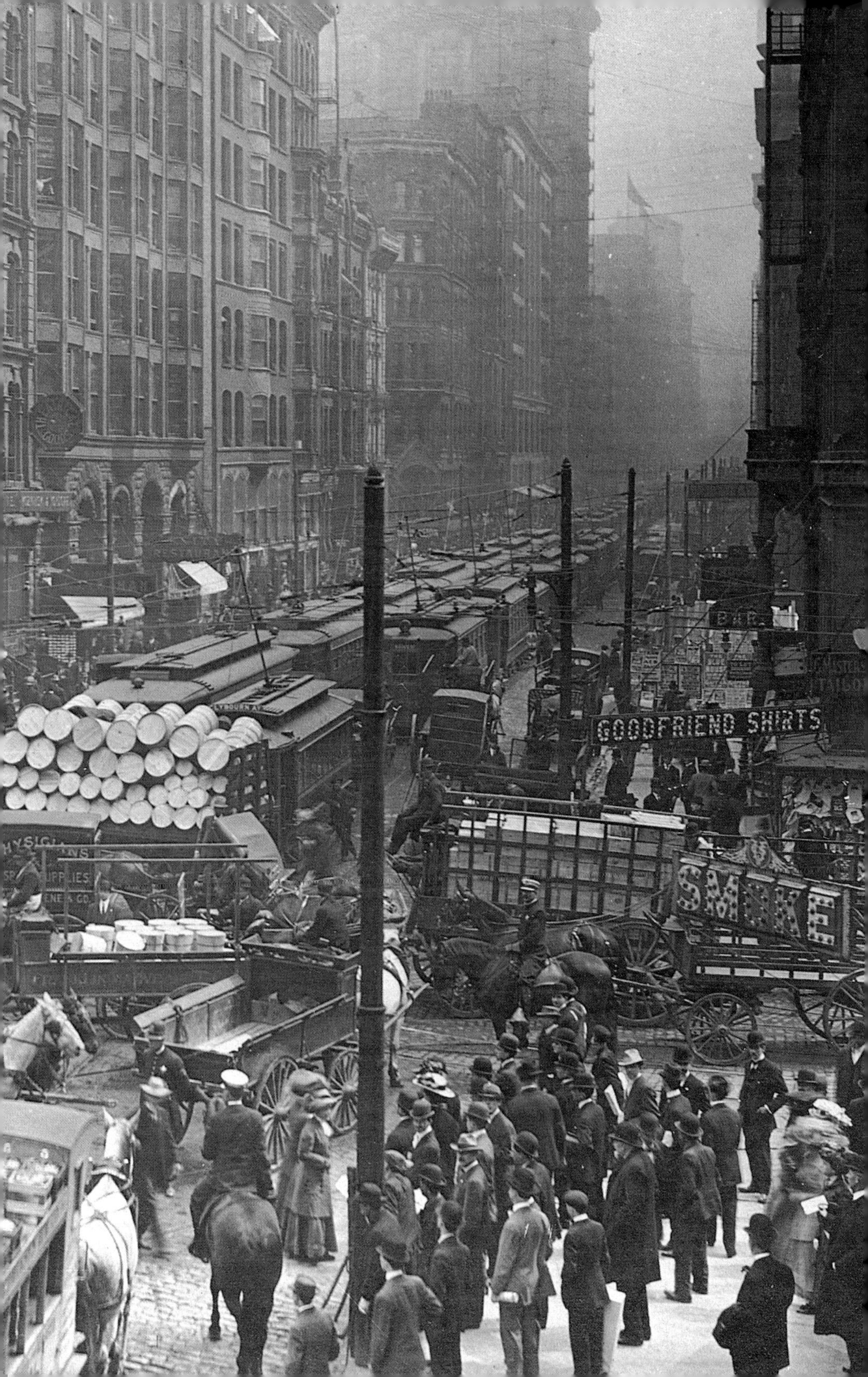
GOODFRIEND SHIRTS
BAR
SMOKE

DECISIVE DATES

BC: Lake Chicago, which covered much of what is now the American Midwest, receded with the glaciers, leaving swamps separating the vast prairies and what is now Lake Michigan.

Pre-1800: Native Americans, the Pottawattomie Indians, used the swampland linking the Great Lakes and the Mississippi River as a trading area. They called it "Checagou" in reference to the stink of rotting wild onions.

1673: Jolliet, a gold-seeking explorer, and Marquette, a Jesuit priest, canoed together into the marshland that would become Chicago.

1779: Jean Baptiste Point DuSable, son of a black slave and a Quebec merchant, established a trading post on the north bank of the Chicago River, located at what is now Michigan Avenue.

1795: General "Mad Anthony" Wayne led troops that overran the Indians and forced them to give up tribal lands, including much of what is now downtown Chicago.

1803: Federal soldiers built Fort Dearborn at the location known today as Lower Wacker and Michigan Avenue.

1812: In an Indian insurrection, 52 men, women and children at the fort were slain in what came to be called the Fort Dearborn Massacre. Troop reinforcements soon put down the uprising and also rebuilt the fort.

1825: The Erie Canal opened, creating a new water route for shipping between Chicago and the East Coast.

1831: First bridge was erected over the Chicago River, linking the North and South sides of town.

1833: During the population and property boom, a downtown plot that had sold for $300 in the previous year was resold for $60,000.

1837: With a population that had grown to 4,170 from a mere 50 only seven years before, Chicago was incorporated as a city. William B. Ogden won the election as Chicago's first mayor.

1848: A group of businessmen formed the Chicago Board of Trade, the world's oldest and largest futures exchange, and launched Chicago as the world center for commodities trading.

1871: The Great Chicago Fire, reputedly begun in Mrs O'Leary's barn when her cow kicked over a lantern, killed 300, left 100,000 homeless and destroyed 18,000 buildings.

1886: Years of discontent among workers, including a riot outside the Pullman plant, culminated in the bombing deaths of seven policemen in the Haymarket Riot. Four anarchists were hanged for the bombing.

1889: Frank Lloyd Wright, the architect, built his much-admired Home and Studio on Chicago Avenue in suburban Oak Park.

1889: Jane Addams, a volunteer social worker, founded Hull House and began the welfare movement that was based on "settlement houses" serving poor communities.

1890: Chicago's population, heavily bolstered by European immigration, passed one million.

1892: The University of Chicago was founded.

1893: The Columbian Exposition was a world's fair that drew the nation's attention, gave Chicago its "Windy City" nickname because of pre-fair boasting, introduced the Ferris wheel and made the exotic dancer Little Egypt both famous and infamous.

1900: Engineers completed a massive project using a series of locks and channels to make the Chicago River reverse its flow so that river waste would no longer run into Lake Michigan.

1905: Wright revealed plans for his architectural masterpiece, Unity Temple, which opened four years later, also in suburban Oak Park.

1906: Upton Sinclair, a crusading journalist, caused a national uproar with his book *The Jungle*, an exposé of unsanitary conditions and cruel labor policies in the stockyards.

1909: Daniel H. Burnham, the architect, unveiled a city plan that called for preservation of the lakefront for public recreation and culture.

1919: After the drowning of a black boy on a public beach, race riots left 38 dead.

1919: The Chicago White Sox, favored to win baseball's World Series, lost. Eight players, including star slugger Joe Jackson, were subsequently banned from the sport for accepting bribes from gamblers to lose.

1920: The Michigan Avenue Bridge opened.

1924: The Union Stock Yard, employing more than 30,000 workers, received more than 18.6 million head of cattle, calves, sheep and hogs.
1929: The seven gangsters killed in the St Valentine's Day Massacre were among more than 400 mobsters eliminated during a five-year period.
1929: The Wall Street stock market crash sent Chicago plummeting into the Great Depression.
1931: Tony Cermak put together the first ethnically "balanced" ticket and laid the groundwork for Chicago's Democratic political machine.
1931: Crime boss Al "Scarface" Capone, after amassing gangland earnings of more than $100 million a year, was convicted of federal income tax evasion and sentenced to eight years in prison.
1933: Despite the Depression, Chicago staged the Century of Progress world's fair, introducing another sexy sensation, fan dancer Sally Rand.
1934: John Dillinger, the bank robber, was gunned down outside the Biograph Theatre by federal agents tipped off by the Lady in Red, the gangster's moll.
1942: As part of the Manhattan Project, a group of physicists achieved the first nuclear chain reaction, providing the technology for nuclear bombs and power.
1947: Capone died of syphilis.
1951: Nelson Algren, winner of the first National Book Award for fiction the previous year for his novel *The Man With the Golden Arm*, published the acclaimed prose poem *Chicago: City on the Make*.
1952: Hugh Hefner, circulation director of *Children's Activities* magazine, borrowed $1,600 to start a new publication called *Playboy*.
1955: Richard J. Daley, a.k.a. "Hizzoner" and "Da Boss," was elected mayor.
1960: Mayor Daley's "late" returns swung the presidential election away from Richard Nixon to John F. Kennedy.
1960: Saul Alinsky, a community organizer, formed the Woodlawn Organization, a grass-roots group that became a focal point for the Chicago civil rights movement.
1966: The Rev. Martin Luther King Jr founded the

Left, "Shoeless" Joe Jackson, 1919. **Right**, Mayor Richard J. Daley, 1975.

Chicago Freedom Movement, which spawned Operation Breadbasket and PUSH, the groups that gave the Rev. Jesse Jackson his national platform.
1968: Divisions in US society over the Vietnam War burst into street violence in what investigators, criticizing Daley and the Chicago police, later called a "police riot" against young demonstrators at the Democratic National Convention.
1969: The Chicago Seven conspiracy trial, which brought demonstrators from the Democratic Convention to court, riveted the nation's attention, along with the "Days of Rage" campaign by militant antiwar factions.
1971: Undercut by competition from smaller Midwestern cities, the Union Stock Yard closed.
1972: The Chicago Mercantile Exchange, begun in 1919 as a tiny butter and egg market, pioneered the financial futures markets.
1974: The world's tallest office building, the 110-story Sears Tower, was opened downtown.
1976: Chicagoan Saul Bellow won the Nobel Prize for Literature.
1976: After 21 tumultuous years, Mayor Daley died in office.
1979: Jane Byrne, having waged a strong "anti-machine" campaign, won the mayoral race against Michael Bilandic, Daley's successor, who was blamed for his inability to clear the streets during the winter's blizzards.
1987: Harold Washington, Chicago's first black mayor, died after four years in office.
1989: Despite decades of opposition, the Chicago Tribune Co., owners of the Cubs, installed lights at Wrigley Field and the baseball team played its first night games at home.
1989: Richard M. Daley, the son of Richard J. Daley, defeated Washington's successor, Eugene Sawyer, as well as several other candidates in a special mayoral election.
1989: Jesse Jackson removed his Rainbow Coalition headquarters and his presidential aspirations to a new home in Washington, DC.
1991: Mayor Daley, re-elected, vowed to fight crime and ease tension as the white population decreased while blacks and Hispanics increased.
1992: Carol Mosely Braun was the first black woman elected to the U.S. Senate.
1993: The Chicago Bulls won the NBA Basketball Championship for the third year in a row.

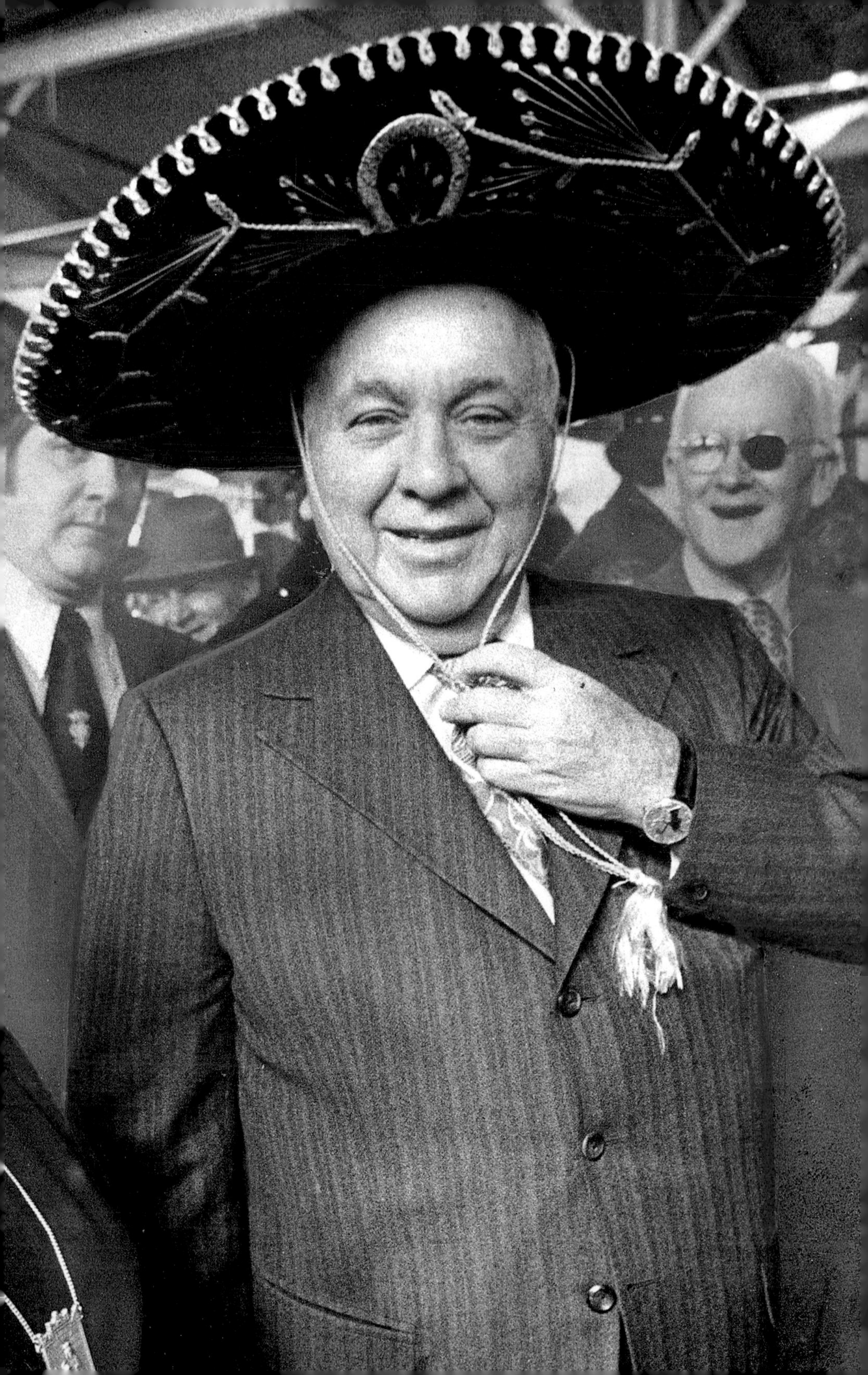

THE WINDS OF POLITICS

In Chicago, the Windy City, the prevailing political breezes come from the fifth-floor City Hall office of the mayor. Blowing through the glass and limestone office canyons of LaSalle Street and the Loop, up along the lakefront and into the neighborhoods, they shape and define Chicago's political character in the mayor's likeness – whoever happens to be the mayor at that particular moment.

Chicago's political winds can, depending on the given mayor, flatten the 50-member City Council like a field of wheat lying in the path of a Midwestern summer storm, or puff up the ambitions of a would-be foe like the spinnaker of a yacht plying Lake Michigan before a zephyr.

Presidents, governors, congressmen and every political wanna-be from the smallest on up have been well advised not to sally far into precincts from Rogers Park to Beverly without first lofting a finger toward City Hall to gauge wind velocity and direction, lest they end up turned as inside-out as an umbrella on State Street in April.

This city of 1.5 million registered voters – a solid three-fourths of them inclined to vote Democratic in major elections – has perhaps the most famous (or infamous depending on one's point of view) reputation for politics of any major US city. And mayors have always been at the center.

Daley duties: Richard J. Daley was the mayor most closely identified with the city. Elected to a record six terms, he died in office after serving 21 consecutive years and pulling the levers of the nation's last partisan political machine.

He also served as Cook County Democratic Party chairman – the only mayor ever to hold both posts at the same time – and handpicked candidates for office. Thus he saw to it that the Machine, fueled by some 40,000 city jobs he controlled and 20,000 more he influenced, churned out sure-bet Democratic pluralities every time. With an accountant's precision, Daley kept tabs on party loyalty and used jobs as a means of rewarding friends and punishing enemies. During Daley's regime, the local political lexicon became salted with terms such as "clout" and "Boss." Cynical slogans such as "Vote early and vote often," became popular clichés for how the Machine succeeded, but the mayor's favorite maxim was "Good politics makes good government." Pithy advice along the lines of "Don't make no waves, don't back no losers," succinctly stated the Machine philosophy.

Daley's accomplishments, however, were not simply raw political power. In the tradition of Chicago's most successful mayors, he was a master builder and the business community loved him. "The City that Works" was coined under Daley as the local motto that Chicago mayors have clung to ever since.

After Daley died in 1976, there were five mayors in 12 years. But the Daley name remained linked with the office in voters'

Left, "Hizzoner Da Mare." **Right**, William B. Ogden, the first mayor.

Politics   45

minds, so much so that his son, Richard M. Daley – also known as Richard II or simply Richie – was elected mayor in 1989.

Punchy quotes: Until landmark federal court rulings curtailed the use of partisan patronage hiring, politics was as avidly participatory in Chicago as playing 16-inch softball, and it continues to rank with Chicago's professional sports franchises as a top spectator activity.

People identify Chicago more with gangsterism than with deep-dish pizza, and so too are they more apt to remember its punch-in-the-nose style of politics than its renowned symphony. It is difficult to know exactly which piece of the legacy is most responsible for Chicago's hurly-burly political reputation.

As for punches in the nose, Chicago politics was typified earlier this century when William Hale Thompson, a three-term mayor, boasted that he would like to sock the King of England in the snoot. While Thompson's comment was reviled by most of the civilized world, Chicagoans laughed it off as a stunt to attract Irish voters and reaffirm the city's "leave us alone" world view. Thompson, who consorted with Al Capone and died with $1.4 million stuffed into safety-deposit boxes, was one in a long line of the larger-than-life characters that Chicagoans are accustomed to having for their mayors.

Another memorable comment came from alderman and saloon keeper Mathias "Paddy" Bauler when Daley was first elected in 1955: "Chicago ain't ready for reform." In 1968, when his police and the military clashed with Yippies and other Vietnam War protesters outside the Democratic National Convention, Daley came up with one of his classic malapropisms, declaring that the National Guard had been called out "to preserve disorder."

The graveyard vote: It is said that Democratic nominee Hubert H. Humphrey lost the election to Republican Richard Nixon that autumn largely because of the convention, as emblematic a Chicago political event as Daley's having "stolen" the presidency for Democrat John F. Kennedy. Illinois was a key state in the 1960 Nixon-Kennedy race, and Daley reputedly withheld Chicago's returns – possibly padding them out with ballots cast in the names of deceased party supporters – until the last moment, when the city miraculously supplied just enough of a margin for Kennedy to carry the state and eventually the nation.

Chicago's tough reputation got tougher during the 1969 "Chicago Seven" conspiracy trial, a legal circus that led to overturned convictions for abuse of the judicial system, and as a result of the "Days of Rage" rampage by a militant faction of Students for a Democratic Society, who took their Weathermen name from the Bob Dylan lyrics – appropriate for Chicago – about not needing a weatherman to tell which way the wind blows.

Nicknames: But Chicago's link with seamy politics was nothing new in the 1960s. For the whole of the previous century, the city reigned as the nation's smoke-filled-backroom capital, playing host to 24 Democratic and Republican national conventions – still more than any other US city. The first was a raucous 1860 Republican Party affair in the historic Wigwam, a temporary structure located near the Chicago River and Lake Street, where dark horse presidential candidate and Illinois native son Abraham Lincoln was nominated.

In a city with several nicknames, it's fitting that Chicago's colorful political characters had colorful nicknames of their own. Daley, of course, was "Da Mare," a linguistic bow to his own syntax, fractured as a result of growing up a sheet metal worker's son in a Back of the Yards neighborhood. The strapping Mayor Thompson was "Big Bill." Six-foot, six-inch, 300-pound Mayor "Long John" Wentworth was one of two newspaper publisher-mayors who served before the turn of the century, the other being Joseph Medill of the *Tribune*. The imperious, mercurial Jane Byrne, swept into office as Chicago's first woman mayor by voters fed up with Michael Bilandic's inept handling of an epic 1979 blizzard, was known as "Lady Jane."

Alderman "Bathhouse John" Coughlin and Michael "Hinky Dink" Kenna were flamboyant lords of the Levee, the downtown vice district, who controlled City Council politics and "boodle," or graft, from the 1890s until Prohibition. "Fast Eddie"

Left, Abraham Lincoln, 1860. **Right**, National Guard jeeps, 1968 Democratic Convention.

Vrdolyak was a latter-day political sharpster who became the City Council kingpin after Daley's death but surrendered his Democratic Party chairmanship for disastrous mayoral candidacies, one as a third-party candidate and the other as the Republican nominee, when Chicago politics began to hinge rather importantly on black-white racial issues in the mid-1980s.

Populist "Walkin' Dan" Walker as a Chicago attorney authored the national report that depicted the 1968 convention fiasco as a police riot. Daley's lasting enmity helped Walker win the governor's office in 1972 after defeating the mayor's handpicked candidate in the Democratic primary. "Big Jim" Thompson, another six-and-a-half-footer, was the federal prosecutor who put some of Daley's closest protégés in jail in the early 1970s, and went on to become Illinois' longest-serving governor.

Lifetime jobs: A handful of governors and US senators from Chicago managed to gain fame – and sometimes infamy – in the shadow of the mayor's office. Otto Kerner, a son-in-law to the late Mayor Anton Cermak, was a popular governor later convicted of corruption by Thompson. Adlai Stevenson II was an ex-governor who lost two successive presidential elections as the Democratic nominee, despite Daley's support. When Daley viewed Stevenson's son and namesake as a potential rival, he helped get Adlai III elected to the US Senate and safely out of town, 700 miles away in Washington, DC.

The mayoralty is viewed by most Chicago politicos as second only to the presidency. But just one Chicagoan – Edward Dunne, elected governor in 1912 – has risen to higher office. While many, particularly the city's early mayors, might have seen City Hall as a beginner's step to the White House, the fifth-floor office has now come to be viewed as a "career cul-de-sac."

Besides, the job carries a relatively low life expectancy: four of Chicago's 41 mayors have died in office, two by assassination. Carter Harrison I, widely viewed as the city's first modern professional politician-mayor, was slain at his home by a disgruntled patronage job seeker. Cermak was in his first term in 1933 when he was felled by a bullet intended for President-elect Franklin Roosevelt. Daley died in 1976 after he was stricken by a heart attack, the same fate that befell Harold Washington, Chicago's first black mayor, in 1987 as he was just beginning a second term.

Jesse's push: Without question the city's most famous non-elected politician has been Jesse Louis Jackson, unsuccessful but highly visible in his campaigns for the Democratic presidential nomination. The peripatetic civil rights activist played an integral role in the establishment of the political dynamics presently at work in Chicago.

Jackson marched with Martin Luther King Jr through Chicago's segregated white neighborhoods in the mid-1960s, and was a prominent minority voice in denouncing Daley's infamous "Shoot to kill" order in the wake of rioting touched off by King's 1968 assassination. In the 1970s and '80s, Jackson used his South Side operation PUSH (People United to Save Humanity) as a revival meeting-cum-political rally venue to mobilize black voters outside the Democratic Machine. He directed voter registration drives and boycotts that helped build a monolithic black electoral movement, supporting Washington and other black candidates – including Jesse Jackson.

Anathema to the white Democratic Party establishment in Illinois and distrusted by black Machine regulars, not to mention some of his own allies in the independent movement, for his "me-first style," Jackson packed up his aspirations for national office and Rainbow Coalition operations in 1989, after 25 years in Chicago, and moved to Washington, DC.

A split city: What Jackson left behind is an overwhelmingly Democratic city; in 1989, for example, the Republican mayoral candidate, "Fast Eddie" Vrdolyak, was slowed to a crawl with barely 3 percent of the vote. But Chicago also remains a city in which the Democratic Party continues to be fractured by race.

White ethnic and black Democrats typically offset each other – there are 19 predominately white wards on the Northwest and Southwest sides and 19 predominantly black wards on the South and West sides. Sometimes, close elections are swung by "lakefront liberals," a nettlesome but inconsequential group during the late Mayor Daley's mayoralty, and Hispanics, the city's fastest growing minority.

Since 1837, when William Butler Ogden became the city's first mayor, the key to winning elections in Chicago has been knitting together a majority coalition from an ethnically diverse populace. For a time in Chicago, Republicans were about as good at it as Democrats.

But the Republican Party lost its domination of the City Council in 1931 when Anton Cermak, a businesslike professional politician, defeated "Big Bill" Thompson, the party's last mayor. Cermak melded, for the first time, white ethnic immigrants and black voters who had previously been Republicans – Lincoln's party. And of no little significance was the fact that the Czech-born Cermak put an end to Irish domination of the Democratic Party melting pot.

Bridgeport bossism: With his untimely death, however, Cermak's new version of the Machine fell into the hands of Irish politicians yet again, specifically those from influential Bridgeport. Born and reared in this Back of the Yards enclave of packing houses, saloons, shops and bungalows were the next four mayors: Edward Kelly, Martin Kennelly, Richard Daley and Michael A. Bilandic. In succession, they occupied the mayor's office from 1933 until 1979.

Jane Byrne's upset of the taciturn and unlucky Bilandic did not end Machine domination or accelerate its demise. The coughing and sputtering, however, had started

Left, thumbs up from Jesse Jackson, 1984. **Right**, the Chicago 7, plus Jerry Rubin's girlfriend.

even before Daley's death. The real end of the old Machine came four years later when Byrne and young Richard M. Daley split the white vote, allowing Harold Washington to win the Democratic nomination.

Washington's winning coalition was built on a strong black turnout and a sufficient showing among Hispanics and the lakefront's "limousine liberals" to capture 52 percent of the vote.

Given Harold Washington's enormous popularity in the community, no black politician, either independent or erstwhile Machine loyalist, dared oppose him. His returns were essentially the same in 1987 in a primary rematch with Byrne.

Daley *redux*: Seven months after his re-election, however, the Mayor's office claimed another victim, and Washington was dead. The city reverberated with shock, and the prospect of a bitter succession battle. Washington's base was split and it was the black political community's turn for a double-barreled shot at the mayoralty in a special 1989 election.

The soft-spoken Eugene Sawyer, Washington's immediate successor and a man who had risen through the Machine ranks, was defeated by Richard the Second in the Democratic primary. Legions of discontented blacks boycotted Sawyer's candidacy, despite the support of Jesse Jackson. Timothy Evans, who had been Washington's floor leader in the City Council, challenged Daley in the general election with a third-party candidacy. With a $7 million campaign treasury and the swing vote solidly in his column, Daley prevailed.

By every indication, however, the city's demographics may be shifting too rapidly – more blacks, and especially more Hispanics – for Mayor Daley to match his father's two decades in office. However, Daley began his tenure by shunning the trappings of bossism that his father took on so eagerly. He won high marks for fairness, and quickly consolidated Hispanic and liberal support beyond that which Washington enjoyed. As a result, Daley, by then known to Chicagoans simply as "Richie," was re-elected in early 1991.

The question that remains blowing in the wind is whether Chicago can approach the year 2000 without the political bluster that has made its reputation for the past century.

Left, heir and mayor apparent, Richard M. Daley, 1990. Right, Mirage Tavern, site of the *Sun-Times* sting, 1977.

Schooled In Scandal

"I too wish to defend my city from people who keep saying it is crooked," author Nelson Algren once wrote. "In what other city can you be so sure a judge will keep his word for $500?"

Scandal is a fact of life in Chicago. Politics, Chicago's favorite pastime, has bred a local strain of unscrupulousness, born of audacity and disrespect for both the public and public office. At the same time, Chicago has a bumptious journalistic community with a long tradition of irreverence toward authority in general and politicians in particular. The result is both more wrongdoing, and more reporting of that wrongdoing, than perhaps anywhere else.

Any "greatest hits" of Chicago scandals and "stings" must include Operation Greylord, the Federal Bureau of Investigation probe into court corruption. Between 1979 and 1983, FBI agents masquerading as defendants, lawyers, prosecutors and even a judge uncovered widespread bribery, extortion and fraud in the courts. The sting led to the convictions of 14 judges and 75 prominent attorneys and court staffers.

The FBI then looked at influence over judges by downtown politicians with ties to organized crime. Operation Koffee Klatsch exploded in late 1989 after federal agents planted electronics bugs and hidden cameras in Counsellor's Row, a popular restaurant across from City Hall.

Corruption is hardly a new phenomenon in Chicago, of course. In the late 1880s, aldermen "Bathhouse" John Coughlin and Michael "Hinky Dink" Kenna offered protection from police interference to vice dealers in exchange for votes. One historian claims that during the 1890s, at least 56 of the 68 aldermen accepted bribes for their votes.

The era of the modern Chicago scandal was probably ushered in by the 1960 Sommerdale Police Scandal, when an arrested thief (the "Babbling Burglar") revealed he was in league with the police in the city's Sommerdale district. Eight policemen were arrested, and the scandal rattled the Democratic political machine.

Political scandal doesn't stop at the city limits, either. A favorite local yarn concerns the 1970 Paul Powell shoebox scandal. A plain cardboard shoebox containing about $800,000 in unaccounted-for cash was found in the hotel-room closet of recently-deceased Democratic secretary of state, Paul Powell.

The cash apparently represented part of the kickbacks Powell took from contractors working on state building projects. A church began annual services on the anniversary of Powell's death to recall the lack of honesty among officials. The collection was taken in shoeboxes.

In the 1977 Mirage Tavern sting, the *Chicago Sun-Times* set up a bar manned by undercover reporters. They discovered that for modest sums – $50, $100 or $200 – building, plumbing, electrical, food, liquor and fire inspectors would overlook violations such as exposed wiring and maggot-infested food. The reporters were able to bribe all but one of the official inspectors they met. Two weeks after the story broke, the same inspectors were again seeking bribes – except that they had raised their prices. Eventually, one-third of all the city's electrical inspectors were convicted.

In 1985, Operation Incubator stung the administration of the late Mayor Harold Washington. An undercover FBI "mole," himself a convicted felon, posed as a representative of a company seeking city contracts. The mole reportedly bribed several city officials, including the city's former deputy revenue director. Several officials and aldermen were convicted, and the public was widely entertained by televised videotapes of one former mayoral aide dickering over the exact amount of his bribe.

A commercial scandal hit the hallowed halls of the Chicago Board of Trade and the Chicago Mercantile Exchange in 1988. Federal undercover agents, wired for sound, went into the trading pits and returned with evidence of fraud: floor traders were trading for themselves at more favorable prices than they traded for their customers. Several traders in each pit admitted guilt and cooperated with the investigation, which focused on the trading of Swiss francs, Japanese yen, treasury bonds and soybeans.

51

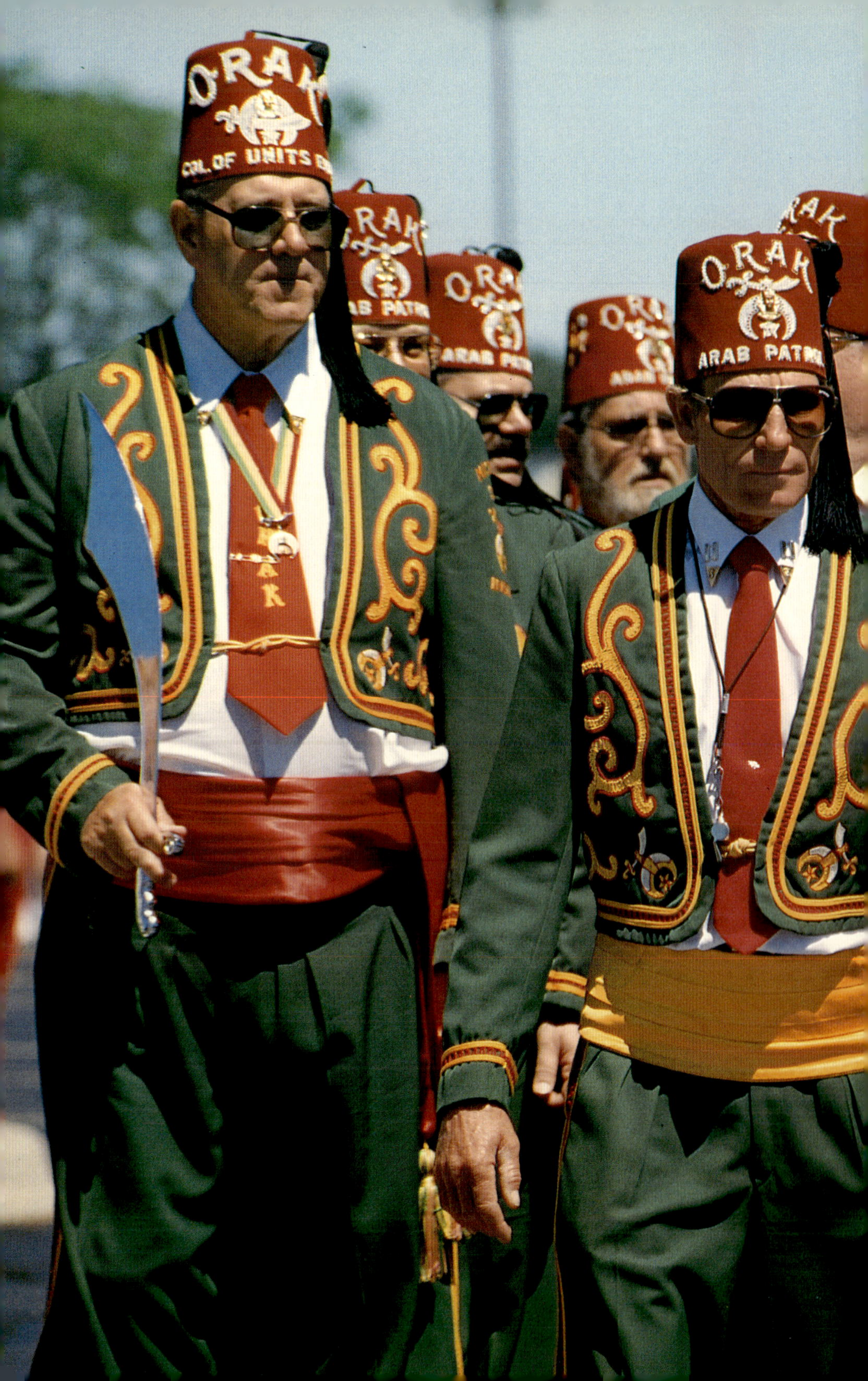
ORAK
COL. OF UNITS

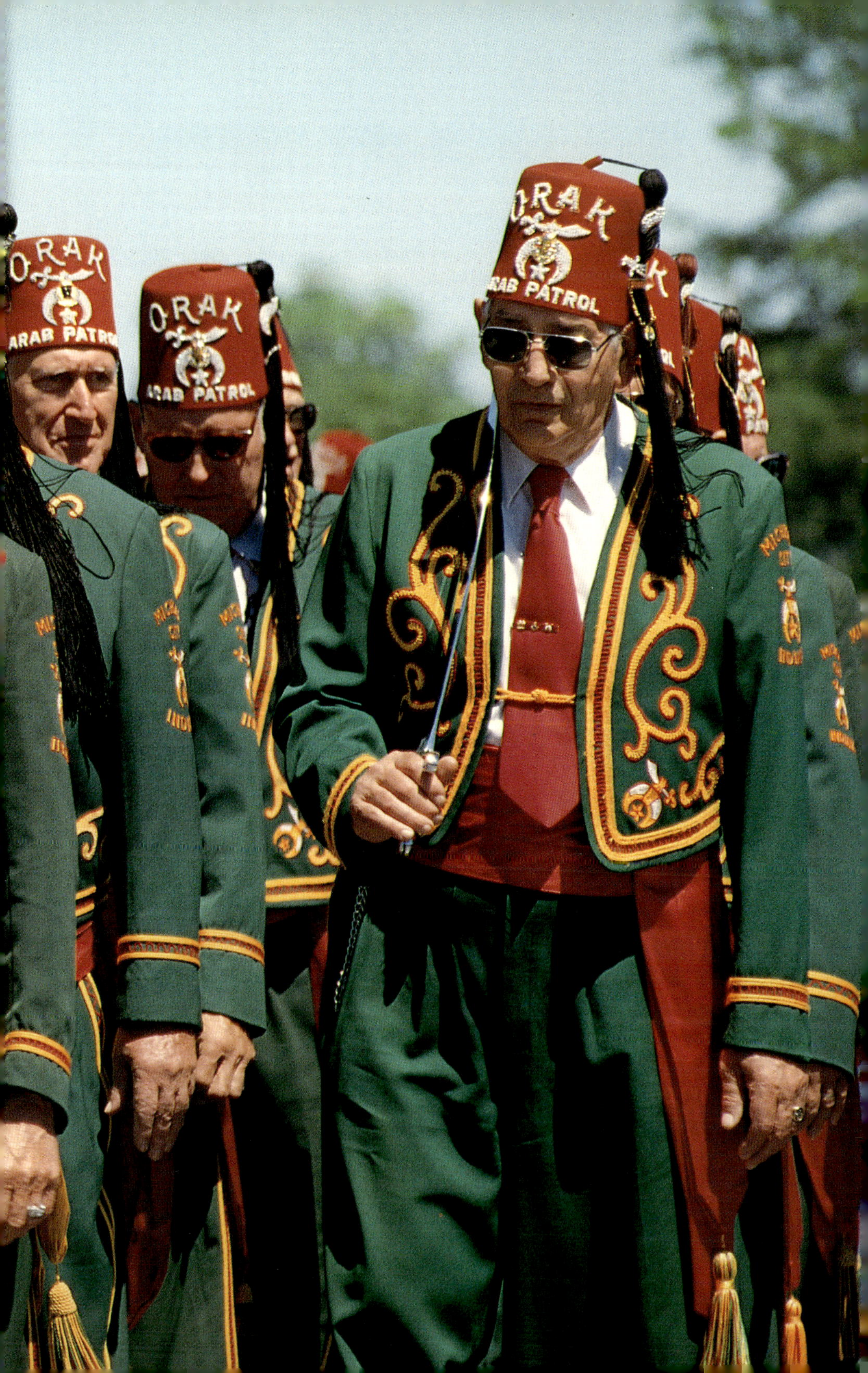
ORAK
ARAB PATROL

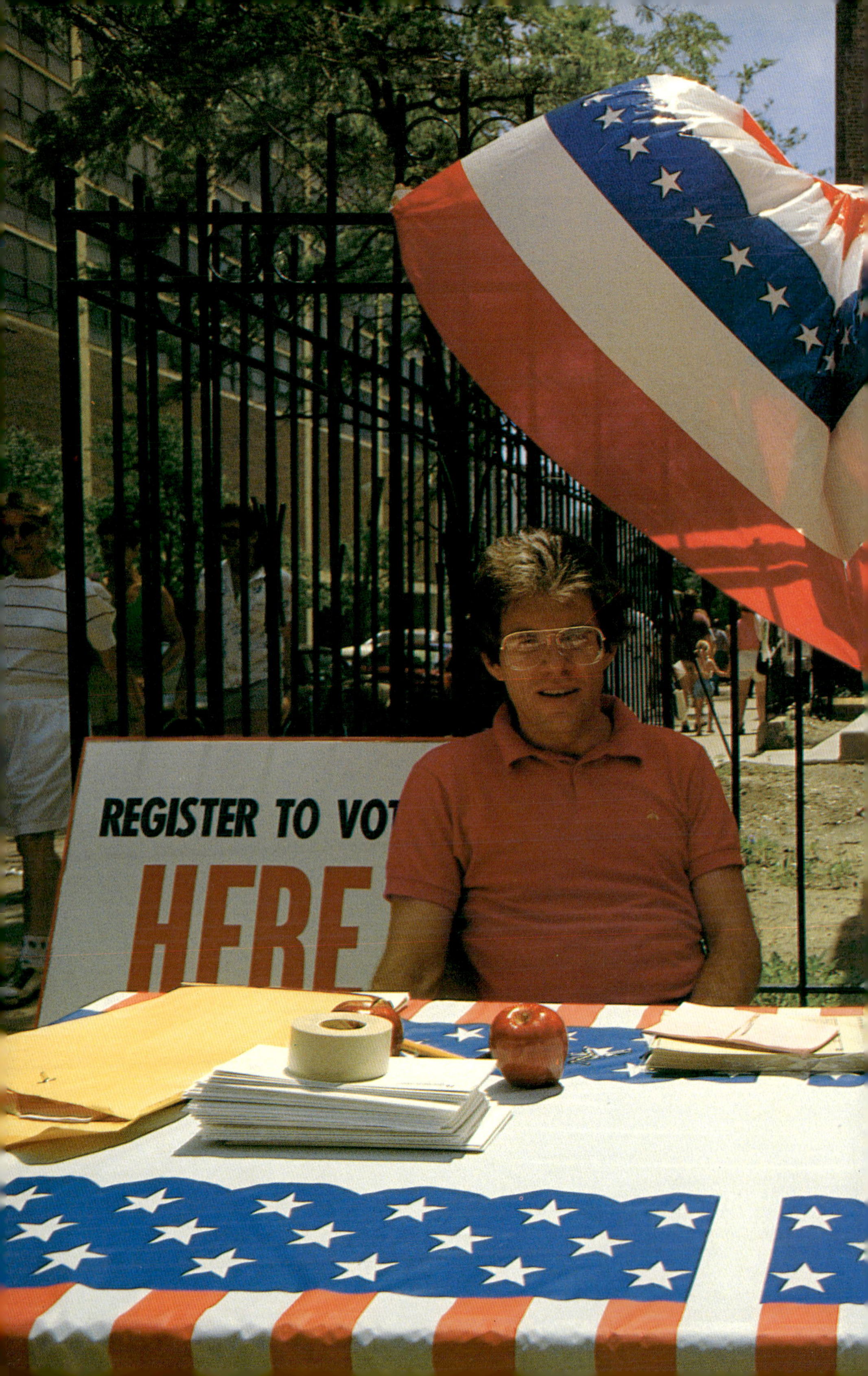
REGISTER TO VOT
HERE

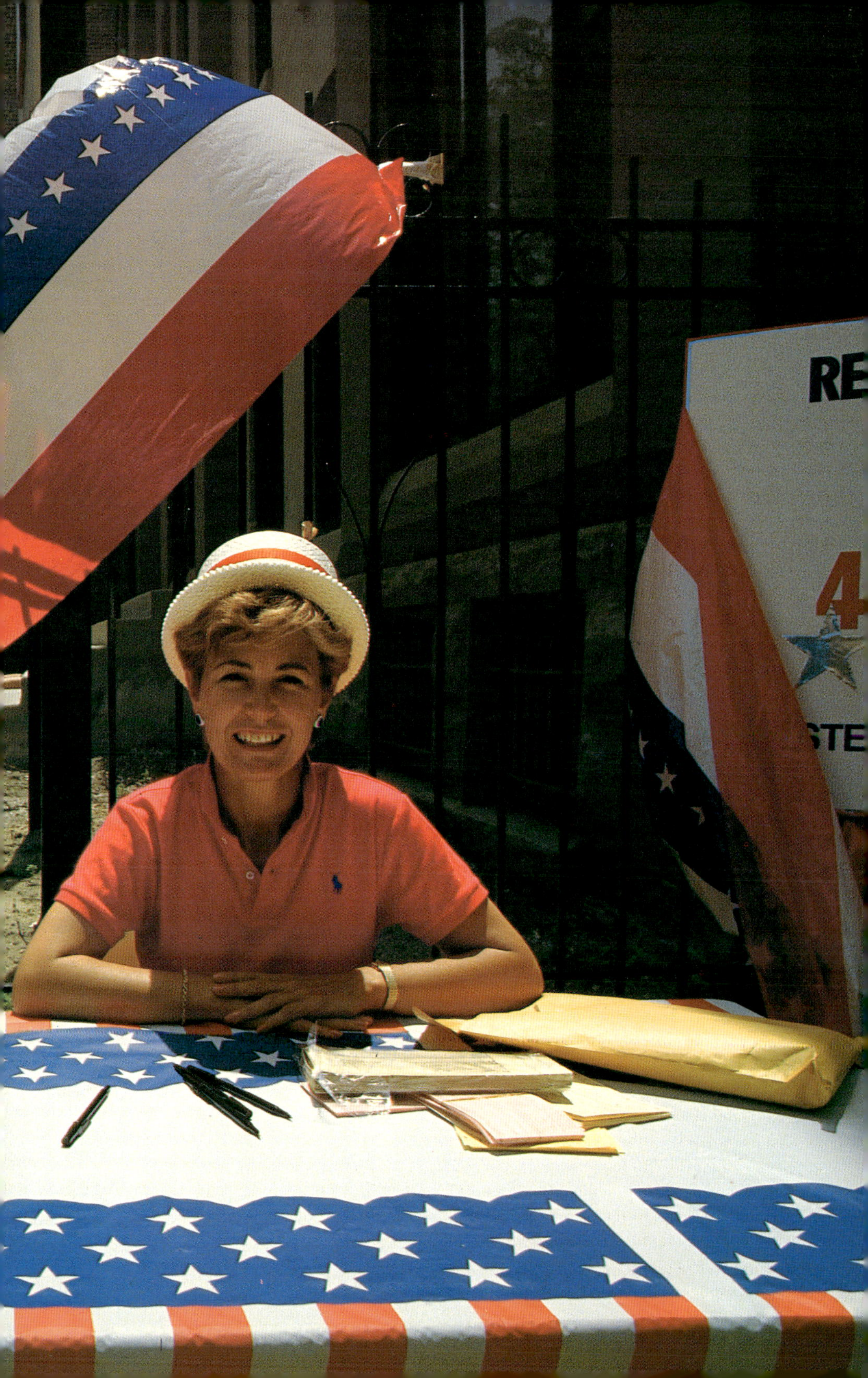
RE
4
STE

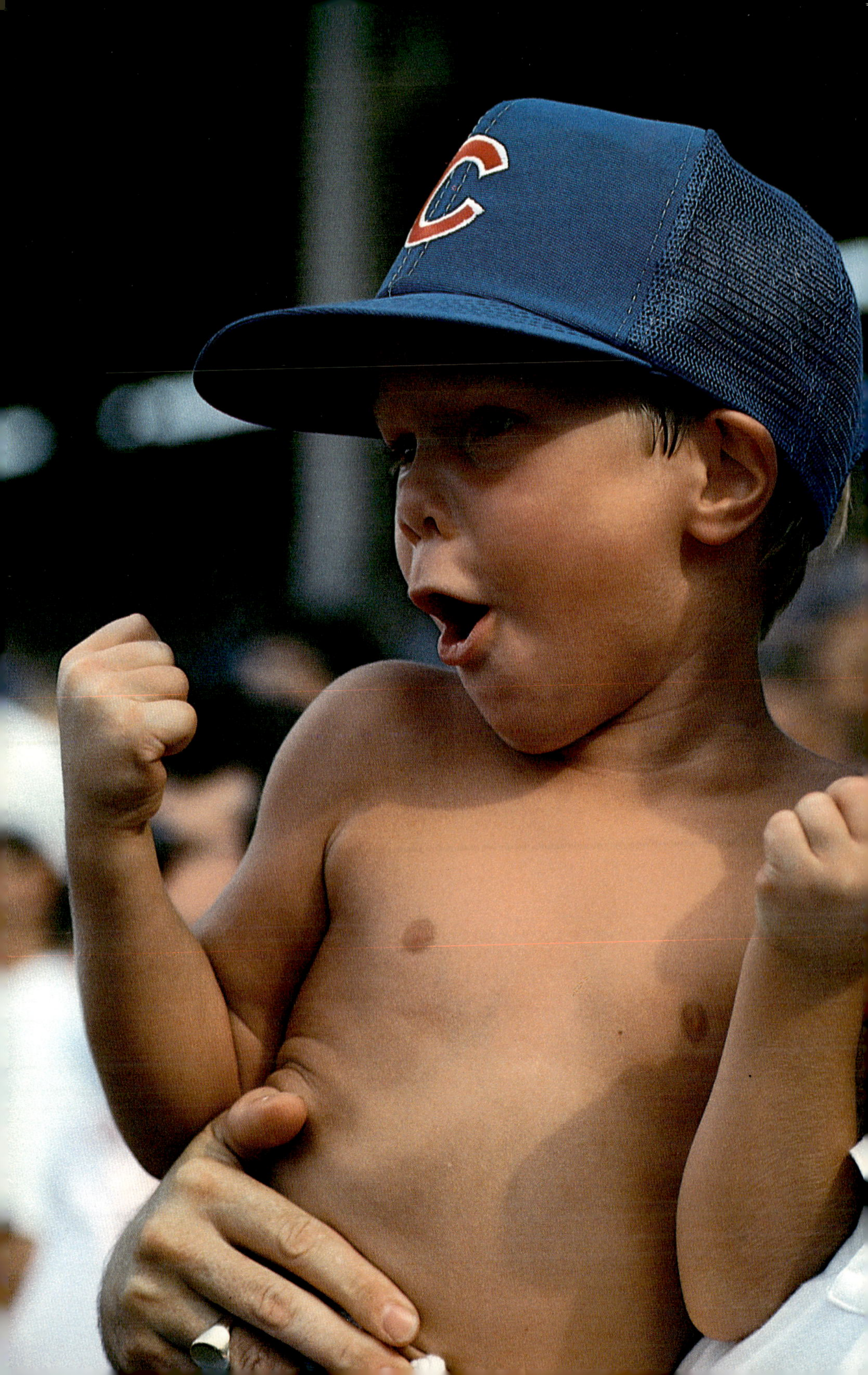

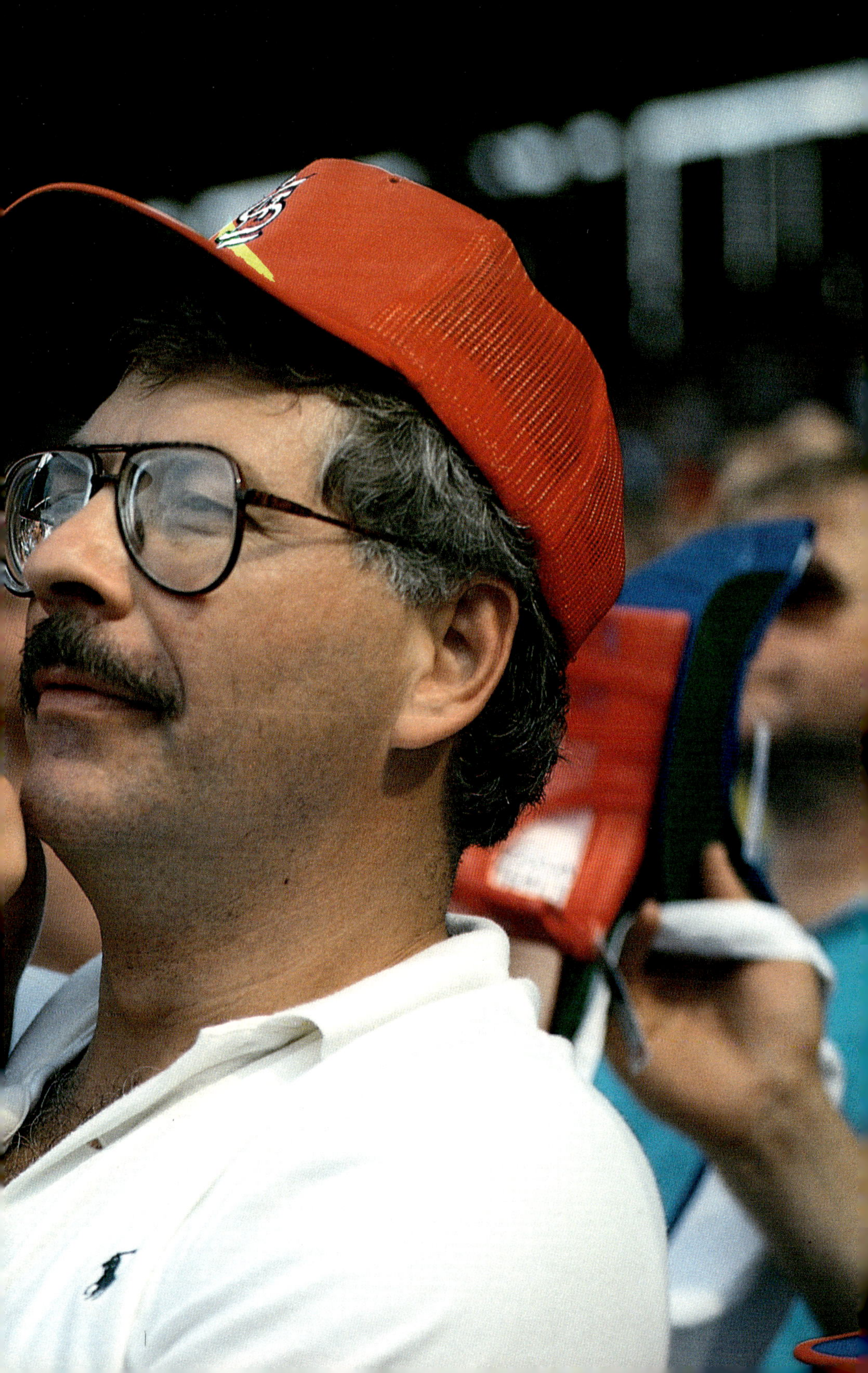

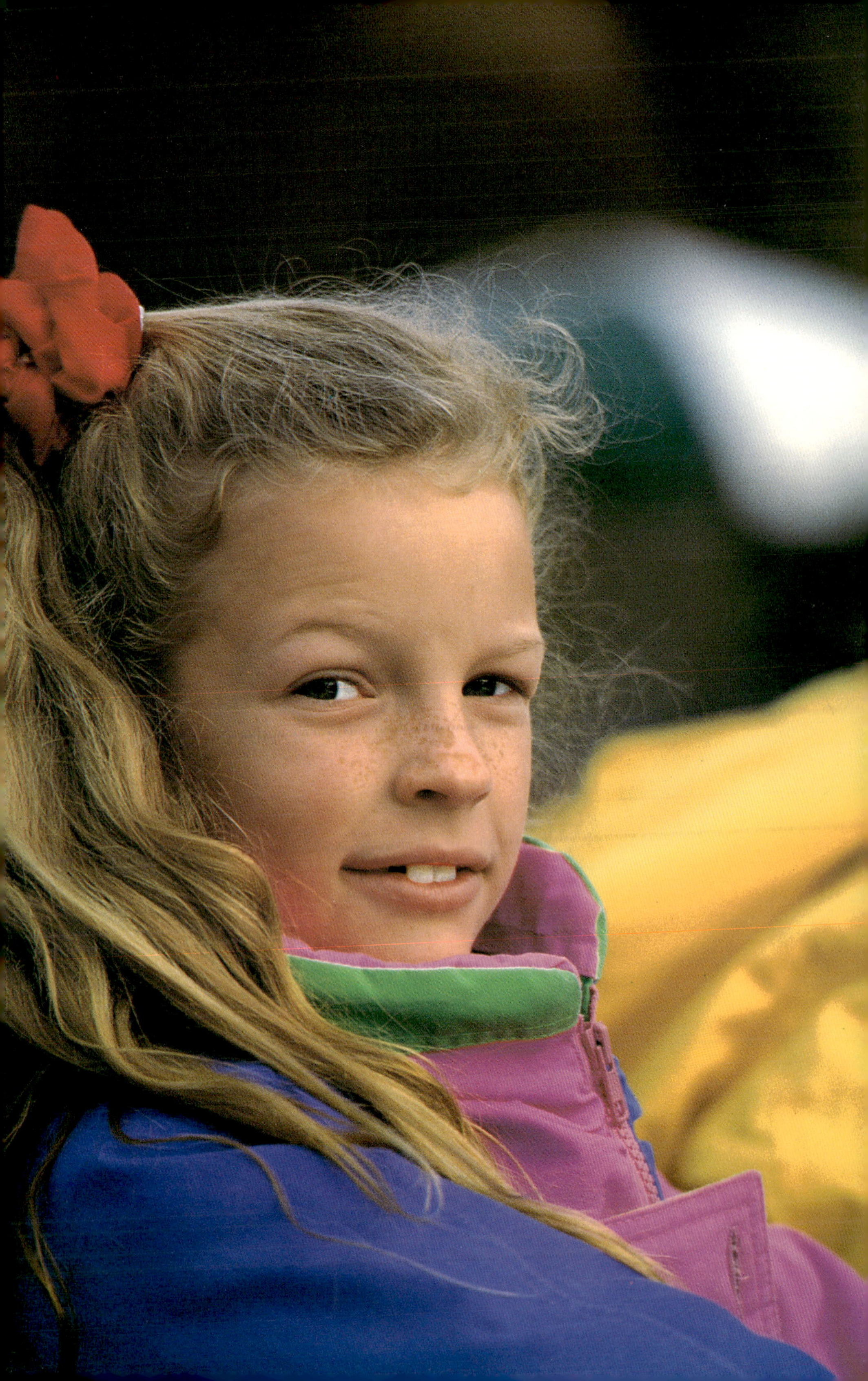

A Hustlin' Town

Chicago was once expected to become the greatest city in America, and hence in the world. It never happened. But for a time it must have seemed a near thing.

Commerce was thriving. Millionaires – in the days before tax write-offs – unbuttoned their pocketbooks for civic halls, museums and monuments of great splendor. Skyscrapers, the first the world had known, pierced the low-lying prairie clouds. Visionary architects such as Louis Sullivan and Frank Lloyd Wright constructed elaborate buildings. H.L. Mencken said that everything interesting in American writing seemed to be coming out of Chicago. With its wonderful central location – in the heart of the Heartland – Chicago seemed certain to grow, to gain, to flourish.

What went wrong? Different people, historians among them, give different reasons: that Chicago lost its hopes of pre-eminence when its businessmen refused to bestir themselves to wrest the automobile industry from Detroit; that air travel deflated the city's aspirations, because with the advent of commercial flights people no longer needed to stop in Chicago en route coast to coast; that the opening of the St Lawrence Seaway, which was supposed to make Chicago a great international port, turned out a failure; that Chicago never really recovered from the Depression, or made up for the loss of the stockyards, or was able to live down its reputation as a crime-syndicate town – and so on and so forth.

Faded rivalry: Other people, other opinions; other historians, other causes. Whatever the opinions, whichever the causes, no one really feels any longer that Chicago is the country's greatest city. Yet the epithet "second city" no longer seems quite accurate. In Chicago nowadays, people feel no more intense a distaste for New Yorkers than the majority of their countrymen outside

New York appear to feel. The old inter-city, one-on-one rivalry between Chicago and New York, which Chicagoans always felt more vividly than New Yorkers, seems to have all but disappeared.

Ah, New York, New York – if you can make it there, the song goes, you can make it anywhere. Of Chicago, the exact reverse used to be said: If you can't make it here, you can't make it anywhere. The sentiment was meant to stand as a tribute to the wide vocational opportunities Chicago then provided. It was probably never very true – to those who work without family money or other nets to catch them, every big city presents the possibility of a dangerous fall – and it may be even less true now. For many who choose to live in Chicago, one of the city's special delights is precisely that it is *not* New York. Judged by its vibrancy, tumult, concentration of talent and sheer excitement, New York is far and away America's greatest city – in fact, the country's only world city. Yet Chicago, for reasons that visitors often find difficult to grasp, nonetheless remains, for

Preceding pages: marching Shriners; voter registration; a chip off the old block. **Left**, fair and freckled. **Right**, a sweet Chicago smile.

Chicago Culture 59

many of those who have lived in it, America's best city.

The city is at its worst, however, when it sets out to imitate New York. It cannot be done, and it is a grave, when not altogether comic, mistake to even try. From "haute cuisine" restaurants to high society social events, pretensions somehow do not work in this town, though that doesn't stop people from trying.

A hustlin' town: Among modern writers, Nelson Algren probably has impressed on the national consciousness the strongest notion of what Chicago is. For Algren, Chicago was above all a hustler's town. "Right from go it was a broker's town and the brokers run it yet," he wrote in a lengthy 1951 prose-poem entitled *Chicago: City on the Make*. Much of the poetry in his prose-poem is of a hopeless sort, yet every once in a while Algren hits a note that resounds with true feeling, as when he remarks that loving Chicago is "like loving a woman with a broken nose, you may well find lovelier lovelies. But never a lovely so real."

To end the litany of clichés about Chicago, one can scarcely do better than consult a volume entitled *Chicago* by Studs Terkel. Self-advertised man of the people, Terkel, with his Uher tape recorder, has become Chicago's recording angel, and hence himself something of a cliché. Slim though Terkel's *Chicago* is, thick and fast fly the clichés that make up its substance. From the Pottawattomies to the Haymarket Riot to the bag lady in Uptown, the history of Chicago, in Terkel's view, is that of big guys screwing little guys, with occasional heroes such as Saul Alinsky popping in for cameo appearances; with plenty of villains such as the general run of businessmen, politicians and, currently, the prosperous young; and with just enough room for a feisty little guy with a cigar and a tape recorder to make a nice living. But then Chicago has always been a hustler's town.

By now, surely America's major-league hustlers must be elsewhere; taking important meetings in Los Angeles, doing power lunches in New York, cutting serious deals in Washington. The notion of Chicago as a powerful organized-crime town no longer seems quite convincing, either. Even in the post-Capone 1940s, the so-called Syndicate was still the behind-the-scenes explanation for everything that went on in the city; it was said to have taken its tribute for every jukebox, case of soda pop, carton of cigarettes and, if rumor were to be believed, nearly every other thing bought and sold in the city.

The Boys themselves were fierce characters, with nicknames (always printed in the press within quotation marks) like "Teets," or "The Camel" or "Big Tuna." Now they mostly seem to be either dead or old bulls gone weak in the knees. Their successors, though doubtless quite as vicious, are younger men with pot bellies and ambitious hairdos who live with their families in gaudily decorated ranch houses in the western suburbs. Chicago no longer seems the mainline crime-boss town it once was.

Perverse pride: Chicagoans generally have taken an old pride in their city's corruption. Not so long ago, when one needed special consideration of one kind or another, somebody always knew somebody who knew somebody else who could fix it, from a broken curb to a black-market baby adoption. In those days, the phrase "everything's on the up and up" was pressed into frequent service, probably because it was difficult to believe many things actually were on the up and up.

The suspicion that things aren't what they seem – aren't quite "on the up and up" – has long seemed one of the qualities that mark people raised in Chicago. In its gentler, and hence more pleasing aspect, it comes across as a humorous dubiety. It also qualifies as part of what is known as the big-city view. In Chicago it doesn't have the hard edge of nastiness that it can take on in New York. This is the Chicago skepticism that takes little or nothing at face value, that gets nervous when a "yes" answer comes a little too quickly, and that checks to see if the wallet is still in place after all large public functions at which a clergyman has been asked to give a benediction.

Chicagoans seem notable among Americans for being deeply suspicious of the next fellow's motives and then being delighted at having these suspicions confirmed. This applies particularly to public life. A large public scandal in Chicago seems to get the salivary glands working like nothing else. The minicams come roaring out onto the streets like fire engines. The editorialists work themselves up into high moral dudgeon. And almost none of it really matters. Black or white, a Chicago politician remains a Chicago politician; and Chicago remains a city that stands in refutation of Lord Acton's maxim by demonstrating, again and again, that only a small amount of power can corrupt absolutely.

Lake tastes: Lake Michigan is the only interesting natural feature in the city, and the Chicago writer Isaac Rosenfeld used to refer to "the lake culture," by which he meant chiefly Hyde Park and the Near North Side with, despite the many differences between the two neighborhoods, their common interest in art, liberal politics and what their denizens take to be good taste. A lake culture persists, although now somewhat shriveled in Hyde Park and somewhat expanded beyond Lincoln Park. Life in Chicago, to adapt the local weatherman's phrase, is somewhat cooler near the lake. Yet the lake culture, though Chicago would be a barbarous place without it, is far from characteristic of the entire city.

Of course it is always the lake that people from out of town see and remember and

<u>Left</u>, a day out in the park. <u>Right</u>, a sidewalk philosopher.

remark upon. And why not? If they come to Chicago "holding," to use the old race track term to describe horse players who had money in their pockets, they might stay at the Drake Hotel, shop amid the glitz of Water Tower Place, dine at some slow-food joint such as the Everest Room, listen to a sumptuous opera at the Lyric, watch Sir Georg Solti do his snug little Central European bow at Orchestra Hall. All of which is fine, splendid even. "Enjoy," as the waitresses love to say at the many Italian restaurants around 26th and Oakley.

Between the Campbell Soup factory and the Fine Arts Building, the Black P-Stone Nation gang and the plummy announcers for WFMT, Chicago provides plenty in the way of extremes. Yet representative Chicago is not found in the extremes between the proud and the profane. It is less likely to be found in a four-bedroom, five-bath condominium in the John Hancock Center than in Jefferson Park (with bachelor Uncle Sven installed in the basement apartment), not in the lockup at 26th and California but on bingo night at Saint Dominic's Parish.

Chicago's solidity may derive from its flatness, an unrelieved stretch of prairie now covered principally by apartments and bungalows, squat factory buildings and shops, and punctuated only by the occasional grandeur of a Catholic church built decades ago. True, there is a magnificent skyline with, to quote Louis Sullivan, its "proud and soaring" qualities, but one generally doesn't live in a skyline.

A city divided: The neighborhood has always been and remains Chicago's chief unit of social organization. Not many people really grew up in Chicago at all; instead they grew up in Austin, or South Shore, or Englewood or Albany Park or Ravenswood or Pullman or Gage Park. To this day there are North Siders who have never been south of the Museum of Science and Industry, and South Siders who have never been north of the Lincoln Park Zoo, and who are perfectly content to be so circumscribed in their local peregrinations.

Growing up in a Chicago neighborhood, the chances are great that one grew up among one's own, among one's fellow Swedes or Poles or Irish or Germans or Jews or blacks or Chinese or Ukrainians or Greeks or (more recently) Koreans or East Indians. As social units go, the neighborhood is long on familiarity and (in most instances) security. It is not strong on imagination; that is to say, growing up in a Chicago neighborhood, it is a bit difficult to imagine life outside the neighborhood. The reigning spirit of the neighborhood is conservative and traditional. Yet it is Chicago's organization around its neighborhoods that gave (and for the most part still gives) the city its feeling of solidity, solidity of a kind not so available elsewhere in the country.

As for physical solidity, Chicagoans, as a general type, tend to be beefier than people in New York (where anxiety peels away pounds) or San Francisco (where elegance is obligatory). Perhaps this is due to the peasant origins of so many of Chicago's early immigrants from Europe. Perhaps it is due to the Chicago diet, which tends to feature such fine and life-threatening items as pizza, ribs and every permutation played on beef. (Much fuss is made over hot dogs in Chicago, but the great, the archetypal Chicago sandwich is the Italian beef and sausage combo. There is no way to eat it without being reminded of one's prehistoric origins; upon finishing it one can almost hear the arteries leading to one's heart creaking to a close; and, unless one's taste buds have been ruined by the food served in spurious French restaurants, it happens to be delicious.)

Somehow, to be overweight – or even homely – in Chicago doesn't seem to be such a bad thing. In New York, if you are homely you had better be smart; in Los Angeles, the capital of cosmetic surgery, homeliness means unhappiness. But in Chicago it's all right to be the way you are.

A city that conveys so emphatic a feeling of solidity tends to induce in its citizens an habitual squinty-eyed realism. Gabble about the rich ethnic diversity of Chicago, for example, is all right coming from politicians, whom no one takes seriously anyhow, but anyone who has grown up in Chicago knows that the Italians don't trust the Jews, who don't think much of the Germans, who tend to be contemptuous of the Irish, who don't care much for the Poles, who could live nicely without the Greeks, who feel the East Indians are a pain, and who themselves wish the city's Spanish-speaking population

Left, slices for four, please. **Right**, campus cheer.

would get their damn kids under some kind of control. Ethnic diversity doesn't get much richer than that.

Still toddlin': The wonder of Chicago is that, despite its endemic corruption, its historic group animosities, its horrifying crime, the city keeps chugging along. Major hospitals and numerous schools and universities dot the cityscape. The Chicago Symphony, the Art Institute and the University of Chicago remain internationally renowned; the Lyric Opera is rapidly entering world-class, if it is not there already. On the debit side, the city is today without a great locally owned department store. Northwestern University has never lived up to its potential to be one of America's elite academic institutions. The Chicago Public Library had been allowed to fall into disarray (although a new main library has now opened), which did not say much for the city's interest in any culture that was lacking in opportunities for snobbish and glitzy display.

The variety of activity in the city remains impressive. It is comforting to think that while the ensemble called The Music of the Baroque gathers in one Chicago-area church for a concert, the members of the group known as Gamblers Anonymous gather in

Chicago Culture 63

another for a meeting. It is reassuring to know that one can eat reasonably and well at Stefani's on Fullerton, walk a few blocks east to an enormous used bookstore on Lincoln Avenue, then go off from there to a basketball game, or a blues bar or a production of a Greek play at the Court Theatre in Hyde Park.

Another wonder is Chicago talent, which keeps cropping up in odd and expected places. The Gilbert and Sullivan Society, for instance, performs elegant operettas in the battered auditorium of Saint Ignatius Church. Amid the ramshackle buildings of East Howard Street just off an alley, one comes upon a shop called Fritz Reuter and Sons, Master Violin Maker, Restorations and Appraisals. Or on 25th Avenue in Melrose Park, on a street doubtless zoned light industrial, a Chinese chef of unsurpassed quality named Ben Moy runs a restaurant frequented by many of the city's best-known artists and intellectuals. Such is Chicago – the figurative width of the place – that its wealth of cultural resources cannot be adequately covered by a single analysis or a single visit.

No surprises: There is a way that Chicagoans speak, and it has nothing to do with giving the letter "a" a harsh sound or reverting from time to time to "dems" and "doses" in the manner of the late Mayor Daley. This way of speaking, this characteristic Chicago voice, combines cynicism with love of life, knowingness with occasional sentimentality. To those that speak it, nothing in the way of corruption comes as news: the language itself has already been "corrupted."

The Chicago voice is a big city voice, and the people who speak with it tend to be old shoe, which is to say familiar and comfortable, for they know that pretensions will take you just so far and that life is a struggle that everyone loses in the end, so you may as well relax and make the best of things. To a serious Chicagoan, life is inexhaustibly interesting, full of secret splendors and, when you come to consider the alternative, a damn fine thing. And Chicago is a good place to view life, a city where the sensible working assumption is that everyone and everything is a fake, except those people and things that one discovers are not, of which Chicago, being the kind of city that it is, has a great deal more than its share.

<u>**Left**</u>**, feathered friends.** <u>**Right**</u>**, Jane Addams, left, and fellow campaigner Mary McDowell, 1917.**

ROOTING OUT PROBLEMS

Despite its reputation as one of the most segregated cities in the United States, Chicago has a long tradition of grass roots movements strong enough to send ripples of liberalism through American society.

That Chicago should have such a tradition of liberal-minded social activism isn't really surprising. For one thing, the University of Chicago, founded in 1892, flourished from its inception as a center for urban sociology. Many of the most important studies of American urban life have come out of this university in Hyde Park. Its scholars historically have been aligned with social, labor and political reform movements.

Community action has been necessary in a city where politicians and employers have always had a vested interest in maintaining the status quo. This environment has encouraged both the rise of radical groups and a tradition of ground-level action aimed at improving social and labor conditions.

As far back as the 1880s, for instance, social worker Jane Addams thrust Chicago to the forefront of the Settlement House movement that sought to improve living conditions, community spirit, education and employment opportunities among immigrants and the urban poor. Addams' Hull House, which began in a mansion-turned-neighborhood center on South Halsted Street, included such features as a day nursery, adult education classes and even an employment bureau for the impoverished.

In contemporary Chicago, community organizer Saul Alinsky came to symbolize grass roots action. Alinsky, who hailed from the University of Chicago's sociology department and worked in the labor movement, helped establish several community organizations bent on social change through self-determination.

In his first effort, Alinsky helped found the Back of the Yards Council, a community group located in the area south of the old Union Stock Yard, where he saw a need for a local coalition to help unemployed workers fight for city services and tackle local crime. The council, now an institution in the neighborhood, still actively addresses public policy issues affecting Back of the Yards residents.

Alinsky is perhaps best known for his role, through his Industrial Areas Foundation, in founding The Woodlawn Organization (TWO), a community-based group organized in 1960 to empower the residents of the deteriorating Woodlawn community south of Hyde Park.

TWO became an important focal point for Chicago's civil rights movement. Its first efforts addressed education, beginning with pickets and leading to school boycotts that raised public awareness of the problems in ghetto schools. TWO also helped bring a branch of the City College into the community. The group battled slum landlords and white retailers who had been swindling their mostly black Woodlawn customers, and obtained federal funds to fight urban blight. While TWO has generally been a positive force in the community, its influence suffered from its dealings with street gangs. During the 1960s, for instance, the group was scandalized by reports that federal housing funds obtained by TWO had been funneled to a radical black street gang in exchange for protection from crime.

Nevertheless, Chicago's grass roots movement was important in the civil rights arena. When the Rev. Martin Luther King Jr expanded his crusade from the South to the northern US in the mid-1960s, he aligned his cause with the local Coordinating Council of Community Organizations (CCCO), a coalition already actively demonstrating against segregation.

In essence, King's Southern Christian Leadership Conference merged with the CCCO when, in 1966, King created the Chicago Freedom Movement with the aim of promoting improved housing, better education and more jobs. The Rev. Jesse Jackson was placed in charge of the movement's Operation Breadbasket, which boycotted stores and products in order to pressure employers to create jobs. From that base, Jackson went on to become one of America's most prominent and influential black political figures.

65

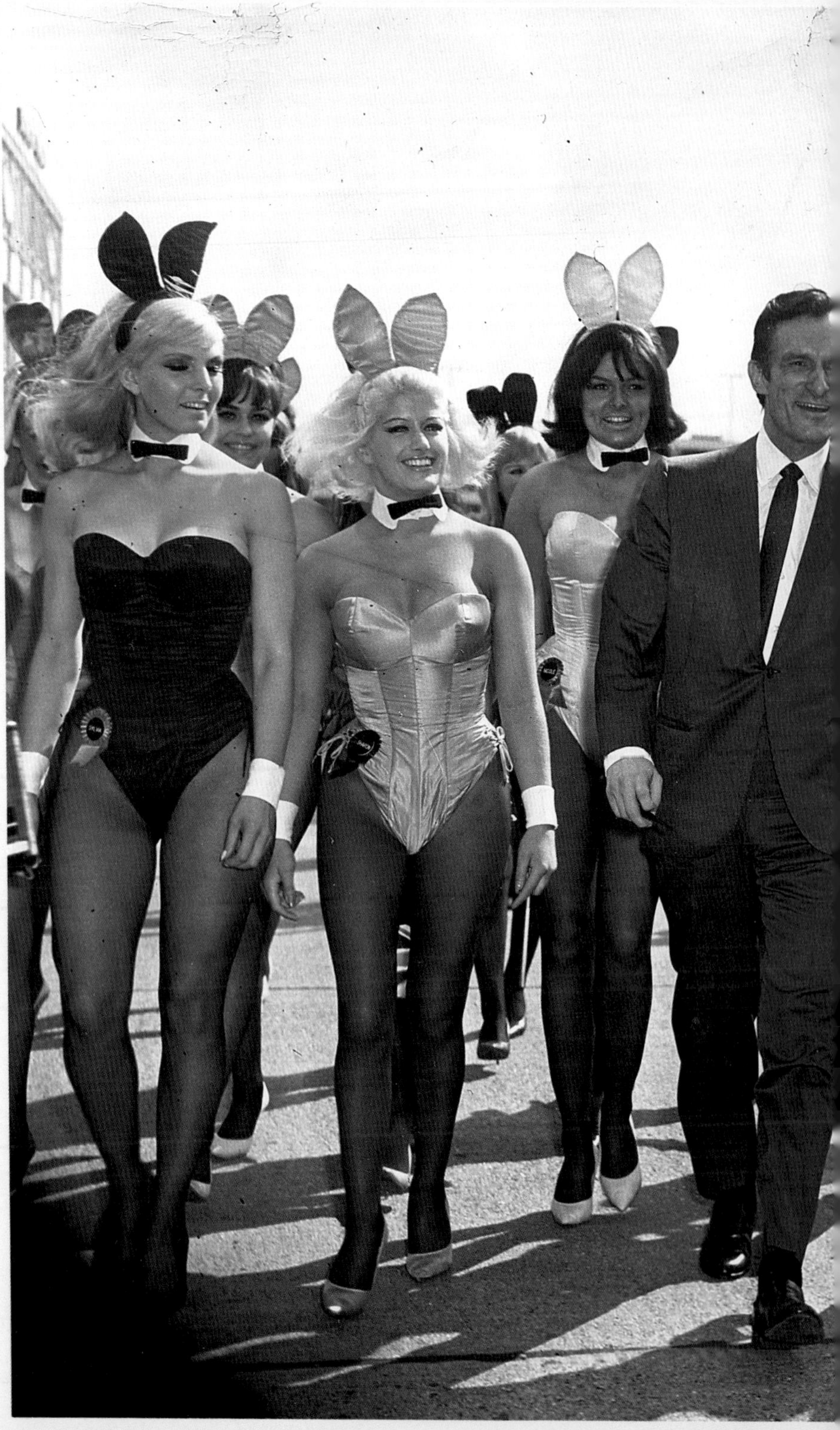

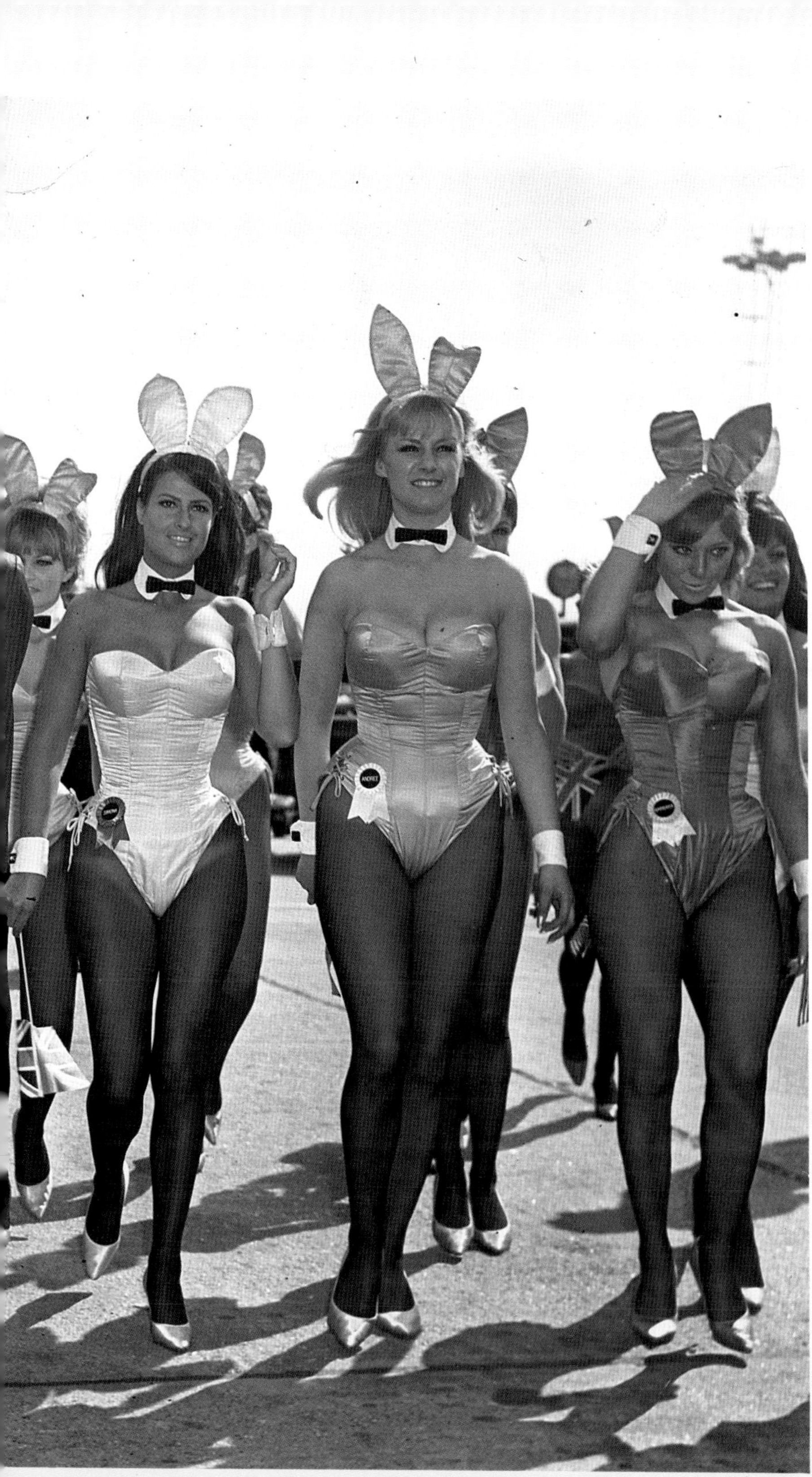

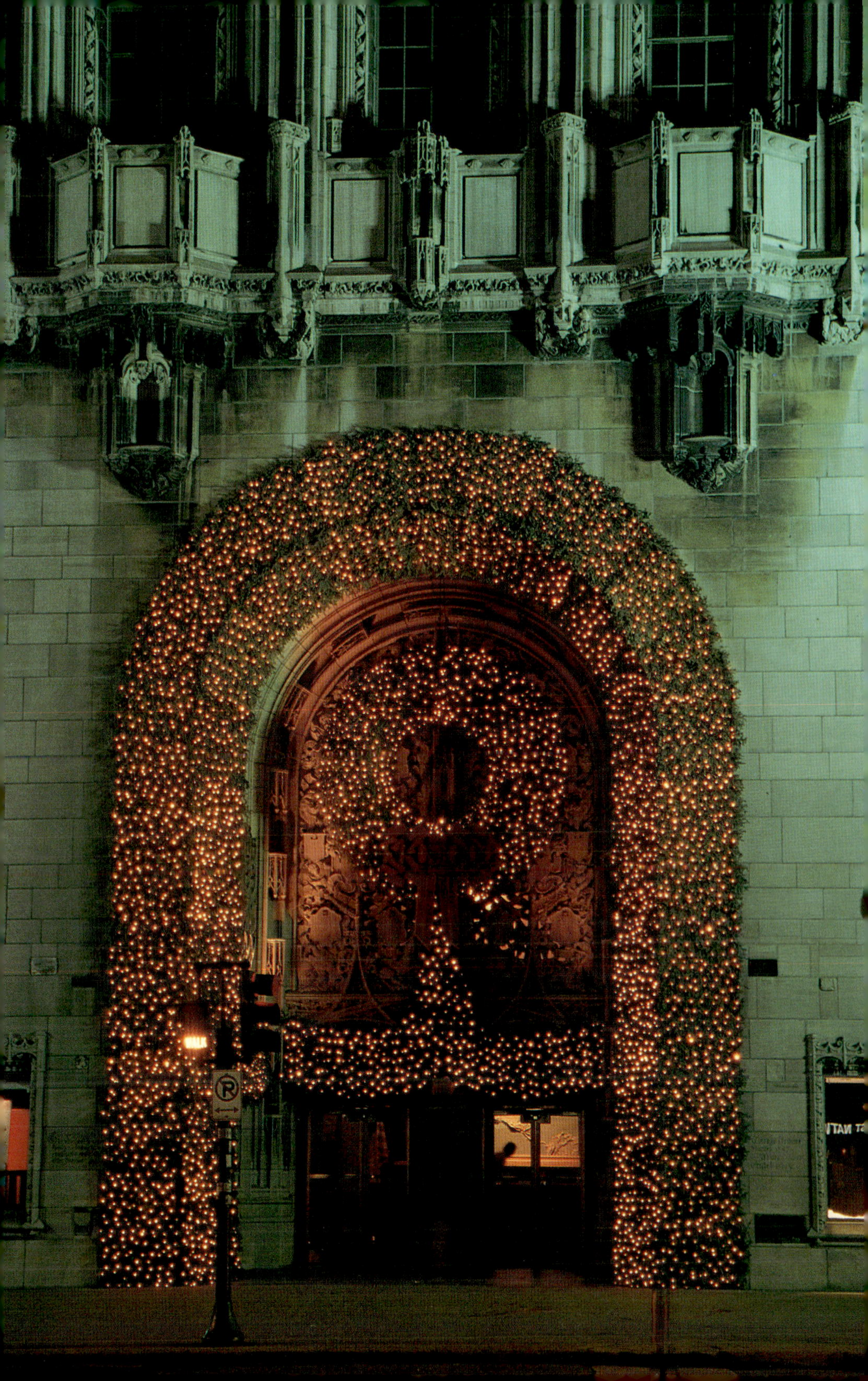

VOICES OF CHICAGO

Chicago's premier columnist is Mike Royko, who writes five times a week for the *Chicago Tribune*. He trades in small words, short sentences and acerbic wit. He talks tough and aims at fat targets. He is the man who gave the city its unofficial motto: "Where's mine?"

Royko is something of a civic treasure in Chicago, celebrated among newspaper readers for his uncommon wealth of common sense. Royko fans, especially wide-eyed young men from the suburbs, sometimes drop by his favorite tavern, the Billy Goat on Hubbard Street, just to watch him drink.

But for all his skill, Royko is something less than a complete original. To the contrary, he writes in a Chicago literary voice that has been evolving for some 100 years, a voice that can be traced directly to earlier notable Chicago newsmen and writers and the penny newspapers of the 1890s.

Touch of gold: Before Royko there was the writer Nelson Algren, best known for his novel *The Man With the Golden Arm*, for which he won the first National Book Award for fiction in 1950; the prose-poem *Chicago: City on the Make*; and an excellent collection of short stories, *The Neo Wilderness*. Algren's most famous words of advice easily could have been written by Royko: "Never play cards with a guy named Doc. Never eat at a place called Mom's. And never sleep with someone whose problems are greater than your own."

Before Algren there was that master of the short story, Ring Lardner, who developed his style as a Chicago sportswriter. Lardner, the model for Abe North in F. Scott Fitzgerald's *Tender is the Night*, is best remembered for his two collections of baseball stories, *You Know Me Al* and *Alibi Ike*.

And before Lardner there was the syndicated Chicago newspaper columnist Finley Peter Dunne, whose literary alter ego, Martin J. Dooley, an Irish immigrant saloonkeeper of droll wit, entertained readers across the nation. Dooley had a knack for slicing through pretense, much in the manner of Royko's own alter ego, Slats Grobnik. It was Dooley who first said, "Trust iv'rybody, but cut the cards."

Like Royko, these earlier Chicago writers wrote for regular Joes, with bluntness and humor, in the language of the common man. Lardner, in particular, is credited by H.L. Mencken with "reducing the American language to print." While East Coast writers in the years before World War I still adhered dutifully to every rule of proper syntax and grammar, Lardner was banging out dialogue such as: "I didn't used to eat no lunch in the playing season except when I knowed I was not going to work."

Vividness: From about 1890 to 1925, Chicago was a national hub of literary bustle, prompting critics to proclaim a "Chicago Renaissance." Mencken, writing in 1917, declared Chicago "the literary capital of the United States" and insisted that all the great

Preceding pages: Hugh Hefner and multiplying bunnies, 1966. **Left**, Tribune Tower entrance. **Right**, Mike Royko.

Personalities 69

American writers of his day had lived at least for a time in Chicago.

"Chicago has drawn them in from their remote wheat towns and far-flung railroad junctions, and it has given them an impulse that New York simply cannot match – an impulse toward independence, toward honesty, toward a peculiar vividness and naivete," he wrote. "New York, when it lures such a recruit eastward, makes a compliant conformist of him, and so ruins him out of hand. But Chicago, however short the time it has him, leaves him irrevocably his own man, with pride sufficient to carry through a decisive trail of his talents. Witness (Sherwood) Anderson, (Theodore) Dreiser, (Edgar Lee) Masters, (Carl) Sandburg and (George) Ade."

Some historians say Chicago's reputation as a writer's town is rooted in the newspaper circulation wars of a century ago, when the morning papers dropped their prices from two cents to a penny. With the price cut, newspapers found their way into the hands of more average Chicagoans than ever before.

Blooming times: Many of the major papers, such as the *Daily News* and the *Inter-Ocean*, attempted to cater to their expanded readership by adopting a more democratic editorial tone. Even the staid *Tribune* made adjustments, such as giving news coverage for the first time to the plebeian sport of boxing and coming out in favor of the shocking new fad of bloomers.

The papers courted journalists who could write in an entertaining and personal style, almost always employing elements of spoken American English. One such pioneer, Eugene Field, wrote both journalism and poetry in his "Sharps and Flats" column for the *Daily News*. He used contractions, slang and offensive words like "ain't" in his poetry. His most enduring works are his children's poems "Little Boy Blue" and "Wynken, Blinken and Nod."

George Ade was another pioneer. He came to Chicago from Indiana in 1890, got a job alongside Field at the *Daily News*, and within three years was a star columnist. In his own words, he showed a "criminal preference for the Midwest vernacular."

But Chicago newspapers did more for literature than play a role in getting plain speech down on paper. In an age before writers' conferences and creative writing fellowships, the papers offered aspiring writers a sort of hardball literary apprenticeship. Dreiser, Sandburg, Field, Edna Ferber and Ben Hecht were among those who put in time on Chicago newspapers, happy for the paycheck and camaraderie.

Until the day it folded in 1978, the *Daily News* remained Chicago's most literate newspaper, conscientiously nurturing such talents as Field, Ade, Sandburg, Hecht and Royko, even when it meant allowing them to freelance a bit on company time. Henry Justin Smith, editor of the *News* during the first third of the century, referred to his stable of writers as "budding Balzacs" and cut them a good deal of slack.

Sandburg covered the 1919 Chicago race riots for the *Daily News* and wrote a book about the tragedy. He later won three Pulitzer Prizes – two for poetry and one for his biography of Abraham Lincoln – and wrote the poem that would become a Chicago cliché: "Hog Butcher for the World, Tool Maker, Stacker of Wheat, Player with Railroads and the Nation's Freight Handler, Stormy, Husky, Brawling, City of the Big

Shoulders." Today, the stockyards are gone and the big shoulders wear Brooks Brothers, but the poem is still quoted and the old image still sticks.

Creative nonfiction: Smith hired Sandburg as much for his poetry as his journalism, so he assigned him the easy task of reviewing "picture plays" for the *News* and left him free to write poetry the rest of the day. Smith prized good writing above all else, possibly even facts. He once hired a reporter who had faked a story about a local resident living to a prodigious age, explaining, "Accuracy can be taught, imagination cannot."

Hecht worked at the *Daily News* alongside Sandburg. It was Hecht, in fact, who got Sandburg the job. Hecht was an outstanding reporter and columnist, but notoriously lazy about doing his legwork. When a deadline loomed, he sometimes made up material. On one occasion he and a *News* photographer cajoled a police captain into posing for a picture aboard a police boat, gun in hand. To explain the picture in the paper, Hecht concocted the totally unsubstantiated headline: "Police Pursue River Bandits."

It made for bad journalism, but good times. Hecht immortalized the Chicago school of high-jinks journalism in his smash play *The Front Page*, which later became a movie that has been remade again and again.

Outside the city's newsrooms, Chicago's literary scene in the 1910s and '20s was anchored by the poet and editor Harriet Monroe. The magazine she founded, *Poetry*, was the official organ of the American Modernist movement and the first to publish T.S. Eliot, Marianne Moore, William Carlos Williams and Ezra Pound.

Literary obsessions: During the next three decades, while the nation struggled through the Great Depression and another world war, Chicago produced four more nationally important writers, all of a proletarian bent: Algren, Richard Wright, Jack Conroy and James T. Farrell. They shared a fascination with Marxism politics and an obsessive interest in the underdog.

Wright, who moved up to Chicago from Mississippi in the 1920s, worked as a postal clerk by day and wrote by night. His best works, including the novel *Native Son*, which was set in Chicago, were strongly influenced by Dreiser's naturalistic fiction.

Conroy, a writer and editor in Chicago for some 40 years, is best remembered today for his 1933 proletarian novel *The Disinherited*. As editor of several leftist literary journals in the 1930s and '40s, he also published the early work of Wright and Algren. Of Algren, Conroy once said: "The gates of his soul opened on the hell side."

Farrell, a second-generation South Side Irishman, wrote more than 50 books and dozens of short stories. His brutally realistic trilogy of books about Studs Lonigan, an aimless youth growing up in Chicago from the early 1900s to the Depression, holds up well today.

Homeless Papa: Conspicuously absent from this rundown of major Chicago writers is the big daddy of them all, Ernest Hemingway, who grew up in suburban Oak Park. Hemingway skipped town after high school and never looked back. He belonged to Paris and Cuba and the world, but never really to Chicago.

"It's hard to imagine Faulkner not writing about Oxford, Mississippi, or Steinbeck

Left, Nelson Algren. **Right**, Carl Sandburg.

leaving the Salinas Valley out of his fiction," observes Michael Reynolds, a Hemingway biographer. "It is almost axiomatic that American authors write about their home towns, yet Hemingway did not." His heroes were all homeless men, wasting few words and traveling light.

It is equally axiomatic that almost all Chicago writers eventually leave town, though seldom with Hemingway's haste. Dunne, Lardner, Dreiser, Sandburg, Hecht, Wright, Farrell and Algren are among those who moved on, lured away by the energy of New York and the big money of Hollywood.

In Algren's case, it was also a matter of hurt feelings. In his introduction to *The Neo Wilderness*, Algren groused that his books could be found in translation "in the libraries of all the large cities of Europe," but not "in the library of the city about which they were written."

Streets seen: Shortly after Algren's death, an alderman proposed to honor him by changing the name of West Evergreen Street to West Algren Street. But folks on the street objected, so the alderman abandoned the plan. The living sometimes vote in Chicago, while the dead usually don't. On the other hand, stretches of two downtown streets are named after two well-known columnists and broadcasters, Irv Kupcinet and Paul Harvey. Those streets, however, are not residential.

Chicago remains a writer's town, if no longer a literary titan. Among the critically acclaimed writers making their homes in Chicago in the 1990s are Pulitzer Prize winner Gwendolyn Brooks, National Book Award recipient Larry Heinemann, Cyrus Colter, Harry Mark Petrakis, Charles Dickinson, Bill Granger, Sara Paretsky, Richard Stern, Stuart Kaminsky and Stuart Dybek. And David Mamet developed his craft as a playwright in Chicago; it's doubtful that anyone has ever captured the profane, hustling attitude of Chicago in crisper dialogue than his real estate salesmen in *Glengarry Glen Ross*.

Over the past quarter-century, however, Chicago has been able to boast of only one *bona fide* literary superstar: Saul Bellow, who in 1976 won the Nobel Prize for literature. Before his recent move to Boston, he was constantly being asked why he did not leave the city. It's not just a matter of "roots," he said on several occasions. "It's more like a lot of old wires."

<u>Above</u>, the film *The Front Page*, 1974 version.

A Faded Playboy

The year was 1952 and Hugh Hefner was earning $120 a week as circulation director of a magazine called *Children's Activities*. In the evening he lived out his fantasy of starting a men's magazine full of bare breasts.

"Hef" borrowed $1,000 from his parents, hocked his furniture for $400 and talked a Chicago bank into lending him $200 to get his fledgling *Stag Party* magazine off the kitchen table of his Hyde Park apartment and into the hands of the newly liberated male.

After objections from *Stag*, a hunting magazine, Hef changed the magazine's title to *Playboy*. A friend and artist designed the now famous rabbit-head trademark in a few minutes. Hef wisely paid $500 for never-before-seen nude pictures of Marilyn Monroe for the launch (or die) issue. With that, the Playboy party officially began in November of 1953.

No one anticipated the success of *Playboy* magazine. It was as if the nation had been waiting for something so out of the mainstream. Within three years, the magazine's circulation hit 500,000 and Hef bought mansions in Los Angeles and Chicago. His Chicago residence, at 1340 N. State Parkway, was a 72-room Victorian mansion with many bars, including one that had an underwater window for viewing the indoor pool.

He sank another $5 million into a DC-9, the *Big Bunny*. He opened Playboy Clubs around the country, generally enjoying his life as the pipe-smoking, pajama-clad guy who really had it made. However, Hef's lifestyle didn't sit well with his wife and the mother of his two children. In 1959, after 10 years of marriage, they were divorced.

The Playboy party lasted for about 30 years, but then it turned into a pumpkin as the public lost interest and the Playboy philosophy became passé. In 1986, Chicago-based Playboy Enterprises Inc. lost $62 million. The magazine's circulation, which peaked at 7.2 million in 1972, plummeted to 3.6 million.

A man of some wisdom, Hef appointed his daughter, Christie Hefner, as chairperson and chief executive officer of the company. She cleaned house in a major way, firing 100 executives and shutting down most of the Playboy Clubs. She even sold daddy's Chicago mansion and his airplane.

Today, Christie has moved her staff into a new headquarters at 680 N. Lake Shore Drive, a modern corporate spread bearing little resemblance to the hedonistic trappings of the past, except for a reception-area bronze sculpture of a Playboy bunny head by artist Richard Hunt.

The current building, formerly the American Furniture Mart, features a coolly modern atrium, which includes skylights, steel catwalks and translucent fiberglass panels – architecture that is hardly in keeping with a den of iniquity.

In 1989, 63-year-old Hef finally settled down and married a former centerfold, 26-year-old Kimberley Conrad. He declined a bachelor party, saying he'd "been at one for 30 years." They had a baby and called themselves an "old-fashioned" couple after they agreed that he would not be in the delivery room.

Even though Hef still controls about 67 percent of Playboy stock and is reportedly writing his autobiography, Christie is clearly wearing the trousers in the family, trying to reposition Playboy Enterprises to be a more profitable organization.

While the magazine is still the mainstay of the corporation, the firm has been having some success licensing products bearing the Playboy, Playmate and bunny-head trademarks. In fact, 80 licensees and 45 countries sell leisure apparel and trinkets, bringing in revenues to the company of about $260 million a year.

Otherwise, *Playboy*'s major excursions into the American consciousness these days come from its explicit photographs. Joan Collins, Jessica Hahn and LaToya Jackson have all stripped for the magazine in recent years. Christie Hefner has convinced her dad that Playboy, both the company and its magazine, must evolve in order to prosper in the future. But it's still not clear exactly what changes can be made to a naughty, libertine philosophy that is no longer either as naughty nor as libertine as it was in the 1950s and '60s.

73

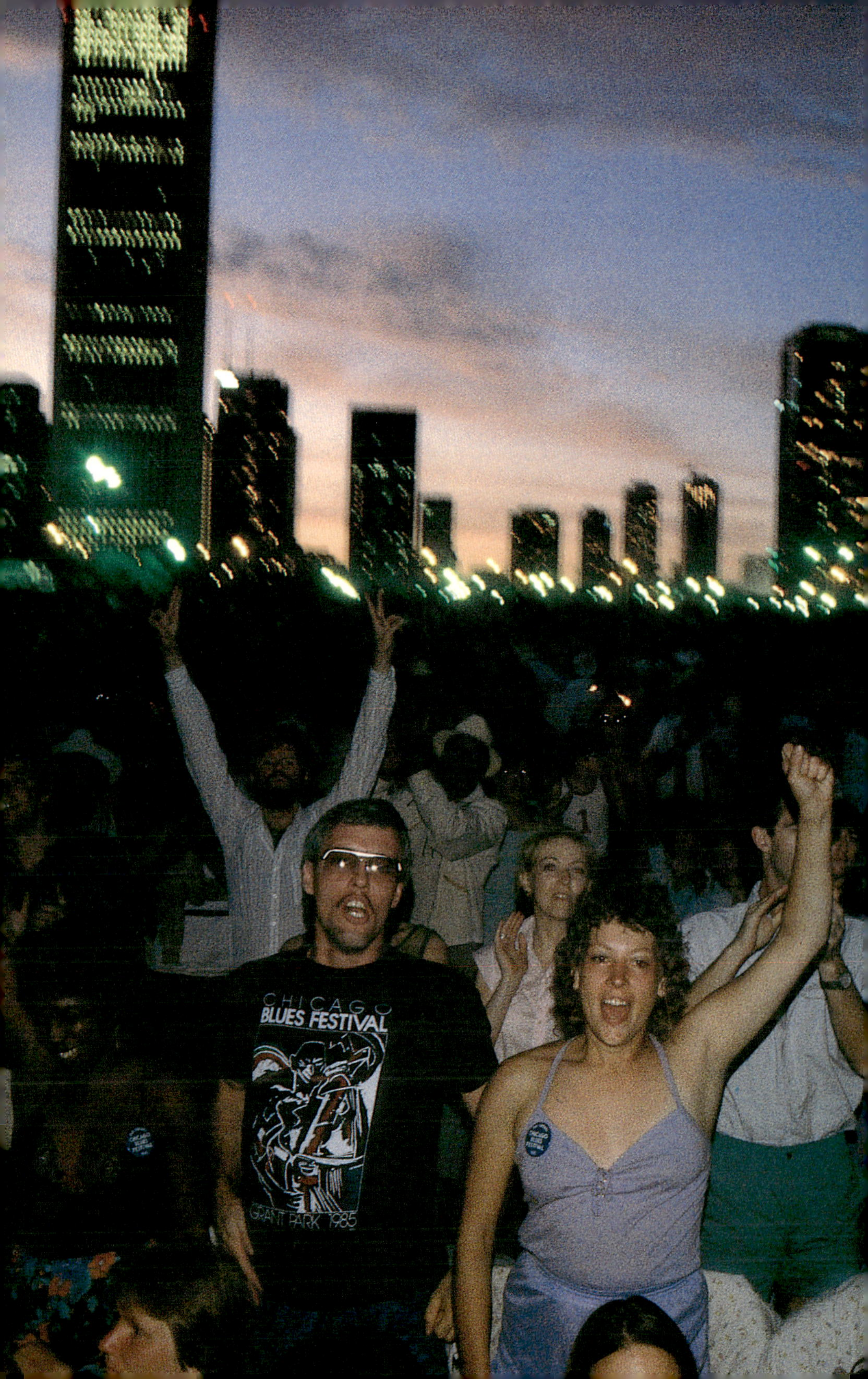
CHICAGO
BLUES FESTIVAL
GRANT PARK 1985

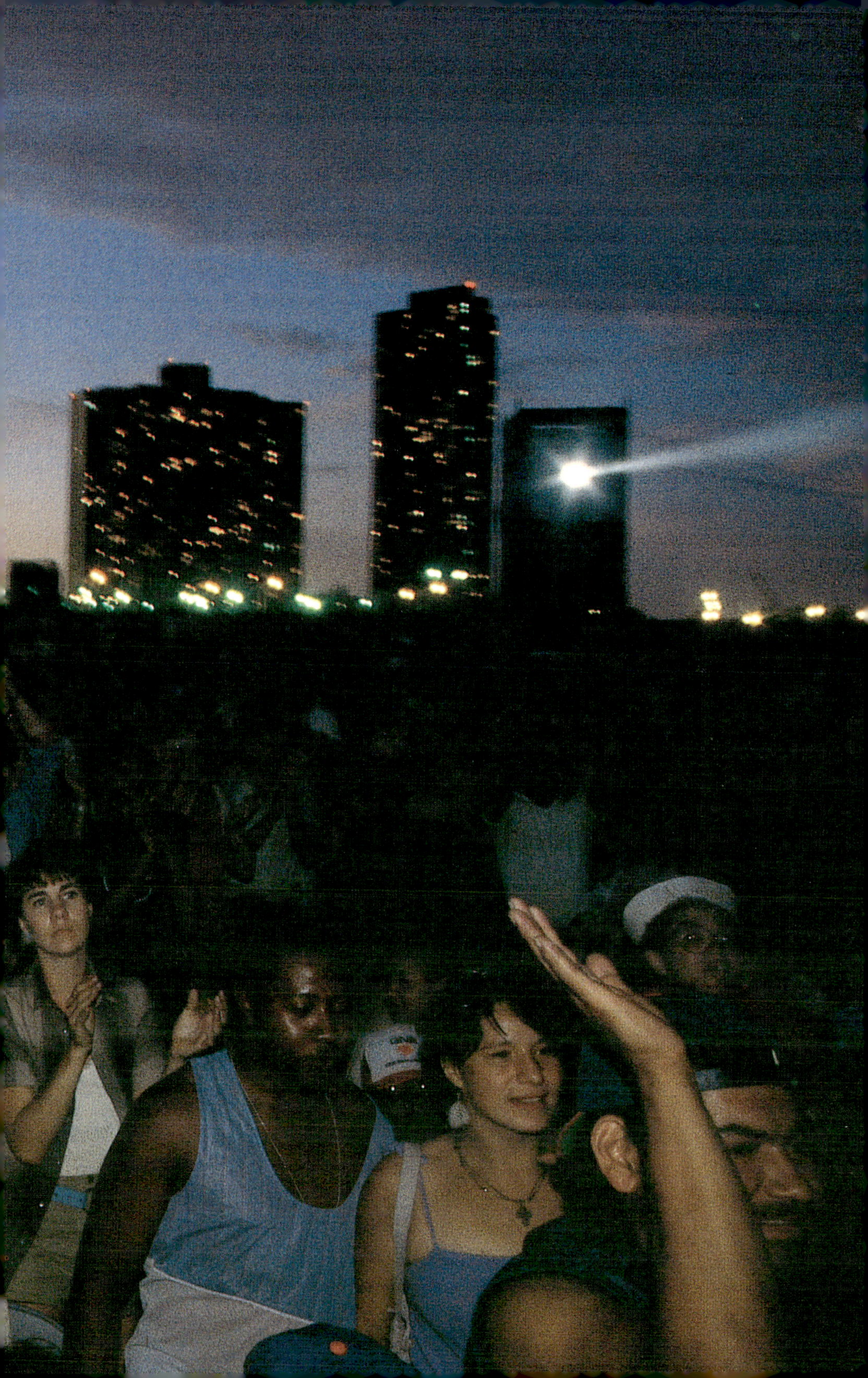

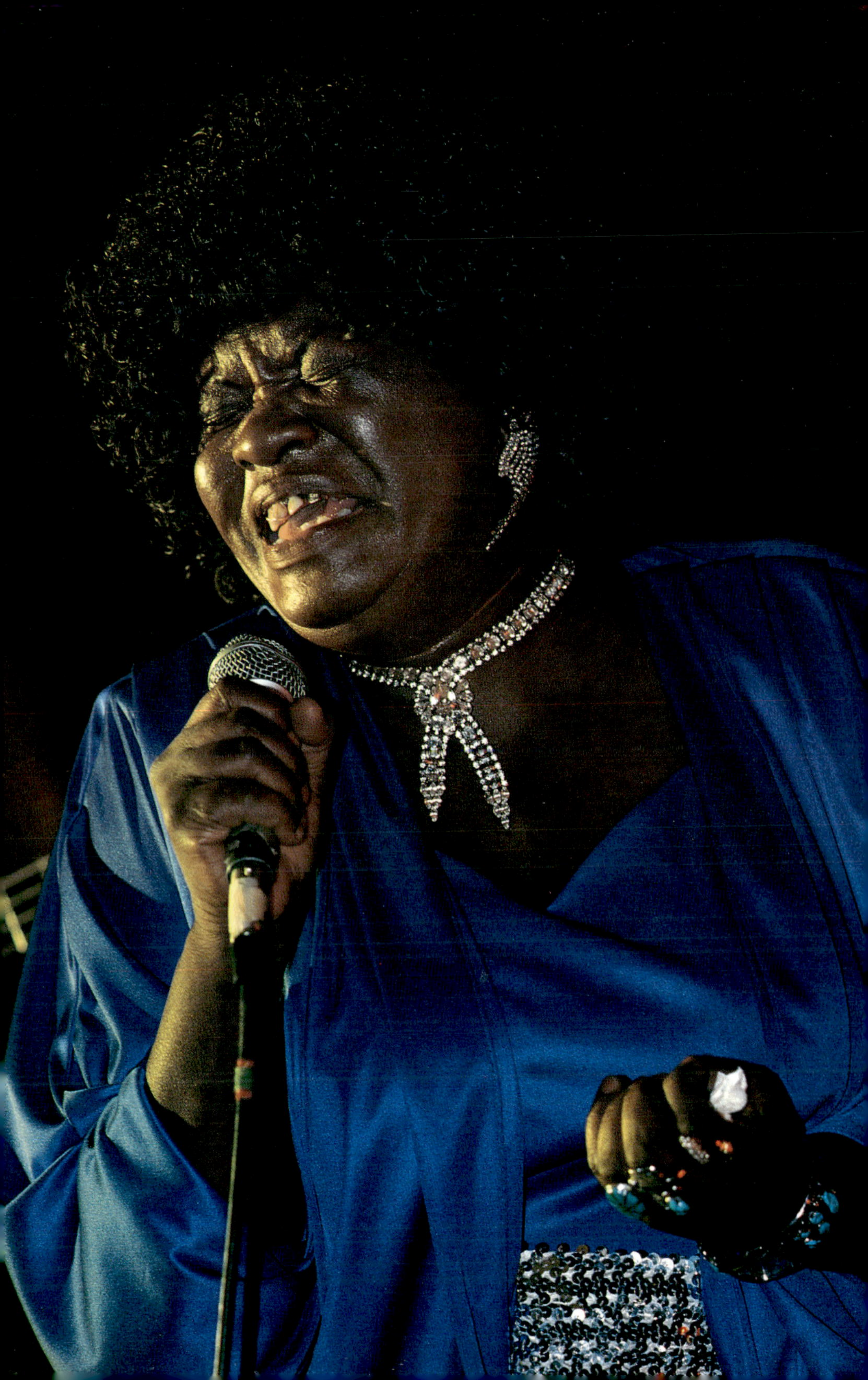

THE CHICAGO BLUES

The long blond-wood bar of the neighborhood tavern was propping up only a few people. Three older black guys in short-sleeved shirts and snappy straw hats trash-talked and cackled back and forth as they sipped their beer, while a younger, thinner black guy in an identical hat looked around coolly as he nursed a fruit juice. A fat white man wearing a plaid shirt and a paisley tie grinned at the three old black guys as he worked on a whisky.

A newcomer, a Hispanic wearing baggy trousers and several earrings, made straight for the older black guys. After a few minutes of chatting and laughing, the whole group gradually migrated to the far end of the room. Two of the men nonchalantly slung guitars over their shoulders, while another settled behind a drum kit. Another adjusted a mike and yet another blew a few tentative notes on his harmonica.

Their music hit the ground running: the heavy beat, the surging bass, the overlay of harp and, leading it all, the whine and squeal of the lead guitar. They grinned at each other. It didn't matter that there were only half a dozen people in the bar. Within minutes, however, the place was jammed with people: more old black guys, nodding their heads in time, and a bunch of young whites who were shouting along, clapping and boogying on their stools. Some started dancing in front of the band, pausing between songs to shake hands with the musicians or offer some words of approval.

It was 3:30 on a Wednesday afternoon in a residential neighborhood. Welcome to the blues, Chicago style.

Blue notes: The Chicago blues hold a secure niche in both the annals of American music and today's popular entertainment, as much a part of the town as Dixieland jazz is to New Orleans. It is a loud, showy, rocking type of music that takes traditional blues themes, chords and bent notes, and then juices them up with amplification. Musicologists could go on and on about the characteristic 12-bar, three-chord schematics and "the dominant seventh," with split quarter tones.

To music scholars, blues music does not refer to "blue" themes in lyrics, but to the "blue" notes that have been played natural or flatted, often deliberately out of tune. It's a style that has been described as getting music out of the cracks between the keys on the piano. To non-experts, the overriding musical feature of the Chicago blues is that the music is guitar-driven.

It would be difficult to overstate the influence of the Chicago blues and Chicago bluesmen on today's popular music, particularly mainstream rock 'n' roll. Anyone who listens to a set of live blues anywhere in Chicago is sure to mark it as the roots of rock. "Musicians treat the blues like gospel; it's a kind of honesty meter, a measure of belief," according to Paris-based music critic Mike Zwerin. "'He can't even play the blues,' is to

Preceding pages: rockin' all night long. **Left,** KoKo Taylor, Chicago's Queen of the Blues. **Right,** backyard barbecue blues.

The Blues 77

say he's hopeless… Chicago remains the point of reference – a mecca."

African roots: Everyone has a personal interpretation and feel for the blues, as with any other art form. But to appreciate the development of Chicago blues, it is important to understand the people who created it. The genesis of the blues can be traced back to Africa, where tribes developed strong oral traditions of passing down their lessons and legends. In some African cultures, one sign of masculinity was the falsetto singing that has become such a part of modern blues, rhythm and blues, soul and rock music.

The Africans who became slaves in America brought their traditions with them, and hung onto vestiges of those traditions despite the cultural influences that led them to speak the language, wear the clothes and use the manners forced on them by white owners. The blues grew out of the "field hollers" of slave times, when the workers bending over cotton or other crops would communicate with each other in long slow chants and songs. Many owners refused to let their slaves talk to each other, but didn't mind them singing while they worked. For many, the holler messages passed from field to field, from plantation to plantation, were the only way of keeping in touch with their African traditions, and sometimes the only way of tracking down family members lost when sold into slavery.

As African rhythms melded with European styles of harmony, the field hollers led to the Negro spirituals and hymns that looked toward happiness some day, but probably not in this lifetime. The early blues, often referred to as the "downhome" or "country" blues, came out of the Mississippi delta, and featured songs that were typically more personal than spiritual. They were songs about loving and leaving, about loyalty and betrayal, about desire and temptation. They were sung for friends at home, for cellmates in prison or for tips on the street.

Accompanied at first by finger-snapping, stomping, "hambone" thigh-slapping and other crude forms of percussion, the downhome blues ultimately became associated with the acoustic guitar, particularly the homemade "bottleneck" style. Some black freemen became wandering minstrels, taking the field hollers and early blues on the road to entertain slave and master alike.

Moving north: In the post-slavery industrial era, the expanding mills and factories of the North brought many blacks up the Mississippi Valley to Chicago. The migration varied between a trickle and a steady stream for much of the first half of this century, but after World War II it became a positive flood as young blacks, often with their families, sought out the bright lights and higher-paying jobs.

Using the government aid for returning servicemen, many came to Chicago to be educated and to become professionals. Thousands took up the jobs – generally menial, but relatively high paying – offered by the ever-growing stockyards. Chicago's two large black-dominated neighborhoods developed because the migrants from the South typically got off the trains at one of two stops. If they got off at the 63rd Street station, they usually settled right there on the South Side; if they got off at the 12th Street station, they generally ended up on the West Side. The Southern musicians, naturally, followed their audience.

One of the men who acted as a bridge between the delta and the city, from Mississippi to Chicago, from downhome to urban blues, was Big Bill Broonzy. He was also one of the first American artists to take the blues to Europe, where it was embraced by sophisticated audiences. Chicago performers often bracket dates in small clubs in their home neighborhoods with tours of big halls in Europe, and a handful of Chicago blues expatriates, notably Paris-based guitarist Luther Allison, have resettled in Europe to take advantage of the enthusiastic audiences. In Chicago, visiting Europeans often seek out the blues bars and clubs, and the annual Chicago Blues Fest has become a focus for many foreign tourists.

Electrifying: Though still popular after World War II, the rural, relatively simple downhome blues – typically one man with one guitar, mourning the love he done lost – eventually gave way to a faster, more raucous, often joyful music. When the electric guitar came along in the 1950s, it was embraced wholeheartedly in the black clubs and living rooms and back yards, and Chicago blues was born.

The man with the guitar not only had an amplifier, but he also had an electric bass player, a drummer, a harmonica player, a saxophone player and perhaps even a lady – sometimes slim and sultry, sometimes wide and wailin' – to sing the blues. The resulting

Left, Junior Wells, the "godfather" of the blues scene. **Right**, Ruth Brown, wide and wailin'.

Chicago blues, however, retained and intensified many of the features experts use to characterize downhome blues: vocal moans and drones, for example, along with "constant repetition of melodic figures, harmonica tremeloes, a heavy sound and rough intensity," according to noted blues author Charles Keil.

The delta bluesmen who defined and refined the new style in the 1950s included J.B. Lenoir, Jimmy Reed, Little Walter, Howlin' Wolf, Sonny Boy Williamson, John Lee Hooker and Muddy Waters, who became the single performer most identified with the earthy, vibrant, driving style of Chicago blues. Waters' songs, such as *Hoochie Coochie Man*, *Got My Mojo Workin'* and *I'm Ready* epitomize the rollicking sexual boastfulness that often replaced the theme of sorrow and helplessness so common in the downhome blues. In *Tiger in Your Tank*, Waters sang:

I can raise your hood.
I can clean your coils.
Check the transmissions,
And give you the oils.
I don't care what the people think,
I want to put a tiger,
You know, in your tank.

Many of the themes and lyrics have become more sophisticated, of course, and humor has become one of the strongest undercurrents in the Chicago blues, as when the singer complains about a straying spouse or a meddling mother-in-law. A modern bluesman – or woman – may complain about a lover who cheats, but may also threaten to kick that lover's ass. Willie Dixon sang many of his own songs, but his true legacy will be the hundreds of blues songs he wrote for other artists, often tailoring the themes, lyrics and rhythms to a performer's individual style. To Dixon, who said, "The wisdom of the blues is the true facts of life," everything that did and could happen was fair game for a blues song.

Chess game: One of the cornerstones of the development of the Chicago blues in the 1950s and '60s was Chess Records, the recording company operated by Leonard Chess, his brother Phil and Leonard's son Marshall. Many of the leading talents in blues cut records with the Chess family. Muddy Waters was with them for years with no contract beyond a handshake. Willie Dixon, who as well as writing songs was an accomplished upright bass player, was a Chess stalwart who often used his basement to audition new talent for the Chess family.

Today, more than 20 years after guiding light Leonard Chess died and the studio was closed, the debate continues in Chicago over the role of the Chess family. Were they whites who exploited black talent? Would the Chicago blues have become so popular if they hadn't given so many unheard artists a chance to record?

One thing not in doubt is that many of the architects of modern rock 'n' roll made formative pilgrimages to the tiny Chess studio on South Michigan Avenue. Prominent rock singers and guitarists, particularly the leaders of the 1960s "English invasion" such as the Rolling Stones, paid personal homage to Chess's blues artists. For a time, Marshall Chess managed the Rolling Stones, who took their name from a Muddy Waters song. They and other modern rock stars not only re-recorded many Chicago blues songs to create international hits, but often borrowed or stole outright individual guitarists' distinctive riffs.

When Howlin' Wolf recorded Willie Dixon's *Little Red Rooster*, for example, it sold 20,000 copies, a big hit for a local blues record. When the Rolling Stones re-recorded the song in a nearly identical manner, it sold more than 500,000 copies. Tom Marker, a longtime Chicago blues disc jockey, recalled that the English rockers, especially the Stones, were "just crazy" about the blues. "Those guys were big fans of the Chicago sound when they were getting their blues thing together themselves," he said. "They were just trying to copy the stuff. Sometimes they would copy the song lick for lick." The black bluesmen made the music, and the white rockers made it famous.

Many blues performers literally sang for their supper and not much more. Even name performers often lived on a shoestring – and still do. For example, Koko Taylor, known in Chicago as the Queen of the Blues, needed the receipts of a benefit thrown by friends and fellow performers to pay the bills after she and several band members were injured in a 1988 auto accident. "Musicians all over Chicago are working hard, but they're working for almost nothing," Taylor told the *Chicago Tribune*.

"You sing the blues, die and they have a benefit to bury you. That's the pattern,"

Left, bassist and songwriter Willie Dixon and Muddy Waters. **Right**, Marshall Chess with classic vinyl.

added Valerie Wellington, another leading lady blues singer in Chicago. That's why Wellington and a number of other performers formed the Chicago Blues Artists Coalition, a sort of blues-rights organization that aims to help performers learn how to handle their own business and financial affairs. The group is also providing self-help counseling and drug-awareness programs. "In this business, it's very easy to get caught up in things of that nature," Wellington said.

Blues survivors: Not all blues artists end up down and out, of course. The Chicago blues have made a lot of money for some artists who have reclaimed the traditions from the white-dominated world of rock. Though not from Chicago, the influence of the Chicago style is heard in many of the tunes of artists B.B. King and Robert Cray. The Chess recording studio is gone, and so are some of the classic South Side blues clubs such as Theresa's, but the Chicago blues scene remains as lively in the 1990s as ever. Following the death of Muddy Waters, guitarist Buddy Guy and singer-harpist Junior Wells share the unofficial title of greatest living Chicago bluesmen. Buddy Guy, for instance, is the man Eric Clapton nominates as the world's greatest guitarist.

But there's a second rank that includes many fans' favorites, including patriarchs such as Sunnyland Slim and Jimmy Walker. Two popular tradition-minded blues guitarists who seem to be playing somewhere in Chicago almost every day are Lefty Dizz, who used to tutor Jimi Hendrix on blues licks, and Muddy Waters Jr, who is actually no relation to "the old man" but has declared himself an unofficial adopted son and continues the raunchy tradition with lyrics such as, "If you wouldn't have kicked the door down, you wouldn't have caught me in bed with your wife."

For visiting blues fans who seek out the music, an added benefit is the musicians, even the headliners, who typically mingle with the crowd before and after shows. They are often happy to have a chat and maybe a drink; more than any other music, the Chicago blues remain of and for everyday people, with all the highs and lows and worries of everyday life. As Purvis Spann, the old Chicago blues disc jockey, used to say, "If you don't like the blues, you got a hole in your soul."

<u>Left</u>, Aretha Franklin testifies for *The Blues Brothers*. <u>Right</u>, John Lee Hooker.

BLUES JOINTS

In the city that created a blues style in its own image, one of the best places to hear the music is on downtown street corners, where individual performers and sometimes whole bands set up to play for donations from passersby. On a Sunday morning, the Maxwell Street market often features a variety of street blues performers, both individuals and entire bands.

There are a number of popular blues clubs on the North Side of Chicago, in neighborhoods that feel safer and more familiar to both visitors and the Chicago middle-class and young professional types who favor the music. The best North Side and downtown clubs include Blue Chicago, B.L.U.E.S., B.L.U.E.S. Etcetera, the Wise Fools Pub, Kingston Mines and Buddy Guy's Legends. It's always advisable to check in advance with these popular clubs to see if booking is necessary; on weekends or when well-known performers are playing there, tickets can be tight.

But that's on the North Side and downtown. You cannot book or make advance reservations on the South Side. For a real plunge into urban blues, nothing compares with the South Side, particularly the Checkerboard, also known recently as the New Checkerboard Lounge. For years, the Checkerboard has been the unofficial headquarters of the Chicago blues for the South Side bluesmen themselves, but it's in a tough neighborhood where visitors should take care. Most white people prefer to arrive at the club in cabs, though frequent visitors drive themselves and then park in the club's own off-street parking lot, which is located nearby and even has a security guard in attendance.

The cover charge at the Checkerboard is usually only a few dollars. Once inside, the club is remarkably small for having such a big reputation. It has seats for perhaps 100 and standing room (which is more usual) for about 300, but in fact it only takes about 30 people to make the place look crowded.

Though the neighborhood outside may be threatening to some, once inside it's easy to make friends among the locals and the bluesmen themselves, who especially appreciate out-of-towners and love the idea of someone crossing an ocean to hear them play.

For the hard-core late-night prowlers, Kingston Mines, with its two alternating stages, can be a gold mine for the blues. One of Chicago's northernmost blues clubs (on North Halsted Street), it's not exactly a fancy club, but it's one of those places that looks better as the night goes on. And the night does go on at Kingston Mines, usually until 4 a.m. On Saturday nights and Sunday mornings, the music rolls until 5 a.m. Other blues performers around the city finish their regular gigs at two or three in the morning and then head for Kingston Mines, where they jam and "talk country" at each other, much to the delight of aficionados.

One of the best places to catch the blues is at Wrigley Side, on Clark Street just around the corner from baseball's Wrigley Field. A specialty here are the shows, often by top Chicago bluesmen such as Lefty Dizz, that begin as soon as the last score is registered in afternoon games at Wrigley Field. Some fans leave the game before it's over to make sure they get a good stool near the band.

In 1990, the city granted landmark status to the building at 2120 South Michigan Avenue that once housed well-known Chess Recording Co. and its legendary music studios.

A former Chess studio musician, Gerald Sims, bought the building and announced plans to turn it into a "living music museum where artists can record, where the public can hear lectures on the blues and where tourists can visit." Interested fans should check to see if it's open.

Another blues stop that isn't in most of the official tourist information is the Old Town School of Music, situated at 909 West Armitage, which not only has a blues school, but features a shop, workshops and occasional acoustic performances.

And, of course, the Chicago Blues Fest has become an avidly awaited annual tradition in early June. It's free, held in downtown's grassy Grant Park, and typically features dozens of artists from both Chicago and elsewhere.

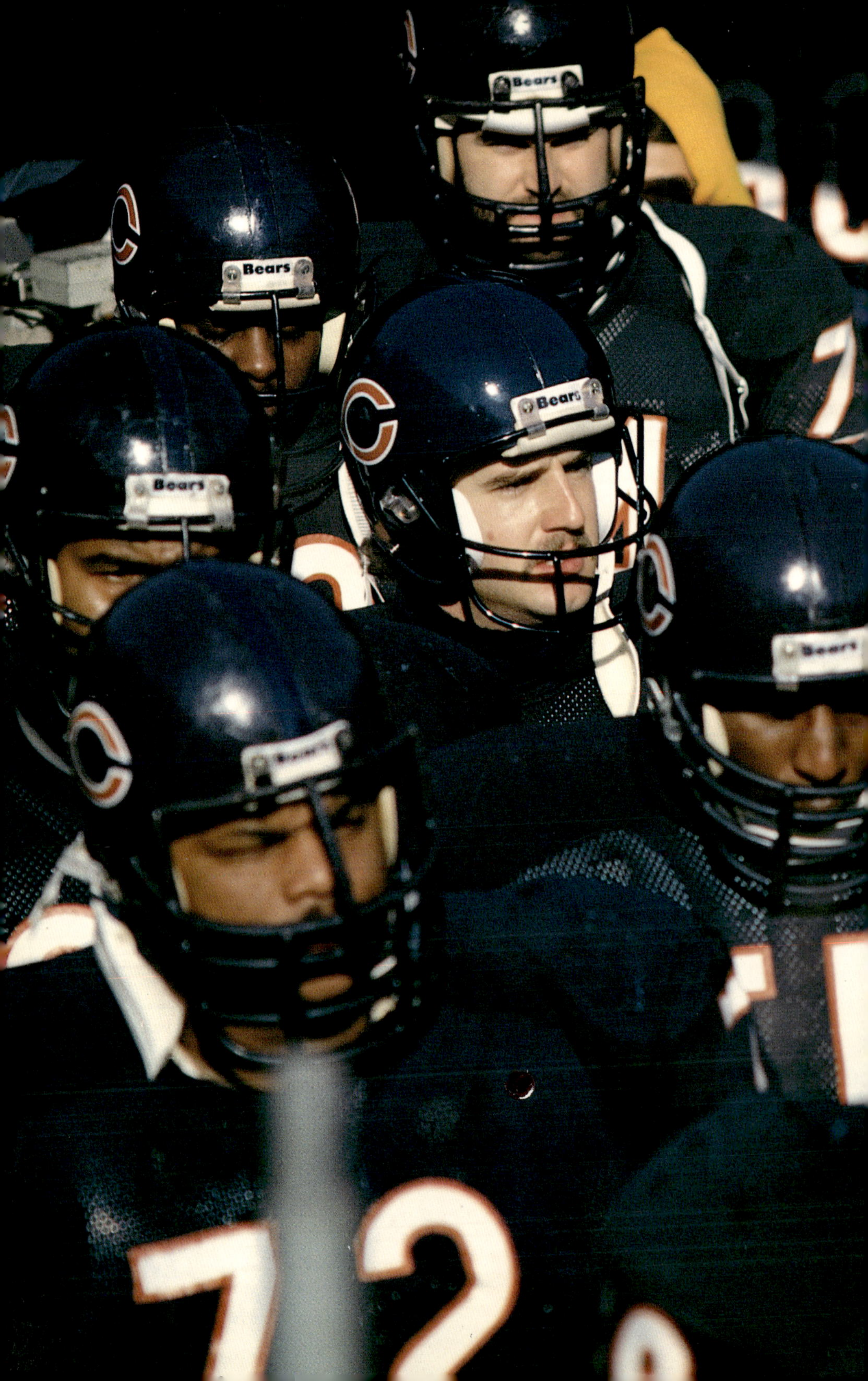
Bears
Bears
Bears
Bears
Bears
Bears
72

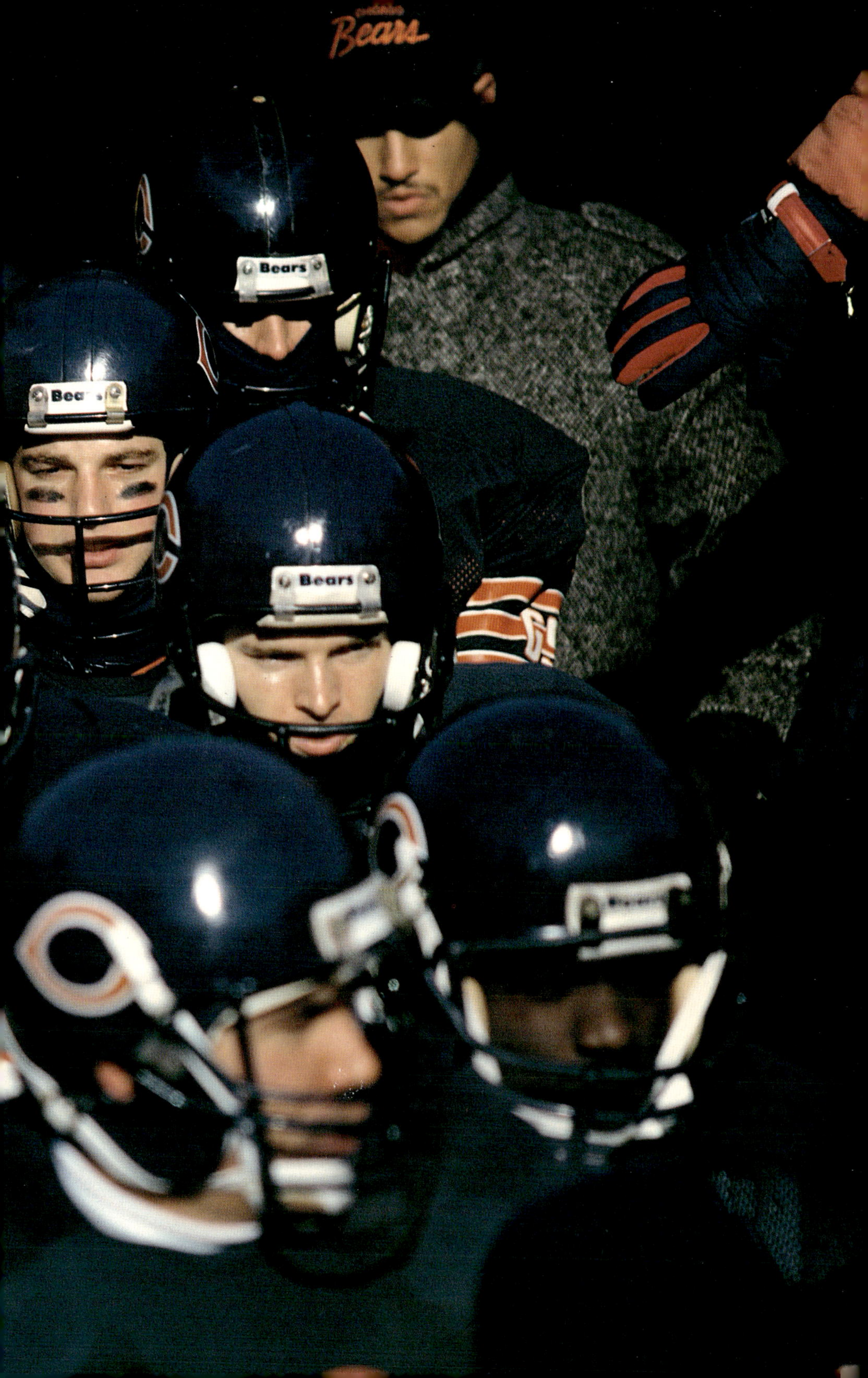
Bears
Bears
Bears
Bears

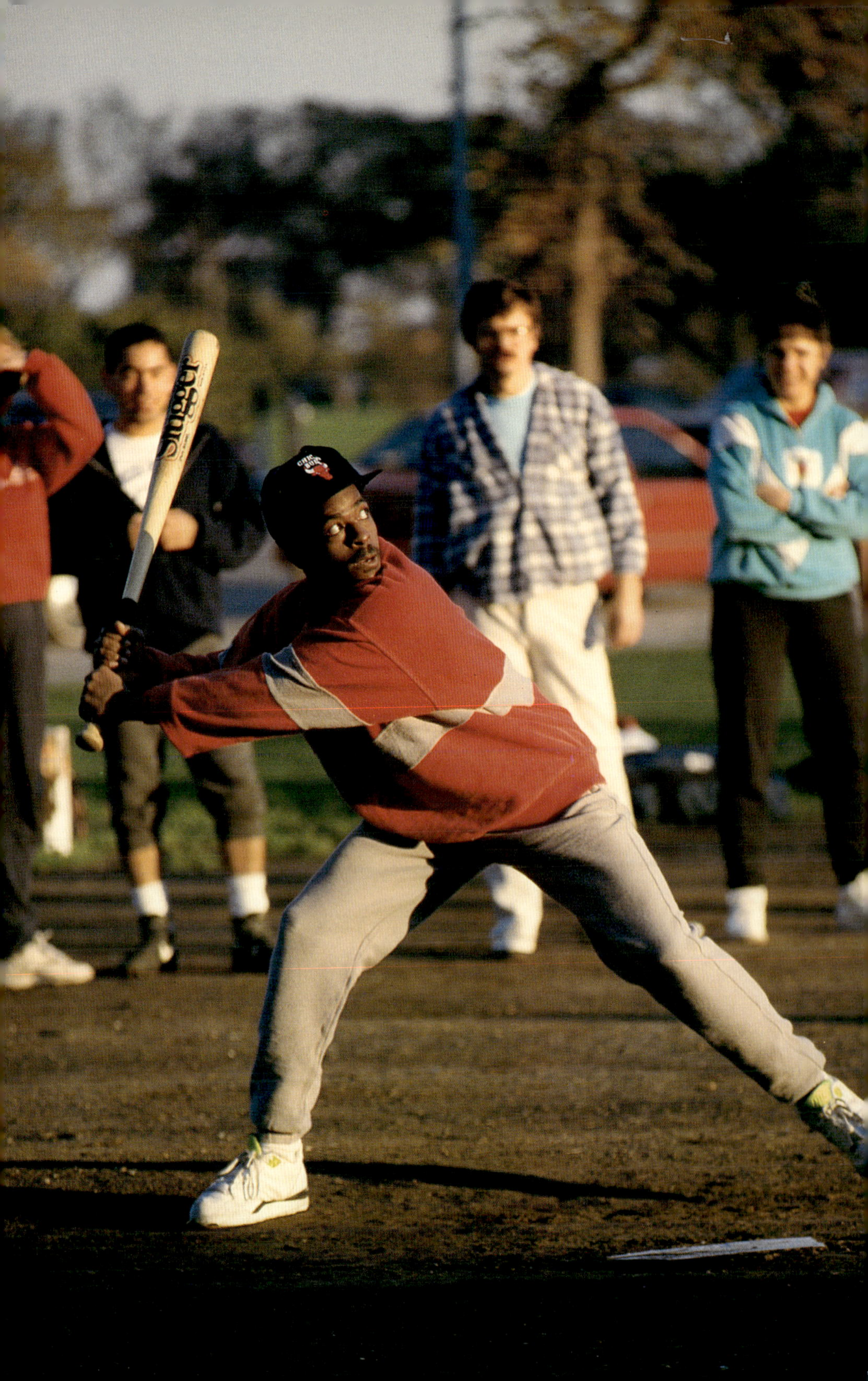
Slugger

A Sports-Mad Town

Chicago is a sporting kind of town, from what people read in the morning newspaper and what they talk about during the day to what they do after work and where they eat and drink at night. In the city's poorer neighborhoods, many young people see a career in sports as their best hope of claiming a slice of the American dream. Public officials recognize the importance of sports in Chicago, from the millions in tax money that helped build a new baseball stadium for the White Sox to the late-night basketball leagues aimed at keeping kids off the streets between the hours of 10 p.m. and 1:30 a.m.

Chicagoans love their professional teams – baseball's Cubs and White Sox, football's Bears, ice hockey's Black Hawks and basketball's Bulls – but they love to play themselves, too. The South Side pick-up basketball games are known for their "no autopsy, no foul" style of rough play, and the lakefront is a haven for runners, cyclists, bodybuilders and volleyball players. Parks all over Chicago feature a popular local variation of softball, baseball's slower cousin, that features a balloon-sized 16-inch ball compared with the 12-inch regulation softball and the 9-inch baseball. (It's probably fitting that since the players are fatter, the ball should be, too.)

Back in time: For many visitors, and for many Chicagoans as well, the quintessential Chicago sporting experience is an afternoon baseball game at Wrigley Field, home of the Chicago Cubs. A Cubs game is a high priority for visiting Americans because it's a chance to savor the national game, to step back in time to the days before World War II when all baseball games were played in the afternoon instead of at night, under lights. Wrigley Field is one of the oldest baseball parks in the major leagues, and fans revel in its ivy-covered walls where balls sometimes become lost and entangled in the vines, and in the way its erratic breezes can turn harmless fly balls into important home runs.

For foreign visitors, even those who know or care little about baseball or sports in general, a visit to Wrigley is a prime opportunity for people-watching, for sizing up the style of these ruddy creatures who call themselves Chicagoans. Perhaps more than any other big US city, the people of Chicago represent the great middle class of America – in size, shape, apparel, speaking voice, economic standing, political attitudes and social concerns – or lack thereof. And there is perhaps no better place than an afternoon baseball game at Wrigley Field to observe folk who are so cheerfully, relentlessly, unabashedly *American*.

Wrigleyville is a middle-class, aspiringly gentrified North Side neighborhood of large, solid-brick apartment blocks and one-time family homes that have been carved into flats and unassuming duplexes. It is also not the most accessible place Chicago could have put a ballpark. But for many fans, the El (elevated railway) ride to Addison, a short walk from the park – it never seems right to

Preceding pages: Bear-faced battle. **Left**, eye on the ball. **Right**, kicking kiddie.

call this little bandbox a stadium – is as much a part of the game as hot dogs and popcorn and beer.

Safe at home: Most afternoon games are sellouts, due to the remarkable allegiance that Cubs' fans show for their long-suffering team. Yet tickets can be had, and usually for not much more than $5 to $20 above face value, depending on the location of the seats. Ticket scalping is illegal, but there are usually plenty of touts slyly making deals across the street or around the corner from the official ticket windows.

Also, people without tickets can strike up a conversation with one of the Cubs' usher-guards outside the entrances; these guys have the uncanny ability to scan the entering crowd for people with extra tickets who will sell them at face value or sometimes simply give them away.

For visitors who just want to sample the atmosphere and look around a bit, the best bargain is probably a standing-room-only ticket, purchased even on sellout days for a few dollars from the regular ticket windows. These tickets do not guarantee a seat (though seats are often available due to no-shows) but they do afford decent views from the many aisles. Many people with SRO tickets prefer to catch a couple of innings from the lower grandstand, a couple more from the upper deck and a couple more from the underground stands where they can munch nachos, pizza, bratwurst, burgers and other fast food while watching the game on overhead closed-circuit TV. For the worst view of the game but perhaps the most fun, adventurous fans prefer the outfield bleachers, where the infamous Bleacher Bums cheer maniacally, strip off their shirts at any hint of sunshine and typically end up soaked in beer, inside and out.

The real show at Wrigley Field is not the baseball on the field, but the fans themselves.

Huge men bearing trays of beer and junk food carefully belly their way through the crowds. Bespectacled, serious young men concentrate on the game, scribbling in their scorebooks as they chart the action play by play. Seemingly oblivious to both the game and the cheers of young men, buxom young women strut confidently up and down the aisles just ahead of the broad-beamed, child-dragging matrons they will probably eventually become.

No one should leave before the middle of the seventh inning, the famous "stretch," when Harry Caray, the venerable Cubs TV and radio announcer, sticks his head out of the overhead broadcasting booth and leads the crowd in singing a horribly off-key version of "Take Me Out to the Ballgame." Caray, a hoary septuagenarian whose words have become a little slowed and slurred since he suffered a stroke a few years ago, is not a typical American glib, blow-dried sportscaster. But his common-man looks and plain-speaking enthusiasm have helped qualify him as one of Chicago's all-time sports personalities.

Local heroes: There are other sports heroes, of course, and they say a lot about Chicago and its makeup. In the 1950s, the baseball heroes were the Cubs' Ernie Banks and the White Sox's Minnie Minoso, a pair of black sluggers known as much for their sunny dispositions as their home runs. In the 1960s, the Chicago Black Hawks had two of the greatest ice hockey players ever, Bobby Hull and Stan Mikita, both team-oriented players who were also prolific scorers and tough guys who comported themselves as gentlemen in a game known for its thugs. In the 1970s, the Chicago Bulls basketball team was led by a combination of smooth black players such as Chet Walker and Bob Love and hard-nosed, scrappy white players such as Jerry Sloan.

The heroes of the 1980s and '90s have been the Cubs' (now-retired) white Ryne Sandberg and black Andre Dawson (now traded to another team), both quiet sluggers known for their off-field charity work; the now-retired Bears' football player Walter Payton (rightly nicknamed "Sweetness") and the Bulls' ex-star Michael Jordan, whose high scoring and soaring slam-dunks made him perhaps the most exciting basketball player of his era.

Drinking in sports: The Chicago Bulls' former coach, Dick Motta, once used a backhanded reference to opera to describe his team's hope in the face of despair: "It ain't over 'til the Fat Lady sings." Nowadays, after the Fat lady sings she is likely to be seen, along with other fans of both food and sports, at one of Chicago's many influential "sports" bars.

The sports bar, as originated in Chicago, was once merely a neighborhood tavern that had a TV installed so that afternoon customers could watch the Cubs in dark, air-conditioned comfort. Now, however, the sports bar has become an American "concept,"

<u>Left</u>, baseball buddies. <u>Right</u>, the Wrigley wave.

much expanded and imitated across the country but still not done anywhere as well as in Chicago.

The modern sports bar still has TV, but there are likely to be several large screens that may show taped highlights or past games when nothing live is being broadcast. Besides the usual theme decorations of sports equipment, photos and memorabilia from hats to bats, many sports bars offer participation in the form of pay-per-play sports trivia games, miniature bowling, little basketball hoops and even indoor baseball batting cages. But what keeps people coming back to the most prominent sports bars are the large quantities of good food, mainly burgers and pasta dishes or pizza, served up from the kitchens.

The Black Sox: Chicago, of course, wouldn't be Chicago without its history of scandal, and that extends to sports, too. The Chicago "Black Sox" baseball bribery scheme discredited the national pastime and is still America's biggest sporting outrage.

In October 1919, the Chicago White Sox arrived in Cincinnati to play the first World Series – the annual championship between the winners of the rival National and American leagues – since the end of World War I. Fans across the nation prepared to follow the games, play by play, as relayed by telegraph to rented halls.

The White Sox were the overwhelming favorites. Pitcher Eddie Cicotte had won 29 games, but the hero of Chicago was "Shoeless" Joe Jackson, an illiterate former cotton-mill worker from South Carolina who wielded a huge, fearsome bat he called "Black Betsy" and had a league-leading .356 batting average.

The bribery plot was initiated by White Sox first baseman Arnold "Chick" Gandil, according to Eliot Asinof, who wrote a book that was the basis for one of the several movies that have been made on the subject. Gandil met with a bookmaker in a Boston hotel three weeks before the series began. For $80,000 to be provided by a group of gamblers, he agreed to arrange for the White Sox to lose.

Gandil recruited Cicotte and five other White Sox players with the $80,000: third baseman George "Buck" Weaver; shortstop Charles "Swede" Risberg; outfielder Oscar "Happy" Felsch; pitcher Claude "Lefty" Williams, and utility infielder Fred McMullin. Jackson demanded $20,000 for his participation and the gamblers agreed, bringing the total figure up to $100,000.

Rumors that Chicago was going to throw the series were so widespread that the dozens of gamblers crowding into the team's Cincinnati hotel room waved $1,000 bills at the players before the first game. Ultimately, the White Sox lost five games to three (the World Series was then a best of nine games, instead of today's best of seven) in contests marred by bobbled catches and bad throws. The White Sox reportedly won their three games only out of anger when the gamblers were slow in making their bribe payments.

Gandil was eventually paid $35,000. Cicotte got $10,000 which he found under his pillow in the hotel the night before the first game. Risberg and Williams got $10,000 each, while Felsch and McMullin got $5,000 each. Jackson, too, only ended up with $5,000, despite his $20,000 demand. Weaver apparently decided not to help throw the games, and there is a strong argument that he in fact played to win. He was paid nothing.

The next year, under the goading of newspaper reporters, a Chicago grand jury indicted the eight ballplayers on nine counts of conspiracy to defraud. The scandal devastated the baseball world. Team owners, under pressure to clean up the game, appointed Judge Kenesaw Mountain Landis as the first commissioner of baseball.

Say it ain't so: The scandal also triggered a wave of bitterness and cynicism. A Chicago newspaper reported that a young boy clutched at Jackson's sleeve as the fallen hero left the grand jury hearing and pleaded, "Say it ain't so, Joe. Say it ain't so."

"Yes, kid, I'm afraid it is," Jackson is said to have replied.

Like so many good Chicago newspaper stories of the era, this one turned out to be a fabrication by a reporter. But the bitterness was real. Chicago kids began to cry sarcastically, "Play bail!" to start sandlot games. The players were acquitted of the criminal charges, but Landis nonetheless suspended them from professional baseball for life. For a time they knocked around in semi-pro and "outlaw" leagues, sometimes playing under pseudonyms.

For betraying the sport, and casting it into disgrace for several years until New York Yankee slugger Babe Ruth caught the fans' fancy, the 1919 White Sox have become forever known as the Black Sox.

<u>Left</u>, rugby mud. <u>Right</u>, Loop cycling.

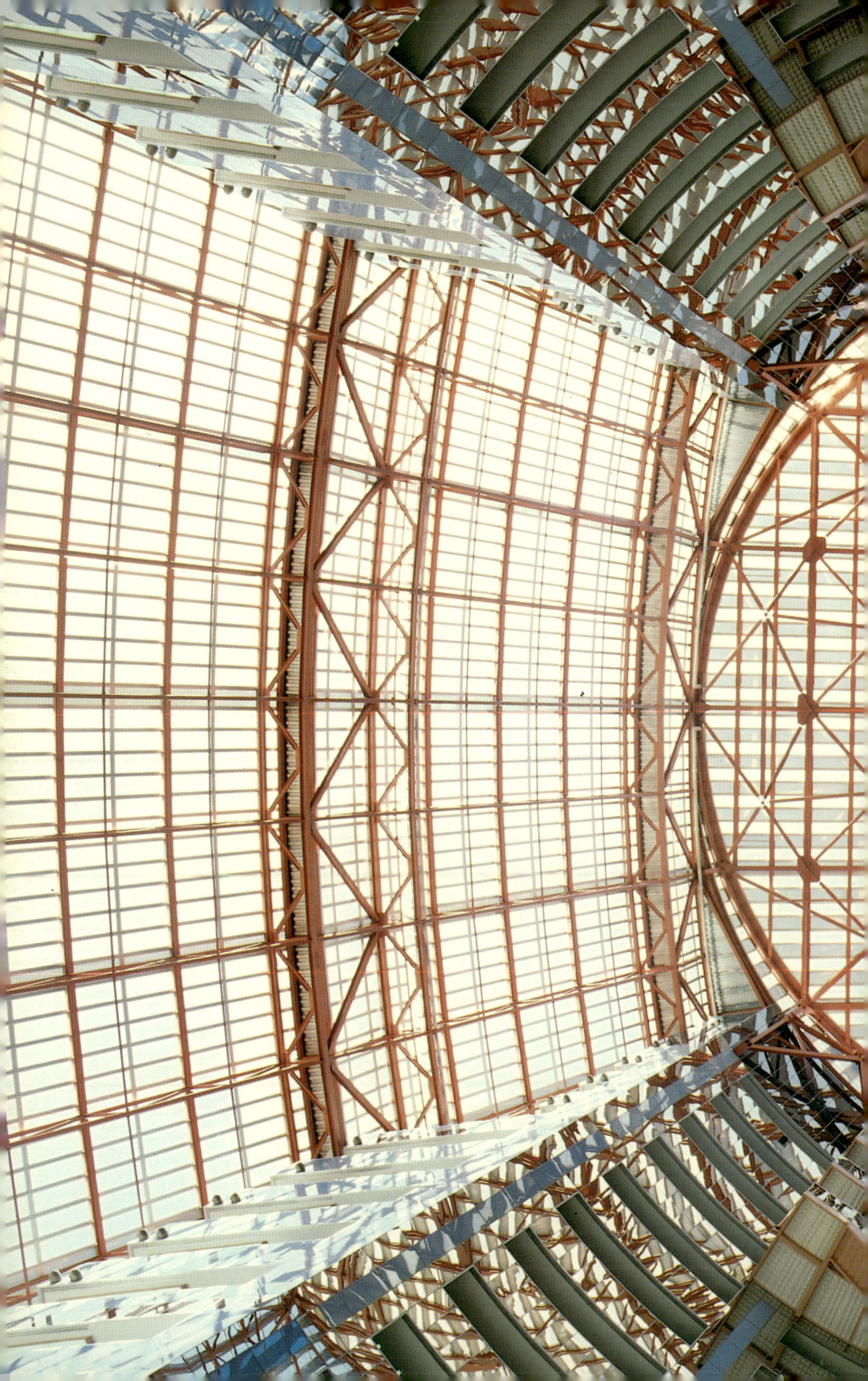

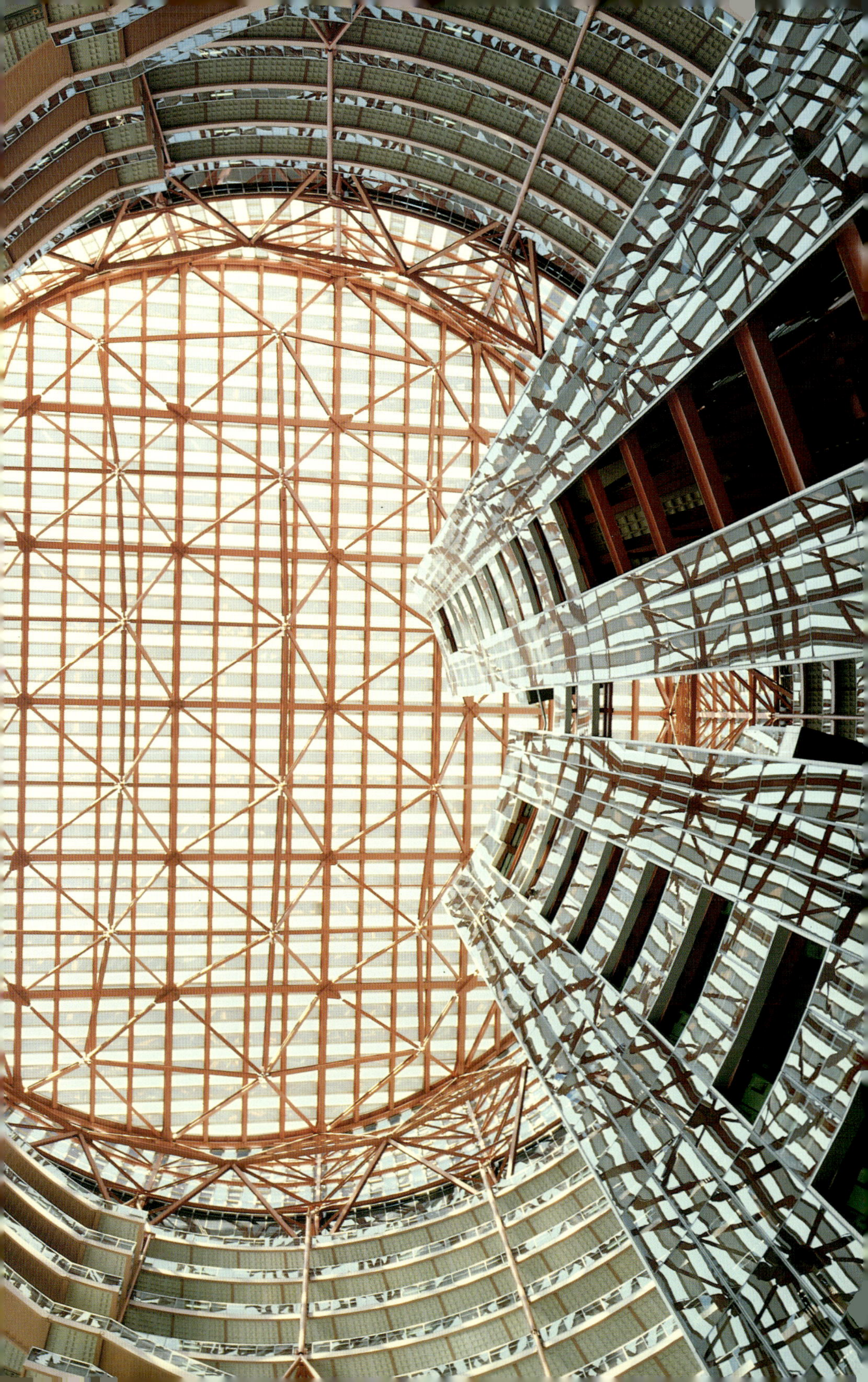

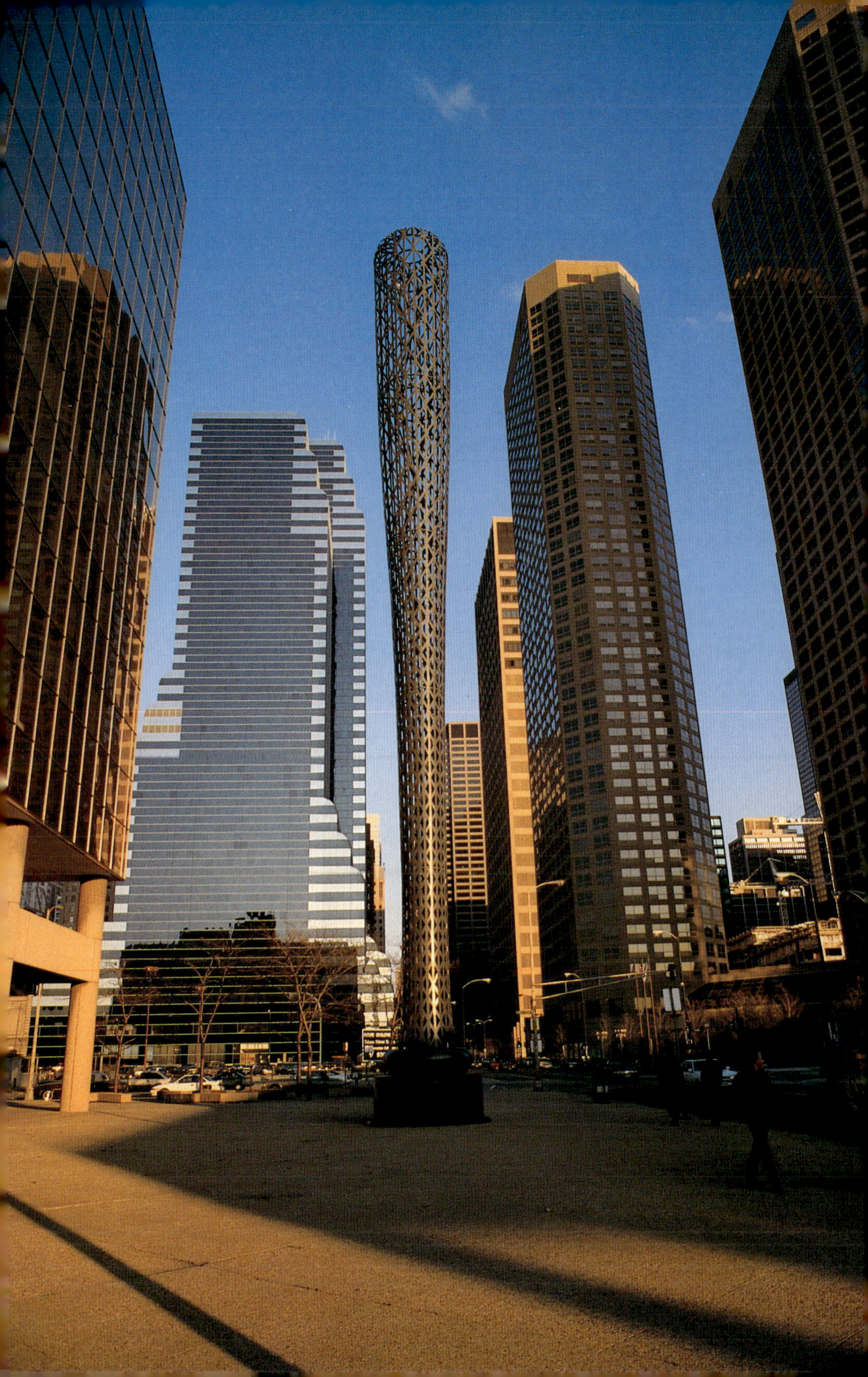

AN ARCHITECT'S PHOENIX

The collective psyche of Chicago has never recovered from the fire of 1871; one look at the city's architecture confirms it. One look up, that is.

Those rows of towering skyscrapers – from the sinewy steel spires of the John Hancock Center to the illuminated turrets of the romantic 900 N. Michigan Building – might never have been erected if Mrs O'Leary's infamous cow hadn't kicked over a lamp and started the fire that levelled the city a century ago. Today, the urge to build bigger, taller and faster hasn't abated. Another fire, these giant buildings seem to say, won't wipe *us* out.

Long after other major American cities have gasped in horror at the faceless glass slabs populating once-pleasant boulevards – and gotten fed up with the shrinking space left for people – Chicago continues to be a place where few if any obstacles are put in the way of really big real estate developments. Los Angeles might compel developers to build art museums, Boston may insist on low-income housing and New York may champion the greater good of historic preservation, but here, builders are still sitting pretty – and high.

Scraping the sky: The miracle is that, considering the running room granted developers, Chicago has any good buildings at all, let alone a collection of museum-quality edifices. The integrity of the cityscape was ensured by the early marriage of big building to cutting-edge architecture: Chicago didn't just rebuild after the fire, it invented the skyscraper – the architectural form that was to define American cities.

From that day forward, good – or a least interesting – architecture has gone hand in hand with big building. Ask Chicago developers why they hired famous architects like Cesar Pelli, Helmut Jahn or Ricardo Bofill, and they'll look at you uncomprehendingly.

<u>Preceding pages</u>: State of Illinois Center atrium. <u>Left</u>, Oldenburg's *Batcolumn*. <u>Right</u>, the Picasso.

The reason is self-evident: this is Chicago.

Perhaps no one epitomizes this phenomenon like local-boy-made-good Paul Beitler, a professional descendant of the men who rebuilt Chicago after the fire. Beitler started his career as a salesman before becoming a leasing broker and making the extremely rare leap to developer. In a city that already has the world's tallest building (Sears Tower: Wacker and Adams, 1,468 feet, 110 stories, built in 1974), the world's fourth-largest building (Amoco Building: 200 E. Randolph, 1,136 feet, 97 stories, 1979) and the world's fifth-largest building (John Hancock Center: Michigan and Chestnut, 1,105 feet, 97 stories, 1969), Beitler announced plans to build a new world's tallest building. Before anyone can outdo the birthplace of the skyscraper by building an inch taller than Sears Tower, Beitler hopes to head them off at the lofty pass with a reed-thin tower that locals are already calling the Sky Needle: Madison and Wells, 1,999 feet, 125 stories, sometime in the 1990s (maybe).

Beitler has already contributed some fu-

Architecture 95

ture landmarks to the city's skyline. For his Madison Plaza buildings, also at Madison and Wells, he hired Skidmore Owings and Merrill's Bruce Graham, of John Hancock Center fame, and Cesar Pelli, the architect for the planned Sky Needle.

Suburban shadows: In 1987 Beitler built the only high-rise in the Chicago suburbs, a 31-story office building in Oakbrook, for which he engaged Helmut Jahn, one of the city's and the world's most famous and controversial architects.

"Tower" is a relative term in Chicago. Examples from the dawn of the skyscraper are clustered in the city's South Loop along Dearborn Street, a group of buildings fewer than 20 stories tall, with masonry facades. Here are the protruding bays, the spare, unornamented surfaces, the penchant for expanses of glass that would characterize Chicago building for the next century. Here are the "Chicago windows," grouped in sets of three.

These proto-skyscrapers look squat and somewhat inelegant today, sooty and down on their luck. But these buildings embody the spirit of post-fire Chicago: no-nonsense, sturdy, dependable structures with a minimum of fuss. If more of their ilk have not been saved – and Chicago has an appalling track record on historic preservation – it's because Chicago is much better at building new landmarks than preserving old ones.

For example, all that's left of the facade of one of the city's most famous landmarks, the Stock Exchange Building designed by Louis Sullivan, is the entrance arch, saved when the building was demolished in 1972 and resettled, sculpture-like, behind the Art Institute of Chicago. There it remains, a reminder of how much the city has lost and continues to lose.

This is the double-edged sword of Chicago architecture, with its go-for-broke mentality that spurs architects and developers to stretch the limits of the skyscraper form, but also obliterates the city's history in its path.

Building history: Of course, many early buildings still stand. The 16-story Monadnock Building at 53 W. Jackson Blvd, built in 1891 by John Root, is the world's tallest building bearing its own weight; the walls are six feet thick at the bottom. Although constructed using outmoded technology, the building has a modern sensibility. The straightforward, clean lines are what architecture critics call "honest," meaning the building doesn't pretend to be anything it isn't. Chicago architecture, if not its politics, is known for honesty.

Across the street along Dearborn are the Pontiac (14 stories, built in 1891), Old Colony (16 stories, 1894) and Fisher (18 stories, 1896) buildings, some of the earliest examples of the steel-frame skyscraper. Steel frames opened up the sky for architects, allowing them the freedom to design true high-rises.

Ironically, the Fisher Building is less modern-looking than the older Monadnock. It exhibits a nostalgia for old-fashioned forms, however, with an ornamented facade designed to disguise the swarthy steel construction beneath. The quintessential Chicago skyscraper is characterized by simplicity, a lack of "unnecessary" ornamentation; style is secondary to structure. These buildings aren't ashamed of the steel skeleton beneath the facade.

Early skyscrapers that flaunt their construction technology still stand on State Street, where the 15-story Reliance Building and 12-story Carson Pirie Scott department store exude the confidence and the skill of Chicago's architectural pioneers. Although the Reliance Building at 36 N. State is in terrible disrepair, its elegance and strength are apparent: crumbling terra-cotta, the loss of its cornice and the ugly ground-floor men's shop can't rob this Daniel Burnham building of its art.

Glass houses: The Reliance Building was built in 1895; Carson's, one of Louis Sullivan's most famous designs, in 1899. It is startling, given their age, that such a high percentage of the facades are made of glass. These are show-off buildings, bragging that so many stories can be held up by such thin tendons of steel. They are only a stone's throw in spirit from the glass towers of the modernists, for which Chicago architecture is probably best known.

It is no accident that Chicago, where the value of new construction has always come before the less tangible good of saving the old and treasured, was the refuge for Bauhaus architects fleeing wartime Germany. Ludwig Mies van der Rohe was the most prominent of these architects to settle in Chicago, which proved a receptive canvas for his daring new buildings.

Perhaps nowhere is Mies' glass and steel

Left, shimmering skyscrapers. Right, architectural contrasts.

vocabulary better articulated than in his buildings here, from the famous 860–880 Lake Shore Drive apartments to the IBM Building at the Chicago River and Wabash Street. As these two structures prove, Mies' goal was an international style of architecture that didn't distinguish among residential, office, industrial or public uses. These are prisms, faceted jewels, beautiful in their craftsmanship and precision, but cold.

With Mies leading the way, Chicago developed an architectural style that can only be described as macho: strong and sinewy was in; warm and flowery was out. The street grid is peppered with these monumental office buildings, and the major federal and city buildings are also cut from modernist cloth.

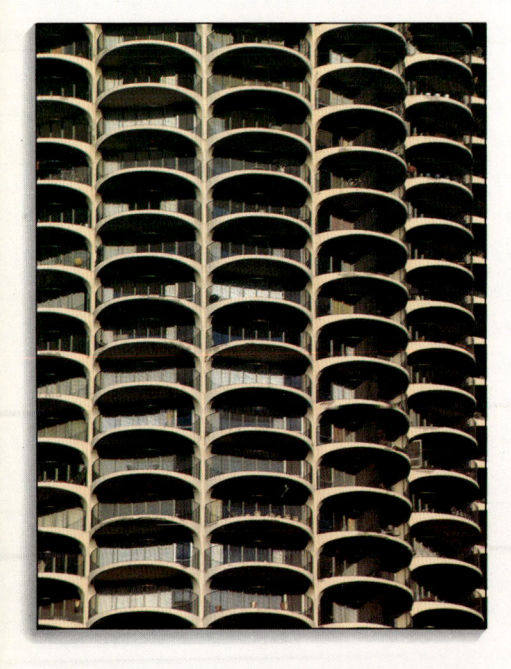

Modernist influence: Some of the city's best modernist buildings are the least famous – Time-Life at 541 N. Fairbanks, Inland Steel at 30 W. Monroe, First National Bank at Madison and Clark streets – and the idiosyncratic: Marina City (dubbed Corncob Towers by locals) at the river and Dearborn, plus the Metropolitan Detention Center at Van Buren and Clark, a downtown jail with slits of windows splayed outward, so the prisoners get the maximum view.

Chicago's modernist buildings are energizing – dynamic and daring essays in construction. They provide a shimmering backdrop for the latest round of tower-building, in which this hard-edged city has acquired a slightly more romantic, certainly less masculine ambience. Everything the modernists believed in has been turned on its ear by the post-modernists, and while Chicago was slow to acquire some of these new designs, it has caught up with a vengeance. The result: a skyline with a little less brawn and a little more grace.

The other nice thing about these new towers is the echo of an architectural aesthetic that made Chicago famous for its building. Details like the tri-partite Chicago window, a 10-story cornice line along Michigan Avenue and a preference for rough-hewn stone at ground level are cropping up in these new designs as the architects pay homage to their building's local antecedents.

Architecture has always been one of the city's greatest exports. No more. New York architects, most notably Kohn Pedersen & Fox, have contributed some of the city's most stunning buildings in recent years; KPF's 333 W. Wacker Drive is one of the best buildings in the city. The 36-story office tower makes a virtue of its triangular site, curving along the bend of the Chicago River on its west facade and presenting a jutting, angular face to the rugged city to the east. The reflective glass, long a favorite of the modernists, is here transposed into a skin as warm as it is taut, lit up daily by the reflection of the setting sun.

There's no question that the out-of-town architects have effected a change in tone. Suddenly, for example, there's a skyline to light up. The flat tops of the Miesian buildings didn't offer much in the way of drama. But the new round of towers – 900 N. Michigan Avenue, 123 N. Wacker, the AT&T Corporate Center (100 S. Franklin), NBC Tower (200 E. Illinois) – boast distinctive tops, often fanciful turrets or spires, that lend themselves to night lights.

Night skyline: Some of the old-timers are lighting up, too. The Chicago Board of Trade (Jackson and LaSalle) and 919 N. Michigan (formerly the Palmolive and then the Playboy Building) have joined the Wrigley

Building and Tribune Tower, both located north of the river on Michigan Avenue, which have long been illuminated at night.

Chicago is lucky to have so many wonderful buildings, because it has precious few wonderful open spaces. The city has less parkland per capita than any other major city in America, and the relentless street grid precludes the grand vistas of European and East Coast cities. This is a place whose children would be startled by the sound of birds and for whom a special farm-in-the-park was built to show them where milk comes from.

While developers can produce great buildings, great spaces require planning, which necessitates putting the brakes on development. And the same zeitgeist that has nurtured the construction of tall buildings has stifled city planning in Chicago. American city planning was born here, with Daniel Burnham's 1909 plan, but it was a stillbirth. Planning may get in the way of development and, as such, has always been suspect.

Planning in Chicago has almost always, therefore, happened by accident. For example, one would think the city's magnificent front yard, Grant Park, was the result of a grand scheme. In fact, it is the consequence of retailer Montgomery Ward's irritation in the late 1890s over plans to build a small city of public buildings – museums and the like – in Grant Park. The building would have obscured the lake view from his corporate headquarters on N. Michigan Avenue, so Ward dug up an old clause in the city code that decreed the lakefront should be "forever free and clear." Ward prevailed, preserving his view, and one of the city's great amenities, forever.

Although Burnham's name is invoked regularly, very little of his ambitious city plan was ever implemented. The Buckingham Fountain made it, as did the layout for the museums along the lakefront. But there's no Civic Center, few of the tree-lined boulevards and not much of the system of southern lakefront lagoons and islands that Burnham once envisioned.

Instead, it is the great planner's credo – "Make no little plans" – that is invoked, and that philosophy has shaped the city. Developers make no small plans, either, and by some magic the result is one of the world's great architectural mosaics.

Left, Marina City. Right, helicopter plies Sears Tower airspace.

Architecture 99

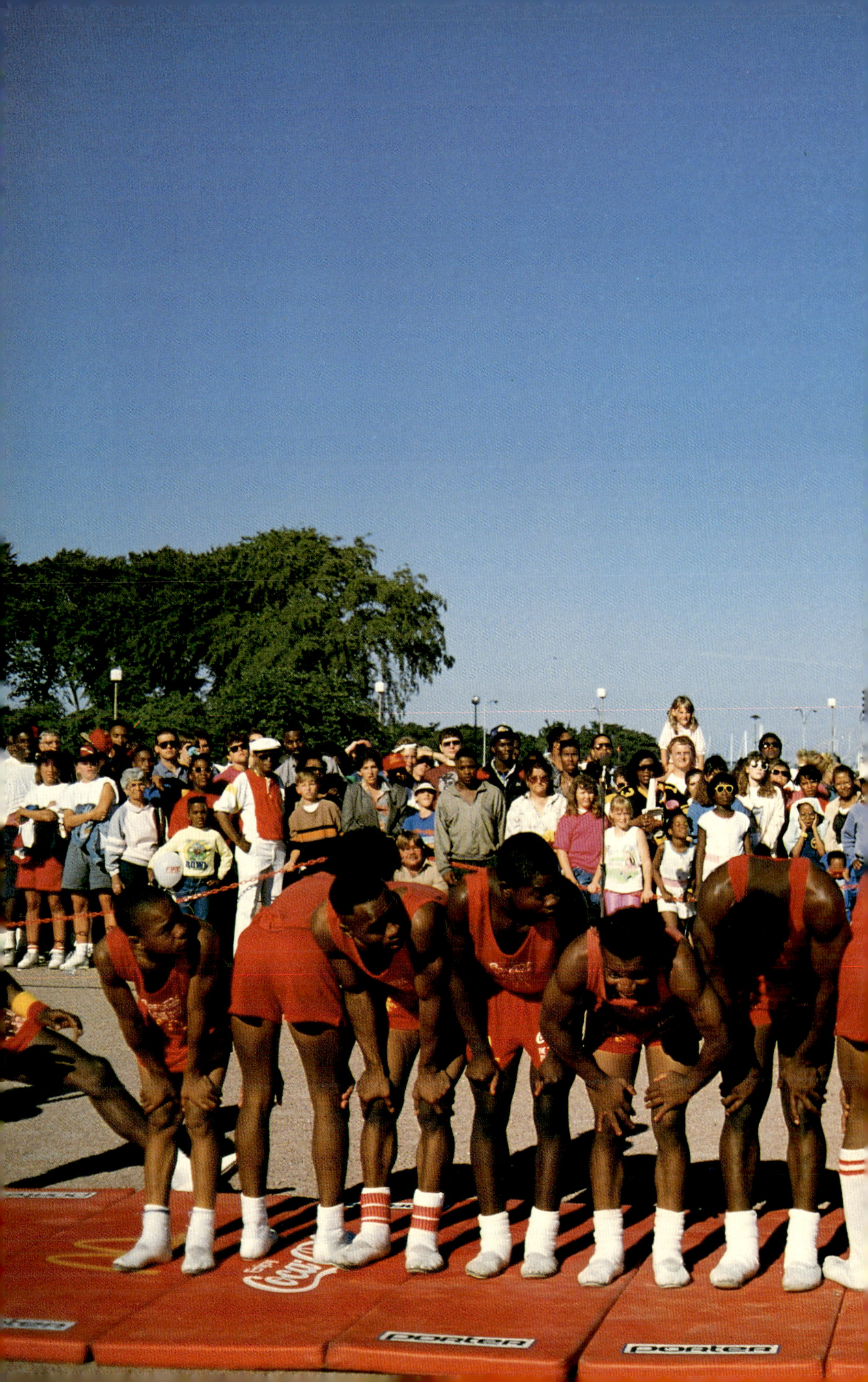
porter
porter

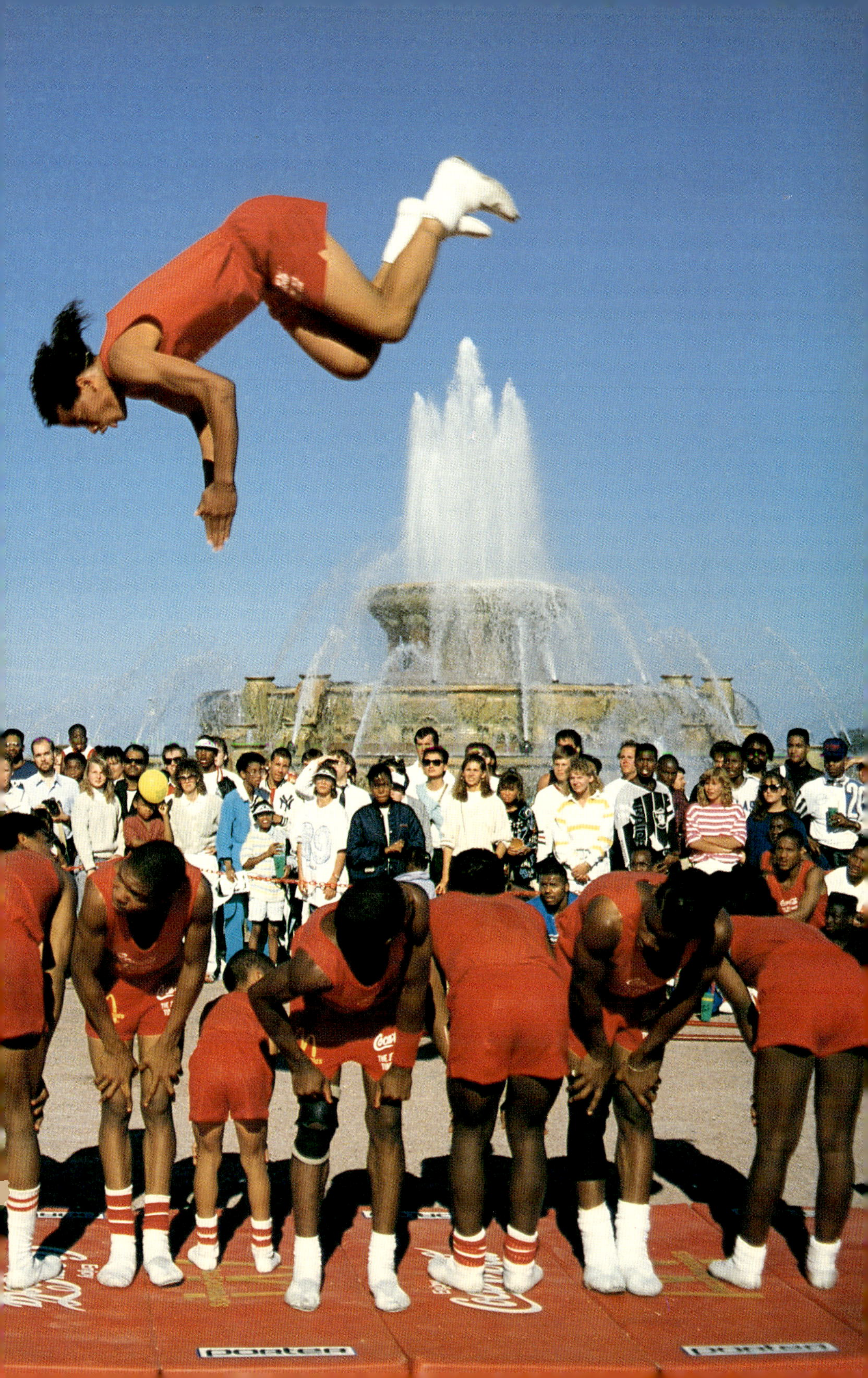

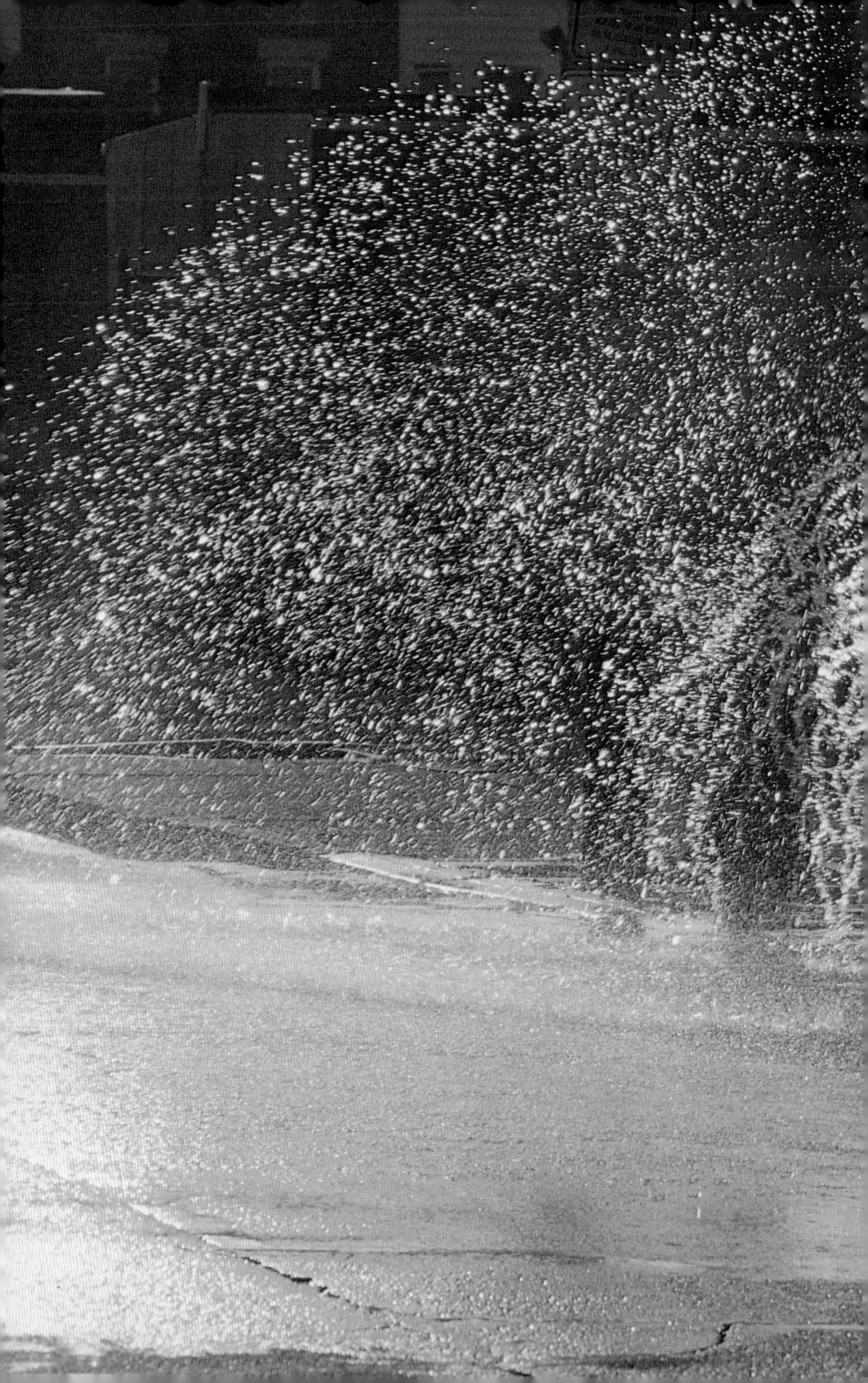

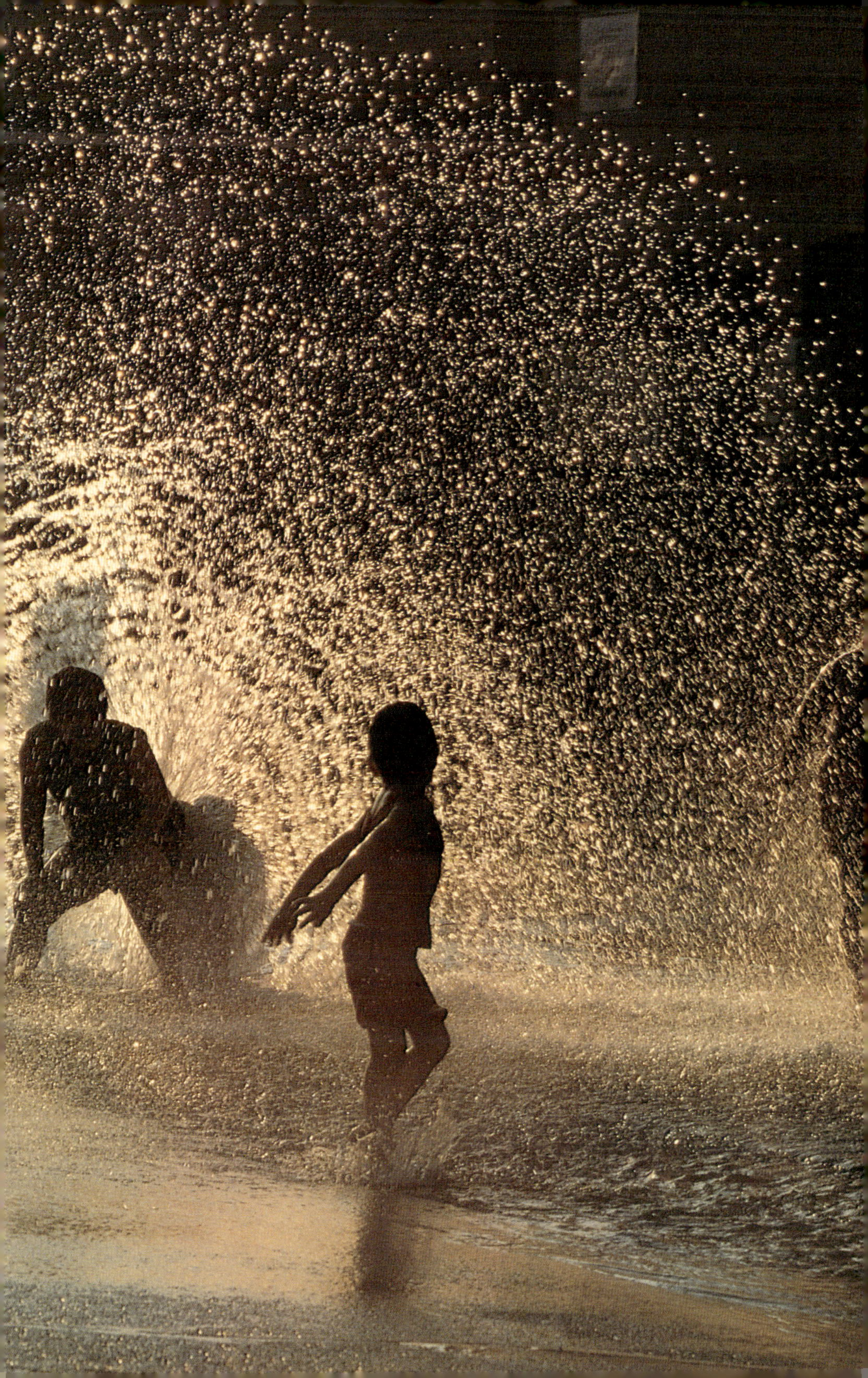

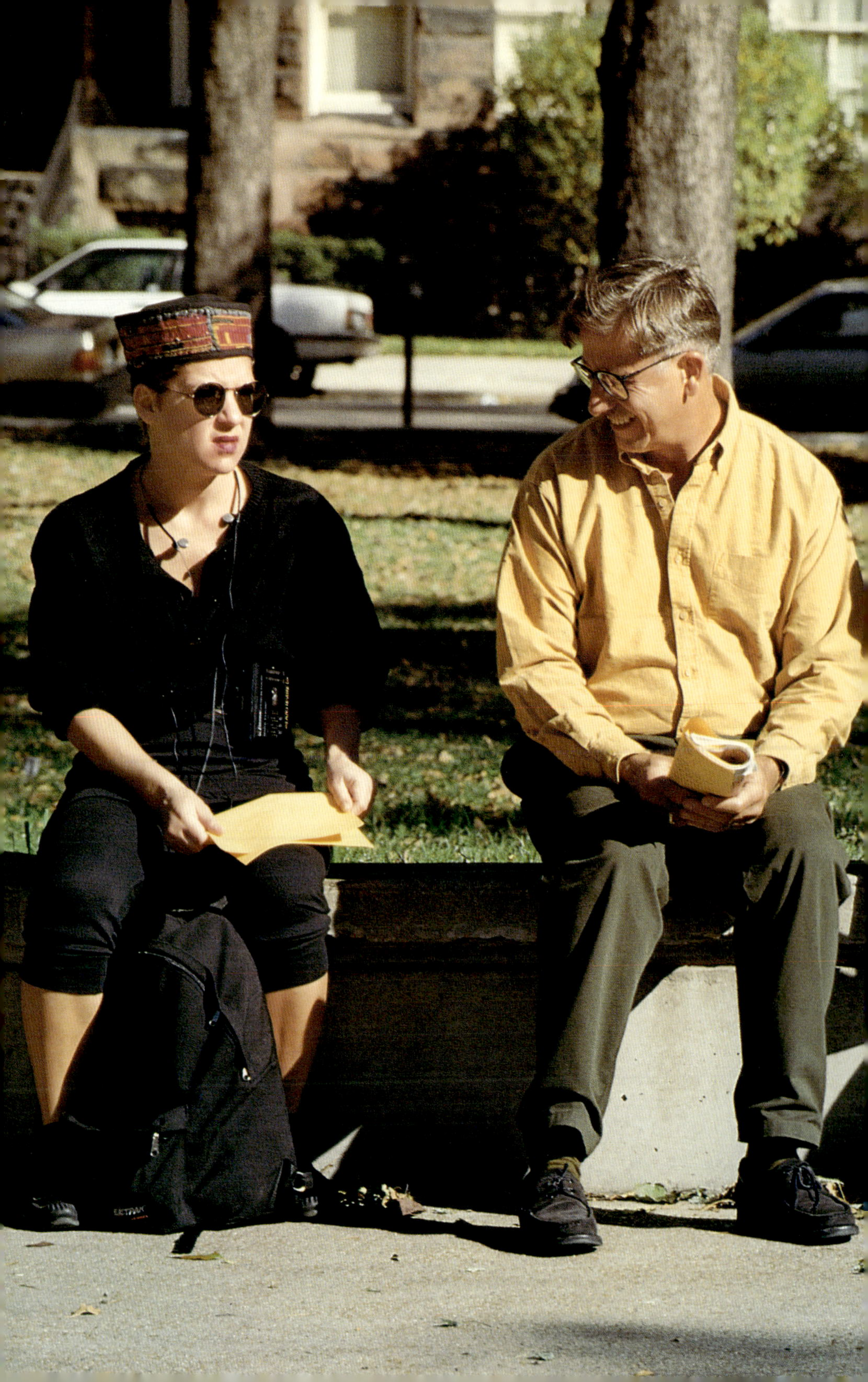

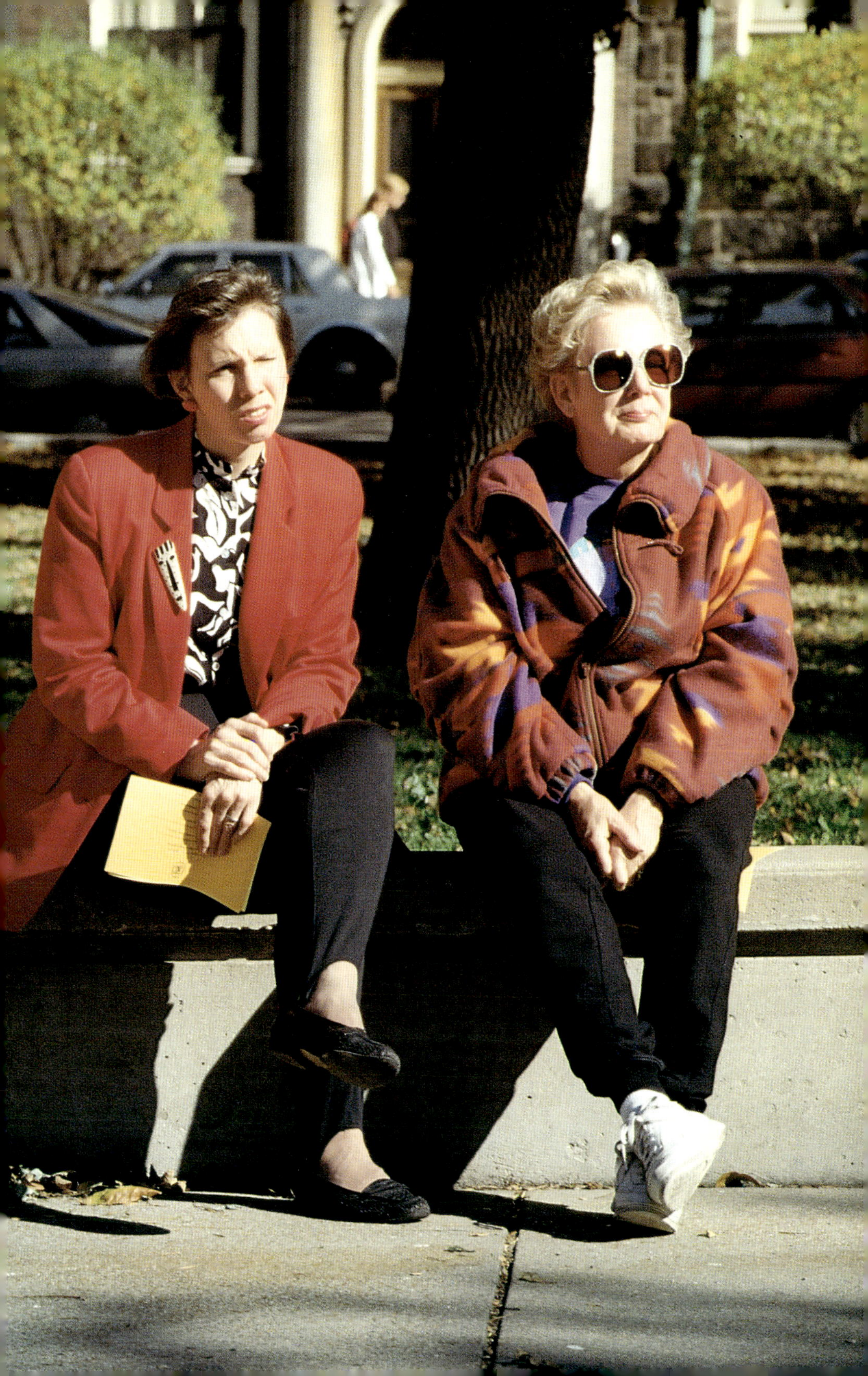

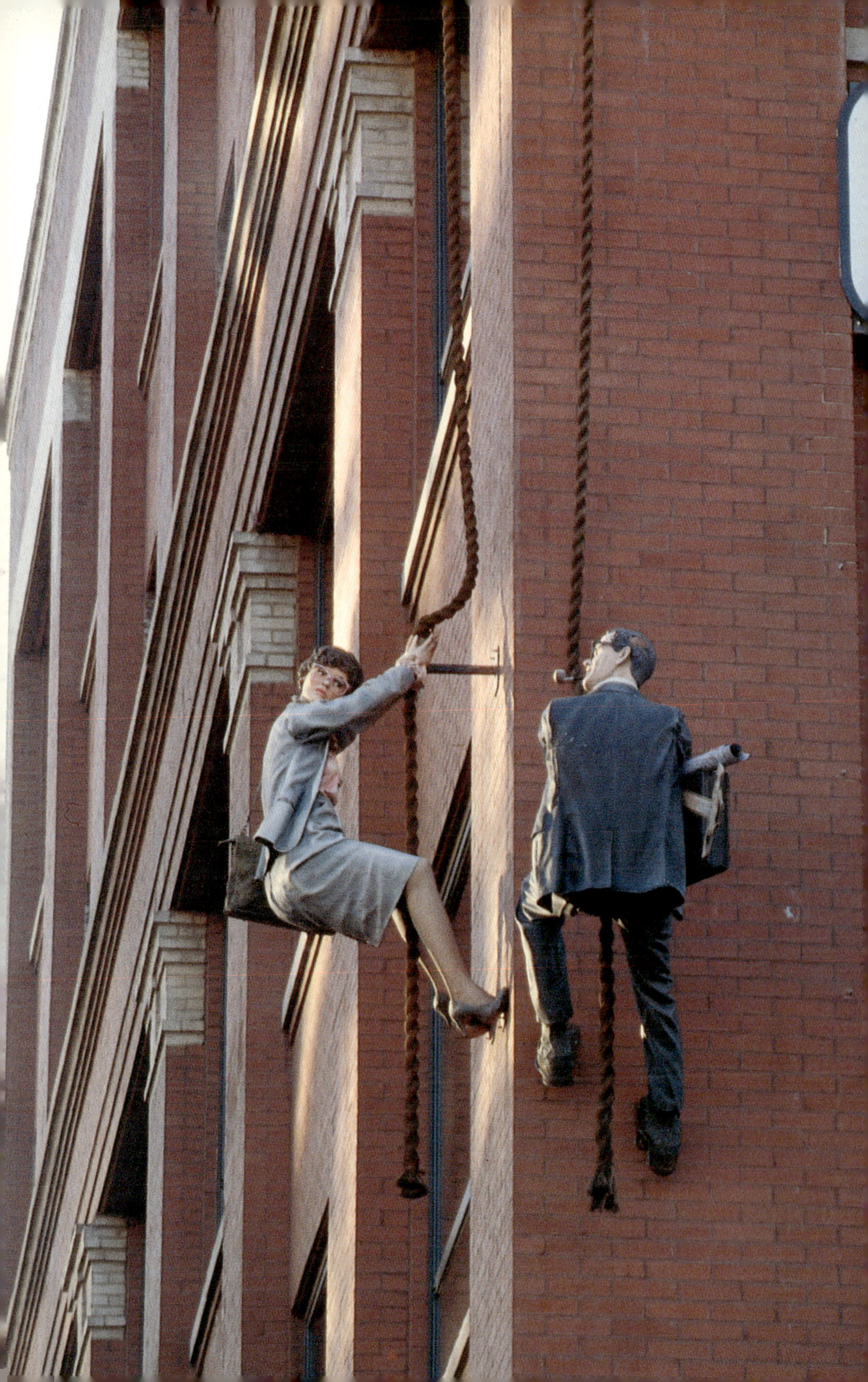

THERE MUST BE AN EASIER WAY IN!!

Chicago
1 mile / 1,6 km
Lake Michigan
Irving Park Rd.
GRACELAND CEMETERY
WRIGLEY FIELD
Bird Sanctuary
Addison St.
Addison St.
WRIGLEYVILLE
Lake Shore Drive
Western Ave.
Ashland Ave.
Clark St.
BELMONT HARBOR
Belmont Ave.
Belmont Ave.
Halsted St.
Racine St.
Chicago Yacht Club
Elston St.
John F. Kennedy Expressway
Diversey Pkwy.
Diversey Pkwy.
North Lagoon
LINCOLN PARK
Damen Ave.
Lincoln Ave.
PARK WEST
North Pond
Pavillion
Fullerton Ave.
Fullerton Ave.
FULLERTON BEACH
Clybourn Ave.
SHEFFIELD
Clark St.
Lincoln Park Conservatory
ZOO
South Lagoon
Milwaukee Ave.
BUCKTOWN
LINCOLN PARK
Armitage Ave.
Armitage Ave.
Chicago Academy of Sciences
South Pond
NORTH AVE. BEACH
Farm in the Zoo
North Ave
North Ave.
HUMBOLDT PARK
OLD WICKER PARK
OLD TOWN
Chicago Historical Society
CABRINI GREEN
GOLD COAST
California St.
Division St.
Division St.
OAK ST. BEACH
John F. Kennedy Expwy.
Ogden Blvd.
LaSalle St.
State St.
Michigan Ave.
OUTER HARBOR
Chicago Ave.
Chicago Ave.
Cathedral
Milwaukee Ave.
Orleans St.
UKRAINIAN VILLAGE
Grand Ave.
Grand Ave.
Merchandise Mart
STREETERVILLE
WEST TOWN
Racine Ave.
Washington Blvd
Randolph St.
City Hall
Randolph Dr.
Warren Blvd.
Washington St.
Randolph St.
Northwestern St.
Sears Tower
LOOP
Adams St.
Adams St.
Art Institute
Jackson Blvd.
Union St.
Jackson St.
CHICAGO HARBOR
Dwight D. Eisenhower Expressway
LaSalle St.
Congress Pkwy.
GRANT PARK
Lake Shore Drive
MEDICAL CENTER
Univ. of Illinois at Chicago
Halsted St.
Dan Ryan Expressway
Shedd Aquarium
Adler Planetarium
Roosevelt Rd.
Roosevelt Rd.
S. Br. Chicago R.
DOUGLAS PARK
UNIVERSITY VILLAGE
Canal St.
Field Museum
South Water Market
Ogden Blvd.
Blue Island Ave.
SOUTH LOOP
Indiana Ave.
NORTHERLY ISLAND
18th St.
18th St.
BURNHAM PARK YACHT HARBOR
Marshall Blvd.
HEART OF CHICAGO
Ashland Ave.
PILSEN
Archer Ave.
Cermak Rd.
Cermak Rd.
Western Ave.
McCormick Place
Blue Island Ave.
California Blvd.
26th St.
Damen Ave.
Adlai E. Stevenson Expressway
26th St.
Lake Shore Drive
California St.
Chicago San. & Ship Canal
31st Blvd.
31st Blvd.
31st Blvd.
State St.
Michigan Ave.
King Dr.
31ST ST. BEACH
Adlai E. Stevenson Expressway
S. Branch Chicago R.
BRIDGEPORT
WHITE SOX PARK
Dan Ryan Expwy.
NEAR SOUTH SIDE
LAKE MEADOWS
M. Luther
Archer Ave.
Ashland Ave.
Racine Ave.
Halsted St.
Indiana Ave.
35th St.
35th St.
35th St.
BURNHAM PARK

PLACES

Chicago is a city of extremes, from the weather to the politics to the architecture. Given its rambling, rambunctious history, it's not surprising that the city retains much of the spirit of individualism upon which it was built.

That individualism is reflected in the city's different districts, from the gloss of the Gold Coast and the Magnificent Mile to the dozens of neighborhoods that fan out from the city's focus, the downtown lakefront. Sociologists debate whether or not Chicago is America's "most segregated" city, but no one disagrees that it is the major city best defined as a collection of neighborhoods.

Many of the ethnic barriers of the old immigrant neighborhoods have broken down, but enough remain to make Chicago a living exhibit of the American melting pot. Fires, riots, booms and busts, strikes, atomic experiments – the landmarks of events that shaped America are literally underfoot throughout Chicago.

Another distinct aspect of Chicago is its North-South divide. The side of the river on which one is born has relatively little influence on future wealth and happiness, but everything to do with a lifelong disdain for people born on the other side.

Both North and South Siders agree, however, that the downtown lakefront is Chicago at its most extreme: a vast lake, tall buildings, great museums, popular beaches, glittering shops, renowned theaters, famous hot dog stands, classy restaurants and the Midwestern Americans who use these aspects of their city daily.

Chicago's sense of irony is reflected in the way that, after years of trying to shrug off the gangster legacy, there are now guided tours showing where who did what to whom.

Rush Street is Chicago's best-known district for nighttime revelry, but today the action has spread much wider and is more varied. Comedy and cabaret clubs are a specialty, from the Second City troupe that has produced so many TV and movie stars to the smaller spots that feature local comics and singers.

Finally, Chicago offers more festivals and celebrations of music, food and people than perhaps any other American city. Chicago is a town to be celebrated for what it is now rather than for its past, and Chicagoans are only too happy to do that kind of celebrating almost every day.

Preceding pages: flipping at the fountain; fire hydrant fun; waiting for a bus; climbing the corporate ladder.

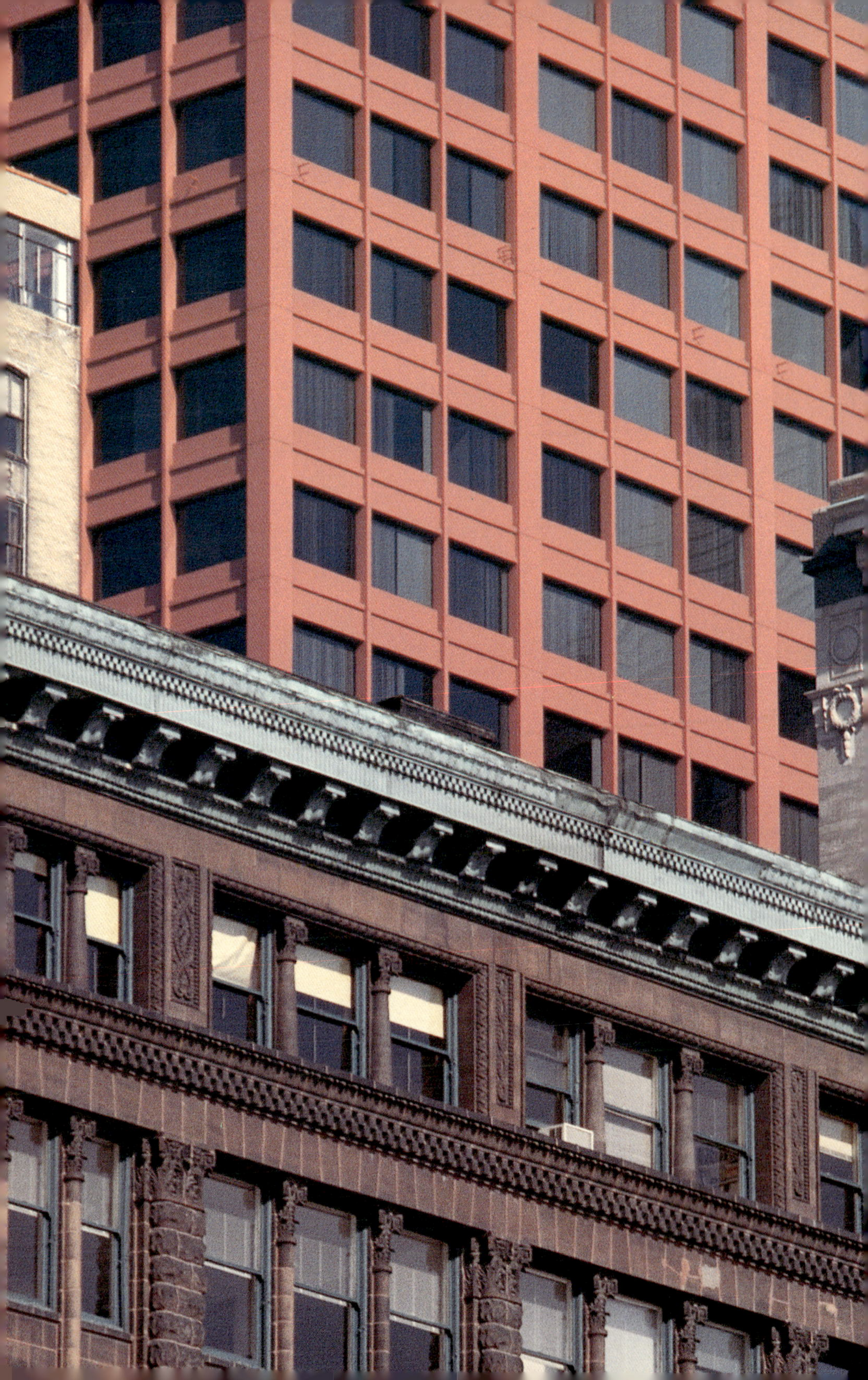

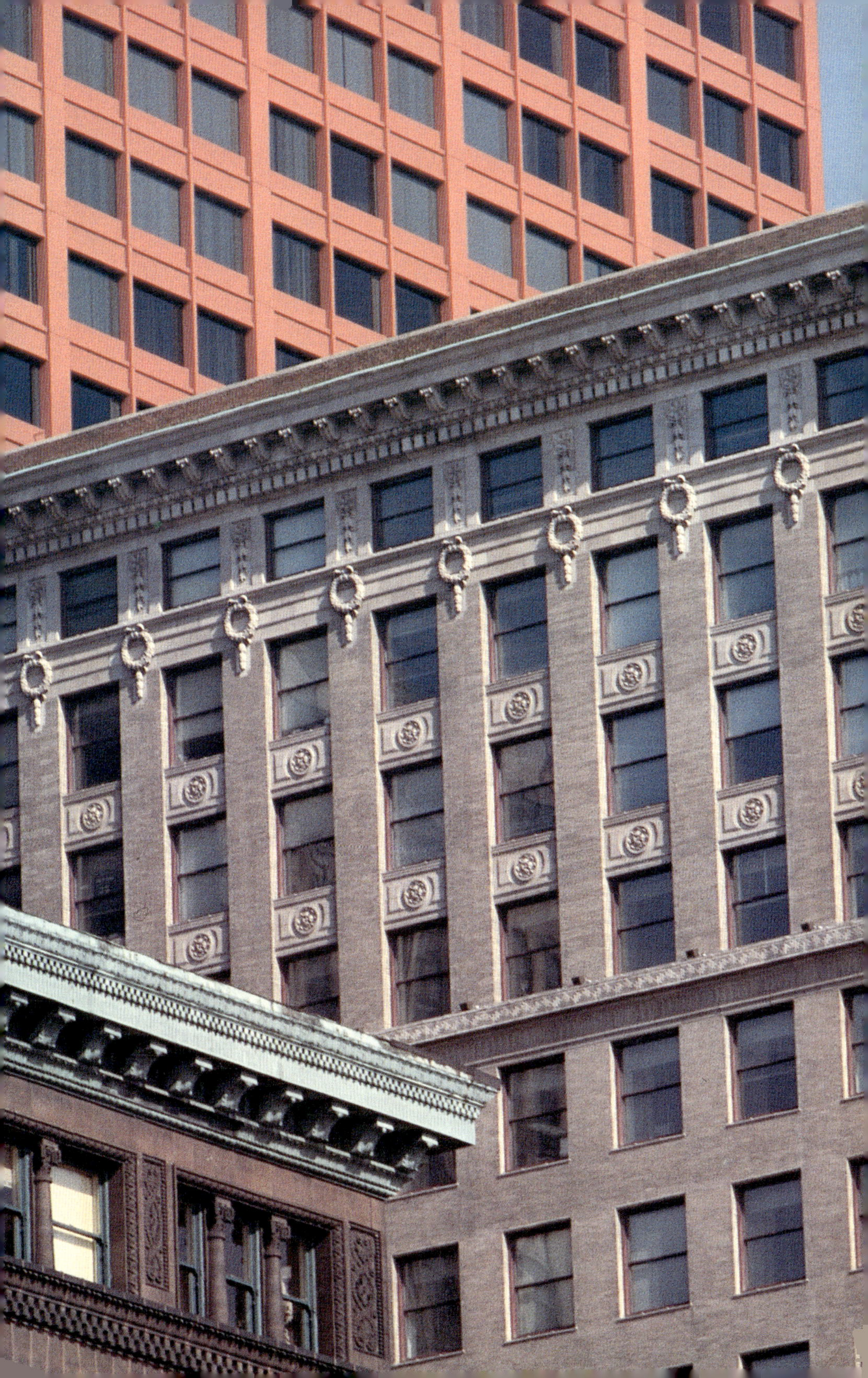

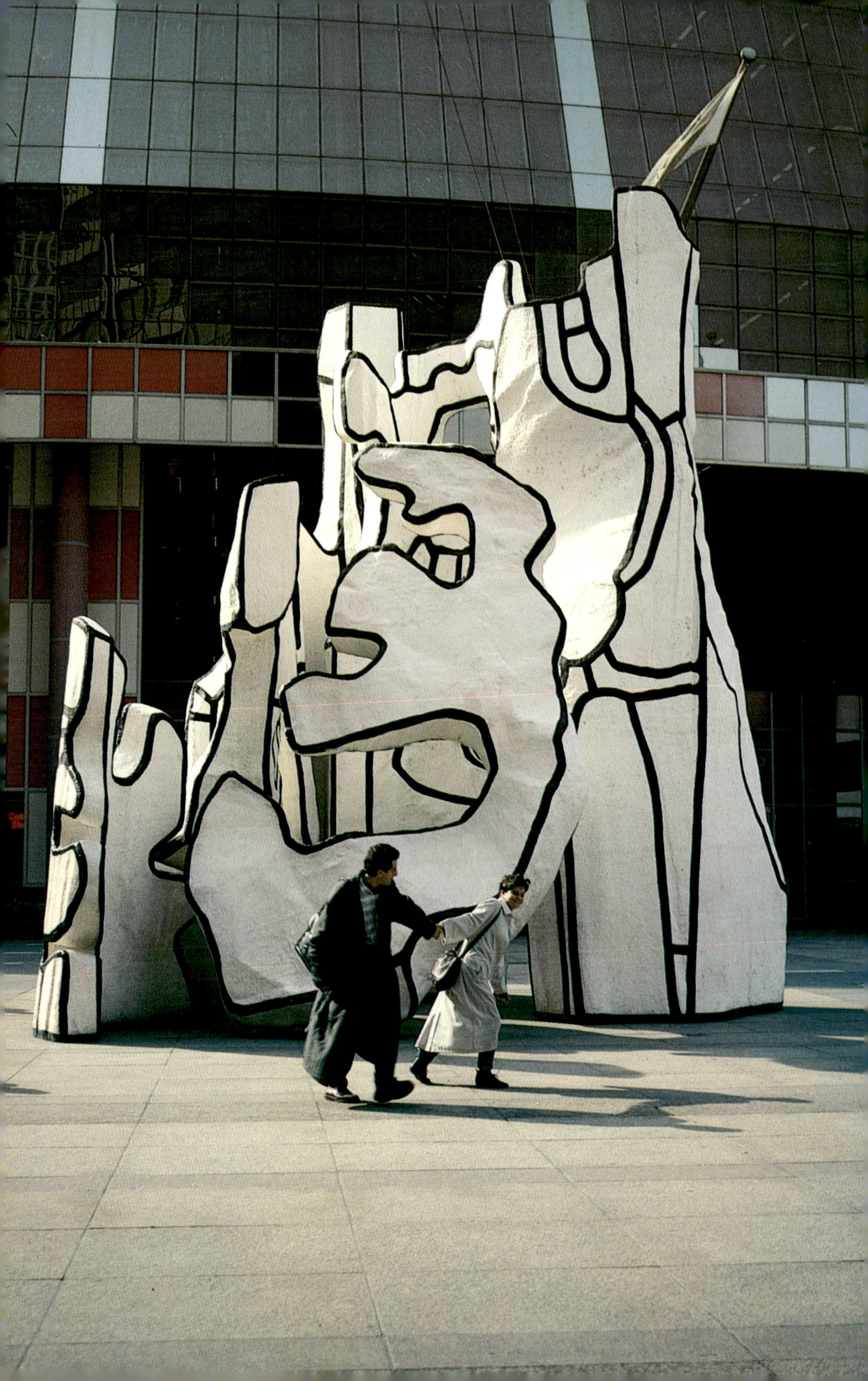

LOOPING THE LOOP

The Loop, a reference to the circumnavigations of the elevated train system, or the El, is how Chicagoans refer to their downtown, the heart of the city.

The Chicago River, spanned by 10 bridges from Lake Shore Drive to Franklin Street, affords a good introduction to the Loop. Cruise boats, Chicago's answer to the *bâteaux mouches* that ply the Seine, dock at North Pier and Michigan and Wacker. One 90-minute Architectural Cruise chugs past Chicago's famous "corncobs," **Marina City**, the graceful trefoil curve of **Lake Point Tower**, the powerful steel-banded **John Hancock building**, and the lopsided steel-and-glass, balloon-like **State of Illinois building**.

On another worthwhile cruise, a guide provided by the Chicago Architecture Foundation covers the city's famous downtown architects from Mies van der Rohe to Helmut Jahn, and then cantilevers to energy consumption, commenting on or pointing out some 100 notable structures in the course of the journey. Less scholarly but operating more frequently, non-specialist boat tours offer 60-minute, 90 minute and two-hour cruises throughout the day and into the evening, when the light-dotted cityscape is often silhouetted against a velvety sky.

Museum buses: Another way to get a sense of the Loop is to take one of the Chicago Transit Authority (CTA) air-conditioned **Culture Buses** that stop at many of the city's most significant museums, neighborhoods and monuments. There are three non-overlapping routes, North, South, and West, and though they all begin at the Art Institute on Michigan Avenue, they ramble in and out of the Loop before returning. Culture vultures and their long-suffering companions may board the bus at one museum, get off to tour another and then catch a later bus to a third.

As an adjunct to boat and bus, or just for its own flawed charm, visitors ought to consider a loop around the Loop via the El. It won't be a quiet experience. The wheels wring banshee shrieks from the tracks as they take the curves, teenagers scream deliriously into each other's rock-deafened ears, the motorman calls out stops over a muddy public-address system and the occasional lurching drunk or wacko extemporizes for the benefit of one and all. But that's Chicago, and the El is about as non-touristy as Chicago gets.

El on Wheels: On the El, a good place to begin a Loop tour is at the **Merchandise Mart** between Wells and Orleans streets, north of the river. The Mart, closed except to the trade, wears a skin of limestone and terra cotta ornamentals, but these do little to soften its brooding magisterial aspect.

Those who board the southbound Ravenswood train one stop earlier, at Chicago, should keep an eye out for the "climbers" on the right, a startling sight

Preceding pages: old skyscrapers against modern backdrop. *Left,* Dubuffet's *Monument with Standing Beast. Right,* doormen's changing of the guard.

Looping the Loop 113

even for seasoned riders. **The climbers** (see page 106) are life-sized models, a man and woman, dressed in business suits. They appear to be pulling themselves up or, possibly, letting themselves down the somber face of a building not much more than 30 feet from the passing trains. Each clutches a realistic briefcase in one hand, and a rope that trails from an overhead fixture in the other. A cartoon balloon sagging from the man's mouth declaims, "There must be an easier way in."

It's worth a few minutes to leave the train and look around the El's **Quincy-Wells station**. Dating from 1897 but recently restored and repainted, it rises above the platforms like an art-deco bungalow. Back on the El, heading east on Van Buren, the odd but dramatic triangular building on the right is the **William J. Campbell US Courthouse Annex**, but the inmates know it better as the Metropolitan Detention Center. This innovative 27-story building, designed for prison efficiency, maximizes the number of cells, each with its own window, in the given space. It also minimizes the hall space necessary to reach them. All in all, the center is a scientific rather than a humanistic exercise in incarceration.

Fizzy facades: Just down the street on the left is the **Fisher Building**, built in 1896 and extended in 1907. From the El, the building's facade, tiers of tall windows gathered into triplets by rounded masonry arches, appears to shimmer gently. The **Automat Building**, also on the left, acquired its jazzy facade of polychromed terra cotta in 1917 when Horn and Hardart converted it from a seedy hotel into a haven for people who didn't mind putting nickels into machines in order to get their food from behind automated windows. What they saw was what they got.

As the train swings left entering Wabash on its northward run, it passes the **CNA Center**, a deep, almost oxblood-red pair of buildings supported on steel columns – Mies van der Rohe's

Loop lines.

Downtown Chicago

1 Univ. of Chicago Campus
2 Time Life Bldg.
3 Tribune Tower
4 Wrigley Bldg.
5 Sun Times Bldg.
6 Merchandise Mart
7 Illinois Center
8 Prudential Bldg.
9 Amoco Bldg.
10 Chicago Theatre
11 Randolph St. Station
12 City Hall & Cook County Bldg.
13 Daley Center
14 Marshall Field
15 Chic. Public Library & Cultural Center
16 Civic Opera House
17 First National Bank
18 Carson Pirie Scott & Co.
19 Palmer House
20 Goodman Theatre
21 Union Station
22 Sears Tower
23 Dirksen Bldg.
24 Art Institute
25 Petrillo Music Shell
26 Post Office
27 Roosevelt University
28 Lincoln Statue
29 Buckingham Fountain
30 Chicago Hilton & Towers
31 Northwestern Station
32 La Salle Station

114

influence. On the left are glimpses of students poring over books at DePaul University's Loop campus, and on either side office buildings flow by as, through the windows, draftsmen move T-squares across slanted boards, dancers spin, and typists punch.

Unless you are determined to complete the loop, exit at **State Street**. "That great street," converted to a pedestrian mall, has lost some weight while gaining in breadth. Widened for its renaissance as a mall, the street gained stalls selling popcorn and fruit. But major retailers such as Wieboldt's, Lytton's, Goldblatt's, Steven's, and Montgomery Ward pulled up stakes in the 1980s, leaving a swath of schlock storefronts advertising cheap electronics and kitsch.

Amid the junk, a few oldtimers remain. Evans, selling women's clothing just south of Madison, tries to ignore the occasional anti-fur picketers. **Marshall Field's** is still an anchor, along with rival department store **Carson Pirie Scott & Co**. Designed by Louis H. Sullivan and built by Daniel Burnham, the Carson Pirie Scott Building retains the architectural tension and grace which made it revolutionary at the turn of the century. Wide, light-embracing windows on the terra-cotta facing rise above cast-iron reliefs that lend strength to the lower floors. The grill on the southwest corner recreates, in metal, swirling floral fantasies reminiscent of Art Nouveau calligraphy.

On Michigan Avenue, just outside the southern boundaries of the Loop proper, are the Museum of Contemporary Photography and the Spertus Museum. The **Museum of Contemporary Photography**, a Columbia College project, takes light-sensitive emulsions – not to mention 19th-century coated glass plates and contemporary electronic adjuncts – seriously. Special exhibits usually complement the internationally-respected Permanent Collection and Print Study Room.

The **Spertus Museum** has a split

Buckingham Fountain, Grant Park.

personality. Part of the collection celebrates the survival of the Jewish people as embodied in their art: the gilt Torah pointers and needlepoint Torah covers of the medieval *stetl* (village), parchment manuscripts and tableware, and modern Israeli festival lamps alongside 300-year-old Passover dishes. The rest of the Spertus collection mourns the horrors of the Holocaust, with numbing mounds of clothing, heaps of buttons and piles of human hair retrieved from the death camps. The museum is unified, however, in its drive to explain Jewish history and celebrate Jewish people.

School daze: Heading north up Michigan Avenue, the **Auditorium Building** once housed a hotel and offices as well as a major theater. The theater and its magnificent tiered ceiling remain, but **Roosevelt University**, a prime example of a city school, has taken over the rest. Theatergoers reach the steeply-banked gallery via an elevator and corridor shared with the school, and a wrong turn may lead to Sociology 101 rather than the opening curtain of *Les Sylphides.*

Further north on Michigan, the granite-and-limestone **Fine Arts Building**, originally a showcase for the Studebaker Carriage Co., now produces budding artists like Jackson Pollack and Virgil Thomson.

The nearby Santa Fe building houses the **Chicago Architecture Foundation's Shop and Tour Center**. This bookstore-cum-gallery is devoted to the history of Chicagoan architecture, The Foundation also maintains the Glessner House and the Clarke House in the Prairie Avenue Historic District, and offers more than 50 tours of architectural highlights in and around Chicago.

Two blocks on is **Orchestra Hall**, home to the Chicago Symphony Orchestra since 1904. A short walk over the green lawns of **Grant Park** east of Michigan Avenue leads to **Buckingham Fountain** which, during the summer, throws jets of water as high as 135

An engineering dedication, Daley Center.

feet. At night, concealed lights turn the jets yellow, pink, blue and green, creating one of the lakeside's more spectacular kinetic effects. Outdoor concerts are a pleasant feature of the nearby **Petrillo Band Shell**.

A tree-dotted park leads to the **Art Institute of Chicago**. Inside, the Art Institute offers a wide range of exhibits, including ancient Chinese bronzes, neolithic Ban Chiang pottery from Thailand, Arthur J. Rubloff's eye-popping collection of paperweights, some of America's choicest examples of French Impressionists and Post-Impressionists, arms and armor, textiles and pre-Columbian pottery as well as hugely popular temporary exhibits.

Founded in 1879, the Art Institute moved to its present French Renaissance-style quarters in 1892, just in time for the 1893 Columbian Exposition. The famous **stone lions** that flank the building's main entrance have, according to legend, occasionally been "sold" to unwary newcomers by hustling locals. In January 1986, when the Chicago Bears went to American football's Super Bowl, the lions found themselves in oversized football helmets fashioned from barbecue kettles.

Glorious protests: Extensive renovations and additions to the Institute over the past 15 years have added a new 1,000-seat auditorium, plus the entire **Trading Room** from the now dismantled Adler and Sullivan's Chicago Stock Exchange, which dates back to 1893. In recent years, the School of the Art Institute has been the center of considerable controversy. One student gained national attention when his painting of the late Mayor Harold Washington, decked out in bra and panties, was unceremoniously yanked from the wall by a group of irate aldermen.

In 1989, another student placed an American flag on the floor, leading some unconcerned museumgoers to walk on it. Protesters crowded the front steps, and motorists, invited to "honk if you love Old Glory," created a ca-

Mao by Warhol, Art Institute of Chicago.

Looping the Loop 117

cophony of patriotism on Michigan Avenue. Some legislators threatened to revoke public funding, but the furor eventually flagged and died down.

The Art Institute regularly offers special exhibits and lecture series. It is also associated with the adjacent **Goodman Theater**, which most nights presents classical and contemporary drama, along with new works and training for would-be playwrights and actors.

A few blocks from the river, the **Chicago Cultural Center** flaunts Tiffany mosaics and domes resplendent with stained glass. Vast public spaces connected by vaulted arches and sweeping staircases create a satisfying interior for a public building. The Center offers programs and exhibits in the performing, visual and literary arts; architectural tours are available.

On **LaSalle Street**, roughly between Madison and Jackson but spilling over onto Wacker Drive three blocks farther from the lake, is a financial district that could well be called Wall Street West. One landmark is the Board of Trade Building, its lobby an Art Deco tone poem in variegated marble, nickel steel and glass. The Lyric Opera's home on Wacker Drive, the **Civic Opera House**, is nicknamed Insull's Throne, so-called for both backer Samuel Insull and its fancied resemblance to a chair of monumental proportions.

Also on Wacker Drive is the 333 West Wacker Drive Gallery, part of the **Chicago Athenaeum**, a museum that aims to show how design can positively impact the human environment in architecture, industrial and product design, graphics and urban planning. Its resource center is at the Daniel H. Burnham Center, 1165 N. Clark Street and Gallery I is at 515 N. State Street.

Plaza art: The **Dirksen Building** and the **Kluczynski Building and Post Office**, both on Dearborn Street and named after prominent native sons, are frequently cited as two examples of Mies van der Rohe's most successful designs. Alexander Calder's *Flamingo*,

Alexander Calder's *Flamingo*.

a series of deep-red arcs whose lightness and grace belie the work's 50 tons, occupies a large, open square between the two buildings.

Meanwhile, at the **Daley Center Plaza**, 162 tons of rusted steel rise 50 feet high. Known only as *The Picasso Sculpture*, it has been the butt of jokes and the subject of criticism since it was first erected in 1967. What is it? The consensus says a woman, though some say a bird, a dog or a range of obscene suggestions. On the south side of Washington Street, directly across from the Picasso, stands **Joan Miró's** *Chicago*, a highly-stylized female figure formed from steel-reinforced concrete. Her skirt is a lively mosaic, and she shows no signs today of the vivid red spray paint with which vandals greeted her controversial arrival in 1981.

Scraping skies: The tallest bank building in the world, the **First National Bank**, soars in a gentle, pale-gray arc above a plaza that opens a few steps down from street level in the fibrillating heart of Chicago's commercial center on Dearborn and Madison. Around noon, on sunny days, the plaza around the **Hamal Fountain** rapidly fills up with office workers, lunching al fresco.

On the Dearborn Street side, **Marc Chagall's** *Four Seasons* mosaic mural, 70 feet of multi-colored marble, glass and stone, squats uncomfortably. It's best seen at night, illuminated, when it doesn't have to compete with the graceful curves of the building or the plaza's spacious sweep.

The 16-story **Monadnock Building**, on Dearborn between Van Buren and Jackson, built in 1891, is the highest ever erected using wall-bearing masonry construction instead of the modern metal-frame method of construction. Named after a picturesque mountain in northeast Vermont, the Monadnock Building remains a personal triumph for architect John Root, and one of the last great examples of a now obsolete technology.

Sears soars: In describing the world's

Arty student.

Looping the Loop 119

tallest office building, one is tempted to borrow from Alexander Pope, who wrote that he "lisped in numbers for the numbers came." Completed in 1974, the **Sears Tower**'s 110 stories soar 1,454 feet, enclose more than 4 million square feet of floor space and accommodate some 16,500 people daily. From the 103rd-floor **Skydeck**, 1,353 feet above the ground, you can see four US states on a clear day (a rarity in Chicago). Roughly 16,000 bronze-tinted glass windows and 28 acres of black anodized aluminum cover a framework of 76,000 tons of steel – and enough concrete for a five-mile long, eight-lane highway.

Admission to the Skydeck includes a multi-image slide show, *The Chicago Experience*, and a brief lecture on the building's main features with the help of a nine-foot model, built to 190th scale, that illustrates and elucidates its nuts-and-bolts workings. Go for the view and the lecture; the slide show is disappointingly uninformative, though mercifully short. Stop in on the Calder level to see **Alexander Calder's** *Universe*, a sculpture 55 feet wide, 33 feet high, consisting of a series of geometric shapes in red, yellow, orange and black, that swing and turn independently.

If hunger pangs strike in the Sears Tower, and a hot dog or doughnut will not do, pop into Mrs Levy's delicatessen for some gefilte fish, or a bagel with cream cheese and lox. Should a south-of-the-border flavor be more appealing, amble over to Dos Hermanos for tacos and enchiladas. Those who cannot leave without a tote bag, ashtray, T-shirt or souvenir mug will find 30 accommodating shops in the tower.

On the hot track: Walking east to Clark and then north brings you to the **State of Illinois Center**, which finally opened on May 6, 1985 amid negative publicity, escalating costs and many design and maintenance problems. Some called it designer Helmut Jahn's homage to megalomania. Others merely noted that 17 stories of glass encircling a huge rotunda topped by a shortened glass cylinder could be expected to play havoc with internal temperatures. And it does. Office workers on upper floors, forced to wear sunscreen and dark glasses on bright days, suffer from temperatures in the high 90s F during the steaming summer months, despite an air-conditioning system working to capacity. And when the air-conditioning breaks down, the building has to be virtually evacuated.

More than 50 state agencies are housed in the center, as well as three levels of restaurants and shops. An art gallery exhibits primarily Illinois artists and artisans, and is well worth a visit. So is the building itself, despite its drawbacks as a place to work. A glass-enclosed elevator provides a thrilling, stomach-lurching ride to the top floor, not recommended for acrophobes. A tour of the building may be had by asking at the information booth. Outside, at the main entrance, **Jean Dubuffet's** *Monument With Standing*

Field Museum of Natural History.

Beast, 10 tons of white fiberglass outlined in black, stands guard.

The museum district: South of the formal boundaries of the Loop, the Field Museum of Natural History, Shedd Aquarium and Adler Planetarium draw crowds of travelers and scholars. The **Field Museum**, whose classical lines separate the north and southbound lanes of Lake Shore Drive with majestic calm, contains more than 19 million artifacts. Named after Marshall Field I, a principal benefactor, the museum was built in 1921 from a Daniel Burnham design, and is regarded as one of the best museums in the world for anthropology, botany, zoology and geology.

A pair of enormous dinosaurs welcome visitors to the high-ceilinged entrance hall, along with an African elephant that, for many Chicagoans, is a symbol of the museum. One of the most spectacular exhibits, the life-sized **tomb of Unisankh**, scion of the Fifth Dynasty Pharaoh, has been carefully reconstructed, down to two original tomb chambers excavated in 1908. The labyrinth's display cases, including faïence amulets, tools and mummies, merge into a human-scale model of an ancient Egyptian village.

Elsewhere, there's a full-scale reproduction of a South Pacific island. Gem lovers gravitate through the extensive array of precious stones to gawk at the **Chalmers Topaz**, resplendent in all its 5,890 carats. The jade room has a superb collection of Orientalia, tempered by a small sampling of ancient jade. This stone comes not only in green but also in rich oxblood red, mustard-seed yellow and white flecked with carmine.

In the swim: Nearer the lake, in the **Shedd Aquarium**, 90,000 gallons of sea water provide a home for sharks, eels, sea turtles and other denizens of the Caribbean deep in the world's biggest public fishbowl. Divers swim among the creatures twice a day, doling out food as spectators crowd around, cameras ready to snap a hammerhead shark or moray eel literally eating out of

Detail from the ancient Egyptian *Book of the Dead*, Field Museum.

Looping the Loop 121

a diver's hand. In all, more than 6,600 specimens inhabit 200-plus separate environments. The Shedd Aquarium's **Oceanarium** duplicates a Pacific Northwest environment for whales, dolphins, sea otters and seals.

The **Adler Planetarium** peers up at the heavens from the northern point of **Northerly Island**, a five-minute walk from Lake Shore Drive via Achsah Bond Drive. The planetarium can project pictures of the night sky as it appeared when Tyrannosaurus Rex and his ilk roamed the Cretaceous swamps and forests of the American Midwest. The show suggests events that scientists believe may have occurred in the first few seconds of Time, and it also casts a speculative eye forward, up to 20 billion years in the future.

Friday nights, weather permitting, which, unfortunately, it seldom does, the show culminates with a closed-circuit TV panorama of the sky through a direct feed from the 20-inch **Doane Observatory telescope**. There's also a three-story museum that includes a **moon rock** collected by the *Apollo 15* astronauts, and the telescope through which Sir William Herschel first sighted the planet Uranus.

Those in need of sustenance might like to return to Michigan Avenue for elegant *cucina Italiana* amid the restaurant La Strada's lushly overstated ambience. Or they could mosey on over to **Printer's Row**, a place and a restaurant, the latter showcasing the skill and talent of Michael Foley, whose combination of traditional French and American nouvelle styles yields some of the most satisfying serious dining in the Loop. A spiffy, up-and-coming area it would be churlish to brand yuppified, Printer's Row does offer the young and affluent a neighborhood to call their own. Outdoor sculpture is all around, and the **Printing Museum** on South Plymouth makes an enjoyable low-key interlude from the likes of the highbrow Art Institute with its display of ponderous bronzes.

Left, Chicago photographed by NASA. **Right**, Dan Aykroyd, left, and John Belushi in *The Blues Brothers.*

CHICAGO IN THE MOVIES

The human drama, comedy and crime of Chicago, along with a cityscape ranging from lovely lakefront and soaring skyscrapers to grim ghettos and sordid stockyards, has been a fertile playground for American filmmakers.

The play *The Front Page* by Ben Hecht and Charles MacArthur described the comic rough and tumble of Chicago newspaper life in a style that has spawned several movie versions, including a largely unfunny Burt Reynolds-Kathleen Turner vehicle, the 1988 *Switching Channels*, that had the stars working in cable television news.

The original 1931 film *The Front Page* was one of the best of the early talkies, starring Pat O'Brien as an ace reporter and Adolphe Menjou as his editor, doing battle against civic corruption and one another. But a 1940 remake, *His Girl Friday*, directed by Howard Hawks, became one of America's favorite movies of the era by making the ace reporter a young, attractive woman (played by Rosalind Russell) with whom the editor (Cary Grant) falls in love while trying to stop her retiring from the paper.

The Front Page spawned a tradition of transforming Chicago's vibrant experimental theater onto the big screen. One of the more successful examples in recent years was local playwright David Mamet's modern romance-comedy of manners, *Sexual Perversity in Chicago*, which was the basis for the 1986 movie *About Last Night*. That film provided springboard roles for several rising young actors, including Demi Moore, Rob Lowe, Jim Belushi and Elizabeth Perkins, and brought to the screen a vivid picture of yuppie life in Chicago, from the sports bars to the softball along the lakefront. Later, when Mamet began writing and then directing his own screenplays, he set much of the 1988 mob comedy *Things Change* in Chicago.

Another 1986 flick that used Chicago locations well was *Ferris Bueller's Day Off*. The John Hughes comedy – one of several he has directed locally about Chicago's suburban teenagers – starred Matthew Broderick as the truant living out everyone's dreams of the way high school should have been but rarely was. Other John Hughes teen-screen hits filmed in Chicago include *Sixteen Candles* in 1984, *The Breakfast Club* and *Weird Science* in 1985 and *She's Having A Baby* in 1988.

Perhaps the quintessential Chicago movie in recent years, however, has been *The Blues Brothers*, the 1980 comedy starring John Belushi and Dan Aykroyd as Jake and Elwood Blues. The story – the outlaw boogie brothers must save their old orphanage – is corny and there are too many car crashes, but the two stars are at their best and some classic music scenes are provided by Aretha Franklin, James Brown and Ray Charles.

In 1987, *The Untouchables* was a blockbuster depiction of the Chicago story that the rest of the world knows best: crime fighter Eliot Ness's battle against the Capone mob.

One of the interesting things about the cinema in Chicago is the way big talents who came up in the town – the Belushis, Aykroyd, John Candy, David Mamet and others – return to their roots when they acquire the kind of creative control needed to dictate where their movies are shot.

Well-known movies in recent years that were filmed in or around Chicago include *Silver Streak* in 1976, *Looking for Mister Goodbar* in 1977, Robert Altman's *A Wedding* in 1978, and *Somewhere in Time* and *My Bodyguard* in 1980. *Ordinary People*, the film directed by Robert Redford that won an Oscar for best picture in 1980, was filmed in its entirety in Chicago and its North Shore suburbs.

Other locally made films include: *Four Friends* in 1981; *Endless Love* and *Continental Divide* in 1981; *Doctor Detroit*, *Bad Boys* and *Risky Business*, another teen movie that made a star of Tom Cruise in 1983, and *Streets of Fire* in 1984. Also filmed in Chicago were *The Color of Money*, the Paul Newman-Tom Cruise sequel to *The Hustler*, and Cruise-vehicle *Top Gun* in 1986; a rare John Hughes non-teen comedy, *Planes, Trains and Automobiles*, in 1987; *Major League*, *Uncle Buck* and *Music Box* starring Jessica Lange in 1989, and another Jessica Lange film, *Men Don't Leave*, released in 1990.

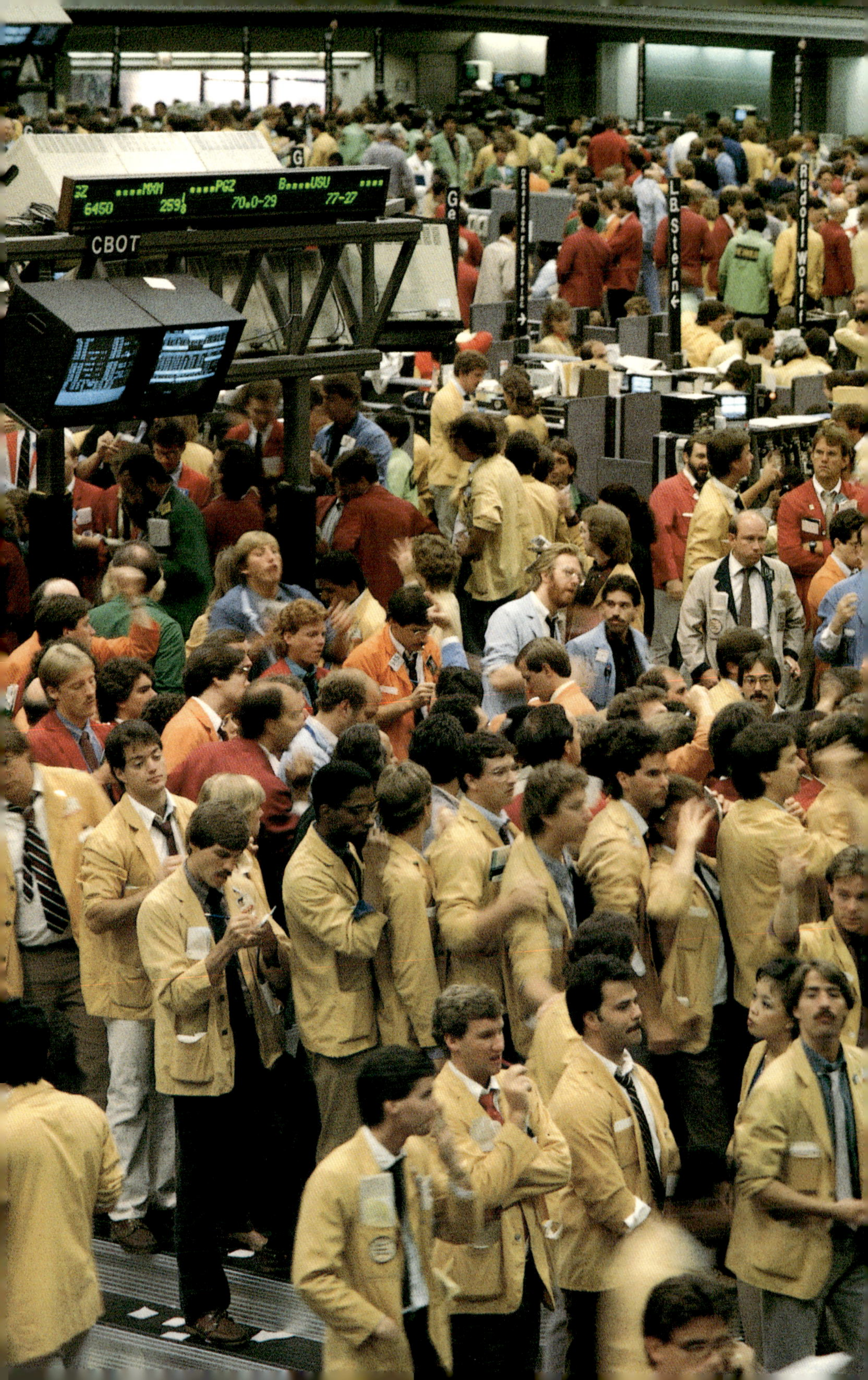
CBOT
L.B.Stern
Rudolf Wolff

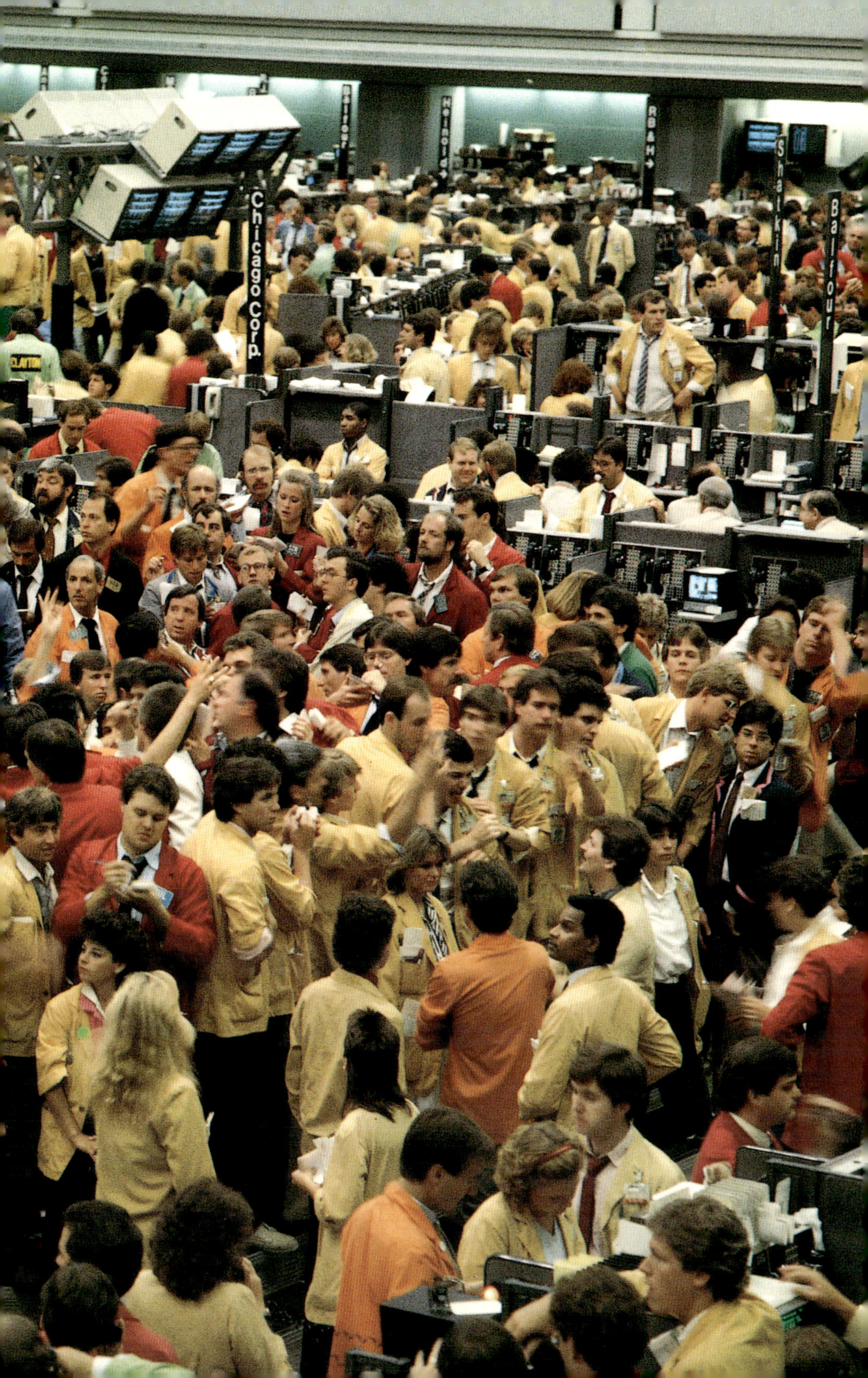
Chicago Corp.
Shatkin
Balfour
CLAYTON

CHICAGO BOARD OF TRADE

THE FINANCIAL DISTRICT

Chicago's financial district is best known for its colorful, raucous futures markets. Amid the seemingly manic action of the trading pits, world prices are set for corn, wheat, soybeans, pork bellies and live cattle, to name just a few of the commodities involved. These century-old markets have become increasingly sophisticated and now include financial instruments such as US Treasury bonds, foreign currencies from Japanese yen to German marks, Eurodollars, stock options and stock indexes.

LaSalle Street is Chicago's answer to Wall Street, lined by somber bank buildings and glistening skyscrapers that are filled with brokerages and law offices. The financial district runs from roughly **Madison Street** on the north to **Jackson Street** on the south, where LaSalle stops at the foot of the towering **Chicago Board of Trade** to form an architectural canyon. The district has been expanding westward to **Wacker Drive**, where the **Chicago Mercantile Exchange** occupies a newer 40-story twin tower.

It makes sense that commodity trading was invented in Chicago, which grew up as a transportation crossroads nestled in the Midwestern breadbasket. In the 1800s, wagons, oxcarts, barges, canalboats and railroads hauled crops here from fields across the prairie. At harvest time the streets and waterways were choked with loads of grain as local farmers scrambled to find buyers. Often there were surpluses in which case spoiled grain was often dumped into Lake Michigan. The exchanges evolved to provide an orderly marketplace for agricultural commerce.

Pit bulls: With the growth of financial futures, futures trading has spread to New York, Tokyo, London, Hong Kong and other international cities. But Chicago remains the industry's center.

Traders are easy to spot, their bright-colored trading jackets unmistakable in the financial district's bars and coffee shops, such as **Lou Mitchell's Restaurant** on W. Jackson Boulevard, where they gather to brag about their trading acumen or debate whether grain prices are heading up or down.

Inside the exchanges, traders and brokers gather in octagonal, stair-stepped rings called "pits," which allow buyers and sellers to see one another. Each pit is for a specific commodity and the biggest are crammed with hundreds of traders who at first glance seem to be simply jumping up and down, frantically waving their arms and shrieking at each other. The activity looks chaotic, but there's method to the madness. Fortunes are at stake here and millions of dollars have been made and lost in a split second.

This fast-moving game lures high-rollers: a seat on the Board of Trade, for example, costs about $400,000. But the prospect of a big score has attracted

Preceding pages: Chicago Mercantile Exchange. **Left**, Chicago Board of Trade. **Right**, John Hancock Tower.

Financial District 127

players from practically every background: ex-cops, former football players, lawyers, teachers, doctors, even professional gamblers have tried their luck in these trading pits. The Jaguars and Porsches parked in surrounding lots attest to the success of many. The unlucky lose their seats and sometimes, literally, their shirts.

On the exchange floors, there are legendary tales of brash traders who won or lost huge sums trying to corner the markets. Traders still tell stories about the time the action in the soybean pit got so crazy that a trader's leg was broken – and no one noticed him writhing on the floor in pain until after the closing bell had sounded, ending trade for the day. Or the one about the time a fire broke out on the Chicago Mercantile Exchange floor and the traders refused to stop buying and selling.

Crying out loud: The physical commodities – wheat, corn and so forth – don't actually change hands. Instead, trading takes place in the form of futures contracts, which are agreements to deliver or take delivery of a certain commodity during a specific month at a price agreed upon in the pit.

It all happens under the open-outcry method, a free-form auction in which each trader shouts out a bid or offer, often red-faced and screaming to be heard over the din. They bellow in pit lingo unintelligible to outsiders: "Ten July at a quarter!" To attract other traders' attention as they try to make themselves understood, they gesture with hand signals symbolizing their prices and the number of contracts they want to buy or sell. Traders stand in specific areas of each pit according to the contract delivery month for which they're trading.

Surrounding the pits are banks of telephones operated by brokerage houses. Most trade orders originate from customers outside the exchange and are phoned in. They are recorded by order-takers, time-stamped and then rushed by floor runners to brokers in the pits.

Continental Illinois Bank Building.

Though it seems little more than a game of dice, the daily hysteria performs a necessary economic function. Traders are buying and selling futures contracts on farm products that may not yet have been planted or harvested. The business is largely speculative and highly risky. But futures trading makes it possible for farmers, processors and wholesalers to lock in a price for their products; they can sleep soundly at night knowing they are protected against damaging price swings regardless of drought or flood.

Future money: Since the 1970s, the biggest growth has come in the area of financial futures, now accounting for more than half the futures exchanges' business. Stock-index futures, used by traders to speculate on general stock market trends rather than specific share prices, came under the spotlight of controversy during the Wall Street market crash of 1987; some argued that the futures' pessimism made the crash worse than it might have been. Today, the relationship between futures trading and stock market volatility is still a subject of debate among experts.

To accommodate their enormous growth, the Chicago exchanges have built shiny new trading floors with video and electronic signboards enabling traders to monitor developments in stock, bond and futures markets around the world. Despite the high-tech surroundings, floor trading practices actually have changed little since the 1800s. But historic changes are in the making. The exchanges are developing automated systems so that trading can take place via computer screens as well as in the pits, a contemporary development which may have unforeseen effects on transactions.

At the heart of the district, at 141 W. Jackson Boulevard, lies the venerable **Chicago Board of Trade**, the world's oldest and biggest futures exchange, founded in 1848 by a group of local businessmen. Even for those bored by financial matters, this landmark Art-Deco skyscraper is worth a look. Designed by Holabird & Root and built in 1930, its lobby elevator doors are graced by golden bundles of wheat. A 32-foot statue of Ceres, the Roman goddess of agriculture, sits at the building's very top.

Just off the lobby is the **Ceres Café** (formerly the Sign of the Trader), a bar and restaurant where traders gather to drown their sorrows, celebrate their profits, or simply take a break, their eyes glued to the commodity prices flashing by on electronic boards punctuating the walls.

Night trading: The Board of Trade is one of the few exchanges open at night. Evening trading sessions are held Sunday through Thursday, catering to businessmen in the Far East dealing in US Treasury bond contracts.

The **Chicago Mercantile Exchange**, established in 1919, began as a tiny butter and egg market and grew into the world's largest trading center for livestock and foreign currencies. In 1972,

Hailing a cab that never comes. Following pages: braced for the financial future.

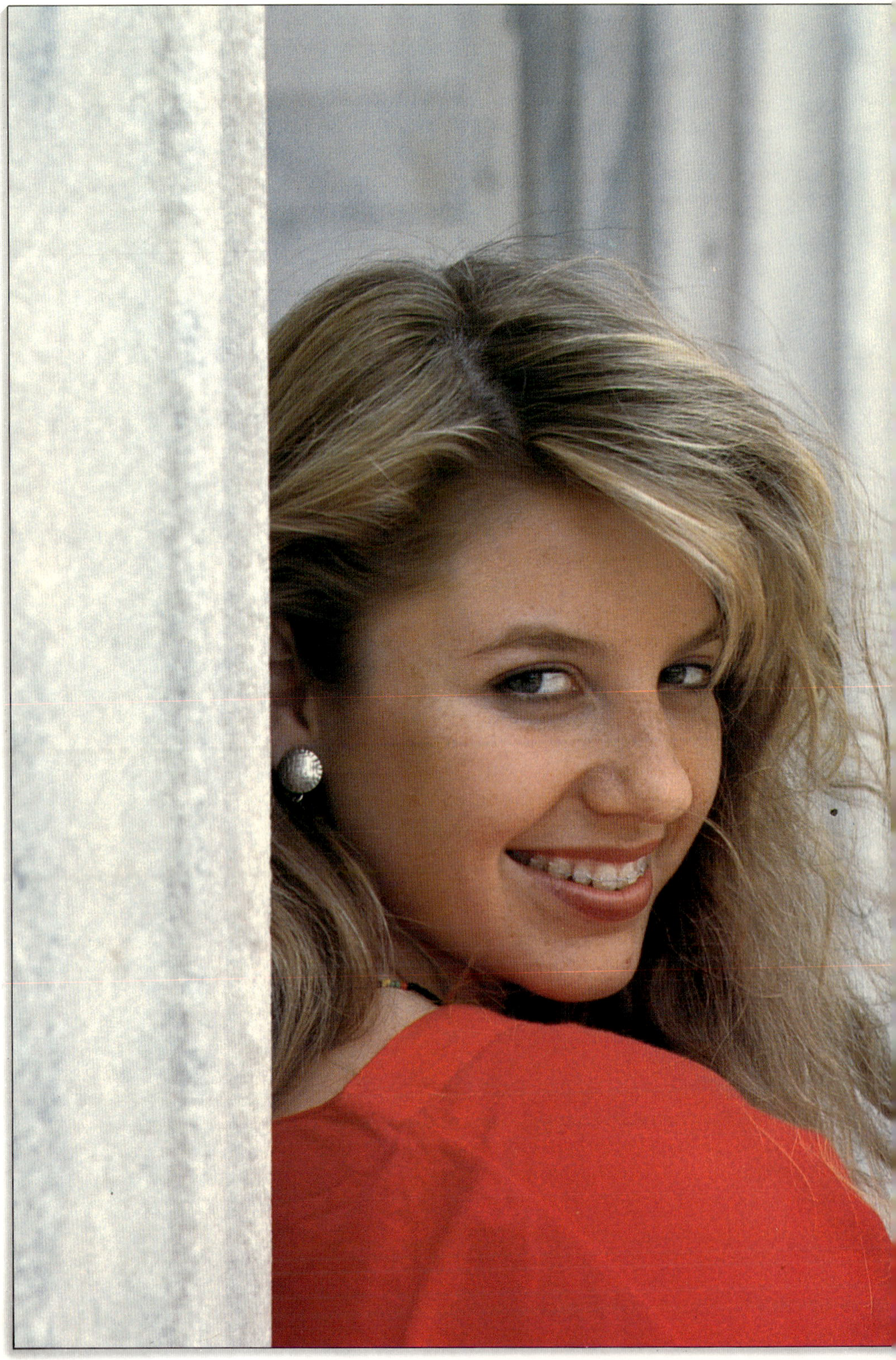

the Merc pioneered financial futures, used by banks and investors to manage risk. Its stock-index market, based on the Standard & Poor's 500, is the industry's biggest.

Several years ago the Merc moved to a new, glitzier home on South Wacker. In a corner of the exchange, butter and egg prices are still recorded, though only out of nostalgia. The brass spittoons once used by cattle traders are now gone. But the jargon of the pits lives on: a popular gathering spot at the Merc is the **Limit Up** bar, its name taken from the traders' term for a big swing in price that causes a market to temporarily shut down.

Just south of the Board of Trade on LaSalle and linked by bridge is a red, polished-granite complex known as **Exchange Center**. This houses the city's two securities exchanges, the Chicago Board Options Exchange and the Midwest Stock Exchange.

The **Chicago Board Options Exchange** is a mere youngster compared to the city's other exchanges. Founded in 1972 as an offshoot of the Board of Trade, it is the birthplace of stock options trading. Some traders maintain that trading options to buy and sell shares requires more tactical finesse and knowledge of mathematical theory than the futures game. Traders in the pits can be seen clutching notes outlining complicated strategies devised by computer.

Compared to the rollicking commodities markets, the 104-year-old **Midwest Stock Exchange** is almost church-like. Its more staid atmosphere, however, belies a thriving activity level. It is the nation's largest stock exchange after New York's.

Other points of interest in the area include the **Continental Illinois Bank and Trust Building** on South LaSalle, a massive block-square building with a "classic" design said to be copied from early Roman baths. It's Chicago's oldest bank. Across the street is the **Federal Reserve Bank of Chicago**.

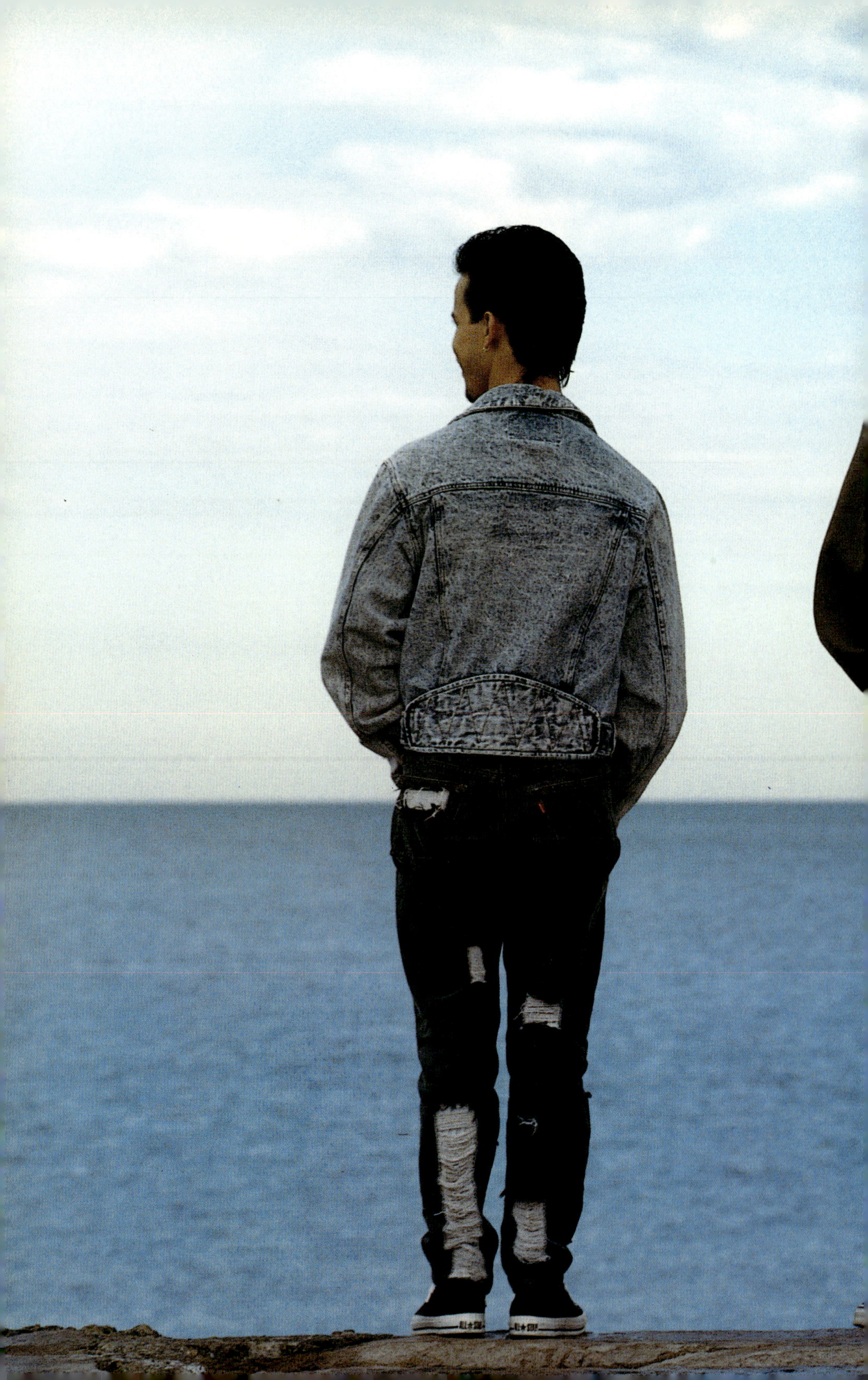

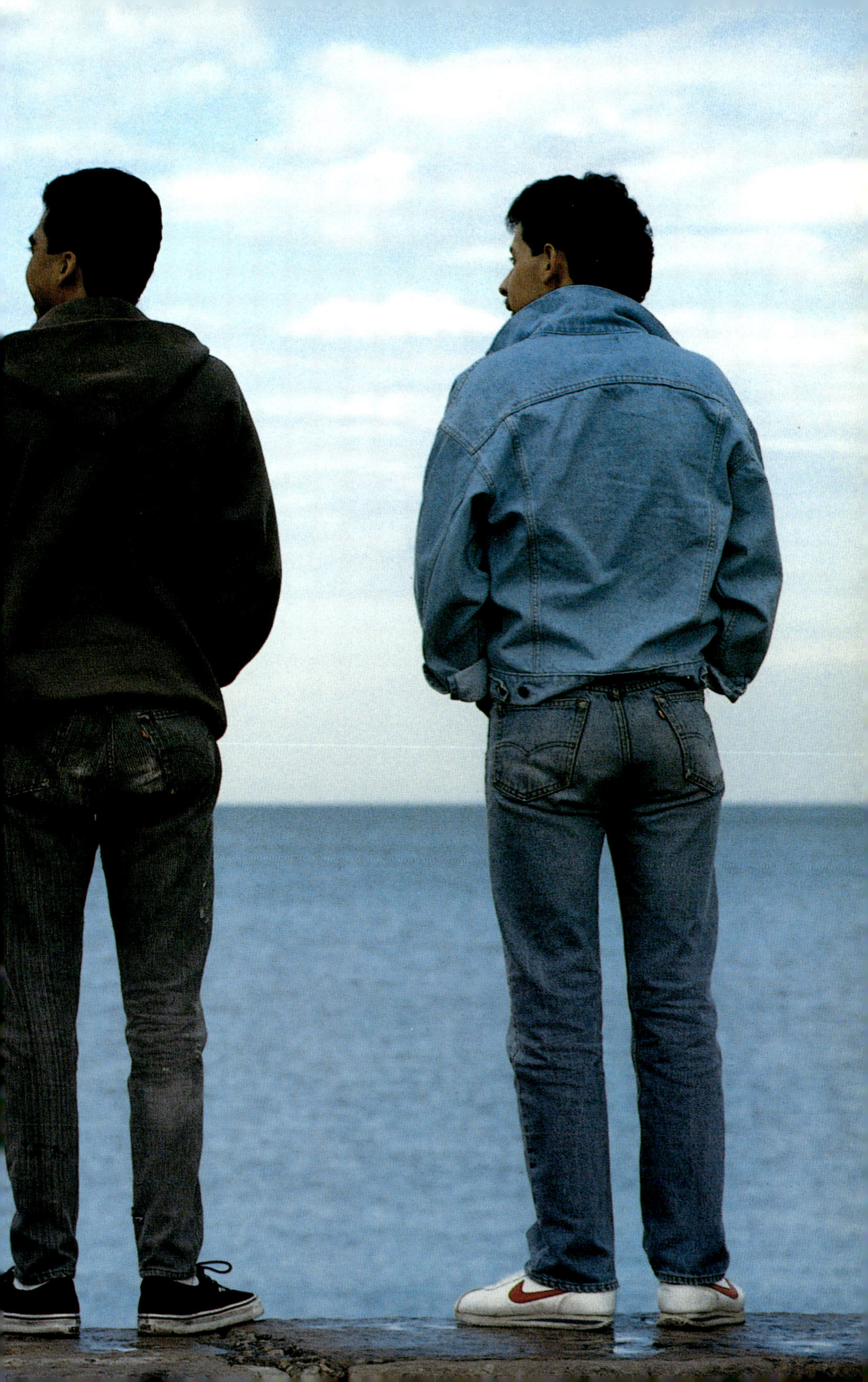

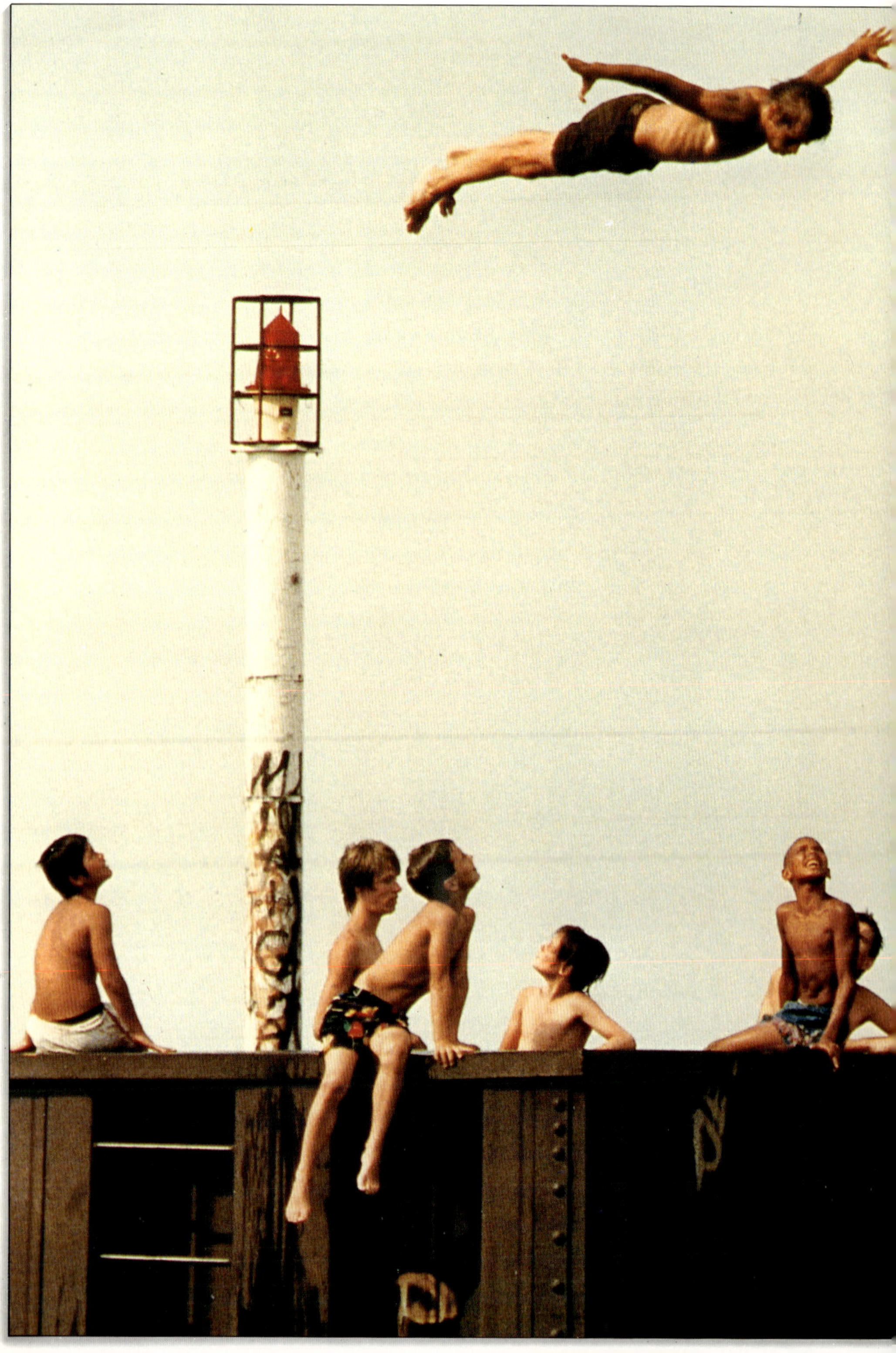

COOLER BY THE LAKE

Nothing defines Chicago more than its lakefront. **Lake Michigan** is the city's front yard: an urban vacationland, outdoor sports playground and important cultural center.

Chicago is situated at the southern tip of Lake Michigan, one of the five freshwater Great Lakes formed by melting glaciers at the end of the last Ice Age. With the coming of the European explorers in the 17th century, the site quickly became a trading center because of the transportation crossroads formed between the lakes and nearby inland rivers.

More than 900 feet deep in places, 300 miles long and 118 miles across, Lake Michigan is the second largest of the Great Lakes. It has a profound effect on the city's weather, acting as a sort of insulating blanket that keeps lakefront neighborhoods cooler in summer and a bit warmer in winter. It unleashes fierce winds that come sweeping down over the water, picking up moisture and sometimes dumping "lake effect" snow on the city.

Coasting: In the minds of Chicagoans, the city's 29-mile **lakefront** is the country's third coast. Visitors are surprised by its breadth and beauty. Other cities may boast waterfronts that are in fact more magnificent, but die-hard Chicagoans will argue, with good reason, that none surpasses their own in terms of sheer fun.

Chicagoans make the most of mild (and sometimes hot) summer temperatures by flocking to the lake for a day of play. Even in the coldest weather, when steam rises eerily from the icy water, some hardy souls regularly bundle up in their heaviest winter gear for a peaceful lakefront stroll. In the chill of spring, smelt fishermen along the shore huddle to keep warm.

Weather permitting, Chicagoans can lie on a beach, sail, visit a zoo, picnic,

Lakeside 135

windsurf, hear a concert, see a play, watch a ballet, hit a bucket of golf balls, play chess, eat brunch, jog, roller skate, ride a bike or see an airshow, all within a few square miles.

Architect Daniel H. Burnham in the early 1900s was the first to visualize the lakefront's possibilities as a recreational center. He rejected the typical waterfront development pattern which was dominated by shipping and other industrial users.

The immense scale of the lake inspired Burnham to draw an ambitious plan for a chain of parks, beaches, cultural facilities and pleasure boat harbors along the shore.

A trip along **Lake Shore Drive**, a thoroughfare skirting the shoreline on one side and skyscrapers and parks on the other, is a glorious way to take in the lakefront, city skyline and nearby sights. The drive stretches 124 blocks from Hollywood Avenue on the north to Jackson Park on the south.

But better yet, those with the time should take a walk or a bike ride. The lakefront is laced with jogging paths and bicycle trails scenic enough to entice even the most dedicated couch potato into at least a little exercise. There are many museums, harbors and historic points along the way.

Bikes can be rented in Lincoln Park at **Fullerton Avenue** just west of Lake Shore Drive. The bike path pretty much parallels the course of Lake Shore Drive on its east side. But beware: bike paths and beach areas often become dangerously crowded in the summer. It will take a little practice to avoid all the roller skaters, runners and sun worshippers. The best time to escape the mob scene is early in the morning or late in the afternoon.

Another picturesque way to enjoy the lakefront is to view it from the water itself. There are a half-dozen or so good **boat tours** of the city, including several offering lunch or dinner cruises. They leave from Navy Pier at Grand Avenue and the lake, and from the Chicago

Preceding pages: waiting for a ship to come in; pier approval. **Below,** Lincoln Park Lagoon.

River, next to the Wrigley Building (410 N. Michigan Avenue).

On the edge of the Loop, **Grant Park** is home to several of the city's most famous museums (see the preceding chapter of this book, on the Loop, for more on the Art Institute, Field Museum and Shedd Aquarium). The center of the violent 1968 antiwar riots during the Democratic National Convention, Grant Park's biggest crowds these days come to the **Petrillo Band Shell** (Columbus Drive and Jackson Boulevard) for its lively array of free concerts. The Grant Park Symphony performs here on weekends during the summer. Its weekend-long music festivals – the **Blues Fest** in early June and **Jazz Fest** in late August – draw fans from around the world.

Thousands of picnickers bring blankets and candles to enjoy the music, dance and savor one of the finest views of the city's skyline. In the week leading up to the Fourth of July, scores of local eateries sell their Chicago-style and ethnic cuisine at the **Taste of Chicago** festival. On Independence Day itself, fireworks light the sky and the symphony plays a rousing version of Tchaikovsky's 1812 Overture.

Another nearby draw is the opulent **Buckingham Fountain**, with a colorful light show each evening at 9pm. Modeled after a fountain at Versailles, it was given to the city by heiress Kate Buckingham in memory of her brother, Clarence, a director of the Art Institute.

Varied past: To the north, at Grand Avenue, **Navy Pier** stretches almost two-thirds of a mile into the lake. Its tip provides what some people claim is the best lakefront vantage point in the city. A multi-million dollar facelift begun in 1990 changed dilapidated to dazzling. The city spruced up the pier's image with picnic tables and flowers. Art classes, puppet shows and free concerts under the canopy are just a few of the pier's expanded summertime programs. Bicyclists, skateboarders, roller skaters and fishermen are welcome. The public can also tour US Navy and Coast Guard vessels which are docked at the pier.

Olive Park, surrounding the city water filtration plant at Ohio Street, has a small but good beach and tree-shaded area for lounging on the grass. It was named for a soldier, Pfc. Milton Olive Lee, who died in Vietnam in 1966 by throwing himself on a hand grenade to save the lives of four friends.

Farther north, the 1,000-acre **Lincoln Park**, Chicago's largest park, borders the lake between North and Hollywood avenues. The park has been called Chicago's Central Park, and in fact the two were designed by the same landscape architect, Frederick Law Olmstead. It's a fine grassy park suited for strolling and picnicking, complete with rambling walks, lagoons and ponds, footbridges, gardens, bronze statues, two museums and a zoo. Three cafés are tucked among the trees and ponds: Café Brauer at the south end of the zoo, Park Place Café at Deming Place and Brett's at Waveland Avenue by the golf course.

At the park's southern tip, at North Avenue and Clark Street, sits the redbrick **Chicago Historical Society**. Its exhibits highlight the city's colorful history and characters, including pioneer life, the Fort Dearborn Massacre, the Chicago Fire and the gangster era. Especially good are its collection of materials on Abraham Lincoln and the Civil War, and copies of the inaugural gowns of US presidents' wives.

Nearby, half hidden by shrubbery, is the **Couch family mausoleum**, a reminder of the days when the park was a municipal cemetery. At the time of the Chicago Fire, the city was moving coffins to private cemeteries. When the fire roared north, families took refuge here, climbing into open graves to escape the blistering inferno.

A little farther north on Clark Street is the **Chicago Academy of Sciences**. Its exhibits focus on the natural history and wildlife of the Great Lakes region, depicting Chicago as the dense coal forest that it was 350 million years ago.

The free zoo: The park's best-known attraction is **Lincoln Park Zoo**, which is open daily. Remarkably, admission is free. The zoo is home to more than 2,000 mammals, reptiles and birds, from koala bears to elephants to giraffes. It's famous for its great ape house, with the world's largest collection of gorillas.

The **Farm-in-the-Zoo** consists of several big red barns that offer visitors a sample of rural life, including cows being milked and chicks hatching. The **Zoo Rookery** provides a peaceful respite for a variety of land and water birds that come to feed and nest. Located south of the regular zoo is a children's petting zoo, open most days during the summer months.

The park is also home to some of the city's nicest gardens: the **Lincoln Park Conservatory**, lush with ferns, palms, flowers and other plants; and the **Grandmother's Garden**, between

Chrysanthemum display, Lincoln Park Conservatory.

Stockton Drive and Lincoln Park West which is full of old-fashioned flowers.

Not far away is an unexpected find: an interesting, if somewhat age-worn, **Viking ship**. Dating from the Columbian Exposition of 1893, it is a copy of a 10th-century ship built by Norway for the exposition and sailed across the Atlantic by a crew of 12.

At Fullerton Parkway, right on the lakefront, is the **Theatre on the Lake**, which stages Broadway plays in the summer months. Strictly community theater, it's nonetheless delightful on a warm evening under the stars.

Sports: The park has something to offer sports enthusiasts of all kinds, whether their interest is in tennis or 16-inch softball, Chicagoans' favorite.

At Diversey, west of Lake Shore Drive, is a **driving range** for golfers. The **golf course** itself is just north of Addison Street.

The Chicago Park District maintains **30 sandy beaches** along the lakefront, bordering some of the city's richest and poorest neighborhoods. They are officially open (that is, manned by lifeguards) from June 15 to September 15. But swimmers can plunge in at their own risk any time the weather allows. The beaches are free, easy to find and very accessible – they are generally named for the nearest cross-street. On peak summer sunning days, finding nearby parking may be impossible, so walking, taking a cab or using public transportation is a good idea.

The city's most famous stretch of sand is **Oak Street Beach**. Located across Lake Shore Drive from the posh high-rises of the city's Gold Coast neighborhood and only steps from Oak Street's exclusive boutiques, this is where the beautiful people go. There is also some serious beach volleyball played here. To get to the beach, use the pedestrian underpass at Michigan Avenue and Oak Street.

Other popular beaches at North Avenue and Fullerton Avenue are frequented by the youthful, arty and so-

Bald eagle, the US national symbol, in Lincoln Park Zoo.

Lakeside 139

phisticated residents of the nearby Lincoln Park neighborhood. A bit south of the North Avenue beach house (hard to miss because it resembles a steamship) is an open-air **chess pavilion** where aficionados come to test their gamesmanship. Farther north, Foster Avenue Beach, popular among urban youths, is known for its **pick-up basketball**.

The most crowded weekend of the season is in mid-July, when Chicago holds its yearly **air-and-water show**. Hordes of spectators jam the beaches to view the aerial parade featuring daredevil stunts and aircraft of all kinds.

Just south of Grant Park are two of the city's most-visited facilities: **Soldier Field**, home of the Chicago Bears football team, and the enormous **McCormick Place**, convention capital of the world.

Shipping: Visible out in the lake just north of Grant Park is the system of locks which enabled engineers to reverse the flow of the Chicago River. In the late 19th century, sewage from the river flowing into the lake had so polluted the water that there were frequent typhoid outbreaks. A massive digging project lowered the river level below that of the lake, diverting its flow into the Illinois River and downstream to the Mississippi River.

Today, most shipping is done by rail or air. But Lake Michigan remains a vital part of the city's life and commerce. Most important, Chicago pumps its drinking water from the lake through intake cribs located two miles offshore. Grain, ore, chemicals and other bulk commodities still move through Chicago's busy docks to other ports around the world.

The **Port of Chicago** is located near the steel mills of the industrial southeast side at the Calumet River. The St Lawrence Seaway connects the Great Lakes to the Atlantic, making the city a midcontinent port for ocean-going vessels. Inland, barge traffic on the Illinois and Mississippi rivers links Chicago to the Gulf of Mexico.

Beach bubbles.

STUDS TERKEL

Studs Terkel is best known for his five books of oral history including Working *and* The Good War. *But Chicago also knows Studs for his daily radio interviews on* WFMT. *Here, speaking into someone else's tape recorder for a change, is Studs Terkel talking in his inimitable style about the lake and the neighborhoods of his adopted city.*

"Chicago is the double-headed city. Our god is Janus, the two-headed god. Nelson Algren, of course, spoke of that often, most eloquently in *Chicago: City on The Make*. He spoke of the city of the night and the city of the day. He wrote of the winners and the losers, of the Jane Addamses and the Al Capones.

"I'm just reading a book now about the Chicago Fire, and what came out of the fire. The myth, the legend, of course, is that after the fire they – all the people of Chicago – worked together. Nonsense. The fact is there was a split, a big split. Why, the Haymarket Riot came just 15 years later.

"Chicago has always been split. The first fur traders – prototypes for our great robber barons – were gypping the Pottawattomies. It was a new land, a new country. Then John Kinzie and his Anglo-Saxon Protestant crowd came here from back East, and the immigrants shortly after that, and everybody was stepping on the next guy.

"The Germans had a tough battle against the WASPS, fighting for Sunday beer. And the Irish had it tough – 'No Irish Need Apply.'

"Who came to Chicago? Hands. I call Chicago a city of hands. 'Hands' is an old-time word for working person. 'Fifty hands wanted.' You read that in rural communities. Farm hand. Hired hand... also factory hands, industrial hands. Chicago is a city of hands, not paper. Some other city, let's say Washington, is a city of paper.

"And yet a crazy thing happened here with the rich men and their wives at the turn of the century. Mrs Potter Palmer and the other wives longed for culture. Whether or not they knew what it was, they wanted it. And so Chicago became a center for culture because of the wives of guys who were meatpackers.

"A guy named Alson J. Smith, a writer, he used the word 'seedbed.' He said Chicago has been a seedbed of various art forms. Take jazz and blues. Back in those early days, before the two big black migrations to Chicago, jazz and blues only had one audience – black people. But when the audience moved north the artists moved north, so Louis Armstrong and King Oliver came to Chicago. And young white kids, like Bud Freeman and Jim McPartland and the whole Austin High gang, heard these guys play. They learned and went East, where all the dough was. Chicago was a seedbed of jazz.

"So what's to see in Chicago? Well, let me tell you. You've got to see the lake, the goddam lake, so magnificent.

"And just stand on the corner of Oak and Michigan, where you've got this crazy juxtaposition. You've got this magnificent lake, and right next to it are these crazy buildings where Xerox copies of things are being made. There is no other city that has a lake, this natural wonder, right in the heart of it. And there's the beach, a common beach, a democratic beach. The poor, the middle class, blacks and whites – they're all on the beaches.

"And you should take an automobile ride through the bungalow neighborhoods and maybe, as Mike Royko would say, go *fast* down South State Street. Drive down there and see the biggest housing complex in the world. It could be an asylum, an orphanage, a prison; it's all these thrown into one.

"And the Art Institute. Go there. Isn't it remarkable? And look at the goddam buildings, the architecture. Isn't it remarkable?

"You know, I was born in New York City and I had asthma as a kid. But I was cured of asthma when I got to Chicago. It was a summer day. I remember. We had a rooming house at Ashland and Flournoy. And I could smell the south wind from the stockyards.

"I just needed something, I think, and Chicago had the energy I wanted, and the feeling. Just something.

"And then it got exciting."

141

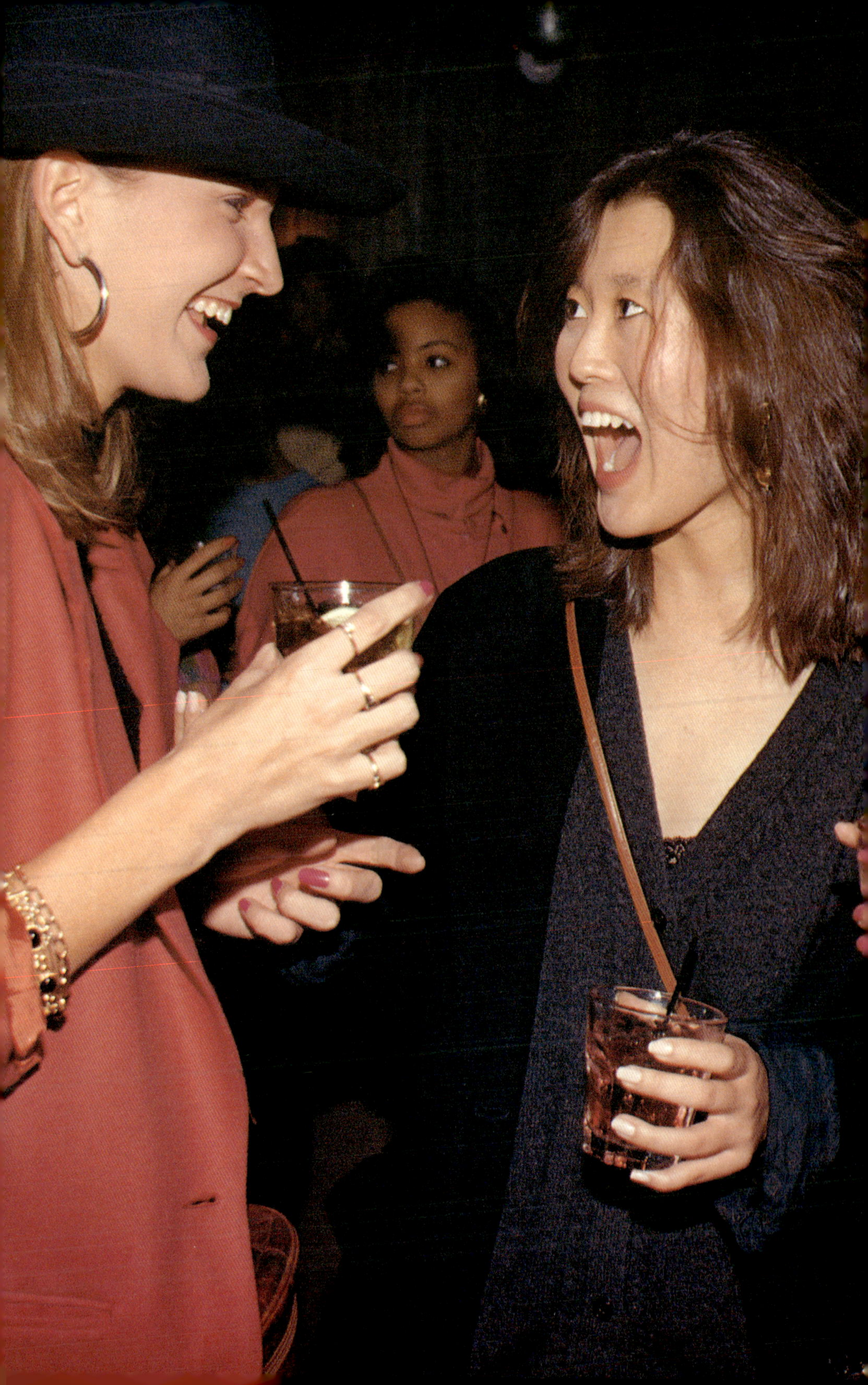

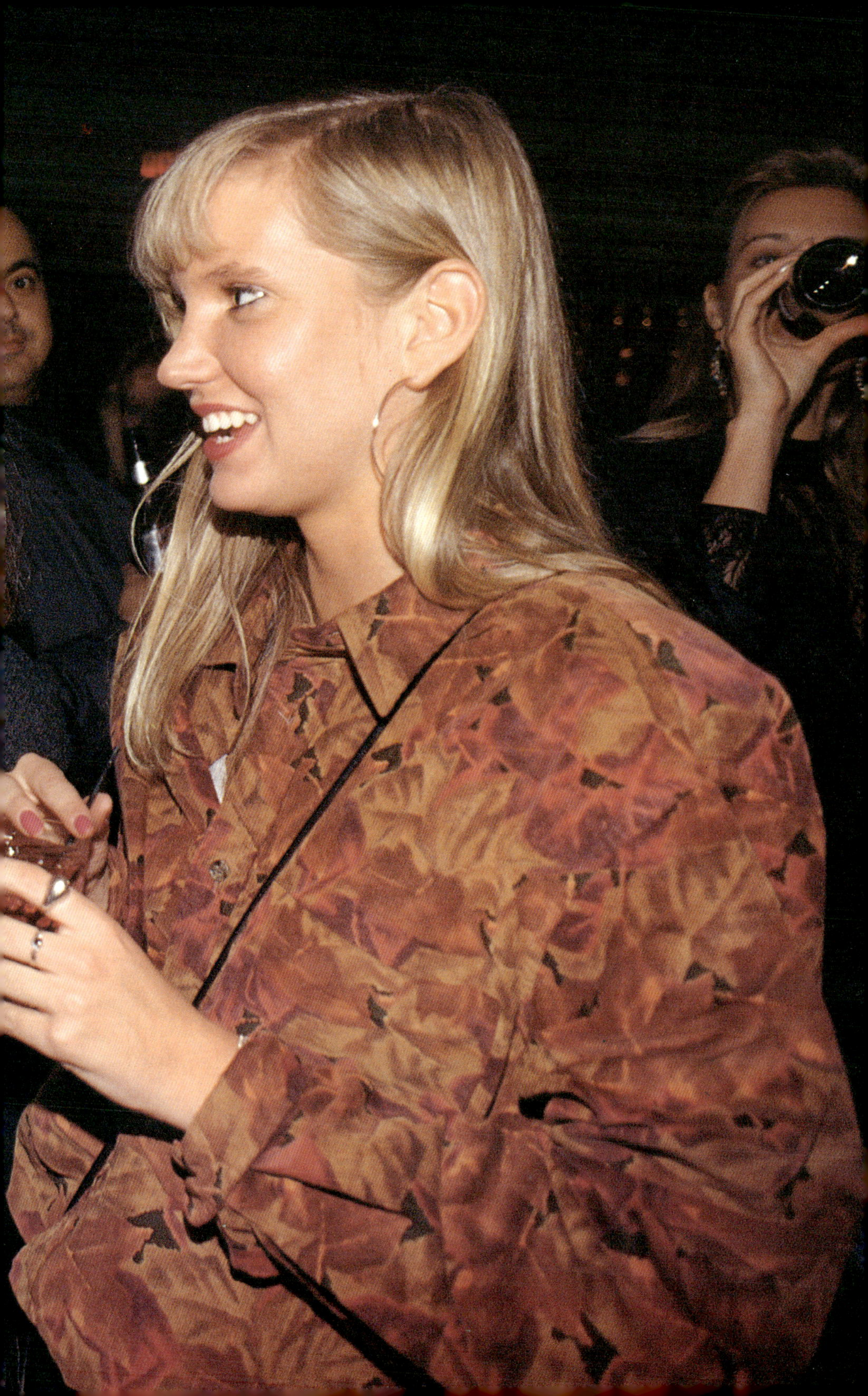

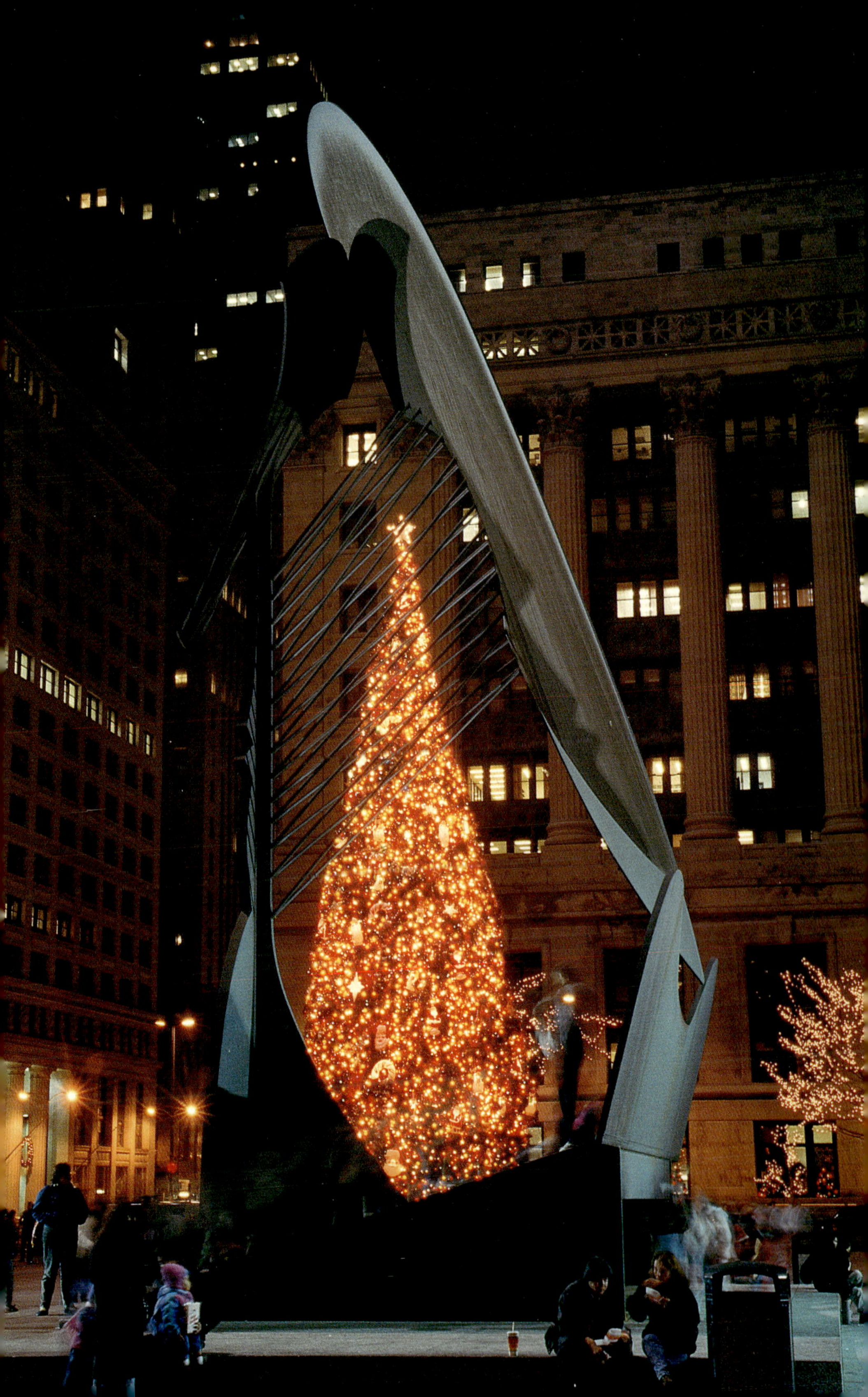

THE MAGNIFICENT MILE

Chicago's **Magnificent Mile**, the city's premier, high-class shopping and strolling street, stretches along N. Michigan Avenue between the Chicago River and Oak Street.

The mile earned its nickname largely because of the array of shops that are the match of any upscale retail area: Tiffany, Cartier, Elizabeth Arden, Burberry, Brooks Brothers and on and on and on. Within five blocks are five of the world's best-known department stores: Saks Fifth Avenue, Neiman-Marcus, Marshall Field's, Lord & Taylor and I. Magnin.

In any season, the only way to sample the Mag Mile is to promenade with thousands of others; even in the dead of winter, the tiny white lights on the branches of the leafless trees give the avenue a warm holiday feeling.

A little history: Start at the **Michigan Avenue Bridge** over the Chicago River, and with some history. Near the northeast pylon of the bridge is a plaque commemorating the passage through the Chicago River in 1673 of the first white men – Jesuit missionary Father Jacques Marquette and Canadian-born explorer Louis Jolliet. On their way north from their explorations on the Mississippi River, they entered the Des Plaines River. There, friendly Native Americans guided them through the Chicago Portage, a stretch of mud that the explorers realized connected the Great Lakes with the Mississippi River and the Gulf of Mexico.

Across the street a plaque near the bridge's southwest pylon notes the passage in 1681 through the Chicago River of Cavalier Robert René de La Salle and Henry Tonty on their way to the Mississippi River and the Gulf of Mexico. During that trip they claimed the Mississippi Valley for France, naming it Louisiana after their king, Louis XIV. La Salle built a fort near the present site of Chicago, and in a letter referred to its location for the first time on record as "Checagou."

On the north bank of the river and the east side of Michigan Avenue, now the site of a wide pedestrian plaza, the city's first non-native settler built his cabin in 1781. He was Jean Baptiste Point DuSable, a French-speaking black man. He established the city's first commercial enterprise, a river trading post.

Set in the sidewalks on the bridge's south end, across Wacker Drive, are markers outlining the site of Fort Dearborn, the first US Army garrison in Chicago, which was built in 1803. In 1812 the fort was destroyed, and about two-thirds of its settlers and soldiers were killed by Indians incited by the British army during the War of 1812. A bas-relief on the southwest bridge pylon commemorates the event. The three other pylons have bas-reliefs commemorating Jolliet and Marquette, fur trader John Kinzie and the rebirth of the city after the Great Fire of 1871.

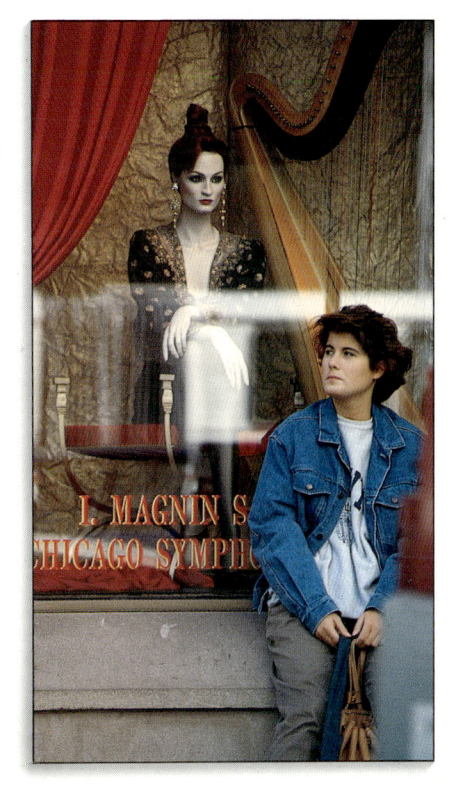

Preceding pages: night clubbers in the Loop. **Left,** the Picasso on Christmas Eve. **Right,** waiting for someone on the Mag Mile.

The Magnificent Mile was originally a dirt path called Pine Street, used primarily by lumber wagons that loaded at the Chicago River. Once lined by warehouses, by the 1880s the area farther north of the river had become a popular building site for merchants' large homes; the streets were lined with wooden paving blocks.

Bridgeworks: The building of the Michigan Avenue Bridge, accomplished with great civic fanfare in 1920, ignited the spectacular growth of the street, by then attached to Michigan Avenue and thus renamed. The bridge itself is a fine example of the double-leaf trunnion bascule bridge, so common over the Chicago River that it is known internationally as a "Chicago style" bridge. "Bascule" is from the French for "see-saw," which is what a bascule bridge does. Its two halves rotate up and down on a pair of horizontal shafts called trunnions. The movement of the two sides, or leaves, can be accomplished with a relatively small motor because the weight of the leaves is precisely balanced by iron or concrete counterweights sunk into a pit below street level. The double-decker Michigan Avenue Bridge's leaves weigh 6.7 million pounds each. The counterweights are balanced so finely that they must be rebalanced every time the bridge is repainted.

Engineering aside, the bridge is a stellar attraction when it is raised and lowered, a frequent occurrence around midday during the spring and summer, enabling tall-masted sailboats to pass to or from their winter storage yards up the river. The sight of the roadbed hovering at nearly a 90-degree angle is astounding to visitors, although office workers impatiently waiting to cross to the other side find it infuriating.

Standing sentry at the south end of the Magnificent Mile are two landmark buildings constructed at the same time as the Michigan Avenue Bridge. On the west side, just north of the river, is the **Wrigley Building**, built in 1921 with an

North Michigan Avenue from the bridge.

annex added in 1924. Its lacily decorated white terra-cotta facade, modeled after the Giralda Tower of Seville Cathedral, is floodlit at night, making it resemble an ornate wedding cake.

Pressing business: Across Michigan Avenue to the east is the **Tribune Tower**, a Gothic revival skyscraper complete with a topping of flying buttresses. Built in 1925, its design was chosen by a nationwide competition held in 1922. It houses the offices of the *Chicago Tribune*, but the newspaper's printing plant is along the north branch of the Chicago River, at Chicago Avenue and Halsted Street. To see the giant presses rolling, cross Michigan Avenue, pass between the two Wrigley Building halves and enter the home of Chicago's other major daily newspaper, the *Chicago Sun-Times* **Building**, where a glass-walled corridor overlooks the press room.

The Tribune Tower, on the other hand, offers a marble lobby inscribed with quotations from famous personages ranging from Euripides to the powerful former *Tribune* publisher Robert R. McCormick. And the sides of the building are studded with hunks of famous buildings and historical sites around the world, including the Parthenon, the Taj Mahal, Westminster Abbey and the Mosque of Suleiman the Magnificent in Istanbul. The stone fragments were gathered by *Tribune* foreign correspondents at the request of McCormick, who reportedly asked them to pursue only "honorable means" in acquiring these invaluable and irreplaceable stone fragments.

Just east of Tribune Tower is **NBC Tower**. Its similarities to Rockefeller Center in New York are no coincidence. The architect Adrian Smith, of Skidmore, Owings and Merrill, studied the Art Moderne-style Rockefeller Center complex, along with nearby Chicago buildings including the Tribune Tower, before designing the NBC Tower. The result, wrote architecture critic Paul Gapp, is "the best-looking

The Water Tower.

Magnificent Mile 147

masonry-clad skyscraper constructed in Chicago since the 1930s."

A pier-less detour: Descend the stairs just north of the NBC Tower, and walk three blocks on Illinois Street to **North Pier Chicago**. It is not really a pier, but was originally a nondescript brick warehouse built between 1905 and 1920 for lake boats to tie up in the adjacent slip and unload their cargo. Today's cargo consists of tourists, for the warehouse has been transformed into a complex of restaurants, exclusive shops, art galleries and leisure attractions, including an indoor golf course. Enjoy a snack on a porch overlooking the water, or munch fresh fudge while walking along the landscaped waterfront promenade.

Parents traveling with fidgety children will find the nearby **Chicago Children's Museum** a godsend, with exhibits aimed at children from pre-schoolers to age 14. Toddlers can play on a big wood fantasy vehicle, crawl through squares lined with various touchable treasures or play in a miniature kitchen or Three Bears' House. For older children, there are child-sized versions of a post office and the Art Institute of Chicago, and a hands-on bubble-making exhibit. Diaper-changing areas are provided in both the men's and women's rest rooms.

North Pier Chicago also offers the **Chicago Maritime Museum**, with exhibits on Midwestern maritime history, including shipping on the Great Lakes and the St Lawrence Seaway, and navigation on Midwest rivers and canals. North Pier also offers 90-minute boat tours focusing on Chicago architecture. Just east of North Pier, past Lake Shore Drive, is **Lake Point Tower**, a curving, three-lobed condominium building whose architects took their inspiration from a 1921 Mies van der Rohe proposal for a Berlin skyscraper.

Elder citizens: The Magnificent Mile has seen such a dizzying pace of development in recent years that it is difficult to picture what it looked like in more

Leafy lunch on the Mag Mile median.

genteel, bygone times. But a few elegant buildings remain on the west side of N. Michigan Avenue, featuring mansard roofs and neoclassical detailing. And history can be seen in more ways than one at the **Hotel Inter-Continental**. Built in 1929 as the Medinah Athletic Club, it features a gilded onion-shaped dome and a floor-by-floor history of the world in interior design, from the Assyrian lions carved into marble balconies on the second floor to the 13th-century Florentine mosaics in the stairwell to the Renaissance paintings above the elevators on the fifth floor.

A touch of modern elegance can be found at the **Terra Museum of American Art**. This narrow building, with a marble facade interrupted by several simple expanses of windows, houses a compact museum of American paintings from the collection of industrialist Daniel J. Terra, who opened the museum in 1987. The museum specializes in 19th-century paintings.

The surrounding blocks, between Grand and Chicago avenues, and St Clair Street and the lake, are known as **Streeterville**. The area is named after George Wellington Streeter, who claimed squatter's rights here for more than 30 years. Streeter and his wife were excursion boat operators whose boat ran aground in 1886 in the lake south of Chicago Avenue. Instead of freeing the boat, they decided to fill up the lake around it. Nearby residents brought dirt, garbage and trash, and soon built a 180-acre shantytown. Streeter "sold" some of the real estate to other squatters, and it was not until 1918 that he was forced out by court order.

At Chicago Avenue, on the west side of N. Michigan, is the **Water Tower**, one of Chicago's most famous landmarks – and possibly one of the least attractive. It is an elaborate, pseudo-Gothic tower surrounded by crenellated medieval turrets. Oscar Wilde, on visiting Chicago in 1882, called it a "castellated monstrosity with pepper boxes stuck all over it." The tower was built to

Playing for passersby.

conceal a standpipe that equalized the pressure of the water pumped from the **Pumping Station** to the east, a less elaborate structure made of the same yellow Joliet limestone. Both structures were built two years before the devastating Chicago Fire of 1871, and are among the few buildings in the area that survived the fire. The tower is locked and empty, but the pumping station is still in use. It also serves as a tourist information center.

The area near the Water Tower seems to attract Chicago street artists. One notable example in recent years has been Lee Godie, a gray-haired, toothless bag lady earning a nice living from selling her childlike drawings to passersby. She even made a deal with a nearby high-fashion boutique to cash checks from her customers, including a number of major art galleries and prominent private collectors.

But it's not just street artists who come to this area. In 1996, the **Museum of Contemporary Art** moved from its cramped location a few blocks away into an exhilerating modern building designed by Berlin architect Josef Paul Kleihues. With five times the space as previously, the museum has thrown itself whole-heartedly into promoting the city's rich collection of contemporary visual arts. As well as exhibits there are lectures, artists' talks and courses.

Good views: North of the Water Tower, between Pearson and Chestnut streets, is **Water Tower Place**, renowned as an upscale downtown shopping mall. Just north of Water Tower Place is the **John Hancock Center**. The third-tallest building in Chicago (and fifth-tallest in the world), it is a tapered black tower marked with external X-shaped braces that support the building against wind. At 1,105 feet, the John Hancock offers a lower observation deck than that of the 1,468-foot Sears Tower. But some aficionados say the view is better, for it includes vast panoramas of lake, with tiny white dots which are sailboats. On a clear day,

Sleeveless; strolling.

150

visitors can see the states of Wisconsin to the north, Indiana to the south, and Michigan straight across the lake.

At the junction of Michigan Avenue, and Chestnut Street is **Fourth Presbyterian Church**, an elegant Gothic church built in 1912 and featuring a cloistered walk and a quiet courtyard with a stone fountain. Farther north are some of the more spectacular examples of recent North Michigan Avenue development. The **900 N. Michigan Building** houses Bloomingdale's and an atrium which includes elegant shops such as Christofle, purveyors of fine silver, and Cacharel, French designer clothing. **One Magnificent Mile**, at the corner of Michigan Avenue and Oak Street, has several shops and fine, somewhat expensive restaurants.

Once a guiding light: For a blast from the past, there's the former Playboy Building, now known as the **919 N. Michigan Building**. This 37-story Art Deco-style skyscraper was built in 1930 with a revolving beacon on top that was used to guide airplanes until taller buildings rendered it obsolete.

At the northernmost foot of the Magnificent Mile, at Michigan Avenue and Walton Street, is the **Drake Hotel**. Built in 1920, it faces Lake Michigan and Oak Street Beach on the north, and offers the weary walker a lobby in the manner of the grand hotels of Europe. For a relatively inexpensive taste of perhaps the best view in all of Chicago, have breakfast or lunch in the hotel's Oak Terrace dining room.

On its north side, the hotel anchors **E. Lake Shore Drive** – a one-block street said to be the single wealthiest block in Chicago, and one of the wealthiest in the world. Some of the amenities in the elegant buildings, constructed between 1912 and 1929, include bedroom vaults for furs at 209 E. Lake Shore Drive; a turntable on the garage floor of the Drake Tower, just east of the Drake Hotel, to turn incoming cars around swiftly so they can drive right out again; and refrigeration for garbage at the

A Mag Mile toy shop.

SHOPPING CENTERS

Once you've got them by the malls, their hearts and minds are sure to follow. Indeed, nowhere has the "malling" of America been more apparent – or accepted more enthusiastically – than in the shopping centers of Chicago.

To those who study such trends, the American mall – a collection of stores under one roof – is variously seen as a shrine to the national urge to acquire, or perhaps as the new "town square," where elderly people walk, teenagers loiter and people with causes set up their petition tables and hand out their leaflets.

There is no doubt, however, that most Americans see their local mall – and, indeed, any mall they encounter – as a place to explore: "Let's go check out the mall." Studies show that more and more families now regard shopping as a leisure activity and view a trip to the mall as a "day out" for the entire family, especially as malls add skating rinks, cinemas, bowling alleys and amusement centers.

Within Chicago, the crown jewel is Water Tower Place. Buttressed by Marshall Field's to the north and Lord & Taylor to the south, this vertical shopping emporium features seven levels with 125 boutiques, salons, eateries, and cinemas in a dazzling array of steel, glass and marble.

The best way to tackle Water Tower Place is to take one of the glass elevators to the top floor, and then work down by escalator, floor by floor: jewelry by Christian Bernard; shoes by Pappagallo, Connie and Florsheim; luggage by Louis Vuitton, and cookies by Mrs Fields.

Other shops offer whatnots for the bath, the dining room, the office or the person for whatever kind of statement one wishes to make. And for the child who has everything but a handmade, 6-foot tall stuffed toy giraffe, FAO Schwartz will happily supply one for a mere $5,000 or so.

Go for the glitter, the crowds, the variety of vendibles, the upper-crustiness of it all. For the exhausted, the Ritz-Carlton Hotel rises 859 feet above the east wing of the complex.

Across Michigan Avenue, Bloomingdale's bestows its aura on more than 50 shops. Despite a colorful 60-foot mural in its atrium and the Four Seasons Hotel looming 58 stories tall in the same structure, despite even Gucci and Henri Bendel, this mall has neither the panache nor the stylish elegance of its Water Tower counterpart.

Nearby, at 700 N. Michigan Avenue, is a newer but equally glitzy mall called Chicago Place. The 80 shops, spread over eight levels and 320,000 square feet, include stalwarts such as Saks Fifth Avenue and high-ticket emporia such as CD Peacock and Luis Vuitton. An eighth-floor food court wraps around an indoor garden. The barrel-vault dome and Prairie School-inspired trappings provide visual relief for shoppers jaded by the relentless retail landscape.

Northwest of the city, the suburb of Skokie offers the Old Orchard Center, an outdoor, low-slung, neatly arranged set of boutiques and department stores. A pool, stone islands, delicate Japanese bridges, flower beds and welcoming benches add a cool touch during hot summer months.

Arcades protect shoppers from the elements and afford a rambling path past the stores, and the whole complex is kept scrupulously clean by workers who seem to scoop up gum wrappers before they hit the ground. Old Orchard's 60-plus shops include Saks Fifth Avenue and Marshall Field's.

Farther north, Northbrook Court is a grande dame of malls – enclosed, bi-leveled, unmistakably tennis-set suburban. The 144 stores arrayed around broad intersecting aisles and plazas with modernist sculpture include Neiman-Marcus, Circle Gallery, I. Magnin and Mark Shale.

Toward the center of the Northbrook mall, an interesting design concept is realized by an interlocking set of steel polygons, painted canary yellow, that form an angular spheroid looking up toward clouds drifting over the skylit roof.

Finally, for the truly dedicated who do not mind the long trek to Schaumburg, there's Woodfield Mall, a granddaddy of US malls containing 235 shops. During the summer, up to 200 buses a day bring in customers from a four-state area to shop at Schaumburg's stores.

Mayfair Regent Hotel, lest it develop a smell. Advice columnist Ann Landers lives here. TV personality Oprah Winfrey lives here. Nancy Reagan lived here as a girl. Abra Wilkin, a granddaughter of John D. Rockefeller, lives in the Drake Tower penthouse, and once hired helicopters to bring up materials for a redecorating job.

Walk east, then turn back south on Lake Shore Drive to see **860 and 880 N. Lake Shore Drive**, two apartment buildings designed in 1952 by Mies van der Rohe. To reach **Oak Street Beach**, double back to the southeast corner of Michigan Avenue and E. Lake Shore Drive, and duck down the pedestrian underpass beneath Lake Shore Drive. Return to the underpass, this time veering right to the west side of Lake Shore Drive. Emerge at the corner of the drive and **Oak Street** for a stretch of high-fashion shops, most notably Ultimo Ltd and the Giorgio Armani boutique.

Rushing out: At the end of the block, turn right and head north on **Rush Street**. Once known as Chicago's nightclub district, it is now popular with suburban teenagers who pack taverns near Rush and Division streets. Some of the bars play great rock 'n' roll, and often have hundreds of patrons singing raucously along. If that sounds good, try some of the bars on Division Street such as She-Nannigans, Butch McGuire's Tavern or Mother's.

Just north of Division Street, on State Parkway, is a charming Art-Moderne apartment building constructed in 1938 with glass blocks wrapped around its curved corners. This area along Lake Shore Drive is known as the **Gold Coast**, a preserve of wealth and elegant architecture. On the lakefront itself are a mixture of modern high-rises and beautiful old apartment buildings where some of Chicago's oldest families have lived. One block west is Astor Street, and the **Astor Street District**, the heart of the Gold Coast. The six-block walk is filled with elegant townhouses.

Lunchtime looking.

Magnificent Mile 153

At the northwest corner of Burton and Astor streets stands the district's largest building, **Patterson House**, a Renaissance revival home designed by New York architect Stanford White. It was commissioned in 1892 by *Chicago Tribune* publisher Joseph Medill as a wedding gift for his daughter and son-in-law. Also notable are the **James Charnley House**, at 1365 N. Astor Street and designed by Frank Lloyd Wright; the **James Houghteling houses** at 1308-12 N. Astor, designed in neo-Elizabethan style by architect John Wellborn Root in 1887, as well as the French Renaissance revival **Joseph T. Ryerson House** at 1406 N. Astor, built in 1922.

There is also the Art-Deco **Edward P. Russell House** at 1444 N. Astor Street, designed by Holabird and Root in 1929, and two Art-Deco apartment buildings at 1301 and 1260 N. Astor Street. At the northern end of Astor at **North Boulevard**, is the earliest house on the block, a large Queen Anne mansion designed by Alfred F. Pashley in 1880 as the residence for the Roman Catholic Archbishop of Chicago.

Around the corner, at 1524 N. Lake Shore Drive, is one of the city's more unusual museums. The **International Museum of Surgical Science** tells the history of surgery using graphic paintings of tumors and amputations and a gruesome variety of surgical instruments, not to mention a death mask of Napoleon.

Heading back west, do not miss the lovely, lacey apartment building at **1550 N. State Parkway**. It was designed in 1912 by Benjamin Marshall and Charles E. Fox, who also designed the Drake Hotel, among other prominent local buildings. The building features enormous, high-ceilinged apartments with *petits salons, grands salons* and *orangeries*, and once housed such well-known families as the Fields and the Shedds.

Old Town: Walk west on North Boulevard, which becomes North Avenue. One block past La Salle Street is Wells Street and the heart of **Old Town**, a neighborhood that has veered from wealth to seediness and back up to wealth again. The side streets north and west of the intersection are lined with pretty townhouses that have been lovingly restored.

Just north of North Avenue, on Wells Street, is the longtime home of **Second City**, the innovative comedy improvisation club that served as a training ground for such stars as Elaine May, Alan Arkin, Joan Rivers, John Belushi and John Candy.

South of North Avenue, is **Wells Street**, which was once Chicago's hippie haven, a place to buy cigarette papers, water pipes, psychedelic magazines and tie-dyed T-shirts. Now Wells Street is a strip of fancy shops and restaurants. For a slight whiff of the past, visit Uno's Bizarre Bazaar, which has been in the area since 1966. The shop still sells tie-dyed T-shirts and peace-sign jewelry.

Left, modern Lisa. **Right**, getting directions outside one of the newer Mag Mile malls.

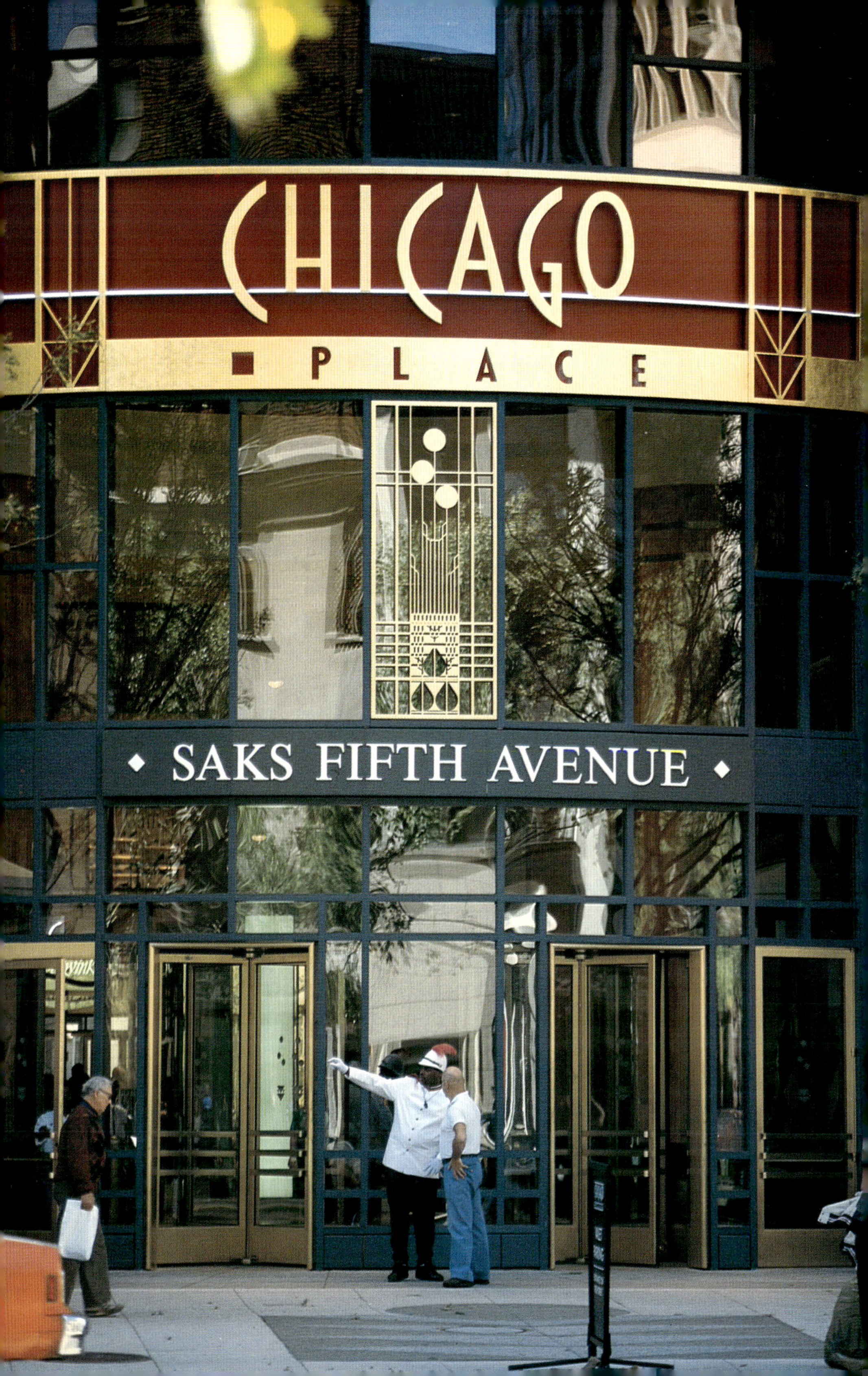
CHICAGO
PLACE
SAKS FIFTH AVENUE

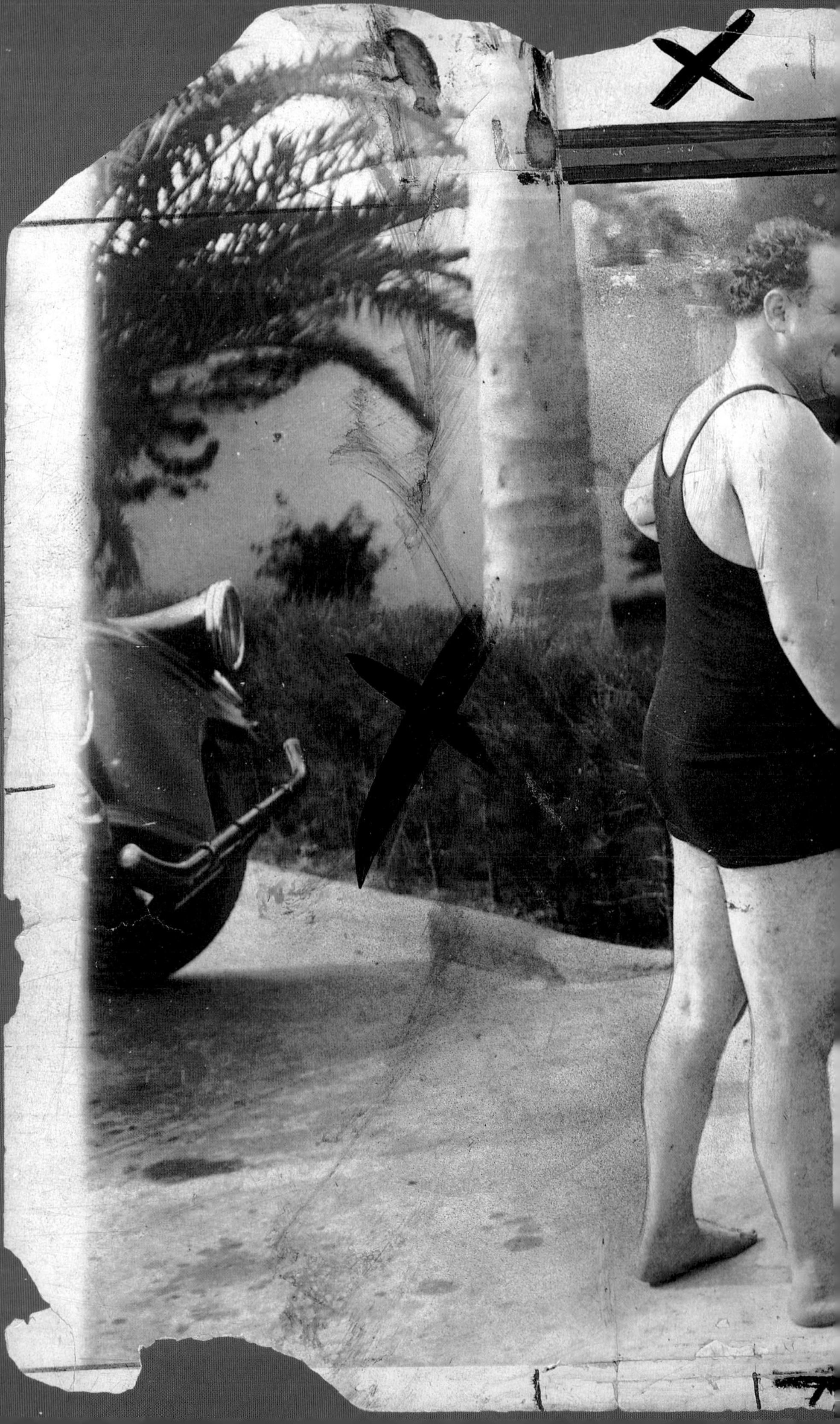

Above—The Capone-Guzik-Fusco wildcat brewery at 1642 South 48th avenue, Cicero, that was raided yesterday by prohibition agents under Elliott Ness, aid of W. E. Bennett, chief of the special prohibition corps.

Ness Raiders 'Knock Out' Capone Breweries in Quick Succession

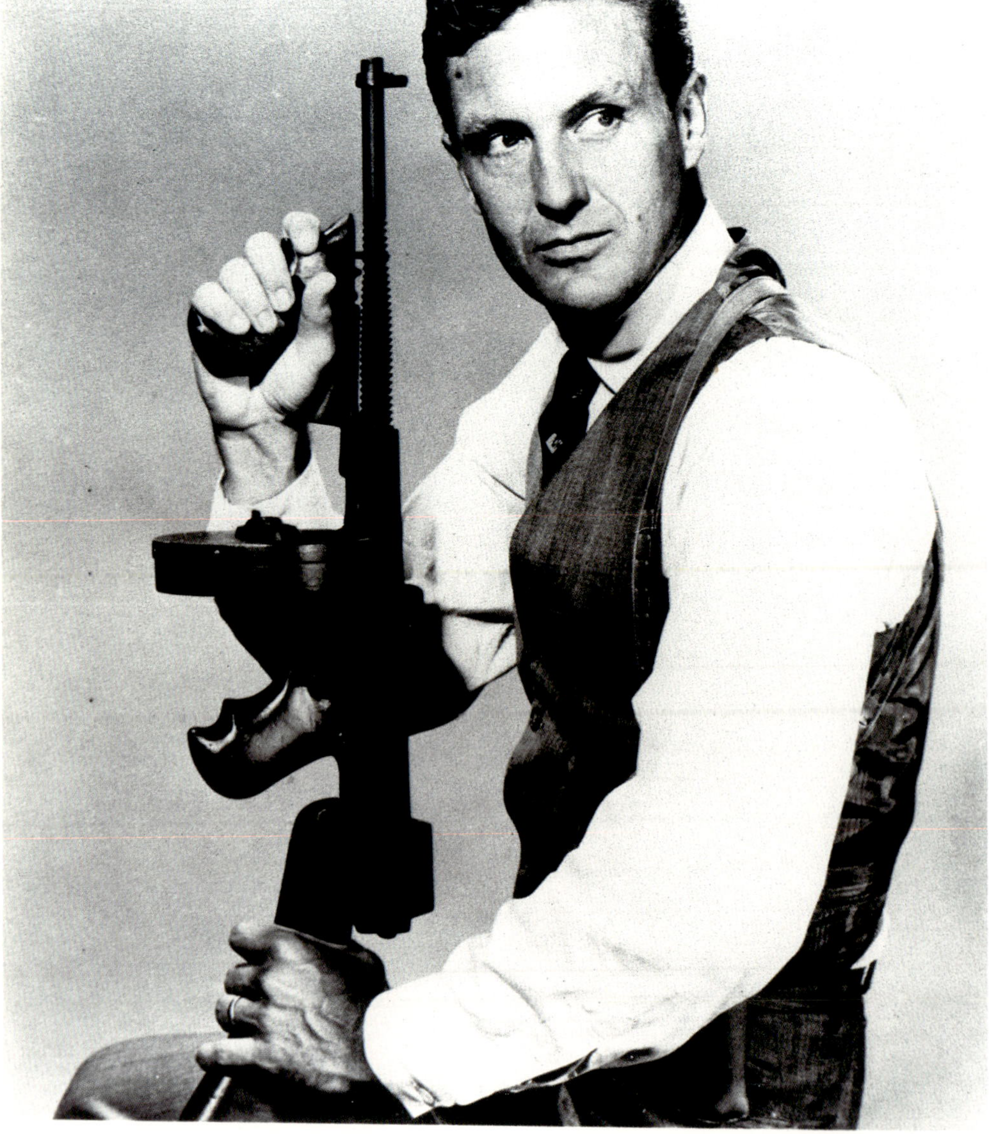

THE GANG'S ALL HERE

Crime historian William J. Helmer said that those people concerned about Chicago's image never had a chance when they tried to purge the city of its association with gangs and gangsters, with firebombs and tommy guns.

"I think that Americans have always had a rebellious streak that permits them to identify with certain kinds of lawbreakers," Helmer suggested. "Gangsters, like Capone, and outlaws, like Dillinger, seem enviably self-confident, unafraid of authority and unafraid of death, and to have an admirable ability to handle stress. If they also have style and élan, they discover that crime may not pay, but it can be a shortcut to immortality."

In the 1950s and '60s, Mayor Richard J. Daley and other city fathers tried to make the world forget about "Scarface" Capone and the Thompson submachine guns that made the Twenties roar.

But times have changed and today the city is no longer demolishing any site associated with gangland lore, and the Chicago Historical Society no longer answers Capone queries with a blank, "Al who?"

Biograph ambush: In the last few years, Chicago has begun learning to live with, if not love, its gangland reputation through tours, exhibits and restaurants. Ironically, the city's only structure with **National Historic Landmark** status and a link to gangster lore has nothing to do with the infamous Capone.

The **Biograph Theatre** at 2433 N. Lincoln Avenue became famous on July 22, 1934 when bank robber John Dillinger was gunned down by federal agents. Dillinger was not part of any crime syndicate; he was a freelancer who resembled Humphrey Bogart and came across as a regular guy. His dramatic flair in relieving banks of their money, the gallantry he sometimes displayed and his success at playing cat-and-mouse with law enforcers contributed to his popularity. Dillinger's brooding good looks and reputation as a dashing playboy only enhanced his standing among women admirers all over America.

When he was betrayed by the "Lady in Red" and ambushed by G-men, Dillinger died in an alley, just south of the Biograph. Women reportedly rushed to the scene to dip their handkerchiefs in the pool of his blood.

Tourists interested in the pivotal events and colorful personalities of Chicago's most exciting and dangerous era can visit **Capone's Chicago**, a museum of the Roaring Twenties, at 605 North Clark Street.

Gang society: Hardcore gangster enthusiasts can even join the John Dillinger Died for You Society, a tongue-in-cheek fan club started in 1966 for followers of gangster lore. "Some called him Public Enemy Number One," noted Horace Naismith, the society president. "Actually, John

Preceding pages: often-reprinted Chicago Sun-Times Rogues Gallery photo of Al Capone at his winter retreat in Florida. **Left,** *Robert Stack as Eliot Ness.* **Right,** *the real Eliot Ness.*

Dillinger was a prominent economic reformer with unorthodox banking methods."

Applicants to the society receive a membership card, a history of the group, a catalog of gangster accoutrements and notices of meetings where an empty chair is always left for the club's namesake.

Chicago's oldest crime structure stands at Dearborn and Hubbard streets. It is the old **Criminal Courts Building**, an imposing, gray stone fortress that has been renovated for private offices. Behind it, where a firehouse now stands, was the old jail where executions were carried out.

It was here, on November 12, 1887, that the four celebrated Haymarket anarchists went to the gallows. (Eight activists were originally charged with incitement to murder after a political riot which ended in several deaths. But sympathy for the accused led to the pardoning of the four survivors.)

In all, 92 prisoners were hanged in the old jail between 1882 and 1929. It would have been 93, but in 1921 "Terrible" Tommy O'Connor, condemned to hang for murdering a police detective, escaped four days before his date with the hangman's knot.

The perpetrators of gangland murders were rarely arrested by the police, however, let alone sentenced to death. Their courtrooms were the smoke-filled headquarters of gangster bosses, and their executions were carried out in public or private by gunmen whose own days were numbered.

Flavored death: During the 1920s, most of the death sentences delivered by gangsters were the result of territorial wars that began over bootlegging and quickly expanded to extortion, gambling, prostitution, labor racketeering and corruption of public officials. The methods of punishment were swift and often ingenious, like rubbing the bullet tips with garlic so that if they missed a vital organ the victim could still die of gangrene.

The aftermath of the St Valentine's Day Massacre, 1929...

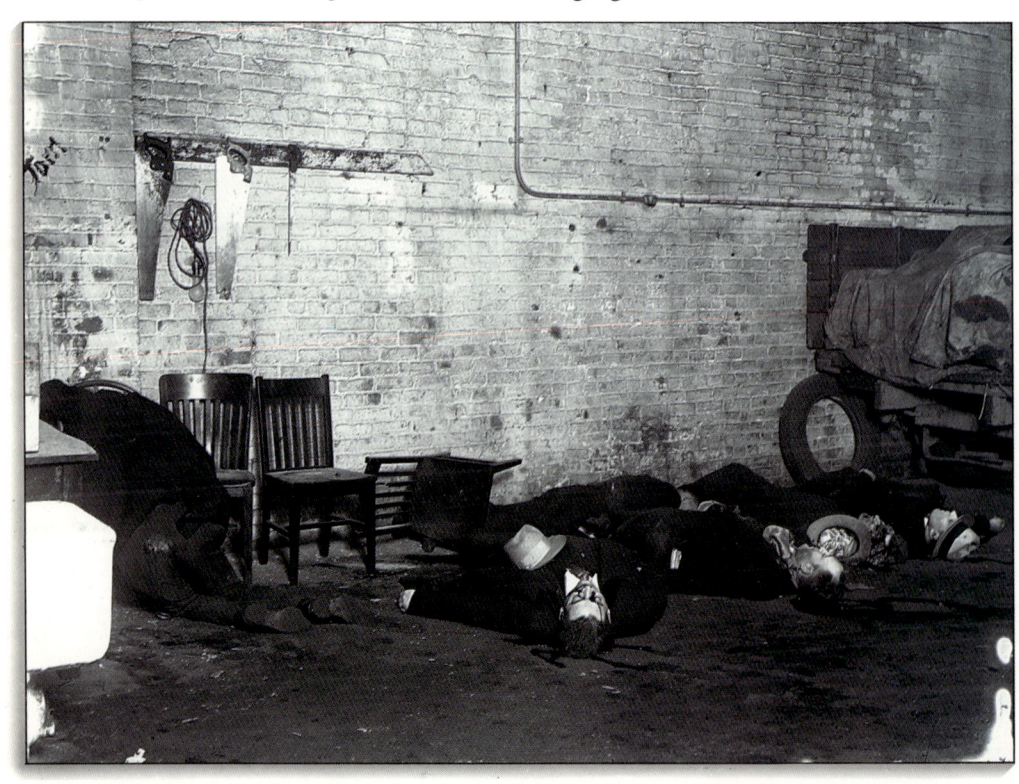

At first, the gangs were content to keep to their own sides of town, but greed got the best of them and entrepreneurs sparked open warfare.

In July of 1921, independent businessman Steve Wisniewski hijacked a beer truck belonging to Dion O'Banion. Deanie, as close friends knew him, had been an altar boy and a singing waiter. But by 1921, O'Banion was the undisputed crime boss of the city's North Side. His top lieutenant, Earl "Hymie" Weiss, forced Wisniewski into a car at gunpoint at the corner of **Halsted** and **14th streets**, now the edge of the Maxwell Street flea market district. Wisniewski got his brains blown out and made history by being the first victim to be "taken for a ride."

O'Banion ran his operation from a flower shop at 738 N. State Street, now a parking lot. He himself had become a thorn for South Side crime boss Johnny Torrio. On November 10, 1924, Capone – who at the time was Torrio's top lieutenant – sent a trio of killers into O'Banion's flower shop to silence the Irish tenor forever.

Weiss took over O'Banion's gang, but not for long. On October 11, 1926, Weiss and his driver, Sam Peller, died in a storm of machine gun bullets on the steps of **Holy Name Cathedral** at 735 N. State Street. Both Weiss and O'Banion were taken to a mortuary at 703 N. Wells Street, now an art gallery. Back then, it was the site of some of Chicago's most lavish gangster funerals. O'Banion's funeral procession included 122 cars and 26 trucks loaded with flowers.

Scarface surfaces: By now, Al Capone had taken over from Torrio, who survived an assassination attempt and decided to retire amid the city's longest running gang war. Its violence was so blatant that Tony Lombardo, Capone's *consigliere*, was gunned down on a Friday afternoon, September 7, 1928, walking east on the south side of Madison, between State and Dearborn. At the time, **State and Madison** was known as

...and a police recreation shortly after the massacre.

Gangland 161

"the world's busiest corner."

But the most notorious of all gangland attacks, the one that would forever burn Capone into Chicago's history, came on St Valentine's Day in 1929. At 2122 N. Clark Street, now a grassy lot in front of a senior citizens' home, stood the SMC Cartage Co. It was at this garage that Capone's boys, masquerading as cops, lined seven members and associates of the rival Bugs Moran gang against a brick wall and riddled them with machine gun bullets. Moran, who had inherited the O'Banion-Weiss organization, was not present at the massacre, and so lived to learn what others already knew: Chicago had become Capone's city.

Capone, whose estimated income surpassed an astonishing $105 million in 1927 – still a Guinness world record six decades later – was finally convicted in 1931 of income tax evasion and served eight years in prison.

His final headquarters were at the corner of Michigan Avenue and 22nd Street, now a vacant, 10-story eyesore building with a sign over the boarded entrance that reads the **New Michigan Hotel**. It used to be the Lexington Hotel, where Capone's office was on the fourth floor, behind the rounded turret windows at the front corner. Several would-be developers over the years have managed to keep the wrecker's ball out, but haven't brought in enough capital to restore the hotel.

Capone died in 1947 in Florida, his body ravaged by syphilis because he was deathly afraid of needles, even those backed by penicillin. He is buried in the family plot at **Mount Carmel Cemetery** in the western suburb of Hillside, about 40 minutes from downtown Chicago.

As for "Machine Gun Jack" McGurn, who masterminded the St Valentine's Day Massacre, his life came to a close on the seventh anniversary of the event. The building at 805 N. Milwaukee Avenue now houses an office furniture store. In 1936, it was a bowling alley, where two remnants of the Moran gang mowed McGurn down with tommy-guns. Into his lifeless left hand, they pressed a blood-red valentine.

Guided tours: Untouchable Tours, a theater on wheels, offers a nostalgic two and a half hour trip to many gang-era landmarks.

The tour's dinner package winds up at **Tommy Gun's Garage**, 1237 S. State Street. Tommy Gun's, a block from Chicago Police Headquarters, offers dinner and an entertaining floor show set in the 1920s. There's a machine gun-toting bouncer and plenty of flappers. The place is usually packed with both locals and visitors from around the globe who buy up the "I Got Massacred" T-shirts.

"Any place in the world, people will associate Chicago with Al Capone. That's what Chicago's known for, like it or not," says Sandy Mangen, proprietor of Tommy Gun's Garage. "Right now, it's a negative image. Let's make it a fun one."

Left, John Dillinger, the people's favorite outlaw, 1934. **Right**, Evelyn Whitney, flapper, 1929.

163

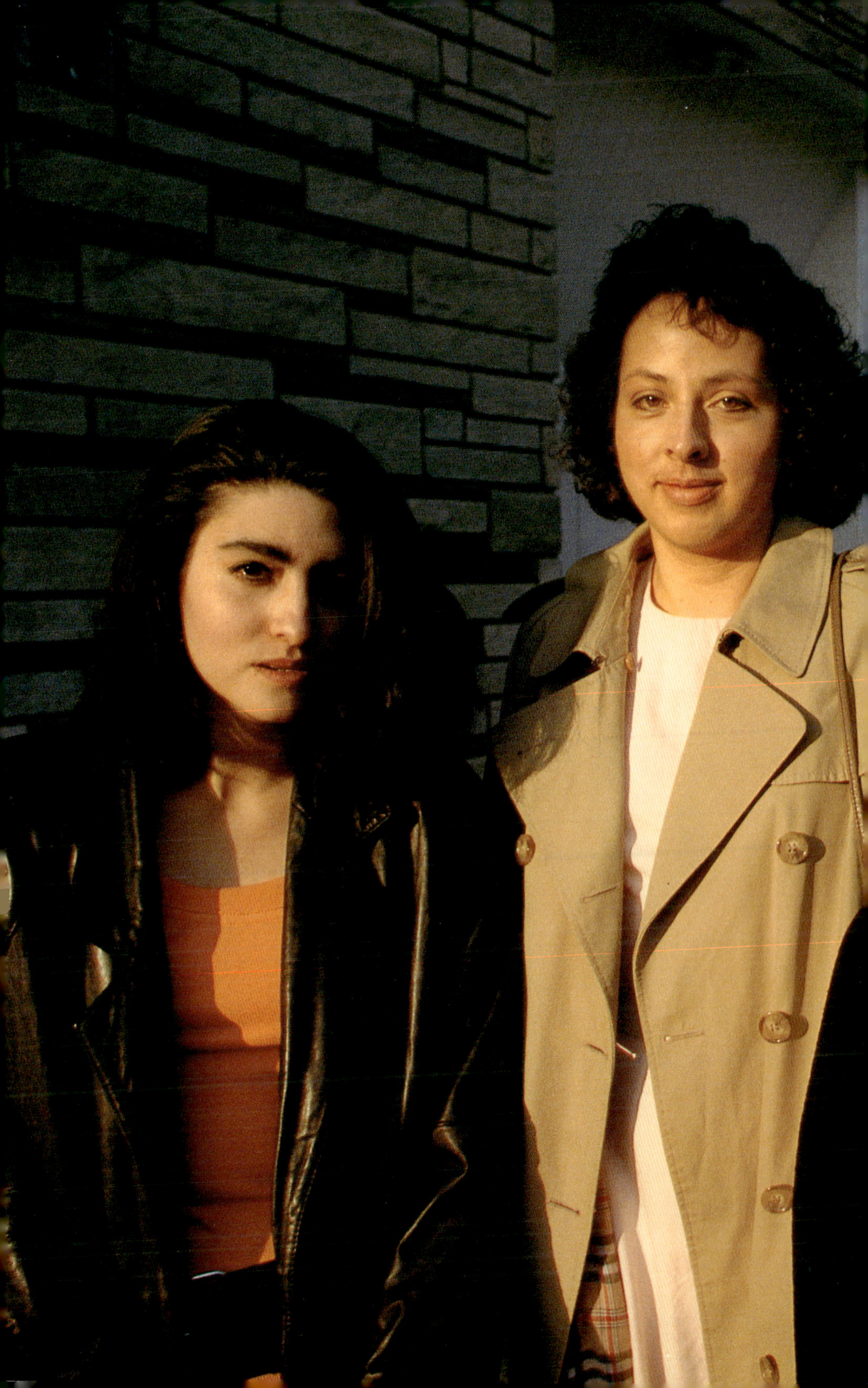

CHURCH
OF THE GREATER
CHICAGO

THE NORTH SIDE

In the 1860s, the fattest madam on Chicago's North Side was Gentle Annie Stafford, who weighed 300 pounds and liked to put on airs. So successfully did she drill her prostitutes in proper manners and refined conversation that, at the opening-night party of a new brothel, one backslapping girl bellowed at every man she met: "Who's your favorite poet? Mine's Byron."

More than 130 years have passed since Gentle Annie's day, but the North Side remains Chicago's classy side of town, flush with restaurants, nightclubs, galleries, theaters, concert halls and people who like to put on airs. Naturally, this tends to grate on South Siders, who talk about North Siders the way some Canadians talk about Americans – all the time, with great emphasis on the "us" and "them," defining themselves by the contrasts. North Siders, on the other hand, talk about South Siders the way Americans talk about Canadians – almost never. They forget the South Side exists.

Diverse lifestyles: But, if truth be told, Chicago's North Side is by no means a uniform world of wine snobs and effete theatergoers. To think so is to think like a South Sider. The North Side is a collection of diverse neighborhoods, ethnic groups and lifestyles, from the third-generation bungalow dwellers of the far Northwest Side to the Vietnamese of Argyle Street to the Koreans of Lawrence Avenue to the Poles of Milwaukee Avenue.

One good way to tour Chicago, especially north of Lincoln Park, is to follow old Indian trails. Most of the major diagonal streets, such as Clark and Milwaukee, run along the former trails. Because they are among Chicago's earliest roads, they bisect many of the city's oldest and most interesting neighborhoods.

The first neighborhood as you ven-

North Side

Chicago and Suburbs

Preceding pages: North Side churchgoers; Wrigley Field. **Below**, casual weekend elegance on the North Side.

ture north of Lincoln Park on Clark Street is **Wrigleyville**, perhaps Chicago's most torridly trendy residential district. Everything about Wrigleyville – roughly bounded by Diversey Parkway, Irving Park Road, Ravenswood Avenue and the lake – has changed in recent years. Even its name.

Fifteen years ago the neighborhood was rough and gritty and called Lake View. But then young white-collar professionals, priced out of comfortable Lincoln Park, began moving in. Older blue-collar Germans, Swedes, Hungarians and Puerto Ricans began moving out. Fashionable espresso bars and restaurants staked claims, like squatters in a gold rush, on seemingly every corner.

Gentrification marches on, but Wrigleyville remains – if only for the moment – one of Chicago's most varied neighborhoods, a place where people of different tongues, colors and incomes live side by side. The cultural heart of Wrigleyville is **Wrigley Field**, a baseball park as quaint as any corner café.

Wrigley Field, more than any other ballpark in the nation, is an integral part of its community, crowded on all sides by houses, apartment buildings and bars. Rooftop Cub fans along Waveland Avenue enjoy a free and unobstructed view of every game, and home runs sometimes break front windows.

For more than a decade, a majority of Wrigleyville residents fought all efforts by the Chicago Tribune Co. – owners of the Cubs – to bring lights and night baseball to the old ball park. They worried that drunken fans might rock the night with noise, urinate on lawns and tie up traffic.

They feared, at bottom, the Great Wrigleyville Revival might falter. As it happened, the Tribune prevailed, and night baseball came to Wrigley Field in the summer of 1989. It did, indeed, create a good deal of noise, rowdiness and gridlock. But the Great Revival never missed a beat. Property values continue to soar in the 1990s.

For a pleasantly refined dining experience after a game, try Thai Classic for seafood, at 3332 N. Clark.

One of the best bars in Wrigleyville is Sheffield's Wine and Beer Garden at 3258 N. Sheffield. This bar somehow manages to strike a pleasant and improbable balance between the yuppie need for fancy bottled beers and jazz music and the old neighborhood's traditional informality.

The 3700 block of N. Clark Street is one of Chicago's most avant garde. Check out Cabaret Metro for cutting-edge rock music; or Pravda Records next door for the sort of independently-recorded music you might not get back home; or the Ginger Man for its big pool tables and exotic imported beers, or the Smart Bar for the hipsters with hair dyed jet-black, chalk-white complexions and dark clothing.

Victoriana: A block north of Wrigley Field is a one-block stretch of Victorian England, incongruously out of place and out of time. **Alta Vista Terrace**, listed on the National Register of His-

North Side 169

toric Places, is a narrow side street of 40 striking houses, built in 1900 and modeled after a street in London. The ornate facades of the houses are paired, one on each side of the street. A few blocks farther up the old Indian trail, at Clark Street and Irving Park Road, lies **Graceland**, Chicago's most stately and historically significant cemetery. You can pick up a map at the front office and walk through Chicago's past. (Foreign visitors should not confuse this Graceland with the Memphis mansion of the same name which is the final resting place of its former owner, Elvis Presley.)

The tombs at Chicago's Graceland include those of John Kinzie (1763–1828), the city's most prominent early settler, farm-machinery inventor Cyrus H. McCormick, meatpacking mogul Phillip D. Armour, heavyweight boxing champions Jack Johnson and Bob Fitzsimmons, retailing giant Marshall Field, architect Louis Sullivan and the founder of baseball's National League, William A. Hulburt. Near **Lake Willowmere** in Graceland stands perhaps the most impressive monument in the cemetery, the intricately detailed **Carrie Eliza Getty Mausoleum**, designed by Sullivan and built in 1890. The limestone monument is considered by many to be a landmark of modern architecture.

Home of the stars: Graceland's elegance stands in dramatic contrast to the shabbiness of the community immediately to the north: **Uptown**. Until about 1950, Uptown was one of Chicago's most exclusive communities. Wealthy businessmen lived in spacious Victorian, Prairie, Queen Anne and Georgian-style homes in Uptown's most exclusive lakefront neighborhoods. Movie stars of the silent era, including Charlie Chaplin, Gloria Swanson, Douglas Fairbanks and Mary Pickford, worked at the Essanay Film Studio on West Argyle Street. Big Band-era stars such as Tommy Dorsey, Glenn Miller and Frank Sinatra per-

Graceland Cemetery.

formed regularly in the famous **Aragon Ballroom**, 1106 W. Lawrence.

But Uptown's glamorous image was shattered by a post-World War II housing shortage. Many of its finest homes and apartment buildings were converted into low-rent rooming houses. The community was flooded with penniless newcomers, including Appalachian coal miners and Native American Indians. Uptown today remains synonymous with winos, the immigrant and migrant poor, flophouses for the homeless and half-way houses for the mentally ill.

Like Wrigleyville, however, Uptown has been rediscovered of late by the forces of gentrification – real estate speculators, housing rehabilitators and young professionals. The Aragon, serving up professional wrestling for many years, is once again a hot concert and dance hall. The lakefront neighborhoods, particularly, are luring back a moneyed crowd. Former Illinois Governor James Thompson, for one, makes his home here. Thanks to gentrification and the recent arrival of thousands of remarkably ambitious immigrants from the Far East, Uptown is making a comeback. Two Uptown neighborhoods in particular stand out: Andersonville and New Chinatown.

Swedish models: Centered at Foster and Clark streets, **Andersonville** is Chicago's last Swedish community and a fast-disappearing one at that. Swedish bakeries, delis and restaurants still dot Clark Street, but have been joined by Japanese, Thai, Korean and Assyrian establishments. When Andersonville celebrates *Midsommarfest* nowadays, blocking off Clark Street for an all-day Old Country summer fair, it assumes something of an international flavor. Walking down Clark, you can nibble on Swedish meatballs, Assyrian *falafel* or Turkish *baklava*, washed down with Thai iced coffee.

At one time Chicago had more Swedes than Stockholm. They settled in five neighborhoods, founded more than

A cyclist about to interrupt a fashion shoot.

50 churches and printed several daily newspapers. But their grandchildren moved to the suburbs. Now, by some estimates, as many as 50,000 Chicago-area residents – including former Governor Thompson – can claim predominantly Swedish ancestry. But relatively few still live in Andersonville.

When touring the neighborhood – as the king and queen of Sweden did in 1988 – stop by Svea Restaurant, at 3258 W. Foster, an Andersonville landmark known for its authentic Swedish pancakes with lingonberries, herring salad, *limpa* bread and boysenberry cobbler. The 5300 and 5400 blocks of Clark Street have many Swedish landmarks, such as Wikstrom's Scandinavian American Gourmet Foods, at 5247 N. Clark, which features a spicy potato sausage called *potatis korv*, and Nelson's Scandinavian Bakery, known for its *limpa* bread and buns.

Also on Clark Street, a good Turkish restaurant is Konak, where Turkish carpets and tapestries decorate the walls. Try the eggplant salad and a kebab. Then there's Beirut Restaurant, known, like Konak's, for its great kebabs.

A hip place to relax and browse for travel books, maps and wearables – many from Third World countries – is Kopi, A Traveler's Café, at 5317 N. Clark in Andersonville. It has a full espresso bar and offers snacks, hearty soups and fresh-baked desserts which you can enjoy while sitting at a hand-painted table.

The best stop-off for souvenirs in Andersonville might be the gift shop of the **Swedish American Museum**, at 5211 N. Clark. The museum features a permanent exhibit illustrating, through pictures and artifacts, the Swedish contribution to the building of Chicago. In the next block, the Swedish Style Gift Shop and the Swedish Style Knit Shop are two other good stops.

For those last-minute gifts, head to The Landmark of Andersonville at 5301 N. Clark, a cooperative with three floors of shops selling country kitsch,

Dual focus; Baha'i Temple.

172

clothing, ethnic crafts and collectibles.

Chinatown: Four blocks east of Andersonville lies an immigrant settlement that is as new to Chicago as Andersonville is old: **New Chinatown.** This two-block stretch of Argyle Street, bounded by Broadway on the west and Sheridan Road on the east, pulsates with the verve and entrepreneurial spirit of Vietnamese and Cambodian refugees, a majority of whom are ethnic Chinese. Vietnamese and Chinese restaurants, grocery stores and clothing stores line the street. Thousands of Asian customers, ignoring seedy Uptown drifters, pour into the area on weekends for the good prices on 150-pound bags of rice among other things, and the authentic smells and sights of home.

Argyle Street is a microcosm of the American immigrant experience. After the Vietnam War, Vietnamese and ethnic Chinese living in Vietnam fled to America and Chicago, choosing to settle on Argyle because rents were cheap. They pooled their meager resources and opened small stores and restaurants. Thousands now live in Uptown's tenements. A few have moved on to better city neighborhoods and the suburbs.

Trung Viet Grocery offers a wide selection of traditional Vietnamese foodstuffs. The store was started by a family that came to Chicago from Saigon in 1979. Kinh Do's Gift Shop, a few doors away on West Argyle, is crammed from floor to ceiling with imported Chinese wares, including exquisite Chinese silks. Two critically acclaimed Vietnamese restaurants in New Chinatown are Pasteur, a café-style establishment, and Lao Vien, a long and narrow storefront restaurant. The food is good, and you can stare out the windows as all of Uptown straggles by. Chinese carry-out dinners and desserts are available all along Argyle Street.

The other Chinatown, first settled by Chinese immigrants around 1912, is centered around Cermak Road and Wentworth Avenue and continues to serve as a Midwestern receiving area

Chinatown twins.

for immigrants from mainland China.

Around the corner from Argyle Street is one more Uptown treat – the **Green Mill Jazz Club**. The Green Mill, at 4802 N. Broadway, is a legendary Chicago late-night jazz and jam-session bar once owned by "Machinegun Jack" McGurn and frequented by Al Capone. In the 1940s, when Big Band musicians and torch singers finished a job at the Aragon or the Edgewater Beach Hotel, they would shed their tuxes and jam til dawn at the Green Mill. Among those who sat in were Frank Sinatra, Billie Holiday, the drummer Gene Krupa, trumpeter Roy Eldridge and drummer Claude "Hey Hey" Humphrey, who later died homeless, frozen in a grocery store parking lot in Uptown.

The Green Mill went sour in the 1960s and '70s, when Uptown was at its seediest, but has come back strong. It offers excellent jazz on almost every night except Monday, when the Poetry Slam is featured. The Slam is a Green Mill original, where local poets with strong constitutions take the stage and serve up their best verse for the mixed crowd of locals and tourists. When they're good, the crowd cheers. When they're not, the crowd jeers.

Devon divide: Argyle Street is one of Chicago's most homogeneous immigrant strips – virtually everybody here is Vietnamese or Cambodian. In contrast, **Devon Avenue**, two miles to the north, is perhaps Chicago's most culturally diverse – not to say confusing – strip. To walk down Devon between Oakley Boulevard and Kedzie Avenue is to wander through another land. But which land?

On the east side of the strip are the shops of the New Guard – Indians, Pakistanis, Greeks, Turks, Palestinians, Syrians, Lebanese and Filipinos. On the west are the shops of the Old Guard – Eastern Europeans and Russian Jews. In between, everything is up for grabs.

The best time to visit Devon Avenue is on a Sunday morning, when the sidewalks are jammed with crates of

A Milwaukee Avenue restaurant.

produce and men in *yarmulkes* and women in saris. In summer, the air is spiced with the intermingled odors of the Arab fruit markets, Jewish bakeries, tandoori chicken, hummus and espresso. For urban romantics, there is no better place to be.

Jews were among the first and last immigrants to settle on Devon. The first wave came from Eastern Europe in the early decades of the century. The most recent poured in from Russia in the 1980s, when the Soviet Union relaxed restrictions on immigration. Asians began settling along Devon in the early 1970s. Devon is known informally as Sari Row because it is lined with stores carrying Indian saris, fabrics, chiffon scarves and jewelry. Taj Sari Palace, at 2553 W. Devon, is one of the largest. Devon also boasts quite a few Jewish and Arab butcher shops.

On the west end of the strip, Miller's Meats and Poultry sells meat that has been slaughtered and prepared in accordance with Jewish kosher law. On the other end of the strip, Sawzi Suleiman and his brothers, the proprietors of Farm City Meats, supply fellow Arabs with meat butchered according to Islamic dietary law.

In the 2900 block of W. Devon, the Shaevitz Meat Market claims a cult following for its kosher hot dogs and salami. The Midwest Fish Market still smokes its own white fish and grinds fillets for gefilte fish.

By general consensus among the local critics, Devon's best Indian restaurant is Standard India, an unpretentious and relatively inexpensive purveyor of subcontinental specialties.

While in the neighborhood, especially if you have children, consider venturing a few blocks further north to **Indian Boundary Park**, at 2500 W. Lunt. The 13-acre park, two blocks west of Western Avenue, has a terrific playground and its own small zoo which features alpacas, yaks, reindeer, swans, and goats, among other animals.

Poles apart: A second old Indian trail

A Polish neighborhood bakery.

in Chicago – Milwaukee Avenue – embodies the history of the single largest ethnic group in the Chicago area, Polish Americans. An estimated one million Poles and people of Polish descent live in the six-county Chicago area, the greatest concentration of Poles outside of Warsaw. Within the city, they have tended to settle in five geographically dispersed areas, the largest number historically have made their homes on or around Milwaukee Avenue.

The heart of America's Polish diaspora, **Polonia**, is on Milwaukee Avenue from Belmont Avenue to Central Park Avenue. Here, in an area called Jackowo, live Chicago's newest Polish immigrants, the best-educated and most sophisticated in the city's history. They love jazz and never learned to polka. Typically, these people may be certified accountants who are often forced to work as janitors.

The intersection of Milwaukee Avenue and Division Street, immediately northwest of the Loop, was called Chicago's **Polish Downtown** after the first Poles moved into the area in the 1860s. Unskilled laborers, they worked in the tanneries and factories along Milwaukee and the banks of the Chicago River. As Scandinavians and Germans worked their way northwest up Milwaukee Avenue, moving on to better lives in better neighborhoods, the Poles followed them through the neighborhoods.

Today, the old Polish downtown is gone. Its last landmark is a gourmet Polish restaurant, the Busy Bee, at 1550 N. Damen, frequented by people who live somewhere else. Second and third-generation Polish-Americans still live along Milwaukee, but in suburban-style neighborhoods on the far edge of town and beyond.

The biggest Polish restaurant on Milwaukee – and in all the Midwest – is in suburban Niles. Przybylo's White Eagle Banquet Hall, at 6845 N. Milwaukee, claims that it can handle around seven wedding receptions at one

A fruit and vegetable shop.

time, and is frequently put to the test.

The new Polish Downtown is the **Jackowo** business district. Polish bakeries, taverns and restaurants crowd the streets. Jackowo (pronounced *yahts-koh-voh*), is Polish for "hyacinth neighborhood." It takes its name from **St Hyacinth**, the local Roman Catholic Church. The Orbit, at 2940 N. Milwaukee, is a popular and boisterous restaurant in Jackowo, known particularly for its *pirogi*.

The **Polish Museum of America** hangs on in the old Polish Downtown, at 1000 N. Milwaukee. It features paintings of famous Polish patriots, as well as exhibits of traditional Polish crafts and Polish weaponry. And for a sense of Chicago Polonia then and now, visit **St Stanislaus Kostka Catholic Church**, at Evergreen and Noble in the old neighborhood. This majestic Renaissance-style church, built in 1881, served more than 8,000 Polish families in 1890. Today, it tends to fewer than 850 families, a testament to changing neighborhood boundaries rather than changing values.

EVANSTON: The first town north of Chicago's city limits is **Evanston**, the city's most cosmopolitan suburb. It has a racially diverse population, a famous university, superior restaurants, unique shops, a tradition of progressive politics, big-city sophistication and small-town warmth. It's an all-round good town, especially now that you can buy a beer there.

Evanston is the national headquarters of the Women's Christian Temperance Union, the folks who gave America Prohibition, the national alcohol ban that perhaps inadvertently allowed the gangsters to flourish. Until only a few years ago, it was illegal to sell packaged alcohol in Evanston and, even now, the town has no taverns.

Local legend has it that, thanks to Evanston's teetotalers, the ice-cream sundae was invented here. Seltzer water was banned on Sundays in the 1880s, so when the local druggists removed it

After services at St Vladimir's.

from their ice-cream sodas, they called what was left – ice-cream with syrup – a "sundae."

Evanston is also special because of **Northwestern University**, its cultural and economic anchor. Founded by Chicago Methodists in 1855, the university has grown from 10 students in one three-story building to almost 11,000 students and more than 160 buildings. Its football team, the Wildcats, is perennially unlucky, but its academics are superior. In the area, only the University of Chicago has a better reputation and Northwestern surpasses the school downtown in several areas.

On campus, **Pick-Staiger Hall** offers regular classical, folk and pop concerts. Its acoustics are excellent. A lesser known treat on campus is the lush **Shakespeare Garden**, just south of the Technological Institute. It is as peaceful as it is beautiful.

Evanston is a walker's town, with miles of stately mansions along its lakefront. One of the finest is open for public viewing, the 28-room **Charles Gates Dawes House**, at 225 Greenwood Avenue. Dawes was America's vice president from 1925 to 1929 under President Calvin Coolidge. The **Evanston Historical Society**, which has offices in the mansion, offers a list of other landmark homes that are also worth viewing.

For good French provincial dining in Evanston, try the stylish Café Express, at 615 Dempster, a slightly bohemian favorite of both students and townies. For a store with a difference, check out Dave's Down To Earth Rock Shop, at 704 Main Street, which sells rocks, precious and otherwise. If you're looking for a semi-precious stone or just a nice paperweight, it's worth a visit.

The **Baha'i Temple**, at Linden and Sheridan in Wilmette, is just over the Evanston town line. This 1953 architectural masterpiece by Louis Bourgeois, with its lacy walls and delicate bell-like shape, is on the National Register of Historic Places.

On the Northwestern University campus.

Urban Woodlands

Loosely ringing Chicago along much of its north, south and west borders is a green belt of natural lands, known as the forest preserves, set aside for conservation and recreation.

While other large cities have dedicated land to similar purposes, the Cook County Forest Preserves, comprising 66,746 acres of woodlands, recreation facilities and open space, is probably the oldest and largest forest preserve system in any US metropolitan area.

In addition to forests and fields, the preserves boast 13 golf courses and driving ranges, 33 fishing lakes and ponds, plus swimming pools, boat ramps, bicycle trails and picnic areas.

Unlike the preserve systems in other cities, where forest land was set aside only after urban populations began moving away from the central downtown areas in the 1950s, the concept of a forest preserve system for Chicago began before the turn of the century on the initiative of some of the city's most prominent citizens.

Their mission was to establish nearby areas where city dwellers could find the pastoral recreation and peace afforded by open space filled with natural flora and fauna. Rather than simply acquiring open tracts, they were interested in preserving naturally beautiful areas "for their own sake and... scientific value, which, if ever lost, cannot be restored for generations."

Only three forest preserves – the Edgebrook/Caldwell woods and the Indian Boundary preserves, both on the northwest side of the city, and the Dan Ryan Woods on the South Side – are actually located within the city limits.

Run as a separate government agency, independent of both the city and the county, the Cook County Forest Preserve District is funded by taxes levied on all county property owners, and by small fees charged to those who use its facilities.

However, the Forest Preserve District board is made up of the same people who are elected to the County Board of Trustees. As a result, the district, like the City of Chicago and the County of Cook, has long been a haven of patronage for the local Democratic party. In Chicago, even when you escape to nature, it's hard to leave behind the political machine.

Until the mid-1970s, the forest preserves were used mostly on Sundays for family outings, company picnics and the like. With so much of the metropolitan population moving into the suburbs, however, the demand for picnic groves, bike and bridle paths is now creating crowds for much of the week, and district managers are trying to cope with overcrowding.

In fact, one problem the district faces is that many suburbs with nearby forest preserves have foregone setting aside extra open space within their own municipalities, relying instead on adjacent forest preserves to provide recreational space for their residents.

Overcrowding isn't the only problem caused by encroaching urbanization. Once-rural roads that in past decades had little impact on natural life within the preserves have been expanded into major highways to serve the ever-growing outlying population and dormitory communities. At the same time, housing and commercial developments have been built around forest preserve district holdings.

Fortunately, about 5 percent of the Cook County Forest Preserve District is set aside as part of the Illinois Nature Preserve system, which is even more conservation-oriented than the forest preserves. The nature preserves, spread throughout the forest areas, are protected regions of unique natural, geological or environmental habitat, crucial to such processes as spring seepage or home to endangered species.

But the preserves aren't used for daytime family fun alone. In the evening they are a favorite place for teenagers to find romantic privacy, and are occasionally dumping grounds for murder victims. Some preserves have also become known for the sale of drugs.

The district has its own police force and, even in the thickest woods, civilization is never far away. Still, for safety's sake, it's best not to visit the forest preserves alone, especially when hiking or biking wooded paths.

179

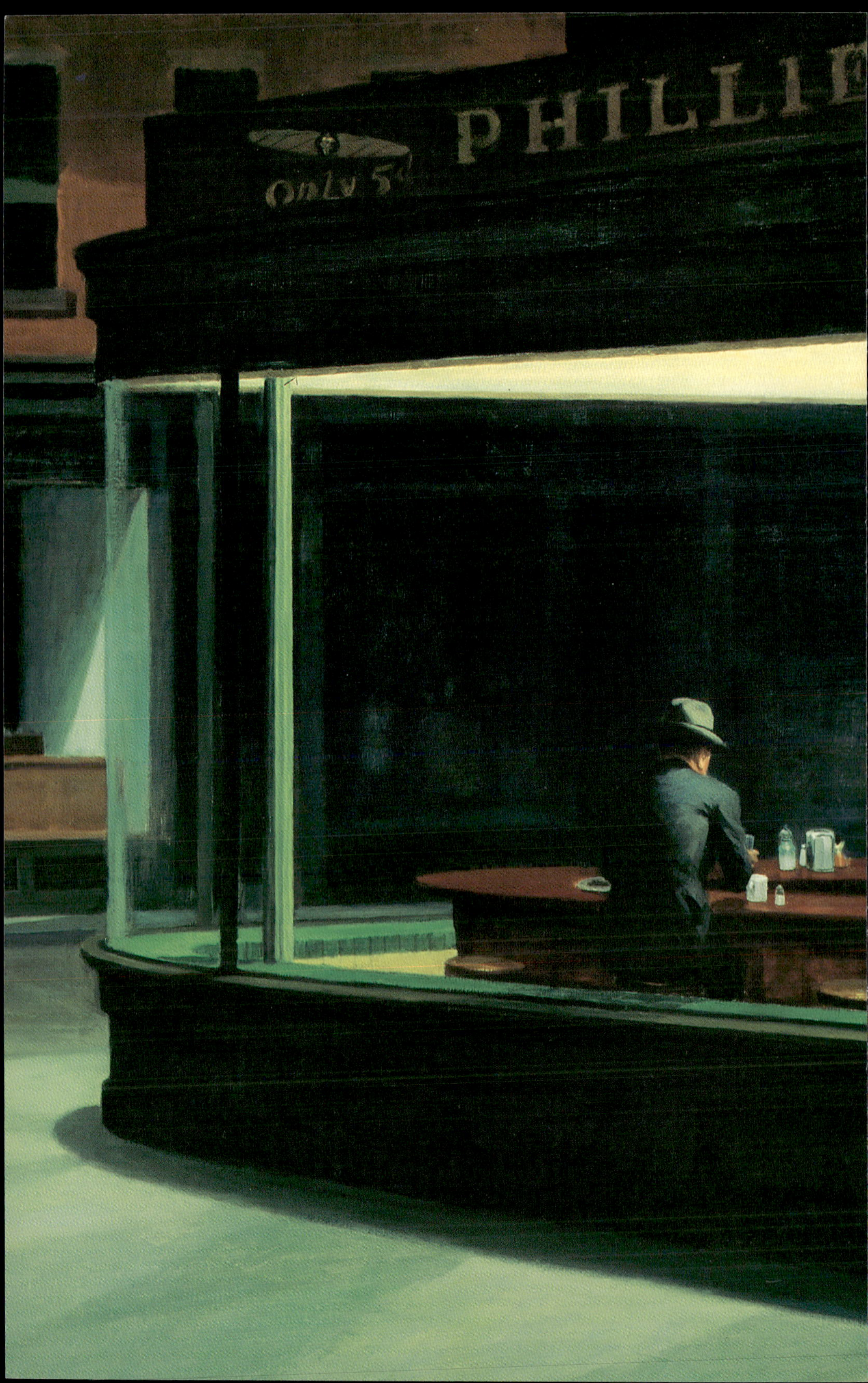

PHILLIE
Only 5¢

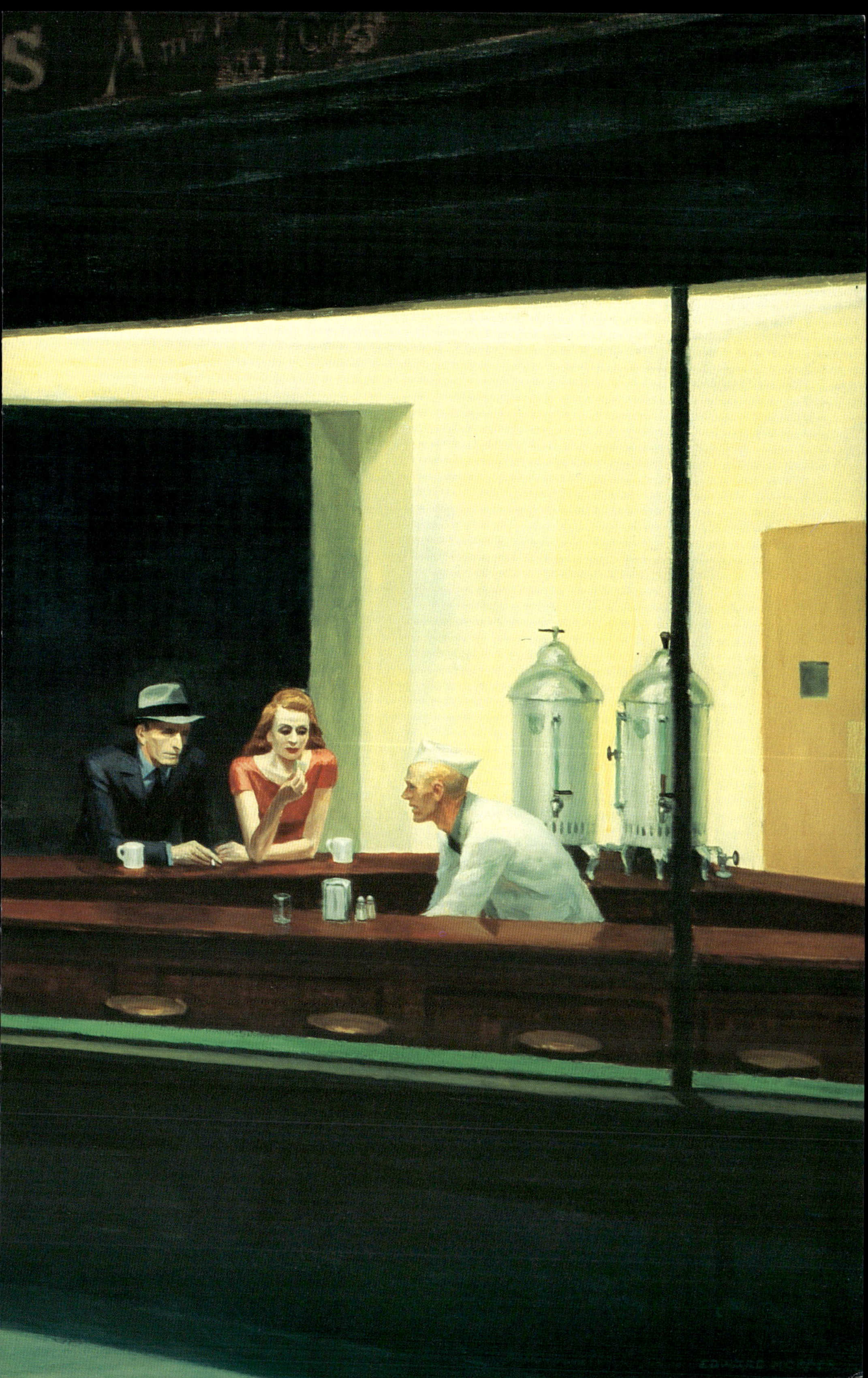

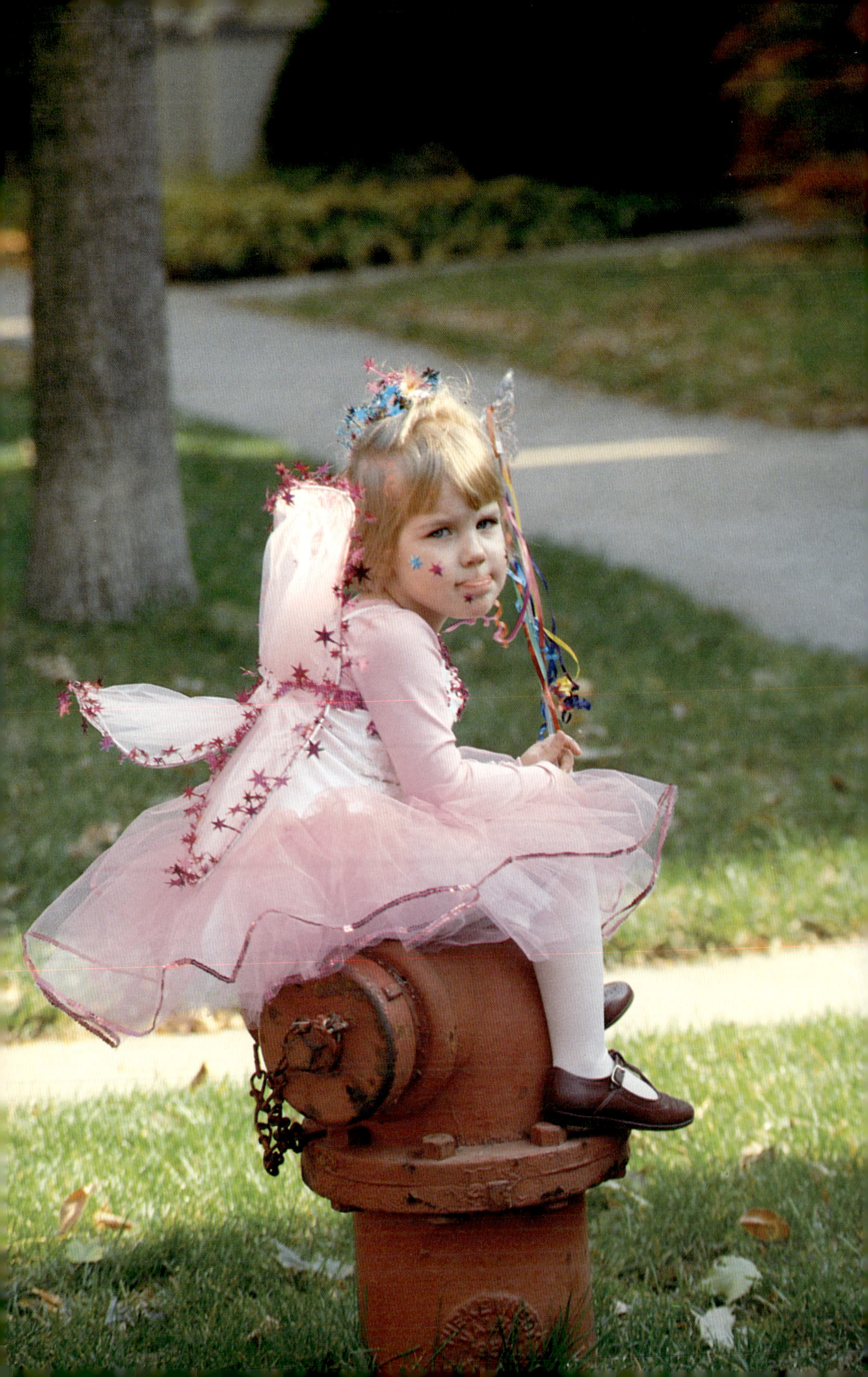

YEAR-ROUND PERFORMANCES

There is no slow season on the Chicago entertainment scene. Whether large theaters or small cabarets, whether lavish ballet and opera productions or one-man shows, Chicagoans are accustomed to a wide choice for a night out. They are also accustomed to seeing live people on stage; in much of the Loop and its neighboring downtown areas, it's much easier to find a play or a music act on stage than it is to find a movie house. Cinema-goers typically head for outlying residential areas and the multi-screens at the shopping malls.

Despite the January-to-October nature of Chicago entertainment, a few attractions are necessarily seasonal. Some of Chicago's 120 theater companies, for example, concentrate on **summer stock** or **Shakespeare in the parks** during June, July and August. Similarly, the summer brings many concerts, day and night and often free, at the band shell in **Grant Park**.

The **Blues Fest** in early June and **Jazz Fest** in August are enormously popular weekend events, attracting internationally known stars like Dizzy Gillespie and John Lee Hooker. Another summer highlight are the outdoor concerts, from big bands and touring symphonies to jazz and pop stars, at **Ravinia** in the north shore suburb of Highland Park. The autumn cultural offerings include the **Lyric Opera of Chicago** and the **Chicago Symphony Orchestra**.

For many Chicagoans and visitors alike, however, the ultimate night out in the Windy City includes the theater and one of the handful of swanky nightclubs or cabarets that serve up sophisticated songs along with the nightcaps.

Stepping out: A few years ago a *New York Times* reviewer wrote: "What is the current state of the American theater? Illinois!" Because there is so much theater in Chicago at any one time, at any time of year, it's best to plan ahead. Both major dailies, the *Chicago Tribune* and the *Chicago Sun-Times*, have extensive Friday entertainment listings for the weekend. In addition, there's a lengthy theater guide in the *Reader*, a 150-page free Chicago weekly found in downtown and lakefront bookstores and coffee shops.

Theater bargains for those who don't plan ahead are available from **Hot Tix booths**. The booths are run by the League of Chicago Theatres, a trade association for 123 theaters and theater companies in the Chicago area. The booths are at 24 S. State Street in the Loop; 1616 Sherman Avenue in Evanston, and 1020 Lake Street in Oak Park. Theater and dance tickets are available the day of the performance at half price, on a cash-only basis. The booths also sell full-price advance tickets for theater, concerts, sports and other events.

The Hot Tix booths offer free copies of the *Theatre Chicago Guide*, with its current listings of productions, ad-

Preceding pages: Edward Hopper's *Nighthawks*. *Left*, waiting in wings. *Right*, a vaudeville landmark.

dresses and telephone numbers for member theaters and detailed maps of playhouse locations.

Long history: Many of the best known Chicago companies of the 1990s started in the 1960s and '70s, but the city's stage history goes back more than 150 years. The first plays were presented in 1837, when Chicago was incorporated as a city. By the time Abraham Lincoln won the Republican nomination in Chicago in 1860, the city had several permanent theaters. The waves of immigrants who came to a brawny Chicago brought with them spirited productions in their native tongues and the city was soon a port of call for an international roster of performers – a tradition that continues today with touring troupes from Broadway and London shows.

However, there's much more to Chicago theater than touring shows in Loop playhouses. In the early 1960s, controversial, avant garde director Bob Sickinger came to Chicago to create a community-based theater for Hull House, seeking a company in the city's heart, nurtured by neighborhoods. From among those artistic roots came actor Mike Nussbaum and playwrights David Mamet and Alan Bates.

The **Body Politic Theatre** was created in the mid-1960s, offering theater games for actors to learn body language. Its executive director, Jim Shiflett, had been taught by the legendary improvisationist Viola Spolin. One of its first program directors was Paul Sills, Spolin's son and a master of improvisation in his own right.

Sills had been a director of The Compass Players in 1955, a group that borrowed from *commedia dell'arte*, a Renaissance style in which actors improvised on scenarios. The Compass Players were characterized by an explosion of creative energy, rehearsing scenarios during the day, performing at night, then taking audience suggestions for more improvisations. From this group, which spawned the Second City improv group, came Mike Nichols,

A T-shirt display; *The Nutcracker* at the Aire Crown.

Elaine May, Shelley Berman and Barbara Harris.

Variety of venues: By the mid-1970s, there was rich competition for the Body Politic. **Victory Gardens Theater** focused on Chicago playwrights and made a commitment to black and Hispanic theater. **Wisdom Bridge Theatre** vibrated with youth, originality and inventiveness. The Evanston Theatre Company, now the **Northlight Theatre**, performed contemporary works, fresh interpretations of classics and forgotten plays with ambitious, thought-provoking productions. And there was David Mamet's **St Nicholas Theater Company**, producing early, highly praised works by the playwright. There was also the irreverent **Organic Theater**, which created a living cartoon on stage with *Warp*, a campy, science-fiction serial.

The number of Off-Loop theaters increased rapidly and by the time they exceeded 100, critics were saying Chicago theater was becoming a major force. Emerging in the late 1970s was a distinctively gritty, visceral mode of performance and in-your-face directional style that came from the **Steppenwolf Theatre Company**. Productions left audiences spent and critics raving. From this theater of realism have come the later writings of Mamet and the acting of John Malkovich and Glenne Headley.

While the Steppenwolf style of lean linguistic vernacular and intense acting has often been used interchangeably with the phrase "Chicago theater," this is not the case. And while the dramatic community still argues over a definition of "Chicago theater," its basic components consist of an energizing strength and a collective heart.

"Chicago theater artists were unable to succeed, and they were unable to fail. And both those things were blessings," wrote Robert Falls, artistic director of the Goodman and former artistic director of Wisdom Bridge. "You couldn't really fail, because it didn't really mat-

Pavement piper; Fernando Jones' tribute to Junior Wells.

ter, whereas in New York or Los Angeles if you failed, that was it. In Chicago, people approach it more as their work, as their art. They're continually writing, acting, designing and directing plays. They're interested in a body of work."

Second to none: One of the things that makes the term "Chicago theater" so immensely difficult to nail down is that it must also include Second City, without doubt its most famous company. The city's theaters of realism and improvisation have links in language and situations. They both make profound use of colloquialisms and of placing the common man in uncommon situations. But whereas one plays for intensity, the other does so for sophisticated laughs.

There's a full history of the homegrown genre available in the **Chicago Theater Collection** for reading and viewing at the Chicago Public Library. It's open to the public and includes original scripts and videotapes of famous performances. In the meantime, there's plenty of live theater to enjoy.

Steppenwolf productions should not be missed. Victory Gardens, Wisdom Bridge, Northlight and the Organic also have reliable productions. There are also several noteworthy companies. The **Court Theatre** in Hyde Park has a repertory which includes innovative productions of classics, rarely-seen masterpieces and significant works by contemporary authors. The season of the **Pegasus Players** in Uptown might include modern and classical productions, a musical and a new script.

For more traditional performances, there's the **Shubert Theatre**, just off State Street in the Loop. Most of the Broadway touring companies play here for longer runs. For shorter runs, of perhaps a week, they play the **Aire Crown** at McCormick Place. But unless you're absolutely dying to see the show, skip the Crown. Its enormous layout loses the intimacy of theater past the first several dozen rows, and theatergoers have always complained of the hall's acoustics.

John Lee Hooker at the Chicago Blues Festival.

There are several theaters in the round and dinner theaters within driving distance of the city. Among the best is the **Candlelight Dinner Playhouse** in southwest suburban Summit. It's about a 15-minute expressway drive from downtown and worth the journey for those fond of musicals.

Tough tickets: Two on the city's "must see" list are usually among the toughest tickets in town to come by: the Goodman and Second City. Virtually any production at the **Goodman Theater**, located behind the Art Institute of Chicago on Michigan Avenue, will be difficult for non-season ticket holders. Recent seasons were nearly sold out, but tickets are sometimes available through agencies and touts.

Opened in 1925, the Goodman is Chicago's oldest and largest resident theater. Its stage has hosted the American premieres of Mamet's Pulitzer Prize-winning *Glengarry Glen Ross* and Nobel Laureate Wole Soyink's *Death and the King's Horseman*. The Midwestern premiere of August Wilson's Pulitzer Prize-winning *Fences* was also performed at the Goodman. An annual sellout and Chicago tradition is *A Christmas Carol*, adapted from Charles Dickens. As a last resort, try going directly to the Goodman for occasional returns from season holders. Another option for those with the time or with budget constraints, especially if in town for at least a few weeks, is to call the Goodman and offer to be a volunteer usher.

Also tough to get are seats for **Second City**, where improvisation became a household word. The setting is a simple one. Six or seven actors work the stage with a few chairs and very limited props. They create topical sketches in a slice-of-life environment and throw in some original songs. The very first show in 1959 took on President Eisenhower, grand opera, the medical profession and the cultural pretensions of FM radio. The troupe never stopped breaking ground and television's *Saturday*

Dizzy Gillespie at the Chicago Jazz Festival.

Night Live might never have become so successful without the influence of Second City and a cast that included so many former Second City regulars.

The acting is called improv because current revues were put together with improvisations that came from audience suggestions after the regular show. Those who stay after the revue for the late improv show can add their suggestions for the actors to tackle. The Second City atmosphere is a pleasant one, with cabaret-style seating and drinks.

Located in **Old Town**, some of the country's best comedic talent developed here. Alumni include Alan Arkin, Dan Aykroyd, John and Jim Belushi, Peter Boyle, Barbara Harris, Bill Murray, Joan Rivers, David Steinberg and many more whose faces on television and in movies are more familiar than their names. The secret to good seats here is to go to performances during the week. Plan on staying for the late improv show, and moving up for better seats when the revue crowd departs.

Theater's future in Chicago looks bright. Several large new theaters are under construction, and the Goodman plans to move into a new North Loop theater complex by the end of 1998.

Cabaret: Sure-bet cabarets are more difficult to recommend in Chicago, not because they are few, but because they open and close like matchbook covers. The tiny cabaret where the willowy singer interpreted Gershwin may have closed because it was never discovered. The elegant room where long-familiar names were booked may have closed because its coziness meant they couldn't charge a big enough cover to pay the performers and still make a healthy profit. Again, check the newspaper listings and call the clubs for more information. Here is a couple of nightspots that are worth mentioning, depending on the entertainment.

The **Park West**, 322 W. Armitage Avenue, will sometimes book cabaret as well as rock groups; and **The Improv**, 504 N. Wells Street, the larg-

Night lights.

188

est club in Chicago, features nationally recognized stand-up comics and a variety show for children on Saturday afternoons. Here, however, is a solid trio of the city's best cabarets that have been around for years and look set to last years more.

The granddaddy of them all is **Milt Trenier's Lounge** in the basement of 610 N. Fairbanks Court, the building that once housed the legendary Chez Paree nightclub. Milt, who always wears a tuxedo and ranks among the best lounge hosts in the country, has been in the business more than 40 years. He started singing with his brothers as a teenager in the vanguard of rock 'n' roll in the early 1950s, preceding the Temptations and the Four Tops. His brothers settled in Las Vegas, where they have won awards performing show tunes, swing and blues. The Treniers, a band which now includes sons and nephews, usually play Milt's club in June and shouldn't be missed. Milt made Chicago his home, and with his wife, Bea, offers a warm and welcoming gathering place for entertainers and lounge fans.

Because of the late-hour license – the joint is often open till near dawn – this is the place where musicians come to unwind after their gigs. There's a wall of photographs near the entrance, a sort of Who's Who of national nightlife, that testifies to past guests. Della Reese, Dizzy Gillespie and Bill Eckstine have "sat in." Bill Cosby once did a two-hour act and Sammy Davis Jr took away Milt's mike and did a whole show. Regular performers include singer and impressionist Bill Acosta and songstylist Paula Ramsey. But whoever's playing, don't leave until Milt himself sings. Backed by the Classic Swing Trio, "mellow and laid-back" were terms coined for Milt and his place.

The **Gold Star Sardine Bar**, in a chic building at 680 N. Lake Shore Drive, was named for its elegance and tiny size. But co-owner and impresario Bill Allen wouldn't have it any bigger. He wanted a cozy café that paid homage to

Before they're packed in at the Gold Star Sardine Bar.

Entertainment 189

the sleek spots of New York, *circa* 1940. He's also particular about who performs and what is sung.

Frequent acts include Tony Bennett, Chicago comedian Tom Dreesen and jazz-artist-in-residence Patricia Barber. But Allen's uncanny knack for success has to do with taking entertainment risks that regularly show big payoffs. Shelley MacArthur, a high-demand runway model and a prominent Chicago socialite, was first booked at the Gold Star and developed by Allen, recalling the notable socialites featured in Manhattan's café society of the 1930s and 1940s. Her *Embraceable You* and *Unforgettable* are fine, but Bill won't let her sing *Fly Me to the Moon* because it doesn't fit the room's style. One night he might feature a young jazz pianist from the Soviet Union, and the next a university women's *a cappella* group. The Gold Star always makes for an entertaining evening.

And finally, because it's often one of the best ways to wind up an evening of theater or an elegant dinner, there's **Pops for Champagne**, 2934 N. Sheffield Avenue, a short cab ride from Michigan Avenue. This elegant room has a rose and green motif with a low bar that forms a crescent around the raised stage. Upholstered chairs surround the bar, so patrons can relax without having their legs dangle from stools. The rest of the room is given to comfortable table seating. And when the weather's warm, there's a romantic outdoor garden.

Pops has a light menu and delicious desserts such as fresh berries and mousse to fill the little holes in a late-night sweet tooth. Local performers take to the tiny stage nightly, weaving through the crowded tables to thank music lovers for coming. Sometimes it's a veteran jazz pianist. At other times, it may be a trio or a stylish blues vocalist. The giant bottles of champagne near the entrance make it clear that the club is serious about bubbly – serious to the tune of 120 varieties on the menu, many available by the glass.

Dancing at the Loop.

Getting Into "Oprah"

"Do you know how to get on national TV?" George the audience coordinator asks the crowd of about 200 people, mostly women, who want to do exactly that.

"Act like you're very excited to be here, and hang on to the edge of your seat," says George. "See that cameraman behind me? He's looking for interesting reactions. So ask a question. Look interested."

George works for Oprah. In most circles, no more identification is needed. Talk-show host Oprah Winfrey is known worldwide, an industry unto herself.

While George loosens up the crowd, the TV lights go on to brighten the studio where *The Oprah Winfrey Show* is taped twice a day, three times a week, and aired a week later for around 15 million viewers.

The subject of this morning's taping is bachelor parties. Oprah, barely 5 feet tall, slips into the studio unnoticed, encircled by producers and assistants. She is busy scanning blue note cards when the audience sees her and immediately begins clapping.

Oprah looks slightly embarrassed, smiles, makes a small wave and says, "How y'all doing?"

She is, after all, a Chicago celebrity, adored for her wit, her empathy, her charm, and most of all, her curiosity and eagerness to ask the most personal questions. Oprah is allowed to say what everyone else is thinking but wouldn't dare say.

To her obvious dismay, a makeup man dabs at her face with a sponge. "May I have some water, please?" she asks no one in particular. The bottle arrives promptly and she sips through a straw while the audience watches intensely. "I hate water. I really do." They laugh, having suffered with her as she shed 65 pounds in a nationally-monitored diet and then regained most of it.

Now Oprah is ready. She clears her throat, the theme music plays and she starts reading from the teleprompter.

"We'll talk to one woman who found out there were prostitutes at her husband's bachelor party," says Oprah. She turns to the woman in the audience who sent her fiancé off to his prenuptial bash with long underwear taped to his body.

Things are off to a good start, the audience provides plenty of zest and then there's a commercial break. More sips of water, more dabs at the face and the show resumes, with Oprah questioning a couple on stage. The wife says she was seriously traumatized upon hearing that strippers were at her husband's bachelor party. "It was a violation. I couldn't be intimate with him for a while," she says.

Now Oprah runs up the aisle with her microphone to where three strippers have been planted in the audience. "I'm a performer and I'm not there to do anything else," one declares. "It's clean, dirty fun," another says firmly, to the obvious dismay of some of the wives nearby.

Oprah encourages this kind of provocative banter because she knows it works. It's good theater. Since September 1986 when the program went into national syndication, she has logged more than 1,000 shows.

An hour passes quickly and the producer tells Oprah there is just one minute left. "Do you want the last word?" he asks. She doesn't. She opts instead to let members of her audience argue among themselves – and they do – as the credits roll.

The producer thanks the audience and then invites everyone to shake Oprah's hand on the way out. Most take up the offer, if only to get a closer look at their idol. One Oprah addict is teary-eyed after the experience.

Oprah moved to Chicago in 1984 at the age of 30 to host a faltering local talk show called *AM Chicago*. By 1985, it was the top show in its time slot and had been renamed, appropriately, *The Oprah Winfrey Show*.

In 1988 her HARPO (Oprah spelled backwards) Productions Inc. took over ownership and all production responsibilities, making her the first woman to own and produce her own talk show.

HARPO Studios, where the TV show is filmed, is located at 110 N. Carpenter Street. There is usually a week-long wait for audience reservations, but admission to the show is free.

JUSTICIA
TRIUNFAR
OVERCOME
ALL PEOPLE
ASSOCIATION HOUSE
BOB SOLARI
TONY MURPHY

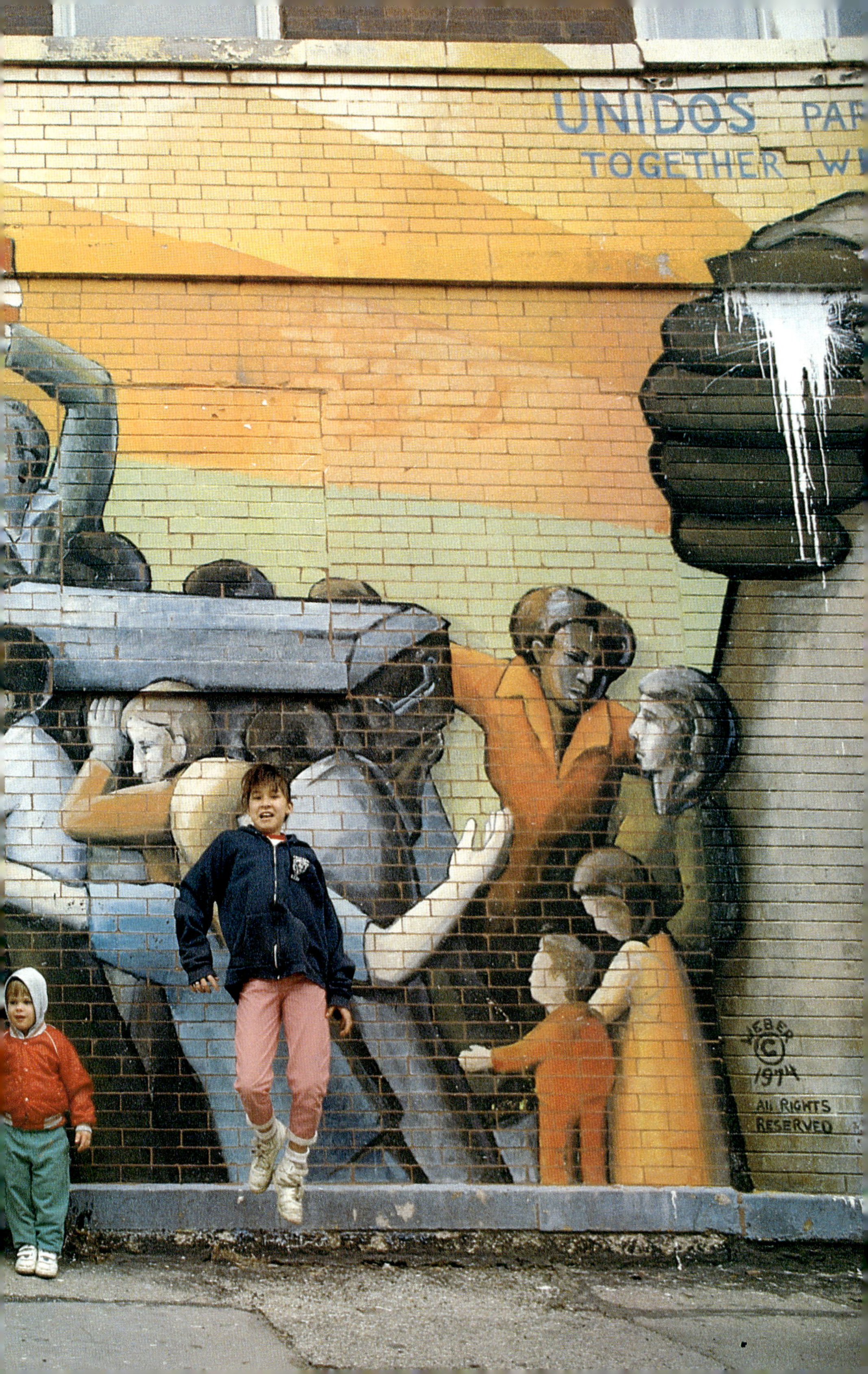
UNIDOS PAR
TOGETHER W
WEBER
©
1974
ALL RIGHTS
RESERVED

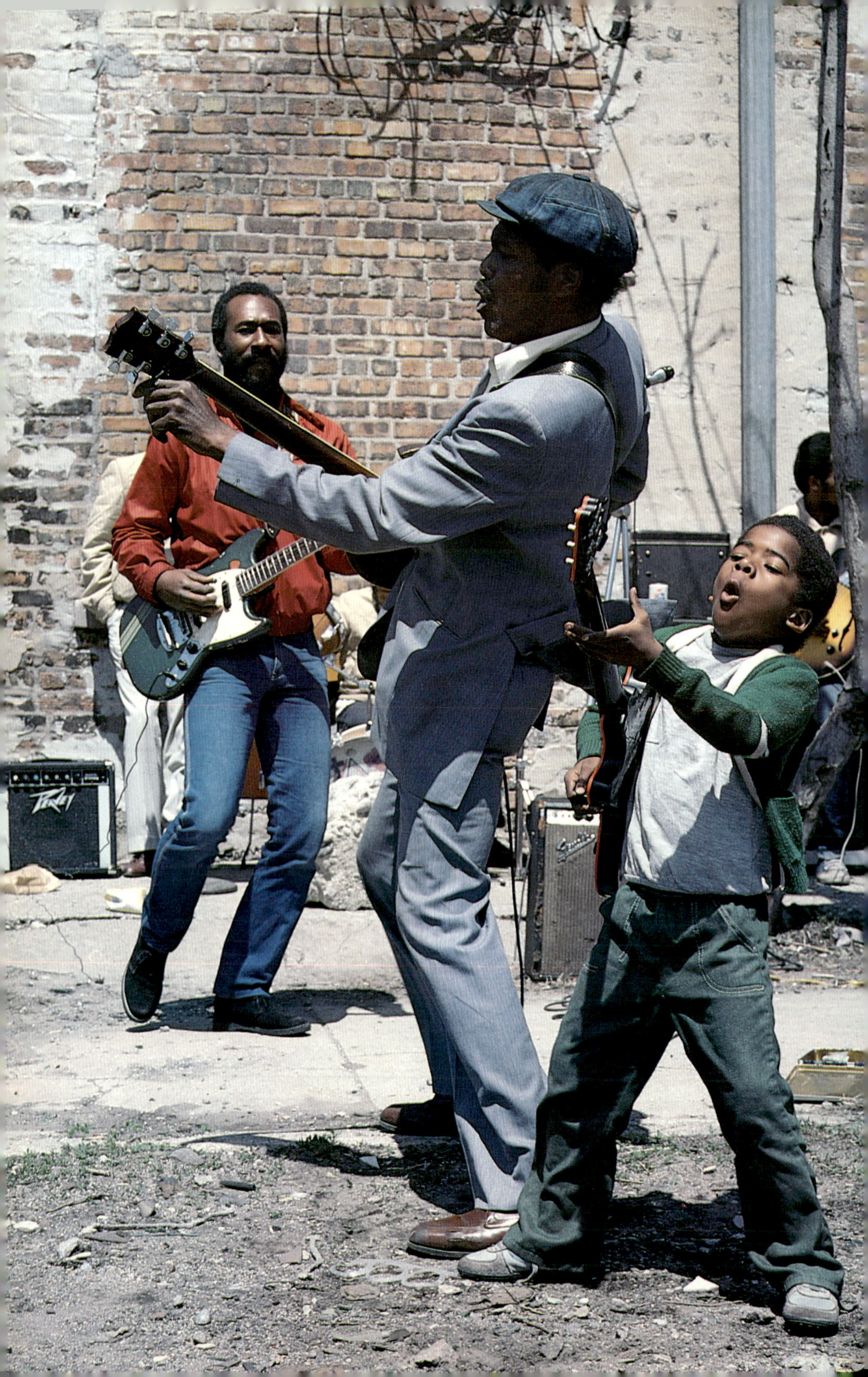

THE WEST SIDE

Lacking a true center, Chicago's West Side offers students of urban development different focuses. Taylor Street at times resembles Lower Manhattan, complete with street eats and a carnival atmosphere each June when Taste of Italy erupts for a three-day gastronomic orgy of pizza, pasta, zuppa and vino. Wicker Park's perennial dilemma is whether to yuppify its aging frame house and gray stone ambience and set itself up as Newtown South, or to become a nest for the artistically and culturally dispossessed.

Maxwell Street, Greektown and Ukrainian Village are remnants of an ethnic Chicago that, urban renewal notwithstanding, retain some of their original color and character. Haymarket Square played a pivotal role in the early struggles of the American labor movement. The University of Illinois at Chicago nibbles away at the surrounding community. Cabrini-Green is a failed experiment in public housing where an unchaperoned elevator ride is risky during the day and downright dangerous at night.

The **University of Illinois at Chicago** began in 1946 at Navy Pier as a collection of temporary classrooms catering primarily to returning veterans. The move into the nucleus of today's campus at Harrison and Halsted, something akin to Godard's Alphaville or one of the more extreme Wagnerian stage sets, took place in 1965 amid hopes of establishing "a Harvard of the Midwest." The reigning pundits recruited a crop of promising young scholars to make it happen. Alas, it was not to be.

When money got tight in the early 1970s, threatened senior faculty members dismissed – though not without a fight – their brighter, more productive juniors who were approaching tenure. The English Department, a bastion of aging fellows, male and female, jettisoned 19 junior staff in one year against the recommendation of the university's own faculty Senate, which prompted a flurry of student protests.

Dominated by an inverted ziggurat that houses administrators and some faculty, the campus is a hodgepodge of structures. The **Behavioral Science Building** spirals like a labyrinthine concrete bunker, leading one professor to remark that he always expected a pellet of food to appear when he found his way to his office. Suspended walkways connecting the ziggurat, **University Hall**, with modular classrooms were supposed to provide cover during wet weather. As in so many Chicago projects, politics intervened. Substandard materials gave the walkways a sieve-like quality, and they leaked water from the beginning.

Settled in: Amid the stylistic mishmash, **Hull House** seems an oasis of dignity. A square brick 19th-century home now in the shade of the university,

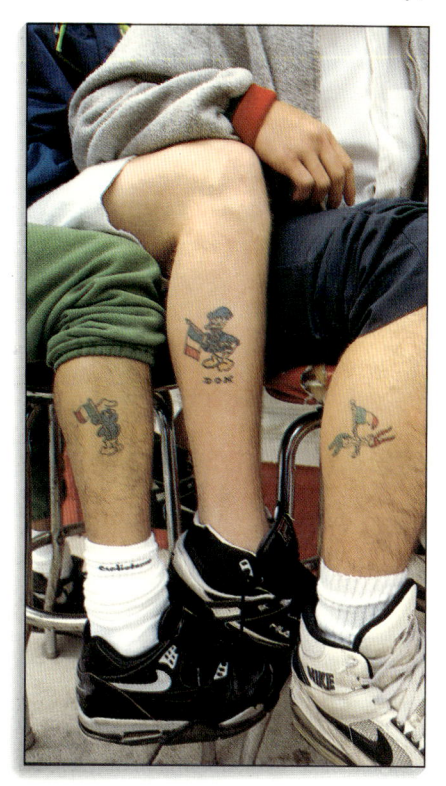

Preceding pages: a Hispanic neighborhood. Left, back yard boogie. Right, leg men.

West Side 195

its gabled two stories rising over white colonnades, Hull House started life at 800 S. Halsted. Jane Addams and Ellen Gates Starr converted the stately edifice into a settlement house in 1889. Now a museum, Hull House unfolds the history of the West Side's ethnic population, from Jews at the turn of the century, through the enclaves of German, Bohemian and Irish immigrants who contributed to the area's colorful melting pot.

West of the university, the thoroughfare of Taylor Street is known as **Little Italy**. Italian ice can be purchased on the sidewalks in summer and fine Italian food can be had year-round at some of the 30 restaurants spread through this community of about 8,000 Italians. Two of these are Rico's Restaurant at 626 S. Racine Avenue and the Rosebud Café at 1500 W. Taylor Street. There's another superb Italian dining area nearby, around 24th and Oakley.

Street shopping: Say the two words "Maxwell Street" in Chicago and an image of ethnic urbanites haggling over prices comes to mind. **Maxwell Street** is less a location than it is a culture, which began as a push-cart produce market that miraculously survived the Chicago Fire of 1871, said to have been started by Mrs O'Leary's cow kicking over a lantern.

While Maxwell Street has been home and shopping district to many nationalities and ethnic groups, immigrant Russian Jews who came in the late 1880s provided the most pronounced ethnic flavor to the area. Licensed vendors from most Chicago neighborhoods sell everything from hubcaps and bicycles to second-hand clothing and old record albums here.

The **Maxwell Street Market** is worth a walk-through, particularly on a Sunday morning, if only to watch a grassroots laissez-faire economy transcend racial and cultural barriers. From behind stalls and out of doorways, blacks and whites, Jews and Greeks, Latinos and Latvians conduct business.

A Ukrainian Village wedding.

Though bargains may exist, *caveat emptor* rules. The gold chain may be 24-carat, as claimed, but the gold isn't likely to be more than a few microns deep, and the "Rolex" or "Patek Phillipe" watches lining a hairy forearm are almost certainly from a Korean or Taiwanese factory.

Locals and nostalgic suburbanites shop for kitchenware, garden tools and the other prosaic stuff of daily life. Lounging Chicago policemen add their bit to the scene at Jim's Hot Dog Stand, 1320 S. Halsted, a stopping-off point for cheap franks or a Polish sausage traditionally washed down with orange soda or root beer.

Bows to Kiev: Another holdover from the past, **Ukrainian Village**, occupies a chunk of territory in the vicinity of Chicago Avenue and Oakley Boulevard south of Wicker Park. Pride of place in the community goes to **St Nicholas Ukrainian Catholic Cathedral** on Rice and Oakley, an exotic, Byzantine construction among the humdrum wood-frame and brick family houses that predominate in the area. Surmounted by a fanfare of ornate cupolas modeled on a Kiev original, the cathedral, built in 1913, embodies the community's continued commitment to traditional values and virtues.

The Milwaukee corridor, a onetime Indian trail that waves of immigrants gradually turned into a bustling mercantile microcosm of the developing city, leads northwest to **Wicker Park**, an island of substantial gray stone buildings saddled with the description "mansion" by their original owners. A magnificent example of "gingerbread," the **Hermann Weinhardt House**, has been impressing passersby at 2137 W. Pierce since 1893.

The Wicker Park Association has touted its turf for a decade or so as an integrated, socially advanced center for alternative lifestyles, but not much along the lines of Oak Park's ethnic sangfroid has emerged. Yuppies buy and renovate buildings along Logan

A noisy Revolutionary War re-enacted.

Boulevard to live in or to rent out, while blue-collar workers and the young unemployed gather in bars on Leavitt, Wabansia and Concord Place.

Polish pride: A mile from Wicker Park, **St Stanislaus Kostka Church** is called "the mother church of all Polish Roman Catholic congregations in Chicago." Considering that Chicago's Polish population reputedly has been – and still may be – second only to Warsaw's, that's no small matter. Like St Nicholas, St Stanislaus reflects an Old World prototype, in this case a church in Krakow. Noble Street is also home to **Holy Trinity Church**, the focal point of fights, physical in more than one case, among parishioners of St Stanislaus and Holy Trinity over parish rights, as well as the German Catholic **St Boniface Church**.

Although burritos and pizza are now more common street food than kielbasa, two prominent repositories of Slavic culture fit comfortably into the area. To the west, on Chicago Avenue, the **Ukrainian National Museum** displays the intricately colored Easter eggs and bright folk costumes that Ukrainians remembered and reproduced in their new homes.

Documentary photographs of the life they left and the life they found in the New World promote a sense of unified cultural history that gives life to Ukrainian customs and provides a context for the folk art.

Reversing on Milwaukee and stopping at Augusta, the **Polish Roman Catholic Union of America** shares a building with the **Polish Museum of America**. Here, special exhibitions and film festivals explore and help maintain the sense of ethnic identity shared by Chicagoans of Polish ancestry. A library of archive material draws historians of diverse interests to this scholarly cubbyhole just off the expressway.

Riot history: A few blocks south and east of the museum, **Haymarket Square** straddles Jefferson Street. The square was the site of an 1886 bomb

Annual Greek-American Parade.

blast that killed 10 people, including seven policemen, and provoked Chicago's most sensational and agonizing display of civic unrest before the 1968 Democratic National Convention and the Days of Rage. The Haymarket Statue, however, having twice (in 1969 and 1970) been knocked from its pedestal by student radicals, no longer adorns the historic patch of ground. The old statue, a likeness of policeman Thomas Birmingham, left hand raised in an age-old gesture of admonition, with helmet and belted coat reminiscent of London's bobbies, now holds court at the **Police Training Academy** on Jackson Boulevard.

Another statue of more historic than artistic interest is the "Pillar of Fire" at the **Chicago Fire Academy**, at Jackson and DeKoven. History is still unclear on whether Mrs O'Leary's cow did or did not kick over an oil lamp that started the great Chicago Fire in 1871. It is indisputable, however, that the O'Leary barn, originally on the site of the Fire Academy, did go up in flames, along with the buildings covering 1,600 acres of the city. Curiously, Mrs O'Leary's adjacent home was spared.

Urban failure: Though hardly a source of civic pride, the **Cabrini-Green housing project** must be included in any survey of the West Side. The present 15-building high-rise cluster replaced a two-story project raised in the early 1940s and leased mainly to returning servicemen and war workers. Black and Italian families, fairly representative of the neighborhood, also rented apartments in Cabrini Houses, as they were then named.

The Cabrini Extension high-rises and William Green housing project were linked in the early 1960s, creating an island of low-income, chronically unemployed and underemployed tenants. The surrounding area, defined roughly by Division, Halsted, Chicago and Wells, deteriorated into a segregated slum that is regarded as one of the worst neighborhoods in the United States.

A Pilsen neighborhood bar.

The quality of life in the ghetto has continued to worsen as a result of several factors: the West Side riots in 1968, following the assassinations of Malcolm X and Dr Martin Luther King Jr; the development of gang fiefdoms; the isolation of the homes from nearby residential communities by a series of small stores and the commercial-industrial properties to the west on Halsted. Former Mayor Jane Byrne's two-week stay in the Cabrini-Green projects during the early 1980s had no effect on the problems, though it amused some tenants and garnered national publicity for the mayor.

But things have deteriorated since then. Nowadays, police do not rush into Cabrini-Green when shooting is reported. Instead, they close off the area until the gunfire stops and then go in to tally up the dead and the wounded. This policy surprises no one. Not tenants, not the media and certainly not other cops. Unfortunately, it's one of the facts of life in Chicago.

Rail, post: Nearer the lake, in a corridor bounded east and west by Wacker and Clinton, are three major Chicago centers for transportation and communication: Union Station on Adams, the Northwestern Station used by Metra at Washington, and the main **Post Office** facing north on Van Buren.

Union Station was intended to form the foundation of a high-rise, but the project never got that far off the ground. The station is worth seeing, however, for its exterior arcade supported by massive stone columns beneath a facade of rectangular windows, and for its somewhat seedy waiting room where the steel truss-and-plaster vault soars overhead to combine grace with grandeur in mid-air.

The **Northwestern Station** on West Madison is a relatively new replacement for the old Chicago and North Western Railway Terminal, an architectural landmark where the classical portico and tesselated barrel vaulting in the main waiting room gave dignity to

Freight train.

the whole idea of rail travel. In contrast, the present structure acts merely as a place for trains and passengers to meet.

Hard underbelly: The belly of Chicago, **South Water Market**, extends from 14th to 15th streets between Miller and Racine. Bays for refrigerated trucks, called "reefers," face each other across a boulevard-wide space where produce distributors take delivery of Georgia peaches, Maine cranberries, Texas and Florida oranges, Chilean grapes, lettuce and almonds from California, and broccoli, green beans and asparagus from all over the country. While primarily wholesalers, some distributors are not averse to a quick cash transaction, and early morning visitors often trudge back to their cars clutching a tray of dew-glistening raspberries or a hundred-pound sack of new potatoes.

Not so much a complement to the South Water Market as an addendum, the **South Loop Marketplace**, at 509 W. Roosevelt, has become the scene of an interesting social and economic experiment. The National Black Farmers Harvest and Business Corporation, the "Black Farmers' Market" in common parlance, rents space at SLM on weekends from which it sells produce trucked in by black farmers from a 10-state region. Prices are low, fruits and vegetables are fresh and the goal is a laudable effort to reduce and eventually reverse the decline in land farmed by blacks. In addition to produce, bargain hunters pick through shelves and tables of oddments at the adjacent flea market, discovering battered Coca-Cola trays and faded tintypes, mechanical banks and Barbie dolls, yesterday's junk that has experienced a sea change and emerged as today's antiques and collectibles.

Greek eateries: Nearby **Greektown**, also known as the Delta due to its triangular shape, lies east of the University of Illinois. For immigrants working in the markets on Randolph Street, Greektown offered a comfortable enclave of coffee houses, compatriots,

Watching baseball through the fence.

shops dealing in Greek Orthodox vestments, candles, sacred images, Greek books and newspapers, but most of all a lively group of restaurants that remind them of their former homes.

Visitors today often seek out those restaurants, a dense patch along Halsted where the Dan Ryan and Eisenhower expressways wind about each other like fishing line before continuing their headlong flight into the suburbs. In restaurants with names like the Parthenon, Greek Islands, Dianna's Island Opaa and Rodity's, food and "neoclassical" theater mix well and customers join with waiters in celebrating the joys of eating, and smashing crockery, in good company.

Saganaki, Greek cheese doused with brandy and set aflame, is extinguished by lemon juice squeezed at the table, eliciting a loud shout of "Opaa!" in unison from staff and clientele. Most restaurants offer a family meal for four at very reasonable prices.

Staples include *taramasalata*, a tangy pink fish roe spread; Greek olives and marinated eggplant; lamb braised with string beans or cauliflower, or baked; *pastitsio* and moussaka, noodle and potato-eggplant casseroles, respectively; and, finally, walnut-studded, honey-soaked *baklava* or rosewater-scented *galactoboureko* washed down with minuscule cups of sweetened Greek coffee.

Along the way, of course, there'll be ouzo, the anise-based aperitif that prepares the palate for the feast – or, some say, deadens it to the assault. Retsina wine, young and bracing, and spiked with resin, is a common dinner drink, along with the frankly sweet Mavrodaphne for the faint of heart. There'll also be lots of talk and smoke, perhaps some singing and once in a while even some spontaneous dancing and plate-smashing.

Bohemia: Neither **Pilsen**, near the southern edge of the West Side, nor Heart of Chicago, a few blocks farther south and west, present such ebullience. Pilsen's mostly bohemian population contributed significantly to Chicago's history during the freewheeling period of labor unrest in the 1870s. Today, the **Pilsen East Artists Colony** at 18th and Halsted provides a quieter avenue of expression for graphic artists, sculptors, actors and writers, who hold individual exhibitions throughout the year and take to the streets in October for their annual art fair.

Walkers will also find Mexican culture in contemporary Pilsen, notably at **Casa Aztlan**, 1831 S. Racine. Over a three-year period, Ray Pattan painted an exuberant panoply of Mexican themes halfway up the building's face. But it is **St Paul Church** that makes the strongest impression in this essentially residential area. Buttressed, vaulted, and topped by five needle-fine spires, Henry J. Schlacks' Gothic fantasy at 22nd Place and Joyne Street embodies a passionate vision more usually associated with Gaudí or Horta than a 19th-century Midwestern church architect.

Left, after pumping iron. **Right**, fire escapes.

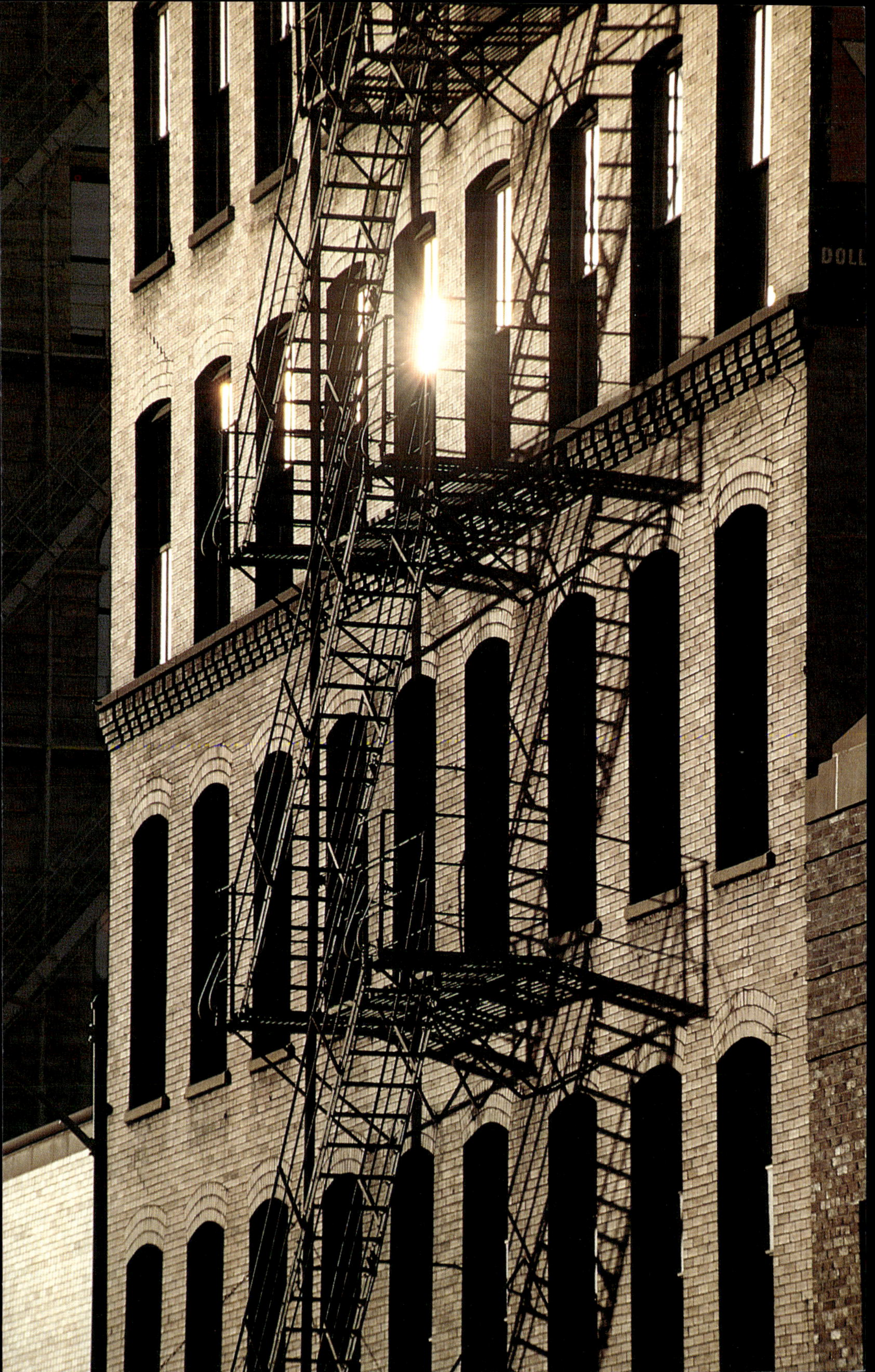

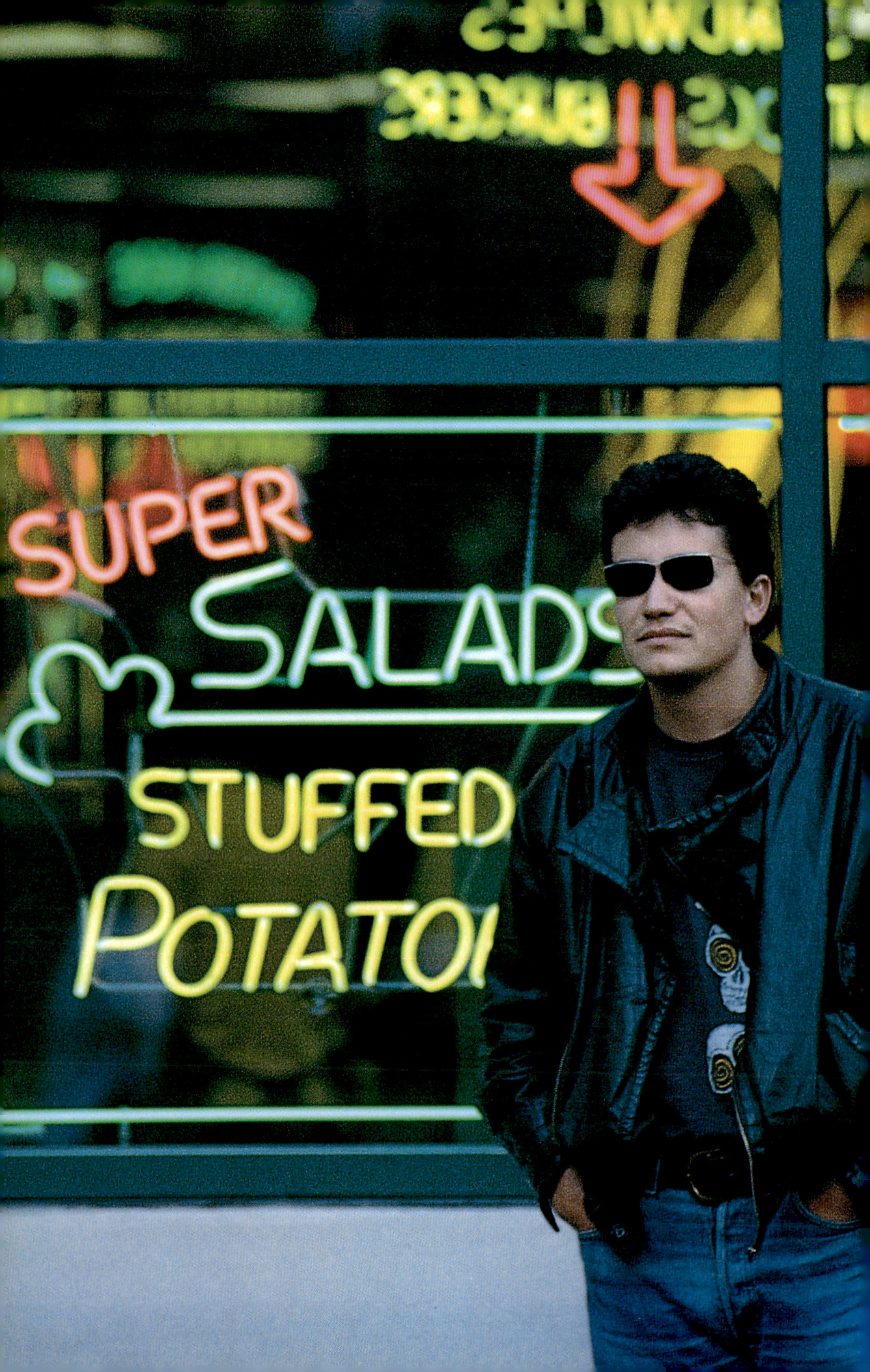
SUPER
SALADS
STUFFED

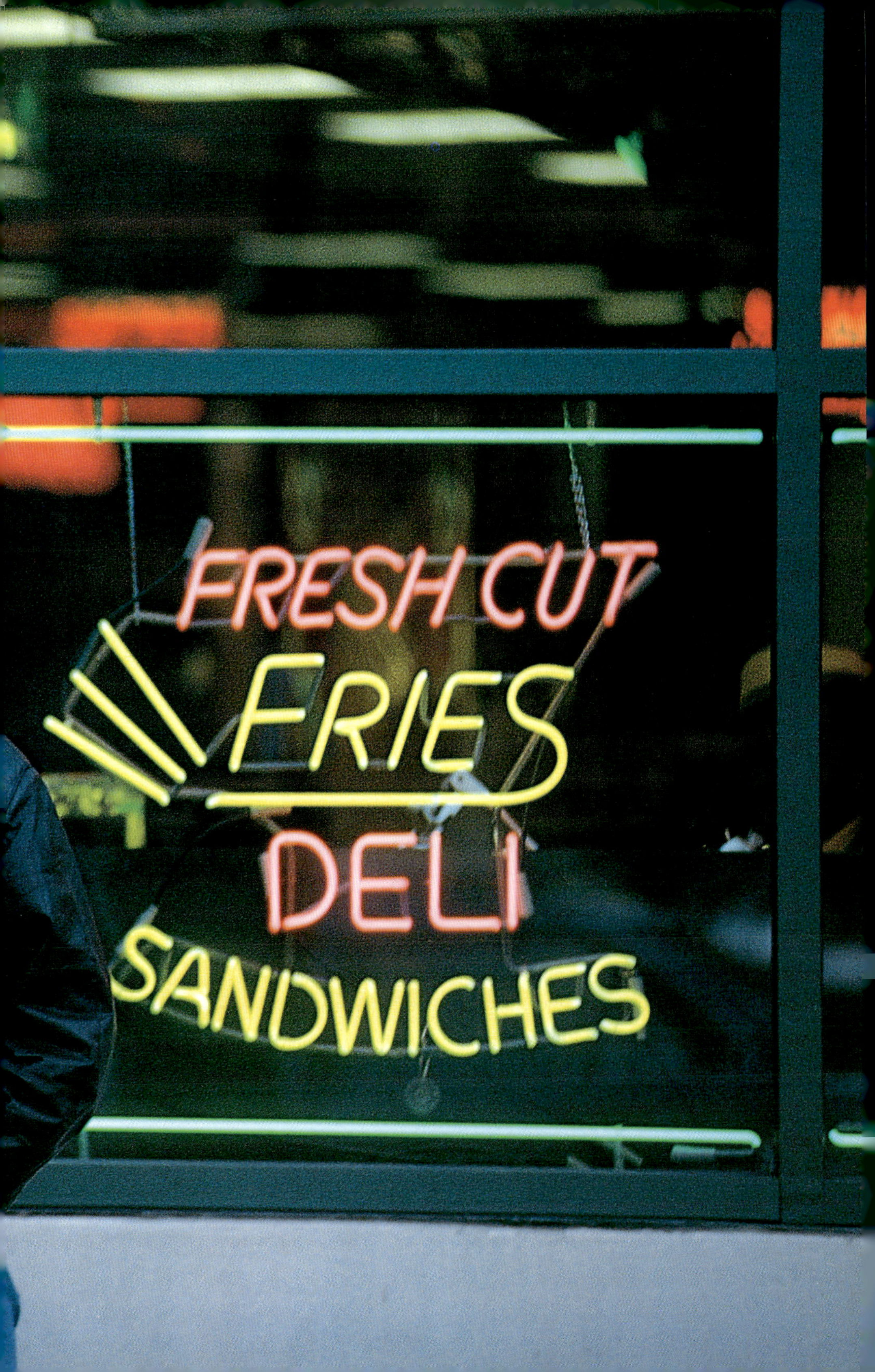
FRESH CUT
FRIES
DELI
SANDWICHES

SUBS
SOFT FROZEN YOGURT ON TAP
scrumptious
ice cream cones
PLAYS

TASTES OF CHICAGO

Befitting a citizenry that considers eating out a serious business – right up there with sports and politics – Chicago is home to hundreds of unusual, interesting and otherwise just plain good restaurants ranging from elegant eateries to simple hot dog stands.

That's why **Taste of Chicago** has proven so successful since getting started in 1982. This annual downtown lakeside party, attended by hundreds of thousands of people, features live entertainment and dozens of restaurant booths, allowing feasters to wander the grassy grounds sampling barbecued ribs, pizza and egg rolls. Taste, which runs from the end of June through July 4, is considered the largest food festival of its kind in the world.

Generations ago, when Chicago's stockyards were in their prime, the city was known as a steak town. Though new immigrant groups have left their culinary marks on the city and diners are more diet conscious, one restaurant that still prides itself on the perfect cut of beef is **Morton's of Chicago**. On Rush Street, the steak house takes its name from Arnie Morton, a colorful city restaurateur who founded Taste of Chicago. Morton is the third of four generations in the Chicago wining and dining business. His namesake reflects those decades of experience.

Morton's offers a clubby atmosphere with dark wood, celebrity photos, white table cloths and an intoxicating aroma of grilled meats. Fork-tender porterhouse steak is the house specialty. But the double fillet, charcoal dark outside and moist red inside, is another favorite cut among beef lovers. "Giving people a good deal seems to have paid off," says Morton, the grandson of a West Side saloon keeper.

Hullo, I'm Your Waiter: Humorist and gourmand Calvin Trillin once noted that Italian restaurants in America can be divided into those whose waiters have names like Vinnie and those that hire fellows named Travis or Dwayne. **Bravissimo**, one of Chicago's finest Italian restaurants, lives up to its name and those who doubt the heritage can discuss it with owner Nick Corey over *grappa*, the potent, colorless Italian brandy.

While some Italian restaurants in Chicago favor the heavy cream of northern Italy and others feature the tomato sauces to the south, Bravissimo pays homage to both with creative flair. The fresh roast duck ravioli comes with a red pepper cream sauce and the traditional spaghetti Napoletana is served with fresh spinach, tomatoes and a homemade pork-and-beef sausage. The list goes on, but two items are the best in the city – the flavorful Wyoming rack of lamb and the calamari, squid lightly fried in peanut oil.

Corey selects his own meats and produce, often from the Randolph Street market. Together with his partner

Preceding pages: light choices. **Left**, submarine sandwich duty. **Right**, a businessman's lunch.

Dining 207

Robert Fink, the pair provide diners with inspired cuisine and a warm atmosphere in a two-level dining room, graced at the entrance by white columns. Be sure to save room for the *tiramisu*, a happy marriage of sweet mascarpone cheese, Kahlua and shaved chocolate. Fink swears he eats one daily and manages to stay slim.

Fiesta: For Mexican food, the hot spot in town is the **Frontera Grill**, in the trendy River North area. They won't take lunch reservations for fewer than six, and dinners need to be booked several days in advance. Owners Rick Bayless and his wife Deann opened their tribute to South of the Border fare in 1987, simultaneously publishing a book, *Authentic Mexican: Regional Cooking from the Heart of Mexico*.

Don't lose confidence due to the couple's non-Hispanic names. They spent eight years researching food in Mexico, and a taste of their cooking in the earth-tone restaurant wins over any skeptics. Rather than limit the menu to Northern Mexican dishes such as tacos and enchiladas, they offer a full range of Mexico's grand cuisine. From Oaxaca, they serve a *sabaroso*, seared turkey breast in rich red *mole*, a sweetened chili sauce. From Central Mexico comes charcoal grilled swordfish with a light cream sauce. The menu changes weekly, but diners always find something delightful to go with the homemade tortillas.

Eastern Europe: Hungarian restaurateur Ivan Kenessey, of **Kenessey's**, is another liberator of cuisine. He notes that culinary recipes created for wealthy families disappeared in Eastern Europe after World War II because of constant food shortages and political repression. "We're going back before war time and bringing back recipes from the good old days of Hungary," says Kenessey, who with his wife, Katalin, look the part of an aristocratic couple.

Their rediscovered recipes are tasty. The fillet mignon Eszterhazy, named for a famous Hungarian family, graces the beef with a white wine cream sauce. The Palacsinta family is honored by walnut-filled crepes, covered with a rich chocolate sauce and served in rum *flambé*. There is also the traditional lamb shank with *letcho* – green peppers, tomatoes and onion with smoked Hungarian sausage in a light paprika sauce.

Kenessey has the most impressive wine list in Chicago: 1,500 different varieties, all stored on wall-to-floor shelves around the grotto-style dining room. Walk around and pick vintage merlot, mersault or Hungarian Siklosi chardonnay. Then pay retail, plus a small uncorking fee. It's the best wine bargain in town. Located across from Lincoln Park, Kenessey's will also put together a variety of picnic lunches, from bread, cheese and wine, to pâté, caviar and Dom Perignon.

Dining in style: Old timer: For four-star gourmet fantasy, Chicagoland has its share, including the legendary **Le Francais** in suburban Wheeling. But perhaps the most outstanding is The

Chicago's classic German restaurant-brewery.

Everest Room, which takes both diners and food to elegant heights.

Located in the city's financial district, **The Everest Room** commands a spectacular, 40th floor view of Chicago's West Side. It is gorgeous at sunset and powerful at night, when cars on the Eisenhower Expressway create an expansive, twinkling vista.

Inside, the nationally acclaimed restaurant surrounds its guests in an ivory-toned ambience of understated elegance and attentive service that remains unobstrusive. The cuisine is inspired. Award-winning chef and owner Jean Joho has drawn on his Alsatian roots to present the magical and magnificent from his kitchen.

There may be light, Maryland crab salad in a thinly sliced cucumber box; succulent Maine lobster with Alsace Gewurztraminer and ginger; exquisite wild pheasant, wrapped in cabbage with basil; and flavorful venison medallions, served with a tart huckleberry sauce.

Don't leave without sampling a dessert. Some recent favorites include lovingly sautéed raspberries in Alsatian raspberry liqueur and the chocolate fantasy, an assortment that includes chocolate-honey sorbet in a molded, maple syrup basket.

Old timer: With restaurants opening and closing in Chicago like menu covers, an exception is the **Berghoff Restaurant**, scheduled to celebrate its 100th anniversary in 1998. Across the street from the elegant Palmer House in the heart of the Loop, the Berghoff offers the best German meals in the city.

The huge dining rooms, with oak paneling and tables, are always crowded, no easy feat for a restaurant that seats 800 diners. Service? The term "hustle and bustle" could have been coined for the Berghoff waiters who always seem to be carrying several plates of tart *sauerbraten*, smoked *thuringer* with sauerkraut, tender *weiner schnitzel* and savory German pot roast, or delivering foaming steins of Berghoff beer.

Sausage making.

Dining 209

The Berghoff serves some 2,500 meals plus 3,000 steins of their Dortmunder-style beer daily. Actually, it sold the beer first. Herman Joseph Berghoff, a German immigrant, opened an Indiana brewery in 1887 and brought his beer to the 1893 World's Columbian Exposition. It was such a success that he opened the Berghoff and was issued Chicago Liquor License No. 1, now on display in the main dining room. The Berghoff also makes its own root beer.

Picking winners: In terms of new restaurants, it's impossible to predict what will be trendy, or even open next month. Some chic spots have been packed one day and literally closed down the next. But if you had to pick, any venue owned by restaurant genius Richard Melman would be an odds-on favorite.

Two of his restaurants, **Shaw's Crab House** and **Shaw's Blue Crab Lounge & Oyster Bar**, next to each other just off State Street, serve some of the best seafood in Chicago. The House offers white tablecloths and 1930s decor, with daily specials such as grilled *mahi mahi* and soft-shelled crabs. The Lounge puts diners on wooden stools for gumbo, chowder or stew. Fresh oysters and clams vary daily and the Maryland crabcakes are always moist.

Bub City Crabshack & Bar-B-Q, another Melman creation, is a lively and spacious eatery fixed up to look like a roadside honky-tonk in Texas. There's even Lone Star and other Texas beers. The cookin' includes stuffed *jalapeno* peppers, oyster and hot sausage po' boys, pick 'n' lick shrimp, blackened fish, dungeness crab, steamed with or without garlic, and plenty of barbecue. Ordinarily in the Midwest, barbecue means ribs. But at Bub's, as in the American South, barbecue means a delicious smoked beef brisket.

Rib tickling: If you're looking for Chicago barbecue – meaty pork ribs slathered in a very messy and zesty sauce – **Twin-Anchors Restaurant and Tavern** has none other than "the chairman of the board" singing its praise. When Frank Sinatra comes to his kind of town, he asks Twin-Anchors, which doesn't ordinarily deliver, to bring him plenty of ribs. Naturally, it's an offer they can't refuse.

Opened in 1932 in a former Old Town speakeasy, Twin-Anchors seems to get better with age. Many consider the ribs the best in Chicago because they are picked with care, served as a slab that overhangs the plate and can be easily pulled from the bone. The friendly, bustling tavern also serves a great burger.

For something completely different, **Mama Desta's Red Sea Restaurant** serves some excellent authentic Ethiopian fare not far from Wrigley Field. The savory food is that of the Amhara and Tigrean peoples, the ruling classes, whose cuisine is among the most sophisticated in East Africa. The spices are reminiscent of East Indian curries, but savory, not sweet.

The more guests at a Mama Desta's table, the better to try more dishes. On each table, the waitress places a pan

Fish formation.

covered with spongy bread called *injera*, which resembles unbaked pizza crust but tastes something like sourdough. Orders are then spooned onto the bread in a decorative arrangement. Diners tear some bread from a side serving and pinch the food with it, rather like making a taco, and then eat with their hands. It's part of the fun.

Couples would do best to order the *Alitcha* combo and the hot combo. The *Alitcha* dish offers chicken, lamb and beef, cooked separately in a thick, mild green sauce. The hot combo has the same meats, but they are cooked in a spicy, red pepper sauce. Cold beer goes very well with the meal, as does a glass of honey wine.

Chinese choice: For Chinese food, also more enjoyable with larger parties, go to Chinatown. Cermak and Wentworth streets are the starting point. Walk through the ornate arch on Wentworth and take in the groceries, kitchen supply houses and souvenir shops. The aroma of garlic and ginger is heady.

A local favorite that is all but unknown among tourists is the **Three Happiness Restaurant** on Cermak. It's a tiny storefront with a few formica tables and cheap prices for, among other things, the best Singapore fried-rice noodles in Chicago. The noodles, which look like spaghetti, are fried in a pan with Szechuan peppers and aromatic spices. Barbecued pork, shrimp and green peppers are added to this to make up a huge single serving. For those preferring Cantonese, Three Happiness offers plump *egg foo yong*, tasty chicken with pea pods and several good beef dishes.

Get along, little doggies: The best hot dogs can be found at **Demon Dogs**, under the Fullerton Avenue El stop. Owner Peter Schivarelli uses top-line Vienna beef hot dogs. The difference is that the better dogs come in a casing that keeps them from shrinking while they're being steamed. Besides the clearer flavor, there should be a slight crunch when that first bite breaks the

Butcher shop.

casing. Chicago has many Vienna stands, but not all have the firmer, non-shrink casing.

A true Chicago dog must be loaded with "the works" – mustard, relish and onions. The tiny peppers are optional and very hot. Demon Dogs, named for the Blue Demon mascot of nearby DePaul University, sells 5,000 hot dogs a week. The french fries, cooked in vegetable oil instead of animal fat, are also excellent. Demon Dogs, opened in 1982, is regarded by many as the best hot dog stand in Chicago because it hasn't diluted its identity by adding salads or grilled chicken sandwiches to the menu. It also has free parking in a congested part of town. The decor is appealing: Schivarelli grew up with members of the rock group Chicago and has decorated his place with many of their gold and platinum records.

Deep dish original: Chicago is famous for deep-dish pizza, a hefty concoction of chunky tomato sauce over a thick baked crust with plenty of mozzarella cheese. Add favorite ingredients, such as pepperoni, sausage, green peppers or mushrooms, and call it a meal.

A pizza war has been running in Chicago for decades among restaurants, critics and customers all claiming different winners. Visitors might want to begin their own research by returning to where it all started back in 1943. **Pizzeria Uno**, a couple of blocks from Michigan Avenue, is the birthplace of Chicago-style deep dish pizza. **Pizzeria Due**, established in 1955, is the sister restaurant and just as good. Creator Ike Sewell, the man most responsible for teaching Americans that pizza could be a meal rather than just a snack, makes pizza with a coarse, crunchy crust, a thick layer of mozzarella and a natural, perfectly seasoned sauce – a good foundation to build on.

No chips: A great burger and a correspondingly great character – or maybe it should be characters – are the attraction at **Billy Goat Tavern & Grill**, a neighborhood bar on lower Michigan

Big hot dog, with relish; a doorman-chef-babysitter welcomes customers of all ages.

212

Avenue that is the city's hangout for newspapermen and women. They simply call it "the Goat" and their legions include Pulitzer Prize winner Mike Royko, the *Chicago Tribune* columnist whom many regard as Chicago's conscience. Visitors often order cheeseburgers in groups, so they can hear the Greek grillman shout, "cheezborger, cheezborger, cheezborger," as he slaps patties on the sizzling grill, just like in the famous *Saturday Night Live* TV skits featuring the late John Belushi.

The burgers are juicy and excellent value. Try the double cheeseburger, served on a Kaiser roll. Take it over to the counter, load it up with pickles, onions, ketchup and mustard, and then survey the tavern's history on its walls. Way before *Saturday Night Live* the place was famous for William "Billygoat" Sianis, who opened the tavern in 1934 and welcomed sportswriters to drink there. One day a goat wandered in and was adopted as a mascot. Sianis, his goatee and goat made good pictures for the several daily newspapers of the day and many of those snaps are displayed along the walls of the tavern. The original Billygoat's nephew, Sam Sianis, runs the place now and keeps the publicity going.

The juice is loose: The best Italian beef sandwich can be found at **Mr Beef** on Orleans. What's an Italian beef? Thinly sliced roast beef is slowly cooked in its own juices with a hint of garlic and packed into a fresh slice of Italian bread. On this, Mr Beef piles sautéed green peppers, hot peppers or both, and offers the choice of "wet," with extra juices, or "dry," without. Owners Dominic and Joseph Zucchero, who opened the beef stand years before the River North area got trendy, use fresh sirloin tip roasts. Their fans, who always pack this daytime-only place, include local and national celebrities alike, such as comedian Jay Leno, who once showed up on a nationwide talk show eating Mr Beef sandwiches. The Italian beef sandwich is a Chicago classic.

A burger with all the trimmings.

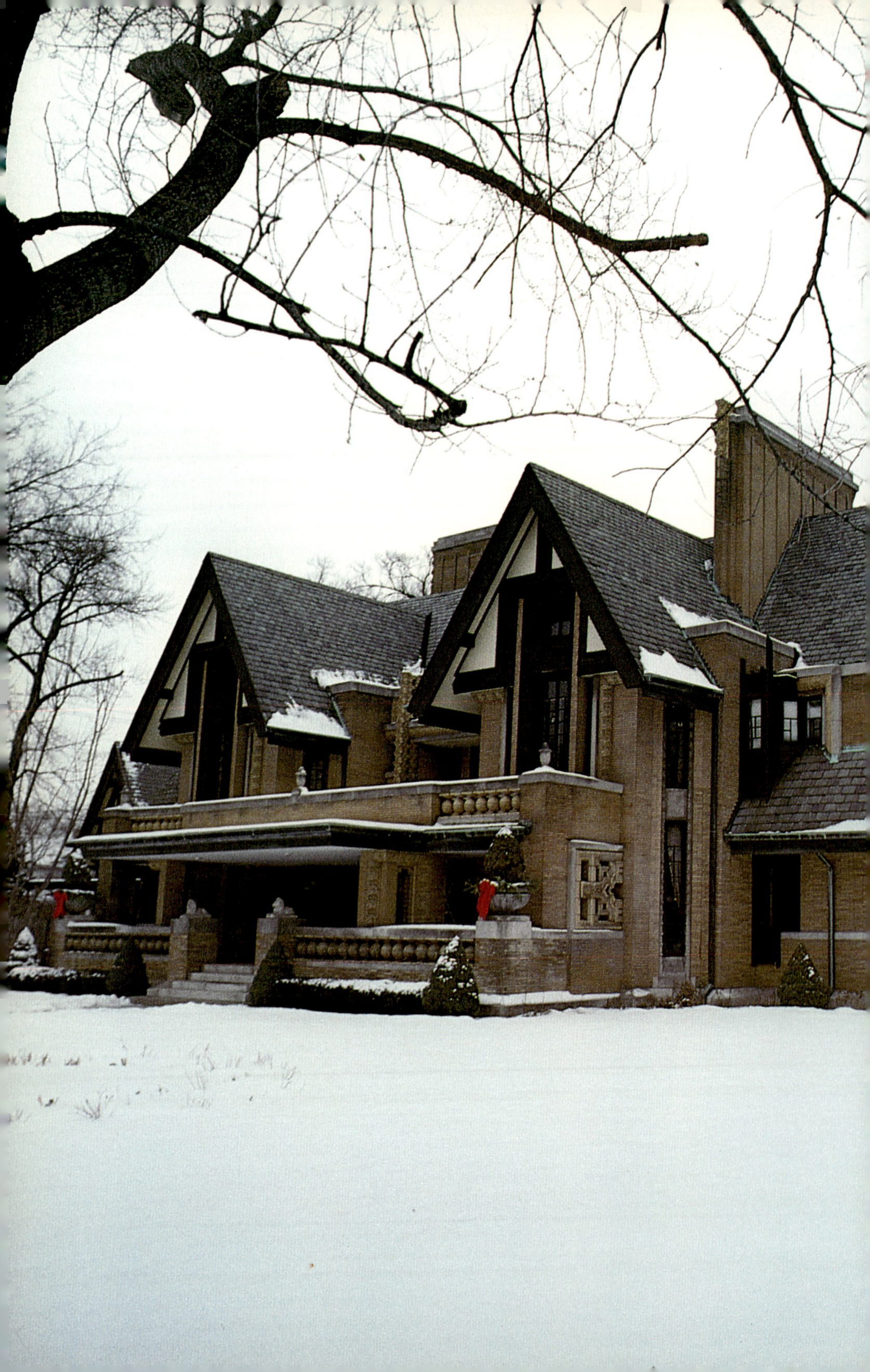

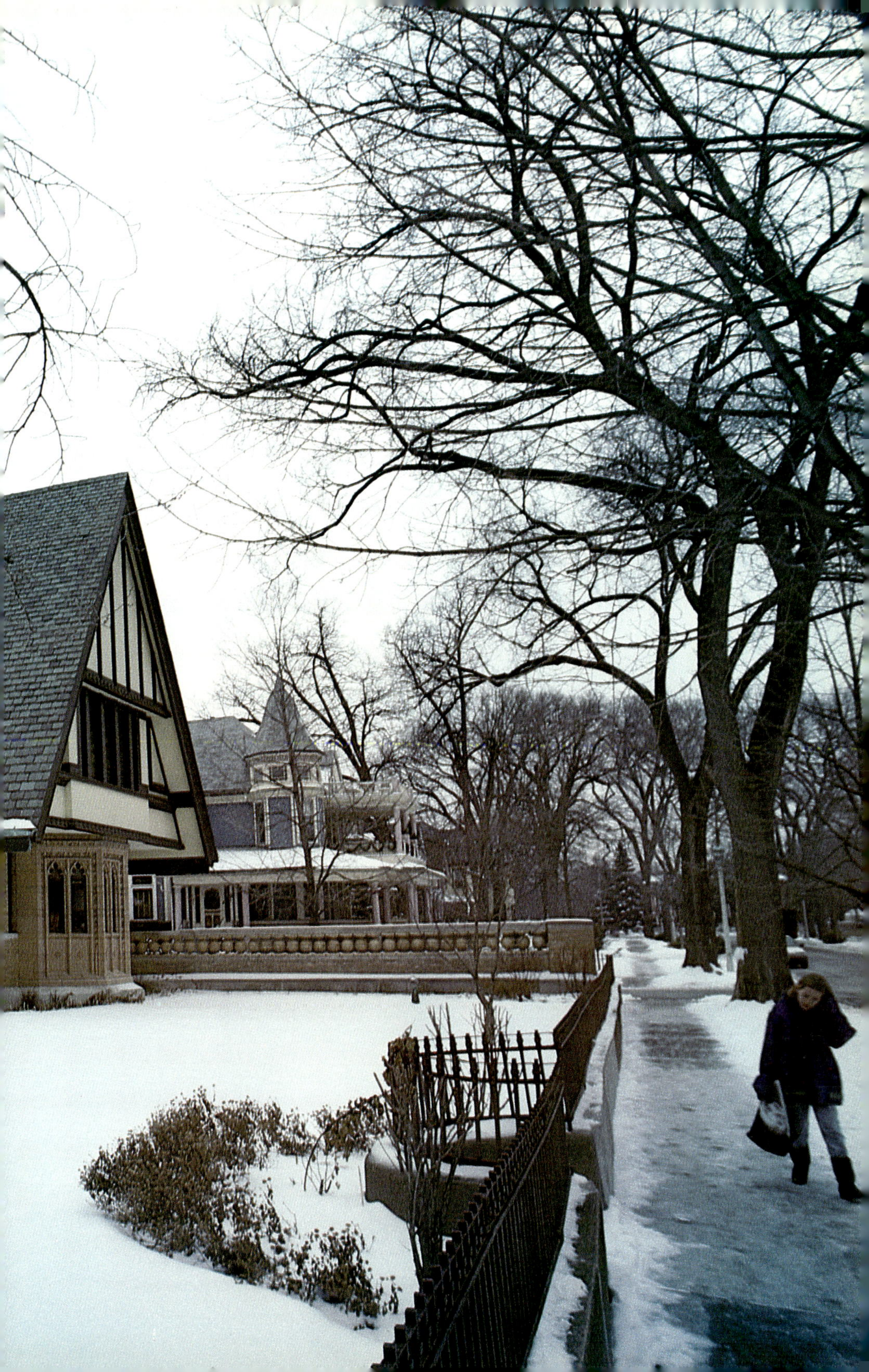

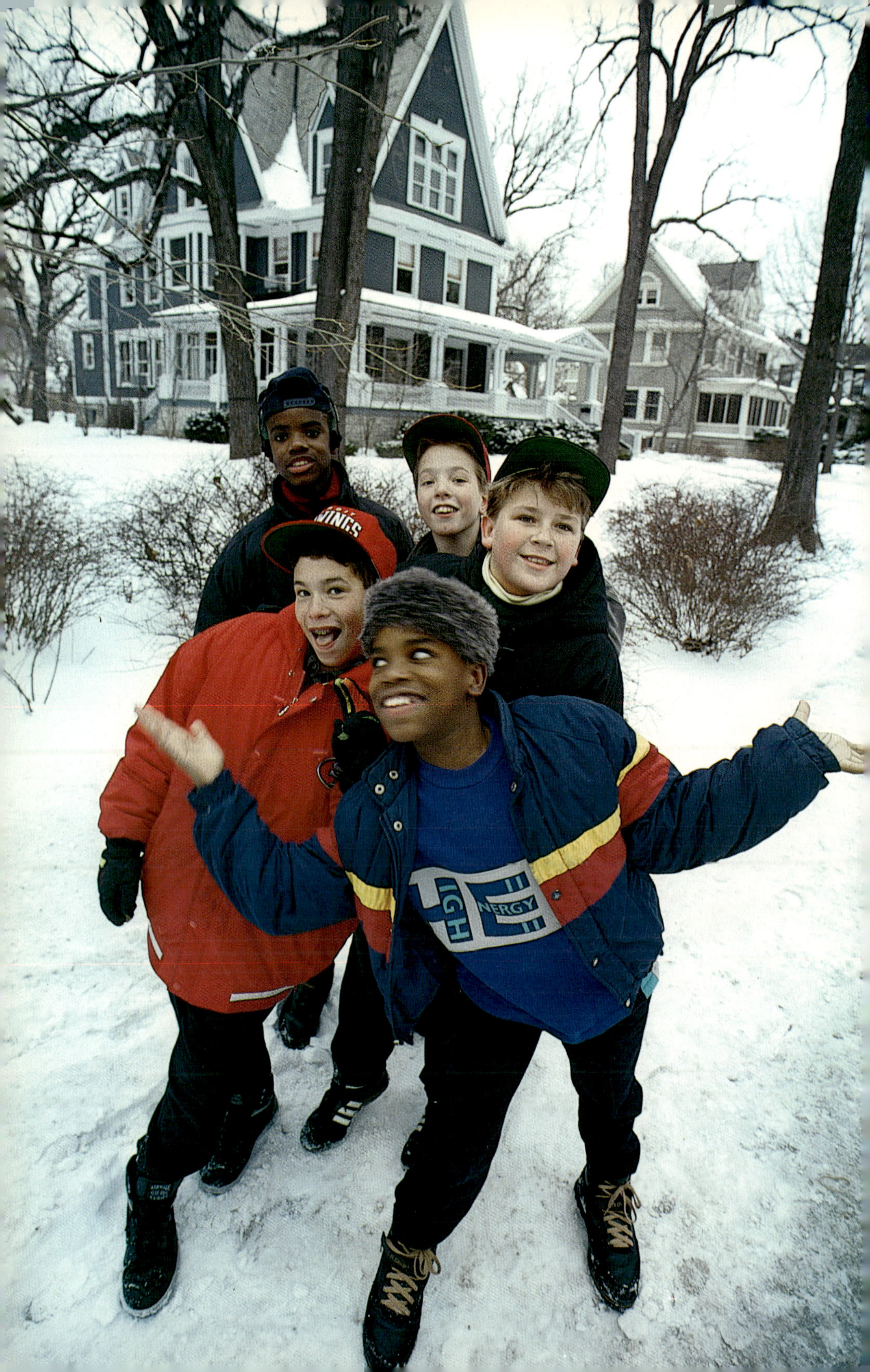
WINGS

OAK PARK

Oak Park is a curious place – or perhaps two places. The inhabitants of this suburb 10 miles due west of Chicago's Loop divide into two groups. One group includes all the normal citizens who get up, get dressed, go to work, clean the house, yell at the kids and run red lights when the street seems clear of police. The second, smaller group is a priestly class, the dead-serious Frank Lloyd Wright fans for whom Prairie School architecture ranks no lower than second or third in the history of great ideas.

Norman Mark, a Chicago broadcaster and a member of the latter group, reverently proclaimed, "To walk through Oak Park is to touch genius." He continues: "Oak Park reverberates with the ghost of Frank Lloyd Wright, an architectural genius who lived there, [and who] revolutionized residential building design…"

Which is true as far as it goes. Mark and other Wright advocates often fail to mention how dark and constricting his interior spaces may be as living quarters, how the flat roofs he gave to some Midwest houses implode under the weight of repeated snowfalls, or how ergonomically unsatisfactory some of his built-in chairs and tables appear on close acquaintance.

Wright turns: Most visitors reach Oak Park via the suburban Metra commuter line from downtown. Near the station in Oak Park, the **Oak Park Visitor's Bureau** rents taped talks for self-guided tours, an ingenious idea for those who prefer a leisurely stroll to the frenetic pace often adopted by zealous tour leaders. A quick count of shelves at the Visitor's Bureau reveals 26 books devoted exclusively to FLW, his designs and his philosophy, including a *Frank Lloyd Wright Home and Studio* coloring book for children. On sale are numerous postcards and posters, as well as mugs, T-shirts and shopping bags, clear indication that FLW has blossomed from mortal architect to immortal souvenir industry.

The reason for the adulation, of course, is the conspicuous near-absence of almost anything other than the Wright and the Queen Anne and Stick houses that make a walk through "historic" Oak Park a must for architecture buffs and an agreeable diversion for the rest of us.

But there are a few other things in Oak Park, which has long been studied by sociologists who view the neighborhood as a classic American suburb, not least for the way its more liberal-minded white residents encouraged middle-class blacks to become their neighbors in the 1950s and '60s.

The Children's Curiosity Corner of the **Oak Park Conservatory and Earth Shelter Classroom** (at 617 Garfield Street) keeps smaller youngsters happy while dad and mom and the older siblings immerse themselves in exhibits that explore desert and tropical

Preceding pages: a Wright house in Oak Park. Left, mugging in Oak Park. Right, Frank Lloyd Wright with a model apartment building, 1930.

Oak Park 217

flora and the specialized biology of ferns. Collections of exotic plants, a waterfall and gardens of herbs combine with native Illinois prairie plants in this richly diverse and undeservedly neglected part of Oak Park.

Cool diversions: Opposite the Visitor's Center, **Austin Garden** is equipped with benches and lots of shade trees which can be a godsend in the heat of July and August. A trio of casual ice-cream parlors cluster nearby on Lake Street: A Taste of Culture Frozen Yoghurt, Phoebe's Frozen Yoghurt and Baskin-Robbins. The first two feature homebaked cakes and muffins as well, to be washed down with non-alcoholic potables, while A Taste of Culture also offers soup.

Oak Park and contiguous River Forest share the **Village Players**, an air-conditioned and comfortable theater small enough to foster a sense of intimacy and engagement. As the view is good from anywhere in the house, tickets only a few dollars and productions usually light and contemporary (*A Funny Thing Happened on the Way to the Forum*, *Stepping Out*, an angst-free *Chorus Line* with tapdancing instead of high kicking), a walking tour can segue pleasantly into a light supper and show.

Oak Park has its share of special events in the summer, many devoted to the arts, or arts and crafts, or to historic buildings, or to literati such as Ernest Hemingway, who was born here, and Edgar Rice Burroughs, author of *Tarzan of the Apes*, who lived and worked in the suburb.

Art fairs punctuate the summer calendar, along with occasional special tours that take visitors into landmark homes, including some of Wright's, that are normally closed to the public. There's also a summer country fair and the **Kettlestrings Festival**, a jamboree named after the settler who established Oak Park as a discrete urban entity back in 1839.

The pedestrian mall sandwiched between the Oak Park Metra station and

Wright's house for Mrs Thomas H. Gale.

Lake Street has gone down sadly since its halcyon days, though there are still a few specialty and fashion shops.

Housing history: Still, Oak Park's main attraction for outsiders, apart from air refreshingly free of pollutants and a social fabric notably unrent by civic dissension, are the walking tours. An entire district, the area lying between Chicago Avenue and Randolph Street on the north and south and Linden and Marion streets east and west, has been given a listing in the *National Register of Historic Places*. Almost all of the houses are private homes, so the interiors have to be imagined from descriptions or viewed via photographs and line drawings that embellish books and pamphlets.

One can, however, tour the **Frank Lloyd Wright Home and Studio**, 947 Chicago Avenue, and Unity Temple, 875 Lake Street. The former's initial structure, dating from 1889, did double duty as workshop and home until 1898, when Wright built a brick-and-shingle house next door to accommodate his expanding needs. All aspects of his architecture business, from conception to artistic design to drafted plans, were carried out here until 1909, the period to which the building – made over into a residence by Wright in 1911 – has been restored.

The 1889 home, the product of Wright's tradition-bound vision, is dominated by a bold pitched-roof second floor, an equilateral triangle pierced by diamond-pane casement windows set in a rectangular array. The studio features a squat octagonal library to go with a two-story drafting room and an inconspicuous side entrance, the latter consistent with Wright's belief, later developed and elaborated upon, that movement from an outer environment to an interior space should be an experienced transition, not an abrupt change. Furnishings designed by Wright fill the house, for which a one-hour tour is available.

The **Gingko Tree Bookstore** downstairs sells tour tickets, also available at the Visitor's Bureau, and any number of books on architecture in general and Wright in particular. Mostly technical works or essays in secular hagiography, at least one volume deserves singling out for its amusing sidelights on Wright's prickly personality, *Letters to Clients* – which also includes letters *from* them. To a 1934 query about thresholds and keeping flies from getting into the house under the door, Wright replies, "Dear Nancy Willey: The screen doors can be cut on the slope and filled with leather flap. A half-inch clearance at the center and about half way back is all that will be needed. The rest will be in the clearance anyway. Let us have no thresholds. Amen. Frank Lloyd Wright."

The Wright church: The construction of Wright's 1905 magnum opus, **Unity Temple**, began in 1906 and wound to a close three years later. A scarcity of money in the church coffers enabled Wright to get the commission and dic-

A "bootleg" house.

tated, in part, his use of poured concrete, which was cheap but relatively untested. The construction has stood the test well, though visitors are cautioned not to stand under the overhanging eaves, which 80 years of weathering have rendered crumbly.

From the street, Unity Temple presents a set of cubic masses whose jutting horizontal slabs and fret-ornamented vertical blocks only in part overcome an essential stolidity and heaviness. A skylight and windows send natural light flooding over the soft earth tones of the church. The sanctuary's muted yellow, green, gray and white interior, plus hanging lamps, heating ducts in quasi-sculptured columns and ribbons of wood trim help to move the eye rhythmically from space to space.

A walk west on Chicago from Forest to Marion passes two **"bootleg" Wright houses**, at 1019 and 1027 Chicago. These are examples of architectural moonlighting for which Louis Sullivan, who had Wright under contract, fired his young associate in 1892. Nearly identical Queen Anne houses whose octagonal bays thrust out from a rectangular box, they suggest the simplification Wright's work was undergoing. The following year saw the construction of the **Walter H. Gale House** a few doors down at 1031 Chicago, in which Wright moves from straight lines to curved forms within the Queen Anne format, yet introduces decorative complexity in the roof shingles and lead glass windows.

Triangles: Kenilworth Avenue unfolds a pastiche of styles in 14 houses, most built between 1880 and 1910, Queen Anne and Prairie School predominating. The overall effect is harmonious despite the many differences – notably from the Colonial Revival at 312 Kenilworth, sporting Ionian corner capitals and a centered doorway, to 417 Kenilworth, whose third floor is an intersection of steeply pitched isosceles triangles and deep dormer windows

Unity Temple interior.

over a boxy second floor set on a central square rimmed by a colonnaded porch.

At 217 Home Avenue, the **Farson House**, a dramatic example of Prairie School architecture (1897–99) by George Washington Maher, looms at the end of a landscaped approach. The building retains its original furniture and fixtures, designed by the architect, as well as antique toys and memorabilia of Hemingway and Wright. The **Historical Society of Oak Park and River Forest** is based in the building, which is open for touring a couple of afternoons a week.

Forest Avenue from Chicago past Pleasant contains several important buildings beginning with four row houses circa 1888–89 (200–206 Forest) and culminating in the **Arthur Heurtley House** (318 Forest), built by Wright in 1902. Particularly noteworthy are the modified gable roof, like a Chinese coolie hat that caps the upper floor casement windows, and alternating light and dark horizontal bands of brick cut only by ground floor windows and a circular arched entrance behind an open porch. Not much fancied by the public, the Heurtley House drew considerable praise from architects and remained one of Wright's personal favorites years later.

Open interior: The flattened S-curve of **Elizabeth Court** connecting Forest and Kenilworth makes an enjoyable departure from straight streets and avenues. Next to a rather overblown Queen Anne structure, the modest statement of the **Mrs Thomas Gale House** at 6 Elizabeth Court achieves a quiet dignity. Its open interior space permits passersby to look through the front ground floor windows to the green yard in back. The **William G. Fricke House** at 540 Fair Oaks Avenue, at first glance similar, hedges the uncompromising horizontals with handsome vertical masses, and a varied, complex use of abrupt corners and multiple flat gable roofs almost suggest the flaring rooflines of pagoda architecture.

Christmas Eve candlelight service at Unity Temple.

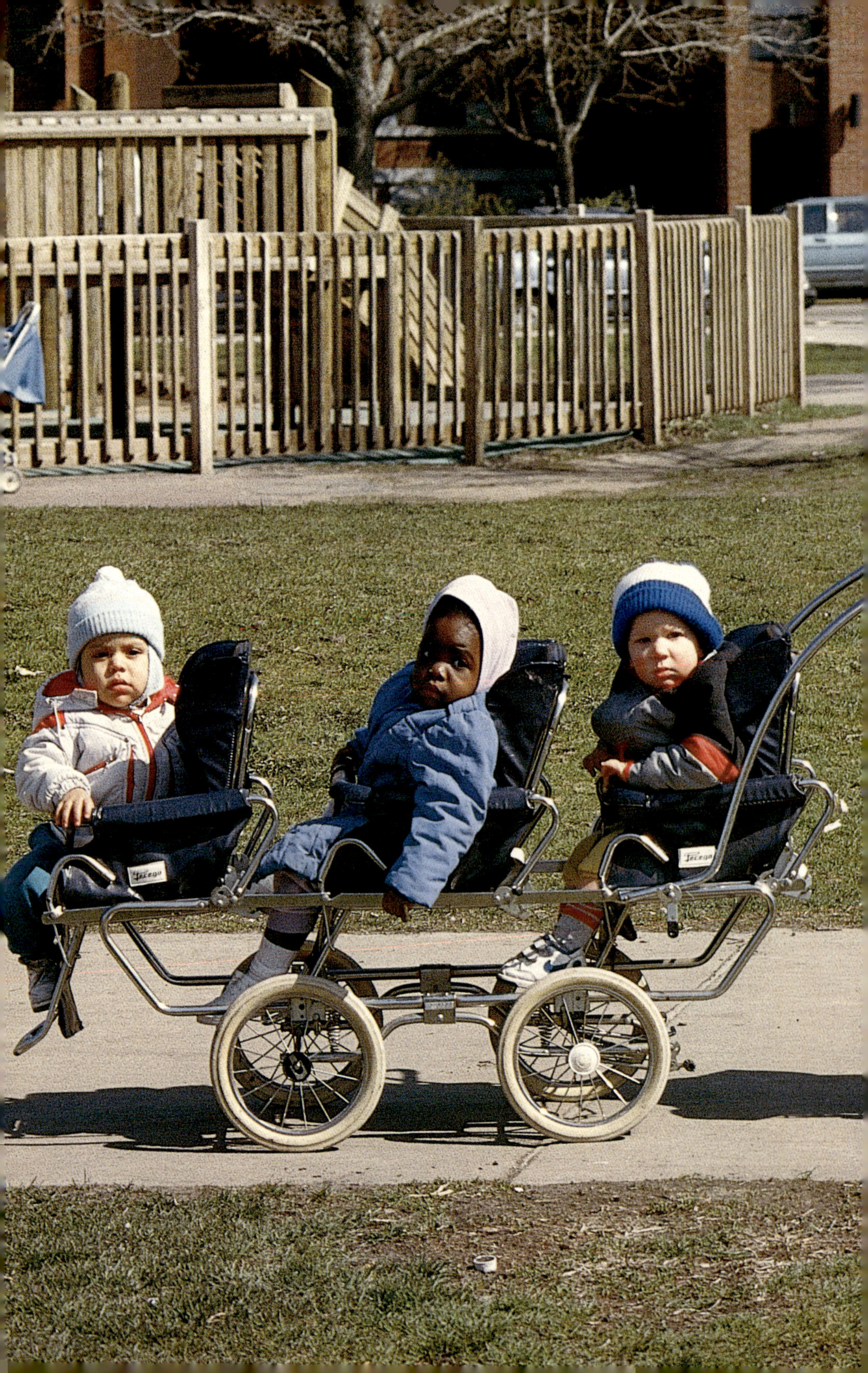

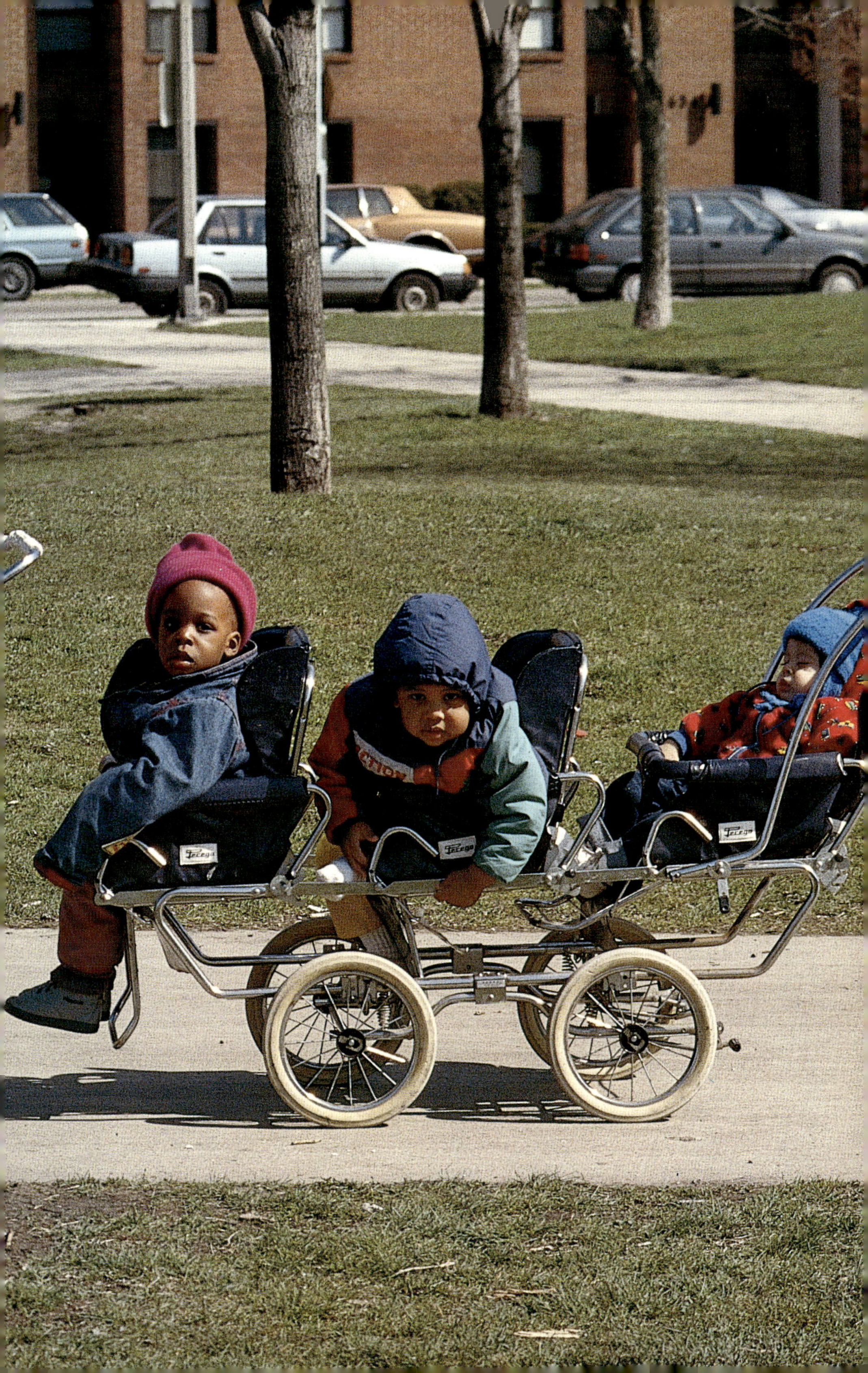

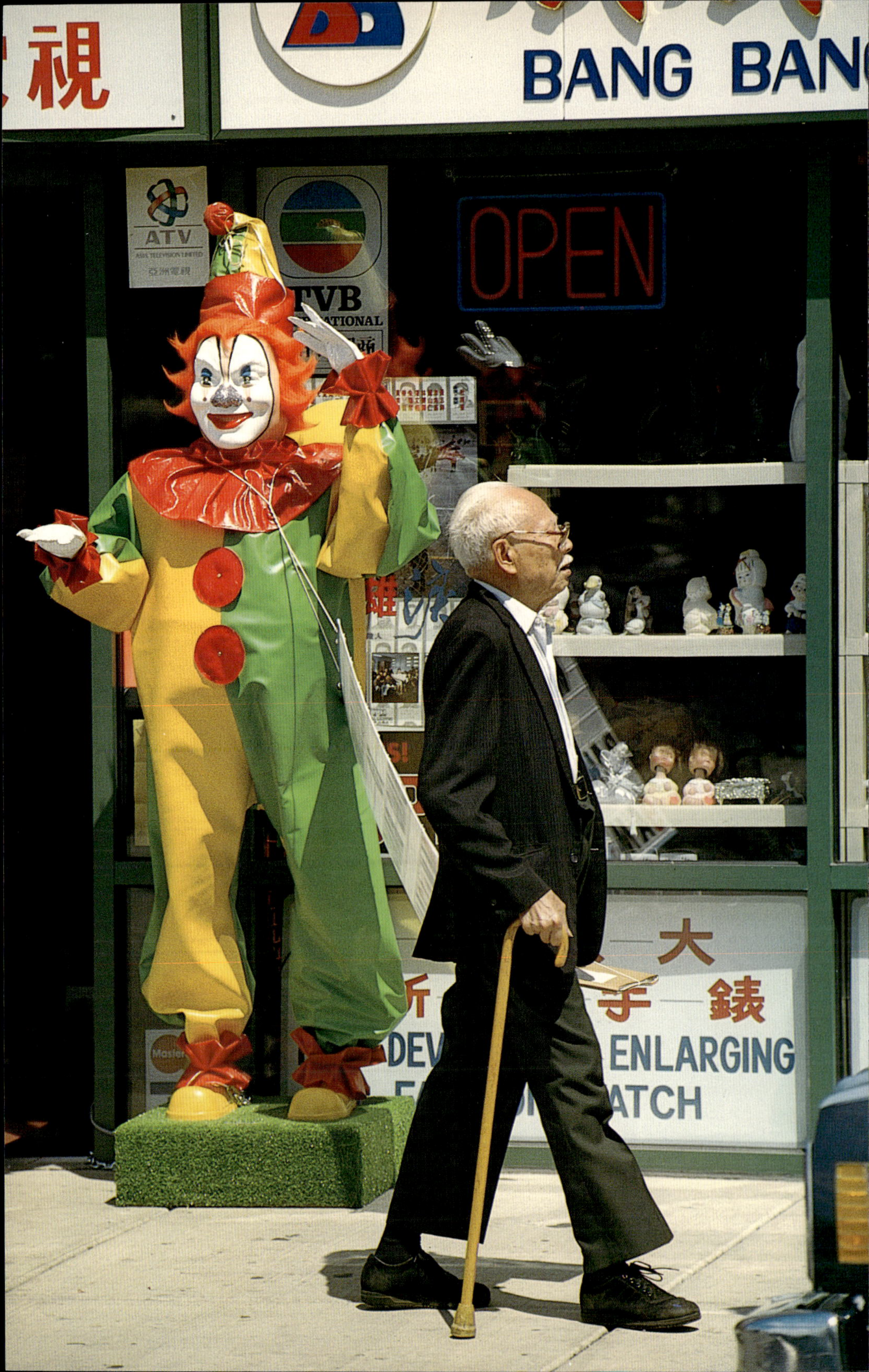

視
BANG BAN
ATV
TVB
OPEN
大
錶
ENLARGING
ATCH

The South Side

Chicago's South Side was the home of the "Mickey Finn," the doctored drink that Michael Finn, the unscrupulous owner of the long-defunct Lone Star Saloon and Palm Garden, used to serve unwitting patrons in the 1890s so that he could rifle their pockets after they passed out.

Visitors to the South Side today have a considerably better chance of remaining alert, but not if they happen to mention anything at all positive about the North Side. Any true South Sider within earshot will quickly inform the visitor that there isn't *anything* good about the North Side.

Such is the thinking on the South Side. As with any neighborhood rivalry or urban turf war, the roots of this north-south division are tangled in the past. But it comes down to this: South Siders think North Siders are arrogant twits who say "Ciao." Of course, South Siders don't just argue with North Siders; if no North Siders are available, they'll happily squabble among themselves over anything and everything, including the definition of the South Side. Some say it's all of Chicago south of Madison Street, which would include half of the Loop. Others insist it includes Grant Park and its museums, which are more generally (and in this book) regarded as part of downtown and the Loop. South Siders also tend to claim well-known areas such as Little Italy and Maxwell Street that are southwest of the Loop and are treated by the official University of Chicago mapmakers (and, again, this book) as part of the West Side.

It's difficult to explain the North-South friction in Chicago, but it dates back at least to 1839. That's when Chicago's first South Side pioneers settled in what is now downtown Chicago. They did this to be near the safety of Fort Dearborn and the trade of the Chicago River. Most of the early settlement was on the south bank of the river, west of what is now Michigan Avenue – making, for argument's sake – the first settlers South Siders.

Troubled waters: In 1831, the city fathers thought it would be a good idea to put a bridge across the Chicago River. The river runs east to west through the center of present-day downtown Chicago and eventually splits north and south. The bridge was designed to open commerce to the North Side, an idea that the South Siders immediately deemed senseless.

Since the bridge was repeatedly rammed by boats trying to navigate the narrow river, the City Council eventually ordered it dismantled in 1839. Pioneer South Siders were jubilant. So much so, they splintered the bridge with axes before North Siders could organize to save it. That animosity has remained in various forms throughout the city's history, particularly when it comes to important matters. Like baseball.

Preceding pages: a daycare convoy. **Left,** Chinatown shop. **Right,** waiting for the tooth fairy.

The Cubs play in a cute little ballpark on the North Side referred to as "the friendly confines" and named for a chewing gum manufacturer. For decades, the White Sox, long regarded as the city's workingman's team, toiled on the South Side in a park named for a first baseman called Comiskey. The park, at 35th and Shields, was built in 1910 and was the oldest in the major leagues until the White Sox built a new one across the street to open the 1991 season. The old stadium was knocked down shortly afterwards to create parking spaces. The new **White Sox Park** is easily reached via CTA, the 35th street station.

In the mid-19th century the South Side was a place where worker and boss lived side by side. It was not unusual to see an early and perhaps sensorily impaired meatpacker build his home right next to the slaughterhouse and its stench. By the late 1800s, however, the captains of Chicago industry had become a little more particular about their neighbors. Still, the very wealthy lived on the South Side, albeit separate from the masses.

Mansion Row: "Millionaires' Row," in the days when a million was really something, was **Prairie Avenue** between 16th and 22nd streets. It was the unofficial home roosting ground for the city's first entrepreneurs to make it big, including George Pullman of the Pullman railroad car, department store magnate Marshall Field, meatpacking mogul Phillip Armour and about 50 others who built mansions there.

There is little here now to attest to the area's former pedigree, but the Prairie Avenue Historic District has preserved some of the old glory. An example is the **Glessner House** at 1800 S. Prairie, a bulky Romanesque mansion – the only remaining H.H. Richardson-designed building in Chicago that is open to public tours. A block away is the city's oldest building, the **Widow Clarke House**, at 1855 S. Indiana Avenue. This Greek revival house was originally built in 1836 about two blocks from where it

A South Side boxing club.

stands now.

Bertha Palmer, a major mover in Chicago society and the wife of Potter Palmer, founder of the Palmer House hotel, helped bring status to the North Side when she convinced her husband to move away from Prairie Avenue. They built a gaudy mansion on North Lake Shore Drive, and the elite of Prairie Avenue eventually followed. With the millionaires moving north, the South Side's animosity toward the North Side grew.

All in the numbers: South Siders then and now believe that their side of town is where "real people" live, the unpretentious folk who still rely on numbered streets – 95th Street is 95 blocks south of the Madison Street north-south dividing line in the Loop, for instance – instead of the named streets on the North Side.

The South Side also has machine shops, steel mills, can factories and, fittingly, the **Museum of Science and Industry** at 57th Street and Lake Shore Drive. Children love this museum for its clear explanations, demonstrations and hands-on exhibits of scientific principles and how they are applied to industrial uses and everyday life. The space center and Omnimax Theatre, with its stunning nature and science films, are also popular attractions.

The cultural center of the South Side is the University of Chicago and the neighborhood known as **Hyde Park**. One local jewel is the **Oriental Institute**, a museum of antiquities at 1155 E. 58th Street. The institute has galleries representing many ancient societies, their art and artifacts: Egyptian, Assyrian, Mesopotamian, Persian and Palestinian. Each gallery is filled with hundreds of exhibits, including a famous 40-ton Assyrian statute of a winged bull.

Within walking distance from the Oriental Institute is the **Robie House**, 5757 S. Woodlawn, a Prairie School architectural masterpiece designed by Frank Lloyd Wright in 1909. Not far

Neighborhood liquor store.

away is the country's first black history museum, **DuSable Museum of African American History**, at 740 E. 56th Street. Founded in 1959, the museum has a permanent exhibit entitled "Up From Slavery" that describes the development of US slavery and includes documents and artifacts of slavery. The museum also has traveling exhibits in addition to memorabilia, sculptures, paintings and photos of and by African Americans.

Ghost yards: The **Chicago Union Stock Yard** once employed 40,000 workers scattered over 500 acres to slaughter cattle and pigs to feed the nation. With just a couple of rendering plants still in operation, the old stockyards are all but gone. The stockyards are now commemorated by the limestone gate erected in 1865 and still standing at Exchange Avenue and Peoria Street (about 41st and Halsted). Now, however, the gate is about the only thing to see, and it leads nowhere.

Like the stockyards, the once-mighty Chicago steel mills have also faded away. Wisconsin Steel, on 106th Street on the southeast side, is nothing but a corrugated steel corpse where weeds and rust have replaced its 3,500 workers. A drive by the deserted plant provides an eerie reminder of American industrial muscle gone soft.

US Steel's South Works has also withered. Founded in 1880, the mill still stands, though mostly empty, on Lake Michigan's southwestern shore, starting at about 79th Street. At its height during World War II, the mill employed more than 18,000 workers. Now, fewer than 1,000 people work at the mill that produced the steel framing for many of Chicago's greatest skyscrapers, including the Sears Tower and the John Hancock Center.

For the flavor of the steel-mill neighborhoods – not to mention a good meal and a good time drinking Niksico beer and eating American-Yugoslavian cuisine – seek out the **Golden Shell**, restaurant. The atmosphere is casual

Wall mural on Japanese-American Friendship Center.

and festive amid strumming minstrels and waitresses jockeying for position with platters of stuffed peppers, cabbages and *muckalica*, a pork tenderloin sautéed with green peppers and onions. No matter what else is consumed, however, the dessert is a must: *krem pita*, a lighter-than-air pudding between two layers of pastry with a vanilla whipped topping.

Pulled out: Farther south and west is another industrial ghost. The Pullman plant no longer manufactures luxury railroad cars in **Pullman**, a neighborhood once referred to as "the most perfect city in the world." That was over a century ago, when Pullman had 8,000 residents, about a third of whom labored in the plants of George Pullman's Palace Car Company.

Pullman was a model industrial town, where the company owned everything. Workers were housed, according to their position, in tidy company homes on streets that were paved and landscaped by the company. Plant managers had larger houses than foremen; foremen had larger houses than laborers.

The village, located between 111th Street and 115th Street from **Cottage Grove** to **Langley Avenue**, is today a national landmark where even North Siders are known to visit, perhaps for an enjoyable brunch at the historic **Hotel Florence**, 11111 S. Forrestville. Some of the beauty of Pullman's public buildings, fountains and reflecting ponds can still be seen, but restoration is a continuing battle. It's the kind of area that must be walked through, lingeringly, to be appreciated.

Despite the well laid plans of Pullman's corporate order, several years after the town was founded the workers began to feel squeezed. To them, it didn't seem fair that the company set rents and controlled prices at its local stores. In 1894, a precedent-setting strike brought violence and federal intervention to Pullman. Eventually, the Illinois Supreme Court ruled the company couldn't own the town. Employ-

Pullman, the ultimate company town, around the turn of the century.

ees were allowed to buy homes, but company support for the town disappeared. It was never the same. The last Pullman car was manufactured in 1981.

Fair tales: Another bit of South Side history was the World's Columbian Exposition of 1893, a giant fair that included: the first Ferris wheel (250 feet in diameter with a capacity of 1,400 passengers, designed by George W. G. Ferris); "Little Egypt," a belly dancer who became a national sex icon of the Gay Nineties; the **Midway Plaisance**, a strip one mile long and 300 feet wide that was lined with examples of the architecture of the world (now a wide grassway on 59th Street that runs through the University of Chicago); and grounds laid out and landscaped by Frederick Law Olmsted, who also designed New York City's Central Park.

Other legacies of the exposition include **Jackson Park**, the Museum of Science and Industry (originally the fair's Fine Arts building), and the name "Windy City," bestowed by the East Coast press because Chicago had been so loud and strident – also well-known South Side traits – in lobbying to host the fair. In the end the event was a roaring success, claiming 27 million admissions.

Just as the 1893 Columbian Exposition celebrated humankind's past, the next big fair in Chicago, the Century of Progress World's Fair of 1933, looked to the future. This expo, built amid man-made islands and lagoons along the South Side lakefront, used new building materials and modernistic designs to project a bold future despite the bleakness of the Great Depression. Meigs Field was later built on Northerly Island, which was part of the fair's site of 598 acres built into the lakefront with sand and fill. The 1933 fair unleashed another sex-bomb to titillate the American public – Sally Rand, the fan dancer who became famous for her glimpse-of-flesh routines in the fair's Italian village, especially popular among the high-rolling hoodlums of the day.

The university: Along the majestic Midway Plaisance sits another South Side landmark, the **University of Chicago's Rockefeller Chapel**. Built in the mid-1920s, its modified Gothic design was intended "to remove the mind of the student from the busy mercantile condition of Chicago and surround him with the peculiar air of quiet dignity." The university today strives to maintain this theme of quiet dignity. Modeled after England's Oxford University, the gray stone buildings and the quadrangles they form can make for serene strolls with stops at some of the university's other sights such as the **Smart Museum**, 5550 S. Greenwood Avenue, where exhibits feature quality art from ancient to contemporary. For fans of the very latest in art, there's the **Renaissance Society** on the fourth floor of the university's **Cobb Hall** at 5811 S. Ellis. This nearly 80-year-old museum has no permanent collection, but it is famous for helping to launch the careers of many contemporary artists by giving

Buddy Guy, blues guitarist *extraordinaire*, hanging out outside the Checkerboard.

230

them their first shows.

The University of Chicago also played a large role in the dawning of the atomic era. Beneath the stands of an athletic field at the University of Chicago, the first sustained and controlled production of atomic energy took place on December 2, 1942. A group of scientists, headed by Enrico Fermi, created the first nuclear reactor, and with it the technology that led to the dropping of two atomic bombs on Japan in 1945 to hasten the end of World War II and, ultimately, usher in the four-decade-long Cold War. The Chicago experiments are commemorated by a **Henry Moore sculpture**, *Nuclear Energy*, on the site of old Stagg Field at 57th Street and Ellis Avenue.

Beverly's hill: The nation's largest urban historic district, containing 3,000 buildings with national register status, is also on the South Side. The **Beverly** neighborhood is situated on a ridge 30 to 40 feet above the rest of the city. Its residential architecture includes two homes designed by Frank Lloyd Wright and 17 houses designed by his student, Walter Burley Griffin, who designed Canberra, the capital of Australia, and who created the standard for the classic Chicago bungalow. **Walter Burley Griffin Place** (10432 South from 1600 West to 1756 West) in Beverly contains several examples of his houses, marked with signs.

The homes of Beverly run the architectural gamut, from Queen Anne to Prairie School to bungalow to modern suburban ranch. There's even the **Irish Castle**, 103rd Street and Longwood Drive, built in 1886 by a Chicago real estate developer who modeled it after one he had seen on the River Dee. North and south of the castle, mansions preside over the neighborhood from atop a glacial ridge.

To get a bit of local South Side flavor, stop in Top Notch Beefburger, 2116 W. 95th Street, for 1950s-style cheeseburgers and fries with thick chocolate shakes served in stainless steel. Reser-

Comiskey Park, opening day of the White Sox baseball season, April 1974.

vations are required, but good New Orleans-style cuisine is available at the Maple Tree Inn, 10730 S. Western Avenue. The restaurant is housed in a converted apartment building, part sports bar and part outdoor beer garden. At night the top floor is a wonderfully dark and mellow jazz club.

Chinatown: One of the South Side's most distinctly ethnic neighborhoods is **Chinatown**, a meandering gaggle of oriental architecture, restaurants and shops that was first settled by Chinese immigrants around 1912. **Cermak Road** and **Wentworth Avenue** is the main intersection of Chinatown. The neighborhood continues to serve as a Midwestern receiving area for immigrants from mainland China and Taiwan. Beneath the cheerful, crowded streets lined with many good restaurants, Chinatown sometimes seethes with crime and gang tensions. Even the On Leong building, considered the **Chinese City Hall**, has been raided for gambling in recent years by federal agents. Of course, this is not all that unusual for the South Side – the home of Al Capone in his heydey.

Not far from Chinatown is Capone's one-time headquarters at the old **Lexington Hotel** at Michigan Avenue and Cermak Road (2200 South). Capone had a suite on the corner, where he could keep an eye on the intersection below from his turret-like office. If and when the decrepit hotel opens to the public – which is scheduled for sometime in the 1990s, when developers are finished – inside there are reputedly a secret "escape" stairway and a long narrow room used by Capone's hoods as a tommy gun target range as if they didn't get enough practice on the streets.

Bridge to City Hall: Since 1933, there has only been one mayor from the North Side. Richard J. Daley was almost canonized as "Hizzoner da Mare" for his 21 years (1955 to 1976) in office. During the Daley era, Chicago saw the building of O'Hare Airport and the **Dan Ryan Expressway**, the vehicular spine of the

University of Chicago.

South Side that was named for one of Daley's longtime political cronies.

Another South Sider, Harold Washington, who was elected in 1983 and died in office in 1987, enjoyed nearly Daley-like status in the black community when he became the city's first black mayor after an election scarred by race baiting.

Daley's son, Richard M. Daley, became mayor in 1989 and, like his father, continued to live in the old neighborhood: **Bridgeport**. While typical of the South Side's working-class roots, Bridgeport is not so typical politically. This small and otherwise insignificant neighborhood has produced five mayors, including three of the last six. A favorite watering hole of Bridgeport and its movers and shakers of the 11th Ward is **Schaller's Pump**, 3714 S. Halsted Street. Over a century old, this tavern is nothing fancy but it's full of the local color of the neighborhood, right down to Frank Sinatra singing "Chicago" on the juke box.

Bridgeport, which is north of Pershing Road and outlined by the south branch of the Chicago River, was originally settled by German and Irish immigrants working on the **Illinois and Michigan Canal**. The I&M was a federal public works project designed to link Lake Michigan to the Mississippi River via local rivers connected to the canal. Bridgeport, named for the low bridge near Ashland Avenue that caused barges to unload and have their cargo portaged, became a boomtown by the time the canalworks were finished in 1848.

Later, Bridgeporters labored in the Union Stock Yard, as did the residents of neighboring Back of the Yards, named for its proximity to the stockyards. Here thousands of immigrants came to work, often in appalling conditions. Upton Sinclair's 1906 exposé *The Jungle* told of spoiled meats and miserable working conditions that caused a national uproar and brought about eventual reforms. The Back of the Yards

Cooling off at the university's Laredo Taft sculpture.

South Side 233

Council, incorporated in 1939, is the country's oldest community council.

Racial tensions: These South Side working-class neighborhoods also figure in a problem that has plagued Chicago for decades: racial unrest. When strikes occurred in places like the stockyards, blacks were often hired from southern states such as Alabama, Georgia and Mississippi to work as strike breakers or scabs. The two world wars also encouraged black migration to Chicago for jobs and in the end the economic competition led to friction and distrust between the blacks and white immigrant workers.

On July 27, 1919, a stone-throwing incident at the 29th Street beach led to the drowning of a black youth and the worst race riot in the city's history. It left 38 people dead and 537 injured. It is also part of a legacy of racism with which the city still struggles.

The South Side has had a black population of varying sizes since the mid-1800s. That black population grew within the city as a separate Chicago, creating over the years a separate economy and a separate society. It was a kind of second city within the second city, a black metropolis, and as off limits to whites as some parts of New York's Harlem.

The separateness of the city can best be seen through the lives of people such as Jesse Binga, a black man who came to Chicago with $5 in his pocket to look for opportunity at the 1893 Columbian Exposition. By the early 1900s he owned a bank and more than 1,000 feet of frontage on South State Street around 34th Street. He became a millionaire philanthropist, respected in the black community. But when he moved into a white neighborhood to fulfill the American dream of a spacious home, his house was repeatedly bombed. The Great Depression ransacked his fortune and his future. He was indicted for actions he took to save his bank and spent some time in jail. He died impoverished, working as a church janitor.

Black spokesmen: Nonetheless, Jesse Binga was representative of a long line of black South Side millionaires who because of their race were often unknown to the white public. He was also one of a long line of South Siders who have offered strong and sometimes controversial leadership to the black community. Notable contemporary examples of spokesmen include Jesse Jackson and Louis Farrakhan, the separatist Black Muslim.

When Jackson resigned as national director of Operation Breadbasket, an aid group for the mainstream civil-rights movement, he was quoted as saying, "I need air. I've got to grow." With those words he founded People United to Save Humanity, commonly known to Chicagoans and throughout the nation as Operation PUSH.

PUSH was Jackson's launching pad. From the stage and pulpit of a converted temple at PUSH **headquarters**, 930 E. 50th Street, Jackson and just about every other major American black

Selling cotton candy on the South Side.

leader of the past quarter century has spoken to enthusiastic audiences. They are often accompanied by swaying, hand-clapping choirs and peppery percussion sections. Whites are welcome to visit and Saturday morning programs are perhaps the best time, particularly if Jackson is making one of his occasional visits from his new headquarters in Washington DC.

Black leadership has been especially important on the South Side because of the racial divisions in a city called the most segregated in America. The South Side has often been portrayed as the base of the black political movement. It has been portrayed just as often as the poor side of town.

The projects: Certainly Chicago has its share of poverty. Driving south on the Dan Ryan Expressway past 35th Street, visitors see row after row of high-rises looming to the east – the Chicago Housing Authority developments, known locally as "the projects."

This, the so-called **State Street Corridor**, is one of the poorest neighborhoods in the entire United States. These developments house some 37,000 residents, most of whom are black and 75 percent of whom are on welfare. It is a neighborhood of relentless poverty where drug abuse, violence and teenage pregnancy are commonplace. It is not a place to stop and sightsee.

But only 50 blocks south is perhaps one of the largest black middle-class enclaves in the nation. **Chatham**, which runs east of the Dan Ryan around 87th Street, is a neighborhood of perfectly landscaped lawns and houses so neat and orderly they look as though they've been audited. Here, the black residents themselves joke that Chatham would seem like a typical middle-class white neighborhood – if the homeowners would stay indoors. Chatham is worth a visit for what many consider to be one of the finest soul food restaurants in America: Army's and Lou's, at 422 E. 7th Street. The ribs, chitlins and grits just don't get any better than here.

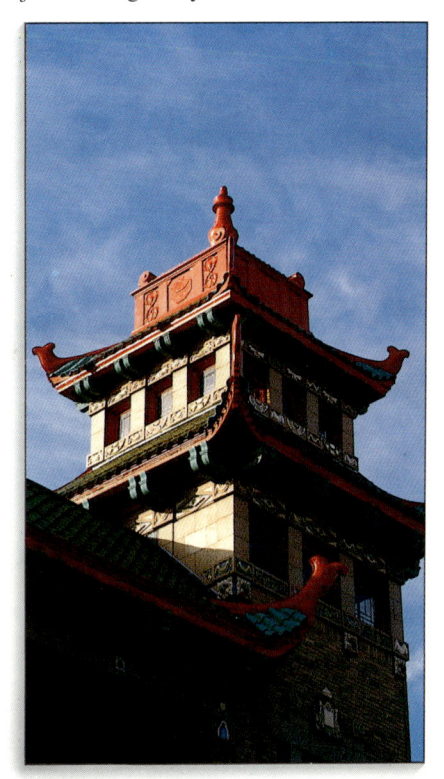

Chinatown.

South Side 235

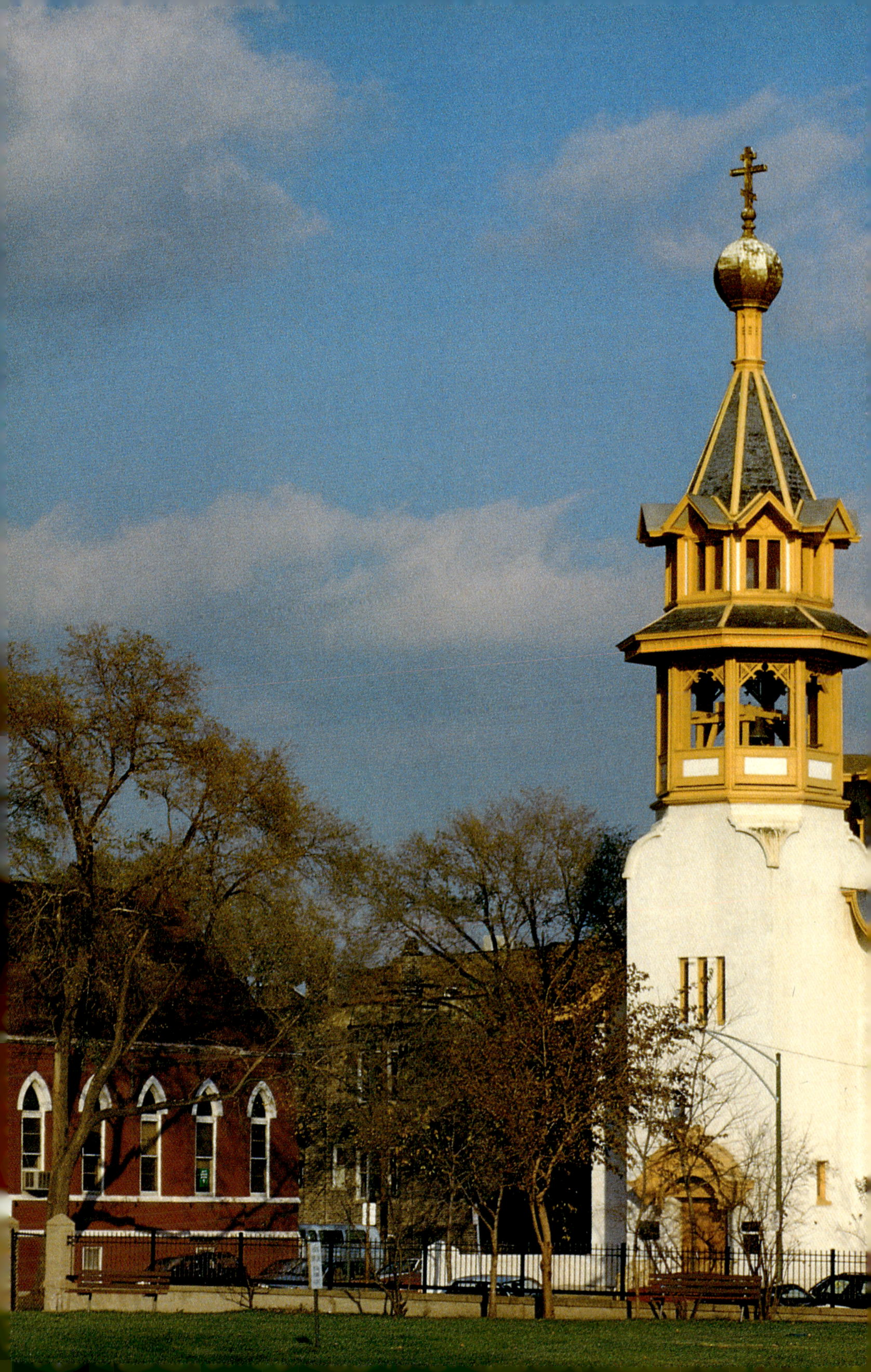

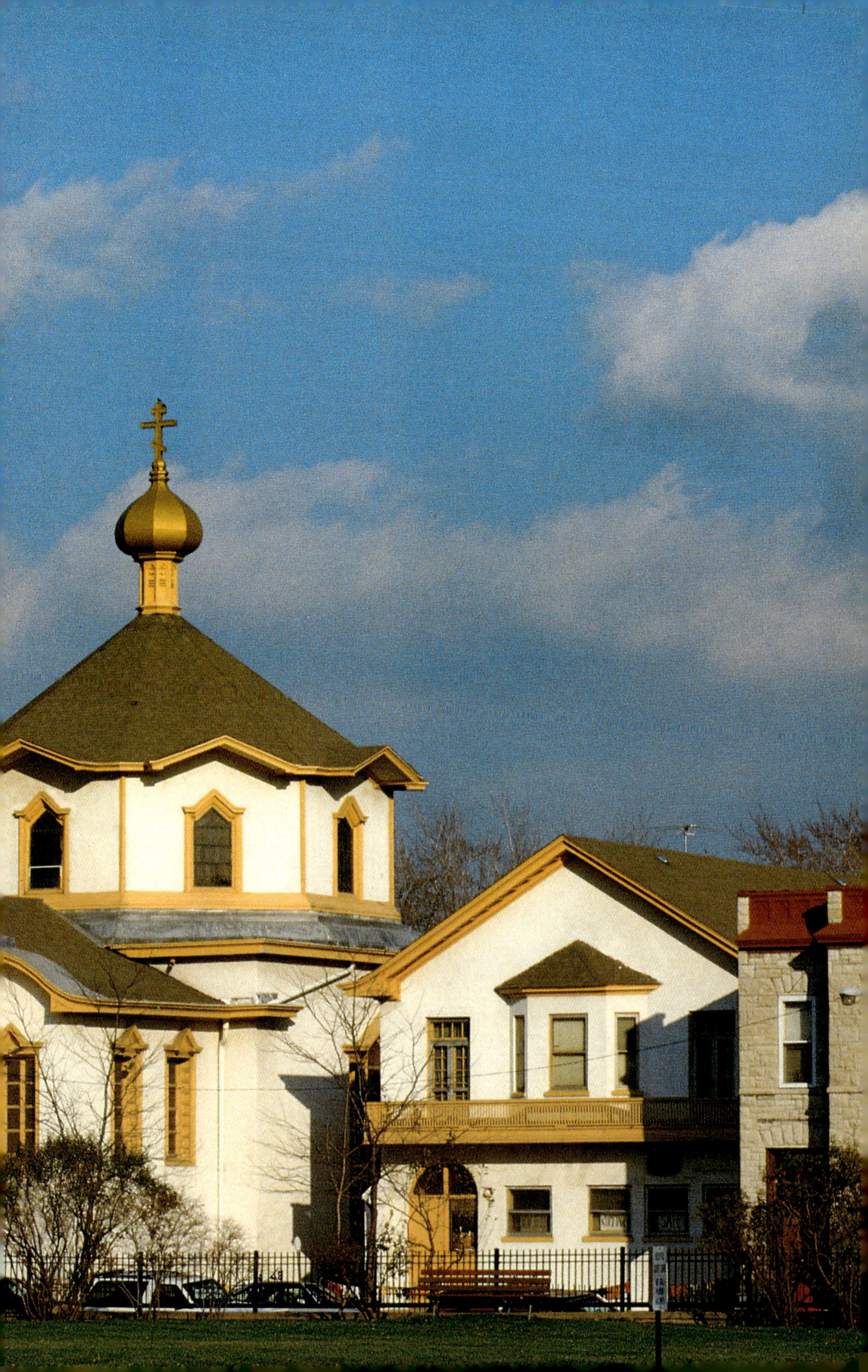

238

DAY TRIPS

A lifelong New Yorker on his first trip to the Midwest had several meetings that took him to small towns outside Chicago. He returned home with the idea of someday moving to one of those towns himself. "I just couldn't believe the relaxed lifestyles, and the way people were so nice to each other," he said. "Sure, they were the type that said 'Have a nice day' to everyone. But you know what? They really meant it. They were friendly and helpful, especially to strangers."

Many travelers, particularly those from abroad whose image of America has been shaped by films, television programs, books and magazines focusing on the big US cities, are pleasantly surprised by their forays beyond the well-beaten concrete paths of the major urban centers. Chicagoans themselves are devoted to what they call day trips, and joining them for a day out is a fine way to rub shoulders. The Loop shows how Chicagoans work; a day trip shows how they play.

Any Chicagoan's list of favorite day trips is likely to include the **Chicago Botanic Garden**. Even the most frenetic commodities trader will be calmed by the 300 peaceful acres of landscaped hills, lakes, wooded areas and many, many gardens.

Romantics may choose the spacious **Rose Garden**, which exhibits some 5,000 rosebushes representing 100 varieties, including All American Rose Selections. Depending on the season, there are rose-growing demonstrations and gardening tips. For those who seek solitude, there is the **Japanese Garden**, set on three serene islands.

Prairie strolls: For the strollers interested in Illinois, there's the **Naturalistic Garden** exhibiting native plants and landscaping, presented in woodland and bird gardens illustrating how the Prairie State used to look.

Children will enjoy the **Natural Trail**, a scenic one-mile path that winds through the oak-hickory forest. There are wild flowers in the spring, brilliant foliage in the fall and frozen beauty in the winter.

From May through September, musicians come from all over the world to play the **Theodore C. Butz Memorial Carillon**. During the concerts, visitors spread blankets on the lawn south of the greenhouses and enjoy a rare treat. A carillon is a musical instrument made up of at least two octaves of cast-bronze bells. The carillonneur plays the bells with his or her hands and feet from a console. The Butz carillon is one of only about 150 true carillons – those played without electrical assistance or amplification – in North America.

For lunch, the Botanic Garden has the Food for Thought Café on the premises, which features healthy snacks such as a fresh seasonal fruit plate and a vegetable-garden submarine sandwich. Those who would rather sit than walk can take

<u>Preceding pages</u>: suburban church. <u>Left</u>, Grant Wood's *American Gothic*. <u>Right</u>, beads and braids.

the **tram tour**, perfect for first-time guests. The 45-minute narrated tour encompasses most of the Botanic Garden. In the winter, the trams are enclosed and heated. There are also bicycle paths throughout the area.

Despite its name, the Chicago Botanic Garden is located 25 miles north of the city in suburban **Glencoe**, a half-mile east of the Edens Expressway on Lake-Cook Road. It picked up its Windy City tag because the park is managed by the Chicago Horticultural Society.

Brookfield: More than 30 years later, a middle-aged Londoner still regales his children – and anyone else who might happen to mention either America or zoos – with stories of his first visit as a boy to Chicago and the big zoo in the suburbs. Particularly vivid are his tales of the giant Kodiak bears, standing on their hind legs to a height of 9 feet and roaring. Several teenagers were tossing slices of bread across the rocky ravine setting off the bear's "natural habitat" enclosure. The boy opened his brown paper bag and handed one of the teenagers a peanut-butter sandwich that promptly went sailing towards a Kodiak. The bear stretched its massive neck a foot or so, snagged the sandwich in its sharp teeth and swallowed the boy's lunch in one gulp. "It was worth missing a meal to see that," the man still says today.

Only 16 miles west of the Magnificent Mile, **Brookfield Zoo** is one of the most respected in the United States. More than 2,000 animals reside on 200 acres. Habitats include the **Small Mammal House** with more than 375 bats and the **Lion House**, one of the original buildings unveiled to the public when the zoo opened in 1934.

Among the most popular exhibits are the **Seven Seas Panorama** and Tropic World. Dolphins perform daily at the Seven Seas complex, a 2,000-seat indoor "dolphinarium" that features tropical plants and interconnected pools holding more than a million gallons of

Chicago Botanic Garden.

saltwater. Outside the arena, strollers can explore the naturalistic rocky shores created to resemble the Pacific Northwest. There, seals and sea lions provide more aquatic entertainment.

Although it's always pleasurable, winter may be the best time to take in **Tropic World** because of the warm indoor temperatures. It is located in a huge building, the size of one-and-a-half football fields. Within are three separate exhibits, each representing rain forests in Asia, South America or Africa, complete with rocks, cliffs and waterfalls. Tropic World was completed in the summer of 1984 at a cost of $11 million. Unlike many zoos, where visitors walk up to the animal cages and then walk away, Tropic World strives for a total environment. Here more than 100 mammals and three dozen birds interact with one another – and with the visitors. Zoological purists may argue that it is not perfectly authentic because there aren't any mosquitos, but few visitors complain.

A recently opened exhibit is the **Fragile Kingdom**. Again, the idea behind the two-acre setting of desert, rain forest and rocky grottos is to create realistic exhibits. These, in turn, aim to help viewers appreciate the African and Asian environments and the animals that inhabit these delicate ecosystems, depending on their surroundings and on one another for survival. Here are the black-backed jackal, the Burmese python and the Siberian tiger, among many other residents.

The size of the Brookfield Zoo is apparent in some of the background statistics. For example, Zoo veterinarians see more than 1,000 patients a year and still make house calls – or rather, cage and cave calls. More than 20,400 bales of hay are used each year – which, if placed end to end, would stretch almost 12 miles. Brookfield visitors consume half a million hamburgers and hot dogs and sip 850,000 soft drinks a year. The gift shops sell more than 50,000 stuffed toy animals

Ice fishermen.

annually for those who want a cuddly memory of the wilds. Brookfield Zoo is located at **1st Avenue** and **31st Street** in west suburban Brookfield and open every day of the year. By car, take either Interstate 55 or Interstate 290 and watch for exit signs for the zoo. By train, take the **Burlington/Metra** to the Zoo Stop at Hollywood Station.

ARLINGTON: Race tracks have never been regarded as the ideal place for children – until the new **Arlington International Racecourse** opened a few years ago. The grand plan has been to make racing a sporting event that brings excitement to sophisticated couples and entire families rather than a gathering place for down-and-outs scuffing their way dejectedly through discarded betting stubs. Richard L. Duchossois, chairman of Arlington since 1983, has not only dedicated himself to rebuilding the racing and breeding industry in Illinois, but to making his racecourse a center for international racing.

Arlington opened in 1927 and had its first full season the following year. For several decades, it stayed ahead of its time with new designs and electronic equipment. By 1941, the course was packing them in and set a one-day attendance record of 50,638 that remains unbroken to this day. Eddie Arcaro became the first American jockey to win 3,000 races with a victory in 1953. And in 1980, Spectacular Bid helped the racecourse set a single-day betting record of $3.5 million.

Tragedy struck on July 31, 1985, when Arlington was destroyed by fire. But out of the ashes came hope and fierce determination and, like Chicago itself, Arlington was rebuilt bigger and better. Duchossois borrowed from Arlington's history of innovations, including air-conditioning and the photo-finish camera. He sent architects touring other international racecourses to determine what was best about them. The result is the present Arlington, reopened in 1989 as an attractive blend of convenience and style. By the end of its first week, the racing industry was already calling it the best in the world.

The racecourse offers free parking and valet parking. There's a great grandstand area, where there's still plenty of room for anxious bettors to press up against the rail on the finishing straight. The green marble floors lead to plushly-appointed private suites and orderly, fast-moving queues for the betting windows. There's warm popcorn and cold beer, plus hot grilled steaks and chilled champagne. Tidiness is ensured by uniformed attendants who scurry around scooping up discarded betting tickets and other litter.

The main theme of the racepark is convenience, as evidenced by 750 television monitors. These are scattered around the grounds and in the stands where visitors cannot see the finishing post. Even the post call is the best around – trumpet player Joe Kelly, who for years led the famous house band at the old Gaslight Club mansion in Chicago, makes the call.

Thrills at Six Flags Great America.

242

Day tripper.

Newcomers feel welcome due to racing exhibits and video programs which help them learn the basics of betting. Duchossois has also created a sense of involvement with special events such as the International Festival of Racing. The biggest races are the Arlington Million, the first Sunday in September, and the Arlington Challenge Cup, in mid-summer.

Arlington International Racecourse is located off Route 53 on **Euclid Avenue**. The season runs from May through early October. Sunday is family day with a petting zoo, puppet shows and pony rides. From downtown Chicago, take Interstate 90 northwest to Route 53. Go north, then exit on Euclid and go east, following the signs. For mass transit, the racetrack can provide information on the special trains and buses operating from downtown Chicago during the racing season.

SIX FLAGS: Among the memories of those Chicago residents over 30 is Riverview Park, a long-time amusement center at Western and Belmont avenues in the heart of the city. In place of those heart-stopping, creaking old wooden roller coasters, which cranked up for the last time in 1967, stands a shopping mall.

But nine years after Riverview closed, **Six Flags Great America** opened. The adventures keep getting better every year. Here's the official description for the **Iron Wolf**, the nation's tallest and fastest looping, stand-up roller coaster, inaugurated in 1990: "Riders who accept the standing challenge will travel down a 90-foot drop reaching speeds up to 55 miles per hour entering a hair-raising 360-degree vertical loop, towering 80 feet into the sky. Dashing from the loop, riders spiral through intertwining hairpin curves, culminating in a spine-tingling corkscrew-type single loop that takes riders nearly parallel to the ground."

If that's not enough, there are plenty of other rides that keep fans lined up. The Demon does an 82-foot vertical

Day Trips 243

drop, a double corkscrew and several vertical loops. The Tidal Wave accelerates to high speeds, then hits a 76-foot-tall vertical loop, forward and then backward.

There are also rides that are only slightly more sedate, such as the Rue Le Dodge bumper cars, or the White Water Rampage rubber boats – great for cooling off in hot weather. For the little ones, there are attractions such as **Bugs Bunny Land** and the grand double-deck carousel with more than 100 gaily-colored animals.

The park is divided into regional theme areas such as **Hometown Square**, **Yankee Harbor** and **Orleans Place**. The colors of the various attractions are vibrant against the bright blue sky, and people watchers will have a great time. For more structured, non-riding entertainment, Great America features the **Pictorium Theatre**, one of the world's largest screens, showing fast-paced action movies of rushing rapids or men in flight. Several theaters around the park offer singing and dancing cartoon characters, high diving acts and Broadway-style reviews.

To get the most out of Great America, a few pointers may prove helpful. Avoid Saturdays and Sundays if at all possible. Get there early. When school's in session, hundreds of children seem to be on field trips. Pick up a map and note the rides and attractions that are most appealing. The park is circular in design, so go in one direction instead of back and forth. Even on what seem to be mild days, bring sun block and a light jacket: the weather can change quickly.

Finally, pack a lunch or pick up some food on the way and leave it in the car for a picnic in the parking lot. The park – and the parking lot – have many food stands, but the prices are high and the quality is probably not as good as whatever you might bring. However, Great America does offer one taste treat, for those who don't mind waiting in lines: the **Funnel Cake Foundry**, located in

Rural Illinois barn.

the County Fair area. Fried dough is funneled into a circle and covered with chocolate, strawberry, cherry, hot caramel or – the favorite – powdered sugar.

Six Flags Great America is located in **Gurnee**, halfway between Chicago and Milwaukee, just off Interstate 94 at Route 132 (Grand Avenue). The season runs from late April through early October. Pets are not allowed at Six Flags, but the park has a boarding facility for a nominal fee. Strollers and wheelchairs are also available on a first-come, first-serve basis for a nominal fee. Cameras can be borrowed with a security deposit.

MILWAUKEE: It's another city and another state, but it's worth a trip of a couple hours into another world: **Milwaukee, Wisconsin**. If driving, take Interstate 94 and just head north. Around **Lincolnshire**, there's an exit sign for **Half Way Road**. It got its name because during the horse-and-buggy days the road marked the half-way point between Chicago and Milwaukee. Drivers today can just follow the signs; downtown to downtown, the journey is only about 90 miles. There's also the train. Amtrak schedules several trains back and forth each day.

Milwaukee is a compact city of 640,000 people. Short walks and cab rides open up a city of old-world charm, uncrowded streets, great German food and beer. For a glimpse of a bygone era, stop off at the **Milwaukee Public Museum**. The Streets of Old Milwaukee exhibit and the European Village offer a respectful sense of the spirit that built this northern city of immigrants. Outside the museum, check out Third Street, between State Street and Highland Avenue, for the **Old World section** of town with its vivid 19th-century architecture.

Across the street from Usinger's Sausage store sits **Mader's**, a Milwaukee classic for more than 90 years. Visited by presidents and presidential candidates, Mader's ranks as one of the most famous German restaurants in North America and has won scores of dining

The Milwaukee horticulture domes.

Day Trips 245

awards. Complete dinners are no longer 20 cents with tip, as they were in 1902, but they remain high in quality and are good value for money. There are several brewery tours in Milwaukee, but if you'd rather hoist a stein, Mader's has a large selection.

Another good place to eat is **Karl Ratzsch's Old World Restaurant**, which provides even more hearty German fare, as well as continental cuisine. From here, head west on Mason to **Water Street**. At 779 N. Front Street, an alley west of Water, between Mason and Wells, there's a tiny office marked "International Exports Limited." Go into the office, follow the instructions and a bookcase will slide open to reveal a secret passage that takes you to the Safe House, a nightclub shrine to Agent 007, spies and espionage. Each area of this unusual bar has a different decor, such as the Mata Hari booth and the Checkpoint Charlie room.

Sports fans can check out the action with the Milwaukee Brewers (baseball) and the Green Bay Packers (football) at **County Stadium**. The Milwaukee Bucks (basketball) and the Milwaukee Admirals (ice hockey) are at the **Milwaukee Exposition, Convention Center and Arena**. Locals tend to call it "the Mecca."

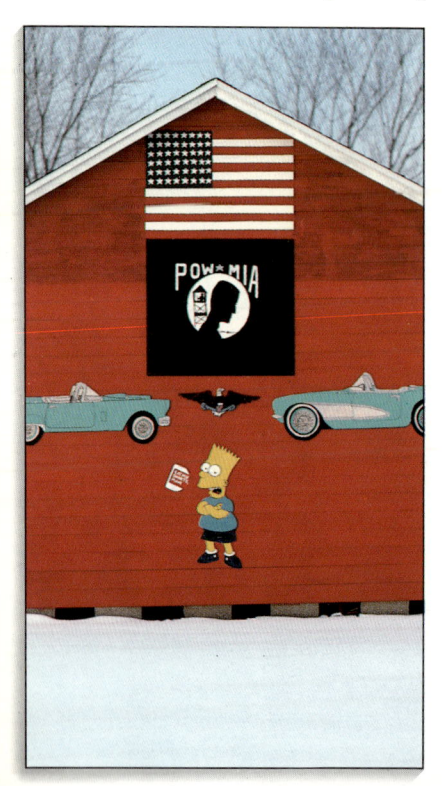

The **Performing Arts Center** showcases theater, ballet and several other cultural events. For outdoor activities, **Summerfest** in early July is an 11-day outdoor party on the lakeshore with plenty of Wisconsin foods, such as roast corn on the cob and grilled bratwursts, and a impressive lineup of well-known entertainers at its jazz, rock, country and main stages.

The **Mitchell Park Horticultural Conservatory** features three massive glass domes, each seven stories high. Inside are tropic, arid and seasonal displays, great for taking pictures. The **Milwaukee County Zoo** rates among the finest zoological parks in the world with some 4,500 animals on exhibit. The **Annunciation Greek Orthodox Church** was the last major building to come off Frank Lloyd Wright's drawing board, and is the scene of an annual July Greekfest.

LAKE GENEVA: One section of Wisconsin, northwest of Chicago on the Illinois-Wisconsin state line, is a walker's dream come true. A gorgeous 26-mile footpath completely circles the glistening waters of **Lake Geneva**. Many hikers choose the sweet-smelling springtime to follow the old trail, tramped out by the original Indian inhabitants; others opt for the season of winter snows to crunch along the icy, but still walkable path.

The trail occasionally cuts through private property, though the courts have ruled that common law over generations has made the path a public right of way. Legally, however, entrance to the footpath itself must come through public property. Veterans suggest **Big Foot Beach Park**, **Lake Geneva Library Park**, **Williams Bay** and **Fontana Beaches** as good entry points.

Left, farmyard art. Right, retired farmer.

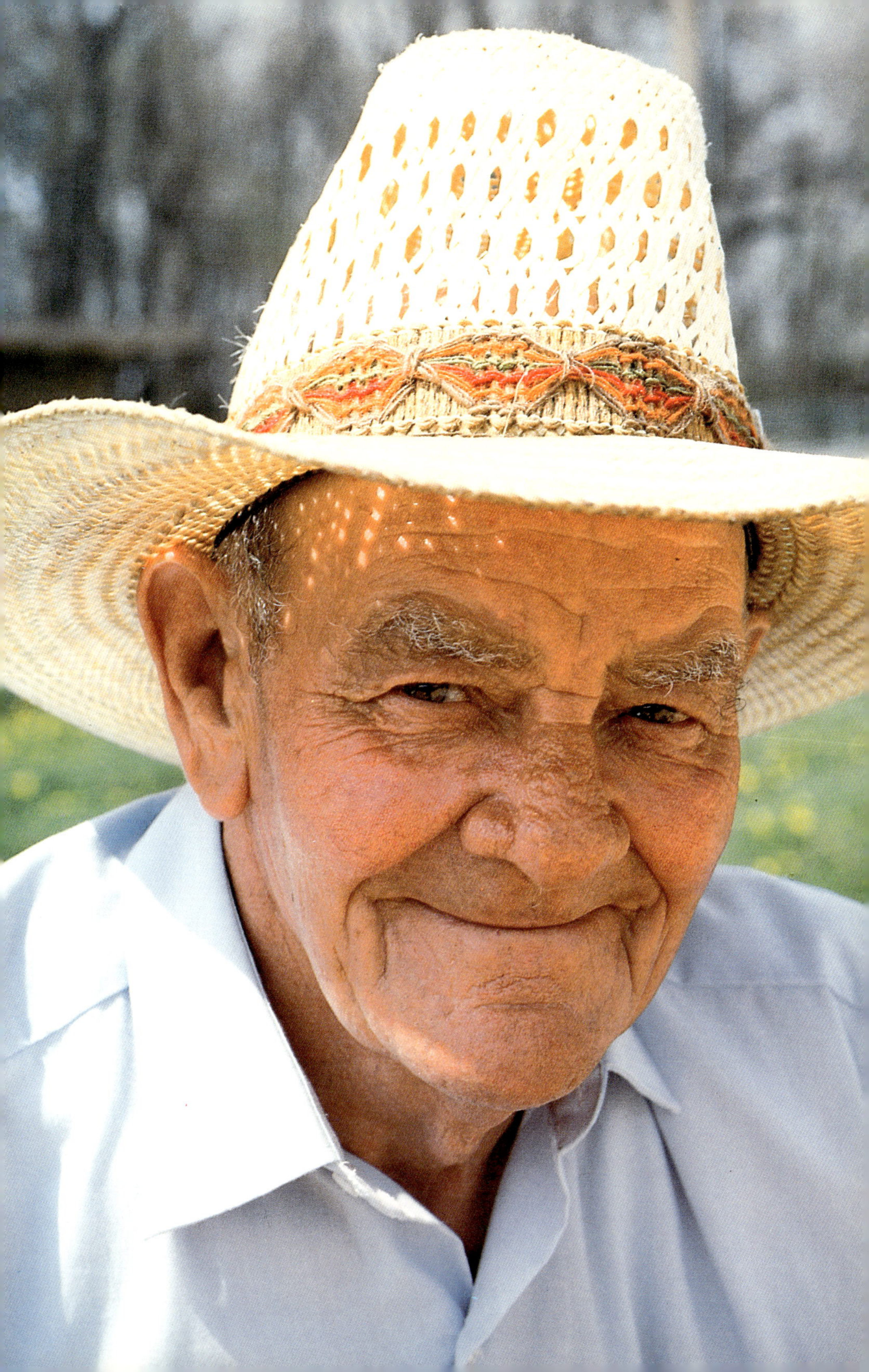

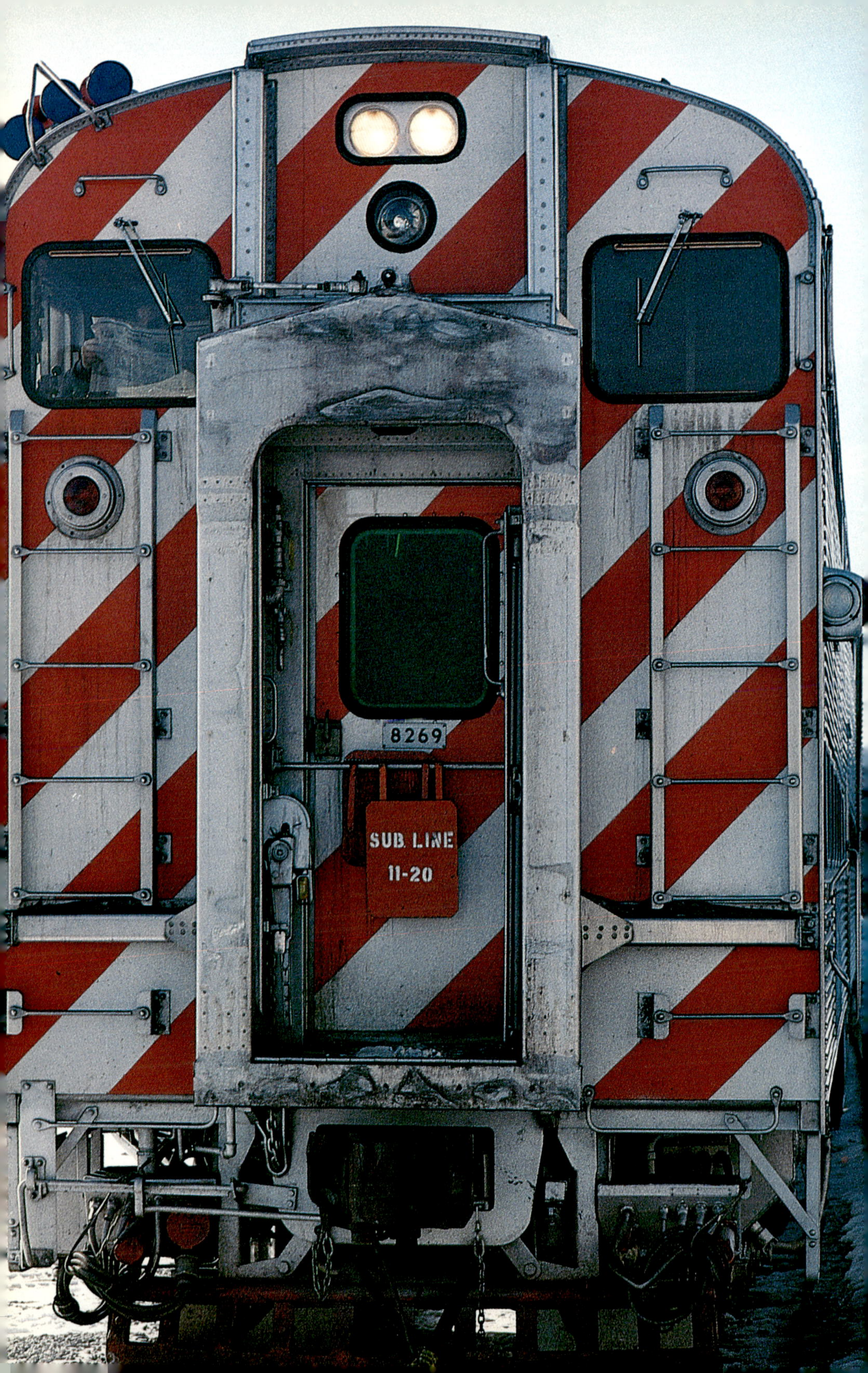
8269
SUB LINE
11-20

INSIGHT GUIDES
Travel Tips

FOR THOSE WITH MORE THAN A PASSING INTEREST IN TIME...

Before you put your name down for a Patek Philippe watch *fig. 1*, there are a few basic things you might like to know, without knowing exactly whom to ask. In addressing such issues as accuracy, reliability and value for money, we would like to demonstrate why the watch we will make for you will be quite unlike any other watch currently produced.

"Punctuality", Louis XVIII was fond of saying, "is the politeness of kings."

We believe that in the matter of punctuality, we can rise to the occasion by making you a mechanical timepiece that will keep its rendezvous with the Gregorian calendar at the end of every century, omitting the leap-years in 2100, 2200 and 2300 and recording them in 2000 and 2400 *fig. 2*. Nevertheless, such a watch does need the occasional adjustment. Every 3333 years and 122 days you should remember to set it forward one day to the true time of the celestial clock. We suspect, however, that you are simply content to observe the politeness of kings. Be assured, therefore, that when you order your watch, we will be exploring for you the physical—if not the metaphysical—limits of precision.

Does everything have to depend on how much?

Consider, if you will, the motives of collectors who set record prices at auction to acquire a Patek Philippe. They may be paying for rarity, for looks or for micromechanical ingenuity. But we believe that behind each $500,000-plus bid is the conviction that a Patek Philippe, even if 50 years old or older, can be expected to work perfectly for future generations.

In case your ambitions to own a Patek Philippe are somewhat discouraged by the scale of the sacrifice involved, may we hasten to point out that the watch we will make for you today will certainly be a technical improvement on the Pateks bought at auction? In keeping with our tradition of inventing new mechanical solutions for greater reliability and better time-keeping, we will bring to your watch innovations *fig. 3* inconceivable to our watchmakers who created the supreme wristwatches of 50 years ago *fig. 4*. At the same time, we will of course do our utmost to avoid placing undue strain on your financial resources.

Can it really be mine?

May we turn your thoughts to the day you take delivery of your watch? Sealed within its case is your watchmaker's tribute to the mysterious process of time. He has decorated each wheel with a chamfer carved into its hub and polished into a shining circle. Delicate ribbing flows over the plates and bridges of gold and rare alloys. Millimetric surfaces are bevelled and burnished to exactitudes measured in microns. Rubies are transformed into jewels that triumph over friction. And after many months—or even years—of work, your watchmaker stamps a small badge into the mainbridge of your watch. The Geneva Seal—the highest possible attestation of fine watchmaking *fig. 5*.

Looks that speak of inner grace *fig. 6*.

When you order your watch, you will no doubt like its outward appearance to reflect the harmony and elegance of the movement within. You may therefore find it helpful to know that we are uniquely able to cater for any special decorative needs you might like to express. For example, our engravers will delight in conjuring a subtle play of light and shadow on the gold case-back of one of our rare pocket-watches *fig. 7*. If you bring us your favourite picture, our enamellers will reproduce it in a brilliant miniature of hair-breadth detail *fig. 8*. The perfect execution of a double hobnail pattern on the bezel of a wristwatch is the pride of our casemakers and the satisfaction of our designers, while our chainsmiths will weave for you a rich brocade in gold *figs. 9 & 10*. May we also recommend the artistry of our goldsmiths and the experience of our lapidaries in the selection and setting of the finest gemstones? *figs. 11 & 12*.

How to enjoy your watch before you own it.

As you will appreciate, the very nature of our watches imposes a limit on the number we can make available. (The four Calibre 89 time-pieces we are now making will take up to nine years to complete). We cannot therefore promise instant gratification, but while you look forward to the day on which you take delivery of your Patek Philippe *fig. 13*, you will have the pleasure of reflecting that time is a universal and everlasting commodity, freely available to be enjoyed by all.

Should you require information on any particular Patek Philippe watch, or even on watchmaking in general, we would be delighted to reply to your letter of enquiry. And if you send us

fig. 1: The classic face of Patek Philippe.

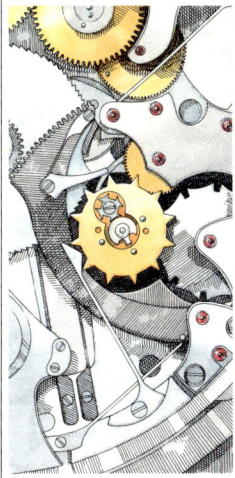

fig. 2: One of the 33 complications of the Calibre 89 astronomical clock-watch is a satellite wheel that completes one revolution every 400 years.

fig. 3: Recognized as the most advanced mechanical regulating device to date, Patek Philippe's Gyromax balance wheel demonstrates the equivalence of simplicity and precision.

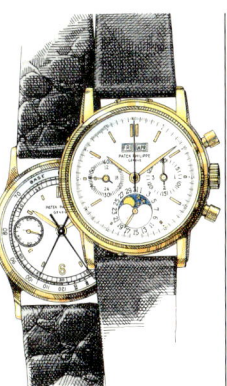

fig. 4: Complicated wristwatches circa 1930 (left) and 1990. The golden age of watchmaking will always be with us.

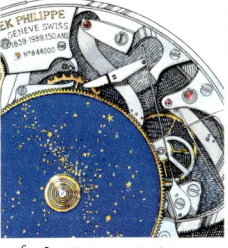

fig. 5: The Geneva Seal is awarded only to watches which achieve the standards of horological purity laid down in the laws of Geneva. These rules define the supreme quality of watchmaking.

fig. 6: Your pleasure in owning a Patek Philippe is the purpose of those who made it for you.

fig. 7: Arabesques come to life on a gold case-back.

fig. 8: An artist working six hours a day takes about four months to complete a miniature in enamel on the case of a pocket-watch.

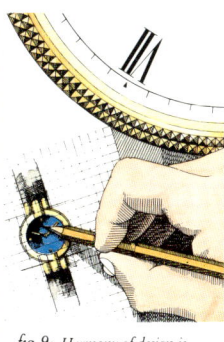

fig. 9: Harmony of design is executed in a work of simplicity and perfection in a lady's Calatrava wristwatch.

fig. 10: The chainsmith's hands impart strength and delicacy to a tracery of gold.

fig. 11: Circles in gold: symbols of perfection in the making.

fig. 12: The test of a master lapidary is his ability to express the splendour of precious gemstones.

PATEK PHILIPPE
GENEVE
fig. 13: The discreet sign of those who value their time.

your card marked "book catalogue" we shall post you a catalogue of our publications. Patek Philippe, 41 rue du Rhône, 1204 Geneva, Switzerland, Tel. +41 22/310 03 66.

INSIGHT GUIDES

COLORSET NUMBERS

North America
160 **A**laska
173 **A**merican Southwest
184I **A**tlanta
227 **B**oston
275 **C**alifornia
180 **C**alifornia, Northern
161 **C**alifornia, Southern
237 **C**anada
184C **C**hicago
184 **C**rossing America
243 **F**lorida
240 **H**awaii
275A **L**os Angeles
243A **M**iami
237B **M**ontreal
184G **N**ational Parks of America: East
184H **N**ational Parks of America: West
269 **N**ative America
100 **N**ew England
184E **N**ew Orleans
184F **N**ew York City
133 **N**ew York State
147 **P**acific Northwest
184B **P**hiladelphia
172 **R**ockies
275A **S**an Francisco
184D **S**eattle
 Southern States of America
186 **T**exas
237A **V**ancouver
184C **W**ashington DC

Latin America and The Caribbean
150 **A**mazon Wildlife
260 **A**rgentina
188 **B**ahamas
292 **B**arbados
251 **B**elize
217 **B**ermuda
127 **B**razil
260A **B**uenos Aires
162 **C**aribbean
151 **C**hile
281 **C**osta Rica
282 **C**uba
118 **E**cuador
213 **J**amaica
285 **M**exico
285A **M**exico City
249 **P**eru
156 **P**uerto Rico
127A **R**io de Janeiro
116 **S**outh America
139 **T**rinidad & Tobago
198 **V**enezuela

Europe
155 **A**lsace
158A **A**msterdam
167A **A**thens
263 **A**ustria
107 **B**altic States

219B **B**arcelona
1187 **B**ay of Naples
109 **B**elgium
135A **B**erlin
178 **B**rittany
109A **B**russels
144A **B**udapest
213 **B**urgundy
122 **C**atalonia
141 **C**hannel Islands
135E **C**ologne
119 **C**ontinental Europe
189 **C**orsica
291 **C**ôte d'Azur
165 **C**rete
226 **C**yprus
114 **C**zech/Slovak Reps
238 **D**enmark
135B **D**resden
142B **D**ublin
135F **D**üsseldorf
149 **E**astern Europe
148A **E**dinburgh
123 **F**inland
209B **F**lorence
154 **F**rance
135C **F**rankfurt
135 **G**ermany
148B **G**lasgow
279 **G**ran Canaria
124 **G**reat Britain
167 **G**reece
166 **G**reek Islands
135G **H**amburg
144 **H**ungary
256 **I**celand
142 **I**reland
209 **I**taly
202A **L**isbon
258 **L**oire Valley
124A **L**ondon
201 **M**adeira
219A **M**adrid
157 **M**allorca & Ibiza
117 **M**alta
101A **M**oscow
135D **M**unich
158 **N**etherlands
111 **N**ormandy
120 **N**orway
124B **O**xford
154A **P**aris
115 **P**oland
202 **P**ortugal
114A **P**rague
153 **P**rovence
177 **R**hine
209A **R**ome
101 **R**ussia
130 **S**ardinia
148 **S**cotland
261 **S**icily
264 **S**outh Tyrol
219 **S**pain
220 **S**pain, Southern
101B **S**t. Petersburg
170 **S**weden
232 **S**witzerland

112 **T**enerife
210 **T**uscany
174 **U**mbria
209C **V**enice
263A **V**ienna
267 **W**ales
183 **W**aterways of Europe

Middle East and Africa
268A **C**airo
204 **E**ast African Wildlife
268 **E**gypt
208 **G**ambia & Senegal
252 **I**srael
236A **I**stanbul
252A **J**erusalem-Tel Aviv
214 **J**ordan
270 **K**enya
235 **M**orocco
259 **N**amibia
265 **N**ile, The
257 **S**outh Africa
113 **T**unisia
236 **T**urkey
171 **T**urkish Coast
215 **Y**emen

Asia/Pacific
287 **A**sia, East
207 **A**sia, South
262 **A**sia, South East
194 **A**sian Wildlife, Southeast
272 **A**ustralia
206 **B**ali Baru
246A **B**angkok
234A **B**eijing
247B **C**alcutta
234 **C**hina
247A **D**elhi, Jaipur, Agra
169 **G**reat Barrier Reef
196 **H**ong Kong
247 **I**ndia
212 **I**ndia, South
128 **I**ndian Wildlife
143 **I**ndonesia
278 **J**apan
266 **J**ava
203A **K**athmandu
300 **K**orea
145 **M**alaysia
218 **M**arine Life in the South China Sea
272B **M**elbourne
211 **M**yanmar
203 **N**epal
293 **N**ew Zealand
205 **P**akistan
222 **P**hilippines
250 **R**ajasthan
159 **S**ingapore
105 **S**ri Lanka
272 **S**ydney
175 **T**aiwan
246 **T**hailand
278A **T**okyo
255 **V**ietnam
193 **W**estern Himalaya

TRAVEL TIPS

Getting Acquainted
The Place 250
Time Zones 250
Climate 250
The People 250
The Government & Economy ... 250

Planning the Trip
What to Bring 251
What to Wear 251
Entry Regulations 251
Health 251
Currency 251
Public Holidays 251
Getting There 252
Special Facilities 253

Practical Tips
Emergencies 254
Business Hours 254
Tipping 254
Religious Services 254
Media 255
Postal Services 255
Phones & Faxes 255
Tourists Information 256
Consulates 256

Getting Around
Orientation 256
From the Airport 257
Domestic Travel 257
Public Transportation 257
Walking & Cycling 257
Hitchhiking 258
On Departure 258

Where to Stay
Hotels 258
Bed & Breakfast 259
Youth Hostels 259

Eating Out
What to Eat 259
Where to Eat 259
Drinking Notes 263

Attractions
Culture 263
City 265
Suburbs 266
Tours 266
Recommended for Children 267
Diary of Events 268
Nightlife 269

Shopping
Shopping Areas 270

Sports & Leisure
Participant 271
Spectator 271

Further Reading
General 272
Other Insight Guides 272

Art/Photo Credits 273
Index 274

Getting Acquainted

Unless otherwise stated, all telephone numbers are preceded by the area code (312). Attractions in the suburbs have various codes; it's always a good ideal to check. The number (800) indicates a toll-free call.

The Place
Geography & Population

Chicago is located in the northeast corner of Illinois in the section of the United States referred to as the Midwest. It's situated on the Great Lakes, at the southwest tip of **Lake Michigan**, which makes up the city's entire eastern border. The city's other large waterway is the Chicago River. About 100 years ago a decision was made to reverse the river's flow, so now water flows to the Illinois River, instead of into the lake. (On St Patrick's Day, the river is dyed green, though some say they can't tell any difference).

Most of the land in and around Chicago is flat, as is much of the Midwest. Perhaps it was the lack of hills that contributed to the desire for tall buildings, and eventually led to the much-recognized skyline of Chicago.

Although Chicago is the best-known city in Illinois, it is not the capital. That honor goes to **Springfield**, located 200 miles to the south in the middle of the state. Of approximately 11.5 million people in Illinois, 7.5 million live in the Chicago area. The population of Chicago alone is almost 3 million.

For inhabitants of a big city, Chicagoans are often surprisingly friendly and an encounter with a foreign visitor is almost always reason enough to stop and have a chat. The makeup of the city is a reflection of its many neighborhoods. The most recent available analysis breaks the population down as follows: whites 38 percent, African-Americans 39 percent, Hispanics 20 percent, Asians and others 4 percent. The Hispanics represent the fastest-growing ethnic group.

Time Zones

Chicago is in the **Central Time Zone**, which is one hour behind New York, two hours ahead of California and six hours behind Greenwich Mean Time. On the last Sunday in April the clock is moved ahead an hour for daylight savings time, and on the last Sunday in October it's moved back an hour to return to standard time.

When it's noon in Chicago (Standard Time) it is:
8am in Hawaii
10am in California
1pm in New York and Montreal
6pm in London
10pm in Moscow
2am (the next day) in Singapore and Hong Kong
3am (the next day) in Tokyo

Climate

Chicago is a great place to experience all four seasons. Summers get quite hot and humid, but it's usually cooler near the lake (as mentioned in almost every weather forecast) because of cooling breezes coming off Lake Michigan. Winter in Chicago means cold temperatures, often with snow. Spring brings its share of rain, but the temperatures are usually moderate, as in the autumn.

Average daily Fahrenheit high temperatures in Chicago:

Month	Temperature
January	29°F
February	34°F
March	44°F
April	59°F
May	70°F
June	79°F
July	85°F
August	82°F
September	75°F
October	64°F
November	48°F
December	35°F

Updated recorded weather reports can be heard by calling 976-1212.

To convert Fahrenheit to Centigrade temperatures, deduct 32, multiply by 5, divide by 9. To convert Centigrade to Fahrenheit, multiply by 9, divide by 5, and add 32.

Centigrade	Fahrenheit
0	32 (Freezing)
15	59
20	68
25	77
30	86
37	99
100	212 (Boiling)

The People
Culture & Customs

Chicagoans are often friendly, but their forwardness sometimes puts off foreigners, and even visitors from other parts of America, who regard them as brash or harsh in speech and manner. Courtesy is appreciated, but so is bluntness – getting to the point, saying what you mean and meaning what you say. Conversations with strangers can sometimes take surprisingly personal turns.

Good service is expected and received throughout Chicago, and visitors should never hesitate to ask for assistance, even if it is for something out of the ordinary. Unusual requests may deserve a tip or gratuity of some sort. Even if "something extra" is declined, Chicagoans won't take offense that it has been offered.

Reservations

Chicago is generally an informal town, but it's also the kind of place where people go out a lot. That means reservations are recommended – sometimes well in advance – for the most popular theaters, restaurants and special events with limited seating.

The Government & Economy

Chicago has a city council form of government. The city council is headed by the mayor. The city is divided into 50 wards, based on the population, each with about 60,000 residents. Each ward is represented by an elected alderman, who is part of the council. In theory, this is a "strong council, weak mayor" system. In reality, the mayor of Chicago wields a great deal of power.

The entire city of Chicago is located in **Cook County**. Cook County is governed by the Cook County Board, which is made up of 17 members; 10 from Chicago, and 7 from the suburbs. The board is headed by a president, who is one of the 17 members.

Both Chicago and Cook County have "home rule," which allows them to decide many local issues, such as taxation, without approval from the state Legislature in Springfield, Illinois.

Although the southern part of Illinois has a lot of agriculture, Chicago's economy is based on big business. **The Loop** is generally regarded as the business and commercial district. LaSalle Street is the financial district, regarded as the "Wall Street" of the Midwest and the home of the commodities exchanges that influence world production and prices of agricultural and other products.

Besides white-collar industries such as insurance, accounting, publishing and state-government administration, Chicago is also one of the retail capitals of America, which is demonstrated vividly along wealthy shopping streets such as Michigan Avenue's "**Magnificent Mile**."

As in most large cities, there is a wide gap between the richest and the poorest people in Chicago, though the overall standard of living is quite high. Much of Chicago depends on a service economy, and good, prompt service is regarded as the norm rather than something out of the ordinary.

Planning the Trip

What to Bring

Maps

Rand McNally has a number of good maps of Chicago, and most bookstores and souvenir shops offer a variety. Especially recommended is *Chicago, Illinois: Visitors Guide and Birds-Eye View*.

The CTA publishes a transit map that can also serve as a good guide to the streets in the city. It can be requested from CTA (Chicago Transit Authority), Merchandise Mart, Chicago, Illinois 60654.

Electricity

The standard for the United States is 110 volts DC. Electrical plugs have two flat pins. European appliances may need converters, but some hotels supply them. Guests staying in hotels that supply in-house hair dryers can leave theirs at home.

What to Wear

It's pretty much "anything goes" for clothing in Chicago. For daytime sightseeing and casual meals, shorts and a T-shirt in summer or jeans and a sweatshirt in winter are acceptable. Comfortable walking shoes are an absolute must.

Somewhat dressier clothes are recommended for some dinner and nighttime activities. For the smarter restaurants or theaters, men should wear jackets and ties, and women dresses.

In summer, bring a bathing suit to enjoy the beaches along Lake Michigan, and be prepared for hot, humid weather. Because it's cooler in the evening, especially near the lake, a light jacket is recommended. In winter, everyone needs a warm coat, hat, gloves, and, in case of snow, a pair of good boots.

Entry Regulations

Visas and Passports

To enter the United States, travelers must have a valid passport. Before departing from their own countries, foreign visitors should contact the nearest United States Embassy or Consulate for information on whether a visa is necessary.

Customs

After picking up their baggage, visitors need to present customs documents which are usually passed out on planes but can be picked up at the customs desks. The time it takes to clear customs can be anywhere from a few minutes to an hour, depending on how many travelers are arriving at the same time and how many agents are on duty.

Narcotics and many foods cannot be brought into the United States. Other items might not be permitted depending on the traveler's origin. Pets are allowed, though they must have proof that their inoculations are current. Personal possessions are not normally liable for duty for US visitors, provided they intend to take them out of the country with them. There are limits, however, on tobacco, alcohol and certain foreign products; Cuban cigars are banned, for example, because of a US trade embargo. Visitors who are not sure should check with their travel agents or US consulates before leaving home.

Health

Chicago can be extremely hot and humid in summer, and extremely cold and snowy in winter. The weather can change dramatically within minutes in any season, so it's best to be prepared for anything. During the summer months insects, and particularly pesky mosquitos, can be a problem, especially in areas of woods or ponds. There is no national health service in the United States and some hospitals or clinics will not provide treatment without assurances of payment, so foreigners may want to purchase private medical insurance in advance.

Currency

Bureaux de change are relatively rare in America. To obtain US dollars at **O'Hare Airport**, there is a foreign currency exchange in the International Terminal that is open from 10am–8pm daily and exchanges about 40 of the major currencies. Tel: 686-7965.

Another source for exchanging currency is **American Express**, which has a number of offices in Chicago, including one at 625 N. Michigan Avenue, tel: 435-2570. Some large banks also have currency exchange windows. Take along your passport if cashing travelers checks.

Public Holidays

Many government agencies, local banks and businesses close during the holidays listed:
January 1: New Year's Day
January 15: Martin Luther King's Birthday
February 12: Abraham Lincoln's Birthday
3rd Monday in February: George Washington's Birthday
Last Monday in May: Memorial Day
July 4: Independence Day
1st Monday in September: Labor Day

2nd Monday in October: Columbus Day
1st Tuesday in November: Election Day
November 11: Veterans' Day
4th Thursday in November: Thanksgiving
December 25: Christmas

Festivals

Chicago has many annual festivals, often with an ethnic flavor that combines food, music, entertainment, the arts and culture.

JANUARY

Chinese New Year Parade, Wentworth Avenue and Cermak Road, tel: 326-5320.

MARCH

St Patrick's Day, Parade starts at Dearborn Street and Wacker Drive, tel: 263-6612.
South Side Irish Parade, 103rd Street and Western Avenue, tel: 238-1969. Celebrated the weekend before St Patrick's Day.

JUNE

International Theater Festival of Chicago, various theaters, tel: 644-3370.
Chicago Gospel Festival, Petrillo Band Shell, Grant Park, tel: 744-3315.
Chicago Blues Festival, Petrillo Band Shell, Grant Park, tel: 744-3315.
Water Tower Arts and Crafts Festival, Chicago Avenue between Michigan Avenue and Lake Shore Drive, tel: 991-4748.
Taste of Chicago, Grant Park, tel: 744-3315. June 27–July 4. A very popular event, featuring lots of food from a variety of Chicago restaurants. Music, too.

JULY

Taste of Chicago, continues in Grant Park, tel: 744-3315. This festival culminates with a spectacular fireworks display over Lake Michigan, accompanied by the Grant Park Symphony Orchestra performing Tchaikovsky's 1812 Overture.
Fourth of July, fireworks on the lakefront and in almost every Chicago neighborhood.
Air and Water Show, North Avenue Beach, tel: 294-2200.
Taste of Lincoln Avenue, food fair between Fullerton and Wrightwood Avenues, tel: 472-9046.
Old St Patrick's World's Largest Block Party, Adams and Des Plaines streets, tel: 782-6171.

AUGUST

Venetian Night Boat Parade, Monroe Harbor, tel: 744-3315.
Antique Show, O'Hare Expo Center, tel: (708) 692-2220.
Chicago Jazz Festival, Petrillo Band Shell, Grant Park, tel: 744-3315.
Illinois State Fair, Springfield (not Chicago), tel: (217) 782-6661.

SEPTEMBER

Viva Chicago, Grant Park, tel: 744-3315.
Ribfest, Grant Park, tel: 222-3232. Backyard chefs compete for the title of best barbecue artist in town.
Berghoff Oktoberfest, Adams Street, from State Street to Dearborn Street, tel: 427-3170.

OCTOBER

Columbus Day Parade, Dearborn Street and Wacker Drive, tel: 828-0010.
Chicago International Film Festival, international films shown at various theaters, tel: 644-3400.
History Mystery Bicycle Tour and Festival, 96th Street and Longwood Drive, tel: 233-3100. A puzzle-solving bicycle tour, followed by food, music and games.

NOVEMBER

Christmas Around the World, Museum of Science and Industry, tel: 684-1414. A popular display of Christmas trees as decorated in various countries.
Lighting of the City's Christmas Tree, Daley Center Plaza, tel: 744-3315.
Christmas Parade, Michigan Avenue from Balbo Avenue to Wacker Drive, tel: 935-8747.

DECEMBER

Caroling to the Animals, Lincoln Park Zoo, tel: 294-4662.
Christmas Flower Show, Lincoln Park Conservatory, tel: 294-4770.

Getting There

By Air

Chicago, served by many major American and foreign air carriers, is the home of the world's busiest airport. **O'Hare International Airport** is located about 18 miles from downtown on the Kennedy Expressway (Interstates 90 and 94) at Mannheim Road. It has an international terminal and three domestic terminals. There are information booths on the upper level of each terminal and outside the "Meeter-Greeter" area of the international terminal. There is a foreign currency exchange in the international terminal. Tel: 686-2200 for general airport information. It's ordinarily a 20-minute trip by car between the airport and downtown but traffic is so unpredictable, especially during rush hour, that it's advisable to allow at least an hour for travel time.

Continental Air Transport, tel: 454-7800, provides bus service between the airport baggage claim area and about 35 downtown hotels. Many hotels provide their own shuttle service, so inquire when making reservations. Taxis are available on the lower level of each terminal. Limousine service or car rentals can be arranged in advance or at the booths near the baggage claim area. Probably the cheapest way to get downtown, and the surest way to avoid traffic jams, is the **Chicago Transit Authority** (CTA) Rapid Transit line which is located under Terminal 4. The trains run frequently to and from the Dearborn Street station downtown.

Midway Airport, 5700 S. Cicero Avenue, a smaller, less crowded alternative to O'Hare for domestic flights, is located about 7 miles southwest of downtown. Its one building is divided into three terminals. Information is available at tel: 767-0500. Continental Air Transport provides bus service between this airport and about a dozen downtown hotels. Tel: 454-7800 to find out times. The reservation booth is in Concourse A, while boarding is at the main terminal. Taxis are available in front of the main (middle) terminal. Limos and car rentals are available near the baggage claim area. Some hotels provide their own shuttle service. There is no direct CTA line.

By Rail

Chicago is serviced by **Amtrak**, a passenger line offering nationwide service. Tel: (800)-USA-RAIL. Amtrak comes in to Chicago's **Union Station** at Jackson and Canal streets, tel: 558-1075.

By Bus

Greyhound/Trailways has nationwide service to its main terminal in the Loop (downtown), at Clark and Randolph streets. It also has two neighborhood stations: the 95th Street and Dan Ryan Expressway CTA station on the south side; and the Cumberland CTA station at 5800 N. Cumberland Avenue on the northwest side near **O'Hare Airport.** Tel: 781-2900 for fares and schedule information.

By Car

The major east–west route across northern Illinois is **Interstate 80**, which passes near Chicago from Indiana to the east or Iowa to the west. Coming from the north, the main **interstates** are **90** and **94**, which merge about 10 miles north of downtown to form the **Kennedy Expressway** (I-90/94), a direct route into downtown. **I-57** runs across the state from the south, and connects with the **Dan Ryan Expressway** (I-90/94) for the downtown area.

Special Facilities
Physically Challenged

Chicago tries to make itself accessible to the handicapped. Almost all the museums and many restaurants have wheelchair access. The City of Chicago Department on Aging and Disability offers information and referral at tel: 744-4016 (TDD & Voice), or tel: 744-6777 (TDD only). The city also offers a 24-hour information hotline for those with impaired hearing, tel: 744-8599 (TDD).

Door-to-door transportation can be arranged for those with limited mobility through special services, tel: 521-1154. It can be difficult to get rides at certain times, so try to plan ahead. It would be wise to have a statement from a doctor verifying the disability. Access Living, although aimed primarily at residents, will provide assistance with travel for visitors.

Contact Access Living, 851 W. Van Buren Street, Suite 525, Chicago, IL 60607, tel: 226-5900. Wheelchair Getaways of Illinois, Inc, PO Box 338, Wilmette, tel: (708) 671-3376 leases vans specially converted for wheelchair users.

Alternative Lifestyles

The hub of Chicago's gay community is Lakeview East, or New Town as it's often called. Halsted, Broadway and Clark Streets between Diversey and Addison Streets is the approximate area for many shops owned and supported by gays.

The City of Chicago has a gay liaison officer who can be contacted on 744-4152.

Gay and Lesbian Pride Week is celebrated each year in late June, and culminates with a popular gay and lesbian pride parade.

Gays are very much a part of everyday life in Chicago, but there are also many places, organizations and publications that specialize in gay life.

Gay Publications

Windy City Times, 970 W. Montana, tel: 935-1974.
Outlines, 3059 N. Southport Avenue, tel: 871-7610.
Gay Chicago Magazine, 3121 N. Broadway, tel: 327-7271.

Gay Community Service

Horizons Community Services, Inc., 3225 N. Sheffield Avenue, has a gay and lesbian helpline, tel: 929-4357, offering confidential counseling and references.
Howard Brown Memorial Clinic, 945 W. George Street, tel: 871-5777, provides confidential diagnosis and treatment.

Gay Politics

Illinois Gay and Lesbian Task Force, 615 W. Wellington Avenue, tel: 975-0707, is an organization involved in civil rights issues and educating the public.

Gay Choruses

Chicago Gay Men's Chorus, tel: 275-7295.
Windy City Gay Chorus, tel: 404-9242.

Gay Library

Gerber-Hart Library, 3352 N. Paulina, tel: 883-3003. This is Chicago's premier gay and lesbian library and resource center. Gerber-Hart's circulating collection consists of nearly 6,000 books and periodicals, plus an archive.

Gay Bars

There are many bars in the Lakeview East area. Some are strictly gay or lesbian, others welcome all. Wander through the neighborhood, or pick up one of the publications that lists area bars. Some possibilities:
The Legacy, 3042 W. Irving Park Road, tel: 588-9405. Opened since 1961, formerly the "21 Club."
Lost and Found, 3058 W. Irving Park Road, tel: 463-9617. Opened in 1965, a lesbian bar.
Vortex Nightclub, 3631 N. Halsted, tel: 975-6622. Nightclub and dance bar with light show. Multi-level complex. Theme parties.

Doing Business

If you're interested in doing business in Chicago, or starting a business in Chicago, there are many sources of information:
Illinois Department of Commerce and Community Affairs, International Business Division, tel: (312) 814-7164.
Chicagoland Chamber of Commerce, tel: (312) 580-6900.
International Visitors' Center, tel: (312) 645-1836. Resources and contacts at all levels in business. They can also help you set up itineraries, especially for groups.

Language

Some hotels can provide translators, and many employ a concierge or other staff who may be multilingual.

The following firms can provide translation services or an interpreter:
Advance Language, 333 N. Michigan Avenue, tel: 782-8123.
Berlitz Translation Services, 845 N. Michigan Avenue, tel: 943-5178.
International Language and Communications Center, Inc., 79 W. Monroe Street, tel: 236-3366.

Complaints

For help with a problem, or to file a complaint, some contacts are:
Better Business Bureau, tel: 346-3313. 10am–2.30pm.
City of Chicago Consumer Information and Complaints, tel: 744-9400.
Governor's Office of Consumer Affairs, tel: (800) 814-2754.

If the complaint is serious enough to require legal assistance, the following service will make referrals to lawyers who are registered with the service.
Illinois Lawyer Referral Service, tel: (800) 252-8916.

Practical Tips

Emergencies

Security & Crime

Gangsters no longer roam the streets of Chicago with their tommyguns, but there are some very real security risks in the city today – especially in some of the lower income neighborhoods, or in the less populated downtown areas late at night.

Visitors who stick to the main hotel, shopping and tourist areas have little cause for concern. The more adventurous who set off to explore Chicago's neighborhoods should first seek the advice of locals. Most areas are safe and friendly but a few, particularly in the public housing areas of the West Side and South Side, are not.

Hotel rooms and cars should be locked when not in use, of course. Don't leave valuables in hotel rooms; use the hotel safe instead. Joggers should stick to daytime routes in well-populated areas.

As in other big cities everywhere, pickpockets are drawn to large crowds, such as those at festivals, concerts and sporting events. Don't carry large amounts of cash or credit cards. Wallets should be carried in inside pockets, and women should keep a hand on their purses. Similarly, purses should not be hung off the backs of chairs in restaurants. If there is a theft or attack, dail 911. The police are prompt and courteous.

Left Luggage

Most airports, train and bus terminals have left-luggage rooms or coin-operated lockers. Most hotels also have a left-luggage room for that last day of stay when visitors must check out but have a few hours to kill before leaving town.

Medical Services

In an emergency, dial 911.

For Ambulance Dispatch (24-hour), tel: (708) AMT-9898.

For a non-emergency, call the Medical Referral Service, tel: 670-2550.

For **dental care**, the Chicago Dental Society emergency service can help 24 hours a day. Monday–Friday 9am–5pm, tel: 836-7300; all other hours, tel: 726-4321.

Poison control is handled at Rush-Presbyterian – St Luke's, tel: 942-5969. Can also be called toll free on 1-800-942-5969.

AREA HOSPITALS

Loop: Rush-Presbyterian–St Luke's Hospital, 1753 W. Congress Parkway, tel: 942-5000. Cook County Hospital, 1835 W. Harrison, tel: 633-6000.

North: Northwestern Memorial, Superior Street and Franklin Court, tel: 908-2000.

South: Michael Reese, 31st and Lake Shore Drive, tel: 791-2000.

Some pharmacies with long hours are: Walgreens, 757 N. Michigan Avenue, tel; 664-8686; Perry Drugs, 990 W. Fullerton, tel; 975-0339; Cosmopolitan Drugs, 754 N. Clark Street, tel; 787-2152.

Weights & Measures

The United States, unlike most of the world, uses the imperial system for measurements. Although the metric system is slowly working its way into usage, it's still not widespread. Therefore, some basic conversions might prove helpful:

1 ounce = 28.5 grams
1 pound (16 ounces) = 453 grams
1 pint = 0.568 liter
1 quart = 1.137 liters
1 gallon = 4.5 liters
1 inch = 2.54 centimeters
1 foot (12 inches) = 0.3048 meters (30.48 centimeters)
1 yard (3 feet) = 0.9144 meters
1 mile (1,760 yards) = 1.609 kilometers
1 gram = 0.035 ounce
1 kilogram = 2.205 pounds
1 millimeter = 0.039 inch
1 centimeter = 0.393 inch
1 meter = 3.28 feet
1 kilometer = 0.62 mile
1 liter = 1.056 quarts

Business Hours

Businesses and government offices in Chicago are generally open from 9am–5pm Monday–Friday. Because many people from the suburbs and outlying areas commute to work in the city, the hour before 9am and the hour after 5pm are the busiest times on the roads, as everyone hurries to or from jobs at approximately the same time. If plans permit, try to avoid driving during these times.

Banking hours are generally 8.30 or 9am–3pm. Some banks have longer hours; some are open a half-day on Saturday and closed on Wednesday.

Tipping

The actual amount of the tip should depend on satisfaction with the service received. The following can be used as a guideline:
Waiter/Waitress: 15–20 percent.
Bartender: 10–15 percent.
Hotel Doorman: $1–$3 for carrying bags; 50¢–$1 for calling taxi.
Hotel Porter/Bellman: $1–$3 per bag; $1–$2 for opening room.
Room-Service Waiter: 15 percent.
Hotel Chambermaid: $1–$2 per night.
Taxi Driver: 15 percent.

Porter Services

Porter services are available in most airports and other transportation centers, as well as in most hotels. The fee is usually entirely up to the traveler, but most range from $1–$3 a bag, depending on distance and difficulty for the porter. In addition, most airports and transportation centers have self-push baggage carts, sometimes free and sometimes for a rental fee ranging from 25 cents to $1.

Religious Services

For help in locating specific services to attend, try the Chicago Church Federation, tel: 977-9929. The following is a list of churches and synagogues in the downtown and near north area:

Annunciation Greek Orthodox Cathedral (Greek Orthodox), 1017 N. LaSalle Street, tel: 664-5485.
Assumption Church Servite Fathers (Roman Catholic), 323 W. Illinois Street, tel: 644-0036.
Cathedral Church of St James (Episcopal), 65 E. Huron Street, tel: 787-7360.
Central Church of Chicago (Non-denominational), 18 S. Michigan Avenue,

9th Floor, tel: 332-4840.
Central Synagogue of the Southside Hebrew Congregation (Conservative), 30 E. Cedar Street, tel: 787-0450.
Chicago Loop Synagogue (Traditional), 16 S. Clark Street, tel: 346-7370.
Chicago Temple (First United Methodist Church), 77 W. Washington Street, tel: 236-4548.
Christ the King (Lutheran in America), 637 S. Dearborn Street, tel: 939-3720.
Church of the Ascension (Episcopal), 1133 N. LaSalle Street, tel: 664-1271.
Congregation Kol Ami (Reform), 150 E. Huron Street, tel: 664-4775.
First St Paul's Evangelical Lutheran Church (Lutheran), 1301 N. LaSalle Street, tel: 642-7172.
Fourth Presbyterian Church (Presbyterian), 126 E. Chestnut Street, tel: 787-4570.
Grace Episcopal Church (Episcopal), 637 S. Dearborn Street, tel: 922-1426.
Holy Name Cathedral (Roman Catholic), 735 N. State Street, tel: 787-8040.
Lake Shore Drive Synagogue (Traditional), 70 E. Elm Street, tel: 337-6811.
Lubavitch Chabad of the Loop (Orthodox), 401 S. LaSalle Street, Suite 9-770, tel: 427-7770.
Old St Mary's Church (Roman Catholic), 21 E. Van Buren Street, tel: 922-3444.
Second Presbyterian Church (Presbyterian), 1936 S. Michigan Avenue, tel: 225-4951.
Seventeenth Church of Christ (Christian Scientist), 55 E. Wacker Drive, tel: 236-4671.
St Patrick's Church (Roman Catholic), 718 W. Adams Street, tel: 782-6171.
St Peter's Church (Roman Catholic), 110 W. Madison Street, tel: 375-5111.

Media
Newspapers & Magazines
There are two major daily newspapers in Chicago, the *Chicago Tribune* and the *Chicago Sun-Times*. Both are morning papers and are available everywhere: hotels, paper boxes on the street, stores, etc. The papers carry local, national and international news. They also have weekend sections (check Friday editions) with up-to-the minute information on entertainment events in Chicago.
Chicago Tribune, 435 N. Michigan Avenue, tel: 222-3232.
Chicago Sun-Times, 401 N. Wabash Avenue, tel: 321-3000.
The *Chicago Defender* is another daily paper with emphasis on the black community, 2400 S. Michigan Avenue, tel: 225-2400.
The Reader is a liberal free weekly, available on Thursday primarily on the north side. 11 E. Illinois Street, tel: 828-0350.
Crain's Chicago Business is a weekly paper for Chicago's business news and other issues. 740 N. Rush Street, tel: 649-5200.
Streetwise is a paper sold by, and benefiting, the homeless of Chicago. It can be bought from individuals throughout the Loop 62 E.13th, tel: 554-0060.
Chicago is a monthly magazine that contains a good guide to restaurants and events in addition to its feature articles. 414 N. Orleans, tel: 222-8999.

NEWSSTANDS
Chicago Main Newsstand, Main Street and Chicago Avenue, Evanston, tel: 864-2727. A large selection of local, national and international papers can be obtained from:
Krochs & Brentanos, 29 S. Wabash Avenue, tel: 332-7500. Some out of town and foreign newspapers.

Radio
Radios pick up two frequencies, AM and FM. The most popular stations include:

AM
670	WMAQ	News
720	WGN	Variety, Talk
780	WBBM	News
820	WSCR	Sports Talk
890	WLS	Talk
1000	WMVP	Sports

FM
93.1	WXRT	Progressive Rock
93.9	WLIT	Light Favorites
94.7	WLS	News, Talk
95.5	WNUA	Smooth Jazz
96.3	WBBM	Top 40
97.9	WLUP	Personality/Entertainment
98.7	WFMT	Classical, Fine Arts
99.5	WUSN	Country
100.3	WPNT	Rock/Contemporary
101.9	WTMX	70s, 80s & 90s
103.5	WFYR	Soft Hits
104.3	WJMK	Oldies
105.9	WCKG	Classic Rock
107.5	WGCI	Black Contemporary

Television
The main channels available on all television sets are:
Channel 2	WBBM	CBS
Channel 5	WMAQ	NBC
Channel 7	WLS	ABC
Channel 9	WGN	Independent
Channel 11	WTTW	PBS
Channel 32	WFLD	Fox

In hotels that offer cable (and most of them do), a listing will likely be provided showing what programming is available on each channel. Some specialty channels include:
ESPN	National sports
CNN	News
TMC	Movies
HBO	Movies
Showtime	Movies
Disney	Family fare
Max	Movies
Nickelodeon	Children's
Sportschannel	Local sports
VH-1	Music Videos
MTV	Music Videos
HLN	News
TWC	Weather

Postal Services
The main post office is located at 433 W. Van Buren Street, tel: 765-4357. It is open from 7am-9pm Monday-Friday, 8am-5pm Saturday. There's also an O'Hare Airport post office that is open 24 hours.
The post office has 67 full service branches in or around Chicago. Most are open from 8.30am–5pm, Monday–Friday, and 8.30am–1pm Saturday. Check the phone book for the nearest location. The post office offers a postal answer line with different recordings depending on the information that is required. Tel: 427-5960.

Phones & Faxes
Telephones
Public telephones are located everywhere, both on the street and in major buildings. The city of Chicago is in area

code **312**, the suburbs in **708**. When calling within the same area code, dial only the seven-digit phone number; when calling the other area code, dial 1-three digit area code-seven digit phone number. Calls between these two area codes are charged as local calls. (If unsure about the area code, go ahead and dial without it and a recording will advise on the proper area code.)

To find out local phone numbers call information at 411. For US long distance numbers the area code can be obtained from the operator (dial 0), then dial 1-(area code)-555-1212. Most overseas cities can be dialed direct. If you require assistance, dial 00 for a long-distance operator.

Telex & fax

Most hotels and many copy or printing shops and other businesses have fax machines that visitors can use for a fee. Telexes can also be sent through most hotels, and telegrams can be sent through Western Union or the telephone companies.

Tourist Information

Information on Chicago is readily available by mail, phone, or in person from:
Chicago Convention and Tourism Bureau, McCormick Place on the Lake, 2301 S. Lake Shore Dr, Chicago IL 60611, tel: 567-8500. Groups and conferences only.
Chicago Offfice of Tourism, Chicago Cultural Center, 77 E. Randolph, Chicago, 60602, tel: 744-2400. Handles general questions from the public.
Illinois Office of Tourism, 100 W. Randolf Street, Suite 3-400, Chicago, IL 60601, tel: 814-4732 or (800) 223-0121.
International Visitors' Center, 520 N. Michigan Avenue, Chicago, IL 60611, tel: (312) 645-1836.
Visitor Information Center, Historic Water Tower, 806 N. Michigan Avenue, Chicago IL 60611. Walk-in facility only.
Mayor's Office of Special Events, 121 N. LaSalle Street, Chicago, IL 60602, tel: (312) 744-3315.
General Information, tel: (312) 744-3370, 24-Hour Hotline.

Consulates

Argentina: 20 N. Clark Street, tel: 263-7435.
Australia: 321 N. Clark Street, tel: 645-9440.
Austria: 400 N. Michigan Avenue, tel: 222-1515.
Belgium: 333 N. Michigan Avenue, tel: 263-6624.
Brazil: 401 N. Michigan Avenue, tel: 464-0244.
Canada: 310 S. Michigan Avenue, tel: 427-1031.
Chile: 333 N. Michigan Avenue, Suite 728, tel: 726-7097.
China, People's Republic of: 104 S. Michigan Avenue, tel: 346-0287.
Colombia: 122 S. Michigan Avenue, tel: 341-0658.
Costa Rica: 8 S. Michigan Avenue, tel: 263-2772.
Denmark: 360 N. Michigan Avenue, tel: 329-9644.
Ecuador: 612 N. Michigan Avenue, tel: 642-8579.
Egypt: 505 N. Lake Shore Drive, tel: 670-2633.
Finland: 35 E. Wacker Drive, tel: 346-1150.
France: 737 N. Michigan Avenue, tel: 787-5359.
Germany: 104 S. Michigan Avenue, tel: 263-0850.
Greece: 168 N. Michigan Avenue, tel: 372-5356.
Guatemala: 333 N. Michigan Avenue, tel: 332-1587.
Haiti: 919 N. Michigan Avenue, Suite 3311, tel: 337-1603.
Iceland: 221 N. LaSalle Street, tel: 236-7600.
India: 150 N. Michigan Avenue, tel: 781-6280.
Ireland: 400 N. Michigan Avenue, tel: 337-1868.
Israel: 111 E. Wacker Drive, tel: 565-3300.
Italy: 500 N. Michigan Avenue, tel: 467-1550.
Jamaica: 188 W. Randolph Street, tel: 372-1202.
Japan: 737 N. Michigan Avenue, tel: 280-0400.
Korea: 500 N. Michigan Avenue, tel: 822-9485.
Liberia: 423 E. 60th Street, tel: 643-8635.
Lithuania: 10000 S. Bell Street, tel: 233-9122.
Luxembourg: 180 N. LaSalle Street, tel: 726-0354.
Mexico: 300 N. Michigan Avenue, tel: 855-1380.
Monaco: 1 E. Superior Street, tel: 642-1242.
The Netherlands: 303 E. Wacker Drive, tel: 856-0110.
Norway: 503 W. Golf, Arlington Heights, tel: 956-6969.
Panama: 1150 N. State Street, tel: 944-5759.
Peru: 180 N. Michigan Avenue, Suite 700, tel: 853-6170.
Philippines: 30 N. Michigan Avenue, tel: 332-6458.
Poland: 1530 N. Lake Shore Drive, tel: 337-8166.
South Africa: 200 S. Michigan Avenue, tel: 939-7929.
Spain: 180 N. Michigan Avenue, tel: 782-4588.
Sri Lanka: 11 S. LaSalle Street, tel: 236-3306.
Sweden: 150 N. Michigan Avenue, Suite 1250, tel: 781-6262.
Switzerland: 757 N. Michigan Avenue, tel: 915-0061.
Thailand: 35 E. Wacker Drive, tel: 236-2447.
Turkey: 360 N. Michigan Avenue, tel: 263-0644.
United Kingdom: 33 N. Dearborn Street, tel: 346-1810.
Uruguay: 79 W. Monroe, tel: 236-3369.
Venezuela: 20 N. Wacker Drive, tel: 236-9655.
Yugoslavia: 307 N. Michigan Avenue, tel: 332-0169.

Getting Around

Orientation

The numbering system in Chicago makes it easy to find your way around. The city is laid out in a grid pattern. The corner of **State and Madison** streets (downtown) is the center point. Any address N., S., E., or W., is north, south, east, or west of that point. Each block is equal to 100 address numbers, so 800 N. State Street, is a point eight blocks north of Madison. Keep in mind that Lake Michigan is to the east.

The lakefront in Chicago has been developed for public use. Starting from the lake, the first area of land is the parkland, consisting of beaches, recreational lands, gardens and some of the popular museums. Heading west away from the lake, the next area is the downtown, with its stores, businesses and hotels. Here are the skyscrapers and interesting buildings that make up Chicago's famous skyline.

To the north, west, and south of the downtown are residential areas. Chicago is a city of diverse neighborhoods: Beverly, Bridgeport, Hyde Park, Lincoln Park, Rogers Park and so on — each a part of the same city, yet with its own name and identity, and often its own ethnic or racial flavor.

Surrounding Chicago in an everwidening band are the suburbs. Primarily residential areas, they usually have a street or two (strips), a specific area (district) or malls for business and shopping. There are often excellent family restaurants in the suburbs. Each suburb may use its own numbering system for streets and addresses, but many follow the pattern begun in the city.

From the Airport

It's ordinarily a 20-minute trip by car between O'Hare Airport and downtown but traffic is so unpredictable, especially during rush hour, that it's advisable to allow an hour for travel time. Taxis are readily available, but are fairly expensive.

Continental Air Transport, tel: 454-7800, provides bus services between the airport baggage claim area and about 35 downtown hotels. Many hotels provide their own shuttle service, so inquire when making reservations. Taxis are available on the lower level of each terminal. Limousine service or car rentals can be arranged in advance or at the booths near the baggage claim area.

Probably the cheapest way to get downtown, and the surest way to avoid traffic jams, is the **Chicago Transit Authority** (CTA) Rapid Transit line under Terminal 4. The trains run frequently to and from the Dearborn Street station downtown.

Midway Airport, 5700 S. Cicero, is a smaller, less crowded alternative to O'Hare, located about seven miles southwest of downtown. Its one building is divided into three terminals. For information, tel: 767-0500.

Domestic Travel

O'Hare Airport, besides its international terminal, has three domestic terminals with flights and connections to all parts of the United States. Call 686-2200. Midway Airport, 5700 S. Cicero Avenue, has three domestic terminals, call 767-0500.

In addition to O'Hare and Midway airports (see Traveling to Chicago), **Meigs Field**, just south of downtown at 12th Street and the lakefront, provides commuter flights to downstate Illinois and Wisconsin. Call 744-4787 for information.

Some budget travelers prefer to see America by bus, "riding the dog" with passes that allow unlimited trips during a certain period of weeks. **Greyhound/Trailways** has nationwide services from its main terminal in the Loop (downtown), at Clark and Randolph streets. Call 781-2900 for fare and schedule information.

America's rail network has been dramatically reduced in recent decades, and the prices are often not much better than airfare. Nonetheless, long-haul **Amtrak** passes for travelers can still be a bargain, and many still prefer the romance of the rails. General information on Amtrak trains and fares for the entire country is available toll-free at (800) USA-RAIL. Amtrak's main Chicago terminal is Chicago's **Union Station** at Jackson and Canal streets, tel: 558-1075.

Public Transportation

Chicago's public transportation network includes buses and rapid transit trains, both subway and elevated (or the "El," as everyone will call it). An excellent transit system map can be requested free from CTA (Chicago Transit Authority), Merchandise Mart, Chicago, IL 60654.

Bus stops are marked with signs which indicate the bus routes they serve. Buses run about every 15 minutes during the day, less often at night.

The RTA (Regional Transportation Authority), tel: 836-7000, will provide travel information 24 hours a day except on major holidays. The RTA service provides commuter trains to the suburbs and exurbs via the Metra lines that leave the city from four central stations.

Taxis

Taxis in Chicago are metered. Fares begin at under $1.50 for the first one-fifth of a mile (or fraction of that). It also costs extra for each additional one-sixth of a mile or 60 seconds of waiting time. There's a charge for each additional passenger between the ages of 12 and 65. A 15 percent tip is standard for the driver. A taxi ride to or from O'Hare Airport will cost between $25 and $30; the ride to or from Midway Airport costs between $18 and $22. A shared ride program is available for a flat rate of $15 (O'Hare) or $10 (Midway) for each person with a maximum of four people.

Here are some of the taxi services in Chicago (Check the Yellow Pages under taxicabs for many more):
Yellow Cab Co, tel: 829-4222.
Checker Taxi Co, tel: 243-2537.
Flash Cab Co, tel: 561-1444.

Car Rentals

Visitors concentrating on the downtown area probably don't need a car. Between public transportation and a little walking, the usual tourist areas are all accessible. Also, taxis are plentiful. There are quite a few parking lots, including underground parking at Grant Park, but these can be expensive. Cheaper on-street parking is difficult to find.

Here is a small sample of rental agencies (Check the Yellow Pages of the phone book under Automobile Rentals for more). Reservations are advised:
Alamo, tel: (800) 327-9633.
Budget, tel: (800) 527-0700.
Hertz, tel: (800) 654-3131.
Avis, tel: (800) 331-1212.
Dollar, tel: (800) 800-4000.
Enterprise, tel: (800) 325-8007.

Walking & Cycling

Chicago is a great walking town for those who are fit, but like most American cities it is much more spread out than most European cities. Visitors who aren't used to extensive walking shouldn't try to hit all of Chicago's downtown landmarks on foot.

Besides using bicycles for cruising along the lakefront, some visitors find that – if they can brave the traffic – cycling is an efficient and cheap way to see a lot of the city very quickly. Bicycle rentals are available at:

Lincoln Park, Fullerton Avenue west of Lake Shore Drive.
Village Cycle Shop, 1337 N. Wells Street, tel: 751-2488.

Hitchhiking

Besides being dangerous, hitchhiking is strictly illegal in and around Chicago, as it is over most of the United States. The practice is regarded as too risky by both drivers and travelers, particularly in urban areas.

On Departure

Remember to check with the airline or the airport before departure to confirm flight numbers and times, and to make seat reservations in advance if possible. Also check the terminal and the time you should check in. Most airlines now require international travelers to check in two hours before scheduled departure, and checking in late can mean losing even confirmed or assigned seats.

Where to Stay

Hotels

Chicago can be a fairly expensive city for accommodation, but there is also a wide variety of hotels and motels in different price ranges. Most hotels – and all the better ones – have restaurants and bars. Seasonal bargains and packages with both overseas and domestic flights are often available, along with "weekender" rates offered by hotels that cater to expense-account business travelers during the week. Tourists trying to save money may find the best bargains a few blocks away from downtown, but still within an easy bus or taxi ride. Here are some of the recommended hotels in Chicago:

Luxury

The Barclay Chicago, 166 E. Superior Street, 60611, tel: 787-6000 or toll free (800) 621-8004. All suites, multilingual concierge, and in a good location.

The Drake Hotel, 140 E. Walton Place, 60611, tel: 787-2200 or toll free (800) 527-4727. Lavish lobby, worth a visit even if not staying at the hotel. Shopping arcade on first floor. Three restaurants including the Cape Cod Room.

Fairmont, 200 N. Columbus Drive, 60601, tel: 565-8000 or toll free (800) 332-3442. Located at the Illinois Center. Complete business services. High tea served.

Four Seasons Hotel, 120 E. Delaware Place, 60611, tel: 280-8800 or toll free (800) 332-3442. Located above Bloomingdales. Indoor pool and health center.

Hotel Nikko, 321 Dearborn Street, 60610, tel: 744-1900 or toll free (800) NIKKO-US. Fitness center. Business services.

Hyatt Regency Chicago, 151 E. Wacker Drive, 60601, tel: 565-1234 or toll free (800) 233-1234. At Illinois Center. Over 2,000 rooms. Atrium Lobby, comedy club nightly, shuttle buses to airports.

Le Meridien Chicago, 21 E. Bellevue Place, 60611, tel: 266-2100 or toll free (800) 443-2100. Penthouse suites available. Jazz pianist. Business services.

Omni Ambassador East, 1301 N. State Street, 60610, tel: 787-7200 or toll free (800) THE-OMNI. Old fashioned elegance. Home of the Pump Room and Byfields.

Park Hyatt, 800 N. Michigan Avenue, 60611, tel: 280-2222 or toll free (800) 233-1234. Lavish contemporary style. Multilingual concierge and staff. Home of La Tour Restaurant.

The Ritz-Carlton Chicago, 160 E. Pearson Street, 60611, tel: 266-1000 or toll free (800) 332-3442. Located above Water Tower Place. Grand lobby. Nightly entertainment and dancing in the "The Bar."

Swissôtel Chicago, 323 E. Wacker Drive, 60601, tel: 565-0565 or toll free (800) 65-GRAND. At Illinois Center. Aims for quiet European ambience. Health spa with indoor lap pool. Also offers jazz and classical music.

Expensive

Blackstone, 636 S. Michigan Avenue, 60605, tel: 427-4300 or toll free (800) 622-6330. Plenty of gangster history and ambience of bygone days.

Chicago Hilton and Towers, 720 S. Michigan Avenue, 60605, tel: 922-4400 or toll free (800)-HILTONS.

Chicago Marriott Downtown, 540 N. Michigan Avenue, 60611, tel: 836-0100 or toll free (800) 228-9290.

Executive Plaza, A Clarion Hotel, 71 E. Wacker Drive, 60601, tel: 346-7100 or toll free (800) 621-4005.

Holiday Inn Chicago City Centre, 300 E. Ohio Street, 60611, tel: 787-6100 or toll free (800) 465-4329.

Holiday Inn Mart Plaza, 350 N. Orleans Street, 60654, tel: 836-5000 or toll free (800) 465-4329.

Hotel Inter-Continental, 505 N. Michigan Avenue, 60611, tel: 944-4100 or toll free (800) 628-2112.

The Knickerbocker Chicago, 163 E. Walton Place, 60611, tel: 751-8100 or toll free (800) 621-8140.

Lenox House Suites, 616 N. Rush Street, 60611, tel: 337-1000 or toll free (800) 44-LENOX.

The Mayfair Regent, 181 E. Lake Shore Drive, 60611, tel: 787-8500 or toll free (800) 545-4000.

The Palmer House Hilton, 17 E. Monroe Street, 60603, tel: 726-7500 or toll free (800) HIL-TONS.

The Radisson Plaza Ambassador West, 1300 N. State Parkway, 60610, tel: 787-7900 or toll free (800) 333-3333.

Sheraton Chicago Hotel & Towers, 301 East North Water Street, 60611, tel: 464-1000 or toll free (800) 325-3535.

Sheraton Plaza, 160 E. Huron Street, 60611, tel: 787-2900 or toll free (800) 325-3535.

Tremont, 100 E. Chestnut Street, 60611, tel: 751-1900 or toll free (800) 621-8133.

The Westin Hotel, 909 N. Michigan Avenue, 60611, tel: 943-7200 or toll free (800) 228-3000. At north end of Magnificent Mile. Health club.

Whitehall, 105 E. Delaware Place, 60611, tel: 944-6300 or toll free (800) 621-8295.

Moderate to Expensive

Ascot House, 1100 S. Michigan Avenue, 60605, tel: 922-2900 or toll free (800) 272-4220.

Avenue Hotel, 1154 S. Michigan Avenue, 60605, tel: 427-8200 or toll free (800) 621-4196.
Congress Hotel, 520 S. Michigan Avenue, 60605, tel: 427-3800 or toll free (800) 635-1666.
Claridge Hotel, 1244 N. Dearborn Street, 60610, tel: 787-4980 or toll free (800) 245-1258.
Gold Coast Group (small hotels in renovated older buildings). Toll free (800) 621-8506. Group includes: **The Talbott**, 20 E. Delaware Place, tel: 944-4970. **The Delaware Towers**, 25 E. Delaware Place, tel: 944-4245. **The Elms**, 18 E. Elm Street, tel: 787-4740.
Midland, 172 W. Adams Street, 60603, tel: 332-1200 or toll free (800) 621-2360.
The Raphael, 201 E. Delaware Place, 60611, tel: 943-5000 or toll free (800) 821-5343.
River North Hotel, 125 W. Ohio Street, 60610, tel: 467-0800 or toll free (800) 528-1234.

Bed & Breakfast

Bed and Breakfast Chicago is a clearinghouse of available bed and breakfast facilities in the Chicago area. Rather than a European-style inn that includes breakfast as part of the payment, a B&B in Chicago is more likely a family which opens its home to guests. Reservations must be made. Contact Bed & Breakfast Chicago, PO Box 14088, Chicago, IL 60614, tel: 951-0085.

Youth Hostels

There is only one hostel in the Chicago area, and it is located well away from the downtown area: **Chicago International Hostel**, 6318 N. Winthrop Avenue, tel: 262-1011.

Eating Out

What to Eat

As the major city in America's heartland, Chicago boasts a wide variety of regional, ethnic and foreign cuisine. The city is known, however, for several specific types of food. Beef of all kinds, particularly prime rib and steaks, have been a specialty of the city since its days as the nation's stockyards, the US butchering capital. An influence from the southern black migration has been "barbecue ribs," the large meaty spare ribs slathered in tangy sauce. Chicago claims to have invented the deep-dish pizza – one of the few items of native fare that vegetarians can enjoy, too – and to have refined the form of Vienna sausage known as the Chicago hot dog. But whatever the style of food, diners in Chicago can almost always be assured that the portions will be large – even by American standards.

Where to Eat

The following restaurants, grouped by style of food, are recommended:

American

Barney's Market Club, 741 W. Randolph Street, tel: 372-6466. One of Chicago's oldest restaurants, specializing in prime rib, steak and lobster.
Mr Beef on Orleans, 666 N. Orleans Street, tel: 337-8500. Offers the best beef sandwich in Chicago. Very casual. Celebrity photos on the wall.
Bigsby's Bar and Grill, 1750 N. Clark Street, tel: 642-5200. Lincoln Park location. Part-owner Michael Jordan, the basketball star, is frequently in the restaurant.
Billy Goat Tavern & Grill, 430 N. Michigan Avenue, tel: 222-1525. Lower level Michigan Avenue. Hangout for the city's press corps. Cheeseburgers are a must.
Binyon's Restaurant, 327 S. Plymouth Court, tel: 341-1155. A popular spot for bankers, attorneys, traders. Famous for its turtle soup.
Blackhawk Lodge, 41 E. Superior Street, tel: 280-4080. American cooking with an emphasis toward healthy choices.
Blackie's, 755 S. Clark Street, tel: 786-1161. Traditional family fare – soups, salads, chili. Specialty is cheeseburgers.
Bub City Crabshack & Bar-B-Q, 901 W. Weed Street, tel: 266-1200. Fun-filled, spacious eatery decorated as a Texas honky-tonk. Plenty of seafood and barbecue selections. Great for garlic lovers.
Butch McGuire's, 20 W. Division, tel: 337-9080. Lunch, dinner and weekend brunch in a lively saloon atmosphere.
City Tavern, 33 W. Monroe Street, tel: 280-2740. Cherrywood paneling and soft lights, across from the Shubert Theatre. Features include homemade sandwiches, omelettes and grilled steaks.
Demon Dogs, 944 N. Fullerton Avenue, tel: 281-2001. Best hot dog stand in the city. Among the best fries.
The Eccentric, 159 W. Erie Street, tel: 787-8390. House specialties: Prime Rib and Rice Crusted Tuna. Homemade desserts.
Ed Debevic's, 640 N. Wells Street, tel: 664-1707. A campy, upbeat '50s diner known for its homestyle food and sassy service.
Entre Nous, 200 N. Columbus Avenue (Fairmont Hotel), tel: 565-8000. An intimate restaurant with "classique" cuisine.
The Fireplace Inn, 1448 N. Wells Street, tel: 664-5264. Ski lodge atmosphere. Barbecued ribs, steaks, seafood, sandwiches. Outdoor dining available.
Gold Coast Dogs, 418 N. State Street, tel: 527-1222; 804 N. Rush Street, tel: 951-5141; 2100 N. Clark, tel: 327-8887. Chicago hot dogs, also burgers and sandwiches.
Gordon, 500 N. Clark Street, tel: 467-9780. Seasonal New American menu highlighting fresh seafood. Brunch on Sundays.
Hamburger Hamlet, 44 E. Walton Street, tel: 649-6601. A Gold Coast institution offering a variety of made to order hamburgers, chili *fajitas*, salads and more.
Hard Rock Café, 63 W. Ontario Street, tel: 943-2252. Mick Jagger's guitar, George Harrison's Beatles suit, Michael Jackson's platinum records and yes, even food, especially hamburgers.
Harry Caray's Restaurant, 33 W. Kinzie Street, tel: 465-9269. Baseball memorabilia decorate the walls while steaks and chops dominate the menu.
Houston's Restaurant, 616 N. Rush Street, tel: 649-1121. Something for everyone here, fish, ribs, soups, steaks, etc, served in a convenient location.
Jim's Hot Dog Stand, 1320 S. Halsted Street. The local police eat here, so it must be filling.

Michael Jordon's Restaurant, 500 N. LaSalle Street, tel: 644-3865. Michael Jordon, the world-famous basketball player, opened this restaurant featuring his favorite foods with a bit of sport thrown in, in the form of a multimedia lounge and memorabilia.

Planet Hollywood, 633 N. Wells, tel: 266-7827. Restaurant and entertainment complex owned and frequented by celebrities.

Red Kerr's, 138 S. Clinton Street, tel: 733-5377. Sports celebrity restaurant owned by Bulls announcer, Johnny "Red" Kerr. Try a barbecue, and maybe see a Chicago sports personality.

Maple Tree Inn, 10730 S. Western Avenue. New Orleans cajun food in a neighborhood Beverly restaurant with a jazz club and an outdoor garden.

Prairie, 500 S. Dearborn Street, tel: 663-1143. Open for breakfast, lunch and dinner. Modernized basic recipes.

The Pump Room, 1301 N. State Parkway, tel: 266-0360. A famous restaurant, known since the 1930s for its "Booth One," which is reserved for celebrities.

Signature Room at the 95th, 875 N. Michigan Avenue, tel: 787-9596. Enjoy elegant dining and a great view of the city from the 95th floor of the John Hancock Building. The menu changes with the seasons.

That Steak Joynt, 1610 N. Wells Street, tel: 943-5091. Steaks and ribs. Offers a Second City dinner/theatre package.

Top Notch Beefburger, 2116 W. 95th Street, tel: 445-7218. 1950s-style burgers and milk shakes in a classic diner in the classic neighborhood of Beverly.

Arab

Old Jerusalem, 1411 N. Wells, tel: 944-0459.

Armenian

Sayat Nova, 157 E. Ohio Street, tel: 644-9159. Romantic restaurant with a reputation for good food. Authentic Armenian-Middle Eastern dishes include *mezzas*, *kebabs* and vegetarian specialties.

Barbecued Ribs

Army's and Lou's, 422 E. 7th Street, tel:483-6550. Many consider this to be one of the finest soul food restaurants in America. The ribs, chitlins and grits just don't get any better than here.

Carson's Ribs, 612 N. Wells Street, tel: 280-9200. Won a *Chicago* magazine contest for the best ribs in town. Meaty ribs in a tangy sweet sauce. Other entrées also available.

Fireplace Bar & Grill, 1960 N. Racine, tel: 528-4300. Ribs, pizza and more. TVs for sporting events.

Miller's Pub, 134 S. Adams, tel: 263-4988. Popular spot for sports and theatergoers. Casual atmosphere. Possible celebrity sightings.

Twin-Anchors Restaurant and Tavern, 1655 N. Sedgwick Street, tel: 266-1616. Among the best ribs in Chicago. Great burgers too. Pleasant neighborhood watering hole.

Chinese

House of Hunan, 535 N. Michigan, tel: 329-9494.

Haylemon Restaurant, 2201 S. Wentworth Avenue, tel: 225-0891.

Jade East Restaurant, 218 W. Cermak Road, tel: 362-4224.

King Wah Restaurant, 2225 S. Wentworth Avenue, tel: 842-1404.

Mandar-Inn Restaurant, 2249 S. Wentworth Avenue, tel: 842-4014.

65 Seafood Restaurant, 2414 S. Wentworth Avenue, tel: 225-7060.

Szechwan House, 600 N. Michigan Avenue, tel: 642-3900. Good location and food, from the spicy foods of Szechwan Province to the delicately flavored dishes of Taiwan.

Three Happiness Restaurant, 209 W. Cermak Road, tel: 842-1964. This is a tiny storefront with limited seating. Serves very good Cantonese and Szechuan food.

Triple Crown Seafood, 211 W. 22nd Place, tel: 790-1788.

Continental

Arnie's, 1030 N. State Street, tel: 266-4800. Gold Coast glitz. This award-winning restaurant has an a la carte menu featuring rack of lamb, Sicilian veal chop and prime steaks. Has a great Sunday brunch.

Crickets, 100 E. Chestnut Street, tel: 280-2100. Varied menu featuring international and American dishes. A place to "see and be seen" for many.

The Rafael, 201 E. Delaware Place (Raphael Hotel), tel: 943-5000. Intimate setting, reasonable prices.

Delicatessen

The Bagel Restaurant, 3107 N. Broadway, tel: 477-0300. North Side. Traditional deli, serves bulging sandwiches and award-winning soups.

D.B. Kaplan's Delicatessen, 845 N. Michigan Avenue (Water Tower Place, 7th Floor), tel: 280-2700. More than 150 creative deli options. Carryout and delivery available. A mural of celebrity caricatures throughout the restaurant.

Manny's Coffee Shop & Deli, 1141 S. Jefferson Street, tel: 939-2855. Near south. Dine in or carry out, a complete breakfast menu, plus sandwiches, homemade soups and salads for lunch. The specialty is corned beef.

Moe's Deli & Pub, 611 N. Rush Street, tel: 828-0110. Near North. Triple decker sandwich creations, homemade soups and desserts, daily specialties. Delivery and carryout services are available.

Ethiopian

Mama Desta's Red Sea Restaurant, 3216 N. Clark Street, tel: 935-7561. Ethiopian cooking. Diners eat with their hands. Bring several friends.

French

Ambria, 2300 N. Lincoln Park West, tel: 472-5959. Serving Chef Gabino Sotelino's cuisine LeGere.

Bistro 110, 110 E. Pearson Street, tel: 266-3110. Hospitable and comfortable, specialties include angel-hair pasta, oven-roasted chicken and *crème brûlée* for dessert. Extensive French-American wine list.

Café Bernard, 2100 N. Halsted Street tel: 871-2100. Country French cuisine. Located in the heart of Lincoln Park.

Charlie Trotter's, 816 W. Armitage, tel: 248-6228. Contemporary multicultural cuisine.

Chez Paul, 660 N. Rush Street, tel: 944-6680. Quiet elegance in the McCormick Mansion.

The Dining Room, 160 E. Pearson Street (Ritz-Carlton), tel: 227-5866. Beautiful setting, daily specials, *foie gras* salad is a specialty.

Everest Room, 410 S. LaSalle Street, tel: 663-8920. One of the top restaurants in the country, with a view to match.

Le Francais, 269 S. Milwaukee Avenue, Wheeling, tel: (708) 541-7470.

Although not located in Chicago, this suburban restaurant is world famous. Contemporary French cuisine in a provincial atmosphere.
Un Grand Café, 2300 N. Lincoln Park West, tel: 348-8886. Authentic Parisian Bistro overlooking Lincoln Park. You can dine on the patio in warm weather.
Yvette Wintergarden, 311 S. Wacker Drive, tel: 408-1242. Art deco Loop bistro located in a tropical atrium. Serves light French-American cuisine.

German

The Berghoff Restaurant, 17 W. Adams Street, tel: 427-3170. Wide selection of meat, poultry and fish items. German fare among the best in the city. They make their own beer and root beer.
Golden Ox, 1578–82 Clybourn Avenue, tel: 664-0780. "Old World" atmosphere, strolling musicians, good German food and a good beer garden.
Zum Deutschen Eck, 2924 N. Southport Avenue, tel: 525-8211. A cozy German restaurant featuring *Schnitzel Dijon* and *sauerbraten*. Live entertainment.

Greek

Denis' Den, 2941 N. Clark Street, tel: 348-8888. A mini-trip to Greece. Live music, dancing encouraged. Homemade Greek food.
Greek Islands, 200 S. Halsted Street, tel: 782-9855. Festive, with room to dance. An exposed steam table showcases many of the house offerings.
Papagus, 600 N. State Street, tel: 642-8450. Features regional Greek cuisine and a variety of *Mezedes*.
The Parthenon, 314 S. Halsted Street, tel: 726-2407. Big and bustling. *Saganaki*, lamb, Greek sausage, suckling pig.

Hungarian

Kenessey's, 403 W. Belmont Avenue, tel: 929-7500. Elegant Hungarian cooking and live gypsy music. Best-priced wine selection in Chicago. Homemade pastries.

Indian

Bukhara Restaurant & Bar, 2 E. Ontario Street, tel: 943-0188. Authentic cuisine from the Northwest Territory of India. *Tandoori* dishes. Glass walled kitchen to view preparations.

Daavat Restaurant, 211 E. Walton Street, tel: 335-1001. Casual atmosphere, curries and *tandoori* dishes.
Gaylord India, 678 N. Clark Street, tel: 664-1700. Traditional *tandoori* specialties.
Kanval Palace Restaurant, 70 E. Walton Street, tel: 787-0400. Intimate and elegant.
Klay Oven Restaurant, 414 N. Orleans Street, tel: 527-3999. Traditional *tandoori* and Karhai dishes.

Italian

Al's No 1 Italian Beef, 169 W. Ontario, tel: 943-3222. Rated Chicago's No 1 Italian beef restaurant by *Chicago* magazine.
Avanzare, 161 E. Huron Street, tel: 337-8056. Focuses on the delicately flavored cuisine of Northern Italy. Tempting seafood and pasta dishes, especially among the daily specials.
Bice Ristorante, 158 E. Ontario Street, tel: 664-1474. Northern Italian cuisine. Homemade pastas. Signature *carpaccio*, *risottos*, mussels, *vongole*, and veal Milanese style. Elegant dining room or outdoor garden.
Bravissimo, 508 N. Clark Street, tel: 644-1427. Inspired Italian cuisine in a relaxed, sophisticated setting. Dishes add creative flair to Northern and Southern classics. The best *calamari* in Chicago.
Carlucci Restaurant, 2215 N. Halsted Street, tel: 281-1220. Regional Italian cuisine. Elegant dining room or outdoor garden.
Centro, 710 N. Wells Street, tel: 988-7775. A serious place for pasta, prime steaks, chops and broiled seafood in the art district.
Coco Pazzo, 300 W. Hubbard, tel: 836-0900. Chef from Bergame, Italy. Elegant loft space.
Como Inn Restaurant, 546 Milwaukee Avenue, tel: 421-5222. Serving Chicago since 1924. Free parking.
Gennaro's Restaurant, 1352 W. Taylor Street, tel: 243-1035. Family business specializing in *gnocchi*, *ravioli*, stuffed eggplant, fried *calamari*.
Gene & Georgetti, 500 N. Franklin Street, tel: 527-3718. For over 50 years this restaurant has offered Italian specialties, steaks and other dishes.
Italian Village, 71 W. Monroe Street, tel: 332-7005. Three restaurants featuring Italian American dishes.

Lino's, 222 W. Ontario Street, tel: 266-0616. Casual but elegant dining in a club-like setting featuring Northern Italian cuisine.
Maggiano's Little Italy, 516 N. Clark, tel: 644-7700. A classic recreation of a New York City pre-war "Little Italy" dinner house. Family-style dining available.
Rico's Restaurant, 626 S. Racine Avenue, tel: 421-7262. Located in the "Little Italy" neighborhood, with home cooking specialties.
The Rosebud Café, 1500 W. Taylor Street, tel: 942-1117. Also located in "Little Italy."
Scoozi, 410 W. Huron Street, tel: 943-5900. The neoclassic atmosphere of a 15th-century artist's studio recreated in the River North gallery district. Italian countryside cuisine.
Spiaggia, 980 N. Michigan Avenue, tel: 280-2754. Main dining room on the 2nd floor offers a view of Lake Michigan; northern Italian cuisine, including homemade pastas and brick-oven pizza. Next door is **Café Spiaggia** (tel: 280-2764), a casual European café with some of the same items and an extensive *antipasto* bar.
Stefani's, 1418 W. Fullerton Parkway, tel: 348-0111. Northern Italian cuisine. Host restaurant for politicians of note from Italy.
Trattoria No. 10, 10 N. Dearborn Street, tel: 984-1718. Charming and warm, featuring a variety of Italian dishes.
Tuscany, 1041 W. Taylor Street, tel: 829-1990. In Little Italy. Open kitchen, woodburning oven and grill remind you of a Tuscan eatery.

Japanese

Benihana of Tokyo, 166 E. Superior Street, tel: 664-9643. One of a US-wide chain, featuring Hibachi-style cooking – the chef prepares dinner at the table.
Benkay, 320 N. Dearborn Street (Hotel Nikko), tel: 744-1900. Authentic Japanese cuisine in an elegant setting. A Sushi Room, a Tatami Room, Teppan-Yaki tables, or Western-style dining rooms.
Hatsuhana, 160 E. Ontario Street, tel: 280-8287. A large *sushi* bar, with many varieties of ocean fish flown in daily.

Lebanese

Beirut, 5204 N. Clark Street. Known for its great *kebabs*.

Mexican

Frontera Grill, 445 N. Clark Street, tel: 661-1434. Wonderful Mexican cooking in a Southwestern setting. Menu changes weekly and represents several regions. Reservations an absolute must.

El Jardin, 3335 N. Clark Street, tel: 528-6775. Mexican cuisine, two outdoor gardens, Sunday brunch.

Hat Dance, 325 W. Huron Street, tel: 649-0066. Good service and value, appealing to upscale young professionals.

Su Casa, 49 E. Ontario Street, tel: 943-4041. In an 18th-century hacienda setting, specialties include chicken *fajitas* and red snapper.

Pizza

Bacino's, 75 E. Wacker Drive, tel: 263-0070. One of the best pizza joints around. Spinach pizza is a specialty.

California Pizza Kitchen, 414 N. Orleans, tel: 222-9030 and Water Tower Place, 7th level, tel: 787-7300. 26 varieties of wood-fired pizzas. Also pastas, salads, soup. Children's menu available.

Edwardo's, 1212 N. Dearborn Street, tel: 337-4490 or 521 S. Dearborn Street, tel: 939-3366. Chicago style stuffed pizza. Dining in, carry out or delivery.

Father and Son Pizza and Italian Restaurant, 645 W. North Avenue, tel: 654-2564. Family-run business with gourmet bakery. Home delivery available.

Gino's East, 160 E. Superior Street, tel: 943-1124. Often a wait to get in.

Pizzeria Uno, 29 E. Ohio Street, tel: 321-1000.

Pizzeria Due, 619 N. Wabash Avenue, tel: 943-2400. Chicago-style, deep-dish pizza was created at Pizzeria Uno in 1943. Pizzeria Due opened in 1955 to handle the overflow. A must-try for pizza lovers.

Polish

Busy Bee, 1500 N. Damen, tel: 772-4433. The last remaining gourmet Polish restaurant in old Polish downtown.

Orbit, 2940 N. Milwaukee Avenue, tel: 276-1355. A popular and boisterous restaurant in the Jackowo (Polish downtown area), known for *pirogi*.

Przybylo's White Eagle Banquet Hall, 6845 N. Milwaukee, tel: (708) 647-0660. The largest Polish restaurant in all the Midwest, it can handle seven wedding receptions at one time.

Seafood

Cape Cod Room, 140 E. Walton Place (Drake Hotel), tel: 787-2200. A famous dining spot with an extensive seafood menu. Specialties include the Bookbinder red snapper soup.

Catch 35, 35 W. Wacker, tel: 346-3500. More than 30 fresh seafood specialties. Oyster bar and display kitchen. Live entertainment.

Nick's Fishmarket, One First National Plaza, tel: 621-0200. Sophisticated atmosphere, good service and wide range of fresh fish and seafood.

Shaw's Crab House and **Shaw's Blue Crab Lounge & Oyster Bar,** 21 E. Hubbard Street, tel: 527-2722. Some of the freshest seafood in the city. The oyster bar has a wide selection. 1930s decor.

Spanish

Café Baba Reeba, 2024 N. Halsted Street, tel: 935-5000. Features a variety of hot and cold tapas. Regional specialties, including *paella*. Outdoor café.

Steak

Barney's Market Club Steakhouse, 741 W. Randolph Street, tel: 372-6466. Double cut prime rib of beef, daily specials. Casual dining in historic Haymarket Square.

Chicago Chop House, 60 W. Ontario Street, tel: 787-7100. Meat and potato place. Specialties include prime rib and a 64 oz. T-bone. Piano bar nightly.

Eli's The Place for Steak, 215 E. Chicago Avenue, tel: 642-1393. Prime aged steaks are the specialty. As famous for its cheesecake as for its steaks and excellent service.

Gibson's Bar & Steakhouse, 1028 N. Rush Street, tel: 266-8999. 1940s style, with supersized steaks. Piano bar with the late night food.

Kinzie Street Chop House, 400 N. Wells Street, tel: 822-0191. Clubby and sophisticated, featuring local art. Serves prime dry-aged steaks, chops, seafood and pasta dishes.

Lawry's the Prime Rib, 100 E. Ontario Street, tel: 787-5000. Roast prime rib carved tableside from a rolling cart, in one of three thicknesses. Huge salad bowls.

Morton's of Chicago, 1050 N. State Street, tel: 266-4820. Clubby atmosphere. "Menu" consists of prime cuts on a platter. Strictly for meat eaters.

Palm Restaurant, 17 E. Monroe Street, tel: 944-0135. Specializing in steak and lobster since 1926.

Ruth's Chris Steak House, 431 N. Dearborn, tel: 321-2725. American prime steaks, lamb veal, pork chops. Fresh fish and select Creole dishes.

The Saloon, 200 E. Chestnut, tel: 280-5454. Comfortable, club-like setting. Its specialties include prime dry-aged steaks, chops, prime rib and seafood.

Swedish

Svea, 3258 W. Foster Avenue, tel: 539-8021. An Andersonville landmark well-known for its authentic Swedish pancakes and excellent boysenberry pie.

Thai

Star of Siam, 11 E. Illinois, tel: 670-0100.

Thai Classic, 3332 N. Clark Street, tel: 404-2000. Spicy Thai fish and other seafood, along with *sate* and other standards.

Turkish

Konak, 5150 N. Clark Street, tel: 271-6688. Kebab and eggplant salad are specialties.

Vegetarian

Reza Restaurant, 432 W. Ontario, tel: 664-4500. *Also* 5255 N. Clark, tel: 561-1898. Persian cuisine served with raw veggies, lentil soup, rice and pita bread.

Vietnamese

Pasteur, 4759 N. Sheridan Road, tel: 271-6673. A critically-acclaimed café situated in Chinatown.

Lao Vien, 1129 W. Argyle Street, tel: 275-1112. A long and narrow storefront restaurant which offers diners good street views through the windows while they dine.

Drinking Notes

Bar, tavern, saloon, pub – in Chicago, all these terms mean someplace to get an alcoholic beverage. Some places serve food, but not all. At most bars, mixed drinks and bottled beer are available, as well as the beers "on tap" or "draft." Beer can often be bought by the pitcher. Soft drinks are always available. Soft drinks and mixed drinks will typically be served with generous amounts of ice, unless otherwise requested.

Some bars allow customers to run a tab; the waitress or bartender keeps track and presents the bill upon departure. Don't forget the tip for the waitress (15–20 percent) or bartender (10–15 percent).

Drinking and driving is dangerous, and the laws on drunk driving are extremely rigid in Illinois.

There are many different types of drinking establishments in Chicago. The neighborhood bar is usually a simple, friendly place, often with a regular crowd, where it might be easy to strike up a conversation. Theme bars have become very popular, and in Chicago the theme is sports. Hotel bars or lounges have traditionally been rather quiet and elegant, sometimes with piano music. But some of the newer ones offer more variety, such as bands or comedy.

Many Chicago bars are open late, until 1am or 2am, and some places that feature entertainment are allowed to remain open until 5am. Many downtown bars are open by midday, although neighborhood taverns are sometimes open at breakfast time.

Sports Bars

Sports bars represent a distinctly American concept that has been raised to an art form in Chicago. Some are owned by sports figures, some are near sports stadiums, others have a sports theme and frequently a big screen TV for watching games.

Some of the well known sports bars are:

Cubby Bear, 1059 W. Addison Street, tel: 327-1662. Across from Wrigley Field, a popular spot for Cubs games. Three 10-foot TV screens and 15 smaller monitors.

Harry Caray's, 33 W. Kinzie Street, tel: 465-9269. This bar and dining room, owned by the Cubs' announcer, is decorated with baseball photos and memorabilia.

Ranalli's Sports Bar and Grill, 1925 N. Lincoln Avenue, tel: 642-9500. Satellite sports TV on an 8-foot screen as well as 10 smaller screens. Popular with famous American athletes, fans and sports personalities.

Sluggers, 3540 N. Clark Street, tel: 248-0055. Located across from Wrigley Field, this place is packed after Cubs games. Try the batting cages for baseball practice.

Attractions

Culture

Museums

Adler Planetarium, 1300 S. Lake Shore Drive, 322-0304. Three floors of exhibits. Multi-media sky show for all over the age of 5. Open: daily 9am–5pm, Friday 9am–9pm. Admission: free Tuesday.

Art Institute of Chicago, S. Michigan Avenue at Adams street, tel: 443-3600. World-famous collection of American and European paintings, sculptures, prints, drawings, etc. A junior museum for children. Open: Monday–Friday 10.30am–4.30pm, Tuesday 10.30am–8pm, Saturday 10am–5pm, Sunday and holidays 12pm–5pm. Admission: free Tuesday.

Chicago Academy of Sciences, 2001 N. Clark Street, tel: 871-2668. Visit life-size wildlife scenes of the Great Lakes area, a walk-through prehistoric coal forest and the dinosaur exhibit. A hands-on children's gallery. Many workshops and programs. Open: 10am–5pm daily. Admission: free Monday.

Chicago Children's Museum, 435 E. Illinois Street (North Pier Building), tel: 527-1000. Hands-on exhibits, workshops and events. Open: Tuesday–Friday 12.30pm–4.30pm, Saturday and Sunday 10am–4.30pm. Preschool section only opens Wednesday, Thursday, and Friday at 10am.

Chicago Historical Society, 1601 N. Clark Street, tel: 642-4600. Museum and research center for Chicago and American history, includes a diorama room depicting scenes from Chicago history. Open: 9.30am–4.30pm Monday–Saturday, noon–5pm Sunday. Admission: free Monday.

Chicago Maritime Museum, North Pier Chicago, tel: 836-4343. Exhibits of Midwestern and Great Lakes maritime history.

DuSable Museum of African-American History, 740 E. 56th Place, tel: 947-0600. History and culture of Africans and Americans of African descent. Open: Monday–Friday 9am–5pm, Saturday and Sunday noon–5pm.

Field Museum of Natural History, Roosevelt Road and S. Lake Shore Drive, tel: 922-9410. Visit an Egyptian tomb including burial chambers, see mummies on display, and explore Egyptian life. There's plenty of hands-on experience in "Place of Wonder" and "Sizes" to make it fun for kids. Open: 9am–5pm daily. Admission: free Wednesday.

Hull House, 800 S. Halsted Street, tel: 413-5353. A museum dedicated to the settlement house movement and its founder, Jane Addams. Open: Monday–Friday 10am–4pm, Sunday noon–5pm.

International Museum of Surgical Science, 1516 N. Lake Shore Drive, tel: 642-6502. An insight to the history of surgery, with lurid graphics on tumors, amputations and Napoleon's death mask.

Museum of Broadcast Communications, Chicago Cultural Center, 78 E. Washington, tel: 629-6000. Tapes of old TV and radio shows are available. Exhibits include the original Charlie McCarthy and Mortimer Snerd Puppets. Open: Monday–Saturday 10am–4.30pm, Sunday noon–5pm.

Museum of Contemporary Art, 220 E. Chicago Avenue, tel: 280-2660. Emphasis on 20th-century painting and performance art. Sculpture garden. Changing exhibits. Open: Tuesday–Saturday 10am–5pm, Sunday noon–5pm. Admission: free Tuesday.

Museum of Contemporary Photography, 600 S. Michigan Avenue, tel: 663-5554. Traces the development of photography, with both special exhibits and a permanent collection.

Museum of Holography, 1134 W. Washington Boulevard, tel: 226-1007. Holographic art from around the world including moving and computer generated holograms. Special exhibits. Open: Wednesday–Sunday 12.30pm–5pm.

Museum of Science and Industry, 57th at Lake Shore Drive, tel: 684-1414. More than 2,000 exhibits, most designed for visitor participation. See the full scale replica of an underground coal mine, a World War II German submarine and hatching chicks. Visit the **Henry Crown Space Center and Omnimax Theater**. Open: Monday–Friday 9.30am–4pm, Saturday, Sunday and holidays 9.30am–5.30pm, Memorial Day–Labor Day 9.30am–5.30pm daily. Admission: free Thursday (except Omnimax).

Oriental Institute, 1155 E. 58th Street, tel: 702-9520. Part of University of Chicago. Five galleries display artifacts of ancient Near East. Open: Tuesday–Saturday 10am–4pm, Sunday noon–4pm. Admission: free.

Peace Museum, 350 W. Ontario, tel: 440-1860. Exhibits and programs related to war and peace. Open: Tuesday–Saturday 11am–5pm.

Polish Museum of America, 984 N. Milwaukee Avenue, tel: 384-3352. Ethnic museum of Polish art and dress. Special events on weekends. Open: daily noon–5pm.

Printing Museum, 731 S. Plymouth Court, tel: 987-1059. A Printer's Row museum with exhibits on the history and development of printing processes.

Shedd Aquarium, 1200 S. Lake Shore Drive, tel: 939-2426. World's largest indoor aquarium with fresh and saltwater fish. Watch the divers hand-feed the sharks, turtles and other fish in the coral reef in the aquarium. Visit Beluga whales and dolphins in the oceanarium. Open: 9am–6pm daily. Admission: free Thursday to aquarium only. Admission tickets can be pre-purchased through Ticketmaster, tel: 559-1212.

Smart Museum, 5550 S. Greenwood Avenue, tel: 702-0200. On the University of Chicago campus: ancient to contemporary art.

Maurice Spertus Museum of Judaica, 618 S. Michigan Avenue, tel: 922-9012. A celebration of Jewish culture through art, along with exhibits recalling the Holocaust.

Swedish American Museum, 5211 N. Clark Sreett. Features pictures and artifacts of Swedish immigrants' contributions to the growth of Chicago. Open: Tuesday–Friday 11am–4pm, Saturday and Sunday 11am–3pm.

Terra Museum of American Art, 666 N. Michigan Avenue, tel: 664-3939. American art from 17th–20th century. Open: Tuesday noon–8pm, Wednesday–Saturday 10am–5pm, Sunday noon–5pm.

Concerts

CLASSICAL

Chicago Symphony Orchestra, Orchestra Hall (September–May), 220 S. Michigan Avenue, tel: 435-8111 for tickets, 435-8122 for schedule. In summer, at Ravina, Highland Park, tel: 728-4642.

Grant Park Symphony Orchestra, Free concerts through the Chicago Park District at Petrillo Band Shell, Grant Park, tel: 294-2420.

Orchestra of Illinois, 506 S. Wabash, tel: 341-1975.

POPULAR MUSIC

Park West, 322 W. Armitage Avenue, tel: 929-5959.

Alpine Valley Music Theater, East Troy, Wisconsin, tel: 899-SHOW.

Poplar Creek Music Theatre, 4777 W. Higgins Road, Hoffman Estates, tel: (708) 559-1212. Outdoor concerts.

Rosemont Horizon, 6920 N. Mannheim Road, Rosemont, tel: 559-1212.

Ravinia, Highland Park, tel: RAV-INIA, features varied music acts (including jazz, classical, R&B, dance) that can be heard and seen from the pavilion, or from the grassy picnic area.

World Music Theatre, 183rd Street and Oak Park Avenue, Tinley Park, tel: 559-1212. Nice suburban location but public transportation is not available.

Ballet

Ballet Chicago, 222 S. Riverside Plaza, tel: 993-7575. Studio at 1016 N. Dearborn Street, tel: 664-6888.

Hubbard Street Dance Co., 218 Wabash Avenue, tel: 663-1642.

Opera

Lyric Opera of Chicago, 20 N. Wacker Drive, tel: 332-2244. (September–February) Hard to get tickets for these popular performances.

Chicago Opera Theatre, 20 E. Jackson Boulevard, tel: 663-0555.

The Light Opera Works, 927 Noyes, Evanston, tel: (708) 869-6300. (June–December). Specializes in Gilbert and Sullivan.

Theaters

For a current listing, phone Curtain Call, 977-1755. Tickets are generally available at the box office, sometimes by mail, and through Ticketron, tel: TICKETS or Ticketmaster, tel: 559-1212. Another ticket source is Hot Tix which sells half-price (plus service charge) tickets for same-day performances, and full-price advance tickets. Call 977-1755 for locations and details on availability.

DOWNTOWN

Arie Crown Theater, 2300 S. Lake Shore Drive, tel: 791-6000. In McCormick Place, primarily road companies of Broadway shows. The place to see *The Nutcracker* at Christmas.

Auditorium Theater, 70 E. Congress Parkway, tel: 922-2110. Great acoustics.

Goodman Theater, 200 S. Columbus Drive, tel: 443-3800. Specializes in contemporary work with many well-known actors.

Kuumba Theatre, 1900 W. Van Buren Street, tel: 461-9000.

Shubert Theatre, 22 W. Monroe Street, tel: 977-1700.

OFF LOOP

Beverly Art Center, 2153 W. 111th Street, tel: 445-3838. An active art center with a Saturday afternoon children's series performed by traveling groups.

Body Politic Theatre, 2261 N. Lincoln Avenue, tel: 871-3000. Comedies and satires.

Court Theatre, 5535 S. Ellis Street (on campus of the University of Chicago), tel: 753-4472. Classics.

Organic Theater Co., 3319 N. Clark Street, tel: 327-5588. Performance art.

Steppenwolf Theater, 2851 N. Halsted Street, tel: 335-1650. National reputation for method acting. Alumni include John Malkovich.

Theatre on the Lake, Fullerton Parkway and the Lakefront. Strictly community theater performing well-known Broadway shows at 8pm Tuesday through Saturday during the summer.

Victory Gardens Theater, 2257 N. Lincoln Avenue, tel: 871-3000. Serious plays. Very professional. **Wisdom Bridge Theatre**, 1559 W. Howard Street, tel: 743-6442.

SUBURBAN

Candlelight Dinner Playhouse, 5620 S. Harlem Avenue, Summit, tel: (708) 496-3000.
Drury Lane/Oakbrook Terrace, 100 Drury Lane, Oakbrook Tce, tel: (708) 530-8300.
Marriott's Lincolnshire Theatre, Route 21 and Milwaukee Road, Lincolnshire, tel: (708) 634-0200.
Pheasant Run Theatre, Route 64, St Charles, tel: (708) 584-6300.
Village Players, shared by the suburbs of Oak Park and River Forest, a small theater with locals taking roles in many of the famous Broadway shows.

Cinema

Cinemas are plentiful in the suburbs. Their numbers have shrunk in the downtown area. Here are the main ones:
Watertower, 845 N. Michigan Avenue, tel: 649-5790.
McClurg Court, 330 E. Ohio Street, tel: 642-0723.
Biograph, 2433 N. Lincoln Avenue, tel: 348-4123 (Note: this is where Dillinger was gunned down by the FBI).
Chestnut Station, Clark and Chestnut streets, tel: 337-7301.
Burnham Plaza, 826 S. Wabash Avenue, tel: 922-1090; 900 N. Michigan Avenue, tel: 787-1988.

All of the above, except the Biograph, are wheelchair accessible; all except the Watertower have sound systems for the hearing impaired. Often children under six are not admitted, so check in advance. For additional theaters, or to check what's currently playing, check a local newspaper.

FOREIGN FILMS

Fine Arts Theatre, 418 S. Michigan Avenue, tel: 939-3700. A good selection of foreign and domestic independent films.
Music Box Theatre, 3733 N. Southport Avenue, tel: 871-6604. Beautiful old-fashioned movie house with premieres, previews and classic American and foreign films.

City

Besides its museums, festivals, sports and special events, Chicago has many attractions and tours. Here are some of the most popular in town:

Animart Puppet Theatre, 3901 N. Kedzie Street, tel: 267-1209. Weekend performances featuring puppets, marionettes and audience participation.
Battletech Center, 435 E. Illinois Street, tel: 836-5977. Experience virtual reality when you slide into a cockpit and battle others on a computer-generated playing field.
Beverly Art Center, 2153 W. 111th Street, tel: 445-3838. A children's theater series on Saturday afternoons for children aged three and older. Varied performances by touring companies include fairy tales and puppet shows.
Buckingham Fountain, Grant Park and Lakefront (Congress Parkway and Lake Shore Drive), tel: 294-2200. A wonderful, large fountain modeled on the Latona Fountain at Versailles. It operates from May 1–October 31 with a multi-colored light display every night from 9–11pm.
Capone's Chicago, 605 N. Clark Street, tel: 654-1919. Witness the pivotal events and personalities that created Chicago's most dangerous era, the Roaring Twenties.
Chicago Board of Trade, 141 W. Jackson Blvd, tel: 435-3590, group tours 435-3625. The largest commodity futures exchange in the world. A viewing gallery, and exhibits are on the fifth floor. Open: Monday–Friday 8am–2pm. Admission: free.
Chicago Board Options Exchange, 440 S. LaSalle Street, tel: 786-5600. Visitor's gallery open: Monday–Friday 8.30am–3.15pm.
Chicago Cultural Center, 78 E. Washington Street, tel: 744-6300. This complex features theaters, concert halls, museums, films, etc. It also offers daily free programs and exhibits covering a wide range of performing, visual and literary arts. For a listing of events dial FINE-ARTS (346-3278). Open: Monday–Thurday 9am–7pm, Friday 9am–6pm, Saturday 9am–5pm. Closed: Sunday and holidays.
Chicago Fire Academy, 558 W. De Koven Street, tel: 744-4728. Located on the site where the Chicago Fire of 1871 is believed to have started. One-hour guided tours of the facilities for training firefighters are offered. Open: Monday–Friday twice a day. Visits by appointment only. Admission: free.
Chicago Mercantile Exchange, 30 S. Wacker Drive, tel: 939-8249. Visitor's gallery open: Monday–Friday 7.30am–3.15pm. Admission: free.
Children's Film Festival, 1517 W. Fullerton Avenue, tel: 929-KIDS. Weekend films for younger and older children.
Citygolf Chicago, 435 E. Illinois Street, tel: 836-5936. Two miniature golf courses depicting Chicago landmarks. For kids and adults of all ages.
Garfield Park Conservatory, 300 N. Central Park Boulevard, tel: 533-1281. Acres of horticultural exhibits featuring four major shows annually. Open: daily 9am–5pm. Admission: free.
John Hancock Center, 875 N. Michigan Avenue, tel: 751-3681. Visit the Observatory to view the area from one of the world's tallest buildings. Open: daily 9am–midnight.
Lifeline Theatre, 6912 N. Glenwood Avenue, tel: 761-4477. This theater is geared toward 5–12 year olds.
Lincoln Park Conservatory, 2400 N. Stockton Drive, tel: 294-4770. Exhibit areas include a palm house and fernery. Features four major flower shows annually. Open: daily 9am–5pm.
Lincoln Park Zoo, 2200 N. Cannon Drive, tel: 935-6700. Highlights include the Koala Exhibit, Great Ape House, Polar Bear Pool with underwater viewing window, and Birds of Prey Exhibit. Be sure to take the kids to the Children's Zoo with Discovery Center and Zoo Nursery, and the Farm in the Zoo. Open: daily 9am–5pm. Admission: free.
Midwest Stock Exchange, 440 S. LaSalle Street, tel: 663-2980. Visitor's gallery open: Monday–Friday 8.30am–3pm.
McCormick Place, 230 S. Lake Shore Drive, tel: 791-7000. The largest indoor exhibit area in the country for trade shows or conventions. **Arie Crown Theatre** is located here, tel: 791-6000. Tours are available.
Merchandise Mart, Wells Street at Chicago River, tel: 527-7600. Home to some of the most beautiful furniture and furnishings. Tours available Monday-Friday at noon. Call 644-4664 for tour information. Admission: free.

Puppet Parlor, 1922 W. Montrose Avenue, tel: 774-2919. Weekend performances including children's classics.
Richard J. Daley Center Plaza, 50 W. Washington Street, tel: 346-3278. Site of Chicago's famous Picasso sculpture. There are frequent outdoor concerts during the summer, and a Christmas tree that will delight young and old in December.
Rock & Roll McDonald's, 600 N. Clark Street, tel: 644-7940. Eat a Big Mac in a pop-music motif.
Saturday's Child, 2465 N. Lincoln Avenue, tel: 248-2665. FAO Schwarz, 835 N. Michigan Avenue (Watertower Place), tel: 787-8894.
Sears Tower, 233 S. Wacker Drive (enter on Jackson Street), tel: 875-9696. The world's tallest building. The 103rd floor skydeck at 1,353 feet above ground is reached by express elevator in just over a minute. The skydeck is open daily March-September 9am–11pm; October–February 9am–10pm.
The Children's Bookstore, 2465 N. Lincoln Avenue, tel: 248-2665. Books for sale, plus activities such as story hours and plays.
United Skates of America, 4836 N. Clark Street, tel: 271-5668. Two roller skating floors. Game room. Food available.
Harold Washington Public Library, 400 S. State Street, tel: 747-4310. One of the world's largest public libraries. Information services, cultural programs, exhibits, art and, of course, books. Closed on Sunday and holidays.
Wacky Pirate Cruise, Mercury Cruiselines, a one-hour cruise departing from the south side of the Chicago River at Michigan Avenue Friday–Sunday at 10am. Also Thursday 10am in July. Reservations are required, tel: 332-1366. Children under 12 must be accompanied by an adult.
Water Tower Pumping Station, Pearson and Michigan streets, tel: 467-7114. Survived the Chicago Fire of 1871. Currently houses "Here's Chicago," a 45-minute sound and sight show about Chicago. Doors open daily at 9.30am with continuous shows.
Oprah Winfrey, HARPO Studios, 110 N. Carpenter Street, tel: 591-9444. Ring at least a week in advance for reservations for seats in the audience of one of America's most popular daytime television talk shows. Free.

Suburbs

Baha'i Temple, Linden Avenue and Sheridan Road, Wilmette, tel: (708) 256-4400. This house of worship is listed in the National Register of Historic Places. There's a visitors' center with displays and presentations. Telephone for tours. Admission: free. Open: October–May 10am–5pm, May–October 10am–10pm. Service daily at 12.15pm and Sunday 3pm.
Brookfield Zoo, First Avenue and 31st Street, Brookfield, tel: (708) 242-2630. A great place to spend a day. See animals in naturalistic settings. Visit Tropic World and see the animals in tropical forest storms three times a day. There are dolphin shows in the new Seven Seas Panorama, and a children's zoo. Open: daily 10am–5pm. Admission: free Tuesday and Thursday.
Chicago Botanic Garden, Lake Cook Road, half a mile off the Edens Expressway, Glencoe, tel: (708) 835-5440. Three hundred acres of gardens, lakes, trails, greenhouses, an education center, museum, library and restaurant. Open: daily 7am–sunset, except Christmas. Admission free, but parking fee.
Drury Lane Children's Theatre, 2500 W. 95th. Street, Evergreen Park, tel: (708) 779-4000. Four children's productions a year performed in the round.
Frank Lloyd Wright Home Studio, 951 Chicago Avenue, Oak Park, tel: (708) 848-1978. A walking tour is offered. The area has over 30 buildings designed by Frank Lloyd Wright. Open: daily 10am–5pm.
Kohls Children's Museum, 165 Green Bay Road, Wilmette, tel: (708) 256-6056. A hands-on museum geared toward children aged 1–10. They call themselves "a place to pretend, invent, touch explore, discover, learn." Open: Tuesday–Saturday 10am–4pm, Sunday noon–4pm.
The Lambs, Interstate 94 and Route 176, Libertyville, tel: (708) 362-4636. A community for the developmentally disabled, there's a restaurant, bakery, ice cream parlor, country store, farmyard, petting zoo, miniature golf, picnic area and special events. Open: daily 9am–5pm, except major holidays.
Marriott's Lincolnshire Theatre for Young Audiences, Lincolnshire, tel: (708) 634-0200. Sometimes includes audience participation.
Medieval Times Dinner and Tournament, 2001 N. Roselle Rd, Schaumburg, tel: (708) 843-3900. Knights on horseback compete in games of skill, combat and jousting while you enjoy a medieval feast at an 11th-century castle. Reservations required. Wednesday–Sunday.
Morton Arboretum, Route 53, Lisle, tel: (708) 719-2400. Has 1,500 acres of plants, gardens, and woodlands. Tours and special programs most Sundays. Restaurant.
Oak Park Conservatory, 617 Garfield Street, Oak Park. Exhibits of desert and tropical flora, collections of Illinois plants and displays on the specialized biology of ferns.
Riverboat Casinos. **Empress River Casino**, Joliet, tel: (708) 345-6789. **Harrah's Casino**, Joliet, tel: (800) 342-7724. **Hollywood Casino**, Aurora, tel: (800) 888-7777.
Santa's Village, Routes 25 and 72, Dundee, tel: (708) 426-6571. See Santa everyday. Amusement rides, shows, waterpark, picnic groves. Young children especially seem to enjoy this. Open: May–September, Monday–Friday 10am–6pm, Saturday and Sunday 11am–7pm.
Show Biz Pizza, in various suburban locations, has video games, preschool rides, skee ball and a stage with a mechanical band singing and entertaining. The kids love it. The pizza is passable.
Six Flags Great America, Interstate 94 at Route 132, Gurnee, tel: (708) 249-1776. Amusement park with over 130 rides and attractions. Don't miss the Rolling Thunder Roller Coaster. Open: May–September 10am–9pm.

Tours

Bus & Walking Tours

Double Decker Bus Tours, Sears Tower, Water Tower and other stops, tel: 922-8919. Narrated tours of Chicago landmarks by Chicago Motor Coach Co. Tours: daily 10am–5pm.
Culture Bus Tours (CTA), Art Institute, Michigan Avenue and Adams Street, tel: 836-7000. Guided bus tours of Chicago neighborhoods and attractions. Three routes, every half hour, 10.30am–5pm, Sunday and holidays (May–September).

Chicago Architectural Tours, 224 S. Michigan Avenue, tel: 922-8687. Walking, bus and boat tours of Chicago's world-famous architecture. There are also exhibitions, lectures, books, gifts and memorabilia dedicated to the art of design.

Chicago Supernatural Tours, PO Box 29054, tel: (708) 499-0300. Ghost tours.

Untouchable Tours, PO Box 43185, tel: 881-1195. Visit Prohibition-era gangster sites. Reservations suggested.

Boat Tours

Chicago From The Lake, North Pier Terminal, 509 E. Illinois Street, tel: 527-1977. Reservations required. 90-minute architectural tour. Also a children's tour.

Mercury, Chicago's Skyline Cruiseline, departs from the South Side of Chicago River at Michigan Avenue, tel: 332-1353. Also a children's cruise, tel: 332-1366.

Shoreline Marine Cruises, tel: (708) 673-3399. 30-minute cruises from north of Shedd Aquarium during the day, from dock just east of Buckingham Fountain in the evening, or Adler Planetarium day and evening.

Spirit of Chicago, South Side of Navy Pier, tel: 321-1241. Reservations required. Lunch, dinner, and moonlight cruises with entertainment. Brunch cruise on Sundays.

Star of Chicago, North Side of Navy Pier, tel: 644-5914. Reservations required. Lunch, dinner, cocktail and moonlight cruises with entertainment. Brunch cruises at weekends.

Wendella Sightseeing Boats, North Side of Chicago River at Michigan Avenue, tel: 337-1446. One to two-hour cruises.

Horse-Drawn Carriages

Chicago Horse & Carriage Ltd, Pearson Street and Michigan Avenue, south of Water Tower Place, tel: 944-6773.

J.C. Cutters, Michigan and Chicago avenues, tel: 664-6014.

The Noble Horse, a block west of Michigan Avenue at Old Water Tower, tel: 266-7878.

Multilingual Tours

Chicago Europe Language Center, 180 N. LaSalle Street, Suite 2510, tel: 276-6683.

Chicago Adventures Inc., 2953 W. Devon Avenue, tel: 338-7310.

On The Scene Tours, 505 N. LaSalle Street, tel: 661-1440.

Recommended for Children

Chicago is a great place to bring kids. Many hotels let children stay in their parents' room for a small charge or for free; ask when making reservations. Many restaurants can provide a special children's menu – usually for children under 12, with smaller portions and lower prices.

Pick up a copy of *Chicago Parents*, a free monthly magazine usually available in libraries or children's bookstores, which lists events of interest to children and their families. Copies or annual subscriptions are available from: Wednesday Journal, Inc., 141 S. Oak Park Avenue, Oak Park, IL 60302, tel: (708) 386-5555.

A dozen things to do with children:

Art Institute's Junior Museum, South Michigan Avenue at Adams Street, tel: 443-3600. The Junior Museum offers an assortment of absorbing activities for children of all ages. There are workshops, tours and demonstrations, including such things as puppet making and calligraphy. Some games send children throughout the museum in search of clues.

Brookfield Zoo, First Avenue and 31st Street, Brookfield, tel: (708) 485-0263. Children especially enjoy the Children's Zoo, where they can touch the animals, watch the cows being milked and just get close. Brookfield has an annual "Teddy Bear Picnic" in June, and an annual Halloween party with a costume parade.

Chicago Children's Museum, 435 E. Illinois Street (North Pier), tel: 527-1000. This museum is made for inquisitive kids, and even has a preschool section. Everything is hands-on. There are family workshops on weekends, and everyday fun such as enclosing yourself in a giant bubble

Chicago Cultural Center, 78 E. Washington Street, tel: 269-2835. The Cultural Center offers a variety of programs for children presented by the Thomas Hughes Children's Library. Call for details.

Field Museum of Natural History, Roosevelt Road and Lake Shore Drive,

tel: 922-9410. There are many exhibits for children, like the giant dinosaurs and Egyptian mummies. The Place of Wonder is specifically for kids, and the Sizes exhibit has lots of fun things to try. Workshops are offered on weekends.

Kohl Children's Museum, 165 Green Bay Road, Wilmette, tel: (708) 251-7781. A hands-on museum geared toward kids. Exhibits rotate throughout the year, plus there are story times and puppet shows. The learning store offers a variety of creative toys.

The Lambs, Interstate 94 and Route 176, Libertyville, tel: (708) 362-4636. Something for everyone. Kids will probably like the ice cream parlor and bakery. There's a farmyard to visit, a petting zoo and miniature golf, plus a picnic area and a restaurant. And special events are held throughout the year.

Lincoln Park Zoo, 2200 N. Cannon Drive, tel: 935-6700. A free zoo right in the city. Children will enjoy everything, especially the Children's Zoo, where they can pet some of the animals, and the Farm in the Zoo. Very popular is the underwater viewing window in the Polar Bear Pool. Paddle boats may be rented on the zoo pond.

Museum of Science and Industry, 57th Street at Lake Shore Drive, tel: 684-1414. There's so much to do here. Favorites include Colleen Moore's Fairy Castle, Hatching Chicks and a giant train set. For the younger children, find the Curiosity Place.

Santa's Village, Routes 25 and 72, Dundee, tel: (708) 426-6751. Amusement rides, especially for younger children, shows that the whole family can enjoy, a water park and picnic groves are among the attractions. But best of all, Santa is always there.

Shedd Aquarium, 1200 S. Lake Shore Drive, tel: 939-2426. The world's largest fishbowl. A favorite spot is the Coral Reef at feeding time as the turtles, sharks and other fish are fed by hand.

Six Flags Great America, I-94 at Route 132, Gurnee, tel: (708) 249-1776. The largest amusement park around. Plenty of rides and shows for one admission fee. (It's fairly expensive so plan on spending the whole day.) For some thrill-seekers, the roller coasters alone make the trip worthwhile.

Diary of Events

There's almost always something going on in Chicago. For the latest information on entertainment and events, turn to the local newspapers, especially on Friday when comprehensive weekend listings are printed. Here are some annual events:

JANUARY

Chicago Boat, Sports and RV Show, McCormick Place, tel: 836-4740.
Chicago Sport Fishing, Travel and Outdoor Show, O'Hare Expo Center, Rosemont, tel: (708) 692-2220.
Chinese New Year Parade, Wentworth Avenue and Cermak Road, tel: 326-5320.

FEBRUARY

Chicago Auto Show, McCormick Place, tel: 791-7000.
Azalea and Camellia Show, Lincoln Park Conservatory, tel: 294-4770. Garfield Park Conservatory, tel: 533-1281.

MARCH

Medinah Shrine Circus, Medinah Temple, 600 N. Wabash Avenue, tel: 266-5050.
Ice Capades, Rosemont Horizon, Rosemont, tel: (708) 635-6601.
St Patrick's Day, parade starts at Dearborn Street and Wacker Drive, tel: 263-6612.
South Side Irish Parade, 103rd Street and Western Avenue, tel: 238-1969. A similar celebration which takes place the weekend before St Patrick's Day.

APRIL

Antique Show, O'Hare Expo Center, tel: (708) 692-2220.
Spring and Easter Flower Show, Lincoln Park Conservatory, tel: 294-4770.

MAY

Chicago International Art Expo, Navy Pier, tel: 787-6858.
Buckingham Fountain Re-Opens, Grant Park, tel: 294-2493.

JUNE

Western Open, Butler Golf Course, Oakbrook, tel: (800) 458-5535.
International Theater Festival of Chicago, includes various theaters, tel: 644-3370.
Chicago Gospel Festival, Petrillo Band Shell, Grant Park, tel: 744-3315.
Chicago Blues Festival, Petrillo Band Shell, Grant Park, tel: 744-3315.
Old Town Art Fair, 1900 N. Lincoln Avenue, tel: 337-1938.
Chicago International Boat Show, Navy Pier, tel: 787-6858.
Water Tower Arts and Crafts Festival, Chicago Avenue between Michigan Avenue and Lake Shore Drive, tel: 991-4748.
Taste of Chicago, Grant Park, tel: 744-3315. June 27–July 4. A very popular event, featuring lots of food from a variety of Chicago restaurants. Music, too.
Printers Row Book Fair, Dearborn and Harrison streets, tel: 987-1980.
Beverly Art Fair, Beverly Art Center, 2153 W. 111th Street, tel: 445-3838.
Ravinia, opens for a summer full of outdoor concerts, Highland Park, tel: RAV-INIA.
Grant Park Concerts, Petrillo Band Shell, Grant Park, tel: 294-2420. Free concerts by the Grant Park Symphony Orchestra.

JULY

Taste of Chicago, continues in Grant Park, tel: 744-3315. The festival culminates with a spectacular fireworks display over Lake Michigan, accompanied by the Grant Park Symphony Orchestra performing Tchaikovsky's *1812 Overture*.
Fourth of July, fireworks on the lakefront and in almost every Chicago neighborhood.
Air and Water Show, North Avenue Beach, tel: 294-2200.
Taste of Lincoln Avenue, food fair between Fullerton and Wrightwood avenues, tel: 472-9046.
Old St Patrick's World's Largest Block Party, Adams and Des Plaines Streets, tel: 782-6171.
Chicago to Mackinac Yacht Races, sailing from Monroe Street Harbor, tel: 861-7777.

AUGUST

Gold Coast Art Fair, River North, Wells and Ontario streets, tel: 280-5740.
Bud Billiken Parade, 35th Street and South King Drive, tel: 225-2400.
Chicago International Sky Nights, Lakefront, tel: 744-3315.
Venetian Night Boat Parade, Monroe Harbor, tel: 744-3315.
Antique Show, O'Hare Expo Center, tel: (708) 692-2220.
Chicago Jazz Festival, Petrillo Band Shell, Grant Park, tel: 744-3315.
Illinois State Fair, Springfield (not Chicago), tel: (217) 782-6661.

SEPTEMBER

Viva Chicago, Grant Park, tel: 744-3315.
Ribfest, Grant Park, tel: 222-3232. Backyard chefs compete for the title of best barbecue artist in town.
Berghoff Oktoberfest, Adams Street, from State to Dearborn streets, tel: 427-3170.
Chicago Bears, season-opening games, Soldier Field, tel: 295-6600.
Lyric Opera, season-opening concerts, Civic Center for Performing Arts, tel: 346-0270.
Chicago Symphony Orchestra, season-opening concerts, Orchestra Hall, tel: 435-6666.

OCTOBER

Columbus Day Parade, Dearborn Street and Wacker Drive, tel: 828-0010.
Chicago International Film Festival, various theaters, tel: 644-3400.
History Mystery Bicycle Tour and Festival, 96th Street and Longwood Drive, tel: 233-3100. A puzzle-solving bicycle tour, followed by food, music and games.

NOVEMBER

Antique Show, O'Hare Expo Center, tel: (708) 692-2220.
Craft Show, O'Hare Expo Center, tel: (708) 692-2220.
Christmas Around the World, Museum of Science and Industry, tel: 684-1414. Christmas trees as decorated in various countries.
Lighting of the City's Christmas Tree, Daley Center Plaza, tel: 744-3315.
Christmas Parade, Michigan Avenue from Balbo to Wacker drives, tel: 935-8747.

DECEMBER

A Christmas Carol, Goodman Theater, tel: 443-3800.
The Nutcracker, Arie Crown Theater, tel: 791-6000.
Caroling to the Animals, Lincoln Park Zoo, tel: 294-4662.
Christmas Flower Show, Lincoln Park Conservatory, tel: 294-4770.

Nightlife

There is plenty of nightlife in Chicago. Most hotels have one or more lounges, many of which are popular spots. The local newspapers and listings magazines have descriptions. Many places never have cover charges, while some do only on weekends.

Night Spots

America's Bar, 219 W. Erie Street, tel: 915-5986. A mainstream dance bar.
Baja Beach Club, North Pier, 401 E. Illinois Street, tel: 222-1992. Disco, cabaret, restaurant. Often a wait to get in.
Cabaret Metro, 3730 N. Clark Street, tel: 549-0203. Dance to rock music.
Excalibur, 632 N. Dearborn Street, tel: 266-1944. Another popular spot, again with long lines. Three floors.
Gamekeepers Tavern and Grill, 1971 N. Lincoln Avenue, tel: 549-0400. Young professionals.
Ginger Man, 3740 N. Clark Street, tel: 787-8141. Exotic beers, big pool tables.
Goose Island Brewing Co., 1800 N. Clybourne Avenue, tel: 915-0071. Serves home-brewed beer.
Ka-Boom, 747 N. Green Street, tel: 243-4800. River West location. Six different environments from hot dance to cool jazz.
Pyramid Room of Cairo, 720 N. Wells Street, tel: 266-6620. River North location. Ambiance of an Egyptian desert oasis.
Sheffields, 3258 N. Sheffield Avenue, tel: 281-4989. An easy-going corner bar, with many brands of beer and a summer beer garden.
Smart Bar, 3730 N. Clark Street, tel: 549-4140. Haven for Chicago's black-clad hipsters.
Whiskey River, 1997 N. Clybourn Avenue, tel: 528-3400. Country nightclub with free dance lessons every night. Live music Wednesday–Saturday.

Singles Bars

The Rush Street area has traditionally been considered the place for singles bars. Caters to the under-40 crowd, and a good number of tourists. Parking is hard to find. Among the most popular bars are:
Bamboo Bernie's, 2247 N. Lincoln Avenue, tel: 549-3900. Tropical drinks. Indoor beach volleyball.
Bootleggers, 13 W. Division, tel: 266-0944.
Butch McGuires, 20 W. Division Street, tel: 337-9080.
Mother's, 26 W. Division Street, tel: 642-7251.
She-Nannigans, 16 W. Division Street, tel: 642-2344.
Snuggery, 15 W. Division Street, 337-4349.

Blues Clubs

As the home of Chicago blues, the guitar-driven music form that evolved from the downhome Mississippi Delta folk music and then had so much influence on modern rock, the city still has a number of clubs and bars devoted almost exclusively to the form, and often featuring many of the legendary bluesmen. They include:
Biddy Mulligan's, 7644 N. Sheridan Road, tel: 761-6532.
Blue Chicago on Clark, 536 N. Clark Street, tel: 661-0100. 1940s-style bar.
BLUES, 2519 N. Halsted Street, tel: 528-1012.
Blues Chicago, 937 N. State Street, tel: 642-6261.
BLUES Etcetera, 1124 West Belmont Avenue, tel: 525-8909.
Kingston Mines, 2548 N. Halsted Street, tel: 477-4646.
Legends, 754 S. Wabash Avenue (owned by guitar great, Buddy Guy), tel: 427-0333.
Lilly's, 2513 N. Lincoln Avenue, tel: 525-2422.
New Checkerboard Lounge, 423 E. 43rd Street, tel: 624-3240. (Considered a rough area. Home of the Blues Hall of Fame.)
Wise Fool's Pub, 2270 N. Lincoln Avenue, tel: 929-1510.

Jazz Clubs

Andy's, 11 E. Hubbard Street, tel: 642-6805.
The Bulls, 1916 N. Lincoln Park West, tel: 337-3000.
Cotton Club, 1710 S. Michigan Avenue, tel: 341-9787.
Gold Star Sardine Bar, 680 N. Lake Shore Drive, tel: 664-4215.
Green Mill, 4802 N. Broadway, tel: 878-5552. A legendary jazz club once owned and frequented by gangsters. Now there's good music every night except Monday, when local would-be poets recite their material for praise or heckling in the "Poetry Slam."
Jazz Showcase, 636 S. Michigan Avenue, tel: 427-4300.
Kiku's, 754 W. Wellington Street, tel: 281-7878.
Milt Trenier's Nite Club, 610 N. Fairbanks Ct, tel: 266-6226. Live jazz/blues nightly.
The Other Place, 7600 S. King Drive, tel: 874-5476.
Oz, 2917 N. Sheffield Avenue, tel: 957-8100.
Pop's for Champagne, 2934 N. Sheffield, tel: 472-1000. Nightly live jazz in champagne bar. Sunday brunch.

Local Bars

Chicago also claims to have invented the American sports bar, though most places now calling themselves such are not the old shot-and-a-beer neighborhood joints, but rather trendy spots popular among both men and women, including some who aren't necessarily interested in the latest scores. See "Drinking Notes" for details.

Cabaret & Comedy Clubs

Funny Firm, 318 W. Grand Street, tel: 321-9500. River North location. Up and coming local talent and national standup comedians.
The Improv, 504 N. Wells Street, tel: 527-3286. Largest club in Chicago. Nationally recognized standup comics. Children's variety show on Saturday afternoons.
Second City, 1616 N. Wells Street, tel: 337-3992. Improvisation. This famous spot was a springboard for Jim and John Belushi, Bill Murray, Dan Akroyd and John Candy, to name a few.
Zanies, 1548 N. Wells Street, tel: 337-4027. First full-time comedy club in Chicago. Local and national talent.

Shopping

Most stores and shops open at 9 or 10am and stay open until at least 6pm; many often remain open until 8 or 9pm.

Shopping Areas

Downtown has its share of boutiques, fashion shops and galleries, along with several of America's best department stores and a myriad of cheaper chain stores, discount houses and manufacturers' outlets. Chicago has enthusiastically embraced the concept of the shopping center, and now the shopping mall. A number of shopping centers and districts can be recommended for the quality and variety of their shops, and for the exciting innovation of their design.

Chicago Place Mall, 700 N. Michigan Avenue, tel: 642-4811. Fifty specialty shops including Saks Fifth Avenue and Louis Vuitton. Eighth floor food court in a tropical garden. European gourmet supermarket.

Gurnee Mills Outlet Mall, Interstate 94 and Route 132, Gurnee, tel: (800) YES-SHOP. Over 200 stores, manufacturers' and retail outlets offering savings on top-name brands.

Magnificent Mile, Michigan Avenue from Chicago River to Oak Street. Glamorous shopping area including Tiffany, Cartier, Chanel, Ralph Lauren, Saks Fifth Avenue, I. Magnin and Bonwit Teller.

Nike Town Chicago, 669 N. Michigan Avenue, tel: 642-6363. Nike shoes, clothes, hats, posters and displays. A one-of-a-kind sport store.

Northbrook Court, in suburban Northbrook, is an enclosed, upscale mall whose 144 shops are aimed at the country-club set.

900 North Michigan Shops, 900 N. Michigan Avenue. This is home to the Chicago branch of Bloomingdales, plus dozens of boutiques and specialty shops, including Gucci. Also restaurants and theaters.

North Pier, 435 E. Illinois Street, tel: 836-4300. A relatively new area offering restaurants, shopping, night clubs, and museums.

Oak Street consists of renovated brownstones, and its outstanding specialty shops emphasize diversity and quality. A fun place to window shop.

Old Orchard, in suburban Skokie, is a large, well-designed mall aimed at providing a pleasing, everyday shopping experience.

State Street, Carson Pirie Scott & Co., at State and Madison Streets, tel: 744-2000, and Marshall Fields, at 111 N. State Street, tel: 781-4917, each have department stores here. Open: Monday and Thursday 9.45am–7.30pm; other days: 9.45am–5.45pm; one Sunday a month.

Water Tower Place, 835 N. Michigan Avenue, tel: 440-3165. An atrium shopping mall with Marshall Fields, Lord & Taylor and seven floors of specialty shops. Plenty of restaurants and movie theaters too. Open: Monday–Friday 10 am–7pm (Marshall Fields until 8pm, Lord & Taylor until 9pm), Saturday 10am–6pm, Sunday 12 noon–6pm.

Woodfield Mall, in suburban Schaumburg, tel: (708) 330-0220, has 235 shops and stores and is reputed to be the second-largest mall in the United States. Buses run regularly from downtown and elsewhere.

Souvenirs

Accent Chicago, 835 N. Michigan Avenue (Water Tower, 7th floor), tel: 944-1354. Complete Chicago themed gift store.

Chicago Tribune Gift Store, 435 N. Michigan Avenue, tel: 222-3080. Unique gifts.

Hello Chicago, 700 N. Michigan, tel: 787-0838. Large selection of T-shirts and sweatshirts with Chicago scenes.

Sales Tax

The sales tax in Chicago is 8 percent: 7 percent for the state of Illinois and another 1 percent for the city of Chicago. The sales tax is added to the listed cost of almost everything, including books, food and clothing. Unlike many European countries, where the value-added tax can be deducted when purchases are being exported, there are no provisions for reimbursement of the sales tax.

Clothing Chart

WOMEN'S DRESSES/SUITS

American	Continental	British
6	38/34N	8/30
8	40/36N	10/32
10	42/38N	12/34
12	44/40N	14/36
14	46/42N	16/38
16	48/44N	18/40

WOMEN'S SHOES

American	Continental	British
4½	36	3
5½	37	4
6½	38	5
7½	39	6
8½	40	7
9½	41	8
10½	42	9

MEN'S SUITS

American	Continental	British
34	44	34
—	46	36
38	48	38
—	50	40
42	52	42
—	54	44
46	56	46

MEN'S SHIRTS

American	Continental	British
14	36	14
14½	37	14½
15	38	15
15½	39	15½
16	40	16
16½	41	16½
17	42	17

MEN'S SHOES

American	Continental	British
6½	—	6
7½	40	7
8½	41	8
9½	42	9
10½	43	10
11½	44	11

Sports & Leisure

Spectator

Baseball
Two major league teams make their homes in Chicago, playing from early April through early October. The Chicago Cubs play in the National League. Their home park is **Wrigley Field**, the oldest park in the major leagues. Located at Clark and Addison Streets (1060 W. Addison Street), Wrigley can be reached by the Howard "El" train. Spend an afternoon or an evening (possible since the highly controversial installation of lights in 1988) amid the ivy-covered walls. For tickets, tel: 559-1212; to reach the office, tel: 924-1000.

The Chicago White Sox play in the American League. They can be seen at **Comiskey Park**, just off the Dan Ryan Expressway at 35th and Shields Streets. The park can be reached on the Dan Ryan "El" Line. To get tickets, tel: 559-1212; for any other information, tel: 924-1000.

Basketball
The Chicago Bulls entertain their fans at **United Center**, 1901 W. Madison Street, which can be reached on the Madison Street Bus No. 20. Tel: 455-4000.

Football
The Chicago Bears play at **Soldier Field**, at 12th Street and the lakefront. Tel: 663-5100.

Ice Hockey
The Chicago Black Hawks play in **United Center**, 1901 W. Madison Street. Tel: 455-7000.

Racetracks
The Chicago area has a number of tracks where horse racing, both thoroughbred and harness, can be enjoyed, including Arlington, which has been completely rebuilt "family style" after it was burnt down a few years ago.
Arlington International Racecourse, Euclid and Wilke Streets, Arlington Heights, tel: (708) 255-4300.
Balmoral Park Racetrack, I-394 and the Calumet Expy, Crete, tel: 568-5700.
Hawthorne Downs Racetrack, 3501 S. Laramie Avenue, Cicero, tel: (708) 780-3700.
Maywood Park Racetrack, North Avenue and 5th Street, Maywood, tel: 626-4816.
Sportsman's Park Racetrack, 3301 S. Laramie Avenue, Cicero, tel: 242-1121.
Off-Track Betting Facilities, 177 N. State Street, tel: 419-8787; 233 W. Jackson Blvd, tel: 427-2300.
Auto Racing: Raceway Park, 130th Street and Ashland Avenue, Calumet Park, tel: (708) 385-4035. **Santa Fe Speedway**, 9100 S. Wolf Road, Hinsdale, tel: (708) 839-1050.
Polo: Oak Brook Polo Club, 2700 S. York Road, Oak Brook, tel: (708) 571-7657.

Participant

The Chicago Park District, tel: 294-2493, is a source of information for most sports.

Bowling
Marina City Bowling Lanes, 300 N. State Street, tel: 527-0747.

Bicycling
A 20-mile path runs along the lakefront. Bicycle rentals are available through Bike Chicago at three locations: Oak Street Beach at Division, Buckingham Fountain, and Lincoln Park Zoo at Fullerton. Tel: (800) 915-2453. Tours available, or use a free self-guided Chicago tour map.

Canoeing
Chicagoland Canoe Base, 4019 N. Narragansett Avenue, is a source for rentals and information, tel: 779-1489. American Youth Hostels (tel: 327-8114) and the Field Museum (tel: 922-9410) arrange trips.

Cross-Country Skiing
Chicago's flat lands are ideal, especially in the parks or in the forest preserves, tel: 261-8400.

Fishing
A license is required to fish in Illinois. It can be obtained at City Hall, 121 N. LaSalle Street, the State of Illinois Center, 100 W. Randolph Street, or some tackle shops or currency exchanges. For information on fishing spots call: Chicago Sportfishing Association, Burnham Park Harbor, tel: 922-1100; the Forest Preserve District, tel: 261-8400; or the Illinois Dept. of Conservation, tel: 814-2070.

Golf
The Chicago Park District, tel: 294-2200, has a number of nine-hole courses and one 18-hole course: Jackson Park, 63rd Street and Stony Island (18 holes); Robert A. Black, 2045 W. Pratt Blvd; Columbus Park, 5700 W. Jackson Blvd; Marquette Park, 6700 S. Kedzie Street; South Shore Country Club, 71st Street and South Shore Drive; Waveland, 3600 N. Lake Shore Drive.

In addition, many of the surrounding suburbs have courses open to the public. They may be a bit more expensive, but they're generally nicer courses.

Ice Skating
McFetridge Sports Complex, 3845 N. California Avenue, has indoor skating, tel: 478-0210. Outdoor skating is available when the weather is suitably cold at Daley Centennial Plaza, 337 E. Randolph Street, tel: 294-4790.

Jogging
The path along the lakefront is shared by bicyclists and joggers. Avoid jogging in deserted areas after dark. For additional information, contact the Chicago Area Runners Association, tel: 666-9836.

Racquetball
Park District and McFetridge Sports Complex, tel: 478-0210.

Swimming
The Chicago Park District has 31 beaches along Lake Michigan. The beaches are open from June 15 to Labor Day, from 9am–9.30pm. Lifeguards are on duty, and no alcohol is allowed. For information, tel: 294-2333.

Tennis

Tennis courts are available throughout the city, generally without charge. The Chicago Park District can advise on the nearest courts, tel: 294-2493.

Tobogganing

A number of toboggan slides are located in the Cook County Forest Preserves, tel: 261-8400. Toboggans can be rented at each location.

☞ ☞ ☞
Further Reading

General

American Apocalypse: The Great Fire and The Myth of Chicago, by Ross Miller, University of Chicago Press, 1990. A look at the rebuilding of Chicago following the fire that destroyed most of the city.

Chicago Architecture 1872–1922, edited by John Zukowsky, Prestel-Verlag, Munich, in association with the Art Institute of Chicago.

Streetwise Chicago, A History of Chicago Street Names, by Don Hayner and Tom McNamee, Loyola University Press, 1988. A fun look at Chicago through the history of its street names.

Sweet Home Chicago: The Real City Guide, by Sherry Kent, Mary Szpur and Tom Horwitz, Chicago Review Press, 1987. A Chicago guide for residents of Chicago.

Something Wonderful Right Away, edited by Jeffrey Sweet, 1978, Avon Books. An oral history of the Second City troupe and the Compass Players.

The Plan of Chicago: 1909–1979, Art Institute of Chicago, 1979, ed. John Zukowsky.

The Chicago School of Architecture, Carl W. Condit, University of Chicago Press, 1964.

Chicago's Famous Buildings, Third Edition, University of Chicago Press, 1980, ed. Ira J. Bach.

Chicago Since the Sears Tower: A Guide to New Downtown Buildings, by Mary Alice Molloy, Inland Architect Press, 1988.

Urban Blues, by Charles Keil, the University of Chicago Press, 1966. Published by Stel-Verlag, Munich, in association with the Art Institute of Chicago.

Other Insight Guides

The widely-acclaimed Insight Guide series includes 190 titles covering every continent. There are also more than 100 Pocket Guides and 60 Compact Guides. The 40-plus titles covering the United States include:

Insight Guide: Crossing America documents three routes by car, vividly portraying the people and places you'll encounter on the way.

Insight Guide: New York City not only covers all the sights worth seeing but also includes some great features, such as the encounters that happen during a typical night-time police patrol.

Pocket Guide: Boston. Contains personal recommendations from a local host, plus detailed itineraries and full-size fold-out map.

Pocket Guide: Atlanta. The practical, personalised guide to the city of the 1996 Olympics. Detailed itineraries and full-size fold-out map.

Insight Compact Guide: Florida. The perfect on-the-spot guides, this series packs an amazing amount of information into a portable format, with text, pictures and maps carefully cross-referenced.

Art & Photo Credits

Photography by
Chuck Berman Cover, 14/15, 16/17, 18/19, 20/21, 27, 52/53, 59, 60, 61, 62, 63, 64, 68, 77, 86, 87, 88, 90, 94, 95, 96, 97, 98, 99, 102/103, 104/105, 106/107, 110/111, 113, 114, 119, 120, 130/131, 132/133, 134/135, 140, 142/143, 144, 145, 148, 149, 150, 151, 152, 153, 154, 155, 164/165, 166/167, 169, 170, 171, 172, 173, 176, 178, 182, 192/193, 195, 196, 197, 199, 200, 201, 202, 203, 204/205, 206, 207, 212, 213, 222/223, 224, 225, 226, 227, 232, 233, 234, 236/237, 239, 243, 247
C & S Chattopadhyay 2, 6/7
Chicago Botanic Garden 240
Chicago Historical Society 26, 28, 29, 30, 31, 33, 34, 35, 36, 37L, 37R, 38, 40/41, 42, 46, 47, 65, 160, 161, 163, 229
Chicago Sun-Times 32, 43, 44, 45, 49, 50, 51, 65, 70, 71, 78, 80R, 81, 156/157, 159, 162, 230, 231
Eddy Posthuma de Boer 54/55, 74/75, 117, 124/125
Field Museum of Natural History 121
Wolfgang Fritz 3
Luke Golobitsh 24/25, 84/85, 116, 184L, 188, 208, 209, 211, 213, 214/215, 216, 220, 241, 244, 246, 248
Raymond W. and Martha Hilpert Gruner 39
Fernando Jones 185R
Cathy Kleiman, Lincoln Park Zoo Society 139
Milwaukee Visitors and Convention Bureau 245
NASA 122
Marc PoKempner 9, 22/23, 56/57, 89, 100/101, 177, 194
James Quinn 76, 79, 83, 91, 92/93, 118, 147, 172R, 184R, 186, 187, 221
Six Flags Great America 242
Topham Picturepoint 48, 66/67
Harry Walker 58, 138, 174, 175, 179, 183, 185L, 210, 228, 235L, 235R
Margaret Wright 112, 115, 126, 127, 128L, 128R, 137, 146, 151, 198, 218, 219

Maps Berndtson & Berndtson

Visual Consultant V. Barl

Index

A

A Wedding 123
About Last Night 123
Addams, Jane *see also* Hull House 34, 42, 65, 141
Ade, George (columnist) 70
Adler Planetarium 122
air-and-water show 140
Aire Crown 186
Algren, Nelson (author) 43, 51, 60, 69, 71–72, 141
Alinsky, Saul 34, 43, 65
Allison, Luther (bluesman) 79
Alta Vista Terrace 169–170
Amoco Building 95
Andersonville 171
Aragon Ballroom 171
Archicenter 119
Architootural Cruise 113
architecture *see also* individual listings 95–99, 145–154
 Alta Vista Terrace 169–170
 Foundation's shop and tour center 116
 architectural cruises 113, 136, 148
 architectural tours 116
 Astor Street houses 153–154
 Bauhaus 97
 Beverly 231
 buildings illuminated at night 98–99, 147
 Chicago style bridge 146
 city plan 33, 99
 modernism 98, 147, 153
 New York architects 98, 154
 Oak Park 217–221
 post-fire 32, 95
Prairie Avenue Historic District 119, 226
Prairie School 152, 220–221, 227
Argyle Street 173–174
Arlington International Racecourse 242–243
Art Institute of Chicago 32, 63, 117
Astor Street District 153
Auditorium Building 116
Austin Garden 218
Automat Building 114
Aykroyd, Dan 123, 188

B

Back of the Yards Council 34, 65, 233
Back of the Yards (ghetto) 35, 47, 49
Bad Boys 123
Baha'i Temple 178
Banks, Ernie 89
"bascule" bridge (Chicago style) 146
baseball *see also* Cubs, White Sox 42, 43, 87–91, 169, 226–227
basketball 87, 89, 140
beaches 136, 139–140, 141
Bears, Chicago 87, 89, 140
Beitler, Paul (developer) 95–96
Bellow, Saul 39, 43, 72
Belushi, Jim 123, 188
Belushi, John 123, 154, 188
Berghoff Restaurant 209
bike paths 136, 179
Bilandic, Michael (mayor) 43, 47, 49–50
Billy Goat tavern 69, 212–213
Binga, Jesse 234
Biograph Theatre 159
"Black Farmers' Market" 201
Black Hawks, Chicago 87, 89
"Black Sox" (baseball scandal) 90–91
Blues Brothers, The 123
Blues Fest 137
blues *see* Chicago blues and individual listings
blues clubs 83
boat tours 113, 136, 148
Body Politic Theatre 184
bootleggers 36–37
Bourgeois, Louis (architect) 178
Bravissimo 207
Breakfast Club, The 123
Bridgeport 233
British, the 28
Brookfield Zoo 240–242
Broonzy, Big Bill (bluesman) 79
Bub City Crabshack & Bar-B-Q 210
Buckingham Fountain 99, 116, 137
Bulls, Chicago 87, 89
Burnham Plan, the 33, 42
Burnham, Daniel H. (architect) 33, 42, 97, 99, 121
Busse, Fred A. (mayor) 38
Byrne, Jane (mayor) 43, 47, 49–50

C

cabaret 188–190
Cabrini-Green housing project 199
Calder, Alexander
 Flamingo 118
 Universe 120
Candlelight Dinner Playhouse 186
Candy, John 123, 154
Capone, Al 36–38, 43, 46, 123, 141, 159–162, 173, 232
Caray, Harry 88–89
carillon 239
Carrie Eliza Getty Mausoleum 170
Carson Pirie Scott Building 97, 115
Carson, Samuel 31
Cavalier, Robert (Sieur de LaSalle) 28

Century of Progress (fair) 38, 230
Cermak, Tony (mayor) 38, 43, 48, 49
Chagall, Marc
 Four Seasons 119
Charles Gates Dawes House 178
Chatham 235
Checkerboard, the (blues club) 83
Chesbrough, Ellis Sylvester 30
Chess Records 80–81
chess pavilion 140
Chess, Leonard 80–81
Chess, Marshall 80–81
Chess, Phil 80
Chicago Athenaeum, 118
Chicago & North Western railroad 30
Chicago Academy of Sciences 138
Chicago Architecture Foundation 113, 116
Chicago Blues Artists Coalition 82
Chicago Blues Fest 83
Chicago blues 77–81, 137, 141
Chicago Board of Trade 42, 51, 127–129
Chicago Board Options Exchange 131
Chicago Botanic Garden 239
Chicago Children's Museum 148
Chicago Coalition of the Homeless 35
Chicago Cultural Center 118
Chicago Fire (Great) 31, 42, 138, 141, 145, 199
Chicago Freedom Movement 43, 65
Chicago Historical Society 138
Chicago Maritime Museum 148
Chicago Mercantile Exchange 43, 51, 127–129, 131
Chicago Place (mall) 152
Chicago Portage 145
Chicago Public Library 63
 Cultural Center 118
Chicago River 31, 42, 113, 140, 145–146, 225
 reversal of 31, 42, 140
Chicago Seven (conspiracy trial) 43, 46
Chicago Sun-Times Building 147
Chicago Symphony Orchestra 33, 116, 183
Chicago Transit Authority (CTA) tours 113
Chicago Tribune 69, 147
"Chicago windows" 96, 98
Chicagoans' accent 64
Chinatown
 New 173
 South Side 232
Chines City Hall 232
churches *see* individual listings
cinema 123
City College 65
City Hall corruption 38
Civic Opera House 118
Civil War 38, 138
climbers, the (sculpture) 114
CNA Center 114
Cobb Hall 230
Color of Money, The 123
Columbian Exposition, of 1893 32, 42, 139, 230

274

commodities trading 42
Conroy, Jack (author) 71
Continental Divide 123
Continental Illinois Bank and Trust Building 131
Cook County Forest Preserves 179
Coordinating Council of Community Organizations 65
"Corncob Towers" (Marina City) 98, 113
Couch family mausoleum 138
Coughlin, "Bathhouse John" (alderman) 47, 51
Court Theatre 64, 186
Criminal Courts Building 160
cruise boats 113
Cubs, Chicago 43, 87–89, 226
Culture Buses 113

D

Daily News 70–71
Daley Center Plaza 119
Daley Richard M. ("Richie") 43, 46, 49–50
Daley, Richard J. (mayor) 39, 43, 45–50, 232
Dan Ryan Woods 179
Darrow, Clarence 34
Dawson, Andre 89
Days of Rage (campaign) 43, 46
de LaSalle, Cavalier Robert René 145
Delta, the 201–202
Democratic National Convention, of 1968 39, 43, 46, 137
Demon Dogs 211
DePaul University 115
Depression, Great 38, 43
Devon Avenue 174–175
Dillinger, John 43, 159
Dixon, Willie (bluesman) 80–81
Dizz, Lefty (bluesman) 82, 83
Doane Observatory 122
Dobmeyer, Douglas 35
Doctor Detroit 123
"downhome" blues 78–79
Drake Hotel 62, 151, 154
Dreiser, Theodore 36, 70
Dubuffet, Jean
  Monument With Standing Beast 120
Dunne, Edward (governor) 48
Dunne, Finley Peter (columnist) 69
DuSable Museum of African American History 228
DuSable, Jean Baptiste Point 28, 42, 145

E

Edgebrook/Caldwell woods 179
El, the 113
Endless Love 123
Erie Canal 29, 42
Evanston Historical Society 178
Evanston, Illinois 177
Everest Room 62, 208–209
Exchange Center 131

F

Farm-in-the-Zoo 138
Farrakhan, Louis 234
Farrell, James T. 71
Farson House 221
Federal Reserve Bank of Chicago 131
Fermi, Enrico (nuclear physicist) 38
Ferris Bueller's Day Off 123
Ferris wheel 32, 42, 230
festivals
  air-and-water show 140
  Blues Fest 137
  Jazz Fest 137
  Kettlestrings Festival 218
  summer stock 183
  Taste of Chicago 137, 207
Field Museum of Natural History 121
"field hollers" 78
Field, Eugene (columnist) 70
Field, Marshall 31, 32, 121, 226
Fine Arts Building 116
First National Bank 119
Fisher Building 97, 114
football 87, 140
Fort Dearborn Massacre 28–29, 42, 138, 145
Fort Dearborn 28–29, 42, 138, 145
Four Friends 123
Fourth Presbyterian Church 151
Fox, Charles E. (architect) 154
Francais, Le 208
Front Page, The 123
Frontera Grill 208
futures markets 43 127–131

G

Gamblers Anonymous 63
gangsterism *see also* Capone 36–37, 43, 60, 159–162
Gilbert and Sullivan Society 64
Gingko Tree Bookstore 219
Glencoe, Illinois 240
Glessner House 226
Gold Coast 153
golf 139, 179
Goodman Theater 117, 187, 188
Graceland cemetery 170
Graham, Bruce (architect) 96
Grant Park Symphony 137
Grant Park 33, 99, 116, 137, 183
Gray Wolves, the 32, 33
Greektown 201–202
Green Mill Jazz Club 174
Griffin, Walter Burley (architect) 231
Guy, Buddy (bluesman) 82

H

Hamal Fountain 119
Harrison I, Carter (mayor) 48
Harvey, Paul 72
Haymarket Riot, of 1886 42, 141, 160, 198–199
Haymarket Square 198–199
Hecht, Ben 36, 71, 123
Hefner, Christie 73

Hefner, Hugh 43, 73
Hemingway, Ernest 71–72
Hermann Weinhardt House 197
His Girl Friday 123
Historical Society of Oak Park and River Forest 221
Holy Name Cathedral 161
Holy Trinity Church 198
horseracing 242–243
hotdogs 211–212
Hotel Inter-Continental 149
Hull House (Jane Addams's) 34, 42, 65, 195–196
Hull, Bobby 89
Hyde Park 61, 64, 227

I

ice hockey 87
ice-cream sundae (origin of) 177
Illinois-Michigan Canal 29
Indian Boundary Park 175, 179
Indians *see* Native Americans
Industrial Areas Foundation 65
International Museum of Surgical Science 154
Irish Castle 231
Italian beef sandwich 213
Italian community 196

J

Jackowo 177
Jackson Park 230
Jackson, Reverend Jesse 43, 48–49, 50, 65, 234–235
Jackson, "Shoeless" Joe 42, 90–91
Jahn, Helmut (architect) 32, 96, 113, 120
James Charnley House 154
James Houghteling houses 154
James T Ryerson House 154
Jazz Fest 137
Jewish heritage *see also* Spertus Museum 174–175
John Dillinger Died for You Society 159
John Hancock Center 95, 113, 150
Jolliet, Louis 27–28, 42, 145
Jordan, Michael 89

K

Kelly, Edward (mayor) 49
Kenessey's 208
Kenna, "Hinky Dink" (alderman) 31, 47, 51
Kennedy, John F. 39, 43, 46
Kennelly, Martin (mayor) 49
Kerner, Otto (governor) 47
Kettlestrings Festival 218
King, Jr, Martin Luther 38, 43, 48, 65, 200
Kinzie, John 28, 30, 141, 145
Kupcinet, Irv 72

L

labor unrest 33–34, 42
Lady in Red, the see also Dillinger 43
Lake Chicago 27, 42
Lake Geneva, Wisconsin 246
Lake Michigan 27, 42, 61, 135–140
Lake Point Tower 113, 148
Lake Shore Drive 136
Landis, Judge Kenesaw Mountain 91
Lardner, Ring 69
LaSalle see de LaSalle
LaSalle Street 118, 127
Lee, Pfc. Milton Olive 138
Limit Up bar 131
Lincoln Park 61, 136, 138-139, 166
Lincoln Park Conservatory 138
Lincoln Park Zoo 138
Lincoln, Abraham 47, 138
literature 69–72
Little Egypt 32–33, 42, 230
Looking for Mister Goodbar 123
Loop, The 113–122
Lyric Opera 62, 63, 118, 183

M

Magnificent Mile 145–154
Maher, George Washington (architect) 221
Major League 123
Mama Desta's Red Sea Restaurant 210
Mamet, David 72, 123, 185, 187
Manhattan Project 43
Marina City 98, 113
Marquette, Father Jacques 27–28, 42, 145
Marshall Field's department store 115
Marshall, Benjamin (architect) 154
Maxwell Street 196–197
mayoral power-politics 45–50
McCormick Place 140
McCormick, Robert R. 147
Men Don't Leave 123
Mencken, H.L. 69
Merchandise Mart 113
Metropolitan Correctional Center 98, 114
Michigan Avenue Bridge 42, 145–6
Midway Plaisance 230
Midwest Stock Exchange 131
Mikita, Stan 89
Milwaukee, Wisconsin 245–246
Minoso, Minnie 89
Miró, Joan (Chicago) 119
Mirage Tavern sting 51
modernism 98, 147, 153
Monadnock Building 32, 96, 119
Monroe, Harriet (poet) 71
Montgomery Ward & Co. 31
Morton's of Chicago 207
Museum of Contemporary Art 149
Museum of Contemporary Photography 115
Museum of Science and Industry 32, 227

museums
 Art Institute of Chicago 32, 63, 117
 Chicago Children's Museum 148
 Chicago Maritime Museum 148
 Cobb Hall 230
 DuSable Museum, African American History 228
 Field Museum of Natural History 121
 International Museum of Surgical Science 154
 Museum of Contemporary Art 150
 Museum of Contemporary Photography 115
 Museum of Science and Industry 32, 227
 Oriental Institute 227
 Polish Museum of America 177, 198
 Printing Museum 122
 Renaissance Society 230
 Smart Museum 230
 Spertus Museum 115–116
 Swedish American Museum 172
 Terra Museum of American Art 149
 Ukrainian National Museum 198
Music Box 123
Music of the Baroque, The 63

N

National Black Farmers Harvest and Business Cooperation 201
Native Americans 27–29, 42, 145
Naturalistic Garden 239
Nature Trail 239
Navy Pier 136, 137
NBC Tower 147
Ness, Eliot 37, 123
New Checkerboard Lounge see Checkerboard
nightlife 188–190
900 N. Michigan Building 95, 98, 151
North Pier Chicago 148
North-South divide 109, 225
Northbrook Court 152
Northlight Theatre 185
Northwestern Station 200
Northwestern University 63, 178

O

O'Leary, Mrs. (and cow) 31, 42, 95, 199
Oak Park (architecture) 42, 217–221
Oak Park Conservatory and Earth Shelter Classroom 217–218
Oak Park Visitor's Bureau 217
Oak Street Beach 139, 153
Oak Terrace dining room see Drake Hotel
Ogden, William B. (mayor) 30, 42, 49
Old Orchard Center, 152
Old Town School of Music 83
Old Town 154, 188
Olive Park 138
Olmstead, Frederick Law 138
Operation Breadbasket 43, 65
Orchestra Hall 62, 116
Ordinary People 123

Organic Theater 185
Oriental Institute 227
Owings, Skidmore (architect) 96

P–Q

Palmer, Potter 31, 227
Pashley, Alfred F. (architect) 154
Patterson House 154
Pegasus Players 186
Pelli, Cesar (architect) 96
People United to Save Humanity (PUSH) 48, 234–235
Petrillo Band Shell 117, 137
pharaoh Unisankh's tomb see Field Museum
Picasso sculpture 119
Pilsen East Artists Colony 202
Pirie, John 31
pizza 212
Planes, Trains and Automobiles 123
Playboy Enterprises Inc. 73
Playboy 73
Poetry Slam, the 174
Police Training Academy 199
Polish community 175–176, 198
Polish Museum of America 177, 198
Polish Roman Catholic Union of America 198
political machine 38, 43, 45–50, 51
Polonia 176
Port of Chicago 140
Pottawattomies 27–29, 42
Prairie Avenue Historic District 119
Prairie Avenue's Millionaires' Row 34, 226
Printer's Row 122
Printing Museum 122
Prohibition 36–38, 177
Pullman neighborhood 229–230
Pullman railcar plant 34, 42
Pullman, George 30, 226, 229
Pumping Station 150
Quincy-Wells Station 114

R

racial unrest 38, 42, 43, 234–235
Rainbow Coalition 43, 49
Rand, Sally 38, 43
Ravinia 183
Reliance Building 97
Renaissance Society 230
restaurants/dining 207–213
Richardson, H.H. (architect) 226
Robie House 227
Rockefeller Chapel 230
Roosevelt University 116
Root, John Wellborn (architect) 32, 96, 119, 154
Rosenfeld, Isaac 61
Royko, Mike (columnist) 69
Rush Street 153

S

St Boniface Church (German Catholic) 198
St Hyacinth's Roman Catholic Church 177
St Nicholas Theater Company 185
St Nicholas Ukrainian Catholic Cathedral 197
St Paul Church 202
St Stanislaus Kostka Catholic Church 177, 198
St Valentine's Day Massacre, of 1929 36, 43, 162
Sandberg, Ryne 89
Sandburg, Carl (poet) 36, 38, 70–71
Sawyer, Eugene (mayor) 43, 50
Scarface *see* Capone
Schaumburg, Illinois 152
Schlacks, Henry J. 202
sculpture (corporate/public)
  Calder, Alexander (*Flamingo*) 118, (*Universe*) 120
  Picasso, Pablo 119
  climbers, the 114
  Miró, Joan (*Chicago*) 119
  Chagall, Marc (*Four Seasons*) 119
  Dubuffet, Jean (*Monument With Standing Beast*) 120-121
  Moore, Henry (*Nuclear Energy*) 231
Sears Tower 43, 95, 119–120, 150
  Skydeck 120
Sears, Roebuck & Co. 31
Second City 154
Sexual Perversity in Chicago 123
Shaw's Blue Crab Lounge & Oyster Bar 210
Shaw's Crab House 210
Shedd Aquarium 121–122
shopping 145–154, 172–173, 196–197
Shubert Theatre 186
Silver Streak 123
Sinclair, Upton (author) 35, 42, 233
Six Flags Great America 243–244
skeet 139
Skokie, Illinois 152
Sky Needle 95
skyscrapers 32, 43, 95, 146–147
Smart Museum 230
Smith, Adrian (architect) 147
social reform 34–35, 233–235
Soldier Field 140
Solti, Sir George 62
Somewhere in Time 123
Sommerdale Police Scandal 51
South Loop Marketplace 201
South Water Market 201
Spertus Museum 115–116
sports bars 89–90
Springfield, Illinois 29
State of Illinois Center 32, 113, 120
Steppenwolf Theatre Company 185
Stevenson II, Adlai (governor) 47–48
Stevenson III, Adlai (senator) 48
stings (FBI) 51
Stock Exchange Building 96
stockyards 35–36, 42, 228

Streeter, George Wellington 149
Streeterville 149
Streets of Fire 123
Students for a Democratic Society (SDS) *see also* Chicago Seven 46
Sullivan, Louis (architect) 32, 62, 96, 97, 170
Swedish American Museum 172
Swedish community 171–172

T

Taste of Chicago 137
Taylor, Koko (blueswoman) 81
Terkel, Studs 60, 141
Terra Museum of American Art 149
Terra, Daniel J. 149
theater *see also* individual listings 183–188
  Aire Crown 186
  Body Politic Theatre 184
  Chicago theater 185–186
  Court Theatre 186
  Goodman Theater 117, 187
  Northlight Theatre 185
  Organic Theater 185–186
  Pegasus Players 186
  Shubert Theater 186
  Second City 154, 187–188
  St Nicholas Theater Company 185
  Steppenwolf Theater Company 185–186
  Victory Gardens Theater 185
  Village Players 218
  Wisdom Bridge Theatre 185
Theatre on the Lake 139
Things Change 123
Thomas, Theodore (conductor) 33
Thompson, "Big Jim" (governor) 47
Thompson, William Hale (mayor) 38, 46, 47, 49
Three Happiness Restaurant 211
Tommy Gun's Garage 162
Tonty, Henry 145
tram tour 240
Tribune Tower 147
Twin-Anchors Restaurant and Tavern 210

U

Ukrainian National Museum 198
Ukrainian Village 197
Uncle Buck 123
Union Station 200
Union Stock Yard 36, 43, 65, 228, 233
Unity Temple 42
University of Chicago 32, 42, 63, 65, 231
  Rockefeller Chapel 230
University of Illinois at Chicago 195
Untouchable Tours 162
Untouchables, The 123
Untouchables, the 37
Uptown 170–174

V

van der Rohe, Ludwig Mies (architect) 32, 97–98, 113, 114, 118, 148
Victory Gardens Theater 184
Vietnamese community 173
Viking Ship 139
Village Players 218
Vrdolyak, "Fast Eddie" 47, 49

W

War of 1812 28
Ward, A. Montgomery 33, 99
Washington, Harold (mayor) 39, 43, 48, 50, 51, 233
Water Tower Place 62, 150, 152
Water Tower 149–150
Waters, Jr, Muddy (bluesman) 82
Waters, Muddy (bluesman) 80–82
Wayne, General "Mad Anthony" 28, 42
Wellington, Valerie (blueswoman) 82
Wells, Junior (bluesman) 82
Wentworth, "Long John" (mayor) 30, 47
White Sox Park 226
White Sox, Chicago 42, 87–91, 226
White, Stanford (architect) 154
Wicker Park 197
Widow Clarke House 226
William J. Campbell US Courthouse Annex 114
"Windy City" nickname 42
Winfrey, Oprah 153, 191
Wisdom Bridge Theatre 185
Woodfield Mall 152
Woodlawn Organization 34–35, 43, 65
World Series of 1919 42, 90–91
World War II 38
world's largest building (Amoco Building) 95
world's tallest bank (First National) 119
world's tallest building (Sears Tower) 95, 119
Wright, Frank Lloyd 32, 42, 217–221
Wright, Frank Lloyd (buildings)
  Arthur Heurtley House 221
  Astor Street houses 154
  Home and Studio 42, 219
  Kenilworth Avenue 220–221
  Oak Park 217–221
  Robie House 227–228
  Unity Temple 42, 219–220
  Walter H. Gale House 220
Wrigley Building 146–147
Wrigley Field 43, 87–89, 169
Wrigleyville 87–88, 169

X–Z

Xerox Building 32
Zoo Rookery 138
zoos
  Brookfield Zoo 240–242
  Lincoln Park Zoo 138